南开英美文学精品教材

美国文学批评名著精读

（上）

The Scholar's Library for the Study of American Literature

常耀信　主编

南开大学出版社

天　津

图书在版编目(CIP)数据

美国文学批评名著精读 / 常耀信主编. —天津:南开大学出版社,2007.3(2007.8重印)

南开英美文学精品教材

ISBN 978-7-310-02674-6

Ⅰ.美… Ⅱ.常… Ⅲ.文学评论－美国－高等学校－教材 Ⅳ.I712.06

中国版本图书馆 CIP 数据核字(2007)第 029440 号

南开大学出版社出版发行

出版人:肖占鹏

地址:天津市南开区卫津路 94 号　　邮政编码:300071

营销部电话:(022)23508339　23500755

营销部传真:(022)23508542　　邮购部电话:(022)23502200

*

天津泰宇印务有限公司印刷

全国各地新华书店经销

*

2007 年 3 月第 1 版　2007 年 8 月第 2 次印刷

880×1230 毫米　32 开本　25.5 印张　726 千字

定价:42.00 元(全二册)

如遇图书印装质量问题,请与本社营销部联系调换,电话:(022)23507125

前　言

　　美国文学评论的发展，至 20 世纪 70 年代，大体经历了三个重要阶段。自 19 世纪 40 年代爱默生的《论诗人》始至 90 年代威廉·狄恩·豪威尔斯的《批评与散文》止的半个世纪，是美国独立文学和文化的炼铸成形时期，是美国作家和评论家为美国独立文学的发展而鸣锣呐喊的时期。第二阶段从 19 世纪末始至 20 世纪 30 年代末止，这是美国文学评论气氛活跃、论争热烈、具有决定意义的阶段。除了 T. S. 艾略特、埃德蒙·威尔逊、艾伦·塔特等"新批评"的声音之外，还有一些不同凡响的声音——凡·威克·布鲁克斯、H·L·门肯以及伦道夫·伯恩等人对美国文学"业已成年"的断言。这是美国文学评论家以全新的目光看待本国文学独特的伟大之处的时代。如果说在这以前，人们习惯于以剖析欧洲和英国文学的思想和方法看待美国文学，因而结论总不外乎"不够伟大"、"不能同欧洲作家的鸿篇巨制相提并论"的话，那么，在这一阶段中，美国评论家已开始从美国的国情出发认识本国文学，认识到美国文学经过近三百年的演变，已于 1901 年至 1920 年间达到"成年"。这一论断开创了美国文学评论的新纪元；它标志着美国文学评论界重新评估美国文学的开端。

　　第三阶段可从 20 世纪 40 年代初 F·O·马西森的《美国的文艺复兴》和艾尔弗雷德·卡津的《在本国土地上》两部文学评论巨著的发表为始。这是一个"重新发现"美国文学的阶段。美国文学评论界一扫过去追随欧洲文学评论的气氛，把精力集中到从本国的文化历史实际出发剖析美国文学上面。如果二三十年代的论断尚需佐证，40 年代后的文学评论则从空泛的议论跃进到从作品的具体实际出发，寻觅出赏析美国文学的理论的阶段。美国文学评论界"重新发现"美国文学的激情在五六十年代升至其"沸腾点"，评论巨著迭相面世，每部新书都立论新颖，给人以一新耳目、发聩振聋的印象，真可谓群芳竞艳，让人目不暇接,读者对评论的兴趣有时竟超过对文学作品本身的兴致。倘然美国文学在 20 世纪前 20 年已趋成年,那么美国文学评论作为文学的一个有机组成部分,在五六十年代业已成年,并以自己的独特风格和欧洲文学评论比肩齐名。这一时期的评论重点在于美国早期文学,即 19 世纪美国文学的主要作家及作品,兼及 20 世纪二三十年代的杰出作家与作品。

20 世纪 70 年代以后,美国文学评论又有了长足发展。在继续探索早期美国文学的内在模式的同时,对 20 世纪以来,即现代和当代文学的评论数目剧增。新一代评论家又独辟蹊径,从不同的角度赏析现当代文学,进一步巩固了美国文学与文学评论在世界文坛上不可小觑的地位。今天美国文学在世界上几乎处于首屈一指的地位,大有取代英国文学的来头,这和美国文学评论界多年来不懈的杰出努力是有密切关系的。

多年来,美国文学评论的突出特点是它的多样性和独创性。正如美国现代诗人华莱士·史蒂文斯的一首诗所说,看山乌鸟的方式可有十三种之多,美国文学评论界自始至今所提出的研究美国文学的理论也是各式各样的。事实上,美国文学评论的基本特点在于它的"多元化";但是透过这些纷然杂陈的观点,人们可以看到评论家都在努力寻觅一种"合成"理论,以诠释几位作家或某一时期内作家的创作活动,使之具有令人信服的理性基础。他们从美国历史或文化发展的角度去赏析本国文学,每人提出的理论都有合理之处。各种理论的总和便使读者有可能在较可靠的基础上看到美国文学的全貌。而且,他们是"百花齐放、百家争鸣",各抒己见,不落窠臼,不肯"吃别人嚼过的馍",有时某些评论家很有"语不惊人死不休"的气势。有人评论说,阅读过去的文学评论,特别是 20 世纪五六十年代的文学评论,其趣味不亚于阅读他们所评论的文学作品。编者本人就很有这种体会。

因此,把这些理论的精粹编选出来以飨读者是非常必要的。

正是出于这种意图,编者编写了《美国文学评论名著精读》,作为大学本科高年级及硕士和博士研究生的美国文学评论课教科书和必备的参考书。由于侧重点不在于反映美国文学评论的历史颠末,因而它的内容主要不是前面所讲的第一阶段和第二阶段，而是第三阶段，即美国文学评论业已成熟的阶段内的各种评论观点。本书共分上、下两册，辑录了美国评论家（除 D·H·劳伦斯外）对早期美国文学的各种评论，收集了评论界关于现当代美国文学的各种颇富影响的评论。所选注的文章皆出自美国学术界所公认的美国文学研究经典著作，都具有一定的经典性，不拘泥于概念的纷争，不玄秘艰涩，兼具科学性与知识性，对美国文学名家和名著进行生动、透辟的分析，视角多变，说理简洁，文字极流畅，在文学评论史上极有可能成为"里程碑"式的作品。它们的出版时间多为 20 世纪五六十年代，但也有相当数量的作品出现在 20 世纪的初年乃至三四十年代（尤其是包括在附件部分的作品）。他们的作者都无疑是美国文学评论界的佼佼者。他们的作品都具有一定的普遍意义及永久性。因而，这些评论文章应是美国文学研究者——本科生、研究生以及社会读者——所必读的"学者文库"中所包括的评论著作。这些作品应有助于增强美国文学学习者和研究者的底蕴和铺垫，应成为美国文学教学与研究工作者的学术基础的中心组成部分。

《美国文学评论名著精读》共选入 23 位著名评论家的专著或专论。每篇选文均由作者介绍、作品介绍、文章节选、注释、讨论题及参考书五部分组成，以利于美国文学的教学。编者相信，本书对美国文学的教学与学术研究工作将有很大的裨益。在美国文学的教学一线工作的教师们，会从本文选中汲取必要的资料，以充实教学的广度和深度，取得更好的教学效果。

在本书的编写过程中，王蕴茹教授在查核资料、对照原文以及通读全文方面，做出了可观的努力和贡献。

尽管编者做了最大努力，书里错讹之处一定仍然不少，敬请各位专家、学者、读者等拨冗不吝指教。

常耀信

2006 年 7 月于南开

Table of Contents

Perry Miller

〔作者介绍〕

佩里·米勒（Perry Miller, 1905-1963），美国文学评论家，生于芝加哥市。1923 年离开大学后流浪三年，在刚果受到启发，找到归宿，自 1931 年起在哈佛大学任教，开始他向 20 世纪解释美国历史的使命。1933 年米勒发表他的文学评论出世作《麻省正统体制》（*Orthodoxy in Massachusetts*），开始认真研究美国清教徒及其传统。之后又发表了《新英格兰的思想》（*The New England Mind*）、《17 世纪》（*The Seventeenth Century*, 1939）及《从殖民区到省制》（*From Colony to Province*, 1953）等重要著作，继续这一专题的研究工作。他的佳作《进入荒野的使命》（*Errand into the Wilderness*, 1956）收集了他的评论名作选品。米勒一生从事美国清教主义的评究，是这一学术领域内的权威学者。他卒世时的未竟之作《美国思想的活动》（*The Life of the Mind in America*, 1965）同他的其他著作一样，是美国文学评论的上乘之作。米勒堪称卓尔不群的美国文化史学家及文学家之一。

Errand into the Wilderness

〔作品介绍〕

《进入荒野的使命》1956 年由纽约哈帕—罗公司出版，是研究美国清教主义及其影响的经典著作。

米勒指出，迄今为止，"社会"史学家们虽对美国文化史进行了认真细致的可贵的研究，但是他们都未抓住问题的根本。他以写《罗马帝国之兴衰》的英国史学家吉本（Edward Gibbon, 1737-1794）为楷模，立志探赜索隐，穷溯美国文化发展的源流。

米勒认为，人类历史的基本因素是人的思想，研究美国历史必须从 17 世纪移居北美的清教徒的思想和信仰着手。美国的清教徒是担负着伟大使命来美洲定居的。《进入荒野的使命》恰切地表达了他们的使命感。他们决心完成在欧洲开始的宗教改革，把北美荒野建成他们理想的、文明的人间乐土。文明和自然的关系是美国民族史的主要因素，也是米勒这部名作的主题。

《进入荒野的使命》回顾了康涅狄格和马萨诸塞两地神权体制侧重清教徒主义的不同原则，在 17 世纪移民初期执政的情况；指出美国清教徒从历史角度看是卡尔文教的信徒，乔纳桑·爱德华兹愿称自己为卡尔文主义者，虽然他因受洛克哲学和牛顿物理学的影响而无法坚持卡尔文的一些基本观点。作者还谈到弗吉尼亚的历史，认为宗教信仰是弗吉尼亚移民的原动力量；那里承认等级和门第，不赞成民主和平等；民主的出现是自然的发展，并非他们的愿望。《进入荒野的使命》还详细探讨了美国清教主义的政教合一政体及清教主义的基本理论，乔纳桑·爱德华兹作为美国清教最后一名"先知"，力求通过北美宗教大觉醒运动重申卡尔文教主张的行动，他对后世，尤其对 19 世纪前期以爱默生为代表的超验主义思想的巨大影响，以及爱默生坚持唯心主义、反对物质主义的基本思想。作者还对"进入荒野的使命"的内涵进行了精辟分析。

米勒自谓，从 1931 年起至 1956 年《进入荒野的使命》发表时止，他潜心研究美国清教思想这一专题长达 25 年之久。其间发表了几部颇富启迪性的专著，写了一些令人震触的文章和讲演辞。《进入荒野的使命》收集了他的文章和演说辞的精粹，展现了美国清教传统的历史及影响，堪称为长期以来，特别是 20 世纪 20 年代以来，对此所进行的研究的总结，奠定了清教在美国文化史上最终的稳定地位。

这里选注的是该书第 1 章，其题目和书名相同。

An Excerpt from *Errand into the Wilderness*

It was a happy inspiration that led the staff of the John Carter Brown Library to choose as the title of its New England exhibition of 1952 a phrase from Samuel Danforth's[1] election sermon, delivered on May 11, 1670: *A Brief Recognition of New England's Errand into the Wilderness*. It was of course an inspiration, if not of genius, at least of talent, for Danforth to invent his title in the first place. But all the election sermons of this period—that is to say, the major expressions of the second generation,[2] which, delivered on these forensic occasions, were in the fullest sense community expression—have interesting titles; a mere listing tells the story of what was happening to the minds and emotions of the New England people: John Higginson's *The Cause of God and His People in New England* in 1663, William Stoughton's *New England's True Interest Not to Lie* in 1668, Thomas Shepard's *Eye-Salve* in 1672, Urian Oakes's *New England Pleaded With* in 1673; and, climactically and most explicitly, Increase Mather's *A Discourse Concerning the Danger of Apostasy* in 1677.

All of these show by their title pages alone—and, as those who have looked into them know, infinitely more by their contents—a deep disquietude. They are troubled utterances, worried, fearful: something has gone wrong. As in 1662 Wigglesworth[3] already was saying in verse, God has a controversy with New England; He has cause to be angry and to punish it because of its innumerable defections. They say, unanimously, that New England was sent on an errand, and that it has failed.

To our ears these lamentations of the second generation sound strange indeed. We think of the founders as heroic men—of the towering stature of Bradford, Winthrop, and Thomas Hooker[4]—who braved the ocean and the wilderness, who conquered both, and left to their children a goodly heritage. Why then this whimpering?

Some historians suggest that the second and third generations suffered a failure of nerve; they weren't the men their fathers had been, and they knew it. Where the founders could range over the vast body of theology and ecclesiastical polity and produce profound works like the treatises of John Cotton[5] or the subtle psychological analyses of Hooker, or even such a gusty though wrongheaded book as Nathaniel Ward's *Simple Cobler*, let alone such, lofty, and right headed pleas as Roger Williams' *Bloody Tenent,* all these children could do was tell each other that they were on probation and that their chances of making good did not seem very promising.

Since Puritan intellectuals were thoroughly grounded in grammar and rhetoric, we may be certain that Danforth was fully aware of the ambiguity concealed in his word "errand." It already had taken on the double meaning which it still carries with us. Originally, as the word first took form in English, it meant exclusively a short journey on which an inferior is sent to convey a message or to perform a service for his superior. In that sense, we today speak of an "errand boy"; or the husband says that while in town, on his lunch hour, he must run an errand for his wife. But by the end of the Middle Ages, errand developed another connotation: it came to mean the actual business on which the actor goes, the purpose itself, the conscious intention in his mind. In this signification, the runner of the errand is working for himself, is his own boss; the wife, while the husband is away at the office, runs her own errands. Now in the 1660's the problem was this: which had New England originally been—an errand boy or a doer of errands? In which sense had it failed? Had it been dispatched for a further purpose, or was it an end in itself? Or had it fallen short not only in one or the other, but in both of the meanings? If so, it was indeed a tragedy, in the primitive sense of a fall from a mighty designation.

If the children were in grave doubts about which had been the original errand—if, in fact, those of the founders who lived into the later period and who might have set their progeny to rights found themselves wondering and confused—there is little chance of our answering clearly. Of course, there is no problem about Plymouth Colony. That is the charm about Plymouth: its clarity. The Pilgrims, as we have learned to call them, were reluctant voyagers; they had never wanted to leave England, but had been obliged to depart because the authorities made life impossible for Separatists. They could, naturally, have stayed at home had they given up being Separatists, but that idea simply did not occur to them. Yet they did not go to Holland as though on an errand; neither can we extract the notion of a mission out of the reasons which, as Bradford tells us, persuaded them to leave Leyden for "Virginia." The war with Spain was about to be resumed, and the economic threat was ominous; their migration was not so much an errand as a shrewd forecast, a plan to get out while the getting was good, lest, should they stay, they would be "intrapped or surrounded by their enemies, so as they should neither be able to fight nor flie." True, once the decision was taken, they congratulated themselves that they might become a means for propagating the gospel in the remote parts of the world, and thus of serving as stepping-stones to others in the performance of this great work; nevertheless, the substance of their decision was that they "thought it better to dislodge betimes to some place of better advantage and less danger, if any such could be found."[6] The great hymn[7] that Bradford, looking back in his old age, chanted about the landfall is one of the greatest passages, if not the very greatest, in all New England's literature; yet it does not resound with the sense of a mission accomplished—instead, it vibrates with the sorrow and exultation of suffering, the sheer endurance, the pain and the anguish, with the somberness of death faced unflinchingly:

May not and ought not the children of these fathers rightly say:
Our fathers were Englishmen which came over this great ocean, and

were ready to perish in this wilderness; but they cried unto the Lord, and he heard their voyce, and looked on their adversitie...

We are bound, I think, to see in Bradford's account the prototype of the vast majority of subsequent immigrants—of those Oscar Handlin[8] calls "The Uprooted": they came for better advantage and for less danger, and to give their posterity the opportunity of success.

The Great Migration of 1630 is an entirely other story. True, among the reasons John Winthrop drew up in 1629 to persuade himself and his colleagues that they should commit themselves to the enterprise, the economic motive frankly figures. Wise men thought that England was overpopulated and that the poor would have a better chance in the new land. But Massachusetts Bay was not just an organization of immigrants seeking advantage and opportunity. It had a positive sense of mission—either it was sent on an errand or it had its own intention, but in either case the deed was deliberate. It was an act of will, perhaps of willfulness. These Puritans were not driven out of England (thousands of their fellows stayed and fought the Cavaliers)—they went of their own accord.

So, concerning them, we ask the question, why? If we are not altogether clear about precisely how we should phrase the answer, this is not because they themselves were reticent. They spoke as fully as they knew how, and none more magnificently or cogently than John Winthrop in the midst of the passage itself, when he delivered a lay sermon aboard the flagship *Arabella* and called it "a Modell of Christian Charity." It distinguishes the motives of this great enterprise from those of Bradford's forlorn retreat, and especially from those of the masses who later have come in quest of advancement. Hence, for the student of New England and of America, it is a fact demanding incessant brooding that John Winthrop selected as the "doctrine" of his discourse, and so as the basic proposition to which, it then seemed to him, the errand was committed, the thesis that

God had disposed mankind in a hierarchy of social classes, so that "in all times some must be rich, some poor, some highe and eminent in power and dignitie; others mean and in subjeccion."[9] It is as though, preternaturally sensing what the promise of America might come to signify for the rank and file, Winthrop took the precaution to drive out of their heads any notion that in the wilderness the poor and the mean were ever so to improve themselves as to mount above the rich or the eminent in dignity. Were there any who had signed up under the mistaken impression that such was the purpose of their errand, Winthrop told them that, although other people, lesser breeds, might come for wealth or pelf, this migration was specifically dedicated to an avowed end that had nothing to do with incomes. We have entered into an explicit covenant with God, "we have professed to enterprise these Accions upon these and these ends"; we have drawn up indentures with the Almighty, wherefore if we succeed and do not let ourselves get diverted into making money, He will reward us. Whereas if we fail, if we "fall to embrace this present world and prosecute our carnall intencions, seekeing greate things for our selves and our posterity, the Lord will surely breake out in wrathe against us, be revenged of such a pericured people and make us knowe the price of the breache of such a Covenant."

Well, what terms were agreed upon in this covenant? Winthrop could say precisely— "It is by a mutuall consent through a specially overruleing providence, and a more than ordinary approbation of the Churches of Christ to seeke out a place of Cohabitation and Consorteshipp under a due form of Government, both civill and ecclesiasticall." If it could be said thus concretely, why should there be any ambiguity? There was no doubt whatsoever about what Winthrop meant by a due form of ecclesiastical government: he meant the pure Biblical polity set forth in full detail by the New Testament, that method which later generations, in the days of increasing confusion, would settle down to calling Congregational, but which for Winthrop was no denominational peculiarity but the very essence of organized Christianity. What a due form of civil government meant, therefore, became crystal clear, a political regime, possessing power, which would consider its main function to be the erecting, protecting, and preserving of this form of polity. This due form would have, at the very beginning of its list of responsibilities, the duty of suppressing heresy, of subduing or somehow getting rid of dissenters—of being, in short, deliberately, vigorously, and consistently intolerant.

Regarded in this light, the Massachusetts Bay Company came on an errand in the second and later sense of the word: it was, so to speak, on its own business. What it set out to do was the sufficient reason for its setting out. About this Winthrop seems to be perfectly certain, as he declares specifically what the due forms will be attempting; the end is to improve our lives to do more service to the Lord, to increase the body of Christ, and to preserve our posterity from the corruptions of this evil world, so that they in turn shall work out their salvation under the purity and power of Biblical ordinances. Because the errand was so definable in advance, certain conclusions about the method of conducting it were equally evident: one, obviously, was that those sworn to the covenant should not be allowed to turn aside in a lust for mere physical rewards; but another was, in Winthrop's simple but splendid words, "we must be knit together in this worke as one man, wee must entertaine each other in brotherly affection," we must actually delight in each other, "always having before our eyes our Commission and community in the worke, our community as members of the same body." This was to say, were the great purpose kept steadily in mind, if all gazed only at it and strove only for it, then social solidarity (within a scheme of fixed and unalterable class distinctions) would be an automatic consequence. A society despatched upon an errand that is its own reward would want no other rewards: it could go forth to possess a land without ever becoming possessed by it; social gradations would remain eternally what God had originally appointed; there would be no internal contention among groups or interests, and though there would be hard work for everybody, prosperity would be bestowed not as a consequence of labor but as a sign of approval upon the mission itself. For once in the history of humanity (with all its sins), there would be a society so dedicated to the holy cause that success would prove innocent and triumph not raise up sinful pride or arrogant dissension.

Or, at least, this would come about if the people did not deal falsely with God, if they would live up to the articles of their bond. If we do not perform these terms, Winthrop warned, we may expect immediate manifestations of divine wrath: we shall perish out of the land we are crossing the sea to possess. And here in the 1660's and 1670's, all the jeremiads (of which Danforth's is one of the most poignant) are castigations of the people for having defaulted on precisely these articles. They recite the long list of afflictions an angry God had rained upon them, surely enough to prove how abysmally they had deserted the covenant: crop failures, epidemics, grasshoppers, caterpillars, torrid summers, arctic winters, Indian wars, hurricanes, shipwrecks, accidents, and (most grievous of all) unsatisfactory children. The solemn work of the election day, said Stoughton[10] in 1668, is "Foundation-work" —not, that is, to lay a new one, "but to continue, and strengthen, and beautifie, and build upon that which has been laid." It had been laid in the covenant before even a foot was set ashore, and thereon New England should rest. Hence the terms of survival, let alone of prosperity, remained what had first been propounded:

If we should so frustrate and deceive the Lords Expectations, that his Covenant-interest, in us, and the Workings of his Salvation be made to cease, then All were lost indeed; Ruine upon Ruine, Destruction upon Destruction would come, until one stone were not left upon another.

Since so much of the literature after 1660—in fact, just about all of it—dwells on this theme of declension and apostasy, would not the story of New England, seem to be simply that of the failure of a mission? Winthrop's dread was realized: posterity had not found their salvation amid pure ordinances but had, despite the ordinances, yielded to the seductions of the good land. Hence distresses were being piled upon them, the slaughter of King Philip's War[11] and now the attack of a profligate king upon the sacred charter. By about 1680, it did in truth seem that shortly no stone would be left upon another, that history would record of New England that the founders had been great men, but that their children and grandchildren progressively deteriorated.

This would certainly seem to be the impression conveyed by the assembled clergy and lay leaders who, in 1679, met at Boston in a formal synod, under the leadership of Increase Mather[12], and there prepared a report on why the land suffered. The result of their deliberation, published under the title *The Necessity of Reformation*, was the first in what has proved to be a distressingly long succession of investigations into the civic health of Americans, and it is probably the most pessimistic. The land was afflicted, it said, because corruption had proceeded apace; assuredly, if the people did not quickly reform, the last blow would fall and nothing but desolation be left. Into what a moral quagmire this dedicated community had sunk, the synod did not leave to imagination: it published a long and detailed inventory of sins, crimes, misdemeanors, and nasty habits, which makes, to say the least, interesting reading.

We hear much talk nowadays about corruption, most of it couched in generalized terms. If we ask our current Jeremiahs to descend to particulars, they tell us that the republic is going on the rocks, or to the dogs, because the wives of politicians aspire to wear mink coats and their husbands take a moderate five per cent cut on certain deals to pay for the garments. The Puritans were devotees of logic, and the verb "methodize" ruled their thinking. When the synod went to work, it had before it a succession of sermons, such as that of Danforth and the other election-day or fast-day orators, as well as such works as Increase Mather's *A Brief History of the War with the Indians*, wherein the decimating conflict with Philip was presented as a revenge upon the people for their transgressions. When the synod felt obliged to enumerate the enormities of the land so that the people could recognize just how far short of their errand they had fallen, it did not, in the modern manner, assume that regeneration would be accomplished at the next election by turning the rascals out, but it digested this body of literature; it reduced the contents to method. The result is a staggering compendium of inquiry, organized into twelve headings.

First, there was a great and visible decay of godliness. Second, there were several manifestations of pride—contention in the churches, insubordination of inferiors toward superiors, particularly of those inferiors who had, unaccountably, acquired more wealth than their betters, and, astonishingly, a shocking extravagance in attire; especially on the part of these of the meaner sort, who persisted in dressing beyond their means. Third, there were heretics, especially Quakers and Anabaptists. Fourth, a notable increase in swearing and a spreading disposition to sleep at sermons (these two phenomena seemed basically connected). Fifth, the Sabbath was wantonly violated. Sixth, family government had decayed, and fathers no longer kept their sons and daughters from prowling at night. Seventh, instead of people being knit together as one man in mutual love, they were full of contention, so that lawsuits were on the increase and lawyers were thriving. Under the eighth head, the synod described the sins of sex and alcohol, thus producing some of the juiciest prose of the period: militia days had become orgies, taverns were crowded, women threw temptation in the way of befuddled men by wearing false locks and displaying naked necks and arms "or, which is more abominable, naked Breasts"; there were "mixed Dancings," along with light behavior and

"Company-keeping" with vain persons, wherefore the bastardy rate was rising. In 1672, there was actually an attempt to supply Boston with a brothel (it was suppressed, but the synod was bearish about the future). Ninth, New Englanders were betraying a marked disposition to tell lies, especially when selling anything. In the tenth place, the business morality of even the most righteous left everything to be desired: the wealthy speculated in land and raised prices excessively; "Day-Labourers and Mechanicks are unreasonable in their demands." In the eleventh place, the people showed no disposition to reform, and in the twelfth, they seemed utterly destitute of civic spirit.

"The things here insisted on," said the synod, "have been oftentimes mentioned and inculcated by those whom the Lord hath set as Watchmen to the house of Israel." Indeed they had been, and thereafter they continued to be even more inculcated. At the end of the century, the synod's report was serving as a kind of handbook for preachers; they would take some verse of Isaiah or Jeremiah,[13] set up the doctrine that God avenges the iniquities of a chosen people, and then run down the twelve heads, merely bringing the list up to date by inserting the new and still more depraved practices an ingenious people kept on devising. I suppose that in the whole literature of the world, including the satirists of imperial Rome,[14] there is hardly such another uninhibited and unrelenting documentation of a people's descent into corruption.

I have elsewhere endeavored to argue that, while the social or economic historian may read this literature for its contents—and so construct from the expanding catalogue of denunciations a record of social progress—the cultural anthropologist will look slightly askance at these jeremiads; he will exercise a methodological caution about taking them at face value. If you read them all through, the total effect, curiously enough, is not at all depressing; you come to the paradoxical realization that they do not bespeak a despairing frame of mind. There is something of a ritualistic incantation about them; whatever they may signify in the realm of theology, in that of psychology they are purgations of soul; they do not discourage but actually encourage the community to persist in its heinous conduct. The exhortation to a reformation which never materializes serves as a token payment upon the obligation, and so liberates the debtors. Changes there had to be; adaptations to environment, expansion of the frontier, mansions constructed, commercial adventures undertaken. These activities were not specifically nominated in the bond[15] Winthrop had framed. They were thrust upon the society by American experience; because they were not only works of necessity but of excitement, they proved irresistible—whether making money, haunting taverns, or committing fornication. Land speculation meant not only wealth but dispersion of the people, and what was to stop the march of settlement? The covenant doctrine preached on the *Arbella* had been formulated in England, where land was not to be had for the taking; its adherents had been utterly oblivious of what the fact of a frontier would do for an imported order, let alone for a European mentality. Hence I suggest that under the guise of this mounting wail of sinfulness, this incessant and never successful cry for repentance, the Puritans launched themselves upon the process of Americanization.

However, there are still more pertinent or more analytical things to be said of this body of expression. If you compare it with the great productions of the founders, you will be struck by the fact that the second and third generations had become oriented toward the social, and only the social, problem; herein they were deeply and profoundly different from their fathers. The finest creations of the founders—the disquisitions of Hooker, Shepard,[16] and Cotton—were written in Europe, or else, if actually penned in the colonies, proceeded from a thoroughly European mentality, upon which the American scene made no impression whatsoever. The most striking example of this imperviousness is the poetry of Anne Bradstreet[17]: she came to Massachusetts at the age of eighteen, already two years married to Simon Bradstreet; there, she says, "I found a new world and new manners, at which my heart rose" in rebellion, but soon convincing herself that it was the way of God, she submitted and joined the church. She bore Simon eight children, and loved him sincerely, as her most Channing poem, addressed to him[18], reveals:

> If ever two were one, then surely we;
> If man were loved by wife, then thee.

After the house burned, she wrote a lament about how her pleasant things in ashes lay and how no more the merriment of guests would sound in the hall; but there is nothing in the poem to suggest that the house stood in North Andover or that the things so tragically consumed were doubly precious because they had been transported across the ocean and were utterly irreplaceable in the wilderness[19]. In between rearing children and keeping house she wrote her poetry; her brother-in-law carried the manuscript to London, and there published it in 1650 under the ambitious title, *The Tenth Muse Lately Sprung Up in America*. But the title is the only thing about the volume which shows any sense of America, and that little merely in order to prove that the plantations had something in the way of European wit and learning, that they had not receded into barbarism. Anne's flowers are English flowers, the birds, English birds, and the landscape is Lincolnshire. So also with the productions of immigrant scholarship; such a learned and acute work as Hooker's *Survey of the Summe of Church Discipline*, which is specifically about the regime set up in America, is written entirely within the logical patterns, and out of the religious experience, of Europe; it makes no concession to new and peculiar circumstances.

The titles alone of productions in the next generation show how concentrated have become emotion and attention upon the interest of New England, and none is more revealing than Samuel Danforth's conception of an errand into the wilderness. Instead of being able to compose abstract treatises like those of Hooker upon the soul's preparation, humiliation, or exultation, or such a collection of wisdom and theology as John Cotton's *The Way of Life* or Shepayd's *The Sound Believer*, these later saints must, over and over again, dwell upon the specific sins of New England, and the more they denounce, the more they must narrow their focus to the provincial problem. If they write upon anything else, it must be about the halfway covenant[20] and its manifold consequences—a development enacted wholly in this country—or else upon their wars with the Indians. Their range is sadly constricted, but every effort, no matter how brief, is addressed to the persistent question: what is the meaning of this society in the wilderness? If it does not mean what Winthrop said it must mean, what under Heaven is it? Who, they are forever asking themselves, who are we?—and, sometimes they are on the verge of saying, who the Devil are we, anyway?

This brings us back to the fundamental ambiguity concealed in the word "errand," that *double entente* of which I am certain Danforth was aware when he published the words that give point to the exhibition. While it was true that in 1630, the covenant, philosophy of a special and peculiar bond[21] lifted the migration out of the ordinary realm of nature, provided it with a definite mission which might in the secondary sense be called its errand, there was always present in Puritan thinking the suspicion that God's saints are at best inferiors, dispatched by their Superior upon particular assignments. Anyone who has run errands for other people, particularly for people of great importance with many things on their minds, such as army commanders, knows how real is the peril that, by the time he returns with the report of a message delivered or a bridge blown up, the Superior may be interested in something else; the situation at headquarters may be entirely changed, and the gallant errand boy, or the husband who desperately remembered to buy the ribbon, may be told that he is too late. This tragic pattern appears again and again in modern warfare; an agent is dropped by parachute and, after immense hardships, comes back to find that, in the shifting tactical or strategic situations, his contribution is no longer of value. If he gets home in time and his service proves useful, he receives a medal; otherwise, no matter what prodigies he has performed, he may not even be thanked. He has been sent, as the devastating phrase has it, upon a fool's errand, than which there can be a no more shattering blow to self-esteem.

The Great Migration of 1630 felt insured against such treatment from on high by the covenant; nevertheless, the God of the covenant always remained an unpredictable Jehovah, a *Deus Absconditus*. When God promises to abide by stated terms, His word, of course, is to be trusted; but then, what is man that he dare accuse Omnipotence of tergiversation? But if any such apprehension was in Winthrop's mind as he spoke on the *Arbella*, or in the minds of other apologists for the enterprise, they kept it far back and allowed it no utterance. They could stifle the thought, not only because Winthrop and his colleagues believed fully in the covenant, but because they could see in the pattern of history that their errand was not a mere, scouting expedition. It was an essential maneuver in the drama of Christendom. The Bay Company was not a battered remnant of suffering Separatists thrown up on a rocky shore; it was an organized task force of Christians, executing a flank attack on the corruptions of Christendom. These Puritans did not flee to America; they went in order to work out that complete reformation which was not yet accomplished in England and Europe, but which would quickly be accomplished if only the saints back there had a working model to guide them. It is impossible to say that any who sailed from Southampton really expected to lay his bones in the new world; were it to come about—as all in their heart of hearts anticipated—that the forces of righteousness should prevail against Laud[22] and Wentworth, that England after all should turn toward reformation, where else would the distracted country look for leadership except to those who in New England had perfected the ideal polity and who would know how to administer it? This was the large unspoken assumption in the errand of 1630; if the conscious intention were realized, not only would a federated Jehovah bless the new land, but He would bring back these temporary colonials to govern England.

　　… In this respect, therefore, we may say that the migration was running an errand in the earlier and more primitive sense of the word—performing a job not so much for Jehovah as for history, which was the wisdom of Jehovah expressed through time. Winthrop was aware of this aspect of the mission—fully conscious of it. "For wee must Consider that wee shall be as a Citty upon a Hill, the eies [eyes] of all people are upon us." More was at stake than just one little colony. If we deal falsely with God, not only will He descend upon us in wrath, but even more terribly, He will make us "a story and a by-word through the word, wee shall open the mouthes of enemies to speake evill of the wayes of god and all professours for Gods sake." No less than John Milton[23] was New England to justify God's ways to man, though not, like him, in the agony and confusion of defeat but in the confidence of approaching triumph. This errand was being run for the sake of Reformed Christianity; and while the first aim was indeed to realize in America the due form of government, both civil and ecclesiastical; the aim behind that aim was to vindicate the most rigorous ideal of the Reformation, so that ultimately all Europe would imitate New England. If we succeed, Winthrop told his audience, men will say of later plantations, "the Lord make it like that of New England." There was an elementary prudence to be observed: Winthrop said that the prayer would arise from subsequent plantations, yet what was England itself but one of God's plantations? In America, he promised, we shall see, or may see, more of God's wisdom, power, and truth "then formerly wee have beene acquainted with." The situation was such that, for the moment, the model had no chance to be exhibited in England; Puritans could talk about it, theorize upon it, but they couldn't display it, could not prove that it would actually work. But if they had it set up in America—in a bare land, devoid of already established (and corrupt) institutions, empty of bishops and courtiers, where they could start *de novo*, and the eyes of the world were upon it—and if then it performed just as the saints had predicted of it, the Calvinist international would know exactly how to go about completing the already begun but temporarily stalled revolution in Europe.

When we look upon the enterprise from this point of view, the psychology of the second and third generations becomes more comprehensible. We realize that the migration was not sent upon its errand in order to found the United States of America, nor even the New England conscience. Actually, it would not perform its errand even when the colonists did erect a due form of government in church and state; what was further required in order for this mission to be a success was that the eyes of the world be kept fixed upon it in rapt attention. If the rest of the world, or at least of Protestantism, looked elsewhere, or turned to another model, or simply got distracted and forgot about New England, if the new land was left with a polity nobody in the great world of Europe wanted—then every success in fulfilling the terms of the covenant would become a diabolical measure of failure. If the due form of government were not everywhere to be saluted, what would New England have upon its hands? How give it a name, this victory nobody could utilize? How provide an identity for something conceived under misapprehensions? How could a universal which turned out to be nothing but a provincial particular be called anything but a blunder or an abortion?

If an actor, playing the leading role in the greatest dramatic spectacle of the century, were to attire himself and put on his make-up, rehearse his lines, take a deep breath, and stride onto the stage, only to find the theater dark and empty, no spotlight working, and himself entirely alone, he would feel as did New England around 1650 or 1660. For in the 1640's during the Civil Wars,[24] the colonies, so the speak, lost their audience. First of all, there proved to be, deep in the Puritan movement, an irreconcilable split between the Presbyterian and Independent wings, wherefore no one system could be imposed upon England, and so the New England model was unserviceable. Secondly—most horrible to relate—the Independents, who the in polity were carrying New England's banner and were supposed, in the schedule of history, to lead England into imitation of the colonial order, betrayed the sacred cause by yielding to the heresy of toleration. They actually welcomed Roger Williams[25], whom the leaders of the model had kicked out of Massachusetts so that his nonsense about liberty of conscience would not spoil the administrations of charity.

In other words, New England did not lie, did not falter; it made good everything Winthrop demanded—wonderfully good—and then found that its lesson was rejected by those choice spirits for whom the exertion had been made. By casting out Williams, Anne Hutchinson, and the Antinomians, along with an assortment of Gortonists and Anabaptists, into that cesspool then becoming known as Rhode Island, Winthrop, Dudlley,[26] and the clerical leaders showed Oliver Cromwell[27] how he should go about governing England. Instead, he developed the utterly, absurd theory, that so long as a man made a good soldier in the New Model Army,[28] it did not matter whether he was a Calvinist, an Antinomian, an Arminian,[29] an Anabaptist or even—horror of horrors—a Socinian! Year after year, as the circus tours this country, crowds howl with laughter, no matter how many times they have seen the stunt at the bustle that walks by itself, the clown comes out dressed in a large skirt with a bustle behind, he turns sharply to the left, and the bustle continues blindly and obstinately straight ahead, on the original course. It is funny in a circus, but not in history. There is nothing but tragedy in the realization that one was in the main path of events, and now is sidetracked and disregarded. One is always able of course, to stand firm on his first resolution, and to condemn the clown of history for taking the wrong turning; yet this is a desolating sort of stoicism, because it always carries with it the recognition that history will never come back to the predicted path, and that with one's own demise, righteousness must die out of the world.

The most humiliating element in the experience was the way the English brethren turned upon the colonials for precisely their greatest achievement. It must have seemed, for those who came with Winthrop in 1630 and who remembered the clarity and brilliance with which he set forth the conditions of their errand, that the world was turned upside down and inside out when, in June 1645, thirteen leading Independent divines—such men as Goodwin, Owen, Nye, Burroughs[30], formerly friends and allies of Hooker and Davenport, men who might easily have come to New England and helped extirpate heretics—wrote the General Court that the colony's law banishing Anabaptists was an embarrassment to the Independent cause in England. Opponents were declaring, said these worthies, "that persons of our way, principall and spirit cannot beare with Dissentors from them, but Doe correct, fine, imprison and banish them wherever they have power soe to Doe." There were indeed people in England who admired the severities of Massachusetts, but we assure you, said the Independents, these "are utterly your enemyes and Doe seeke your extirpation from the face of the earth: those who now in power are your friends are quite otherwise minded, and doe profess they are much offended with your proceedings." Thus early commenced that chronic weakness in the foreign policy of Americans, an inability to recognize who in truth constitute their best friends abroad.

We have lately accustomed ourselves to the fact that there does exist a mentality, which will take advantage of the liberties allowed by society in order to conspire for the ultimate suppression of those same privileges.

The government of Charles I and Archbishop Laud had not, where that danger was concerned, been liberal, but it had been conspicuously inefficient; hence, it did not liquidate the Puritans (although it made half-hearted Efforts), nor did it herd them into prison camps. Instead, it generously, even lavishly, gave a group of them a charter to Massachusetts Bay, and obligingly left out the standard clause requiring that the document remain in London, that the grantees keep their office within reach of Whitehall. Winthrop's revolutionaries availed themselves of this liberty to get the charter overseas, and thus to set up a regime dedicated to the worship of God in the manner they desired—which meant allowing nobody else to worship any other way, especially adherents of Laud and King Charles. All this was perfectly logical and consistent. But what happened to the thought processes of their fellows in England made no sense whatsoever. Out of the New Model Army came the fantastic notion that a party struggling for power should proclaim that, once it captured the state, it would recognize the right of dissenters to disagree and to have their own worship, to hold their own opinions. Oliver Cromwell was so far gone in this idiocy as to become a dictator, in order to impose toleration by force! Amid this shambles, the errand of New England collapsed. There was nobody left at headquarters to whom reports could be sent.

Many a man has done a brave deed, been hailed as a public hero, had honors and ticker tape heaped upon him—and then had to live, day after day, in the ordinary routine, eating breakfast and brushing his teeth, in what seems protracted anticlimax. A couple may win their way to each other across insuperable obstacles, elope in a blaze of passion and glory—and then have to learn that life is a matter of buying the groceries and getting the laundry done. This sense of the meaning having gone out of life, that all adventures are over, that no great days and no heroism lie ahead, is particularly galling when it falls upon a son whose father once was the public hero or the great lover. He has to put up with the daily routine without ever having known at first hand the thrill of danger or the ecstasy of passion. True, he has his own hardships—clearing rocky pastures, hauling in the cod during a storm, fighting Indians in a swamp—but what are these compared with the magnificence of leading an exodus of saints to found a city on a hill, for the eyes of all the world to behold? He might wage a stout fight against the Indians, and one out of ten of his fellows might perish in the struggle, but the world was no longer interested. He would be reduced to writing accounts of himself and scheming to get a publisher in London, in a desperate effort to tell a heedless world, "Look, I exist!"

His greatest difficulty would be not the stones, storms, and Indians, but the problem of his identity. In something of this sort, I should like to suggest, consists the anxiety and torment that inform the productions of the late seventeenth and early eighteenth centuries—and should I say, some there after? It appears most clearly in *Magnalia Christ: Americana*, the work of that soul most tortured by the problem, Cotton Mather: "I write the Wonders of the Christian Religion, flying from the Depravations of Europe, to the American Strand." Thus he proudly begins, and at once trips over the acknowledgement that the founders had not simply fled from depraved Europe but had intended to redeem it. And so the book is full of lamentations over the declension of the children, who appear, page after page, in contrast to their mighty progenitors, about as profligate a lot as ever squandered a great inheritance.

And yet, the *Magnalia* is not an abject book; neither are the election sermons abject, nor is the inventory of sins offered by the synod of 1679. There is a bewilderment, confusion, chagrin, but there is no surrender. A task has been assigned upon which the populace are in fact intensely engaged. But they are not sure any more for just whom they are working; they know they are moving, but they do not know where they're going. They seem still to be on an errand, but if they are no longer inferiors sent by the superior forces of the Reformation, to whom they should report, then their errand must be, wholly of the second sort, something with a purpose and an intention sufficient unto itself. If so, what is it? If it be not the due form of government, civil and ecclesiastical, that they brought into being, how otherwise can it be described?

The literature of self-condemnation must be read for meanings far below the surface, for meanings of which, we may be so rash as to surmise, the authors were not fully conscious, but by which they were troubled and goaded. They looked in vain to history, for an explanation of themselves; more and more it appeared that the meaning was not to be found in theology, even with the help of the covenantal dialectic. Thereupon, these citizens found that they had no other place to search but within themselves—even though, at first sight, that repository appeared to be nothing but a sink of iniquity. Their errand having failed in the first sense of the term, they were left with the second, and required to fill it with meaning by themselves and out of themselves. Having failed to rivet the eyes of the world upon their city on the hill, they were left alone with America.

〔注释〕

1. Samuel Danforth：塞谬尔·丹佛斯（1626-1674），新英格兰牧师。

2. the second generation：指第二代北美移民。

3. Wigglesworth：威格尔斯沃思（Michael Wigglesworth, 1631-1705），北美诗人，以其作品《末日》（*The Day of Doom*, 1662）而著称。

4. Thomas Hooker：托马斯·胡克尔（1586-1647），清教神学家，

观点比较温和。

5. John Cotton：约翰・科顿（1585-1652），新英格兰清教领袖。下文中 Nathaniel Ward：沃德（1568-1652），清教神学家。

6. 引自布雷福德所著《普利茅斯开发史》第九章。

7. The great hymn：指下文的引文。

8. Oscar Handlin：评论家。

9. 引自《基督教博爱的典范》。

10. Stoughton：斯托顿（William Stoughton），北美神学家。

11. King Philip's War：菲利普王战争（1675-1676），地区印第安人与英国殖民者之间最激烈的战争，北美殖民史上代价最高的战争之一。菲利普王为新英格兰地区印第安人部落联盟的首领，1676 年他去世后，印第安人对白人移民的抵抗便以失败而告终。

12. Increase Mather：英克里兹・马瑟（1639-1723），北美神学家。

13. Isaiah or Jeremiad：指《圣经・旧约》中的《以赛亚书》和《耶利米书》。

14. the satirists of imperial Rome：指贺拉斯（Horace, 65-8, BC）、马歇（Martial, 40-104，AD）、波特罗尼斯（Petronius, 66 AD 去世）及朱温纳尔（Jun Juvenal，60-140 AD）。

15. the bond：指《基督教博爱的典范》。

16. Shepard：谢波德（Thomas Shepard，1605-1649），北美神学家。

17. Anne Bradstreet：布拉兹特里特（1612-1672），北美女诗人，著有诗集《美洲最近出现的第十位缪斯》（*The Tenth Muse Lately Sprung Up in America*, 1650）等。

18. 指《写给我的亲爱的丈夫》（"To My Dear and Loving Husband"）。

19. 指《写在我家失火之后》（"Upon the Burning of Our House"）一诗。

20. the halfway covenant：半誓约者，为新英格兰公理教会教徒资格的一种形式，它准许受过洗礼、具有正统信仰的人享受正式成员的一切权利，但不能参加圣餐。

21. the covenant philosophy of a special and peculiar bond：指《基督教博爱的典范》所体现的誓约思想。温思罗普在这次布道中指出，他们移民北美是和上帝约定好的举动，目的在于建立一个纯正的圣经式体制，而不在于积财致富，倘然成功，上帝会奖赏他的选民；倘然改变初衷，而去追求尘世的虚荣，上帝会对毁约者进行报复。

22. Laud：洛德（William Laud），英王查理一世时的坎特伯雷大主教，国王在宗教事务方面的首席顾问。下文中 Wentworth：温特沃思（Thomas Wentworth），是英王查理一世时的爱尔兰总督。二人都是英王的得力助手，后来皆受国会弹劾，被处死。

23. John Milton：约翰·弥尔顿（1608-1674），英国诗人。他在长诗《失乐园》中说："I may assert Eternal Providence，/And justify the way of God to man."

24. the Civil Wars：指英国内战（1642-1649）。

25. Williams：指 Roger Williams。下文中 Anne Hutchinson：安·哈钦森（1591-1643），北美自由派宗教家。Antinomians：信奉反律法论者。Gortonists：戈顿教派，系塞缪尔·戈顿（Samuel Gorton）所创，戈顿后移居罗得岛。Anabaptists:再洗礼派。以上三派皆有反对当时北美政教合一专制政体的倾向。

26. Dudley：托马斯·杜得利（1576-1653），马萨诸塞殖民区总督。

27. Oliver Cromwell：奥利佛·克伦威尔（1599-1658），英国内战时国会军司令，后为共和时期的护国公。

28. the New Model Army：新模范军，1645 年克伦威尔所建的对抗保王派的军队。

29. Arminian：阿明尼乌教派教徒，因荷兰归正会神学家阿明尼乌（Jacobus Arminius，1560-1609）而得名，该派以开明的观点反对加尔文教的命定论，认为上帝的权威和人的自由意志并不矛盾；下文中 Socinian：索西奴斯教派教徒，否认三位一体、耶稣的神性等。

30. Goodwin, Owen, Nye, Burroughs：皆为当时英国清教派教士、神学家。下文中 Davenport：约翰·德温波特（John Davenport, 1597-1670），新英格兰纽黑文殖民区牧师、神学家。

Questions For Discussion:

1. What does the phrase "errand into the wilderness" mean? How did the first generation of settlers view their migration to North America? In what way was the nature of the errand changed in the second and third generations?

2. The synod of 1679 listed twelve kinds of misbehavior of which the Americans were then found guilty. How should these "sins" be viewed in a historical perspective?

3. What effect do you think the sense of mission of the early settlers or "the errand into the wilderness" has had over American literature? Discuss with reference to some major American authors and their works.

For Further Reference:

1. Waller, George M., ed. *Puritanism in Early America*. Boston: D. C. Heath and Company, 1950.

2. Clark, Harry Hayden. *Transitions in American Literary History*. New York: Octagon Books, 1967.

R. W. B. Lewis

〔作者介绍〕

    刘易斯（R. W. B. Lewis，1917-），美国文学评论家，英语及美国文学教授。他研究美国文学与文化多年，著作包括文学批评、传记及编辑的作品。其中有《美国的亚当：19 世纪的天真、悲剧及传统》（*The American Adam: Innocence，Tragedy，and Tradition in the Nineteenth Century*）、《歹徒与天使：当代小说中的代表人物》（*The Picaresque Saint: Representative Figures in Contemporary Fiction*）、《神启的考验：美国文学及人文传统论文集》（*Trials of the Word: Essays in American Literature and the Humanistic Tradition*）及《论哈特·克兰的诗歌》（*The Poetry of Hart Crane: A Critical Study*）、《伊迪丝·沃顿传》（*Edith Wharton: A Biography*）等。此外，刘易斯还与克林斯·布鲁克斯、罗伯特·潘恩·华伦合编《美国文学：创作者和创作过程》（*American Literature: The Makers and the Making*）等书。

The American Adam：Innocence，Tragedy，and Tradition in the Nineteenth Century

〔作品介绍〕

    19 世纪是美国文化及美国文学炼铸成形的时期。文化界谈论的焦点是像克里夫古尔（Hector St. John de Crevecoeur，1735-1813）在其著名的《一个美国农夫的来信》（*Letters from an American Farmer*）中所提到的"新世界的新人"，即美国人。欧洲移民来到北美，看到那一望无垠的长林丰草，重建伊甸乐园的思想便油然而生。这种思想贯穿在 17 世纪初至 18 世纪末近 200 年的文字记载中。然而，美国人清楚地意识到自己正在新世界摆脱历史和传统的羁绊而创造新生活，并将这种意识清楚地表达出来，则是在 19 世纪。在历史、神学和文化领域内，这种意识通过关于亚当的神话讨论得到了简要而透辟的说明。随着时间的推移，"亚当的神话"逐步发展成为"美国的神话"，"亚当的题材"成为美国文坛巨匠的中心题材之一。《美国的亚当：19 世纪的天真、悲剧及传统》这部精辟的文学评论著作，把一个世纪的文化思想史加以总结，并明确指出它对现代美国文化及文学的影响。这部著作 1955 年由芝加哥大学出版社出版。

刘易斯在《序》中说，《美国的亚当》一书谈的是美国神话的起源和发展。19 世纪 20 年代，美国文化界的主要发言人——散文家、评论家、历史学家、小说家、诗人及牧师们——受到新文化正在形成的乐观情绪的感染和激励，对新世界里人的道德、思想及艺术能力进行了全面论述，对美国人的性格及生活作出结论性定义。"美国的神话"——关于亚当的神话——便是在这一时期内逐步形成的。"美国的神话"把世界视为刚刚诞生的天地，人类被赋予第二次机会建立全新的理想的生活。活动在新世界里的新人，从历史的桎梏下解放出来，没有祖先和传统的牵累，孑然一身，自强不息，以本身内在的卓越的能力，迎接着生活的考验和磨炼。人们逐渐认识到，这个新人无疑是堕落前的亚当。他的思想洁白无瑕，举止古朴率真。世界和历史都展现在他的面前。

《美国的亚当》以相当的篇幅叙述了"亚当的题材"在 19 世纪美国文学作品中的运用及发展过程。爱默生（Ralph Waldo Emerson，1803-1882）对新世界充满无限热忱和乐观情绪，是 19 世纪美国乐观派的代表。"这里（指新世界——编者）站立着古朴率真的亚当，以单纯的自我面对着整个世界。"爱默生的这一名言对"美国的神话"的形成起了关键作用。他的好友梭罗（Henry David Thoreau, 1817-1862）只身伫立在华尔腾湖畔面对自然和世界的景状，正是爱默生所形容的亚当形象的体现。他的名著《华尔腾》（Walden）表明，他是他的同代人中对新世界内新人争取自由与新生的潜力了解得最深的人。在小说里描述新亚当在新世界降生和成长的第一位美国作家应推库柏（James Fenimore Cooper，1789-1851）。他的《皮袜子五部曲》（The Leatherstocking Tales）描写北美最初移民的典型——绰号叫"皮袜子"的纳蒂·班波在北美原始森林中的活动，自老与死写起，叙说他走向新生的青春的过程。这正是新世界的开拓者把旧世界的老皮脱落在欧洲，在荒野上开创新生活的新亚当形象的逼真写照。霍桑（Nathaniel Hawthorne，1804-1864）的作品反映出"亚当的题材"在美国文学中的发展。他对"新亚当"在新世界的成长并非抱着盲目的乐观。一方面他认为新大陆必须摧枯拉朽、改弦更张，如他的短篇小说《地球的浩劫》（"Earth's Holocaust"）及其姊妹篇《新亚当和新夏娃》（"The New Adam and Eve"）里所表明的那样；另一方面又对新世界的成长持一定的保留态度：旧世界的陈规陋习和人内心里存在的"恶"，已在新世界生根结蒂，"新亚当"尚须经过一番严峻的考验方能真正成长。《红字》（The Scarlet Letter）、尤其是《玉石雕像》（The Marble Faun），便颇有一种"幸运的堕落"后悲剧性崛起的意味。

麦尔维尔（Herman Melville，1819-1892）的作品，在整体上可被视为"亚当的题材"的最全面、最完整的体现。它所描述的是"天真——失天真——复天真"的人类成长过程。麦尔维尔是一个怀着对新世界的希望和憧憬而开始自己写作生涯的作家。他的前期作品如《泰比》（Typee）、《奥穆》（Omoo）及《莱德勃恩》（Redburn）充满一种激荡人心的乐观精神。美国的发展使麦尔维尔的殷切期望未能实现，他终于感到沉闷、忧郁、不满。而在他的代表作《白鲸》（Moby Dick）里，这种情绪已发展成为幻想破灭后的愤怒了。新亚当因失望而对上帝产生怨恨，似已发疯。面临白鲸所代表的邪恶，天真已不复存在。麦尔维尔经过一生的磨炼和思考，对生活终于采取了平静的肯定和接受态度。这在他的最后一部小说《比利·巴德》（Billy Budd）中表现出来。比利是出现在邪恶的世界里的又一个亚当。他没有祖先，没有历史，是刚站起的野蛮人、还未蒙受撒旦引诱而犯戒的亚当。他是天真的化身。他在绞刑架上徐徐上升的场面令人忆起耶稣在十字架上殉难后升天的景象。小说表明，亚当在堕落后又恢复了失去的天真。惠特曼的《草叶集》（*Leaves of Grass*）堪称为"亚当的歌"，他本人则可被誉为"亚当的歌手"。如果说爱默生和梭罗提出了新世界的轮廓、新亚当的概貌的话，惠特曼则以诗人的笔触，刻画了这个世界的状貌，描绘出新亚当的面目。《草叶集》的世界是一个生机勃勃的世界。它的主人公是一个纯真而富于进取精神的亚当式人物。《草叶集》读来很有《圣经·创世纪》的味道，不过这是叙述新伊甸的"创世纪"，等待亚当的已不是失乐园的经典悲剧，而是亚当以造物主身份出现的喜剧了。诗集的几百首诗可以说是用"亚当的神话"连接成的有机整体。

刘易斯认为，亨利·詹姆斯（Henry James, 1843-1916）一生所描绘的多是亚当式男女主人公。像《美国人》（*The American*）中的纽曼，《苔瑟·密勒》（*Daisy Miller*）中的苔瑟·密勒，《贵妇人的画像》（*Portrait of a Lady*）里的伊莎贝尔，《使节》（*The Ambassadors*）里的兰伯特·斯特雷彻，《鸽翼》（*The Wings of the Dove*）中的米利·西尔，以及《金碗》（*The Golden Bowl*）里的亚当·维渥尔等，都是詹姆斯刻画的代表美国人天真本性的典型形象。詹姆斯的作品在一定程度上表达出美国人亚当式经历的旋律：生就的天真淳朴，面向现实生活，蒙受邪恶的诱骗，经过"不幸的堕落"和痛苦，经受磨炼后获得智慧和成熟。

随着美国现实生活中绝望情绪的增长，反映爱默生式的乐观情绪、具有惠特曼式的引吭高歌特点的文学，逐渐让位于反映绝望情绪的思想模式和文学题材。"美国的亚当"这一形象似乎已失去其对文学创作的原动作用。但是，刘易斯指出，这并非意味着"美国的神话"业已寂灭，并非意味着"新世界的新人"这一题材已从美国文学中消失。事实上，细读美国近几十年来严肃的文学作品便会发现，"美国的亚当"仍以某种形式影响着文学创作，它依然是美国现当代文学中伟大的永恒性作品的创作动力。刘易斯列举出诸如盖茨比、艾萨克·麦卡斯林、《看不见的人》（*Invisible Man*）里的"我"、《麦田里的守望者》（*The Catcher in the Rye*）中的主人公霍尔登以及奥吉·马奇等文学形象，指出"美国的亚当"依然出没在现当代文学中。他认为，这一题材业已经过时间的考验，现在依然、以后也必将继续影响美国文学的创作。

这里选注的是该书几篇重要的章节。

An Excerpt from *The American Adam: Innocence, Tragedy, and Tradition in the Nineteenth Century*

THE AMERICAN ADAM: WHITMAN

I

The fullest portrayal of the new world's representative man as a new, American Adam was given by Walt Whitman in *Leaves of Grass*—in the liberated, innocent, solitary, forward-thrusting personality that animates the whole of that long poem. *Leaves of Grass* tells us what life was made of, what it felt like, what it included, and what it lacked for the individual who began at that moment, so to speak, where the rebirth ritual of *Walden*[1] leaves off. With the past discarded and largely forgotten, with conventions shed and the molting season concluded, what kind of personality would thereupon emerge? What would be the quality of the experience which lay in store for it?

Leaves of Grass was not only an exemplary celebration of novelty in America; it also, and perhaps more importantly, brought to its climax the many-sided discussion by which—over a generation—innocence replaced sinfulness as the first attribute of the American character. Such a replacement was indispensable to Whitman's vision of innocence, though, of course, it did not account for his poetic genius. But the fact was that, of all the inherited notions and practices which the party of Hope[2] studied to reject, by far the most offensive was the Calvinist doctrine of inherited guilt: the imputation to the living individual of the disempowering effects of a sin "originally" committed by the first man in the first hours of the race's history.[3] In New England, where the argument was most intense the traditional view of human character was that of Orthodox Calvinism. And Calvinism, according to the hopeful, not only maintained doctrines of ancient and obscure origin; it even argued in one of them[4] that an ancient and obscure misdemeanor could have a positive effect upon the living man. Traditionally, an inherited taint was postulated coldly in an inherited dogma. It was time to renounce both the taint and the dogma.

The Unitarians—and among them, especially, the Unitarian wit and healer, Dr. Oliver Wendell Holmes[5]—mounted the strongest attack against the doctrine of inherited guilt; and their efforts are to be noted before coming to Whitman. But the Unitarian attitude is not easily disentangled from the general epidemic of confidence in human nature which seemed to be spreading everywhere and which even infected the party of Memory.[6] Indeed, the nostalgic had been watching the new cheerfulness with increasing agitation for a number of years, and thought they could spot it within their own citadels. One of them put the case as follows: "For a considerable time past, it has been unhesitatingly maintained that all mankind are born free from sin and have no moral corruption of nature or propensity of evil—that they are perfectly innocent—that they come into existence in the same state in which Adam was before the fall." One might think, that this polemic was directed against Emerson, who was known to believe that "the entertainment of the proposition of depravity is the last profligacy and profanation," and who smiled his acknowledgment of "each man's innocence"; or perhaps against Thoreau, who found that "the impression made on a wise man is that of universal innocence"; or else against Walt Whitman, the self-styled "chanter of Adamic songs." In fact, its target lay inside its own party; it was a reaction as early as 1828 to the whispers of extremely modified hope which could be heard at Calvinist Yale[7] in the gentle voices of men like Nathaniel Taylor.

It is not easy to imagine that anyone who held, as Taylor did, that "the entire moral depravity of mankind is by nature," that sin is a real and universal thing to be "truly and properly ascribed to *nature* and *not* to circumstances," and that men sin "as soon as they become moral agents...*as soon as they can*," was considered a dangerous radical. But Taylor was regarded as such, and so even was Moses Stuart, professor of theology at relentlessly orthodox Andover.[8] For these men seemed to be retreating some small distance at least from the sound principles of Jonathan Edwards. They seemed to be saying and teaching that, although human beings did observably disobey the commandments of God, they did so on their own, by assertion of their own nature, and not because of a total corruption transmitted at the instant of their conception from a diseased ancestry originally and fatally infected by Adam. They seemed to be embracing the false doctrine which had given rise to all the grievous dissensions of New England Protestantism;[9] they seemed, almost, as bad as the Unitarians.[10]

But there was no stopping the force of the new optimism. Everybody professed a little of it, and everybody complained that his neighbor was professing too much. The march of heresy was punctuated by the blows visited by one combatant upon the head of him next on the left. While Moses Stuart was being chided for yielding an inch on total depravity, he himself was busy replying to the larger yieldings indicated by the sermons and essays of Unitarians Channing and Andrews Norton;[11] and the dismay of Norton at being, as said, so badly misconstrued by Moses Stuart exploded in the rage and fear aroused by Emerson's sublimely confident address to the Harvard Divinity School in 1830. Theodore Parker,[12] in turn, after valiantly reinforcing Channing's hopeful Unitarian gospel, was almost hustled out of the American Unitarian Association, since, as Lowell put it, "from their orthodox kind of dissent, he dissented." The human stock, one might say, tracing the development chronologically, was rising steadily, until it achieved its highest value in the figure of Adam. The status of Jesus declined proportionately, or, at least, it continued to until Emerson, who deified everybody, also deified Jesus once more—thereby, in a characteristic Emersonian paradox, demonstrating the fullness of Jesus' humanity.

The Unitarians, consequently, stood at approximately the middle point in the controversy—between someone like Moses Stuart, on the one hand, and Emerson, on the other. They took their name from their rejection of the Trinity in favor of Unity; but if they could get along without two of three persons of the Trinity, it was because of a prior conviction about the nature of man.

As the Unitarian minister and historian of the movement, George A. Ellis, wrote in 1857, looking back on *A Half-Century of the Unitarian Controversy*, "The doctrine, that God visited the guilt of Adam's personal sin upon the unborn millions of his posterity... was infinitely more objectionable to some liberal Christians than the Trinitarian theory." To the Unitarians, the Calvinist picture of man sounded like this:

A corrupted nature is conveyed by ordinary generation, to all of Adam's posterity, in consequence of his personal sin... If this Orthodox doctrine is not a most shameful trifling with solemnities, as well as with language, it asserts that, by the constitution and appointment of God, the one man Adam had like power to communicate a vitiated nature, like a hereditary disease, not merely to the bodies, but to the souls, of all human beings. This doctrine either contradicts truth and reason, in affirming that any one can be partaker in sin committed before his birth, or it contradicts justice and righteousness, by subjecting us to punishment for the offence of another.

That was the issue, as the Unitarians read it, on the whole correctly, in the contemporary discussion. If all the force and meaning of the old idea of original sin had disappeared from the religious consciousness of the day, it was largely the fault of orthodoxy, the religious element in the party of Memory. For that party, too, argued the case in almost exclusively historical terms, affirming the enslavement of the present by the past as heatedly as the hopeful insisted on its freedom. But the orthodox slowed little awareness of the organic vitality of history, of the way in which the past can enliven the present: the past was simply the place where the issues had been decided, and the decision was all that mattered. The orthodox habit of presenting the end-product of religious belief drained of the spiritual impulses, which had gone into the historical shaping of it, led to a frozen but fragile structure, and one not likely to hold very long against the assaults of the opposition. The energetic hostility of the hopeful to the influence of the past, to the transmission of anything—be it laws, property, or ideas—gathered against the doctrine of transmitted guilt and overwhelmed it.

The stand on the Trinity followed. For if the individual started on his spiritual career with an unsullied conscience, there was no need for expiation; there was no need, as the Unitarians were willing to say quite explicitly, of a propitiation for our sins. The sacrifice of the god[13] satisfied a human yearning for a redemption possible only by a divine action; but the yearning vanished along with the sense of sin. The reason for the divinity of Jesus evaporated; and he became, like Paul,[14] one of the most admirable of the characters in ancient history. The third member of the Trinity was no less rapidly defunctionalized by the hopeful attitude; for in a view which rested upon a freedom from history, upon a lack of communion between one generation and the next, there was no function for a continuing presence in time and history, for a guaranty of the unity of all ages.

The Unitarian *controversy* can be dated, as George Ellis dated it, from about 1805, when the Unitarian theories about man and God were introduced at Harvard by Henry Ware and given some sanction by his position as Hollis Professor of Divinity. Unitarianism itself, of course, went back much farther. Most of its doctrine had been preached by such disciples of Enlightenment and such anti-Edwardseans as Charles Chauncy and Jonathan Mayhew[15] (who died in 1766). The natural goodness of man, the unlikelihood of hell, the benevolence and probable singularity of God were none of them novel propositions. They had made their appearance with the birth of Christianity; and the various heresies about the nature of Jesus, with their shifting corollaries about the nature of man, had been meticulously outlawed one by one in the great church councils of the first Christian centuries. They have recurred since at such regular intervals that their appearance can never be adequately explained in terms of immediate intellectual "background." Perhaps social psychology would be more helpful: what governs the rise and fall of man's evaluation of himself?

...The excitement of life, for the hopeful, lay exactly in its present uniqueness; the burden of doubt and guilt had been disposed of when the whole range of European experience had been repudiated, for the burden was the chief product of that experience. The individual moral course was thus to be plotted—not in terms of readjustment or of identification with any portion of the past, and much less in terms of redemption—but simply in terms of the healthy cultivation of natural, unimpaired faculties.

The American was to be acknowledged in his complete emancipation from the history of mankind. He was to be recognized now for what he was—a new Adam, miraculously free of family and race, untouched by those dismal conditions which prior tragedies and entanglements monotonously prepared for the newborn European. Nathaniel Hawthorne, in his sympathetic and ironic way, had already furnished the working metaphor for this phase in the career of the New World's representative man: in a companion piece to "Earth's Holocaust," a fantasy called "The New Adam and Eve." It was the story of a second pair created after "the Day of Doom has burst upon the globe and swept away the whole race of man"—two pure people "with no knowledge of their predecessors nor of the diseased circumstances that had become encrusted around them." Innocent, cheerful, curious, they start forth on their way to discover, as Adam is made to observe, "what sort of world this is, and why we have been sent hither." Holmes, still insisting on the enabling portion of the past, could not have told them much about their fresh and purified world. But Walt Whitman, in *Leaves of Grass*, was ready to tell them everything.

II

Whitman appears as the Adamic man reborn here in the 19th century [John Burroughs[16] (1896)].

In his old age, Dr. Holmes derived a certain amount of polite amusement from the poetry of Walt Whitman. Whitman, Holmes remarked, "carried the principle of republicanism through the whole world of created objects"; he smuggled into his "hospitable vocabulary words which no English dictionary recognizes as belonging to the language—words which will be looked for in vain outside of his own pages." Holmes found it hard to be sympathetic toward *Leaves of Grass*; it seemed to him windy, diffuse, and humorless; but his perceptions were as lively as ever. In these two observations he points to the important elements in Whitman which are central here: the spirit of equality which animated the surging catalogues of persons and things (on its more earthly level, not unlike Emerson's lists of poets and philosophers, with their equalizing and almost leveling tendency); the groping after novel words to identify novel experiences; the lust for inventiveness which motivated what was for Whitman the great act, the creative act.

Holmes's tone of voice, of course, added that for him Whitman had gone too far; Whitman was too original, too republican, too entire an Adam. Whitman had indeed gone further than Holmes: a crucial and dimensional step further, as Holmes had gone further than Channing or Norton. In an age when the phrase "forward-looking" was a commonplace, individuals rarely nerved themselves to withstand the shock of others looking and moving even further forward than they. Emerson himself, who had gone so far that the liberal Harvard Divinity School forbade his presence there for more than thirty years, shared some of Holmes's feeling about Whitman. When his cordial letter welcoming *Leaves of Grass* in 1855 was published in the *New York Tribune*, Emerson muttered in some dismay that had he intended it for publication, he "should have enlarged the *but* very much—enlarged the *but*." *Leaves of Grass* was pitched in the very highest key of self-reliance, as a friend of its author maintained; but Emerson, who had given that phrase its contemporary resonance, believed that any attitude raised to its highest pitch tended to encroach dangerously on the truth of its opposite.

It would be no less accurate to say that Walt Whitman, instead of going too far forward, had gone too far backward; for he did go back, all the way back, to a primitive Adamic condition, to the beginning of time.

In the poetry of Walt Whitman, the hopes which had until now expressed themselves in terms of progress crystallized all at once in a complete recovery of the primal perfection. In the early poems Whitman accomplished the epochal return by huge and almost unconscious leaps: In later poems he worked his way more painstakingly up the river of history to its source; as, for example, in "Passage to India," where the poet moves back from the recently constructed Suez Canal, back past Christopher Columbus, past Alexander the Great and the most ancient of heroes and peoples, to the very "secret of the earth and sky." In the "beginning," John

Locke[17] once wrote, "all the world was America." Whitman manages to make us feel what it might have been like; and he succeeds at last in presenting the dream of the new Adam—along with his sorrows.

A measure of Whitman's achievement is the special difficulty which that dream had provided for others who tried to recount it. Its character was such that it was more readily described by those who did not wholly share in it. How can absolute novelty be communicated? All the history of the philosophy of language is involved with that question, from *The Cratylus* of Plato[18] to the latest essay on semantics; and one could bring to bear on it the variety of anecdotes about Adam's naming the animals by the disturbingly simple device of calling a toad a toàd.

Hawthorne conveyed the idea of novelty by setting it in an ancient pattern: allowing it thereby exactly to be *recognized*; and reaching a sharpness of meaning also to be found in Tocqueville's[19] running dialectic of democracies and aristocracies. Whitman employed the same tactic when he said of Coleridge that he was "like Adam in Paradise, and just as free from artificiality." This was a more apt description of himself, as he knew:

> I, chanter of Adamic songs,
> Through the new garden the West,
> 　the great cities calling. [20]

It is, in fact, in the poems gathered under the title "Children of Adam" (1860) that we have the most explicit evidence of his ambition to reach behind tradition to find and assert nature untroubled by art, to reestablish the natural unfallen man in the living hour. Unfallen man is, properly enough, unclothed as well; the convention of cover came in with the Fall; and Whitman adds his own unnostalgic sincerity to the Romantic affection for nakedness:

> As Adam, early in the morning,
> Walking forth from the bower refesh'd with sleep,

Behold me where I pass, hear my voice, approach,

Touch me, touch the palm of your hand to my body,

as I pass,

Be not afraid of my body.[21]

For Whitman, as for Holmes and Thoreau, the quickest way of framing his novel outlook was by lowering and secularizing the familiar spiritual phrases: less impudently than Thoreau but more earnestly, and indeed more monotonously, but with the same intention of salvaging the human from the religious vocabulary to which (he felt) it had given rise. Many of Whitman's poetic statements are conversions of religious allusion: the new miracles were acts of the senses (an odd foreshortening, incidentally, of Edwards' Calvinist elaboration of the Lockian psychology); the aroma of the body was "finer than prayer"; his head was "more than churches, bibles and all creeds." "If I worship one thing more than another," Whitman declaimed, in a moment of Adamic narcissism, "it shall be the spread of my own body." These assertions gave a peculiar stress to Whitman's seconding of the hopeful, belief in men like gods: "Divine am I, inside and out; and I make holy whatever I touch." Whitman's poetry is at every moment an act of turbulent incarnation.

But although there is, as there was meant to be, a kind of shock value in such lines, they are not the most authentic index to his pervasive Adamism, because in them the symbols have become too explicit and so fail to work symbolically. Whitman in these instances is stating his position and contemplating it; he is betraying his own principle of indirect statement; he is telling us too much, and the more he tells us, the more we seem to detect the anxious, inflated utterance of a charlatan. We cling to our own integrity and will not be thundered at. We respond far less willingly to Whitman's frontal assaults than we do to his dramatizations; when he is enacting his role rather than insisting on it, we are open to persuasion. And he had been enacting it from the outset of *Leaves of*

Grass.

This is the true nature of his achievement and the source of his claim to be the representative poet of the party of Hope. For the "self" in the very earliest of Whitman's poems is an individual who is always moving forward. To say so is not merely to repeat that Whitman believed in progress; indeed, it is in some sense to deny it. The young Whitman, at least, was not an apostle of progress in its customary meaning of a motion from worse to better to best, an improvement over previous historic, condition, a "rise of man." For Whitman, there was no past or "worse" to progress from; he moved forward because it was the only direction (he makes us think) in which he could move; because there was nothing behind him—or if there were, he had not yet noticed it. There is scarcely a poem of Whitman's before, say, 1867, which does not have the air of being the first poem ever written, the first formulation in language of the nature of persons and of things and of the relations between them; and the urgency of the language suggests that is was formulated in the very nick of time, to give the objects described their first substantial existence.

Nor is there, in *Leaves of Grass*, any complaint about the weight or intrusion of the past; in Whitman's view the past had been so effectively burned away that it had, for every practical purpose, been forgotten altogether. In his own recurring figure, the past was already a corpse; it was on its way out the door to the cemetery; Whitman watched it absentmindedly, and turned at once to the living reality. He did enjoy, as he reminds us, reciting Homer while walking beside the ocean; but this was just because Homer was exempt from tradition and talking at and about the dawn of time. Homer was the poet you found if you went back far enough; and as for the sea, it had (unlike Melville's) no sharks in it—no ancient, lurking, destructible evil powers. Whitman's hope was unspoiled by memory. When he became angry, as he did in *Democratic Vistas* (1871), he was not attacking his generation in the Holgrave[22] manner for continuing to accept the old and the foreign, but for fumbling its extraordinary opportunity, for taking a wrong turn on the bright new highway he had mapped for it. Most of the time he was more interested in the map, and we are more interested in him when he was.

It was then that he caught up and set to music the large contemporary conviction that man had been born anew in the new society, that the race was off to a fresh start in America. It was in *Leaves of Grass* that the optative mood, which had endured for over a quarter of century and had expressed itself so variously and so frequently, seemed to have been transformed at last into the indicative. It was there that the hope that had enlivened spokesmen from Noah Webster[23] in 1825 ("American glory begins at the dawn") to the well named periodical, *Spirit of the Age* in1849 ("The accumulated atmosphere, of ages, containing stale ideas and opinions … will soon be among the things that were")—that all that stored-up abundance of hope found its full poetic realization. *Leaves of Grass* was a climax as well as a beginning, or rather, it was the climax of a long effort to begin.

This was why Emerson, with whatever enlarged "buts" in his mind, made a point of visiting Whitman in New York and Boston; why Thoreau, refusing to be put off "by any brag or egoism in his book," preferred Whitman to Bronson Alcott[24] and why Whitman, to the steady surprise of his countrymen, has been regarded in Europe for almost a century as unquestionably the greatest poet the New World has produced; an estimate which even Henry James would come round to. European readers were not slow to recognize in Whitman an authentic rendering of their own fondest hopes; for if much of his vision had been originally imported from Germany and France, it had plainly lost its portion of nostalgia en route. While European romanticism continued to resent the effect of time, Whitman was announcing that time had only just begun. He was able to think so because of the facts of immediate history in America during the years when he was maturing; when a world was, in some literal way, being created before his eyes. It was this that Whitman had the opportunity to dramatize; and it was this that gave *Leaves of Grass* its special quality of a Yankee Genesis: a new account of the creation of the world—the creation, that is, of a new world; an account this time with a happy ending for Adam its hero; or better yet, with no ending at all; and with this important emendation that now the creature has taken on the role of creator.

It was a twofold achievement, and the second half of it was demanded by the first. We see the sequence, for example, in the development from section 4 to section 5 of "Song of Myself." The first phase was the identification of self; an act which proceeded by distinction and differentiation, separating the self from every element that in a traditional view might be supposed to be part of it; Whitman's identity card had no space on it for the names of his ancestry. The exalted mind which carried with it a conviction of absolute novelty has been described by Whitman's friend, the Canadian psychologist, Dr. R. M. Bucke, who relates it to what he calls Whitman's "cosmic consciousness." "Along with the consciousness of the cosmos [Dr. Bucke wrote], there occurs an intellectual enlightenment which alone would place the individual on a new plane of existence—would make him almost a member of a new species." *Almost a member of a new species*: that could pass as the slogan of each individual in the party of Hope. It was a robust American effort to make real and operative the condition which John Donne[25] once had merely feared:

> Prince, Subject, Father, Son are things forgot,
> For every man alone thinks he has got
> To be a Phoenix, and that then can be
> None of that kind, of which he is, but he.

Whitman achieves the freedom of the new condition by scrupulously peeling off every possible source of, or influence upon, the "Me myself," the "what I am." As in section 4 of "Song of Myself":

> Tripers and askers surround me
>
> People I meet, the effect upon me of my early life, or the
>
>> ward and the city I live in or the nation....
>
> The sickness of one of my folks, or of myself, or the ill
>
>> doing or loss or lack of money, or depressions or exaltations,
>
> Battles, the horror of fratricidal wars, the fever of doubtful
>
>> news, the fitful events,
>
> These come to me days and nights and go from me again,
>
> But they are not the Me myself.
>
> Apart from the pulling and hauling stands what I am;
>
> Stands amused, complacent, compassionating, idle, unitary;
>
> Looks down, is erect; or bends an arm on an impalpable
>
>> certain rest,
>
> Looking with side-curved head curious what will come next,
>
> Both in and out of the game, and watching and wondering
>
>> at it.

There is Emerson's individual, the "infinitely repellent orb." There is also the heroic product of romanticism, exposing behind the mass of what were regarded as inherited or external or imposed and hence superficial and accidental qualities the true indestructible secret core of personality. There is the man who contends that "nothing, not God, is greater to one than one's self."

There, in fact, is the new Adam. If we want a profile of him, we could start with the adjectives Whitman supplies: amused, complacent, compassionating, idle, unitary; especially unitary, and certainly very easily amused; too complacent, we frequently feel, but always compassionate— expressing the old divine compassion for every sparrow that falls, every criminal and prostitute and hopeless invalid, every victim of violence or misfortune. With Whitman's help we could pile up further attributes, and the exhaustive portrait of Adam would be composed of a careful gloss on each one of them: hankering, gross, mystical, nude, turbulent, fleshy, sensual, eating, drinking, and breeding; no sentimentalist, no stander above men and women; no more modest than immodest; wearing his hat as he pleases indoors and out; never skulking or ducking or deprecating; adoring himself and adoring his comrades; afoot with his vision.

> Moving forward then and now and forever,
>
> Gathering and showing more always and with velocity,
>
> infinite and ommigenous. [26]

And announcing himself in language like that. For an actual illustration, we could not find anything better than the stylized daguerreotype of himself which Whitman placed as the Frontispiece of the first edition. We recognize him at once; looking with side-curved head, bending an arm on the certain rest of his hip, evidently amused, complacent, and curious; bearded, rough, probably sensual; with his hat on.

Whitman did resemble this Adamic archetype, according to his friend John Burroughs: "There was a look about him," Burroughs remembered, "hard to describe, and which I have seen in no other face, a gray, brooding, elemental look, like the granite rock, something primitive and Adamic that might have belonged to the first man." The two new adjectives there are "gray" and "brooding" and they belong to the profile, too, both of Whitman and of the character he dramatized. There was bound to be some measure of speculative sadness inherent in the situation. Not all the leaves Whitman uttered were joyous ones; though he wanted them all to be and was never clear why they were not. His ideal image of himself—and it is his best single trope for the new Adam—was that of a live oak he saw growing in Louisiana:

> All alone stood it and the mosses hung down from the
>
> branches,
>
> Without any companion it grew there uttering joyous

> leaves of dark green,
>
> And its lock, rude, unbending, lusty, made me think of
>
> myself.[27]

But at his most honest, he admitted, as he does here, that the condition was somehow unbearable:

> I wondered how it could utter joyous leaves standing alone
>
> there without a friend near, for I knew I could not....
>
> And though the live-oak glistens there in Louisiana solitary
>
> in a wide flat space,
>
> Uttering joyous leaves all its life without a friend a lover
>
> near,
>
> I knew very well I could not.[28]

Adam had his moments of sorrow also. But the emotion had nothing to do with the tragic insight; it did not spring from any perception of a genuine hostility in nature; or lead to the drama of colliding forces. Whitman was wistful, not tragic. We might almost say that he was wistful because he was not tragic. He was innocence personified. It is not difficult to marshal a vast array of references to the ugly, the gory, and the sordid in his verses; brought together in one horrid lump, they appear as the expression of one who was well informed about the shabby side of the world; but though he offered himself as "the poet of wickedness" and claimed to be "he who knew what it was to be evil," every item he introduced as vile turns out, after all, to be merely a particular beauty of a different original coloration: "Evil propels me and reform of evil propels me, I stand indifferent." A sentiment like that can make sense only if the term "evil" has been filtered through a transfiguring moral imagination, changing in essence as it passes.

That sentiment, of course, is not less an expression of poetic than of moral motivation. As a statement of the poetic sensibility, it could have been uttered as easily by Shakespeare or Dante as by Whitman. Many of the very greatest writers suggest, as Whitman does, a peculiar artistic innocence, a preadolescent wonder which permits such a poet to take in and reproject whatever there is, shrinking from none of it. But in Whitman, artistic innocence merged with moral innocence: a preadolescent ignorance of the convulsive undertow of human behavior—something not at all shared by Dànte or Shakespeare. Both modes of innocence are present in the poetry of Walt Whitman，and they are not at any time to be really distinguished. One can talk about this image of moral innocence only in terms of his poetic creation.

"I reject none，accept all，then reproduce all in my own forms." The whole spirit of Whitman is in the line: there is his strategy for overcoming his sadness，and the second large phase of his achievement，following the act of differentiation and self-identification. It is the creative phase，in that sense of creativity which beguiles the artist most perilously into stretching his analogy with God—when he brings a world into being. Every great poet composes a world for us and what James called the "figure in the carpet" is the poet's private chart of that world; but when we speak of the poet's world—of Dostoevski's or Balzac's—we knowingly skip a phrase，since what we mean is Dostoevski's (or Balzac's) selective embodiment of an already existing world. In the case of Whitman，the type of extreme Adamic romantic，the metaphor gains its power from a proximity to the literal，as though Whitman really were engaged in the stupendous task of building a world that had not been there before the first words of his poem.

The task was self-imposed for Whitman's dominant emotion, when it was not unmodified joy，was simple，elemental loneliness; it was a testimony to his success and contributed to his peculiar glow. For if the hero of *Leaves of Grass* radiates a kind of primal innocence in an innocent world，it was not only because he had made that world，it was also because he had begun by making himself. Whitman is an early example，and perhaps the most striking one we have，of the self-made man，with an undeniable grandeur which is the product of his manifest sense of having been responsible for his own being—something far more compelling than the more vulgar version of the rugged individual who claims responsibility only for his own bank account.

And of course he was lonely, incomparably lonely; no anchorite was ever so lonely, since no anchorite was ever so alone. Whitman's image of the evergreen, "solitary in a wide, flat space… without a friend a lover near," introduced what more and more appears to be the central theme of American literature, in, so far as a unique theme may be claimed for it; the theme of loneliness, dramatized in what I shall later describe as the story of the hero in space. The only recourse for a poet like Whitman was to fill the space by erecting a home and populating it with companions and lovers.

Whitman began in an Adamic condition which was only too effectively realized, the isolated individual, standing flush with the empty universe, a primitive moral and intellectual entity. In the behavior of a "noiseless, patient spider," Whitman found a revealing analogy:

> A noiseless, patient spider
> I mark'd, where, on a little promontory, it stood out,
>   isolated,
> Mark'd how, to explore the vacant, vast surrounding,
> It launched forth filament, filament, filament, out of itself,
> Ever unreeling them-ever tirelessly speeding them. [29]

"Out of itself." This is the reverse of the traditionalist attitude that, in Eliot's phrase, "home is where one starts from." Whitman acted on the hopeful conviction that the new Adam started from himself; having created himself, he must next create a home. The given in individual experience was no longer a complex of human, racial, and familial relationships; it was a self in a vacant, vast surrounding. Each simple separate person must forge his own framework anew. This was the bold, enormous venture inevitably confronted by the Adamic personality. He had to become the maker of his own conditions—if he were to have any conditions or any achieved personality at all.

There were, in any case, no conditions to *go back to*—to take upon one's self or to embody. There is in fact almost no indication at all in *Leaves of Grass* of a return or reversion, even of that recovery of childhood detected in *Walden*. Whitman begins after that recovery, as a child, seemingly self-propagated, and he is always going *forth*; one of his pleasantest poems was constructed around that figure.[30] There is only the open road, and Whitman moves forward from the start of it. Homecoming is for the exile, the prodigal son, Adams after the expulsion, not for the new unfallen Adam in the western garden. Not even in "Passage to India" is there a note of exile, because there is no sense of sin ("Let others weep for sin"). Whitman was entirely remote from the view of man as an orphan which motivated many of the stories of Hawthorne and Melville and which underlay the characteristic adventure they narrated of the search for a father. Hawthorne, an orphan himself and the author of a book about England called *Our Old Home*, sometimes sent his heroes to Europe to look for their families; Melville dispatched his heroes to the bottom of the sea on the same mission. This was the old way of posing the problem: the way of mastering life by the recovery of home, though it might require descent to the land of the dead; but Whitman knew the secret of his paternity.

Whitman was creating a world, even though he often sounds as though he were saluting a world that had been lying in wait for him: "Salut au monde." In one sense, he is doing just that, welcoming it, acknowledging it, reveling in its splendor and variety. His typical condition is one of acceptance and absorption; the word which almost everyone who knew him applied to his distinguishing capacity was "absorptive." He absorbed life for years; and when he contained enough, he let it go out from him again. "I... accept all, then reproduce all in my own forms." He takes unflagging delight in the reproductions; "Me pleased," he says in "Our Old Feuillage"; it is the "what I am." But the pleasure of seeing becomes actual only in the process of naming. It is hard to recall any particular of life and work, of men and women and animals and plants and things, of body and mind, that Whitman has not somewhere named in caressing detail. And the process of naming is for Whitman nothing less than the process of creation. This new Adam is both maker and namer; his innocent pleasure, untouched by humility, is colored by the pride of one who looks on his work and finds it good. The things that are named seem to spring into being at the sound of the word. It was through the poetic act that Whitman articulated the dominant metaphysical illusion of his day and became the creator of his own world.

We have become familiar, a century after the first edition of *Leaves of Grass*, with the notion of the poet as the magician who "orders reality" by his use of language. That notion derived originally from the epochal change—wrought chiefly by Kant and Hegel[31]—in the relation between human mind and the external world; a change whereby the mind "thought order into" the sensuous mass outside it instead of detecting an order externally existing. Whitman (who read Hegel and who wrote a singularly flatulent poetic reflection after doing so) adapted that principle to artistic creativity with a vigor and enthusiasm unknown before James Joyce[32] and his associates in the twentieth century. What is implicit in every line of Whitman is the belief that the poet *projects* a world of order and meaning and identity into either a chaos or a sheer vacuum; he does not *discover* it. The poet may salute the chaos; but he creates the world.

Such a conviction contributed greatly to Whitman's ever enlarging idea of the poet as the vicar of God, as the son of God—as God himself. Those were not new labels for the artist, but they had been given fresh currency in Whitman's generation; and Whitman held to all of them more ingenuously than any other poet who ever lived. He supervised the departure of "the priests" and the arrival of the new vicar, "the divine literatus"; he erected what he called his novel "trinitas" on the base of "the true son of God, the poet"; he offered himself as a cheerful, divine scapegoat and stage-managed "my own crucifixion." And to the extent that he fulfilled his own demands for the poet—as laid down in the Preface to *Leaves of Grass* and in *Democratic Vistas*—Whitman became God, the Creator.

This was the mystical side of him, the side which announced itself in the fifth section of "Song of Myself," and which led to the mystical vision of a newly created totality. The vision emerges from those lyrical sweeps through the universe in the later sections of the poem: the sections in which Whitman populated and gave richness and shape to the universe by the gift of a million names. We can round out our picture of Whitman as Adam—both Adam as innocent and Adam as namer—if we distinguish his own brand of mysticism from the traditional variety. Traditional mysticism proceeds by denial and negation and culminates in the imagery of deserts and silence, where the voice and the being of God are the whole of reality. Whitman's mysticism proceeds by expansive affirmation and culminates in plenitude and huge volumes of noise. Traditional mysticism is the surrender of the ego to its creator, in an eventual escape from the limits of names; Whitman's is the expansion of the ego in the act of creation itself, naming every conceivable object as it comes from the womb.

THE FORTUNATE FALL: HENRY JAMES, SR.[33]

James was perhaps the most energetically hopeful man of his generation, with a hope, so to speak, exploding out of the tensions lying behind it. He was possessed of a transcendent cheerfulness derived from the experience and the full knowledge of tragedy. His cheerfulness was consequently less fragile and more solid than the buoyant innocence of the party of Hope. Along with a very few others, James suggested how the drama of Adam should proceed, or how, to put it differently, the young culture should finally achieve its maturity. James was convinced that the story was not yet finished.

This is to say—and it was the elder James's conscious intention—that he began his account of the representative American spiritual adventure where the professedly hopeful left off. His observations about some of them indicate as much: he referred to Emerson as his fair unfallen friend, and he decided later about Thoreau that he was "literally the most childlike, unconscious and unblushing egotist it has ever been my fortune to encounter in the ranks of manhood." The phrases build into a partial statement of James's program for Adam: for in order to enter the ranks of manhood, the individual (however fair) had to *fall*, had to pass beyond childhood in an encounter with "Evil," had to mature by virtue of the destruction of his own egotism. James's entire intellectual effort—the whole burden of what his wife and his children affectionately and vaguely called "father's ideas"—may be described as an immense salvaging of the American Adam. For unless he were salvaged, James felt, he would never be saved; and, unlike Whitman or Thoreau, James did believe that the moral problem was salvation rather than self-development.

James looked forward with no less assurance than Emerson and Whitman to a human achievement of perfection; but the signal difference between James and his unfallen friends is indicated by his statement (in the letter about Whitman) that the perfection he had in mind was one "to which manifestly no one is born, but only *re*-born." His italics emphasized the same conviction in the sentence which followed: "We come to such states not by learning, only by *unlearning*." What had to die, what had to be unlearned, was the proposition, writ so extensively in *Leaves of Grass*, that the individual was the source of his own being. "He lived and breathed," William was to say about his father, "as one who knew he had not made himself." This was the knowledge which led him to his major principles: principles which, like the impulse behind them, were less intellectual concepts than (in William's words) "instinct and attitude, something realized at a stroke and felt like a fire in the breast." Such knowledge, moreover, was an accomplishment, gained through a kind of suffering so comprehensive that it might accurately be called a kind of death. Of his many narrations of this liberating tragedy, perhaps the most succinct occurs in *Society the Redeemed Form of Man* (1879):

> The only hindrance to men's believing in God as a creator is their inability to believe in *themselves* as created. Self-consciousness, the sentiment of personality, the feeling I have of life in myself, absolute and underived from any other save in a natural way, is so subtly and powerfully atheistic, that, no matter how loyally I may be taught to insist upon creation as a mere traditional or legendary fact, I never feel inclined personally to believe in it, save as the fruit of some profound intellectual humiliation or hopeless inward vexation of spirit. My inward afflatus from this cause is so great, I am conscious of such super abounding personal life, that I am satisfied, for my own part at least, that my sense of selfhood must in some subtle exquisite way find itself wounded to death—find itself *become death*, in fact, *the only death I am capable of believing in*—before any genuine resuscitation is at all practicable for me.

This was the view of human development that motivated James's repeated observation that "the first and highest service which Eve renders Adam is to throw him out of Paradise." James regarded the contemporary ideal of man as Adam in Paradise as adolescent rubbish; "every man who has reached even his intellectual teens," he wrote, "begins to suspect that life is no farce… that it flowers and fructifies on the contrary out of the profoundest tragic depths"; and he trained his most trenchant rhetoric on the Adamic figure. The heroic and winsome hero of the idealists appeared, under the eye of the elder James, as "a dull, somnolent, unconscious clod," as an "innocent earthling," as "imbecile, prosaic, unadventurous." James clung to the older ending of the story of creation, just as he continued to prefer the old "virile" pessimistic spirit of religion to the "cuddling-up-to-God" of the "feeble Unitarian sentimentality." In the Book of Genesis he found an allegory of every individual's spiritual adventure, of everyone, that is, who had the energy to grow up. Growing up required the individuating crisis which in Genesis is dramatized as the fall of Adam: the fatal, necessary quickening within the unconscious chunk of innocence of the awareness of self.

The capital sin in the Jamesian universe was just this exclusive *self*-consciousness, egotism, "proprium," or "selfhood," as he variously labeled it. This was about as far as many personalities had the power to travel; this was, for example, the limit of Thoreau's accomplishment; it was about as far as the American culture had come; but James watched expectantly for that "transformation-scene in human affair" (in his son Henry's phrase) which would affect the drama of the culture and which might be observed in the private history of certain individuals. That transformation-scene, the second and greater crisis in experience, led from total self-distrust to a rebirth of the personality as a *social* being: one might say, to rebirth as a citizen of the holy and glorious city of James. The new form of man, "the redeemed form of man," was society; only the sin made possible the rebirth; and, for all its tragedy, it was a necessary sin, and a subject for rejoicing.

James himself had undergone the entire complex experience, from an early self-assertiveness, through the fearful evening in England in the spring of 1844 when he was smitten by "a perfectly insane and abject fear" which reduced him "from a state of firm, vigorous, joyful manhood to one of almost helpless infancy," to a far more vigorous new life dedicated to preaching his own brand of socialism. It was in the light of his own recollections that James could announce the ineluctable requirement of a tragic *fall* in such robustly hopeful accents.

He examined the alternative hypothesis, which seemed to motivate the expressions and the conduct of the Adamists. Supposing, James asked, that their dream was a true dream and that men, in America or anywhere else were truly sinless, truly exempt from the temptation and the fall. The condition they would enjoy would in that case, however pleasant, be aimless and "horticultural"; there would be no rise and no ambition to rise to the nobler condition of genuine manhood. The inadequacy of Adamism was eloquently set forth:

> In Adam, then, formed from the dust and placed in Eden, we find man's natural evolution distinctly symbolized—his purely instinctual and passional condition—as winning and innocent as infancy no doubt, but also, happily, quite as evanescent. It is his purely genetic and *premoral* state, a state of blissful infantile delight unperturbed as yet by those fierce storms of the intellect which are soon to envelope and sweep it away, but also unvisited by a single glimpse of that Divine and halcyon calm of the heart in which these hideous storms will finally rock themselves to sleep. Nothing can indeed be more remote (except in pure imagery) from distinctively *human* attributes, or from the spontaneous life of man, than this sleek and comely Adamic condition, provided it should turn out an abiding one; because man in that case would prove a mere dimpled nursling of the skies, without ever rising into the slightest Divine communion or fellowship, without ever realising a truly Divine manhood and dignity.

That paragraph (it is from *Christianity the Logic of Creation* [1857]) condenses one of the most telling critiques ever formulated of an enduring phase of the American cultural temperament. And its tone is no less revealing that its content. There was nothing in James of that inverted pride in evil that has become almost the national counterpart of the continuing claim of innocence. Someone remarked to a friend of his that James puzzled him because "if he has a preference it is for evil"; but James's response to the conventional embrace of despair was summed up in a comment on Carlyle (Carlyle who, according to James's correspondent, pronounced "his usual putrid theory of the universe" in a series of remarks "interpolated with convulsive laughter"): "Never was anything more false than this worship of sorrow by Carlyle; he has picked it up out of past history and spouts it for mere display... it is the merest babble." James escaped the sterilities of both sides—the arrested development of infantile innocence and the premature old age of a paralyzing absorption with sin—by seeing moral problem in unvarying dramatic terms: as a process, a story, with several grand climacterics.

It was this sense of a plot in experience that gave manifest sincerity to his account of the Fall—of Adam's fall and the fall of "every son of Adam"—as essentially fortunate. "Any one with half an eye," he wrote, "can see... that Adam's fall, as it is called, was not that stupid lapse from the divine favor which it has vulgarly been reputed to have been, but an actual rise to the normal human level." He went on, "We certainly may, if we like, continue to vote this manly act of Adam disastrous... but to the deathless immortal part of man... it is anything but disastrous. It is an every way upward step indeed, pregnant with beatific consequences.... And accordingly every son of Adam... welcomes this puny, silly death, which inwardly is his proper consciousness, as his inevitable and unconscious resurrection to life." James's picture of the falling and the fallen was lit up at each instant by the radiance of the *vita nuova*[34] which the "silly death" alone made possible.

But as we read these passages, we recover some of our original regret over the perverseness of his language. It was an extraordinarily private language; in his manipulation of it, James shows us the Emersonian man, spontaneously marking great truths with no regard whatever for their diversified historical formulations. His friend Garth Wilkinson indicated an important difference between himself and James when he acknowledged his own insistent attention to history. And we are not helped by James's habit of assaulting past doctrines in terms that suggest he must be thinking about their opposites. Even his son William, not the most dependable guide to intellectual history, had to comment upon his father's remarkable ignorance of the past, an ignorance which partly prevented him from communicating his analysis of the present.

For what James had hit on by the sheer force of his speculation was a variation on a very ancient theme: the theme of the "fortunate fall." In the history of Christian theology, the theme can be traced back almost to the fourth century A.D., and its most enduring formulation came in the medieval hymn which is sung during the Holy Saturday Mass. The hymn is exultant; it is known, indeed, as the "Exultet"; it is the most poetic and the most transcendently hopeful answer that Christianity ever contrived to the old puzzle about the existence of evil in a world created by a benevolent God: "O Felix culpa!" the hymn exclaims: "quae talem et tantum meruit habere redemptorem." ("O happy sin!　to deserve so great a redeemer.") The theological implication is that happiness may be predicated of the sin because, as a consequence of it, the world was enlarged and enlightened through the figure of the Redeemer and the joy of the Atonement. It is the imputation to the human event of the quality of the divine action. And the hymn thus paradoxically rejoices in the enforced departure of Adam from Eden: "O certe necessarium Adae peccatum"—certainly Adam's sin was necessary.

The Christian suggestion teeters on the verge of heresy, and, for all its cheerfulness, it has always made its proponents uneasy. But as a metaphor in the area of human psychology, the notion of the fortunate fall has an immense potential. It points to the necessary transforming shocks and sufferings, the experiments and errors—in short, the experience—through which maturity and identity may be arrived at. This was just the perception needed in a generation that projected as one of its major ideals the image of man as a fair unfallen Adam. The claim of newborn innocence for the individual in America inevitably elicited the response that innocence is inadequate for the full reach of human personality; that life, in James's words, "flowers and fructifies… out of the profoundest tragic depths." The ancient theme of the fortunate fall might have conveyed James's meaning with weight and authority.

How it might do so has been demonstrated in a later day by the extraordinarily dense little statement of dreaming Earwicker in Joyce's *Finnegans Wake*: "O foenix culprit! ex nickylow malo comes mickle-massed bonum." Some of the nearly endless suggestions and combinations there are the following: that out of evil (malo), though it is related to the devil (nick) and is itself a nothingness (nickylow-*nihilo*), comes a vastness (mickle, mass) of good, a good symbolized by Michaelmas. Through the experience of evil, the perpetrator of the *culpa*, the culprit, is reborn like the phoenix; and thus the culprit is happy after all (*felix*).

Joyce was the very type of imagination in total communion with the whole of a many-stranded past. Henry James the elder, sharing his age's enthusiastic rejection of the past, was quite the opposite type. He had vaulted to the insight, but he lacked the language to articulate it. James had none of the dour nostalgic belief in inherited depravity; he accepted the principle that men began like Adam. But he went on to ask whether men must remain in the state of Adam—whether life had not more to offer than "this sleek and comely Adamic condition." He could not clearly and finally answer his own question: perhaps just because the insight he had seized upon was essentially dramatic and could therefore be better described in action than argued in syllogisms. The vocabulary he really needed was, one may hazard the language of narrative literature. But James apparently never realized that something like a "fortunate fall"—explained and justified in terms much like his own—was central to the fiction of his friend Hawthorne and of Hawthorne's friend Melville. And he did not live long enough to read in his son Henry's novels a very comparable principle spelled out in extraordinary dramatic detail.

THE RETURN INTO TIME: HAWTHORNE

… The essential continuity of American fiction explains itself through this historic transformation whereby the Adamic fable yielded to what I take to be the authentic American narrative. For much of that fable remained in the later narrative; the individual going forth toward experience; the inventor of his own character and creator of his personal history; the self-moving individual who is made of confront that "other"—the world or society, the element which provides experience. But as we move from Cooper to Hawthorne, the situation very notably darkens; qualities of evil and fear and destructiveness have entered; self-sufficiency is questioned through terrible trials; and the stage is set for tragedy. The solitary hero and the alien tribe, "the simple genuine self against the whole world"—this is still the given for the American novelist. The variable is this: the novelist's sense of the initial tension—whether it is comforting, or whether it is potentially tragic, whether the tribe promises love, or whether it promises death.

Hawthorne was perhaps the first American writer to detect the inevitable doubleness in the tribal promise. For he was able by temperament to give full and fair play to both parties in the *agon*: to the hero and to the tribe as well. And, having done so, he penetrated to the pattern of action—a pattern of escape and return, at once tragic and hopeful—which was likely to flow from the situation as given. In addition, Hawthorne felt very deeply the intimacy between experience and art, and he enacted a change as well in the resources and methods of the narrative art: something which mirrored, even while if articulated, his heroes and heroines' adventures. Finally, it was Hawthorne who saw in the American experience the re-creation of the story of Adam and who, more than any other contemporary, exploited the active metaphor of the American as Adam—before and during and after the Fall. These are the three aspects of Hawthorne that I shall consider.

The opening scene of *The Scarlet Letter* is the paradigm dramatic image in American literature. With that scene and that novel, New World fiction arrived at its first fulfillment, and Hawthorne at his. And with that scene, all that was dark and treacherous in the American situation became exposed. Hawthorne said later that the writing of *The Scarlet Letter* had been oddly simple, since all he had to do was to get his "pitch" and then to let it carry him along. He found his pitch in an opening tableau fairly humming with tension—with coiled and covert relationships that contained a force perfectly calculated to propel the action thereafter in a direct line to its tragic climax.

It was the tableau of the solitary figure set over against the inimical society, in a village which hovers on the edge of the inviting and perilous wilderness; a handsome young woman standing on a raised platform, confronting in silence and pride a hostile crowd whose menace is deepened by its order and dignity; a young woman who has come alone to the New World, where circumstances have divided her from the community now gathered to oppose her; standing alone, but vitally aware of the private enemy and the private lover—one on the far verges of the crowd, one at the place of honor within it, and neither conscious of the other—who must affect her destiny and who will assist at each other's destruction. Here the situation inherent in the American scene was seized entire and without damage to it by an imagination both moral and visual of the highest quality, seized and located, not any longer on the margins of the plot, but at its very center.

The conflict is central because it is total; because Hawthorne makes us respect each element in it. Hawthorne felt, as Brown[36] and Cooper and Bird[37] had felt, that the stuff of narrative (in so far as it was drawn from local experience) consisted in the imaginable brushes between the deracinated and solitary individual and the society or world awaiting him. But Hawthorne had learned the lesson only fitfully apprehended by Cooper. In *The Scarlet Letter* not only do the individual and the world, the conduct and the institutions, measure each other; the measurement and its consequences are precisely and centrally what the novel is about. Hester Prynne has been wounded by an unfriendly world; but the society facing her is invested by Hawthorne with assurance and authority; its opposition is defensible and even valid. Hester's misdeed appears as a disturbance of the moral structure of the universe, and the society continues to insist in its joyless way that certain acts deserve the honor of punishment. But if Hester has sinned, she has done so as an affirmation of life, and her sin is the source of life; she incarnates those rights of personality that society is inclined to trample upon. The action of the novel springs from the enormous but improbable suggestion that the society's estimate of the moral structure of the universe may be tested and found inaccurate.

The Scarlet Letter, like all very great fiction, is the product of a controlled division of sympathies, and we must avoid the temptation to read it heretically. It has always been possible to remark, about Hawthorne, his fondness for the dusky places, his images of the slow movement of sad, shut-in souls in the half-light. But it has also been possible to read *The Scarlet Letter* (not to mention "The New Adam and Eve" and "Earth's

Holocaust") as an endorsement of hopefulness; to read it as a hopeful critic named Loring read it (writing for Theodore Parker's forward-looking *Massachusetts Quarterly Review*) as a party plea for self-reliance and an attack upon the sterile conventions of institutionalized society. One version of him would align Hawthorne with the secular residue of Jonathan Edwards; the other would bring him closer to Emerson. But Hawthorne was neither Emersonian nor Edwardsean; or rather he was both. The characteristic situation in his fiction is that of the Emersonian figure, the man of hope, who by some frightful mischance has stumbled into the time-burdened world of Jonathan Edwards. And this grim picture is given us by a writer who was skeptically cordial toward Emerson, but, for whom the vision of Edwards, filtered through a haze of hope, remained a wonderfully useful metaphor. The situation, in the form which Hawthorne's ambivalence gave it, regularly led in his fiction to a moment of crucial choice: an invitation to the lost Emersonian, the thunderstruck Adam, to make up his mind—whether to accept the world he had fallen into, or whether to flee it, taking his chances in the allegedly free wilderness to the west. It is a decision about ethical reality, and most of Hawthorne's heroes and heroines eventually have to confront it.

That is why we have the frantic shuttling, in novel after novel, between the village and the forest, the city and the country; for these are the symbols between which the choice must be made and the means by which moral inference is converted into dramatic action. Unlike Thoreau or Cooper, Hawthorne never suggested that the choice was an easy one. Even Arthur Mervyn[38] had been made to reflect on "the contrariety that exists between the city and the country"; in the age of hope the contrariety was taken more or less simply to lie between the restraints of custom and the fresh expansiveness of freedom. Hawthorne perceived greater complexities. He acknowledged the dependence of the individual for nourishment upon organized society (the city), and he believed that it was imperative "to open an intercourse with the world." But he knew that the city could destroy as well as nourish and was apt to destroy the person most in need of nourishment. And while he was responsive to the attractions of the open air and to the appeal of the forest, he also understood the grounds for the Puritan distrust of the forest. He retained that distrust as a part of the symbol. In the forest, possibility was unbounded; but just because of that, evil inclination was unchecked, and witches could flourish there.

For Hawthorne, the forest was neither the proper home of the admirable Adam, as with Cooper, nor was it the hideout of the malevolent adversary, as with Bird. It was the ambiguous setting of moral choice, the scene of reversal and discovery in his characteristic tragic drama. The forest was the pivot in Hawthorne's grand recurring pattern of escape and return.

It is in the forest, for example, that *The Scarlet Letter* version of the pattern begins to disclose itself: in the forest meeting between Hester and Dimmesdale, their first private meeting in seven year. During those years, Hester has been living "on the outskirts of the town," attempting to cling to the community by performing small services for it, though there had been nothing "in all her intercourse with society... that made her feel as if she belonged to it." And the minister has been contemplating the death of his innocence in a house fronting the village graveyard. The two meet now to join in an exertion of the will and the passion for freedom. They very nearly persuade themselves that they can escape along the forest track, which, though in one direction it goes "backward to the settlement," in another goes onward—"deeper it goes, and deeper into the wilderness, until... the yellow leaves will show no vestiges of the white man's tread." But the energy aroused by their encounter drives them back instead, at the end, to the heart of the society, to the penitential platform which is also the heart of the book's structure.

In no other novel is the *agon* so sharp, the agony so intense. But the pattern is there again in *The Marble Faun* as Miriam and Donatello flee separately from the city to the wooded Apennines to waste their illicit exultation in the discovery that they must return to Rome and the responsibility for their crime. It is true that Zenobia, in *The Blithedale Romance*, never does return from her flight; because her escape consummates itself in suicide, and she drowns in the river, running through the woods near the utopian colony. Zenobia, who is often associated in the narrator's fancy with the figure of Eve, is too much of an Eve to survive her private calamity. The more usual outcome—more usual, that is, with Hawthorne—is realized in a sort of tremulous parody by the abortive train ride of Hepzibah and Clifford Pyncheon in *The House of the Seven Gables*— "the flight of the two owls," who get only a station or so along the line into the country before limping back to town to confess to a crime which has not after all been committed.

It is poor Clifford who most blatantly gives voice to the contemporary aspirations imitated in these journeys, as he babbles on in an echo of the hopeful language he must have heard from Holgrave, the daguerreotypist. Homelessness, he explains to an embarrassed fellow-passenger, is the best of condition: "the soul needs air: a wide sweep and a frequent change of it." He sees "the world and my best days before me" and is sure the flight has restored him to "the very heyday of my youth." These exclamations comprise the first principles of Adamism. Clifford trembles in the untenable belief that he has fulfilled the action attributed (by Lawrence) to Cooper's Hawkeye—the motion "backwards from old age to golden youth."[39] The ironic context for his babbling and the total collapse that it rapidly leads to reveal that here, for the first time in American fiction, the story of Adam has become an element of the story actually being narrated—and so begins to suffer serious modifications. Clifford, too, wants to make that leap from memory to hope; his Adamic ambition is an ingredient in the novel; but his leap is Icarian.[40]

Many things are being *tested* as well as exemplified in these circular journeys, in the pattern of escape and return. Among them, the doctrine inherited from Edwards that "an evil taint, in consequence of a crime committed twenty or forty years ago, remain[s] still, and even to the end of the world and forever." Among them, too, the proposition, implicit in much American writing from Poe and Cooper to Anderson[41] and Hemingway, that the valid rite of initiation for the individual in the new world is not an initiation into society, but, given the character of society, an initiation *away from* it: something I wish it were legitimate to call "*de*initiation." The true nature of human wickedness is also in question. Hawthorn's heroes and heroines are almost always criminals, according to the positive laws of the land, but Hawthorne presumed all men and women to be somehow criminals, and himself not the least so. The elder James reported to Emerson how Hawthorne had looked to him at a Saturday Club meeting in Boston: "like a rogue who finds himself in the company of detectives"; we can imagine him there: furtive, uneasy, out of place, half-guilty and half-defiant, poised for instant flight. No doubt it was because he appraised his personal condition this way that Hawthorne so frequently put his characters in the same dilemma, James's comment is a droll version of the opening glimpse of Hester Prynne. And no doubt also this was why Hawthorne so obviously sympathized with what he nevertheless regarded as impossible enterprise—the effort to escape.

But if he customarily brought his sufferers back *into* the community, if they submitted most of his rogues to ultimate arrest, if the "evil taint" does turn out to be ineradicable, it was not because Hawthorne yielded in the end to the gloomy doctrine of Edwards. It was much rather because, for all his ambivalence, Hawthorne had made a daring guess about the entire rhythm of experience and so was willing to risk the whole of it. His qualifications as a novelist were at stake, for if the guess had been less comprehensive, he would have been a novelist of a very different kind, an inferior Melville, perhaps, exhausting himself in an excess of response to every tragic, new, unguessed-at collision. But if the guess had been any more certain, he might scarcely have been a novelist at all, but some sort of imperturbable tractarian. As it was, he could share some part of the hope of motivating the flight, he could always see beyond the hope to the inevitable return, and he could even see a little distance beyond the outcome of surrender to the light and strength it perhaps assured.

Beneath the sunshine that illuminates the soul's surface, he once wrote, there is a region of horror that seems, to the inward traveler, "like hell itself," and through which the self wanders without hope; but deeper still there is a place of perfect beauty. He was not often so certain, but that was the substance of his guess about experience. And this is why there is always more to the world in which Hawthorne's characters move than any one of them can see at a glance. There is more than the surface sunshine covering the whole horizon of the hopeful of his day or his fiction—his new Adam and Eve,[42] the comfortable customers of his "Celestial Railroad," in their untested faith in human purity and in a new world all the braver because it had stamped out the past. But there is more too, much more, than the darkness, the monster, and the divers shapes which tormented the souls of the lost and the guilty—Mr. Hooper behind his black veil[43], Reuben Bourne of "Roger Melvin's Burial," young Goodman Brown. There was still some fulfillment of the spirit, some realization of the entire self which it was worth losing one's self to find; only the lost, indeed, were likely to find it on their return journey, though a soul might shrivel, like young Brown's, in the process.

〔注释〕

1. the rebirth ritual of Walden：指梭罗在其名著《华尔腾》最后一章中所讲的 60 年前的虫卵复活的故事。

2. the party of Hope：指 19 世纪美国文化界的乐观派，他们反对原罪说。

3. the first man in the first hours of the race's history：指初生的亚当。

4. one of them：正统的加尔文神学思想可归纳为彻底的堕落、无条件的挑选、有限制的赎罪、不能拒绝的恩惠及圣徒的永远感恩等五条信条，这里指其中第五条"圣徒的永远感恩"，即"上帝的选民得救以后拥有执行上帝旨意的一切能力，自始至终正直地生活"。

5. Oliver Wendell Holmes：霍姆斯（1809-1894），美国诗人、医生、幽默作家。

6. the party of Memory：指 19 世纪美国文化界的传统派；下文的 the nostalgic 同义。

7. Calvinist Yale：耶鲁学院为加尔文宗信仰保守力量据点之一。

8. Andover：安多弗，位于美国马萨诸塞州东北部的一城镇，19 世纪美国宗教保守力量的据点之一。

9. Protestantism：新教，16 世纪宗教改革中产生的基督教各新教派别的统称。新教主张教会制度的多样化，并对天主教的教义作了一些删减，如不承认"炼狱"，否认圣餐实体转化说，反对尊奉玛丽亚为圣母，反对教皇权力等。

10. Unitarians：唯一神论者，指信奉唯一神论（Unitarism）的人。唯一神论反对三位一体说（Trinity, 即神是由圣父、圣子、圣灵组成），认为上帝是一个整体。唯一神论者相信人能自我完善。

11. Channing and Andrews Norton：昌宁（W. E. Channing）与诺顿，19 世纪美国神学家，属乐观派。

12. Theodore Parker：帕克尔（1810-1860），美国学者、教士。

13. The sacrifice of the god：指耶稣遇难。

14. Paul：保罗，即圣保罗（St. Paul，卒于公元前 64 年或 67 年左右）。他是基督教第一位传教士和使徒，为基督教的传播作出了重要贡献。

15. Charles Chauncy：昌西（1705-1787），美国牧师。Jonathan Mayhew：梅休（1720-1766），美国传教士。

16. John Burroughs：布洛斯（1837-1921），美国自然主义者，散文作家。

17. John Locke：洛克（1673-1704），英国哲学家。他批驳"先天知识论"，认为知识基于感觉经验等大脑反射的基础上，是经验主义哲学的奠基人及主要代表之一。他维护英国资产阶级革命，提出了"天生权利"（人的生命、自由、财产等权力）；针对王室的神权，他主张将国家的权力建立在社会契约的基础上，允许人民有反抗的权力。洛克的思想对 18 世纪启蒙思潮及革命运动，尤其是对法国革命和美国革命都产生了深远影响。

18. *The Cratylus* of Plato：柏拉图的《克利梯拉斯篇》。此篇作品和《政治家篇》和《法律篇》等构成，从语言学角度来看具有鲜明特征的一组作品，为柏拉图晚期作品。

19. Tocqueville：托克维尔（Alexis Comte de Tocqueville, 1805-1859），法国政治家，著有《论美国的民主》（*De la democratie en Amerique*）一书。

20. 引自惠特曼《亚当的子孙》（"Children of Adam"）第 8 首诗 "Ages and Ages，Returning at Intervals"。

21. 引自惠特曼《亚当的子孙》第 16 首诗 "As Adam Early in the Morning"。

22. Holgrave：霍桑所著的小说《七个尖角阁的房子》（*The House of Seven Gables*）中的人物。

23. Noah Webster：诺亚·韦伯斯特（1758-1843），美国字典编纂家、作家。

24. Bronson Alcott：阿尔科特（1791-1888），美国先验主义者、牧师、作家。

25. John Donne：唐恩（1572-1631），英国“玄学派”诗人，下面 4 行诗引自他的诗作《世界的剖析》（"An Anatomy of the World"）。

26. 引自惠特曼的诗《自我之歌》（"Song of Myself"）第 32 节。

27. 引自惠特曼的诗《在路易斯安那我看到一株活橡树在成长》（"I Saw in Louisiana a Live Oak Growing"）。

28. 同上。

29. 引自惠特曼的诗《一只无声息的耐心的蜘蛛》（"A Noiseless Patient Spider"）。

30. 指 "There Was a Child Went Forth" 一诗。

31. Kant and Hegel：康德（Immanuel Kant, 1724-1804）及黑格尔（George Wilhelm Friedrich Hegel, 1770-1831），均为德国唯心主义哲学家。

32. James Joyce：乔伊斯（1882-1941），爱尔兰人，现代派作家，主要作品有《尤利西斯》（Ulysses）、《都柏林人》（Dubliners）、《一个年轻艺术家的画像》（The Portrait of an Artist as a Young Man）以及《为芬尼根守灵》（Finnegans Wake）等。

33. Henry James, Sr.：指美国小说家亨利·詹姆斯（Henry James, 1843-1916）之父。

34. vita nuova：新生。

35. William：指 William James（威廉·詹姆斯, 1842-1910），美国哲学家、心理学家。

36. Brown：布朗（Charles Brockden Brown, 1771-1810），美国小说家。

37. Bird：伯德（Robert Montgomerv Bird, 1806-1854），美国小说家、剧作家。

38. Arthur Mervyn：布朗所著小说《亚瑟·莫尔文》（Arthur Mervyn）里的主人公。

39. 参阅 D. H. Lawrence 所著《美国古典文学研究》（Studies in Classic American Literature）第 54 页。

40. Icarian：伊卡尔斯式的，即过于野心勃勃的。据希腊神话，伊卡尔斯与其父狄得拉斯（Daedalus）获罪遭系狱之苦，于是用蜡和羽毛制成翅膀，逃出克里特岛的"迷宫"。伊卡尔斯违父嘱而飞得过高，接近了太阳，致使翅膀融化，堕海而死。

41. Anderson：安德森（Sherwood Anderson, 1876-1941），美国小说家。

42. "New Adam and Eve"：霍桑所著一短篇小说名；下文中"The Celestial Railroad"亦系其一短篇作品名。

43. Mr. Hooper behind his black veil：指霍桑所著的《牧师的黑面纱》（"The Minister's Black Veil"）；下文中"Roger Melvin's Burial"亦为霍桑一短篇小说；Young Goodman Brown 为霍桑所著的短篇小说《年轻的小伙子布朗》（"Young Goodman Brown"）中的主人公。

Questions For Discussion:

1. Review the first impulses that finally gave birth to the myth of America, and the attitudes which the chief intellectual spokesmen of the nineteenth century took toward it.

2. How does Whitman present the image of the American Adam in his *Leaves of Grass*?

3. Define the theme of "fortunate fall," which Henry James, Sr. touched upon and which was central to the fiction of Hawthorne and Melville.

4. Quote your own experience of reading American literature and discuss whether the image of the American Adam is still kept alive.

For Further Reference:

1. Miller, Perry. *Errand into the Wilderness*. New York: 1956.

2. Feidelson, Charles. *Symbolism and American Literature*. Chicago: 1952.

D. H. Lawrence

〔作者介绍〕

D. H. 劳伦斯（David Herbert Lawrence, 1885-1930），英国诗人、小说家、散文家。他一生写了十部长篇小说及大量诗歌。他的文学批评才能在其《美国经典文学研究》(*Studies in Classic American Literature, 1923*) 一书中得到充分发挥。他宛如荒野中的先知一样，以前所未有的精辟论述，揭示了新美国"意识"和美国人的世界观。这本书已成为美国文学评论的经典著作之一，也是研究劳伦斯本人创作思想的最好素材。

Studies in Classic American Literature

〔作品介绍〕

《美国经典文学研究》1923 年由美国托马斯·塞尔策公司出版。劳伦斯写这本书的目的在于"把美国的故事从美国艺术家手中拯救出来"，让人们重新认识霍桑、坡、麦尔维尔和惠特曼所写的"那些小薄册子"。劳伦斯认为艺术家都是些说谎者。他们总是在撒谎，"而谎言经过巧妙的编织即可成为真理"。一般读者往往不能识破这些谎言。劳伦斯建议他们以审慎、甚至怀疑的态度去阅读文艺作品，因为，"真正的艺术总要或多或少找些借口"，而美国人不论做什么事情又"特别爱找借口"。他们"不喜欢直来直去，总是使他们所做的一切表现出某种双重含意"。

　　劳伦斯认为，美国最初的清教徒移民虽然脱离了欧洲的直接束缚，但是到北美大陆后却发现他们仍然不能独立自主地生活。他们还未彻底摆脱欧洲传统的影响。因此，为了不被假象所迷惑，我们必须深入到"美国的灌木丛中"，即美国经典文学中，去仔细搜寻一番。美国经典文学是研究真正美国精神与美国意识的出发点。

　　劳伦斯在书中研究了八位美国经典作家：富兰克林、克里夫古尔、库柏、爱伦·坡、霍桑、达纳、麦尔维尔及惠特曼。

　　劳伦斯认为，富兰克林是彻底的理性主义者，人类至善至美的象征。劳伦斯不喜欢这类人。他认为每个人都是"无数相互矛盾个体的集合"。其中任何一个个体的完善都要以牺牲其他个体为代价，并有损于人的灵魂的整体性。富兰克林在下意识里是痛恨欧洲的。但他又挣脱不了它的束缚，因为他已经被他自己所攒聚的物质财富禁锢住了。他是美国早期真正的实用主义者，他的意识已机械化了。

　　克里夫古尔恰好与富兰克林形成鲜明对照。他是一位富于感情的理想主义者，他热爱大自然，热爱"高尚的野蛮人"。用劳伦斯的话讲，"本杰明没看到大自然，而克里夫古尔早在梭罗和爱默生创造出他们的大自然之前就发现了它。"克里夫古尔的理想是在茫茫荒原之上建立起自己的家园。他的《一个美国农夫的来信》（*Letters from an American Farmer*, 1782）正表达出作者的这种愿望。

　　库柏的愿望是把美国的印第安人介绍给白人。劳伦斯对库柏的《皮袜子五部曲》所进行的评论可谓生动具体、入木三分。他认为库柏的五部曲歌颂了印第安人首领津加谷克与白人移民纳蒂·班波之间所存在的那种新型的"比两性关系更深刻的"人类关系。这个主题后来在惠特曼的诗歌中也有所体现。劳伦斯认为《皮袜子五部曲》从主人公的暮年回溯到他的青年时代，这种安排是为了体现美国神话形成的过程。美国"兴起于垂暮之年，脸上布满了皱纹，松软皮囊包裹着的躯体痛苦地扭动；然而这层松软的皮囊却慢慢蜕掉，这时美国才焕发出青春的活力"。这就是所谓贯穿于整个美国艺术发展史中的双重性。即"一、旧意识的解体与蜕变；二、新意识的随之形成"。

　　在劳伦斯看来，坡只经历了第一个解体的过程。他的旧意识已消失，但新意识却并未随之产生。坡与其说是一位艺术家，还不如说是一位科学家。他把他的人物像拆机器一样逐个进行剖析，结果发现他们都是由于缺少爱情而死去。他的那些"病态的"故事，有助于摧毁欧洲传统加于美国的影响。

劳伦斯认为霍桑的《红字》（The Scarlet Letter，1850）"类似寓言，是一篇充满地狱气息的世俗故事"。美国人所表现出来的意识是美好的，而其下意识却极凶残，时刻准备着去摧毁什么。这又是美国人的双重性所在。劳伦斯认为，《红字》是一部描写原罪取得胜利的伟大的讽喻之作。海丝特的"罪"不但毁掉了牧师狄姆斯台尔，而且也毁掉了她的丈夫奇林沃思。在这部小说中，海丝特相当于夏娃，狄姆斯台尔酷似亚当，而奇林沃思则扮演了诱引亚当和夏娃犯罪的撒旦的角色。

达纳的《两年的海上生活》（Two Years Before the Mast，1840）是一部关于了解知识、了解大海的书。劳伦斯认为，"了解"会导致存在的慢慢消亡。我们的目的是"知道如何不去知道"。两年的海上生活使达纳变得过于精通世故，更接近于他的末日，所以最后只能无聊地度过晚年。

劳伦斯对麦尔维尔极其崇拜，称他为"最伟大的预言家和描写海上生活的诗人"。尽管麦尔维尔喜欢用格言警句、过于自信，但他却是一位伟大的艺术家，一个真正的美国人。他的《白鲸》（Moby Dick，1851)是世界上最神奇的充满神秘与象征意味的著作之一；同时也是一部令人敬畏的书，一部描写毁灭的书。大白鲸就是白色种族的化身，追杀它即等于自杀。劳伦斯指出，这就是人类的厄运，人类的双重性。

劳伦斯对惠特曼也极为推崇，称他为第一位代表北美洲大陆讲话的白色土著。他勇敢地撕下那张使霍桑、坡、爱默生和麦尔维尔都感到惴惴不安的道德假面具。他的道德观就是活的灵魂。对他来说，活的灵魂最为重要。惠特曼在他的诗歌中也讴歌了男人间的关系，男性间的爱。劳伦斯认为这种关系是人类的基本本能，任何正从废墟上崛起的新文化都不能没有它（我们知道，这种思想也贯穿于劳伦斯本人的小说创作中）。

《美国经典文学研究》立论新颖、不落窠臼。它的许多论点已成为现当代美国文学评论的有机组成部分，影响很大。这本书除在论调上多少有些咄咄逼人、结论稍嫌武断以外，不愧为美国经典文学研究的经典之作。

这里选的是该书前言、第 1 章及第 5 章。

An Excerpt from *Studies in Classic American Literature*

FOREWORD

Listen to the States asserting: "The hour has struck! Americans shall be American: The U.S.A. is sow grown up artistically. It is time we ceased to hang on to the skirts of Europe, or to behave like schoolboys let loose from European schoolmasters—"

All right, Americans, let's see you set about it. Go on then, let the precious cat out of the bag, if you're sure he's in.

> *Et interrogatum est ab ommibus:*
> *"Ubi est ille Toad-in-the-Hole?"*
> *Et iteratum est omnibus:*
> *"Non est inventus!"*[1]

Is he or isn't he inventus?

If he is, of course, he must be somewhere inside you, Oh American. No good chasing him over all the old continents, of course. But equally no good *asserting* him merely. Where is this new bird called the true American? Show us the homunculus of the new era. Go on, show us him. Because all that is visible to the naked European eye, in America, is a sort of recreant European. We want to see this missing link of the next era.

Well, we still don't get him. So the only thing to do is to have a look for him under the American bushes. The old American literature, to start with.

"The old American literature! Franklin, Cooper, Hawthorne & Co.? All that mass of words! All so unreal!" cries the live American.

Heaven knows what we mean by reality. Telephone, tinned meat, Charlie Chaplin, water-taps, and World-Salvation, presumably. Some insisting on the plumbing, and some on saving the world: these being the two great American specialties. Why not? Only, what about the young homunculus of the new era, meanwhile? You can't save yourself before you are born.

Look at me trying to be midwife to the unborn homunculus!

Two bodies of modern literature seem to me to have come to a real verge: the Russian and the American. Let us leave aside the more brittle bits of French or Marinetti[2] or Irish production, which are perhaps over the verge. Russian and American. And by American I do not mean Sherwood Anderson, who is so Russian. I mean the old people, little thin volumes of Hawthorne, Poe, Dana, Melville, Whitman. These seem to me to have reached a verge, as the more voluminous Tolstoy, Dostoevsky, Chekhov, Artzibashev[3] reached a limit on the other side. The furthest frenzies of French modernism or futurism have not yet reached the pitch of extreme consciousness that Poe, Melville, Hawthorne, Whitman reached. The European moderns are all *trying* to be extreme. The great Americans I mention just were it. Which is why the world has funked them, and funks them today.

The great difference between the extreme Russians and the extreme Americans lies in the fact that the Russians are explicit and hate eloquence and symbols, seeing in these only subterfuge, whereas the Americans refuse everything explicit and always put up a sort of double meaning. They revel in subterfuge. They prefer their truth safely swaddled in an ark of bulrushes, and deposited among the reeds until some friendly Egyptian princess comes to rescue the babe.[4]

Well, it's high time now that someone came to lift out the swaddled infant of truth that America spawned some time back. The child must be getting pretty thin, from neglect.

CHAPTER I   THE SPIRIT OF PLACE

We like to think of the old-fashioned American classics as children's books. Just childishness, on our part. The old American art-speech contains an alien quality, which belongs to the American continent and to nowhere else. But, of course, so long as we insist on reading the books as children's tales, we miss all that.

One wonders what the proper high-brow Romans of the third and fourth or later centuries read into the strange utterances of Lucretius[5] or Apuleius or Tertullian, Augustine or Athanasius. The uncanny voice of Iberian[6] Spain, the weirdness of old Carthage,[7] the passion of Libya and North Africa; you may bet the proper old Romans never heard these at all. They read old Latin inference over the top of it, as we read old European inference over the top of Poe or Hawthorne.

It is hard to hear a new voice, as hard as it is to listen to an unknown language. We just don't listen. There is a new voice in the old American classics. The world has declined to hear it, and has babbled about children's stories.

Why? Out of fear. The world fears a new experience more than it fears anything. Because a new experience displaces so many old experiences. And it is like trying to use muscles that have perhaps never been used, or that have been going stiff for ages. It hurts horribly.

The world doesn't fear a new idea. It can pigeon-hole any idea. But it can't pigeon-hole a real new experience. It can only dodge. The world is a great dodger, and the Americans the greatest. Because they dodge their own very selves.

There is a new feeling in the old American books, far more than there is in the modern American books, which are pretty empty of any feeling, and proud of it. There is a "different" feeling in the old American classics. It is the shifting over from the old psyche to something new, a displacement. And displacements hurt. This hurts. So we try to tie it up, like a cut finger. Put a rag round it.

It is a cut too. Cutting away the old emotions and consciousness. Don't ask what is left.

Art-speech is the only truth. An artist is usually a damned liar, but his art, if it be art, will tell you the truth of his day. And that is all that matters. Away with eternal truth. Truth lives from day to day, and the marvelous Plato of yesterday is chiefly bosh today.

The old American artists were hopeless liars. But they were artists, in spite of themselves, which is more than you can say of most living practitioners.

And you can please yourself, when you read *The Scarlet Letter*, whether you accept what that sugary, blue-eyed little darling of a Hawthorne has to say for himself, false as all darlings are, or whether you read the impeccable truth of his art-speech.

The curious thing about art-speech is that it prevaricates so terribly, I mean it tells such lies. I suppose because we always all the time tell ourselves lies. And out of a pattern of lies art weaves the truth. Like Dostoevsky posing as a sort of Jesus, but most truthfully revealing himself all the while as a little horror.

Truly art is a sort of subterfuge. But thank God for it, we can see through the subterfuge if we choose. Art has two great functions. First, it provides an emotional experience. And then, if we have the courage of own feelings, it becomes a mine of practical truth. We have had the feelings *ad nauseam*.[8] But we've never dared dig the actual truth out of them, the truth that concerns us, whether it concerns our grandchildren or not.

The artist usually sets out—or used to—to point a moral and adorn tale.[9] The tale, however, points the other way, as a rule. Two blankly opposing morals, the artist's and the tale's. Never trust the artist. Trust the tale. The proper function of a critic is to save the tale from the artist who created it.

Now we know our business in these studies: saving the American tale from the American artist.

Let us look at this American artist first. How did he ever get to America, to start with? Why isn't he a European still, like his father before him?

Now listen to me, don't listen to him. He'll tell you the lie you expect, which is partly your fault for expecting it.

He didn't come in search of freedom of worship. England had more freedom of worship in the year 1700 than America had. Won by Englishmen who wanted freedom, and so stopped at home and fought for it. And got it. Freedom of worship? Read the history of New England during the first century of its existence.

Freedom anyhow? The land of the free! This the land of the free! Why, if I say anything that displeases them, the free mob will lynch me, and that's my freedom. Free? Why, I have never been in any country where the individual has such an abject fear of his fellow countrymen. Because, as I say, they are free to lynch him the moment he shows he is not one of them.

No, no, if you're so fond of the truth about Queen Victoria, try a little about yourself.

Those Pilgrim Fathers and their successors never came here for freedom of worship. What did they set up when they got here? Freedom, would you call it?

They didn't come for freedom. Or if they did, they sadly went back on themselves.

All right then, what did they come for? For lots of reasons. Perhaps least of all in search of freedom of any sort: positive freedom, that is.

They came largely to get *away*—that most simple of motives. To get away. Away from what? In the long run, away from themselves. Away from everything. That's why most people have come to America, and still do come. To get away from everything they are and have been.

"Henceforth be masterless."

Which is all very well, but it isn't freedom. Rather the reverse. A hopeless sort of constraint. It is never freedom till you find something you really *positively want to be*. And people in America have always been shouting about the things they are *not*. Unless, of course, they are millionaires, made or in the making.

And after all there is a positive side to the movement. All that vast flood of human life that has flowed over the Atlantic in ships from Europe to America has not flowed over simply on a tide of revulsion from Europe and from the confinements of the European ways of life. This revulsion was, and still is, I believe, the prime motive in emigration. But there was some cause, even for the revulsion.

It seems as if at times man had a frenzy for getting away from any control of any sort. In Europe the old Christianity was the real master. The Church and the true aristocracy bore the responsibility for the working out of the Christian ideals: a little irregularly, maybe, but responsible nevertheless.

Mastery, kingship, fatherhood had their power destroyed at the time of the Renaissance.

And it was precisely at this moment that the great drift over the Atlantic started. What were men drifting away from? The old authority of Europe? Were they breaking the bonds of authority, and escaping to a new more absolute unrestrainedness? Maybe. But there was more to it.

Liberty is all very well, but men cannot live without masters. There is always a master. And men either live in glad obedience to the master they believe in, or they live in a frictional opposition to the master they wish to undermine. In America this frictional opposition has been the vital factor. It has given the Yankee his kick. Only the continual influx of more servile Europeans has provided America with an obedient labouring class. The true obedience never outlasting the first generation.

But there sits the old master, over in Europe. Like a parent. Somewhere deep in every American heart lies a rebellion against the old parenthood of Europe. Yet no American feels he has completely escaped its mastery. Hence the slow, smouldering patience of American opposition. The slow, smouldering, corrosive obedience to the old master Europe, the unwilling subject, the unremitting opposition.

Whatever else you are, be masterless.

> "Ca Ca Caliban
>
> Get a new master, be a new man."[10]

Escaped slaves, we might say, people the republics of Liberia[11] or Haiti. Liberia enough! Are we to look at America in the same way? A vast republic of escaped slaves. When you consider the hordes from eastern Europe, you might well say it: a vast republic of escaped slaves. But one dare not say this of the Pilgrim Fathers, and the great old body of idealist Americans, the modern Americans tortured with thought. A vast republic of escaped slaves. Look out, America! And a minority of earnest, self-tortured people.

The masterless.

> "Ca Ca Caliban
>
> Get a new master, be a new man."

What did the Pilgrim Fathers come for, then, when they came so gruesomely over the black sea? Oh, it was in a black spirit. A black revulsion from Europe, from the old authority of Europe, from kings and bishops and popes. And more. When you look into it，more. They were black, masterful men, they wanted something else. No kings, no bishops maybe. Even no God Almighty. But also no more of this new "humanity" which followed the Renaissance. None of this new liberty which was to be so pretty in Europe. Something grimmer, by no means free-and-easy.

America has never been easy, and is not easy today. Americans have always been at a certain tension. Their liberty is a thing of sheer will, sheer tension, a liberty of THOU SHALT NOT. And it has been so from the first. The land of THOU SHALT NOT.[12] Only the first commandment is: THOU SHALT NOT PRESUME TO BE A MASTER. Hence democracy.

"We are the masterless." That is what the American Eagle[13] shrieks. It's a Hen-Eagle.

The Spaniards refused the post-Renaissance liberty of Europe. And the Spaniards filled most of America. The Yankees, too, refused, refused the post-Renaissance humanism of Europe. First and foremost, they hated masters. But under that, they hated the flowing ease of humour in Europe: At the bottom of the American soul was always a dark suspense, at the bottom of the Spanish-American soul the same. And this dark suspense hated and hates the old European spontaneity, watches it collapse with satisfaction.

Every continent has its own great spirit of place. Every people is polarized in some particular locality, which is home, the homeland. Different places on the face of the earth have different vital effluence, different vibration, different chemical exhalation, different polarity with different stars: call it what you like. But the spirit of place is a great reality. The Nile valley produced not only the corn, but the terrific religions of Egypt. China produces the Chinese, and will go on doing so. The Chinese in San Francisco will in time cease to be Chinese, for America is a great melting-pot.

There was a tremendous polarity in Italy, in the city of Rome. And this seems to have died. For even places die. The Island of Great Britain had a wonderful terrestrial magnetism or polarity of its own, which made the British people. For the moment, this polarity seems to be breaking. Can England die? And what if England dies?

Men are less free than they imagine; ah, far less free. The freest are perhaps least free.

Men are free when they are in a living homeland, not when they are straying and breaking away. Men are free when they are obeying some deep, inward voice of religious belief. Obeying from within. Men are free when they belong to a living, organic, *believing* community, active in fulfilling some unfulfilled, perhaps unrealized purpose. Not when they are escaping to some wild west. The most unfree souls go west, and shout of freedom. Men are freest when they are most unconscious of freedom. The shout is a rattling of chains, always was.

Men are not free when they are doing just what they like. The moment you can do just what you like, there is nothing you care about doing. Men are only free when they are doing what the deepest self likes.

And there is getting down to the deepest self! It takes some diving.

Because the deepest self is way down, and the conscious self is an obstinate monkey. But of one thing we may be sure. If one wants to be free, one has to give up the illusion of doing what one likes, and seek what IT[14] wishes done.

But before you can do what IT likes, you must first break the spell of the old mastery, the old IT.

Perhaps at the Renaissance, when kingship and fatherhood fell, Europe drifted into a very dangerous half-truth: of liberty and equality. Perhaps the men who went to America felt this, and so repudiated the old world together. Went one better than Europe. Liberty in America has meant so far the breaking away from *all* dominion. The true liberty will only begin when Americans discover IT, and proceed possibly to fulfill IT. IT being the deepest *whole* self of man, the self in its wholeness, not idealistic halfness.

That's why the Pilgrim Fathers came to America, then; and that's why we come. Driven by IT. We cannot see that invisible winds carry us, as they carry swarms of locusts, that invisible magnetism brings us as it brings the migrating birds to their unforeknown goal. But it is so. We are not the marvelous choosers and deciders we think we are. IT chooses for us, and decides for us. Unless, of course, we are just escaped slaves, vulgarly cocksure of our ready-made destiny. But if we are living people, in touch with the source, IT drives us and decides us. We are free only so long as we obey. When we run counter, and think we will do as we like, we just flee around like Orestes pursued by the Eumenides.[15]

And still, when the great day begins, when Americans have at last discovered America and their own wholeness, still there will be the vast number of escaped slaves to reckon with, those who have no cocksure, ready-made destinies.

Which will win in America, the escaped slaves, or the new whole men?

The real American day hasn't begun yet. Or at least, not yet sunrise. So far it has been the false dawn. That is, in the progressive American consciousness there has been the one dominant desire, to do away with the old thing. Do away with masters, exalt the will of the people. The will of the people being nothing but a figment, the exalting doesn't count for much. So, in the name of the will of the people, get rid of masters. When you have got rid of masters, you are left with this mere phrase of the will of the people. Then you pause and bethink yourself, and try to recover your own wholeness.

So much for the conscious American motive, and for democracy over here. Democracy in America is just the tool with which the old master of

Europe, the European spirit, is undermined. Europe destroyed, potentially, American democracy will evaporate. America will begin.

American consciousness has so far been a false dawn. The negative ideal of democracy. But underneath, and contrary to this open ideal, the first hints and revelations of IT. IT, the American whole soul.

You have got to pull the democratic and idealistic clothes off American utterance, and see what you can of the dusky body of IT underneath.

"Henceforth be masterless."

Henceforth be mastered.

CHAPTER V   FENIMORE COOPER'S LEATHERSTOCKING NOVELS

In his Leatherstocking books, Fenimore is off on another track. He is no longer concerned with social white Americans that buzz with pins[16] through them, buzz loudly against every mortal thing except the pin itself. The pin of the Great Ideal.

One gets irritated with Cooper because he never for once snarls at the Great Ideal Pin which transfixes him. No, indeed. Rather he tries to push it through the very heart of the Continent.

But I have loved the Leatherstocking books so dearly. Wish-fulfillment!

Anyhow, one is not supposed to take LOVE seriously, in these books. Eve Effingham, impaled on the social pin, conscious all the time of her own ego and of nothing else, suddenly fluttering in throes of love: no, it makes me sick, LOVE is never LOVE until it has a pin pushed through it and becomes an IDEAL. The ego, turning on a pin, is wildly IN LOVE, always. Because that's the thing to be.

Cooper was a GENTLEMAN,[17] in the worst sense of the word. In the Nineteenth Century sense of the word. A correct, clock-work man.

Not altogether, of course.

The great national Grouch was grinding inside him. Probably he called it COSMIC URGE. Americans usually do: in capital letters.

Best stick to National Grouch. The great American grouch.

Cooper had it, gentleman that he was. That is why he flitted round Europe so uneasily. Of course, in Europe he could be, and was, a gentleman to his heart's content.

"In short," he says in one of his letters, "we were at table two counts, one monsignore, an English Lord, an Ambassador, and my humble self."

Were we really!

How nice it must have been to know that one self, at least, was humble.

And he felt the democratic American tomahawk wheeling over his unconformable scalp all the time.

The great American grouch.

Two monsters loomed on Cooper's horizon:

Mrs. COOPER	MY WORK
MY WORK	MY WIFE
MY WIFE	MY· WORK
The DEAR CHILDREN	MY WORK!!!

There you have the essential keyboard of Cooper's soul.

If there is one thing that annoys me more than a businessman and his BUSINESS, it is an artist, a writer, painter, musician, and MY WORK. When an artist says MY WORK, the flesh goes tired on my bones. When he says MY WIFE, I want to hit him.

Cooper grizzled about his work. Oh, heaven, he cared so much whether, it was good or bad, and what the French thought, and what Mr. Snippy Knowall said, and how Mrs. Cooper took it. The pin, the pin!

But he was truly an artist: then an American: then a gentleman.

And the grouch grouched inside him, through all.

They seem to have been specially fertile in imagining themselves "under the wigwam,"[18] do these Americans, just when their knees were comfortably under the mahogany, in Paris, along with the knees of

> 4 Counts
>
> 2 Cardinals
>
> 1 Milord
>
> 5 Cocottes
>
> 1 Humble self

You bet, though, that, when the cocottes were being raffled off, Fenimore went home to his WIFE.

Wish Fulfilment		Actuality
THE WIGWAM	vs.	My HOTEL
CHINGACHGOOK	vs.	MY WIFE
NATTY BUMPPO	vs.	MY HUMBLE SELF

Fenimore, lying in his Louis Quatorze hotel in Paris, passionately musing about Natty Bumppo and the pathless forest, and mixing his imagination with the Cupids and Butterflies[19] on the painted ceiling, while Mrs. Cooper was struggling with her latest gown in the next room, and the dejeuner[20] was with the Countess at eleven….

Men live by lies.

In actuality, Fenimore loved the genteel continent of Europe, and waited gasping for the newspapers to praise his WORK.

In another actuality he loved the tomahawking continent of America, and imagined himself Natty Bumppo.

His actual desire was to be: *Monsieur Fenimore Cooper le*

grandecrivain am ericain. [21]

His innermost wish was to be: Natty Bumppo.

Now Natty and Fenimore, arm-in-arm, are an odd couple.

You can see Fenimore: blue coat, silver buttons, silver-and-diamond buckle shoes, ruffles.

You see Natty Bumppo: a grizzled, uncouth old renegade, with gaps in his old teeth and a drop on the end of his nose.

But Natty was Fenimore's great wish: his wish-fulfillment.

"It was a matter of course," says Mrs. Cooper, "that he should dwell on the better traits of the picture rather than on the coarser and more revolting, though more common points. Like West, he could see Apollo in the young Mohawk."

The coarser and more revolting, though more common points.

You see now why he depended so absolutely on MY WIFE. She had to look things in the face for him. The coarser and more revolting, and certainly more common points, she had to see.

He himself did so love seeing pretty-pretty, with the thrill of a red scalp now and then.

Fenimore, in his imagination, wanted to be Natty Bumppo, who, I am sure, belched after he had eaten his dinner. At the same time Mr. Cooper was nothing if not a gentleman. So he decided to stay in France and have it all his own way.

In France, Natty would not belch after eating, and Chingachgook could be all the Apollo he liked.

As if ever any Indian was like Apollo. The Indians, with their curious female quality, their archaic figures, with high shoulders and deep, archaic waists, like a sort of woman! And their natural devilishness, their natural insidiousness.

But men see what they want to see: especially if they look from a long distance, across the ocean, for example.

Yet the Leatherstocking books are lovely, lovely half-lies.

They form a sort of American Odyssey,[22] with Natty Bumppo for Odysseus.

Only, in the original Odyssey, there is plenty of devil, Circes[23] and swine and all. And Ithacus is devil enough to outwit the devils. But Natty is a saint with a gun, and the Indians are gentlemen through and through, though they may take an occasional scalp.

There are five Leatherstocking novels: a decrescendo of reality, and a crescendo of beauty.

1. *Pioneers*: A raw frontier-village on Lake Champlain, at the end of the eighteenth century. Must be a picture of Cooper's home, as he knew it when a boy. A very lovely book, Natty Bumppo an old man, an old hunter half civilized.

2. *The Last of the Mohicans*: A historical fight between the British and the French, with Indians on both sides, at a Fort by Lake Champlain. Romantic flight of the British general's two daughters, conducted by the scout, Natty, who is in the prime of life; romantic death of the last of the Delawares.

3. *The Prairie*: A wagon of some huge, sinister Kentuckians trekking west into the unbroken prairie. Prairie Indians, and Natty, an old, old man; he dies seated on a chair on the Rocky Mountains, looking east.

4. *The Pathfinder*: The Great Lakes. Natty, a man of about thirty-five, makes an abortive proposal to a bouncing damsel, daughter of the Sergeant at the Fort.

5. *Deer slayer*: Natty and Hurry Harry, both quite young, are hunting in the virgin wild. They meet two white women. Lake Champlain again.

These are the five Leatherstocking books: Natty Bumppo being Leatherstocking, Pathfinder, Deerslayer, according to his ages.

Now let me put aside my impatience at the unreality of this vision, and accept it as a wish-fulfilment vision, a kind of yearning myth. Because it seems to me that the things in Cooper that make one so savage, when one compares them with actuality, are perhaps, when one considers them as presentations of a deep subjective desire, real in their way, and almost prophetic.

The passionate love for America, for the soil of America, for example. As I say, it is perhaps easier to love America passionately, when you look at it through the wrong end of the telescope, across all the Atlantic water, as Cooper did so often, than when you are right there. When you are actually *in* America, America hurts, because it has a powerful disintegrative influence upon the white psyche. It is full of grinning, unappeased aboriginal demons, too, ghosts, and it persecutes the white men, like some Eumenides,[24] until the white men give up their absolute whiteness. America is tense with latent violence and resistance. The very common sense of white Americans has a tinge of helplessness in it, and deep fear of what might be if they were not common-sensical.

Yet one day the demons of America must be placated, the ghosts must be appeased, the Spirit of Place atoned for. Then the true passionate love for American Soil will appear. As yet, there is too much menace in the landscape.

But probably, one day America will be as beautiful in actuality as it is in Cooper. Not yet, however. When the factories have fallen down again.

And again, this perpetual blood-brother theme of the Leatherstocking novels, Natty and Chingachgook, the Great Serpent.[25] At present it is a sheer myth. The Red Man and the White Man are not blood-brothers: even when they are most friendly. When they are most friendly, it is as a rule the one betraying his race-spirit to the other. In the white man—rather high-brow—who "loves" the Indian, one feels the white man betraying his own race. There is something unproud, underhand in it. Renegade. The same with the Americanised Indian who believes absolutely in the white mode. It is a betrayal. Renegade again.

In the actual flesh, it seems to me the white man and the red man cause a feeling of oppression, the one to the other, no matter what the good will. The red life flows in a different direction from the white life. You can't make two streams that flow in opposite directions meet and mingle soothingly.

Certainly, if Cooper had had to spend his whole life in the backwoods, side by side with a Noble Red Brother, he would have screamed with the oppression of suffocation. He had to have Mrs. Cooper, a straight strong pillar of society, to hang on to. And he had to have the culture of France to turn back to, or he would just have been stifled. The Noble Red Brother would have smothered him and driven him mad.

So that the Natty and Chingachgook myth must remain a myth. It is a wish-fulfilment, an evasion of actuality. As we have said before, the folds of the Great Serpent would have been heavy, very heavy, too heavy, on any white man. Unless the white man were a true renegade, hating himself and his own race-spirit, as sometimes happens.

It seems there can be no fusion in the flesh. But the spirit can change. The white man's spirit can never become as the red man's spirit. It doesn't want to. But it can cease to be the opposite and the negative of the red man's spirit. It can open out a new great area of consciousness, in which there is room for the red spirit too.

To open out a new wide area of consciousness means to slough the old consciousness. The old consciousness has become a tight-fitting prison to us, in which we are going rotten.

You can't have a new, easy skin before you have sloughed the old, tight skin.

You can't.

And you just can't, so you may as well leave off pretending.

Now the essential history of the people of the United States seems to me just this: At the Renaissance the old consciousness was becoming a little tight. Europe sloughed her last skin, and started a new, final phase.

But some Europeans, recoiled from the last, final phase. They wouldn't enter the *cul de sac* of post-Renaissance, "liberal" Europe. They came to America.

They came to America for two reasons：

1. To slough the old European consciousness completely.

2. To grow a new skin underneath, a new form.

The second is a hidden process.

The two processes go on，of course，simultaneously. The slow forming of the new skin underneath is the slow sloughing of the old skin. And sometimes this immortal serpent feels very happy，feeling a new gold glow of a strangely-patterned skin envelop him：and sometimes he feels very sick，as if his very entrails were being torn out of him, as he wrenches once more at his old skin, to get out of it.

Out！Out！he cries，in all kinds of euphemisms.

He's got to have his new skin on him before ever he can get out.

And he's got to get out before his new skin can ever be his own skin.

So there he is，a torn，divided monster.

The true American, who writhes like a snake that is long in sloughing.

Sometimes snakes can't slough. They can't burst their old skin. Then they go sick and die inside the old skin, and nobody ever sees the new pattern.

It needs a real desperate recklessness to burst your old skin at last. You simply don't care what happens to you, if you rip yourself in two, so long as you do get out.

It also needs a real belief in the new skin. Otherwise you are likely never to make the effort. Then you gradually sicken and go rotten and die in the old skin.

Now Fenimore stayed very safe inside the old skin: a gentleman, almost a European, as proper as proper can be. And, safe inside the old skin, he *imagined* the gorgeous American pattern of a new skin.

He hated democracy. So he evaded it and had a nice dream of something beyond democracy. But he belonged to democracy all the while.

Evasion!—Yet even that doesn't make the dream worthless.

Democracy in America was never the same as Liberty in Europe. In Europe Liberty was a great life-throb. But in America Democracy was always something anti-life. The greatest democrats, like Abraham Lincoln, had always a sacrificial, self-murdering note in their voices. American Democracy was a form of self-murder, always. Or of murdering somebody else.

Necessarily. It was a *pis aller*. It was the *pis aller* to European Liberty. It was a cruel form of sloughing. Men murdered themselves into this democracy. Democracy is the utter hardening of the old skin, the old form, the old psyche. It hardens till it is tight and fixed and inorganic. Then it *must* burst, like a chrysalis shell. And out must come the soft grub, or the soft damp butterfly of the American-at-last.

America has gone the *pis aller* of her democracy. Now she must slough even that, chiefly that, indeed.

What did Cooper dream beyond democracy? Why, in his immortal friendship of Chingachgook and Natty Bumppo he dreamed the nucleus of a new society. That is, he dreamed a new human relationship. A stark, stripped human relationship of two men, deeper than the deeps of sex. Deeper than property, deeper than fatherhood, deeper than marriage, deeper than love. So deep that it is loveless. The stark, loveless, wordless unison of two men who have come to the bottom of themselves. This is the new nucleus of a new society, the clue to a new world-epoch. It asks for a great and cruel sloughing first of all. Then it finds a great release into a new world, a new moral, a new landscape.

Natty and the Great Serpent are neither equals nor unequals. Each obeys the other when the moment arrives. And each is stark and dumb in the other's presence, starkly himself, without illusion created. Each is just the crude pillar of a man, the crude living column of his own manhood. And each knows the godhead of this crude column of manhood. A new relationship.

The Leatherstocking novels create the myth of his new relation. And they go backwards, from old age to golden youth. That is the true myth of America. She starts old, old, wrinkled and writhing in an old skin. And there is a gradual sloughing of the old skin, towards a new youth. It is the myth of America.

You start with actuality. *Pioneers* is no doubt Cooperstown, when Cooperstown was in the stage of inception: a village of one wild street of log cabins under the forest hills by Lake Champlain: a village of crude, wild frontiersmen, reacting against civilization.

Towards this frontier-village in the winter time, a negro slave drives a sledge through the mountains, over deep snow. In the sledge sits a fair damsel. Miss Temple, with her handsome pioneer father, Judge Temple. They hear a shot in the trees. It is the old hunter and backwoodsman, Natty Bumppo, long and lean and uncouth, with a long rifle and gaps in his teeth.

Judge Temple is "squire" of the village, and he has a ridiculous, commodious "hall" for his residence. It is still the old English form. Miss Temple is a pattern young lady, like Eve Effingham: in fact, she gets a young and very genteel but impoverished Effingham for a husband. The old world holding its own on the edge of the wild. A bit tiresomely too, with rather more prunes and prisms than one can digest. Too romantic.

Against the "hall" and the gentry, the real frontiers-folk, the rebels. The two groups meet at the village inn, and at the frozen church, and at the Christmas sports, and on the ice of the lake, and at the great pigeon shoot.

It is a beautiful, resplendent picture of life. Fenimore puts in only the glamour.

Perhaps my taste is childish, but these scenes in *Pioneers* seem to me marvellously beautiful. The raw village street, with woodfires blinking through the unglazed window-chinks, on a winter's night. The inn, with the rough woodsman and the drunken Indian John; the church, with the snowy congregation crowding to the fire. Then the lavish abundance of Christmas cheer, and turkey-shooting in the snow. Spring coming, forests all green, maple-sugar taken from the trees; and clouds of pigeons flying from the south, myriads of pigeons, shot in heaps; and night-fishing on the teeming, virgin lake; and deer-hunting.

Pictures! Some of the loveliest, most glamorous pictures in all literature.

Alas, without the cruel iron of reality. It is all real enough. Except that one realizes that Fenimore was writing from a safe distance, where he would idealize and have his wish-fulfilment.

Because, when one comes to America, one finds that there is always a certain slightly devilish resistance in the American landscape, and a certain slightly bitter resistance in the white man's heart. Hawthorne gives this. But Cooper glosses it over.

The American landscape has never been at one with the white man. Never. And white men have probably never felt so bitter anywhere, as here in America, where the very landscape, in its very beauty, seems a bit devilish and grinning, opposed to us.

Cooper, however, glosses over this resistance, which in actuality can never quite be glossed over. He *wants* the landscape to be at one with him. So he goes away to Europe and sees it as such. It is a sort of vision.

And, nevertheless, the oneing will surely take place—some day.

The myth is the story of Natty. The old, lean hunter and back-woodsman lives with his friend, the grey-haired Indian John, an old

Delaware chief, in a hut within reach of the village. The Delaware is Christianized and bears the Christian name of John. He is tribeless and lost. He humiliates his grey hairs in drunkenness, and dies, thankful to be dead, in a forest fire, passing back to the fire whence he derived.

And this is Chingachgook, the splendid Great Serpent of the later novels.

No doubt Cooper, as a boy, knew both Natty and the Indian John. No doubt they fired his imagination even then. When he is a man, crystallized in society and sheltering behind the safe pillar of Mrs. Cooper, these two old fellows become a myth to his soul. He traces himself to a new youth in them.

As for the story: Judge Temple has just been instrumental in passing the wise game laws. But Natty has lived by his gun all his life in the wild woods, and simply childishly cannot understand how he can be poaching on the Judge's land among the pine trees. He shoots a deer in the close season. The Judge is all sympathy, but the *law* must be enforced. Bewildered Natty, an old man of seventy, is put in stocks and in prison. They release him as soon as possible. But the thing was done.

The letter killeth.[26]

Natty's last connexion with his own race is broken. John, the Indian, is dead. The old hunter disappears, lonely and severed, into the forest, away, away from his race.

In the new epoch that is coming, there will be no letter of the Law.

Chronologically, The *Last of the Mohicans* follows *Pioneers*. But in the myth, The *Prairie* comes next.

Cooper of course knew his own America. He travelled west and saw the prairies, and camped with the Indians of the prairie.

The Prairie, like *Pioneers*, bears a good deal the stamp of actuality. It is a strange, splendid book, full of sense of doom. The figures of the great Kentuckian men, with their wolf-women, loom colossal on the vast prairie, as they camp with their wagons. These are different pioneers from Judge Temple. Lurid, brutal, tinged with the sinisterness of crime; these are the gaunt white men who push west, push on and on against the natural opposition of the continent. On towards a doom. Great wings of vengeful doom seem spread over the west, grim against the intruder. You feel them again in Frank Norris[27] novel, *The Octopus*. While in the West of Bret Harte[28] there is a very devil in the air, and beneath him are sentimental self-conscious people being wicked and goody by evasion.

In *The Prairie* there is a shadow of violence and dark cruelty flickering in the air. It is the aboriginal demon hovering over the core of the continent. It hovers still, and the dread is still there.

Into such a prairie enters the huge figure of Ishmael,[29] ponderous, pariah-like Ishmael and his huge sons and his were-wolf wife. With their wagons they roll on from the frontiers of Kentucky, like Cyclops[30] into the savage wilderness. Day after day they seem to force their way into oblivion. But their force of penetration ebbs. They are brought to a stop. They recoil in the throes of murder and entrench themselves in isolation on a hillock in the midst of the prairie. There they hold out like demi-gods against the elements and the subtle Indian.

The pioneering brute invasion of the West, crime-tinged!

And into this setting, as a sort of minister of peace, enters the old, old hunter Natty, and his suave, horse—riding Sioux Indians.[31] But he seems like a shadow.

The hills rise softly west, to the Rockies. There seems a new peace; or is it only suspense, abstraction, waiting? Is it only a sort of beyond?

Natty lives in these hills, in a village of the suave, horse-riding Sioux. They revere him as an old wise father.

In these hills he dies, sitting in his chair and looking far east, to the forest and great sweet waters, whence he came. He dies gently, in physical peace with the land and the Indians. He is an old, old man.

Cooper could see no further than the foothills where Natty died, beyond the prairie.

The other novels bring us back east.

The Last of the Mohicans is divided between real historical narrative and true "romance." For myself, I prefer the romance. It has a myth meaning, whereas the narrative is chiefly record.

For the first time we get actual women: the dark, handsome Cora and her frail sister, the White Lily. The good old division: the dark sensual woman and the clinging, submissive little blonde, who is so "pure."

These sisters are fugitives through the forest, under the protection of a Major Heyward, a young American officer and Englishman. He is just a "white" man, very good and brave and generous, etc. but limited, most definitely *borne*. He would probably love Cora, if he dared, but he finds it safer to adore the clinging White Lily of a younger sister.

This trio is escorted by Natty, now Leatherstocking, a hunter and scout in the prime of life, accompanied by his inseparable friend Chingachgook, and the Delaware's beautiful son—Adonis[32] rather than Apollo—Uncas, The last of the Mohicans.

There is also a "wicked" Indian, Magua, handsome and injured incarnation of evil.

Cora is the scarlet flower of womanhood, fierce, passionate off-spring of some mysterious union between the British officer and a Creole woman in the West Indies. Cora loves Uncas, Uncas loves Cora. But Magua also desires Cora, violently desires her. A lurid little circle of sensual fire. So Fenimore kills them all off, Cora, Uncas, and Magua, and leaves the White Lily[33] to carry on the race. She will breed plenty of white children to Major Heyward. These tiresome "lilies that fester,"[34] of our day.

Evidently Cooper—or the artist in him—has decided that there can be no blood-mixing of the two races, white and red. He kills 'em off.

Beyond all this heart-beating stand the figures of Natty and

Chingachgook: the two childless, womanless men, of opposite races. They are the abiding thing. Each of them is alone, and final in his race. And they stand side by side, stark, abstract, beyond emotion, yet eternally together. All the other loves seem frivolous. This is the new great thing, the clue, the inception of a new humanity.

And Natty, what sort of a white man is he? Why, he is a man with a gun. He is a killer, a slayer. Patient and gentle as he is, he is slayer. Self-effacing, self-forgetting, still he is a killer.

Twice, in the book, he brings an enemy down hurtling in death through the air, downwards. Once it is the beautiful, wicked Magua—shot from a height, and hurtling down ghastly through space, into death.

This is Natty, the white forrunner. A killer. As in *Deerslayer*, he shoots the bird that flies in the high, high sky, so that the bird falls out of the invisible into the visible, dead, he symbolizes himself. He will bring the bird of the spirit out of the high air. He is the stoic American killer of the old great life. But he kills, as he says, only to live.

Pathfinder takes us to the Great Lakes, and the glamour and beauty of sailing the great sweet waters. Natty is now called Pathfinder. He is about thirty-five years old, and he falls in love. The damsel is Mabel Dunham, daughter of Sergeant Dunham of the Fort garrison. She is blonde and in all things admirable. No doubt Mrs. Cooper was very much like Mabel.

And Pathfinder doesn't marry her. She won't have him. She wisely prefers a more comfortable Jasper. So Natty goes off to grouch, and to end by thanking his stars. When he had got right clear, and sat by the campfire with Chingachgook, in the forest, didn't he just thank his stars! A lucky escape!

Men of an uncertain age are liable to these infatuations. They aren't always lucky enough to be rejected.

Whatever would poor Mabel have done, had she been Mrs. Bumppo?

Natty had no business marrying. His mission was elsewhere.

The most fascinating Leatherstocking book is the last, *Deerslayer*. Natty is now a fresh youth, called Deerslayer. But the kind of silent prim youth who is never quite young, but reserves himself for different things.

It is a gem of a book. Or a bit of perfect paste. And myself, I like a bit of perfect paste in a perfect setting, so long as I am not fooled by pretence of reality. And the setting of Deerslayer *could* not be more exquisite. Lake Champlain again.

Of course it never rains: it is never cold and muddy and dreary: no one has wet feet or toothache: no one ever feels filthy, when they can't wash for a week. God knows what the women would really have looked like, for they fled through the wilds without soap, comb, or towel. They breakfasted off a chunk of meat, or nothing, lunched the same, and supped the same.

Yet at every moment they are elegant, perfect ladies, in correct toilet.

Which isn't quite fair. You need only go camping for a week, and you'll see.

But it is a myth, not a realistic tale. Read it as a lovely myth. Lake Glimmerglass.

Deerslayer, the youth with the long rifle, is found in the woods with a big, handsome, blonde-bearded backwoodsman called Hurry Harry. Deerslayer seems to have been born under a hemlock tree out of a pine-cone: a young man of the woods. He is silent, simple, philosophic, moralistic, and an unerring shot. His simplicity is the simplicity of age rather than of youth. He is race-old. All his reactions and impulses are fixed, static. Almost he is sexless, so race old. Yet intelligent, hardy, dauntless.

Hurry Harry is a big blusterer, just the opposite of Deerslayer. Deerslayer keeps the centre of his own consciousness steady and unperturbed. Hurry Harry is one of those floundering people who bluster from one emotion to another, very self-conscious, without any centre to them.

These two young men are making their way to a lovely, smallish lake, Lake Glimmerglass. On this water the Hutter family has established itself. Old Hutter, it is suggested, has a criminal, coarse, buccaneering past, and is a sort of fugitive from justice. But he is a good enough father to his two grown-up girls. The family lives in a log hut "castle," built on piles in the water, and the old man has also constructed an "ark," a sort of house-boat, in which he can take his daughters when he goes on his rounds to trap the beaver.

The two girls are the inevitable dark and light. Judith, dark, fearless, passionate, a little lurid with sin, is the scarlet-and-black blossom. Hetty, the younger, blonde, frail and innocent, is the white lily again. But alas, the lily has begun to fester. She is slightly imbecile.

The two hunters arrive at the lake among the woods just as war has been declared. The Hutters are unaware of the fact. And hostile Indians are on the lake already. So, the story of thrills and perils.

Thomas Hardy's inevitable division of women into dark and fair, sinful and innocent, sensual and pure, is Cooper's division too. It is indicative of the desire in the man. He wants sensuality and sin, and he wants purity and "innocence." If the innocence goes a little rotten, slightly imbecile, bad luck!

Hurry Harry, of course, like a handsome impetuous meat-fly, at once wants Judith, the lurid poppy-blossom. Judith rejects him with scorn.

Judith, the sensual woman, at once wants the quiet, reserved, unmastered Deerslayer. She wants to master him. And Deerslayer is half tempted, but never more than half. He is not going to be mastered. A philosophic old soul, he does not give much for the temptations of sex. Probably he dies virgin.

And he is right of it. Rather than be dragged into a false heat of deliberate sensuality, he will remain alone. His soul is alone, for ever alone.

So he will preserve his integrity, and remain alone in the flesh. It is a stoicism which is honest and fearless, and from which Deerslayer never lapses except when, approaching middle age, he proposes to the buxom Mabel.

He lets his consciousness penetrate in loneliness into the new continent. His contacts are not human. He wrestles with the spirits of the forest and the American wild, as a hermit wrestles with God and Satan. His one meeting is with Chingachgook, and this meeting is silent, reserved, across an impassable distance.

Hetty, the White Lily, being imbecile, although full of vaporous religion and the dear, good God, "who governs all things by his providence," is hopelessly infatuated with Hurry Harry. Being innocence gone imbecile, like Dostoevsky's Idiot, she longs to give herself to the handsome meat-fly. Of course he doesn't want her.

And so nothing happens: in that direction. Deerslayer goes off to meet Chingachgook, and help him woo an Indian maid. Vicarious.

It is the miserable story of the collapse of the white psyche. The white man's mind and soul are divided between these two things: innocence and lust, the Spirit and Sensuality. Sensuality always carries a stigma, and is therefore more deeply desired, or lusted after. But spirituality alone gives the sense of uplift, exaltation, and "winged life," with the inevitable reaction into sin and spite. So the white man is divided against himself. He plays off one side of himself against the other side, till it is really a tale, told by an idiot,[35] and nauseating.

Against this, one is forced to admire the stark, enduring figure of Deerslayer. He is neither spiritual nor sensual. He is a moralizer, but he always tries to moralize from an actual experience, not from theory. He says: "Hurt nothing unless you're forced to." Yet he gets his deepest thrill of gratification, perhaps when he puts a bullet through the heart of a beautiful buck, as it stoops to drink at the lake. Or when he brings the invisible bird fluttering down in death, out of the high blue. "Hurt nothing unless you're forced to." And yet he lives by death, by killing the wild things of the air and earth.

It's not good enough.

But you have there the myth of the essential white America. All the other stuff, the love, the democracy, the floundering into lust, is a sort of by-play. The essential American soul is hard, isolate, stoic, and a killer. It has never yet melted.

Of course, the soul often breaks down into disintegration, and you have lurid sin and Judith, imbecile innocence lusting, in Hetty, and bluster, bragging, and self-conscious strength, in Harry. But there are the disintegration products.

What true myth concerns itself with is not the disintegration product. True myth concerns itself centrally with the onward adventure of the integral soul. And this, for America, is Deerslayer. A man who turns his back on white society. A man who keeps his moral integrity hard and intact. An isolate, almost selfless, stoic, enduring man, who lives by death, by killing, but who is pure white. This is the very intrinsic-most American. He is at the core of all the other flux and fluff. And when *this* man breaks from his static isolation, and makes a new move, then look out, something will be happening.

〔注释〕

1. 拉丁语，大意为

And the question is put to everyone：

"Where on earth is the Toad-in-the-Hole？

And to everyone is answered，

"It is not invented."

下文的 inventus 即英文 invented。

2. Marinetti：马里内蒂（Fllippo Tommaso Marinetti, 1876-1944），意大利文艺理论家，1909 年发起未来主义运动。

3. Artzibashev：阿尔志巴绥夫（Mikhail Petrovich Artzibashev, 1878-1827），俄国作家，作品有《萨宁》（1907）等。

4. 参阅《旧约・出埃及记》第 2 章。埃及法老命令杀掉所有希伯莱女子所生的男婴，以灭其种族。希伯莱先知摩西出生后，母亲无奈，将他放在一蒲草箱内，置于河边的芦苇中。法老的女儿来河边洗澡，发现了箱子和孩子，遂将孩子抱入宫中喂养。

5. Lucretius：卢克莱修（约 99-55BC），古罗马诗人，唯物主义哲学家，伊壁鸠鲁的信徒，著有《物性论》。下文中 Apuleius：阿普列乌斯（约 123-180）古罗马作家、哲学家等。Tertullian：图尔图良（约 160-222），基督教教父之一。Augustine：奥古斯丁（354-430）古罗马帝国基督教思想家，教父哲学的主要代表。Athanasius：阿塔那修斯（328-373），古罗马亚历山大城主教。

6. Iberian：源于 Iberia，伊比利亚，古地名，今西班牙、葡萄牙。

7. Carthage：迦太基，古国名，今北非突尼斯北部。Libya：古希腊语"非洲"之意。作者列举这些，系指古罗马维吉尔的史诗《伊尼埃斯记》（*Aeneid*）。

8. ad nauseam：拉丁语，意为"令人作呕地"。

9. To point a moral and adorn a tale：引自英国 18 世纪作家塞缪尔・约翰逊（Samuel Johnson, 1709-1784）的长诗《人生希望多空幻》（"The Vanity of Human Wishes"）。原文为：

He left a name，at which the world grew pale，

To point a moral，or adorn a tale.

10. 引自莎士比亚《暴风雨》（*The Tempest*）第 2 幕第 2 场，与原文略有出入。原文为：

Ban，Ban，Cacaliban

Has a new master：—get a new man.

11. Liberia：利比里亚，1848 年为共和国。Haiti：海地，1804 年独立。这两个国家中由非洲而来的奴隶很多。

12. Thou shalt not：《旧约·出埃及记》记叙的摩西十诫皆如此行文。下文的 Thou shalt not…系作者模仿《十诫》的语气。

13. 作者以美国国徽上的鹰指代美国。

14. IT：指 the deepest whole self of man，the self in its wholeness, not idealistic halfness。参见下文。

15. 据希腊神话，俄瑞斯武斯（Orestes）为阿伽门农之子，在父为母所杀之后，为父复仇，杀死亲母，因此遭到复仇女神厄里尼厄斯（Erinyes），又名欧墨尼得斯（Eumenides）的追逐，变成疯子。后为女神雅典娜所赦，归国继承父位。

16. pins：指昆虫如蝴蝶等常被人用针穿透，用以制作标本，但死前常频颇振动双翼，嗡嗡作声。这里，作者把"Great Ideal"喻为"pin"。

17. 指徒具一套行为规范的"绅士"。

18. wigwam：北美东部和中部印第安人用兽皮或树皮覆盖的棚屋。

19. Cupids and Butterflies：古罗马爱神丘比特与普赛克（Psyche）相恋，但不准她窥见自己的面貌。普赛克出于好奇，夜里违命挑灯偷视，当她惊于丘比特的美貌之际，丘比特惊醒，离开普赛克。之后，普赛克为寻找丘比特曾历经艰险，两人最后又重归于好。希腊语普赛克为"蝴蝶"之意，也指人的灵魂。此处丘比特和蝴蝶均用复数，泛指以此故事为素材的巴黎旅馆天花板上的美术作品。

20. dejeuner：法语，意为"早餐"或"午餐"。

21. Monsieur Fenimore Cooper，le grand ecrivain americain：法语，意为"库柏先生，美国大文豪"。劳伦斯一语道破库柏思想上的矛盾和双重性。

22. *Odyssey*：《奥德赛》，古希腊史诗，相传为荷马所作，记述奥底修斯（Odysseus）自特洛伊战争后在海上漂泊十年，终于返回家园的艰难经历。在当代，Odyssey 也作"漂流"、"流浪"之意。

23. Circes：出自《奥德赛》。喀尔刻（Circe）为太阳神的女儿，精于巫法，曾将与奥底修斯同行的人变成猪，诱使奥底修斯在她的处所滞留一年之久。Ithacus：指奥底修斯。

24. Eumenides：欧墨尼得斯，复仇女神，参见注 15。

25. Chingachgook, the Great Serpent：“Chingachgook” 为印地安语，意为 “巨蛇”，参阅《最后的莫西干人》(*The Last of the Mohicans*) 第 6 章。

26. The letter killeth：意为 “条文害人”。引自《新约·哥林多后书》第 3 章，原文为：

Not of the letter, but of the spirit; for the letter killeth, but the spirit giveth life (Corinthian 3:6)。

27. Frank Norris：诺里斯（1870-1902），美国作家。下文中 *The Octopus*（《章鱼》）是他的代表作。

28. Bret Harte：哈特（1836-1902），美国短篇小说家。

29. Ishmael：指 Ishmael Bush，《草原》一书中的人物之一。他试图在西部荒原上建立某种文明和民主制度的想法，是纳蒂·班波所不赞成的。

30. Cyclops：赛克洛普斯，希腊神话里的独目巨人族的总称。据荷马在《奥德赛》中描写，他们住在极西方的山洞里，身材庞大，秉性残暴，不习耕作，不信神祇，没有法规。

31. Sioux Indians：美国印第安人部族的联合体，活动范围大至在今日的 Wisconsin，Minnesota 和 Dakota 等州。

32. Adonis：阿多尼斯，在希腊神话中，指腓尼基的自然之神，是植物凋零和复苏的象征。西语中 “阿多尼斯” 常作 “美男子” 的同义词，代表一种令人同情、带有感伤色彩的美，与阿波罗（Apollo）的阳刚之美不同。

33. White Lily：百合花，在西语中象征纯洁。这里指天真无助的爱丽丝。

34. Lilies that fester：引自莎士比亚《十四行诗》第 94 首，原文为：
Sweetest things turn sourest by their deeds
Lilies that fester smell far worse than weeds.

35. A tale told by an idiot：引自莎士比亚悲剧《麦克白斯》第 5 幕

第 5 场。原文为：

> It [life] is a tale
> Told by an idiot, full of sound and fury,
> Signifying nothing.

Questions For Discussion:

1. If every continent has its own spirit of place, what is the spirit of America with its "real, new experience"?

2. D. H. Lawrence seems to suggest that James Fenimore Cooper was torn, psychologically at least, between his longing for a wilderness and for a civilized mode of existence. Discuss.

3. What does D. H. Lawrence see in the Natty and Chingachgook myth?

4. How do the Leatherstocking Tales embody the myth of the essential white America?

For Further Reference:

1. Fussell, Edwin S. *Frontier: American Literature and the American West*. Princeton, N. J.: Princeton Univ. Press, 1957.

2. Smith, Henry Nash. *Virgin Land: The American West as Symbol and Myth*. Cambridge, Massachusetts, Harvard Univ. Press, 1950.

Henry Nash Smith

〔作者介绍〕

亨利·纳什·史密斯（Henry Nash Smith, 1906-1986），美国著名文学批评家、历史学家。他出生在美国得克萨斯州达拉斯城，毕业于美国南部卫理公会大学，后就读于哈佛大学，先后获得硕士和博士学位。1965 年起任美国艺术科学院院士。1950 年他的获奖著作《处女地：作为象征和神话的美国西部》（*Virgin Land: The American West as Symbol and Myth*）出版。该书成为美国文学研究的经典著作之一。史密斯博士是马克·吐温研究专家，写过多部研究马克·吐温的专著。

Virgin Land: The American West as Symbol and Myth

〔作品介绍〕

《处女地：作为象征和神话的美国西部》1950 年由美国哈佛大学出版社出版。

美国西部在美国社会发展过程中所起的作用，以及它对美国文学的影响，一直是美国历史学家和文学评论家所关心的问题。史密斯博士在本书中深入探讨了美国著名史学家弗雷德里克·杰克逊·特纳（Frederick Jackson Turner，1861-1932）在其《边疆在美国历史上的重要性》（"The Significance of the Frontier in American History，" 1893）一文中所提出的"边疆假设"的论点。特纳认为，一个自由区域的存在，它的不断的后退，以及美国向西部的拓殖，是美国社会发展的动力所在。特纳关于美国发展的论断从根本上改变了人们头脑中的旧有观念。史密斯博士在他的《处女地》这部开拓型专著里，谈到美国西部概念的形成过程，它对美国人意识的影响以及这种影响在美国文学与社会思潮中的反映。他还说到美国大陆的早期移民对如何建立美国所持有的截然不同的看法，简述了惠特曼、库柏、梭罗等作家对开拓西部的态度与见解。惠特曼高声讴歌美国开拓者们的西进运动，认为他们到达太平洋海岸之日，便是美国的盛世到来之时。库柏在自己的作品中竭力塑造一位西部开拓者的英雄形象。而在梭罗看来，世界只有在西部那一片荒原上才能存在下去。史密斯进而谈到被开拓出的西部以及由此而产生的"乐园神话"，这一神话成为19世纪美国社会发展的象征性神话，对美国及美国文学的发展都产生过相当影响。作家约瑟夫·柯克兰（Joseph Kirkland, 1830-1894）和哈姆林·加兰（Hamlin Garland, 1860-1940）的作品是美国西部这段历史的出色记录。

美国作家和文学评论家伯纳德·德沃托（Bernard de Voto, 1897-1955）在评论《处女地》一书时说："《处女地》不愧是一部在历史研究和文学批评两方面都有所建树的著作，一部有存在价值的著作。"

这里选注的是该书《前言》、第5章、第6章和第12章。

An Excerpt from *Virgin Land: The American West as Symbol and Myth*

PROLOGUE

Eighteenth-Century Origins

> I discern ... a new power, the People occupied in the wilderness...
> —William Gilpin[1],
> *The Central Gold Region* (1860)

What is an American? Asked St. John de Crevecoeur before the Revolution, and the question has been repeated by every generation from his time to ours. Poets and novelists, historians and statesmen have undertaken to answer it, but the varying national self-consciousness they have tried to capture always escapes final statement. Men of Thomas Jefferson's day emphasized freedom and republicanism as the defining characteristics of American society; the definitions of later thinkers stressed the cosmopolitan blending of a hundred peoples into one, or mechanical ingenuity, or devotion to business enterprise. But one of the most persistent generalizations concerning American life and character is the notion that our society has been shaped by the pull of a vacant continent drawing population westward through the passes of the Alleghenies, across the Mississippi Valley, over the high plains and mountains of the Far West to the Pacific Coast.

This axiom, which was grasped at least in part by Crevecocur, before him by Benjamin Franklin, and subsequently by Emerson, by Lincoln, by Whitman, by a hundred others, comes to us bearing the personal imprint of a Wisconsin historian, Frederick Jackson Turner, who gave it its classic statement in a paper on "The Significance of the Frontier in American History" read before the American Historical Association at the Chicago World's Columbian Exposition in 1893. Although Turner asserted that the westward movement was about to come to an end with what he believed to be the closing of the frontier of free land in the West, a whole generation of historians took over his hypothesis and rewrote American history in terms of it. Despite a growing tendency of scholars to react against the Turner doctrine, it is still by far the most familiar interpretation of the American past.

Brilliant and persuasive as Turner was, his contention that the frontier and the West had dominated American development could hardly have attained such universal acceptance if it had not found an echo in ideas and attitudes already current. Since the enormous currency of the theory proves that it voices a massive and deeply-held conviction, the recent debate over what Turner actually meant and over the truth or falsity of his hypothesis is much more than a mere academic quibble. It concerns the image of themselves which many—perhaps most—Americans of the present day cherish, an image that defines what Americans think of their past, and therefore what they propose to make of themselves in the future.

The present study traces the impact of the West, the vacant continent beyond the frontier, on the consciousness of Americans and follows the principal consequences of this impact in literature and social thought down to Turner's formulation of it. Whatever the merits of the Turner thesis, the doctrine that the United States is a continental nation rather than a member with Europe of an Atlantic community has had a formative influence on the American mind and deserves historical treatment in its own right.

At the opening of the eighteenth century the image of the West beyond the Appalachian Mountains was very dim in the minds of those subjects of the British crown who inhabited the fringe of colonies along the Atlantic coast. The unsettled forest no longer seemed, as it had to Michael Wigglesworth[2] in 1662, a "Devils den,"

> a waste and howling wilderness,
>> where none inhabited
> But hellish fiends, and brutish men
>> That devils worshiped.

Yet few English-speaking colonists had reliable knowledge of the interior of the continent. In so far as the West had come under European control at all, it was French. The English colonists had been engaged in war against this enemy as early as the 1690's, but not even the boldest prophet could imagine a day when the English power would extend over the unmeasured expanse of the Mississippi Valley. The imperial development of Britain was moving in another direction, toward dominion over the seven seas rather than toward the blank and remote hinterland of North America.

The earliest analyses of British policy in the Mississippi Valley proceed from these assumptions. Settlement in the interior might be expedient as a means of defense against the French or as an incident of the fur trade, but it had no meaning in itself. There was no reason for the government to encourage inland colonization because agricultural commodities were far too bulky to be transported from the interior to the seacoast and such colonies could have no part in the sea-borne commerce upon which the British Empire was based. The Council of Trade and Plantations declared in a memorial submitted to George I in 1721 that "all the settlements, that may at any time hereafter be made beyond the mountains, or on the lakes, must necessarily build their hopes of support much more upon the advantage to be made by the Indian trade, than upon any profits to arise from planting at so great a distance from the sea."

Even as late as 1763, when the French had been defeated and it was clear that British sovereignty would be extended over the Mississippi Valley, Lord Egremont, Secretary of State, proposed with perfect logic that Americans with an itch for emigration should be forbidden to move out into the interior. They should be directed instead to Nova Scotia or Georgia, near the sea, "where they would be useful to their Mother Country instead of planting themselves in the Heart of America out of reach of Government where from the great difficulty of procuring European commodities, they would be compelled to commerce and manufactures to the infinite prejudice of Britain…"

This was a rational analysis of the problem of the Empire. Colonies were sources of raw materials for which British merchants could find a market either in the United Kingdom or on the continent of Europe. Europe was still largely self-sufficient in the production of foodstuffs except for specifically subtropical items like sugar. There was a British or a European market for furs, for tobacco, and for "naval stores"—

turpentine, pitch, timber suitable for shipbuilding, and so on, but it seemed unlikely that farmers in the Ohio Valley would be able to produce any commodities worth transporting to a transatlantic market. Hardheaded economic thinking supported the faction in Parliament which opposed taking over the Mississippi Valley from France. And the economic argument was reinforced by the obvious administrative difficulties which would be created by expansion of population beyond easy reach of the seacoast.

But the American West was nevertheless there, a physical fact of great if unknown magnitude. It strongly influenced the debate over the nature of the Empire which preceded the Revolution. The interior of North America was an almost infinite expanse of arable land capable of supporting a large population. It was potential wealth on an unprecedented scale. The magnetic attraction of this untouched natural resource interfered with the conception of an empire based on maritime commerce by suggesting the quite different vision of a populous agricultural society, largely self-contained, in the Mississippi Valley. The West therefore posed a major question: Could the fabric of the Empire be made flexible enough to allow agricultural expansion in North America without breaking the economic and political integration centered in London?

It was possible for a sincere "imperial patriot" to maintain that such a creative development of the British system was both inevitable and desirable. The decision of William Pitt,[3] for example, to take over the French possessions in America at the Peace of Paris in 1763 indicated his acceptance of this general view. And the American colonies had already produced in Benjamin Franklin a far-seeing theorist who understood what a portentous role North America might play in the future development of British power. Franklin's pamphlets[4] on western settlement were occasioned by his interest in various land companies that were seeking grants in the Ohio Valley from the Crown, but his conclusions were a remarkably accurate prevision of what this new force would mean in the development of American society.

First of all, he grasped an elementary principle distilled from more than a century of English colonial experience in the New World: he saw that agriculture would long continue to be the dominant economic enterprise of continental America. Orthodox theory, which presupposed trade as the basis of British power, had been developed from the point of view of the merchant, and in this broad sense may be, for convenience, called mercantilist. Franklin, on the other hand, speaks as an agrarian. He starts out from the "political arithmetic" of John Graunt[5], Sir William Petty, and their followers in the late seventeenth century, a method which showed the first steps toward a statistical study of trends in population. But he realizes that the American birth rate, under the influence of an abundant supply of vacant land waiting always just beyond the frontier, bears no relation to the birth rate of "full-settled old Countries, as *Europe*." Population in the New World doubles every twenty years. Such a geometrical progression leads to staggering consequences. In a hundred years, he asserts, the population of the English-speaking colonies in America will be "more than the people of *England*, and the greatest Number of *Englishmen* will be on this Side the Water."[6]

Here was a new force with which British statesmen must deal. They might strive to suppress it by legislation for bidding settlement in the interior but—as Franklin blandly avoided saying until his patience wore thin under repeated failures to secure the land grants he wanted—such laws were not likely to have much effect. Besides, a brilliant and constructive alternative lay open to the makers of British policy. The merchants of England must realize that colonies like those in North America were vastly more important as potential markets than simply as sources of raw materials. Franklin undertakes to demonstrate that agricultural settlement of the interior, far from being meaningless to imperial trade, will provide the greatest of all outlets for British manufactures. Developing almost as an aside the theory that was to have currency down to our own day as the "safety-valve" doctrine, he points out that free land will constantly attract laborers from the cities and thus keep wages high. Manufacturing will continue to be unprofitable for Americans on this account in any foreseeable future, and the British merchant will enjoy a natural monopoly of a constantly expanding market for exports. The argument is set forth with admirable clarity in a pamphlet prepared in collaboration by Franklin and Richard Jackson, London agent for the colony of Pennsylvania:

> The new settlement will so continually draw off the spare hands from the old, that our present colonies will not... find themselves in a condition to manufacture even for their own inhabitants, to any considerable degree, much less for those who are settling behind them.

> Thus our *trade* must, till that country becomes as fully peopled as *England*, that is for centuries to come, be continually increasing, and with it our naval power; because the ocean is between us and them, and our ships and seamen must increase as that trade increases.

The vision roused Franklin to one of his rare moments of enthusiasm. "What an Accession of Power to the British Empire by Sea as well as Land!" he exclaimed with an emotion that we need not judge insincere. "What Increase of Trade and Navigation! What Numbers of Ships and Seamen!"

Nevertheless, Franklin's blueprint for a new Empire could hardly fail to arouse misgivings in English minds. He exhibits an unaccustomed naiveté in a letter to Lord Kames[7] in 1760: "I have long been of opinion, that the *foundations of the future grandeur and stability of the British empire lie in America....*" It was asking too much of Englishmen to look forward with pleasure to the time when London might become a provincial capital taking orders from an imperial metropolis somewhere in the interior of North America. Yet the idea had found expression long before Franklin seized upon it. Bishop Berkeley[8] had written with gentle melancholy in the 1720's that "Westward the course of empire takes its way," and Englishmen were familiar with his notion of a fated succession of world states. The empire of Greece had given way to that of Rome, Rome had yielded preeminence to northern Europe, the empires of France and Spain had waned as Britain had waxed in power. Was America fated to be the next inheritor of universal sway? By 1774 a contributor to the *Middlesex Journal* noted with disapproval that the idea of America as the future seat of empire was widely current in England, and a humorous skit in *Lloyd's Evening Post*, to which the mid-twentieth century has lent a grim dramatic irony, pictured two Americans visiting London in 1974 and finding it in ruins like Balbec[9] or Rome.

Americans naturally took such ideas more seriously than did Englishmen. The theme, for example, is developed at length in a poem on "The Rising Glory of America" written by Philip Freneau and Hugh Henry Brackenridge for the Princeton commencement of 1771. "Say," exclaim the class laureates,

> shall we ask what empires yet must rise,
> What kingdoms, pow'rs and states where now are seen
> But dreary wastes and awful solitude,
> Where melancholy sits with eye forlorn
> And hopes the day when Britain's sons shall spread
> Dominion to the north and south and west
> Far from th' Atlantic to Pacific shores?

In 1771 the vision was ambiguous: the question of whether Britain's sons on the Pacific shore would still be loyal subjects of the crown was left tactfully vague. But with the achievement of American independence, the belief in a continental destiny quickly became a principal ingredient in the developing American nationalism. In 1784 Thomas Hutchins, a protégé of George Croghan[10] who was interested in western land speculations and had been named "Geographer to the United States," published in his *Historical Narrative and Topographical Description of Louisiana, and West-Florida* a prophecy concerning the future development of the new nation that left little to be added by the philosophers of Manifest Destiny[11] in the 1840's. Using the traditional notion of a series of world empires, he finds in the natural resources of the North American continent promise of a power greater than any in the past. He estimates the habitable area of the continent—including Spanish possessions—at three and a half million square miles, and announces: "If we want it, I warrant it will soon be ours." The inhabitants of the potent empire which had already begun to develop in the New World,

> so far from being in the least danger from the attacks of any other quarter of the globe, will have it in their power to engross the whole commerce of it, and to reign, not only lords of America, but to possess, in the utmost security, the dominion of the sea throughout the world, which their ancestors enjoyed before them.

In a word, "North America… as surely as the land is now in being, will hereafter be trod by the first people the world ever knew."

Even conservative New England responded to the soaring theme when Timothy Dwight[12] included in his *Greenfield Hill* a rhapsody on westward expansion:

> All hail, thou western world! by heaven design'd
> Th' example bright, to renovate mankind.
> Soon shall thy sons across the mainland roam;
> And claim, on far Pacific shores, their home;
> Their rule, religion, manners, arts, convey,
> And spread their freedom to the Asian sea.

Where erst six thousand suns have roll'd the year

O'er plains of slaughter, and over wilds of fear,

Towns cities, fanes, shall lift their towery pride;

·The village bloom, on every streamlet's side;

Proud commerce' mole the western surges lave;

The long, white spire lie imag'd on the wave;

O'er morn's pellucid main expand their sails,

and the starr'd ensign court Korean gales.

There is even a hint of the vision of world brotherhood to be set forth later in Whitman's "Passage to India":

Then to new climes the bliss shall trace its way,

and Tartar deserts hail the rising day;

From the long torpor startled China wake;

Her chains of misery rous'd Peruvia break;

Man link to man; with bosom bosom twine;

And one great bond the house of Adam join;

The sacred promise full completion know,

And peace, and piety, the world o'erflow.

Thomas Jefferson had already made a more concrete analysis of the process by which he believed the entire continent was to be peopled from the "original nest" of the Atlantic settlements. The inhabited parts of the United States, he noted in 1786, had already attained a density of ten persons to the square mile, and "wherever we reach the inhabitants become uneasy, as too much compressed, and go off in great numbers to search for vacant country." The lesson of Daniel Boone's venture beyond the mountains had become clear:

We have lately seen a single person go & decide on a settlement in Kentucky, many hundred miles from any white inhabitant, remove thither with his family, and a few neighbors, & though perpetually harassed by the Indians, that settlement in the course of 10 years has acquired 30, 000 inhabitants, its numbers are increasing while we are writing, and the state of which it formerly made a part has offered it independence.

At this rate, he estimated all the territory east of the Mississippi would be occupied within forty years. Then the people would begin settling beyond the river, and eventually, no doubt, pour into South America as well.

Even before the treaty of peace that officially marked the end of the Revolution, Philip Freneau had elaborated his vision of future glory in the West. The North American empire of the future, he wrote in 1782, would bring agriculture to the summit of perfection and make the nations brothers by disseminating the riches of the New World throughout the earth. The world's great age would begin anew "those days of felicity… which are so beautifully described by the prophetic sages of ancient times." As in a hundred yet unwritten rhapsodies on the West, the physical fact of the continent dominates the scene. The American interior is presented as a new and enchanting region of inexpressible beauty and fertility. Through stately forests and rich meadows roam vast herds of animals which own no master, nor expect their sustenance from the hands of man. A thousand rivers flow into the mighty Mississippi,

who from a source unknown collecting his remotest waters, rolls forward through the frozen regions of the north, and stretching his extended arms to the east and west, embraces those savage groves, as yet uninvestigated by the traveler, unsung by the poet, or unmeasured by the chain of the geometrician; till uniting with the Ohio, and turning due south, receiving afterwards the Missouri[sic] and a hundred others, this prince of rivers, in comparison of whom the Nile is but a Rivulet and the Danube a mere ditch, hurries with his immense flood of waters to the Mexican sea, laving the shores of many fertile countries in his passage, inhabited by savage nations as yet almost unknown, and without a name.

The emotions that have gone into this passage are even more remarkable than its overt content. The stately trees, the buffalo (somehow transformed into mild sweet-breathed dairy herds, perhaps through the connotations of "meadows"), the bland climate, are bathed in a golden mist of utopian fantasy. The Channing hint of frontier-boasting in the comparison between the Mississippi and rivers known to fame in the Old World serves as comic seasoning for the solemn and elevated prose; and the whole is pulled together at the end on a note of remoteness, strangeness, yet haunting potential accessibility. What traveler should penetrate the groves and solitudes, what explorer name the nameless savage tribes, what poet sing the westward-flowing rivers?

The early visions of an American Empire embody two different if often mingled conceptions. There is on the one hand the notion of empire as command of the sea, and on the other hand the notion of empire as populous future society occupying the interior of the American continent. If these two kinds of empire are not mutually exclusive—for we can readily concede that patriots would want to claim every separate glory for their country—they nevertheless rest on different economic base and imply different policies. Engrossing the trade of the world is an ambition evidently taken over from the British mercantilist ideal. On the other hand, creating new states in the dreary solitudes of the West is an enterprise that depends upon the increase of population resulting from agricultural expansion into an empty, fertile continent. This second version of the American Empire, based on agrarian assumptions, more nearly corresponds to the actual course of events during the nineteenth century.

Both these conceptions predict the outcome of the westward movement. Empire conceived as maritime dominion presupposes American expansion westward to the Pacific. The idea draws upon the long history and rich overtones of the search for a northwest passage to

Asia, or, in Whitman's phrase, a "passage to India." It will occupy our attention in Book One. The hunter and trapper who served as the pathfinder of overland expansion and became one of the fixtures of American mythology forms the subject of Book Two. The very different idea of a continental empire dependent upon agriculture, and associated with various images of the Good Society to be realized in the West, may be called the theme of the Garden of the World. Its development will be traced in Book Three.

CHAPTER V

DANIEL BOONE: EMPIRE BUILDER OR PHILOSOPHER OF PRIMITIVISM?

During the summer of 1842, following his sophomore year at Harvard, Francis Parkman[13] made a trip through northern New York and New England. After spending several days admiring the scenery along the shores of Lake George, he noted in his journal: "There would be no finer place of gentlemen's seats than this, but now, for the most part, it is occupied by a race of boors about as uncouth, mean, and stupid as the hogs they seem chiefly to delight in." The tone is even blunter than that of Timothy Dwight's famous description of backwoodsmen in this area a generation earlier, but it embodies a comparable aristocratic disdain. Observers from Eastern cities made similar comments about uncultivated farmers along every American frontier. The class bias underlying the judgment was one of the dominant forces shaping nineteenth-century attitudes toward the West.

When Parkman got away from farms and hogs, out into the forest, his tone changed completely. He wrote, for example, that a woodsman named

James Abbot, although coarse and self-willed, was "a remarkably intelligent fellow; has astonishing information for one of his condition; is resolute and independent as the wind." The young Brahmin's delight in men of the wilderness comes out even more forcibly in the journal of his Far Western trip four years later. *The Oregon Trail* presents the guide Henry Chatillon, a French-Canadian squaw man, as a hero of romance—handsome, brave, true, skilled in the ways of the plains and mountains, and even possessed of "a natural refinement and delicacy of mind, such as is rare even in women."

Parkman's antithetical attitudes toward backwoods farmers and the hunters and trappers of the wilderness illustrate the fact that for Americans of that period there were two quite distinct Wests: the commonplace domesticated area within the agricultural frontier, and the Wild West beyond it. The agricultural West was tedious; its inhabitants belonged to a despised social class. The Wild West was by contrast an exhilarating region of adventure and comradeship in the open air. Its heroes bore none of the marks of degraded status. They were in reality not members of society at all, but noble anarchs owning no master, free denizens of a limitless wilderness.

Parkman's love of the Wild West implied a paradoxical rejection of organized society. He himself was the product of a complex social order formed by two centuries of history, and his way of life was made possible by the fortune which his grandfather had built up as one of the great merchants of Boston. But a young gentleman of leisure could afford better than anyone else, to indulge himself in the slightly decadent cult of wildness and savagery which the early nineteenth century took over from Byron. Historians call the mood "primitivism." Parkman had a severe case. In later life he said that from his early youth "His thoughts were always in the forest, whose features possessed his waking and sleeping dreams, filling him with vague cravings impossible to satisfy." And in a preface to

The Oregon Trail written more than twenty years after the first publication of the book he bewailed the advance of humdrum civilization over the wide empty plains of Colorado since the stirring days of 1846.

Such a mood of refined hostility to progress affected a surprising number of Parkman's contemporaries. Nevertheless, it could hardly strike very deep in a society committed to an expansive manifest destiny. A romantic love of the vanishing Wild West could be no more than a self-indulgent affectation beside the triumphant official cult of progress, which meant the conquest of the wilderness by farms and towns and cities. If there was a delicious melancholy for sophisticated and literary people in regretting the destruction of the primitive freedom of an untouched continent, the westward movement seemed to less imaginative observers a glorious victory of civilization over savagery and barbarism. For such people—and they were the vast majority—the Western hunter and guide was praiseworthy not because of his intrinsic wildness or half-savage glamour, but because he blazed trails that hardworking farmers could follow.

One of the most striking evidences of the currency of these two conflicting attitudes toward the westward movement is the popular image of Daniel Boone. The official view was set forth in a greatly admired piece of allegorical sculpture by Horatio Greenough[14] in the National Capitol, which depicted the contest between civilization and barbarism as a fierce hand-to-hand struggle between Boone and an Indian warrior. George C. Bingham's[15] painting "The Emigration of Daniel Boone" (1851) showed the celebrated Kentuckian leading a party of settlers with their wives and children and livestock out, into a dreamily beautiful wilderness which they obviously meant to bring under the plow.

These empire-building functions were amply documented by the facts of history. Boone had supervised the Treaty of Sycamore Shoals which extinguished the Indian claim to much of Kentucky, he had blazed the

Wilderness Trail through the forest, and after leading the first settlers to Boonesborough in 1775, he had stoutly defended this outpost of civilization against the Indians during the troubled period of the Revolution. His functions as founder of the commonwealth of Kentucky had been celebrated as early as 1784 by John Filson, first architect of the Boone legend, in *The Discovery, Settlement and Present State of Kentucky*. Filson represents Boone as delighting in the thought that Kentucky will soon be one of the most opulent and powerful states on the continent, and finding in the love and gratitude of his countrymen a sufficient reward for all his toil and sufferings. The grandiose epic entitled *The Adventures of Daniel Boone*, published in 1813 by Daniel Bryan, a nephew of the hero, is even more emphatic concerning his devotion to social progress. Complete with Miltonic councils in Heaven and Hell,[16] the epic relates how Boone was chosen by the angelic Spirit of Enterprise to bring Civilization to the trans-Allegheny wilderness. When he is informed of his divine election for this task, Boone's kindling fancy beholds Refinement's golden file smoothing the heathen encrustations from the savage mind, while Commerce, Wealth, and all the brilliant Arts spread over the land. He informs his wife in a Homeric leave-taking that the sovereign law of Heaven requires him to tread the adventurous stage of grand emprise, scattering knowledge through the heathen wilds, and mending the state of Universal Man. Faithful to his mission even in captivity among the Indians, he lectures the chief Montour on the history of the human race, concluding with reflections on

> How Philanthropy
> And social Love, in sweet profusion pour
> Along Refinement's pleasure-blooming Vales,
> Their streams of richest, life-ennobling joy.

By the side of Boone the empire builder and philanthropist, the anonymous popular mind had meanwhile created an entirely different hero, a fugitive from civilization who could not endure the encroachment of settlements upon his beloved wilderness. A dispatch from Fort Osage[17] in the Indian territory, reprinted in *Niles' Register* in 1816, described an interview with Boone and added: "This singular man could not live in Kentucky when it became settled... he might have accumulated riches as readily as any man in Kentucky, but he *prefers the woods*, where you see him in the dress of the roughest, poorest hunter."

Boone's flight westward before the advance of the agricultural frontier—actually dictated by a series of failures in his efforts to get and hold hand—became a theme of newspaper jokes. The impulse that produced Western tall tales transformed him into the type of all frontiersmen who required unlimited elbow room. "As civilization advanced," wrote a reporter in the New York *American* in 1823, "so he, from time to time, retreated"—from Kentucky to Tennessee, from Tennessee to Missouri. But Missouri itself was filling up: Boone was said to have complained, "I had not been two years at the licks before a d-d Yankee came, and settled down *within an hundred miles of me*!!" He would soon be driven on out to the Rocky Mountains and would be crowded there in eight or ten years. Edwin James, chronicler of the Stephen H. Long[18] expedition, visiting Fort Osage in 1819, heard that Boone felt it was time to move again when he could no longer fell a tree for fuel so that its top would lie within a few yards of the door of his cabin. This remark set James, a native of Vermont, to thinking about the irrational behavior of frontiersmen. He had observed that most inhabitants of new states and territories had "a manifest propensity, particularly in the males, to remove westward, for which it is not easy to account." There was an apparently irresistible charm for the true Westerner in a mode of life "Wherein the artificial wants and the uneasy restraints inseparable from a crowded population are not known, wherein we feel ourselves dependent immediately and solely on the bounty of nature, and the strength of our own arm...." The long party came upon a man more than sixty years old living near the farthest settlement up the Missouri who questioned them minutely about the still unoccupied Platte Valley.[19] "We discovered," noted James with astonishment, "that he had the most serious intention of removing with his family to that river."

Seizing upon hints of Boone's flight before the advance of civilization, Byron paused in his description of the siege of Ismail in the eighth canto of *Don Juan* to insert an extended tribute to him. Although Byron's Boone shrank from men of his own nation when they built up unto his darling trees, he was happy, innocent, and benevolent; simple, not savage; and even in old age still a child of nature, whose virtues shamed the corruptions of civilization. Americans quoted these stanzas eagerly.

Which was the real Boone—the standard-bearer of civilization and refinement, or the child of nature who fled into the wilderness before the advance of settlement? An anonymous kinsman of Boone wrestled with the problem in a biographical sketch published a few years after the famous hunter's death in 1820. It would be natural to suppose, he wrote, that the Colonel took great pleasure in the magnificent growth of the commonwealth he had founded in the wilderness. But such was not the case. Passionately fond of hunting, "like the unrefined Savage," Boone saw only that incoming settlers frightened away all the game and spoiled the sport. He would "certainly prefer a state of nature to a state of Civilization, if he were obliged to be confined to one or the other."

Timothy Flint's biography,[20] perhaps the most widely read book about a Western character published during the first half of the nineteenth century, embodies the prevalent confusion of attitudes. Flint says that Boone delighted in the thought that "the rich and boundless valleys of the great west—the garden of the earth—and the paradise of hunters, had been won from the dominion of the savage tribes, and opened as an asylum for the oppressed, the enterprising, and the free of every land." The explorer of Kentucky

> had caught some glimmerings of the future, and saw with the
> prophetic eye of a patriot, that this great valley must soon become
> the abode of millions of freemen; and his heart swelled with joy, and
> warmed with a transport which was natural to a mind so
> unsophisticated and disinterested as his.

Yet we learn only a few pages later that he was driven out of
Kentucky by "the restless spirit of immigration, and of civil and physical
improvement." Even in Missouri, "the tide of emigration once more swept
by the dwelling of Daniel Boone, driving off the game and monopolizing
the rich hunting grounds." In despair,

> he saw that it was in vain to contend with fate; that go, where
> he would, American enterprise seemed doomed to follow him, and
> to thwart all his schemes of backwoods retirement. He found
> himself once more surrounded by the rapid march of improvement,
> and he accommodated himself, as well as he might, to a "state" of
> things which he could not prevent.

On yet other occasions Flint credits Boone with a sophisticated cult
of pastoral simplicity greatly resembling his own which he had imitated
from Chateaubriand.[21] When the frontiersman seeks to induce settlers to
go with him into the new land, he is represented as promising them that
the original pioneers, in their old age, will be surrounded by

> consideration, and care, and tenderness from children, whose
> breasts were not steeled by ambition, nor hardened by avarice; in
> whom the beautiful influences of the indulgence of none but natural
> desires and pure affections would not be deadened by the selfishness,
> vanity, and fear of ridicule, that are the harvest of what is called
> *civilized and cultivated life.*

The debate over Boone's character and motives lasted into the next
decade. The noted Western Baptist minister and gazetteer, John M. Peck,

prepared a life of Boone for Jared Sparks's[22] Library of American Biography in 1847 which repeatedly attacked the current conception of the hero as a fugitive from civilization. Peck says that Boone left North Carolina for the Kentucky wilderness because of the effeminacy and profligacy of wealthy slave owners who scorned the industrious husbandman working his own fields. But by the time the biographer interviewed the aged hero in Missouri in 1818, Boone had become aware of an imposing historical mission. Although he had not consciously aimed to lay the foundations of a state or nation, he believed that he had been "a creature of Providence, ordained by Heaven as a pioneer in the wilderness, to advance the civilization and the extension of his country."

James H. Perkins, of Cincinnati, writing in 1846 in the *North American Review*, was equally interested in the problem of Boone's motives, but inclined to a more modest interpretation. Boone, he said, was a white Indian. Although he and his companions were not at all like the boasting, swearing, drinking, gouging Mike Fink[23] of the later West, they were led into the wilderness not by the hope of gain, nor by a desire to escape the evils of older communities, nor yet by dreams of founding a new commonwealth, but simply, by "a love of nature, of perfect freedom, and of the adventurous life in the woods." Boone "would have pined and died as a nabob in the midst of civilization. He wanted a frontier, and the perils and pleasures of a frontier life, not Wealth; and he was happier in his log-cabin, with a loin of venison and his ramrod for a spit, than he would have been amid the greatest profusion of modern luxuries." If one detects a patronizing note in this account, it goes along with a greater respect for the simple, hearty virtues that are left to the frontiersman. Such a view seems to have become general in the 1840's. William H. Emory of the Army of the West which invaded New Mexico in 1846 invoked the figure of the Kentuckian to convey his impression of an American settler in the Mora Valley northeast of Santa Fe: "He is a perfect specimen of a generous openhearted adventurer, and in appearance what I have pictured to myself, Daniel Boone, of Kentucky, must have been in his day."

Yet the issue long remained unsettled. As a character in fiction Boone could still be made the spokesman of a stilted primitivism. Glenn, the young Eastern hero of John B. Jones's shoddy *Wild Western Scenes* published in 1849, is traveling in the vicinity of Boone's last home in Missouri, and there encounters the venerable pioneer. The highly implausible conversation between the two men indicates to what unhistorical uses the symbol of Boone could be put. The Westerner asks Glenn whether he has become disgusted with the society of men. Glenn, who happens to be just such a rhetorical misanthrope as the question implies, welcomes the opportunity to set forth his views:

> I had heard [he declares] that you were happy in the solitude of the mountain-shaded valley; or on the interminable prairies that greet the horizon in the distance, where neither the derision of the proud, the malice of the envious, nor the deceptions of pretended love and friendship, could disturb your peaceful meditation; and from amid the wreck of certain hopes, which I once thought no circumstances could destroy [it is a matter of disappointment in love], I rose with a determined vow to seek such a wilderness, where I would pass a certain number of my days engaging in the pursuits that might be most congenial to my disposition. Already I imagine I experience the happy effects of my resolution. Here the whispers of vituperating foes cannot injure, nor the smiles of those fondly cherished, deceive.

Boone clasps the young coxcomb's hand in enthusiastic agreement. If, Daniel Bryan's epic represents the limit of possible absurdity in making Boone the harbinger of civilization and refinement, this may stand as the opposite limit of absurdity in making him a cultural primitivist. The image of the Wild Western hero could serve either purpose.

CHAPTER VI

LEATHERSTOCKING AND THE PROBLEM OF SOCIAL ORDER

Although Boone was not exactly the prototype of Cooper's Leatherstocking, there is a haunting similarity between the two figures. Cooper based a part of chapters X and XII of *The Last of the Mohicans* on a well-known exploit of Boone in conducting the rescue of Betsey and Fanny Callaway and Jemima Boone, his daughter, from the Cherokees. Betsey Callaway, like Cora Munro in Cooper's novel, tried to aid her rescuers by breaking twigs to mark the trail, and was detected by her Indian guards. The rescuer also furnished Cooper with several other details for his story.

Near the opening of *The Prairie* Cooper sets his stage by describing the migration of Americans from Ohio and Kentucky across the Mississippi immediately after the Louisiana Purchase. Although Boone actually settled in Missouri in 1799, Cooper names him among the emigrants of 1804:

This adventurous and venerable patriarch was now seen making his last remove; placing the "endless river" between him and the multitude, his own success had drawn around him, and seeking for the renewal of enjoyments which were rendered worthless in his eyes, when trammelled by the forms of human institutions.

In a footnote added to the revised edition, Cooper elaborates this passage with the remark that Boone emigrated beyond the Mississippi "because he found a population of ten to the square mile, inconvenient." The aged Leatherstocking has likewise "been driven by the increasing and unparalleled advance of population, to seek a final refuge against society in the broad and tenantless plains of the west..."

The similarities between Boone and Leatherstocking were analyzed at length by a perceptive writer in *Niles' Register* in 1825, when Leatherstocking had appeared in only one novel, *The Pioneers*. The critic points out that both these heroes love the freedom of the forest, both take a passionate delight in hunting, and both dislike the ordinary pursuits of civilized men. As testimony to the fidelity of Cooper's characterization, the writer quotes a letter from a traveler through the Pennsylvania mountains who came upon herdsmen and hunters reminiscent both of Boone and of Leatherstocking. One of their number, celebrated throughout the West as having once been a companion of Boone, had set out for Arkansas when he was almost a hundred years old, and was reported to be still alive, a solitary hunter in the forest. A nephew of the emigrant who remained in Pennsylvania, himself athletic and vigorous at the age of seventy, shared Leatherstocking's love of hunting and his antipathy for "clearings" to such a marked degree that the traveler felt he must have sat as a model for Cooper. A similar point was made by the poet Albert Pike, who after graduating from Harvard, went out the Santa Fe Trail and later settled in a very primitive Arkansas. "I cannot wonder that many men have chosen to pass their life in the woods," wrote Pike in 1834, "and I see nothing overdrawn or exaggerated in the character of Hawkeye and Bushfiled."[24] He listed as the prime attractions of the lonely hunter's life its independence, its freedom from law and restraint, its lack of ceremony.

For at least one section of the reading public, then, Leatherstocking, like Boone, was a symbol of anarchic freedom, an enemy of law and order. Did this interpretation conform to Cooper's intention in drawing the character?

The original hunter of *The Pioneers* (1823) clearly expresses subversive impulses. The character was conceived in terms of the antithesis between nature and civilization, between freedom and law, that has governed most American interpretations of the westward movement. Cooper was able to speak for his people on this theme because the forces at work within him closely reproduced the patterns of thought and feeling that prevailed in the society at large. But he felt the problem more deeply than his contemporaries: he was at once more strongly devoted to the principle of social order and more vividly responsive to the ideas of nature and freedom in the Western forest than they were. His conflict of allegiances was truly ironic, and if he had been able—as he was not—to explore to the end the contradictions in his ideas and emotions, the Leatherstocking series might have become a major work of art. Despite Cooper's failures, the character of Leatherstocking is by far the most important symbol of the national experience of adventure across the continent. The similarities that link Leatherstocking to both the actual Boone and the various Boones of popular legend are not merely fortuitous.

The Pioneers illustrates these aspects of Cooper's work with almost naive directness. After a negligible first novel, *Precaution*, he had turned to the matter of the American Revolution in *The Spy*, which had a sensational success. The Preface to *The Pioneers*, his next book, has a jaunty air bespeaking the apprentice novelist's growing confidence: Cooper announces that he is now writing to please himself alone. We may well believe him, for the scene is the Cooperstown of his childhood, and the character, of Judge Marmaduke Temple, patron of the infant community, landed proprietor, justice of the peace, and virtual lord of the manor, has much in common with that of the novelist's father William Cooper. Not only did both William Cooper and Judge Temple buy land on the New York frontier and oversee the planting of a town on the shores of Lake Otsego; they resemble one another even in the minor detail of springing from Quaker forebears but having given up formal membership in the sect. When an author turns to autobiographical material of this sort and introduces a central character resembling his father, one does not have to be very much of a Freudian to conclude that the imagination is working on a deeper level than usual. This is certainly the case in *The Pioneers*.

Still very much an amateur in the externals of his craft, Cooper contrived for his story of Cooperstown a flimsy plot that hinges upon a childish misunderstanding about Judge Temple's administration of the property of his old friend Major Effingham, but the plot is merely a framework to hold together a narrative focused about an entirely different problem. The emotional and literary center of the story is a conflict between Judge Temple and the old hunter Leatherstocking which symbolizes the issues raised by the advance of agricultural settlement into the wilderness. In the management of this theme Cooper is at his best. From the opening scene, when Judge Temple claims as his own a deer that Leatherstocking's young companion has shot, until the moment when the Judge sentences the old hunter to a fine and imprisonment because of his resistance to the new game laws, the narrative turns constantly about the central issue of the old forest freedom versus the new needs of a community which must establish the sovereignty of law over the individual. One aspect of the conflict is, of course, the question of a primitive free access to the bounty of nature—whether in the form of game or of land—versus individual appropriation and the whole notion of inviolable property rights. Not far in the background are the further issues of the rough equality of all men in a state of nature as against social stratification based on unequal distribution of property; and of formal institutional religion versus the natural, intuitive theology of Leatherstocking, who has little regard for theological niceties or the minutia of ritual.

The profundity of the symbol of Leatherstocking springs from the fact that Cooper displays a genuine ambivalence toward all these issues, although in every case his strongest commitment is to the forces of order. The social compact, with all its consequences, is vividly and freshly realized, as it had to be realized with every new community planted in the wilderness. And all the aspects of authority—institutional stability, organized religion, class stratification, property—are exhibited as radiating from the symbol of the father. But if the father rules, and rules justly, it is still true that in this remembered world of his childhood Cooper figures as the son. Thus he is able to impart real energy to the statement of the case for defiance and revolt.

But we are not concerned with Cooper's personal relation to his materials so much as with his treatment of the themes arising from the advance of the agricultural frontier. The broader setting for the story is indicated in an exclamation of Elizabeth Temple: "The enterprise of Judge Temple is taming the very forests! How rapidly is civilization treading on the footsteps of nature!" When Elizabeth, with a burst of womanly sympathy for the imprisoned Leatherstocking, declares he must be innocent because of his inherent goodness, her father makes a crucial distinction: "Thou hast reason. Bess and much of it too, but thy heart lies too near thy head." The Judge himself means to pay Leatherstocking's fine, but he cannot brush aside the sentence of imprisonment which he imposed as the spokesman of necessary justice. He sends Elizabeth with a purse to visit the hunter and comfort him: "…say what thou: wilt to the poor old man; give scope to the feelings of thy warm heart; but try to remember, Elizabeth, that the laws alone remove us from the condition of the savages; that he has been criminal, and that his judge was thy father."

Another interesting scene occurs when the sonless Judge Temple invites Oliver Effingham to enter his household as a secretary. Oliver hesitates. Richard, the Judge's pompous factotum, says in an aside to Elizabeth, "This, you see, cousin Bess, is the natural reluctance of a half-breed to leave the savage state. Their attachment to a wandering life is, I verily believe, unconquerable." The Judge remarks that the unsettled life of a hunter "is of vast disadvantage for temporal purposes; and it totally removes one from within the influences of more sacred things." But this rouses Leatherstocking, who bursts out:

No, no, Judge…take him into your shanty in welcome, but tell him the real thing. I have lived in the woods for forty long years, and have spent five years at a time without seeing the light of a clearing, bigger than a wind-row in the trees, and I should like to know where you'll find a man, in his sixty-eighth year, who can get an easier living, for all your betterments, and your deer-laws: and, as for honesty, or doing what's right between man and man, I'll not turn my back to the longest winded deacon on your patent.

This states the issue as succinctly as possible. Cooper is unable to solve it, and resorts to a compromise statement that represents exactly his unwillingness or inability to accept the full implications of the conflict he has stated. The Judge answers, "nodding, good-naturedly at the hunter": "Thou art an exception, Leatherstocking; for thou hast a temperance unusual in thy class and a hardihood exceeding thy years. But this youth is made of materials too precious to be wasted in the forest."

The Judge's reply expresses the unfailing regard for status which qualified Cooper's attitude toward the idea of nature as a norm. Leatherstocking, noble child of the forest, is nevertheless of inferior social status; whereas even in disguise, Oliver's gentle birth is palpable to the Judge's Falstaffian instinct. Leatherstocking began life as a servant of Major Effingham, and he is wholly illiterate. The fact that he speaks in dialect is a constant reminder of his lowly origin. It is true that the social status of the old hunter was not to prove significant during the long passages of adventure in *The Last of the Mohicans* and *The Prairie*, which deal with Indian warfare and the rescue of Cooper's distressed heroines from their captors. Here Leatherstocking's prowess with the rifle, his talents as a strategist, and his skill in following trails could be exploited with little regard for gradations in rank. But the problem of the hunter's status could not be permanently ignored. The response of readers to this symbol of forest freedom and virtue created a predicament for the novelist by revealing to him that his most vital character occupied a technically inferior position both in the social system and in the form of the sentimental novel as he was using it. The store of emotion associated with the vast wilderness in the minds of both Cooper and his audience was strikingly inharmonious with the literary framework he had adopted.

A more self-conscious or experimentally inclined writer might have found in this situation a challenge to devise a new form, proceeding functionally from the materials. But Cooper was not the man to undertake a revolution, either in life or in literature. He chose a different course of action; he set about modifying the traditional form of the novel as far as he could without actually shattering it, and at the same time altering his materials as much as possible to make them fit.

Cooper's efforts to solve his problem can be traced in the last two novels of the Leatherstocking series, *The Pathfinder* and *The Deerslayer*, which appeared in 1840 and 1841. In *The Prairie*, published thirteen years before, he had described the death of Leatherstocking, and had at that time meant to abandon the character forever. This decision seems to have been due in part to the technical difficulty mentioned above, for in later years Cooper told his daughter he wished he had left out of *The Prairie* the genteel hero and heroine, Inez de Certavallos and Captain Middleton, retaining only those characters who properly belonged to the locale. But if the upper-class hero and heroine were to be omitted, and Leatherstocking was to be promoted to the post of official hero, how was the plot to be managed? It is at this point that Cooper's reluctance to break witch the conventions of the sentimental novel becomes most glaringly apparent. A novel, according to canons which he considered binding, was a love story. The hero of the novel was the man who played the male lead in the courtship. If Leatherstocking was to be promoted to this rank, he must be made to fall in love with a heroine. In *The Pathfinder*, Cooper accordingly, sets to work with great good will to exhibit Leatherstocking in love. The problem was to construct a female character, sufficiently refined and genteel to pass muster as a heroine, but sufficiently low in social status to receive the addresses of the hunter and scout without a shocking and indecent violation of the proprieties.

The object of Leathersfocking's affection, Mabel Dunham, is the daughter of a sergeant—not an officer—in the British army. When she is first introduced in the company of Cap, her seafaring uncle, who occupies "a station little, if any, above that of a common mariner," Cooper is careful to point out that Mabel is "a maiden of a class in no great degree superior to his own." She is, therefore, technically accessible to the lower-class Leatherstocking. But before she can qualify as a heroine, Mabel has to be given some of the attributes of gentility. Cooper explains elaborately that upon the death of her mother Mabel had been taken in charge by the widow of a field-officer of her father's regiment. Under the care of this lady Mabel had acquired "some tastes, and many ideas, which otherwise might always have remained strangers to her." The results of this association

> were quite apparent in her attire, her language, her sentiments, and even in her feelings, though neither, perhaps, rose to the level of those which would properly characterize a lady. She had lost the coarser and less refined habits and manners of one in her original position; without having quite reached a point that disqualified her for the situation in life that the accidents of birth and fortune would probably compel her to fill.

In particular, Mabel had acquired a degree of sensibility that caused her to respond in approved fashion to the beauty of landscape—an index in Cooper almost as infallible as that of language for distinguishing the upper classes from the lower.

Ironically enough, the novelist's care in refining Mabel creates a fresh problem for him. The modifications of her character that qualify her for the role of heroine raise her somewhat above the actual range of Leatherstocking's manners and tastes. When Mabel's father proposes the marriage, Leatherstocking is timid about it. He fears that a "poor ignorant woodsman" cannot hope to win the girl's affection. The sergeant compels the scout to admit that he is a man of experience in the wilderness, well able to provide for a wife; a veteran of proved courage in the wars; a loyal subject of the King. But Leatherstocking still demurs: "I'm afeard I'm too rude, and too old, and too wild like, to suit the fancy of such a young and delicate girl, as Mabel, who has been unused to our wilderness ways, and may think the settlements better suited to her gifts and inclinations." Pressed still further, Leatherstockipg makes an avowal that throws a flood of light on: Cooper's conception of the social relationships prevailing within his standard tableau of a captured heroine in the process of being rescued by Leatherstocking and a genteel hero:

> I have traveled with some as fair; and have guided them through the forest, and seen them in their perils and in their gladness; but they were always too much above me, to make me think of them as more than so many feeble ones I was bound to protect and defend. The case is now different. Mabel and I are so nearly alike, that I feel weighed down with a load that is hard to bear, at finding us so unlike. I do wish, sergeant, that I was ten years younger [the scout was then presumably in his early thirties], more comely to look at, and better suited to please a handsome young woman's fancy!

In short, "I am but a poor hunter, and Mabel, I see, is fit to be an officer's lady." She is indeed, as appears in the course of the story when the regimental quartermaster wants to marry her; or is she? Cooper subsequently causes this officer to prove a traitor, perhaps because of an unconscious impulse to punish him, for his subversive disregard of class lines. In any event, when the actual moment of Leatherstocking's proposal arrives, Mabel's superior refinement is so unmistakable that it decides the issue. One or Cooper's very few valid comic inventions causes her, in her confusion, to use a more and more involved rhetoric that Leatherstocking cannot follow at all. He has to resort to his characteristic query, "Anan?"[25] The match is quite unsuitable and in the end Leatherstocking has the exquisite masochistic pleasure of giving his blessing to her union with Jasper Western, the young, handsome, and worthy Great Lakes sailor.

If Leatherstocking could hardly be imagined as married, however, a feeling for symmetry would suggest that he at least might be shown as himself hopelessly beloved. This is the formula of the last novel of the series, *The Deerslayer*, which removes the obstacle of the hero's age by going back to the period of his early youth and thus represents the utmost possible development of Leatherstocking into a hero of romance. In this story he is loved by Judith Hutter, beautiful daughter of a somewhat coarse backwoodsman. But Judith's reputation is stained by past coquetries: she is obviously not an appropriate mate for the chaste Leatherstocking and eventually is consigned to an offstage marriage with a British officer.

Despite these late experiments in depicting Leatherstocking in his youth, the persistent image of the hunter was that of his first appearance, as a man of venerable age. This trait of Leatherstocking was strengthened by whatever parallels were felt to exist between him and Daniel Boone. When John Filson's biography of Boone appeared in1784, the Kentuckian, at fifty, already seemed a patriarchal figure, his active days of fighting in the past. The folk cult of Boone that developed after 1815 emphasized the picturesque conception of an octogenarian huntsman. Cooper himself gives testimony to the popular tendency to exaggerate Boone's age when he remarks in a note to the revised edition of *The Prairie* that the famous hunter emigrated to Missouri "in his ninety-second year." Boone was actually sixty-five when that event occurred. The many Western hunters created in the image of Leatherstocking who people Western fiction through most of the nineteenth century are characteristically of advanced age.

If Leatherstocking was, so to speak, intrinsically aged, this fact hindered his transformation into a hero of romance as seriously as did his low social status. Cooper was thus led to experiment with younger heroes who had Leatherstocking's vital relation to the forest, but were more easily converted into lovers. The character of Oliver Effingham in *The Pioneers* had early suggested the idea of a young hunter, wearing the garb and following the vocation of Leatherstocking. In *The Prairie* the impulse to double the role of the hunter in this fashion yields the character of Paul Hover, who, like Oliver, appears as an associate of Leatherstocking but is a real instead of merely a pretended child of the backwoods. Paul is a native of Kentucky and has a dialect that is the unmistakable badge of lowly status. It is true that he is merely a bee hunter rather than a hunter of deer and bear, but his sentiments concerning the rifle and his skill at marksmanship arouse Leatherstocking's enthusiastic approval. The most interesting thing about Paul is that, despite the presence in this novel of the official genteel hero and heroine, he is treated as an embryonic hero himself. He is young and handsome and virtuous, and in the end is allowed to marry Ellen Wade, who has carefully been given appearance, manners, speech, and sensibility superior to those of her crude companions—a distinct foreshadowing of Mabel Dunham's status and character in *The Pathfinder*. The Paul-Ellen love affair in *The Prairie,* in fact, seems to have furnished Cooper with the germ of his experiments in the two later novels.

Near the end of his life the novelist made a final effort to construct a story with a Western hero in *The Oak Openings* (1898). Like Paul Hover twenty years earlier, Ben Boden is a bee hunter of admirable character. In the absence of a genteel hero，however, he has to be refined somewhat beyond Paul Hover's level. This process is indicated in terms of the significant criterion of language. We are told twice in the first chapter that he used surprisingly pure English for one in his social class, and he has the further genteel trait of highly moral views concerning whiskey. Margaret Waring, the heroine, like Ellen Wade, is related to a coarse frontiersman, but is made as refined as possible within the iron limits of her status. Although *The Oak Openings* is one of Cooper's weakest novels, the fault lies in his uncontrollable tendency to preach on any current topic that happens to come into his mind. The basic conception is very promising.

The novel begins as if Cooper were determined to see what might have been made of *The Prairie* if he had carried out his project of omitting the genteel hero and heroine. If this conjecture is valid, then Ben Boden represents Cooper's ultimate achievement in trying to use a man of the wilderness as a technical hero. After the dangers of Indian warfare in early Michigan have been endured by the young lovers, the novelist feels compelled to add an epilogue that exhibits Ben Boden in his old age as a substantial farmer, a man of influence in the community, and a state senator. This career "shows the power of man when left free to make his own exertions." But if Boden's Jacksonian rise in the world gives retroactive sanction to Cooper's choice of him as a hero, it dissolves whatever imaginative connection he may have had with the mysterious and brooding wilderness.

Cooper's twenty-five years' struggle to devise a Wild Western hero capable of taking the leading role in a novel yielded the following results: (1) Since the basic image of Leatherstocking was too old for the purposes of romance, the novelist doubled the character to produce a young hunter sharing the old man's habits, tastes, skills, and, to some extent, his virtues. (2) The earliest of the young hunter companions of Leatherstocking, Oliver Effingham, could be a hero because he was revealed as a gentleman temporarily disguised as a hunter. That is, the hero retained all his genteel prerogatives by hereditary right, and at the same time claimed the imaginative values clustering about Leatherstocking by wearing a mask, a *persona* fashioned in the image of the old hunter. But this was so flagrant a begging of the question that Cooper could not be satisfied with it. He therefore undertook further development of the young hunter produced by doubling the character of Leatherstocking, and this process yielded (3) the Paul Hover-Ben Boden type of hero, a young and handsome denizen of the wilderness, following the gentler calling of a bee hunter and thus free from even the justifiable taint of bloodshed involved in Leatherstocking's vocation. This young Western hero is given a dialect less pronounced than that of Leatherstocking except in Leatherstocking's most exalted moments. His actual origin is left vague. He is not a member of the upper class, but he is nowhere specifically described as having once been a servant. Finally, the young hero has none of the theoretical hostility to civilization that is so conspicuous in Leatherstocking. These changes make it technically possible for a Wild Westerner to be a hero of romance, but they destroy the subversive overtones that had given Leatherstocking so much of his emotional depth.

CHAPTER XXII

THE MYTH OF THE GARDEN AND TURNER'S FRONTIER HYPOTHESIS

By far the most influential piece of writing about the West produced during the nineteenth century was the essay on "The Significance of the Frontier in American History" read by Frederick Jackson Turner[26] before the American Historical Association at Chicago in 1893. The "frontier hypothesis" which he advanced on that occasion revolutionized American historiography and eventually made itself felt in economics and sociology, in literary criticism, and even in politics.

Turner's central contention was the "the existence of an area of free land, its continuous recession, and the advance of American settlement westward explain American development." This proposition does not sound novel now because it has been worked into the very fabric of our conception of our history, but in 1893 it was a polemic directed against the two dominant schools of historians: the group interpretating American history in terms of the slavery controversy, led by Herman Edouard von Hoist,[27] and the group headed by Turner's former teacher, Herbert B. Adams[28] of Johns Hopkins, who explained American institutions as the outgrowth of English, or rather ancient Teutonic germs planted in the New World. Turner maintained that the West, not the proslavery South or the antislavery North, was the most important among American sections, and that the novel attitudes and institutions produced by the frontier, especially through its encouragement of democracy, had been more significant than the imported European heritage in shaping American society.

To determine whether Turner's hypothesis is or is not a valid interpretation of American history forms no part of the intention of this book. The problem here is to place his main ideas in the intellectual tradition that has been examined in earlier chapters. Whatever the merits or demerits of the frontier hypothesis in explaining actual events, the hypothesis itself developed out of the myth of the garden. Its insistence on the importance of the West, its affirmation of democracy, and its doctrine of geographical determinism derive from a still broader tradition of Western thought that would include, Benton[29] and Gilpin as well, but its emphasis on agricultural settlement places it clearly within the stream of agrarian theory that flows from eighteenth-century England and France through Jefferson to the men who elaborated the ideal of a society of yeoman farmers in the Northwest' from which Turner sprang. Turner's immersion in this stream of intellectual influence had an unfortunate effect in committing him to certain archaic assumptions which hampered his approach to twentieth-century social problems. But one must not forget that the tradition was richer than these assumptions, and that it conferred on him the authority of one who speaks from the distilled experience of his people. If the myth of the garden embodied certain erroneous judgments made by these people, concerning the economic forces that had come to dominate American life, it was still true to their experience in the large, because it expressed beliefs and aspirations as well as statistics. This is not the only kind of historical truth, but it is a kind historians need never find contemptible.

Turner's most important debt to his intellectual tradition is the ideas of savagery and civilization that he uses to define his central factor, the frontier. His frontier is explicitly "the meeting point between savagery and civilization." For him as for his predecessors, the outer limit of agricultural settlement is the boundary of civilization, and in his thought as in that of so many earlier interpreters we must therefore begin by distinguishing two Wests, one beyond and one within this all-important line.

From the standpoint of economic theory, the wilderness beyond the frontier, the realm of savagery, is a constantly receding area of free land. Mr. Fulmer Mood has demonstrated that Turner derived this technical expression from a treatise on economics by Francis A. Walker[30] used as a text by one of his teachers at John Hopkins, Richard T. Ely. In Walker's analysis Turner found warrant for his belief that free land had operated as a safety valve for the East and even for Europe by offering every man an opportunity to acquire a farm and become an independent member of society. Free land thus tended to relieve poverty outside the West, and on the frontier itself it fostered economic equality. Both these tendencies made for an increase of democracy. Earlier writers from the time of Franklin had noted that the West offered freedom and subsistence to all, but Turner restated the idea in a more positive form suggested by his conviction that democracy, the rise of the common man, was one of the great movements of modern history.

In an oration delivered in 1883 when he was still an undergraduate he had declared: "Over all the world we hear mankind proclaiming its existence, demanding its rights. Kings begin to be but names, and the sons of genius, springing from the people, grasp the real scepters. The reign of Aristocracy is passing; that of humanity begins." Although "humanity" is a broad term, for Turner it referred specifically to farmers. He conceived of democracy as a trait of agricultural communities. About this time, for example, he wrote in his Commonplace Book that historians had long occupied themselves with "noble warriors, & all the pomp, and glory of the higher class—But of the other phase of the common people, the lowly tillers of the soil, the great mass of humanity… history has hitherto said but Little." And he fully accepted the theory of small landholdings that underlay the cult of the yeoman. He planned to develop the idea in an "Oration on Peasant Proprietors in U.S." (by which he meant small farmers tilling their own land):

> … the work of the Cobden Club on Land Tenure [he wrote] giving the systems of the various countries the paper on America—opens by showing how uninteresting is the subject being as it is purely peasant proprietorship—In this simplicity of our land system lies one of the greatest factors in our progress. Enlarge on the various systems & show the value of it here—point out the fact that if our lands in the west had not been opened to & filled with foreign emigrant it is not unlikely that they would have fallen into the hands of capitalists & have been made great estates—e.g. Dalyrymple farm—Show effects of great estates in Italy—in Eng.

In systems of land tenure, he felt, lay the key to the democratic upsurge that had reached a climax in the nineteenth century:

> It is not by Contrat Socials that a nation wins freedom & prosperity for its people—it is by attention to minor details—like

this—it is by evolution—

Show place of F. R. [French Revolution]—ring in Shelley's Prometheus this was an awakening but now-in our own age is the real revolution going on which is to raise man from his low estate to his proper dignity (enlarge from previous oration)—in this grand conception it is not an anticlimax to urge the value—the essential necessity of such institutions as the peasant proprietors—a moving force, all the stronger that it, works quietly in the great movement.

This is the theoretical background of the proposition in the 1893 essay that "democracy [is] born of free land," as well as of the celebrated pronouncement made twenty years later: "American democracy was born of no theorist's dream; it was not carried in the Susan Constan[31] to Virginia, nor in the Mayflower to Plymouth. It came stark and strong and full of life out of the American forest, and it gained new strength each time it touched a new frontier."

But while economic theory still underlies this later statement, the change of terminology has introduced new and rich overtones. We have been transferred from the plane of the economist's abstractions to a plane of metaphor, and even of myth—for the American forest has become almost an enchanted wood, and the image of Antaeus has been invoked to suggest the power of the Western earth. Such intimations reach beyond logical theory. They remind us that the wilderness beyond the limits of civilization was not only an area of free land; it was also nature. The idea of nature suggested to Turner a poetic account of the influence of free land as a rebirth, a regeneration, a rejuvenation of man and society constantly recurring where civilization came into contact with the wilderness along the frontier.

Rebirth and regeneration are categories of myth rather than of economic analysis, but ordinarily Turner kept his metaphors under control and used them to illustrate and vivify his logic propositions rather than as a structural principle or a means of cognition; that is, he used them rhetorically, not poetically. The nonpoetic use of a vivid metaphor is illustrated, in a speech he delivered in 1896:

> Americans had a safety valve for social danger, a bank account on which they might continually draw to meet losses. This was the vast unoccupied domain that stretched from the borders of the settled area to the Pacific Ocean... No grave social problem could exist while the wilderness at the edge of civilizations [*sic*] opened wide its portals to all who were oppressed, to all who with strong arms and stout heart desired to hew out a home and a career for themselves. Here was an opportunity for social development continually to begin over again, wherever society gave signs of breaking into classes. Here was a magic fountain of youth in which America continually bathed and was rejuvenated.

The figure of the magic fountain is merely a rhetorical ornament at the end of the paragraph having a rational structure and subject to criticism according to recognized canons. But sometimes, especially when the conception of nature as the source of occult powers is most vividly present, Turner's metaphors threaten to become themselves a means of cognition and to supplant discursive reasoning. This seems to happen, for example, in an essay he wrote for the *Atlantic* in 1903. After quoting a clearly animistic passage from Lowell's Harvard Commemoration Ode[32] on how Nature had shaped Lincoln of untainted clay from the unexhausted West, "New birth of our new soil, the first American," Turner builds an elaborate figurative structure:

> Into this vast shaggy continent of ours poured the first feeble tide of European settlement. European men, institutions, and ideas were lodged in the American wilderness, and this great American West took them to her bosom, taught them a new way of looking upon the destiny of the common man, trained them in adaptation to the

conditions of the New World, to the creation of new institutions to meet new needs; and ever as society on her eastern border grew to resemble the Old World in its social forms and its industry, ever, as it began to lose faith in the ideal of democracy, she opened new provinces, and dowered new democracies in her most distant domains with her material treasures and with the ennobling influence that the fierce love of freedom, the strength that came from hewing out a home, making a school and a church, and creating a higher future for his family, furnished to the pioneer.

It would be difficult to maintain that all these metaphors are merely ornamental. Is it wholly meaningless, for example, that the West, the region close to nature, is feminine, while the East, with its remoteness from nature and its propensity for aping Europe, is neuter?

In the passage just quoted, a beneficent power emanating from nature is shown creating an agrarian utopia in the West. The myth of the garden is constructed before our eyes. Turner is asserting as fact a state of affairs that on other occasions he recognized as merely an ideal to be striven for. Earlier in the same essay, for example, he had summarized Jefferson's "platform of political principles" and his "conception that democracy should have an agricultural basis." The "should" easily becomes "did": Jefferson's agrarian ideal proves to be virtually identical with the frontier democracy that Turner believed he had discovered in the West. To imagine an ideal so vividly that it comes to seem actual is to follow the specific procedure of poetry.

The other member of the pair of ideas which defined the frontier for Turner was that of civilization. If the idea of nature in the West provided him with a rich and not always manageable store of metaphorical coloring, his use of the idea of civilization had the equally important consequence of committing him to the theory that all societies, including those of successive Wests, develop through the same series of progressively higher stages. Mr. Mood has traced this conception also to Ely and to Walker, and back of them to the German economic theorist Friedrich List.[33] But, as we have had occasion to notice earlier in this study, the idea had been imported into the United States from France soon after 1800 and by the 1820's had become one of the principal instruments for interpreting the agricultural West.

Turner's acceptance of this theory involved him in the difficulties that it had created for earlier observers of frontier society, such as Timothy Flint.[34] For the theory of social stages was basically at odds with the conception of the Western farmer as a yeoman surrounded by utopian splendor. Instead, it implied that the Western farmer was a coarse and unrefined representative of a primitive stage of social evolution. Turner's adoption of these two contradictory theories makes it difficult for him to manage the question of whether frontier character and society and frontier influence on the rest of the country have been good or bad. As long as he is dealing with the origins of democracy in the West he evidently considers frontier influence good. A man who refers to "the familiar struggle of West against East, of democracy against privileged classes" leaves no doubt concerning his own allegiance. This attitude was in fact inevitable as long as one maintained the doctrine that frontier society was shaped by the influence of free land, for free land was nature, and nature in this system of ideas is unqualifiedly benign. Indeed, it is itself the norm of value. There is no way to conceive possible bad effects flowing from the impact of nature on man and society.

But when Turner invokes the concept of civilization, the situation becomes more complex. His basic conviction was that the highest social values were to be found in the relatively primitive society just within the agricultural frontier. But the theory of social stages placed the highest values at the other end of the process, in urban industrial society, amid the manufacturing development and city life which Jefferson and later agrarian theorists had considered dangerous to social purity. Turner wavered between the two views. In the 1893 essay, to take a minute but perhaps significant bit of evidence, he referred to the evolution of each successive region of the West "into a higher stage"—in accord with the orthodox theory of civilization and progress. When he revised the essay for republication in 1899, he realized that such an assumption might lead him into inconsistency and substituted "a different industrial stage."

But he could not always maintain the neutrality implied in this revision. For one thing, he strongly disapproved of the Western love of currency inflation, which he considered a consequence of the primitive state of frontier society. "The colonial and Revolutionary frontier," he asserted in the 1893 essay, "was the region whence emanated many of the worst forms of an evil currency," and he pointed out that each of the periods of lax financial integrity in American history had coincided with the rise of a new set of frontier communities. The Populist agitation for free coinage of silver[35] was a case in point.

> Many a state that now declines any connection with the tenets of the Populists [he wrote] itself adhered to such ideas in an earlier stage of the development of the state. A primitive society can hardly be expected to show the intelligent appreciation of the complexity of business interests in a developed society.

In his revision of the essay in 1899 Turner noted with satisfaction that Wisconsin had borne out his principles:

> Wisconsin, to take an illustration, in the days when it lacked varied agriculture and complex industrial life, was a stronghold of the granger and greenback movements[36]; but it has undergone an industrial transformation, and in the last presidential contest Mr. Bryan[37] carried but one county in the state.

Here the evolution of society from agrarian simplicity toward greater complexity is assumed to bring about improvement.

Yet if Turner could affirm progress and civilization in this one respect, the general course of social evolution in the United States created a grave theoretical dilemma for him. He had based his highest value, democracy, on free land. But the westward advance of civilization across the continent had caused free land to disappear. What then was to become of democracy? The difficulty was the greater because in associating democracy with free land he had inevitably linked it also with the idea of nature as a source of spiritual values. All the overtones of his conception of democracy were therefore tinged with cultural primitivism, and tended to clash with the idea of civilization. In itself this was not necessarily a disadvantage; the conception of civilization had been invoked to justify a number of dubious undertakings in the course of the nineteenth century, including European exploitation of native peoples all over the world. Furthermore as we have had occasion to observe in studying the literary interpretation of the agricultural West, the theory of social progress through a uniform series of stages was poor equipment for any observer who wished to understand Western farmer. But Turner had accepted the idea of civilization as a general description of the society that had been expanding across the continent, and with the final disappearance of free land this idea was the only remaining principle with which he could undertake the analysis of contemporary American society.

Since democracy for him was related to the idea of nature and seemed to have no logical relation to civilization, the conclusion implied by his system was that postfrontier American society contained no force tending toward democracy. Fourierists[38] earlier in the century, reaching a conclusion comparable to this, had maintained that civilization was but a transitory social stage, and that humanity must transcend it by advancing into the higher stage of "association." Henry George[39] in Turner's own day had announced that progress brought poverty, that civilization embodied a radical contradiction and could be redeemed only by a revolutionary measure, the confiscation of the unearned increment in the value of natural resources. But Turner did not share the more or less revolutionary attitude that lay back of these proposals. On the contrary, he conceived of social progress as taking place within the existing framework of society, that is, within civilization. Whatever solution might be found for social problems would have to be developed according to the basic principles already accepted by society. This meant that his problem was to find a basis for democracy in some aspect of civilization as he observed it about him in the United States. His determined effort in this direction showed that his mind and his standards of social ethics were subtler and broader than the conceptual system within which the frontier hypothesis had been developed, but he was the prisoner of the assumptions he had taken over from the agrarian tradition. He turned to the rather unconvincing idea that the Midwestern state universities might be able to save democracy by producing trained leaders, and later he placed science beside education as another force to which men might turn for aid in their modern perplexity, but these suggestions were not really satisfying to him, and he fell back at last on the faith he had confided to his Commonplace Book as an undergraduate—a faith neither in nature nor in civilization but simply in man, in the common people. In 1924, after reviewing the most urgent of the world's problems, Turner declared with eloquence and dignity:

> I prefer to believe that man is greater than the dangers that menace him; that education and science are powerful forces to change these tendencies and to produce a rational solution of the problems of life on the shrinking planet. I place my trust in the mind of man seeking solutions by intellectual toil rather than by drift and by habit, bold to find new ways of adjustment, and strong in the leadership that spreads new ideas among the common people of the world; committed to peace on earth and ready to use the means of preserving it.

This statement is an admission that the notion of democracy born of free land, colored as it is by primitivism, is not an adequate instrument for dealing, with a world dominated by industry, urbanization, and international conflicts. The First World War had shaken Turner's agrarian code of values as it destroyed so many other intellectual constructions of the nineteenth century. He continued to struggle with the grievous problems of the modern world, but his original theoretical weapons were no longer useful.

Turner's predicament illustrates what has happened to the tradition within which he worked. From the time of Franklin down to the end of the frontier period almost a century and a half later, the West had been a constant reminder of the importance of agriculture in American society. It had nourished an agrarian philosophy and an agrarian myth that purported to set forth the character and destinies of the nation. The philosophy and the myth affirmed an admirable set of values, but they ceased very early to be useful in interpreting American society as a whole because they offered no intellectual apparatus for taking account of the industrial revolution. A system which revolved about a half-mystical conception of nature and held up as an ideal a rudimentary type of agriculture was powerless to confront issues arising from the advance of technology. Agrarian theory encouraged men to ignore the industrial revolution altogether, or to regard it as an unfortunate and anomalous violation of the natural order of things. In the restricted but important sphere of historical scholarship, for example, the agrarian emphasis of the frontier hypothesis has tended to divert attention from the problems created by industrialization for a half century during which the United States has become the most powerful industrial nation in the world. An even more significant consequence of the agrarian tradition has been its effect on politics. The covert distrust of the city and of everything connected with industry that is implicit in the myth of the garden has impeded cooperation between farmers and factory workers in more than one crisis of our history, from the time of Jefferson to the present.

The agrarian tradition has also made it difficult for Americans to think of themselves as members of a world community because it has affirmed that the destiny of this country leads her away from Europe toward the agricultural interior of the continent. This tendency is quite evident in Turner. Although he devoted much attention to the diplomatic issues arising out of westward expansion, the frontier hypothesis implied that it would be a last misfortune for American society to maintain close connections with Europe. The frontier which produced Adrew Jackson, wrote Turner with approval in 1903, was "free from the influence of European ideas and institutions. The men of the 'Western World' turned their backs upon the Atlantic Ocean, and with a grim energy and self-reliance began to build up a society free from the dominance of ancient forms." It was only later, when he was trying to find a theoretical basis for democracy outside the frontier, that Turner criticized the American attitude of "contemptuous indifference" to the social legislation of European countries.

But if interpretation of the West in terms of the idea of nature tended to cut the region off from the urban East and from Europe, the opposed idea of civilization had even greater disadvantages. It not only imposed on Westerners the stigma of social, ethical, and cultural inferiority, but prevented any recognition that the American adventure of settling the continent had brought about an irruption of novelty into history. For the theory of civilization implied that America in general, and the West *a fortiori*[40] were meaningless except in so far as they managed to reproduce the achievements of Europe. The capital difficulty of the American agrarian tradition is that it accepted the paired but contradictory ideas of nature and civilization as a general principle of historical and social interpretation. A new intellectual system was requisite before the West

26. Frederick Jackson Turner：特纳（1861-1932），美国历史学家。

27. Herman Edouard von Holst：霍尔斯特（1841-1904），生于俄国，1866 年前往美国，任芝加哥大学历史教授。

28. Herbert B. Adams：亚当斯（1860-1897），美国历史学家。

29. Benton：班通（Thomas Hart Benton，1782-1858）美国政治家。

30. Francis A. Walker：瓦尔克（1840-1897），美国经济学家。下文中 Richard T. Ely：艾莱（1854-1943），美国经济学家。

31. the Susan constant：1606 年美国探险家史密斯（John Smith，1580-1631）到弗吉尼亚殖民区去所乘的船名。

32. 该诗全名为"We Recited at the Harvard Commemoration"（1865）。特纳的引文取自该诗第 6 诗节，"New birth of our new soil the first American"为该诗节最后一句。

33. Friedrich List：里斯特（1789-1864），德国经济家。

34. Timothy Flint：弗林特（1780-1940），美国牧师、作家。

35. The Populist agitation for free coinage of silver：平民党运动（the Populist Movement），为 19 世纪后期美国中西部和南部农业改革者的政治联盟，成立于 1872 年，提出自由铸造银币以增加货币流通等要求。

36. the granger and greenback movements：格兰其运动（the granger movement）和绿背纸币运动（the greenback movement）都是 19 世纪后期与美国农业发展有关的运动。前者要求农民联合起来反对铁路公司和谷物仓库的垄断，后者要求发行没有黄金储备的绿背纸币以促进货币流通。两个运动均在 19 世纪 80 年代失败。

37. Mr. Bryan：布莱恩（William Jennings Bryan, 1860-1925）美国政治家，倡导自上铸造银币运动。

38. Fourierists：傅立叶主义者，法国社会理论家傅立叶（Charles Fourier, 1772-1837）的追随者。

39. Henry George：乔治（1839-1897），美国经济学家。

40. a fortiori：拉丁语，意为"更不必说"。

Questions For Discussion:

I. It took a long time and the continual effort of more than one generation of writers to discover the literary values of the West, to realize that Western materials, with their rich folk culture and dialects, could offer interesting and challenging themes for fiction. Discuss this complex literary evolution with reference to the works of such authors as James Fenimore Cooper, and try to define the salient characteristics of American Western literature.

2. Evaluate the influence of the West over the development of American literature both from a thematic and stylistic points of view.

For Further Reference:

Fussell, Edwin S. *Frontier: American Literature and the American West*. Princeton, N.J.: Princeton Univ. Press, 1965.

Mark Twain were all in their different ways preoccupied with certain aspects of social life as it was shaping itself in the America of their times. Of these four, Cooper and Twain were, in some of their works, most directly concerned with the contemporary scene. Though Hawthorne's and Melville's work is seldom characterized by such directness of intention, it presents, perhaps for that very reason, a subtler and more abiding exploration of the very basis of social life and values.

It has always been difficult, however, to define the exact nature of the relation between these novelists' greatest work and the facts of American sociology as we know them. Nor is the difficulty surmounted entirely by reminding ourselves that their most significant themes were transcendent, engaging in but also going beyond the social aspect of life. The works of many of their European contemporaries (Dostoevsky and Balzac for example) also achieve a wider, if not similar, concern for the more ultimate problems of human destiny, and yet it has been comparatively easy to make this correlation in the case of European fiction. If one defines the novel as an art form entirely in terms of English and continental fiction, works like *The Deerslayer, The Scarlet Letter, Moby-Dick,* and *Huckleberry Finn* would represent an achievement which easily measures up to the requirements of great art but at the same time somehow falls below the level of the good novel. This seeming paradox has a great deal to do with the question of the relation between American society and the American novel. Lionel Trilling sees it when he observes in his essay on "Manners, Morals, and the Novel":

> Now the novel as I have described it has never really established itself in America. Not that we have not had very great novels but that the novel in America diverges from its classic intention, which, as I have said, is the investigation of the problem of reality beginning in the social field. The fact is that American writers of genius have not turned their minds to society... the reality

they sought was only tangential to society. [1]

This perceptive formulation has a suggestiveness which goes beyond the requirements of the context in which it appears. Trilling has raised some important questions, and he briefly touches upon at least one of them when he says in a later essay that in America "the real basis of the novel has never existed—that is, the tension between a middle class and an aristocracy which brings manners into observable relief as the living representation of ideals and the living comment on ideas."[2]

To say that these observations are accurate but only negative is not to disparage Trilling, because his purpose is to provide certain fruitful comparisons rather than to argue why the American novel should not exist. It is true that some of the early American novelists themselves repeatedly evaluated their work in terms of the practice of their English contemporaries. Cooper started frankly as an imitator and perhaps never quite shook off the bad influence of Sir Walter Scott. Hawthorne admired Anthony Trollope and deprecated his own inability to write in the popular manner of the English novelists. Nevertheless, in their best work, the American novelists went their own way, and, if they felt uneasy about it, we must remember that they were creating a different kind of novel and did not enjoy our advantage of seeing it established in its own right as a vital and significant body of literature. Hence, whatever excursions we make into the realm of sociology must, in the last analysis, help our understanding of the primary fact of its enduring effectiveness. In the same way, a comparative study of the English and American novel of the nineteenth century can be useful only as a step toward a more positive account of the American novelists' concern with society and social values, even if such a comparison leads us finally to a revision of the accepted assumptions about social reality, the nature of the novelist's intention, and the relation between society and the novel.

One can thus proceed from Trilling's observations and ask: if the

with a complex body of imaginative literature. To quote Karl Mannheim
again:

> Wishful thinking has always figured in human affairs. When
> the imagination finds no satisfaction in existing reality, it seeks
> refuge in wishfully constructed places and periods. Myths, fairy
> tales, other-worldly promises of religion, humanistic fantasies, travel
> romances, have been continually changing expressions of that which
> was lacking in actual life. They were more nearly complementary
> colours in the picture of the reality existing at the time than utopias
> working in opposition to the *status quo* and disintegrating it.[4]

If one accepts this statement, and if one remembers further that, according
to Mannheim's unusual definition of terms, a "utopia" is an idea which is
"situationally transcendent" but also realizable in actuality, one would
conclude that Cooper's Leatherstocking Tales and Melville's *Typee* bear a
closer relation to the social reality of nineteenth-century America than, let
us say, the utopia of Jacksonian democracy which was materially working
against and disintegrating the status quo of the time.

In reality, however, dissatisfaction with existing society did not make
Cooper, Hawthorne, Melville, and even the Mark Twain of *Huckleberry
Finn* wildly fanciful. They did not employ their imaginations in the
construction of fairy tales or fantasies. As for other-worldly promises of
religion, strictly speaking, these can be found only outside the work of the
great novelists, in such fictions as Sylvester Judd's[5] *Margaret: A Tale of
the Real and Ideal, Blight and Bloom*. The four important novelists
mentioned here derived their ideals from another source. In many different
ways, they all leaned over backward and at some points achieved a
sustaining contact with the great myth of America—the complex of ideas
and ideals which had animated the beginnings of the experiment that had
now grown into the social and moral world around them. Since it
recognized the limitations as well as the promises of human existence, it

was not altogether an expansive myth. Nor did its promise represent even to the most sanguine mind anything more than a possibility, a suggestion of potential reality.

I am aware that one of the many dangers implicit in this kind of discussion is that it is always possible to trace many myths in the past of a country, or, rather, a myth by its very nature permits a diversity of implications to be read into it. I might therefore say at once that I am concerned with those components of the American myth which have a bearing primarily on the social concerns of the classic American novel and which, it seems to me, will help to illuminate some of its problems. My contention is that, though this myth grew out of a definite socio-historical moment and was eventually defeated by the historical development of its own paradoxical nature, some of its essential features remained for a long time operative in the American creative sensibility. Accordingly, the best account of the particular set of implications I see in it will be a historical one.

What imaginative men will say in critical times is often revelatory of certain aspects of the national sensibility which in more normal times remain hidden from common view. A good example of this fact is provided by *I'll Take My Stand*,[6] the documentary response of twelve famous Southerners to the great economic crisis in America. Although the whole enterprise was conducted with the air of a political gesture, the document is interesting precisely because its contributors were not politicians but primarily writers, and it is interesting to speculate whether, during the depression years, it would have been possible in any other country of the Western world to collect under a similar banner an equally intelligent set of critics, poets, novelists, sociologists, and historians. To say the least, anywhere else the program and values they advocated would have been considered too impractical to deserve serious or systematic exposition, much less to receive any attention at all. And yet some of their

thought it some indignity and disrespect unto them. And for men's wives to be commanded to do service for other men, addressing their meat, washing their clothes, etc., they deemed it a kind of slavery, neither could many husbands well brook it.

If we compare this passage with the one quoted from Winthrop, we notice that the cause of the failure was precisely the nonobservance of the conduct Winthrop had enjoined: the abridgment of superfluities forth supply of others' necessities; upholding a familiar commerce together in all meekness, gentleness, patience, and liberality; and remembering always the commission and community in the work as members of the same body. The surprising thing then is not that the communitarian experiment at Plymouth failed but that there should ever have been a hope of its success. Indeed, on their departure from Leyden,[10] John Robinson, their minister, had warned the band of Puritans of this danger. "And lastly," he wrote in a letter to "the whole company" which Bradford quotes in full, "your intended course of civil community will minister continual occasion of offence, and will be as fuel for that fire, except you diligently quench it with brotherly forbearance." Winthrop and Robinson were speaking in terms of Christian social ideals, whereas Bradford, in his practical experiment, had to encounter the hard economic reality of the individual's self-interest.

These were indeed the two main drives behind the social movement which led to the settlement of America. It was a continuation of that historical moment in which religious fervor, as Mannheim says, "joined forces with the active demands of the oppressed strata of society." Its animating energy had a dual purpose and a millennial character: "The impossible gives birth to the possible, and the absolute interferes with the world and conditions actual events. This fundamental and most radical form of the modern utopia was fashioned out of a singular material. It corresponded to the spiritual fermentation and physical excitement of the peasants, of a stratum living closest to the earth. It was at the same time robustly material and highly spiritual."

The economic motivation, however, formed no part of the grand design as the Puritan leaders conceived it. It was there from the outset, but it was not acknowledged on the same terms as the religious aspect of the enterprise. Indeed, in the long line of communitarian colonies in America it was not until the nineteenth century that a colony was frankly organized as an economic experiment. Even Cotton Mather,[11] by whose time the original energy of religious dedication was already waning, believed firmly that the earlier colonizing attempts of the English in New England had failed because "the designs of those attempts being aimed no higher than the advancement of some *worldly interests*, a constant series of disasters has confounded them." It is after this observation that Mather relates the well-known story of a preacher of his who urged his congregation in the northeastern regions "to approve themselves a *religious* people" since otherwise "they would contradict the main end of planting this wilderness." Hereupon a well-known person stood up in the assembly and cried out: "Sir, you are mistaken: you think you are preaching to the people at the Bay; our *main end* was to *catch fish*." After suitably deprecating this attitude, Cotton Mather goes on to say how his own colony was "formed upon more glorious aims."

In 1623 Bradford does not seem to have even noticed this Cod-God paradox, this discrepancy between Winthrop's high Christian ideals, which he shared, and the conduct of his fellow colonists. The economic side of the enterprise was important to him (indeed it takes up a great part of his narrative) but it was not allowed to figure in the providential design which had sent the pilgrims across the ocean. He was content to leave the economic predilections of man alone. His final comment on the breakdown of the communitarian experiment is perhaps significant in its farsightedness and definitely more shrewd than Cotton Mater's

archetype of American experience even as it may be taken for the first statement of the American myth. Divested of its endless details about shipping costs, adventurers, beaver-skins, and such other things, the frame of the story presents an epic reference: the solemn exodus of a band of people from a corrupt world and their journey across the ocean to build a New Jerusalem upon a virgin land. The Christ and Virgin whom Cotton Mather later called upon to inspire his own history,[15] combine with effortless ease in the narrative of this literal-minded Puritan to whom the past was represented mainly by the Bible and the future by a great hope. Like the ancient bards, he himself remains anonymous, while the hero of his tale is not man but men, the constant and strangely moving "They" of the narrative.

At the same time, the story is also the unfolding of a phase in the endless drama between God and Satan—the two invisible but primary actors. With this extension we have that supramundane reference, that metaphysical dimension, which, in one form or another, is always present in the great American novels of the nineteenth century but which rarely emerges from the more purely social preoccupation of European fiction. Bradford's history is set in motion by those "wars and oppositions [which]… Satan hath raised, maintained and continued against the Saints, from time to time, in one sort or other." Oppressed in this manner, rather than submit to the machinations of Satan acting through his surrogates in a depraved society, the saints decide to separate themselves from such a society altogether and remove themselves to "some of those vast and unpeopled countries of America" which are "devoid of all civil inhabitants." Once there, with "the mighty ocean which they had passed" separating them "from all the civil parts of the world," they can hope to find no "friends to welcome them nor inns to entertain or refresh their weather beaten bodies; no houses or much less towns to repair to, to seek for succour." All that can sustain the small community is the spirit of God and the inward conviction of the righteousness of their course.

Here we have, in terms of the language and outlook of the early seventeenth century, the basic pattern of the drama which, in other and varying terms, was to find recurrent expression in subsequent American imaginative literature. Put in a simplified form, it may be described as the theme of separation from an established society in search of a more satisfying community life. Society, the individual, and community—the main points of this triadic theme—were variously termed and defined by the various persons with whom I am chiefly concerned. Nevertheless, they figured in the imaginations of all of them. And together with this preoccupation went a brooding sense of forces beyond man's reach and of a reality which is not man-made but which man must take into account: what I have called the metaphysical dimension of their vision.

The first separation from Europe was not the end but only the beginning of a process which was to repeat itself endlessly in America. It is fitting therefore that Bradford, whose narrative began with the first Puritan community's removal to Holland, should describe toward the end of the book, in what is one of its most moving passages, the separation of the younger members from the parent church, not as individuals asserting their freedom but only "like children translated into other families"—the old narrator preserving bravely the intimate imagery of communal feeling while the elegiac note of the passage indicates that its lack of basis in actual social relationships was already becoming apparent.

"God in His wisdom," as Bradford says, had seen "another course fitter" for the Americans. This was the course of individualism, and it was not long before the covenanted community began to feel the strain of the paradox which lay at the center of its life, and the severe unity of the Puritan church itself was disturbed by dissension. By the time we come to Cotton Mather's history, after the turn of the century, the narrator has emerged from communal anonymity and assumed the first-person singular,

decisive importance to him is his being a freeholder. Unlike Wordsworth, he has nothing but pity for the European farmers who live close to the earth but do not own it. And as for the primitive African, he is neither a noble nor an ignoble savage. In the South, where he is kept in bondage and ignorance, the slave is rude and depraved, while in the North, where he is trained in the ways of civilization, he is as decent a human being as his master. In the last letter, Crevecoeur does not expound his scheme of going to live in an Indian tribe without expressing a hope that he may be able to civilize the savages, especially through the art of inoculation in which his wife possesses much skill.

The first eight of Crevecoeur's twelve letters thus provide a discursive answer to his celebrated question ("What then is the American, this new many") mainly in terms of the economic and political differences between Europe and America. The American, Crevecoeur says, is a European or the descendant of a European "who, leaving behind him all his ancient prejudices and manners, receives new ones from the new mode of life he has embraced, the new government he obeys, and the new rank he holds." In the "great American asylum" the poor immigrant is freed from the oppression of a feudal society, from the taxation of landlord, church, and monarch, from involuntary idleness, servile dependence, penury, and useless labour. "Here religion demands but little of him; a small voluntary salary to the minister, and gratitude to God; can he refuse these?" Be he a trader, farmer, craftsman, or a common laborer, he will be rewarded amply for his labor, so that in time he will cast off his servile timidity and acquire the dignity and self-confidence of a true human being. No wonder Crevecoeur should exclaim: "We have no princes, for whom we toil, starve, and bleed, we are the most perfect society now existing in the world."

Here we have struck perhaps for the first time that note of conscious superiority of American over European social institutions, of pride in democratic equality and abundance of opportunity, which we hear again and again in the subsequent literature of the country, though with increasingly critical qualifications. Crevecoeur's own book is far from lacking in critical reference. However, before considering this aspect of it, it would be well to remind ourselves of its contextual breadth by turning a century and a half backward to the pilgrims or about the same number of years forward to modern times. William Bradford had also spoken of Americans as Europeans escaping oppression, when, after describing their landing, he asked whether future generations ought not to remember that their "fathers were Englishmen which came over this great ocean, and were ready to perish in this wilderness" but the Lord "heard their voices" and "delivered them from the hand of the oppressor."[31] It was an inevitable development, but also one with which the American imagination could never wholly reconcile itself. The tensions created by this uneasy sense of disequilibrium have tended to produce a variety of attitudes, ranging from an unreasoned but acute sense of betrayal to more thoughtful criticism. For example, to take a recent formulation, this is how Richard Hofstadter[18] sums up the chief characteristics of American politics in the "Introduction" to his book *The American Political Tradition*:

> However much at odds on specific issues, the major political traditions have shared a belief in the rights of property, the philosophy of economic individualism, the value of competition; they have accepted the economic virtues of capitalist culture as necessary qualities of man. Even when some property right has been challenged, as it was by followers of Jefferson and Jackson—in the name of the rights of man or the rights of the community, the challenge, when translated into practical policy, has actually been urged on behalf of some other kind of property.... American traditions also show a strong bias in favor of equalitarian democracy, but it has been a democracy in cupidity rather than a democracy of

nineteenth century. The American farmer is no longer the unreserved celebrator of democratic man and economic competitiveness, for he sees that human beings share the predatory characteristics as well as the passions of cruelty and violence which, in previous letters, he had discovered everywhere in the animal kingdom. The law of mutual destructiveness, which governs the world of nature, provides also the key to the history of human society. Accordingly, where he had expressed a firm belief in the virtues of civilization, he now regards both society and the wilderness as morally equivocal:

> If from this general review of human nature, we descend to the examination of what is called civilized society; there the combination of every natural and artificial want, makes us pay very dear for what little share of political felicity we enjoy. It is a strange heterogeneous assemblage of vices and virtues, and of a variety of other principles, for ever at war, for ever jarring, for ever producing some dangerous, some distressing extreme. Where do you conceive then that nature intended we should be happy? Would you prefer the state of men in the woods, to that of men in a more improved situation? Evil preponderates in both; in the first they often eat each other for want of food, and in the other they often starve each other for want of room.

This passage, apart from its own significance, provides also the proper background for an understanding of the strange last letter, entitled "Distresses of a Frontier Man," which is in some ways the most interesting of the whole set, and which develops further the theme of "civilized society." In Letter 9 immediately after the lines quoted above, Crevecceur had concluded that for his own part he thought that the vices and miseries to be found in civilization exceed those of the wilderness "in which real evil is more scarce, more supportable, and less enormous." Now, as the attributes of "society"—war, destruction, and pillage—invade his backwoods sanctuary, the paradox acquires the immediacy and urgency of a personal problem, so that he forms and expounds at length the scheme of abandoning his house and farm and seeking refuge in the less complicated life of an Indian tribe. "Yes," he declares, "I will cheerfully embrace that resource, it is a holy inspiration."

It would be easy to form out of this letter a neat little bridge for crossing over to Cooper's Leatherstocking Tales in the next century. It would be equally easy to dismiss it as a vulgar contraption of the romantic writer at his worst. Nevertheless, as I have tried to point out earlier, it is a mistake to regard Crevecoeur as being altogether a literary showman of current attitudes. Not even the most liberal discounting of his obvious posturing for effect can wholly eliminate the imaginative core of his meaning, for, like Cooper after him, he shows a serious if unsophisticated concern for the values implicit in the drama of rival civilizations. Even in this letter he does not at any place suggest an unqualified approval of the primitive tribal life. On the contrary, he consistently maintains his earlier critical ambiguity. He is repeatedly worried by the fear that his young son may slip permanently from the higher agrarian life of his father into the savage hunting state. He insists that the family will maintain their own separate forms of worship under the wigwams. He even hopes that his influence may help the Indians to acquire certain aspects of civilization. And finally he presents his decision as an inevitable but perhaps only a temporary choice.

It is not important to inquire into the actual facts which lay behind the dramatization of this choice. To argue whether these reflections had their origin in the Indian raid on his house or in the conflict of loyalties[19] he experienced during the Revolutionary War would be about as meaningful as to speculate whether Crevecoeur could actually have encountered the caged Negro whose plight he describes with incredible flourishes of melodrama at the end of Letter 9. It is much more important to note that

than that of the father of all men, who requires nothing more of us than what tends to make each other happy."

To ask whether such Indians existed anywhere outside of Crevecoeur's imagination would be as irrelevant as to remember that he never went to live among their tribes. As an imaginative writer, and not unlike some novelists of the next century, his purpose in introducing his example of ideal community life is not to describe an actual people in a factual place but rather to create a set of values by means of which he can evaluate the society of his time.

The thousands of frontier men who succeeded Crevecoeur on the American scene did not share his misgivings about the course America was taking. Individualism, as Ralph Gabriel[21] has pointed out, was the most dominant force behind the developments of the nineteenth century. Its pressure was not only advancing men over the continent along an ever-extending frontier but also breaking down social institutions in the older settled areas. "Aristocracy," Tocqueville observed, "had made a chain of all the members of the community, from the peasant to the king; democracy breaks that chain and severs every link of it." Even in religion there was a shift, as Gabriel points out, from Calvin's monarch-God to Horace Bushnell's conception of Jesus as the divine man, "American Christianity" emphasizing the individual and his emotions rather than institutional observances.

Insofar as individualism represented an advance in human values, its virtues were recognized implicitly or overtly by all thoughtful Americans of the nineteenth century. But it was also creating an atomistic society of isolated human beings which lacked moral and social purpose as much as it did any principle of cohesiveness. Writing in the last decades of the century, Henry Adams[22] reviewed the situation of 1800 in the following words:

In the early days of colonization, every new settlement represented an idea and proclaimed a mission…. No such character belonged to the colonization of 1800. From Lake Erie to Florida, in long, unbroken line, pioneers were at work, cutting into the forests with the energy of so many beavers, and with no more express moral purpose than the beavers they drove away. The civilization they carried with them was rarely illumined by an idea; they sought room for no new truth; and aimed neither at creating, like the Puritans, a government of saints, nor like the Quakers, one of love and peace; they left such experiments behind them, and wrestled only with the hardest problems of frontier life.

It is not surprising, Adams goes on to say, that foreign observers as well as the Americans of the sea coast did not admire this development, asserting that

virtue and wisdom no longer guided the United States! What they saw was not encouraging….Greed for wealth, lust for power, yearning for the blank void of savage freedom such as Indians and wolves delighted in—these were the fires that flamed under the caldron of American society, in which, as conservatives believed, the old, well-proven, conservative crust of religion, government, family, and even common respect for age, education, and experience was rapidly melting away, and was indeed already broken into fragments, swept about by the seething mass of scum ever rising in greater quantities to the surface.[23]

Not all Americans, certainly not the great novelists of the nineteenth century, who were acutely aware of the situation described by Adams, were by any means conservatives. They did not wish to see Tocquevill's hierarchic chain of aristocratic institutions reimposed upon their society. On the contrary, they wanted to preserve the gains of democracy and looked forward to the realization of social possibilities which they believed to be inherent in the democratic principle itself. Nor were many foreign observers necessarily antagonistic to American democracy just because they found themselves among its critics. If Dickens considered the Eastern Penitentiary in Philadelphia an inhuman institution, it was only after he had discovered that the inmates of the many asylums, poor-houses, hospitals, and prisons at South Boston "are surrounded by all reasonable means of comfort and happiness that their condition will admit of, are appealed to, as members of the great human family, however afflicted, indigent, or fallen; are ruled by the strong Heart, and not by the strong... Hand."[24] In "Concluding Remarks"—the last chapter of the *American Notes*, in which he presents his view of "the general character of the American people, and the general character of their social system"—he begins by observing that Americans are "by nature, frank, brave, cordial, hospitable, and affectionate. Cultivation and refinement seem but to enhance their warmth of heart and ardent enthusiasm." He goes on to add, however, that these qualities are "sadly sapped and blighted in their growth among the mass" by that "great blemish in the popular mind of America... Universal Distrust." Linking this distrust itself with the American's "love of 'smart' dealing" he locates the ultimate root of the evil in "the national love of trade."[25] This diagnosis is paralleled by Emerson's criticism in "New England Reformers": "This whole business of Trade gives me to pause and think, as it constitutes false relations between men"[26] or again in "Man the Reformer":

> The ways of trade are grown selfish to the borders of theft, and supple to the borders (if not beyond the borders) of fraud.... I leave for those who have the knowledge the part of sifting the oaths of our custom houses; I will not inquire into the oppression of the sailors; I will not pry into the usages of our retail trade. I content myself with the fact that the general system of our trade (apart from the blacker trades, which, I hope, are exceptions denounced and unshared by all reputable men), is a system of selfishness; is not dictated by the high

and yet the world these men were creating was coming to rest increasingly on the foundations of selfishness, distrust, and crass materialism.

These products of individualism were not only falsifying social relations but abstracting from them all human content, so that the most alarming feature of this society was the isolation of its members. Tocqueville observed that democratic equality "places men side by side, unconnected by any common tie," and Emerson exclaimed in "Society and Solitude": "But how insular and pathetically solitary are all the people we know!" Emerson's position on this question of insularity and social relatedness, as on so many other questions, is interesting partly because of his dialectical manner of arguing both sides of a case. On the one hand, he seems undoubtedly to approve this tendency and to approximate closely his popular image as the champion of the self-reliant individual, of "the great Transcendental fallacy" as Daniel Aaron calls it. Nevertheless, as Aaron points out: "He was both the critic and the celebrator of his and subsequent generations, the Yea-sayer and the Nay-sayer."[28] Many positive elements of his attitude were shared by his contemporaries, not excluding the novelists, because, if their awareness of the limitations of individualism went beyond his, they, as much as he, took individual freedom as their starting point. If he seems to insist more on the individual's standing alone, a part at least of his reason is the same as theirs, for, as he says in his essay on Friendship: "To stand in true relations with men in a false age is worth a fit of insanity, is it not?" And finally, if in "Society and Solitude" he talks of the "necessity of isolation which genius feels," it is, as he goes on to say, a "tragic necessity... irresistibly driving each adult soul as with whips into the desert, and making our warm covenants sentimental and momentary." A little later he adds, as though by way of a conscious comment on the other and better-known side of his own attitude: "But this banishment to the rocks and echoes no metaphysics can make right or tolerable.... A man must be clothed with

sentiments of human nature; is not measured by the exac
reciprocity, much less by the sentiments of love and herois
a system of distrust, of concealment, of superior keennes
giving but of taking advantage.

We can notice here how the principle of self-interes
Crevecoeur had recognized as the strongest allurement that Amer
to the "new man," has degenerated into selfishness and mutual dis
must notice, too, that for Dickens, as well as for Emerse
characteristics of a commercial culture are evil primarily beca
warp natural feelings and destroy human relations, for this wa
main point of the nineteenth-century novelists' criticism of thei
And if Dickens' survey led him to conclude that the America
would be well advised to love "the Real less, and the Ideal s
more" and to encourage "a wider cultivation of what is beautifu
being eminently and directly useful,"[27] we must not forget that a
later, in his story "The Artist of the Beautiful," Hawthorne atte
give imaginative embodiment to precisely the same idea.

These men of imagination thus recognized the relation
economic forces and moral values. But, insofar as the emphasi
the moral consequences rather than the economic machinery of th
they viewed the freedom of the individual as something
meaningful. In the lecture on "New England Reformers," Em
way of illustrating his concept of the sufficiency of the private ma
the story of the individual who was excommunicated by his c
account of his connection with the antislavery movement
thereupon promptly and boldly "excommunicated the church, ir
and formal process." Society thus presented the image of a bod
unfettered by any restrictive pressures, liberated from the res
religious, social, and economic institutions, enjoying a freedom o
and action such as individuals had not known in any other place

society, or we shall feel a certain bareness, and poverty, as of a displaced and unfurnished member."

Thus, while the practical-minded citizens of America were pushing forward to reap the benefits of unrestrained freedom, its philosophers, poets, and novelists were pondering the loss of moral and social values that went with the development. If the former lacked, as Adams said, all sense of moral purpose, the latter were deeply aware of the missionary tradition which had accompanied the settlement of America. No one doubted the necessity of destroying older social institutions. But what had happened to the expectations of a new society, the hope of a regenerated humanity, the vision of New Jerusalem? The American philosophers and poets felt the process of democracy had defeated its promise.

A visionary conception of society provided more than the measuring rod of their criticism; from it came also their positive social values. In this sense the myth of America was still operative in the nineteenth century. An ideal society could be created as soon as the individuals concerned subscribed to the ideal principle which was to inform it. Since Americans were no longer the victims of old institutions but the prospective creators of new ones, the decisive factor was the moral regeneration of the individual. Emerson's answer to "this whole business of Trade" in "New England Reformers" was simple: "Let into it the new and renewing principle of love." For, as he had said in "Man the Reformer": "We must be lovers, and at once the impossible becomes possible." This was also Whitman's answer in 1864 when, after his disillusionment with the workings of practical democracy, he wrote in a characteristic vein: "The final meaning of Democracy through many transmigrations is to press on through all ridicules, arguments, and ostensible failures to put in practice the idea of the sovereignty, license, sacredness of the individual. This idea isolates, for reasons, each separate man and woman in the world;—while the idea of Love fuses and combines the whole. Out of the fusing of these twain, opposite as they are, I seek to make a homogeneous Song."[29]

The visionary aspect of the American tradition was not, however, monopolized by literary artists. The great type of American social experience—separation from a corrupt society to form an ideal community—was receiving practical enactment in the numerous experiments of the contemporary communitarians. The first colonies were settled in the second half of the seventeenth century by foreign sectarians such as the Dutch Mennonites and Labadists[30]. During the eighteenth century the Moravians and the Shakers[31] had great success with their Utopian settlements, illustrating, as Arthur Bestor has said, "the process that was repeated time after time in America in the seventeenth, eighteenth, and nineteenth centuries."[32] In the nineteenth century the movement was considerably accelerated and the number of utopian colonies increased to well beyond 200, the experiments exciting widespread interest, both critical and enthusiastic.

Though the seminal idea of these colonies was in all cases brought over from Europe，the schemes came to full flower only in the new world, showing how persistently America figured in people's imagination as the bright hope of Europe. If Europe represented the hard facts of social reality, America was seen as approximating the possibility of ideal community life. In the nineteenth century, however, the communitarian tradition registered certain developments which were more significant than the quantitative increase in the number of experiments. In the first place, it was no longer restricted to foreign immigrants or to groups which continued to regard themselves as alien. As general social conditions in America itself grew unsatisfactory, American intellectuals, artists, and reformers started experimenting with utopian colonies of their own. A more important development lay in the fact that, in keeping with the general tendency of the nineteenth century, the economic and social implications of the communitarian way of life began to supersede its earlier religious and theological inspiration. Even the older utopian groups regarded themselves increasingly as communitarians first and sectarians second. When the followers of Father Rapp[33] established the third of their villages in 1825, they called it not Harmony, as on both previous occasions, but Economy. The apostles of this new phase of communitarianism were Fourier and Owen.

Nevertheless, in America, unlike Europe, there was a continuity of tradition between the secular communities of the nineteenth century and the religious fervor of the seventeenth. "In America, and America alone, the religious socialism of the seventeenth century evolved without a break into the secular socialism of the nineteenth." This transmission of communitarian tradition is illustrated by Brook Farm[34]. Two years and a half before its establishment, its founder, George Ripley, visited the German sectarian community at Zoar, and his wife wrote enthusiastically about its way of life. The first prospectus of Brook Farm made allusion to the Moravians, the Shakers, and Rappites[35], while Hawthorne, who joined the community early in its career, had already shown interest in the Shakers by publishing two tales about them in the 1830s. "The communitarian tradition influenced Brook Farm," Mr. Bestor concludes, "and Brook Farm, in turn, passed the influence along. The Fruitlands[36] experiment of Bronson Alcott... was in some measure its offshoot, for Alcott had participated in the original plans for Brook Farm, and inaugurated his own experiment only when convinced that the older community was not sufficiently ideal."

Hawthorne, of course, had the strongest critical reservations about the whole communitarian enterprise, and their nature was such that they would be shared by many of his contemporaries who never made the experiment of actually living in a utopian community, or even paid much attention to the movement. But before taking this up, it would be well to note two aspects of communitarian thought which represent the

14. 引自爱德义·T·鲍登《心灵的牢房：人的孤独与美国小说》，纽约麦克米伦出版公司 1961 年版。

15. 指马瑟所著的《基督在美洲的匹绩》。

16. 指富兰克林（参阅《穷理查的历书》）。

17. 《来自一个美国农夫的信》为克里夫古尔（Crevecoeur）所写。

18. Richard Hofstadter：霍夫斯达德（1916-1970），美国历史学家。

19. the conflict of loyalties：美国革命时期，克里夫古尔虽然同意富兰克林的独立思想，但却把自己置于英国殖民军的保护之下，因而曾被捕，获释后回法国，后来又回美国任驻德国领事。

20. Non serviam：不行。

21. Ralph Gabriel：拉尔夫·亨利·盖布利尔所著的《美国民主思想的历程》，纽约罗纳德出版公司 1956 年版，第 33 页。

22. Henry Adams：亨利·亚当斯（1838-1918），美国历史学家，著有《亨利·亚当斯的成长》等书。

23. 引自亨利·亚当斯所著的《美利坚合众国史》，纽约斯克里卜纳出版公司 1890 年版，第 1 卷第 177 至 178 页。

24. 引自狄更斯《美国随笔及意大利见闻》，伦敦牛津大学出版社 1957 年版，第 53 页。

25. 同上，第 244 至 246 页。

26. 引自爱默生《爱默生全集》，波士顿 1888-1893 年版。

27. 同注 38，第 248 页。

28. 引自丹尼尔·爱伦：《前程无量的人们》，纽约牛津大学出版社 1951 年版，第 7 页。

29. 引自 C.J. 福尼斯编：《瓦尔特·惠特曼论集》，哈佛大学出版社 1928 年版，第 127 至 128 页。

30. Mennonites：门诺教派信徒。门诺教是由荷兰宗教改革家门诺·西蒙斯（Menno Simians, 1486-1561）所创建的基督教一新教派别。它拒绝服军役，反对从事公共事务及宣誓，主张通过修身来实现对神灵的追求。Labadists：拉巴迪教派主徒。拉巴迪教派系由法国神学家拉巴迪（Jean de Labadie, 1610-1674）所创建。它主张儿童公有及共产共食。

31. Moravians：摩拉维亚教信徒。摩拉维亚教系基督教新教的一个派别，1772 年建于中欧的摩拉维亚。该教派致力于传教，其教徒多喜爱生活在分散的团体中。Shakers：震颤派信徒。震颤派系美国基督教派别，主张独身、财产公有及公社生活。

32. 引自亚瑟·尤基尼·白斯特：《偏远森林中的乌托邦》，费城宾夕法尼亚大学出版社 1950 年版，第 26 页。

33. George Rapp：拉普，或称 Father Rapp（1757-1874），美国宗教领袖。

34. Brook Farm：布鲁克农场，正式名称为农业和教育社。1841年至 1847 年美国批评家及改革家，该农场的创建者和组织者里普利（George Ripley, 1802-1880）曾于此进行过乌托邦式公社生活实验。

35. Rappites：拉普派信徒，拉普派系乔治·拉普创建的美国基督教一派别。它反对结婚，主张独身的公社生活。

36. The Fruitlands：由美国哲学家阿尔科特（Bronson Alcott，1799-1888）所建，类似 Brook Farm。

37. Albert Brisbane：布里斯倍尼(1809-1890)，美国改革家。

Questions For Discussion:

1. What is it that A. N. Kaul has got to say about American fiction? Why is it not proper to evaluate American fiction in European terms?

2. What is the essence of the American experience that American fiction represents? If, according to A. N. Kaul, what imaginative men say in critical times is often revelatory of certain aspects of the national sensibility, what do you think the works of Cooper, Hawthorne, Melville, and Mark Twain reveal of the national experience of America?

For Further Reference:

1. R. W. B. Lewis. *The American Adam*. Chicago: The Univ. of Chicago press, 1955.

2. *Puritanism in Early America*. George M. Walter，ed. Boston: D.C.: Heath and Company, 1950.

3. Edwin S. Fussell. *Frontier: American Literature and the West*. Princeton, N. J.: Princeton Univ. Press.

Leslie Fiedler

　　莱斯利·菲德勒（Leslie Fiedler，1917- ），美国文学评论家、小说家、诗人。他是二战后美国文学评论界风云人物之一。在文学评论中，他把社会学、心理学与神话熔为一炉，提出一些貌似古怪但却令人耳目一新的观点。使他一举成名的是他撰写的关于《哈克贝利·芬历险记》的评论作品，在这里他指出在哈克和吉姆间存在着同性恋感情的论点。这一论点后来发展为一种理论，认为白人在心理上无法正视有色人种，美国文学及文化乃是对其他种族"爱"与不爱的表现，以及美国白色女人在文化上处于统治地位而男人则竭力逃脱它的控制等等。菲德勒长于创新，但有些观点失于偏颇而不一定非常可靠。他的最富有影响的作品是《美国小说里的爱与死》（*Love and Death in the American Novel*，1960）。此外他还写了诸如《美国小说中的犹太人》（*The Jew in the American Novel*，1950）等评论著作。

Love and Death in the American Novel

　　《美国小说里的爱与死》1960 年由纽约标准书局出版。它对自 19 世纪末至 20 世纪 50 年代末的美国小说进行了别开生面的评论。菲德勒认为，美国小说与欧洲小说相比较，在表现爱与死这种题材的手法上有很大差别。他指出，美国小说未能处理好成人的性爱；它带有浓厚的恐怖和死的气氛。《美国小说里的爱与死》集中探讨了美国小说中的伤感（"爱"）和哥特式（"死"）两种文学传统。

菲德勒指出，美国小说家之所以不能正面描述异性爱，主要是由美国生活本身所存在的追怀童稚时期的特点所致。美国生活中对性的畏惧，对性的各种日常表现的令人费解的视若无睹，使美国小说又返回到"青春期前"去。因此，美国小说的经典作品为回避性爱、结婚及社会责任的事实起见，便有脱离社会的倾向；美国小说家对描述此类问题颇感棘手。菲德勒认为，他们的心理障碍是他们处理异性爱题材不力的症结所在。这也导致他们沉迷于死、乱伦及同性恋等素材，以恐怖代替爱情，以内疚、畏怯和理想化的同性恋去填补因惧怕表现成人异性而留下的空白。菲德勒认为，欧洲哥特式小说英译本对美国小说所产生的影响是决定性的，因为这类小说的基本特点是恐怖，而不是爱情。

《美国小说里的爱与死》以欧美文学为对象，旁征博引，纵横驰骋，主要从英美两国文学的比较角度，论述了爱与死两种传统在文学作品中的体现。书中所涉及的美国作家有布朗、库柏、坡、霍桑、麦尔维尔和马克·吐温，对他们的代表作品进行了繁实详尽的分析。菲德勒对库柏的《皮袜子五部曲》、霍桑的《红字》、麦尔维尔的《白鲸》以及马克·吐温的《哈克贝利·芬历险记》等名著的论述集中表现出他作为文学评论家独辟蹊径、戛戛独造的风格。此外他还对诸如亨利·詹姆斯、豪威尔斯、海明威、福克纳、菲茨杰拉德及索尔·贝娄等现当代作家的某些作品发表了他的独特见解。菲德勒还较详尽地分析了英国作家塞缪尔·理查森、司各特及 M·G·刘易斯的作品，为他对美国文学的论点提供佐证。《美国小说里的爱与死》是一本立意新颖、论证翔实的评论专著，它为阅读美国文学提供一个饶有趣味的全新的视角。

这里选注的是该书的第 1 章和第 11 章。

An Excerpt from *Love and Death in the American Novel*

CHAPTER I　THE NOVEL AND AMERICA

Between the novel and America there are peculiar and intimate connections. A new literary form and a new society, their beginnings coincide with the beginnings of the modern era and, indeed, help to define it. We are living not only in the Age of America but also in the Age of the Novel, at a moment when the literature of a country without a first-rate verse epic or a memorable verse tragedy has become the model of half the world. *The Age of the American Novel*, a French critic calls a book on contemporary writing; and everywhere in the West there are authors who quite deliberately turn from their own fictional traditions to pursue ours—or at least something they take for ours.

We have known for a long time, of course, that our national literary reputation depends largely upon the achievement of our novelists. The classical poetic genres revived by the Renaissance had lost their relevance to contemporary life before America entered the cultural scene; and even the lyric has provided us with occasions for few, and limited, triumphs. Whitman, Poe, and Dickinson—beyond these three, there are no major American poets before the twentieth century; and even about their merits we continue to wrangle. It is Melville and Hawthorne and James (together with such latter-day figures as Faulkner and Hemingway) who possess the imagination of a Europe already committed to the novel as the prevailing modern form. Not only in the United States, though preeminently there, literature has become for most readers quite simply prose fiction; and our endemic fantasy of writing "the Great American Novel" is only a local instance of a more general obsession. The notions of greatness once associated with the heroic poem have been transferred to the novel: and the shift is a part of that "Americanization of culture" which some European intellectuals continue ritually to deplore.

But is there, as certain continental critics have insisted, an "American novel," a specific sub-variety of the form? If we turn to these critics for a definition, we come on such terms as "neo-realist," "hard-boiled," "naive," and "anti-traditional"—terms derived from a standard view of America as an "anti-culture," an eternally maintained preserve of primitivism. This view (notoriously exemplified by Andre Gide)[1] ends by finding in Dashiell Hammett[2] the same values as in William Faulkner, and is more a symptom of European cultural malaise than a useful critical distinction. While America is, in a very real sense, a constantly recreated fact of the European imagination, it is not only, or even pre-eminently, that it is tempting to insist on the part rebuttal that, far from being an anti-culture, we are merely a branch of Western culture; and that there is no "American novel," only local variants of standard European kinds of fiction: American sentimental, American gothic, American historical romance, etc. Certainly no single sub-genre of the novel was invented in United States. Yet the peculiarities of our variants seem more interesting and important than their resemblances to the parent forms.

There is a real sense in which our prose fiction is immediately distinguishable from that of Europe, though this is a fact that is difficult for Americans (oddly defensive and flustered in its presence) to confess. In this sense, our novels seem not primitive, perhaps, but innocent, unfallen in a disturbing way, almost juvenile. The great works of American fiction are notoriously at home in the children's section of the library, their level of sentimentality precisely that of a pre-adolescent. This is part of what we mean when we talk about the incapacity of the American novelist to develop; in a compulsive way he returns to a limited world of experience, usually associated with his childhood, writing the same book over and over again until he lapses into silence or self-parody.

Merely finding a language, learning to talk in a land where there are no conventions of conversation, no special class idioms and no dialogue between classes, no continuing literary language—this exhausts the American writer. He is forever *beginning*, saying for the first time (without real tradition there can never be a second time) what it is like to stand alone before nature, or in a city as appallingly lonely as any virgin forest. He faces, moreover, another problem, which has resulted in a failure of feeling and imagination perceptible at the heart of even our most notable works. Our great novelists, though experts on indignity and assault, on loneliness and terror, tend to avoid treating the passionate encounter of man and woman, which we expect at the center of a novel. Indeed, they rather shy away from permitting in their fictions the presence of any full-fledged, mature women, giving us instead monsters of virtue or bitchery, symbols of the rejection or fear of sexuality.

To be sure, the theme of "love" in so simple a sense is by no means necessary to all works of art. In the *Iliad*[3], for instance, and in much Greek tragedy, it is conspicuously absent; and in the heroic literature of the Middle Ages, it is peripheral where it exists at all. The "belle Aude"[4] of the *Chanson de Boland* is a supernumerary, and the only female we remember from *Beowulf*[5] is a terror emerging from the darkness at the bottom of the waters. The world of the epic is a world of war, and its reigning sentimental relationship is the loyalty of comrades in arms; but by the eighteenth century the notion of a heroic poem without romance had come to seem intolerable. The last pseudo-epics of the baroque[6] had been obsessed with the subject of love, and the rococo[7] had continued to elaborate that theme. Shakespeare himself appeared to the English Augustans[8] too little concerned with the "reigning passion" to be quite interesting without revision. Why, after all, should Cordelia[9] not survive to marry Edgar, they demanded of themselves and they rewrote *King Lear* to prove that she should.[10]

The novel, however, was precisely the product of the sentimentalizing taste of the eighteenth century; and a continuing tradition of prose fiction did not begin until the love affair of Lovelace and Clarissa[11] (a demythicized Don Juan[12] and a secularized goddess of Christian love) had been imagined. The subject par excellence of the novel is love or, more precisely—in its beginnings at least—seduction and marriage; and in France, Italy, Germany, and Russia, even in England, spiritually so close to America, love in one form or another has remained the novel's central theme, as necessary and as expected as battle in Homer or revenge in the Renaissance drama. When the Romantic impulse led in Germany to a technical recasting of the novel form, even the wildest experimentalists did not desert this traditional theme; Schiller's *Lucille* is a dialogue on freedom and restraint in passion. But our great Romantic *Unroman*[13] our typical anti-novel, is the womanless *Moby Dick*.

Where is our *Madame Bovary*, our *Anna Karenian*, our *Pride and Prejudice* or *Vanity Fairy*[14]? Among our classic novels, at least those before Henry James, who stands so oddly between our own traditions and the European ones we rejected or recast, the best attempt at dealing with love is *The Scarlet Letter*, in which the physical consummation of adultery has occurred and all passion burned away before the novel proper begins. Our *Madame Bovary* is a novel about adultery with the adultery offstage; and the child who is its product is so elfin and ethereal that it is hard to believe her engendered in the usual way. For the rest, there are *Moby Dick* and *Huckleberry Finn*, *The Last of the Mohicans*, *The Red Badge of Courage*[15], the stories of Edgar Allan Poe—books that turn from society to nature or nightmare out of a desperate need to avoid the facts of wooing, marriage, and child-bearing.

The figure of Rip Van Winkle[16] presides over the birth of the American imagination; and it is fitting that our first successful homegrown legend should memorialize, however playfully, the flight of the dreamer from the shrew—into the mountains and out of time, away from the drab duties of home and town toward the good companions and the magic keg of beer. Ever since, the typical male protagonist of our fiction has been a man on the run, harried into the forest and out to sea, down the river or into combat—anywhere to avoid "civilization," which is to say, the confrontation of a man and woman which leads to the fall to sex, marriage, and responsibility. One of the factors that determine theme and form in our great books is this strategy of evasion, this retreat to nature and childhood which makes our literature (and life) so Channingly and infuriatingly "boyish."

The child's world is not only asexual, it is terrible: a world of fear and loneliness; a haunted world; and the American novel is pre-eminently a novel of terror. To "light out for the territory"[17] or seek refuge in the forest seems easy and tempting from the vantage point of a chafing and restrictive home; but civilization once disavowed and Christianity disowned, the bulwark of woman left behind, the wanderer feels himself without protection, more motherless child than free man. To be sure, there is a substitute for wife or mother presumably waiting in the green heart of nature: the natural man, the good companion, pagan and unashamed— Queequeg[18] or Chingachgook or Nigger Jim. But the, figure of the natural man is ambiguous, a dream and a nightmare at once. The other face of Chingachgook is Injun Joe[19], the killer in the graveyard and the haunter of caves; Nigger Jim is also the Babo of Melville's "Benito Cereno," the humble servant whose name means "papa" holding the razor to his master's throat; and finally the dark-skinned companion becomes the "Black Man," which is a traditional American name for the Devil himself.

The enemy of society on the run toward "freedom" is also the pariah in flight from his guilt, the guilt of that very flight; and new phantoms arise to haunt him at every step. American literature likes to pretend, of course, that its bugaboos are all finally jokes: the headless horseman[20] a hoax, every manifestation of the supernatural capable of rational, explanation on the last page—but we are never quite convinced. *Huckleberry Finn*, that euphoric boys' book, begins with its protagonist holding off at gun point his father driven half mad by the D. T. 's and ends (after a lynching, a disinterment, and a series of violent deaths relieved by such humorous incidents as soaking a dog in kerosene and setting him on fire) with the revelation of that father's sordid death. Nothing is spared; Pap, horrible enough in life, is found murdered brutally, abandoned to float down the river in a decaying house scrawled with obscenities. But it is all "humor," of course, a last desperate attempt to convince us of the innocence of violence, the good clean fun of horror. Our literature as a whole at times seems a chamber of horrors disguised as an amusement park "fun house," where we pay to play at terror and are confronted in the innermost chamber with a series of inter-reflecting mirrors which present us with a thousand versions of our own face.

In our most enduring books, the cheapjack machinery of the gothic novel is called on to represent the hidden blackness of the human soul and human society. No wonder our authors mock themselves as they use such devices; no wonder Mistress Hibbins in *The Scarlet Letter* and Fedallah in *Moby Dick* are treated half jocularly, half melodramatically, though each represents in his book the Faustian pact, the bargain with the Devil[21], which our author have always felt as the essence of the American experience. However shoddily or ironically treated, horror is essential to our literature. It is not merely a matter of terror filling the vacuum left by the suppression of sex in our novels, of Thanatos[22] standing in for Eros. Through these gothic images are projected certain obsessive concerns of our national life; the ambiguity of our relationship with Indian and Negro, the ambiguity of our encounter with nature, the guilt of the revolutionist who feels himself a patricide—and, not least of all, the uneasiness of the writer who cannot help believing that the very act of composing a book is Satanic revolt. "Hell-fired," Hawthorne called *The Scarlet Letter*, and Melville thought his own *Moby Dick* a "wicked book."

The American writer inhabits a country at once the dream of Europe and a fact of history; he lives on the last horizon of an endlessly retreating vision of innocence—on the "frontier," which is to say, the margin where the theory of original goodness and the fact of original sin come face to face. To express this "blackness ten times black"[23] and to live by it in a society in which, since the decline of orthodox Puritanism, optimism has become the chief effective religion, is a complex and difficult task.

It was to the novel that the American writer turned most naturally, as the only *popular* form of sufficient magnitude for his vision. He was, perhaps, not sufficiently sophisticated to realize that such learned forms as epic and tragedy had already outlived their usefulness; but, working out of a cultural background at best sketchy and unsure, he felt insecure before them. His obligations urged him in the direction of tragedy, but traditional verse tragedy was forbidden him; indeed, a chief technical problem for American novelists has been the adaptation of nontragic forms to tragic ends. How could the dark vision of the American—his obsession with violence and his embarrassment before love—be expressed in the sentimental novel of analysis as developed by Samuel Richardson or the historical romance as practiced by Sir Walter Scott? These subgenres of fiction, invented to satisfy the emotional needs of a merchant class in search of dignity[24] or a Tory squirearchy consumed by nostaligia, could only by the most desperate expedients be tailored to fit American necessities. Throughout their writing lives, such writers as Charles Brockden Brown and James Fenimore Copper devoted (with varying degrees of self-consciousness) all their ingenuity to this task, yet neither Brown nor Cooper finally proved capable of achieving high art; and the literary types invented by both have fallen since into the hands of mere entertainers—that is, novelists able and willing to attempt anything *except* the projection of the dark vision of America we have been describing. The Fielding novel, on the other hand, the pseudo-Shakespearean "comic epic" with its broad canvas, its emphasis upon reversals and recognitions, and its robust masculine sentimentality, turned out, oddly enough, to have no relevance to the American scene; in the United States it has remained an exotic, eternally being discovered by the widest audience and raised to best-sellerdom in its latest imported form, but seldom home-produced for home consumption.

It is the gothic form that has been most fruitful in the hands of our best writers: the gothic *symbolically* understood, its machinery and decor translated into metaphors for a terror psychological, social, and metaphysical. Yet even treated as symbols, the machinery and decor of the gothic have continued to seem vulgar and contrived; symbolic Gothicism threatens always to dissolve into its components, abstract morality and shoddy theater. A recurrent problem of our fiction has been the need of our novelists to find a mode of projecting their conflicts which would contain all the dusky horror of gothic romance and yet be palatable to discriminating readers, palatable first of all to themselves.

Such a mode can, of course, not be subsumed among any of those called "realism," and one of the chief confusions in our understanding of our own literature has arisen from our failure to recognize this fact clearly enough. Our fiction is essentially and at its best nonrealistic, even anti-realistic; long before *symbolisme* had been invented in France and exported to America, there was a full-fledged native tradition of symbolism. That tradition was born of the profound contradictions of our national life and sustained by the inheritance from Puritanism of a "typical"[25] (even allegorical) way of regarding the sensible world—not as an ultimate reality but as a system of signs to be deciphered. For too long, historians of American fiction have mistakenly tried to impose on the course of a brief literary history a notion of artistic "progress" imported from France or more precisely perhaps, from certain French literary critics. Such historians have been pleased to speak of "The Rise of Realism" or "The Triumph of Realism," as if the experiments of Hawthorne or Poe or Melville were half-misguided fumblings toward the final excellence of William Dean Howells!

But the moment at which Flaubert was dreaming *Madame Bovary* was the moment when Melville was finding *Moby Dick*, and considered as a "realistic" novel the latter is a scandalous botch. To speak of a counter-tradition to the novel, of the tradition of "the romance" as a force in our literature, is merely to repeat the rationalizations of our writers themselves; it is certainly to fail to be *specific* enough for real understanding. Our fiction is not merely in flight from the physical data of the actual world, in search of a (sexless and dim) Ideal; from Charles Brockden Brown to William Faulkner, or Eudora Welty[26], Paul Bowles or John Hawkes, it is, bewilderingly and embarrassingly, a gothic fiction, nonrealistic and negative, sadist and melodramatic—a literature of darkness and the grotesque in a land of light and affirmation.

Moreover—and the final paradox is necessary to the full complexity of the case—ours is a literature of horror for boys. Truly shocking, frankly obscene authors we do not possess; Edgar Allan Poe is our closest approximation, a child playing at what Baudelaire was to live. A Baudelaire,[27] a Marquis de Sade,[28] a "Monk" Lewis, even a John Cleland is inconceivable in the United States. Our flowers of evil are culled for the small girl's bouquet, our novels of terror (*Moby Dick, the Scarlet Letter, Huckleberry Finn*, the tales of Poe) are placed on the approved book lists of Parents' Committees who nervously fuss over the latest comic books. If such censors do not flinch at necrophilia or shudder over the book whose secret motto is "I baptise you not in the name of the Father... but of the Devil,"[29] or fear the juvenile whose hero at his greatest moment cries out,

"All right, I'll *go* to Hell,"[30] it is only another irony of life in a land where the writers believe in hell and the official guardians of morality do not. As long as there's no *sex*!

Yet our authors are as responsible as the P. T. A. 's[31] for the confusion about the true nature of their books; though they may have whispered their secret to friends, or confessed it in private letters, in their actual works they assumed what camouflage prudence dictated. They wanted to be misunderstood. *Huckleberry Finn* is only the supreme instance of subterfuge typical of our classic novelists. To this very day, it is heresy in some quarters to insist that this is not finally the jolliest, the *cleanest* of books; Twain's ironical warning to significance hunters, posted just before the title page,[32] is taken quite literally, and the irreverent critic who explicates the book's levels of terror and evasion is regarded as a busybody and scandalmonger. It is at last hard to say which is more remarkable, the eccentricity of American books or our critics' conspiracy of silence in this regard. (Or is it the critics' *unawareness* of the fact?) Why, one is driven to ask, why the distortion and why the ignorance? But the critics, after all, are children of the same culture as the novelists they discuss; and if we answer one question we will have answered both.

Perhaps the whole odd shape of American fiction arises simply (as simplifying Europeans are always ready to assure us) because there is no real sexuality in American life and therefore there cannot very well be any in American art. What we cannot achieve in our relations with each other it would be vain to ask our writers to portray or even our critics to miss. Certainly many of our novelists have themselves believed, or pretended to believe, this. Through *The Scarlet Letter*, there is a constant mournful undercurrent, a series of asides in which Hawthorne deplores the sexual diminution of American women. Mark Twain, in *1601*[33] somewhat similarly contrasts the vigor of Elizabethan Englishwomen with their American descendants; contrasting the sexual utopia of pre-colonial

England with a fallen America where the men copulate "but once in seven yeeres"; and his pornographic sketch, written to amuse a clergy man friend (for men only!), ends on the comic-pathetic image of an old man's impotent lust that "would not stand again." Such pseudo-nostalgia cannot be taken too seriously, however; it may, indeed, be the projection of mere personal weakness and fantasy. Certainly, outside their books, Hawthorne and Twain seem to have fled rather than sought the imaginary full-breasted, fully sexed, woman from whom American ladies had presumably declined. Both married, late in life, pale hypochondriac spinsters, intellectual invalids—as if to assert publicly that they sought in marriage not sex but culture! [34]

Such considerations leave us trapped in the chicken-egg dilemma. How can one say whether the quality of passion in American life suffers because of a failure of the writer's imagination or vice versa? What is called "love" in literature is a rationalization, a way of coming to terms with the relationship between man and woman that does justice, on the one hand, to certain biological drives and, on the other, to certain generally accepted conventions of tenderness and courtesy; and literature, expressing, and defining those conventions, tends to influence "real life" more than such life influences it. For better or for worse and for whatever reasons, the American novel is different from its European prototypes, and one of its essential differences arises from its chary treatment of woman and of sex.

To write, then, about the American novel is to write about the fate of certain European genres in a world of alien experience. It is not only a world where courtship and marriage have suffered a profound change, but also one in the process of losing the traditional distinctions of class; a world without a significant history or a substantial past; a world which had left behind the terror of Europe not for the innocence it dreamed of, but for new and special guilts associated with the rape of nature and the exploitation of dark-skinned people; a world doomed to play out the imaginary childhood of Europe. The American novel is only *finally* American; its appearance is an event in the history of the European spirit—as, indeed, is the very invention of America itself.

II

Though it is necessary, in understanding the fate of the American novel, to understand what European prototypes were available when American literature began, as well as which ones flourished and which ones disappeared on our soil, it is even more important to understand the meaning of that moment in the mid-eighteenth century which gave birth to Jeffersonian democracy and Richardsonian sentimentality alike: to the myth of revolution and the myth of seduction. When Charles Brockden Brown, the first professional American author, sent a copy of his *Wieland* to Thomas Jefferson in 1798, he must, beneath his modest disclaimers, have had some sense of his and the President's kinship as revolutionaries. "I am therefore obliged to hope," Brown wrote, "that... the train of eloquent and judicious reasoning... will be regarded by Thomas Jefferson with as much respect as... me." But if Jefferson ever found the time to read Brown's novel, he left no record; we know only that he expressed general approval of "works of the imagination" as being able, more than history, to "possess virtue in the best and vice in the worst forms possible." It is a chillingly rational approach to art and a perhaps sufficient indication of the hopelessness of Brown's attempting in those sensible years to live by his writing.

Yet despite the fact that no professional novelist of real seriousness was to find a supporting public in America for twenty-five or thirty years more, Brown's instincts had not deceived him. He and Jefferson were engaged in a common enterprise; the novel and America did not come into existence at the same time by accident. They are the two great inventions of the bourgeois, Protestant mind at the moment when it stood, on the one hand, between Rationalism and Sentimentalism, and on the other, between the drive for economic power and the need for cultural autonomy. The series of events which includes the American and the French Revolutions, the invention of the novel, the rise of modern psychology, and the triumph of the lyric in poetry, adds up to a psychic revolution as well as a social one—perhaps first of all to a psychic revolution. This revolution, viewed as an overturning of ideas and artistic forms, has traditionally been called "Romantic"; but the term is paralyzing narrow, defining too little too precisely, and leading to further pointless distinctions between Romanticism proper, pre-Romanticism, *Storm and Drang*,[35] Sentimentalism, *Symbolisme*, etc. It seems preferable to call the whole continuing, complex event simply "the Break-through," thus emphasizing the dramatic entry of a new voice into the dialogue of Western man with his various selves.

The Break-through is characterized not only by the separation of psychology from philosophy, the displacement of the traditional leading genres by the personal lyric and analytic prose fiction (with the consequent subordination of plot to character); it is also marked by the promulgation of a theory of revolution as a good in itself and, most notably perhaps, by a new concept of inwardness. One is almost tempted to say, by the invention of a new kind of self, a new level of mind; for what has been happening since the eighteenth century seems more like the development of a new organ than the mere finding of a new way to describe old experience. The triumph, for instance, of the theory that insanity is not possession by forces outside the psyche but a failure within the psyche itself is a representative aspect of the change-over.

It was Diderot[36] who represented a first real awareness (as Freud represents a final one) that man is *double* to the final depths of his soul, the prey of conflicting psyches both equally himself. The conflict had, of course, always been felt, but had traditionally been described as occurring between man and devil, or flesh and spirit; that the parties to the dispute are both man and spirit was a revolutionary suggestion. In his demi-novel, *Rameau's Nephew*, Diderot projected the conflicting divisions within man's mind as the philosopher and the parasite, the rationalist and the underground man, debating endlessly the cause of the head versus that of the gut. And in his pornographic *Bijoux Indiscrets*, he proposed another version of the same dialogue, the enchanted (and indiscreet) genitals speak the truth which the mouth will not avow, thus comprising an allegorical defense of pornography in the guise of a pornographic work. In the same year in which Richardson's sentimental novel *Clarissa* was published, John Cleland's long-lived dirty book *The Memoirs of Fanny Hill* was making a stir. Pornography and obscenity are, indeed, hallmarks of the age of the Break-through. Not only pious novels but titillating ones show the emergence of the underground emotions (of what the period itself euphemistically called "the heart") into high culture. Quite as influential as Diderot (or Richardson or Rousseau) in the *bouleversement*[37] of the eighteenth century is the Marquis de Sade, who stands almost emblematically at the crossroads of depth psychology and revolution.

Not only did de Sade shed new light on the ambivalence of the inner mind, revealing the true darkness and terror implicit in the drive which the neo-classical age (revolting against Christian notions of sin) had been content to celebrate as simple "pleasure" or polite "gallantry"; he may even have caused that symbolic storming of an almost empty prison with which the French Revolution begins. Himself a prisoner in the *Tour de la liberte* of the Bastille[38], de Sade, through an improvised loudspeaker made of a tube and funnel, screamed to bystanders to rescue his fellow inmates who were having their throats cut—and scattered handwritten leaflets complaining about jail conditions to the crowd he attracted. On July 3, 1789, he was finally transferred elsewhere to insure "the safety of the building," but not before he had started to write *Justine, or the Misfortunes of Virtue*, that perverse offshoot of the Richardsonian novel, and had thus begun to create the first example of revolutionary pornography. Maurice Blanchot, in an essay called *Lautreamont et Sade*, describes his method as follows: "What is striking is this: the language of de Sade is precisely opposite to the cheating language of hangmen; it is the language of the victim; he invented it in the Bastille... He put on trial, reversing the process of his own judgment, the men who condemned him, God himself, and—in general—every limitation against which his frenzy clashed..."

In the Marquis de Sade, the Break-through found its most stringent and spectacular spokesman: the condemned man judging his judges, the pervert mocking the normal, the advocate of destruction and death sneering at the defenders of love and life; but his *reductio*[39] follows logically enough from assumptions shared by Jefferson and Rousseau,[40] Richardson and Saint-Just. Whatever has been suspect, outcast, and denied is postulated as the source of good. Before the Break-through, no one, Christian or Humanist, had doubted the inferiority of passion to reason; of impulse to law; and though it is possible sophistically to justify all eighteenth-century reversals by quoting the verse which says the last shall be first, Christianity is dead from the moment such a justification is made. The Break-through, the triumphant intrusion of the libido into the place of virtue and reason, is profoundly anti-Christian though it is not always willing to appear so. There is a brief age of transition when the Enlightenment and Sentimentalism exist side by side, when it is still possible to pretend that true reason and true feeling, the urgings of passion and the dictates of virtue are identical—and that all are alike manifestations of the orthodox God. But Sentimentalism yields quickly to the full Romantic revolt; in a matter of months, Don Juan, enemy of Heaven and the family, has been transformed from villain to hero;[41] and before the process is finished, audiences have learned to weep for Shylock rather than laugh him from the stage. The legendary rebels and outcasts, Prometheus and Cain, Judas and the Wandering Jew, Faust and Lucifer himself are one by one redeemed. The parricide becomes an object of veneration, and tourists (among them that good American abroad, Herman Melville) carry home as an icon Guido's picture of Beatrice Cenci,[42] slayer of her father!

The process is continuous and nearly universal. Even the values of language change: "gothic" passes from a term of contempt to one of description and then of praise, while "baroque" makes more slowly the same transition; meanwhile terms once used honorifically to describe desired traits—"condescension," for example—become indicators of disapproval. The child is glorified over the man, the peasant over the courtier, the dark man over the white, the rude ballad over the polished sonnet, the weeper over the thinker, colony over mother country, the commoner over the king—nature over culture[43]. At first, all this is a game: the ladies of the court in pastoral dress swing high into the air to show their legs with a self-consciousness quite unlike the abandon of children to which they are pretending. But in a little while, Jean-Jacques Rousseau has fainted on the road to Vincennes and awakened to find his waistcoat soaked with tears;[44] and it is suddenly all in earnest. Whatever was down is now up, as the under-mind heaves up out of the darkness: barricades are erected and the novel becomes the reigning form; the Jew walks openly out of the ghetto, and otherwise sensible men hang on their walls pictures of trees and cattle. The conjunctions are comic in their un-expectedness and variety.

It is hard to say what was cause and what effect in the complex upheaval; everything seems the symptom of everything else. Yet deep within the nexus of causes (gods must die for new genres to be born) was that "death of God" that has not yet ceased to trouble our peace. Somewhere near the beginning of the eighteenth century, Christianity (more precisely, perhaps, that desperate compromise of the late Middle Ages and early Renaissance, Christian Humanism) began to wear out. It was not merely, or even primarily, a matter of the destruction of the political and social power of one Church or another, much less of the lapse of economic control by the priests. The divisions within Christendom surely contributed to the final collapse, but they are perhaps better regarded as manifestations than as causes of the insecurity over dogma that was at work deep within. Institutionalized Christianity at any rate began to crumble when its God began to fail, that is to say, when its mythology no longer proved capable of controlling and revivifying the imagination of Europe.

The darker motive forces of the psyche refused any longer to accept the names and ranks by which they had been demeaned for almost two thousand years; one worshiped as "gods," they had been made demons by fiat, but now they stirred again in discontent. Especially the Great Mother—cast down by the most patriarchal of all religions[45] (to the Hebrews, she was Lilith[46] the bride of darkness), ambiguously redeemed as the Blessed Virgin and denied once more by a Hebraizing Protestantism[47]—clamored to be honored once more. The very distinction between God and Devil, on which the psychic balance of Europe had for so long been staked, was threatened. It did not matter that some people (chiefly women) continued to go to church, or even that there were revivals within the framework of surviving sects; fewer and fewer men lived by the legends of the church, and the images of saints represented not living myths but "mythology" in a literary sense, tales to be read for amusement or "analyzed" in the light of the teachings of anthropology or psychology. There remained only the job of carrying the news of God's death to those who had not yet heard the word.

The effect of the growing awareness (an awareness, to be sure, at first shared by only a handful of advanced thinkers) of this cosmic catastrophe was double: a sense of exhilaration and a spasm of terror, to which correspond two initial and overlapping stages of the Break-through. There was first of all the conviction of the Age of Reason and its spokesmen; the *philosophes*,[48] grave-diggers of the Christian God, that they—and all of mankind—were at last *free*, free of the superstition and ignorance so long sponsored by the priests for their own selfish ends. Those demons into which the early Christian apologists had translated the gods of antiquity seemed to the *philosophes* idle inventions of the Church itself: bugaboos to scare the pious into unquestioning subservience. Even the Christian God seemed to them such a contrivance, demonic and irrational. In the imagined universe presided over by their own "Author of Creation," there could be no place for mystery or blackness. Once *"l'infame,"* the scandalous Church, had been crushed, all monsters would be eliminated forever, and man could take up his long, baffled march toward perfection in a sweet, sunlit, orderly world. Just such a vision; however modified by circumstance, moved the Deist intellectuals, who founded America, especially that Thomas Jefferson to whom C. B. Brown, himself a follower of the *philosophes*, proffered his gothic novel.

Insofar as America is legendary, a fact of the imagination as well as one of history, it has been shaped by the ideals of the Age of Reason. To be sure, the European mind had dreamed for centuries before the Enlightenment of an absolute West: Atlantis, Ultima Thule, the Western Isles[49]—a place of refuge beyond the seas, to which the hero retreats to await rebirth, a source of new life in the direction of the setting sun which seems to stand for death. Dante, however, on the, very brink of an age which was to turn the dream into the actualities of exploration, had prophetically sent to destruction in the West, Ulysses, the archetypal explorer. The direction of his westward journey through the great sea is identified with the sinister left hand; and Ulysses himself comes to stand for man's refusal to accept the simple limits of traditional duty: "not the sweetness of having a son, nor the pious claim of an old father, nor the licit love that should have made Penelope rejoice could quench in me the burning to become familiar with the vice of men and men's valor."[50] It is a fitting enough epigraph to represent that lust for experience which made America. There is, indeed, something blasphemous in the very act by which America was established, a gesture of defiance that began with the symbolic breaching of the pillars of Hercules,[51] long considered the divine signs of limit.

To be sure, the poets of later Catholicism made an effort to recast the dream of America in terms viable for their Counter-Reformation imaginations, to forge a myth that would subserve new political exigencies. It was not accident, they boasted, that the discoverer of America (sponsored by those most Catholic defenders of the Faith) had been called Cristoforo Colombo, "the Christ-bearing dove." Had he not carried orthodoxy into a world of unredeemed pagans, a reservoir of souls providentially kept in darkness until they were needed to replace the lapsed Christians of heretical northern Europe?

It is, however, the Enlightenment's vision of America rather than that of the Church that was written into our documents and has become the substance of our deepest sense of ourselves and our destiny. If North America had remained Latin,[51] the story might have been different; but Jefferson himself presided over the purchase of the Louisiana Territory,[52] which settled that question once and for all. History sometimes provides suitable symbolic occasions, and surely one of them is the scene that finds Jefferson and Napoleon, twin heirs of the Age of Reason, preparing the way for Lewis and Clark,[53] that is to say, for the first actors in our own drama of a perpetually retreating West. Napoleon, it must be remembered, was the sponsor of the painter David[54] and Jefferson the planner of Monticello; good neo-classicists both, they place the American myth firmly in the classicizing, neo-Roman tradition of the late eighteenth century. The New World is, of course, in one sense an older one than Europe, a preserve of the primitive, last refuge of antique virtue; indeed, the writers and artists of the Empire period could never quite tell the difference between Americans, red or white, and the inhabitants of the Roman Republic. The face of Washington, as rendered in bronze by Houdon,[55] is that of the noblest Roman of them all, or, in Byron's phrase (already a cliche) , "the Cincinnatus of the West."[56]

But America is not exclusively the product of Reason—not even in the area of legend. Behind its neo-classical facade, ours is a nation sustained by a sentimental and Romantic dream, the dream of an escape from culture and a renewal of youth. Beside the *philosophes*, with whom he seemed at first to accord so well that they scarcely knew he was their profoundest enemy, stands Rousseau. It is his compelling vision of a society uncompromised by culture, of simple piety and virtue bred by "Nature," i. e. the untended landscape, that has left the deepest impress on the American mind. The heirs of Rousseau are Chateaubriand and Cooper, after whom the world of togas[57] and marble brows and antique heroism is replaced by the sylvan scene, across which the melancholy refugee plods in search of the mysterious Niagara, or where Natty Bumppo, buckskinned savior, leans on his long rifle and listens for the sound of a cracking twig. The bronze face of a bewigged Washington gives way to the image of young Abe[58] splitting logs in a Kentucky clearing.

The dream of the Republic is quite a different thing from that of the Revolution. The vision of blood and fire as ritual purification, the need to cast down what is up, to degrade the immemorial images of authority, to impose equality as the ultimate orthodoxy—these came from the *Encyclopedie*[59], perhaps, as abstract ideas; but the spirit in which they were lived was that of full-blown Romanticism. The Revolution of 1789 (for which ours was an ideological dress rehearsal) may have set up David as its official interpreter, but it left the world to Delacroix;[60] and though it enthroned Reason as its goddess, it prepared for a more unruly Muse.

In Sentimentalism, the Age of Reason dissolves in a debauch of tearfulness; sensibility, seduction, and suicide haunt its art even before ghosts and graveyards take over—strange images of darkness to usher in an era of freedom from fear. And beneath them lurks the realization that the devils which had persisted from antiquity into Christianity were not dead but only driven inward; that the "tyranny of superstition," far from being the fabrication of a Machiavellian[61] priesthood, was a projection of a profound inner insecurity and guilt, a hidden world of nightmare not abolished by manifestos or restrained by barricades. The final horrors, as modern society has come to realize, are neither gods nor demons, but intimate aspects of our own minds.

CHAPER XI

THE BLACKNESS OF DARKNESS[1] : E. A. POE AND
THE DEVELOPMENT OF THE GOTHIC

I

In his harried career as a journalist, book-reviewer, short-storywriter, poet, and critic, Edgar Allan Poe tried twice to write a full length novel, reworking each time chronicles of American exploration on sea and land. Both *The Narrative of A. Gordon Pym* (1937-1938) and *The Journal of Julius Rodman* (1840) strike us as improbable books for Poe to have attempted, concerned as they are with the American scene and the great outdoors. The former is based upon accounts of pioneering expeditions to the South Seas, and, especially a South Polar expedition projected by an acquaintance of Poe called J. N. Reynolds; while the second borrows heavily from the journals of Lewis and Clark,[2] purporting to describe a trip across the Rockies which had preceded theirs. Both long fictions are, superficially at least, full-fledged "Westerns" from the pen of an author none of whose more notable short stories (except the insufferably commercial "The Gold Bug") involve either native problems or a native setting.

There is little doubt that Poe was trying to cash in on contemporary interest in the remote and the unexplored, exploited, on the one hand, by such popular histories as Washington Irving's *Astoria or Adventures of Captain Bonneville*, and on the other, by the Indian novels of James Fenimore Cooper. In the course of a review of the latter's *Wyandotte*, written in 1843, Poe reflects on the Leatherstocking Tales and remarks a little ruefully:

> … we mean to suggest that this theme—life in the wilderness—is one of intrinsic and universal interest, appealing to the heart of man in all phases; a theme, like that of life upon the ocean, so unfailingly omniprevalent in its power of arresting and absorbing attention, that while success or popularity is, with such a subject, expected as a matter of course, a failure might be properly regarded as conclusive evidence of imbecility on the part of the author…

He goes on to add, however, that "the two theses in question," that is, the wilderness and life upon the ocean, are subjects to be avoided by the "man of genius… more interested in fame than popularity," for they belong to the lesser of the "two great classes of fiction," the "popular division" at whose head Cooper stands. Of this category, Poe remarks that "the author is lost or forgotten; or remembered, if at all, with something very nearly, akin to contempt." He considers his own fiction in general part of the other great class, which includes the work of "Mr. Brockden Brown, Mr. John Neal,[3] Mr. Simms, Mr. Hawthorne," of whom it can be said that "even when the works perish, the man survives."

Yet in *Gordon Pym* and *Julius Rodman*, Poe tried his hand at the two popular themes, attempting, for the first time perhaps, to treat the sort of legendary material which had appeared in Leatherstocking Tales with the scrupulous documentation of Irving's nonfictional accounts. The kind of book at which Poe aimed Melville was to produce with eminent success; beginning less than a decade later with the best-selling *Typee* (1846) and *Omoo* (1847), and raising the genre to unexpected power in *Moby Dick*. Poe is considerably less successful, failing completely in the case of the unfinished *Julius Rodman* to lend fictional life to borrowed documents; and achieving in *Gordon Pym* a work so hopelessly unpopular (in America at least!), that only within the last very few years has a major attempt to redeem it been undertaken. Poe himself, some time after its appearance, was willing to write off *Gordon Pym* as a "silly book"; and certainly from the first he had considered it, or pretended to consider it, a shameless bid for popular success—the sort of "Tale in a couple of volumes," which his friend Paulding[4] had assured him would win him the mass audience that had snubbed his collections of short stories.

The whole apparatus which surrounds the anonymous final form of *Gordon Pym* is apologetic, an involved attempt on Poe's part to convince himself that his primary purpose in publishing the tale was to perpetrate a hoax on the reader. But this is an almost compulsive aspect of Poe's art in general, arising from a dark necessity, which dogged not only him among American writers, of remaining in ignorance about his own deepest aims and drives. Just so Cooper was obligated to believe that he was mocking his wife's literary taste before he could become an author,[5] while Melville eternally persuaded himself that he was on the verge of producing a best-seller, and Twain pretended he was a writer of books for boys.

The apologetic and playful preface to *Pym* has for us now chiefly biographical interest, illuminating the author but not the work. Whatever

Poe's ostensible or concealed motives, he created in his only complete longer fiction not a trivial hoax but the archetypal American story, which would be recast in *Moby Dick* and *Huckleberry Finn*. Why, then, did Poe's book not achieve either the immediate acclaim accorded the latter or the slowly growing reputation won by the former? All the attributes of the highbrow Western[6] are present in his novel: the rejection of the family and of the world of women, the secret evasion from home and the turning to the open sea. Only a bevy of black squaws and a few female corpses ("scattered about…in the last and most loathsome state of putrefaction") intrude into the world of pure male companionship which Poe imagines; and they provide no competition to the alliance of Pym either with his boyhood friend and Anglo-Saxon compeer, Augustus Barnard, or with his dusky demon, the "hybrid line-manager," Dirk Peters.

Rioting and shipwreck and rescue at sea do not break the rhythm of the flight that bears Pym farther and farther from civilization toward a primitive isolation, symbolized by the uncharted island and the lost valley, the derelict ship, and the small boat adrift at sea. Even Rip Van Winkle's initiatory draught, the alcoholic pledge to escape and forgetfulness, is represented in *Pym*. Buried in a coffin-like refuge in the black hull of a riot-torn ship, Gordon Pym finds at hand a bottle to console him; and later he and his companions fish up out of the flooded hold a flask of Madeira!

There are totemic beasts to spare in the pages of Poe's Western: a great white bear dramatically slaughtered, as well as legendry and exotic animals, compounded surrealistically out of incongruous familiar forms, and even stranger tabooed birds, who float lifelessly on a tepid and milky sea. And through it all, the outcast wanderer—equally in love with death and distance—seeks some absolute Elsewhere, though more in woe than wonder. Poe's realm of refuge and escape seems finally a place of death rather than one of love: the idyllic American dream turned nightmare as it is dreamed in its author's uneasy sleep.[7] If the West means archetypically some ultimate innocence, there is no West in Poe's book at all—only an illusory hope that draws men toward inevitable disenchantment and betrayal. It is not merely that a gothic horror balances the quest for innocence in *Gordon Pym*; such a balance is the standard pattern of all highbrow Westerns: of *Moby Dick*, in which the sinister figure of Fedallah confronts the beneficent one of Queequeg; and even of *Huckleberry Finn*, in which the threat of Pap's ignorant spite and the shadow of slavery define by contrast the pure peace of Jackson's Island and the raft. Only in Poe's novel, however, is the dark counterpoint permitted to drown out the *cantus firmus*[8] of hopeful joy or to mar a final harmonic resolution.

Huckleberry Finn closes on a note of high euphoria, sustained by rescue and redemption and promises of new beginnings, which quite conceal from the ordinary reader the tragic implications of the conclusion; while *Moby Dick* ends with the promise of adoption, the symbolic salvation of the orphaned Ishmael by the crushing, motherly *Rachel*. Only at the close of *Gordon Pym* is the Great Mother identified with total destruction, a death without resurrection, a sterile, white womb from which there is no exit. "And now we rushed into the embraces of the cataract, where a chasm threw itself open to receive us. But there arose in our pathway a shrouded human figure, very far larger in its proportions than any dweller among men. And the hue of the skin of the figure was of the perfect whiteness of snow." The white whale and the *Rachel* have been fused into a single symbol, the Great Mother as *vagina dentata*; and though Poe's preface has already assured us that Pym somehow escaped to write his story, we know this for a mere device to explain how such a first-person narrative could have been written at all—a gimmick and a lie. In the tone and feeling of the text, which alone have the right to ask an act of faith, there is every assurance the Pym and Peters died.

The book is finally an anti-Western disguised as the form it utterly travesties; and this fact the great public, which will not in such matters be fooled, perceived—and perceiving, rejected the work. From the beginning, a perceptive reader of *Gordon Pym* is aware that every current sentimental platitude, every cliché of the fable of the holy marriage of males is being ironically exposed. Man's best friend, the dog, turns into a slavering monster ready to tear his master's throat to appease his hunger and thirst; a presumably loyal crew, led by the kind of standard black cook who plays the grinning and subservient comedian even in *Moby Dick*, mutinies;[9] a bird flies through the pure blue air to drop "with a sullen splash" at the feet of a half-famished group of sailors "a portion of clotted and liver like substance," a chunk of decayed human flesh; an approaching ship, hailed as a source of rescue, turns out to be a vessel loaded only with human carrion, from which issues "a smell, a stench, such as the whole world has no name for." Even the friendly bottle, traditional symbol of innocent male companionship, induces not joy but the D. T.'s "an indescribable state of weakness and horror! ... a violent ague."

Most disconcerting of the parodies in *Pym* is that of the theme of resurrection itself, which later carries so much symbolic weight in both *Moby Dick* and *Huckleberry Finn*. Like Ishmael or Huck, Gordon Pym is presumably slain only to rise again, immersed and entombed only to be reborn—in his case, not once but over and over. Out of the coffin in the hold and out of a swoon that seems death itself, he is brought to life, but only to face mutiny and a new threat of destruction; and he emerges in the disguise of a ghost; his face coated with white chalk and blotched with blood, his clothes stuffed to resemble the bloated stomach of a swollen corpse. The threat of murder once again avoided, he is the victim of shipwreck; and almost dead once more (his life meagerly sustained by drinking the blood of a murdered shipmate), he is rescued by a passing ship, only to fall victim to a last catastrophe which leaves him buried alive just as in the beginning. A "living inhumation," Poe calls the state of life-in-death, to which his long circle brings him back; and he lingers almost sensuously over the details: "The blackness of darkness… the terrific oppression of the lungs, the stifling fumes from the damp earth… the allotted portion of *the dead*…" But even from this plight, Pym is rescued, this time by his blood-stained, demonic mate, Dirk Peters; and the two together approach the ultimate plunge into a white polar chasm, from which there is no reason to believe either can emerge. Indeed, it is precisely such an end which the pariah poet-sailor[10] has prayed for, has loved in anticipation: "death or captivity among barbarian hordes… a lifetime dragged out in sorrow and tears, upon some grey and desolate rock." The guilt of Pym and of his creator demands of experience not the consolation of love but the delicious punishment of a living death, not the gift of Queequeg but of Fedallah.

Since Pym lusts for Gehenna[11] rather than Eden, the companions he chooses on his quest embody not fertility or patient endurance but impotence and terror. Augustus Barnard, his first specter bridegroom, dies horribly, rots away visibly on a parody before-the-fact of Huck's raft: "His arm was completely black from the wrist to the shoulder, and his feet were like ice… He was frightfully emaciated; so much so that… *he now did not weigh more than forty or fifty* [pounds] *at the farthest*. His eyes were… scarcely perceptible, and the skin of his cheeks hung so loosely as to prevent his masticating any food… without great difficulty." His painful death is not even sacrificial, merely another device to produce a shudder, especially at the point where his entire leg comes off in the hand of the man who is attempting to heave his rotten corpse into the sea! Augustus' impromptu grave-digger is his successor; for it is Dirk Peters who tosses the first good companion over the side, to the sharks who gather with gnashing teeth. But Peters is, as we have already noticed, a very ogre: such a monster, one of Poe's critics describes him, as children draw to scare themselves, a nightmare out of our racial beginnings. In him, the qualities of Queequeg and Fedallah and Captain Ahab are oddly combined; a savior and a beloved primitive, he is also a murderer, a consumer of human flesh, a demi-devil, a madman. He is, in fact, as Marie Bonaparte[12] suggests, the accursed hero who has destroyed the Father, taking on himself the guilt of the artist who only writes or dreams such horror. He protects the artist-surrogate of the plot with almost maternal tenderness, fights his battles like a big brother; and like a lover, holds him safe and warm when the defeated wanderer seeks his bloody embrace, impotent and whimpering. Yet the sought-for embrace is a rape and a betrayal, a prelude to certain death.

The climax of the relationship of Pym and Peters comes at the moment when the two are trapped on the Island of Tsalal, where all their companions have been killed by an artificial landslide contrived by the bloodthirsty black aborigines. The two survivors are trying to find their way out of a cleft in the earth that has providentially sheltered them; and Pym is suspended in fright on a sheer cliff wall.

> For one moment my fingers clutched compulsively upon their hold, while, with the movement, the faintest possible idea of escape wandered, like a shadow, through my mind—in the next my whole soul was pervaded with a *longing to fall*; a desire, a yearning, a passion utterly uncontrollable. I let go at once my grasp upon the peg, and, turning half round from the precipice, remained tottering for an instant against its naked face. But now there came a spinning of the brain; a shrill-sounding and phantom voice screamed within my ears; a dusky, fiendish and filmy figure stood immediately beneath me; and, sighing, I sank down with a bursting heart, and plunged within its arms.

The "dusky, fiendish... figure" is, of course, Peters, the half-breed; and the studied ambiguity of the passage, in which the language of horror becomes that of eroticism, the dying plunge becomes a climactic embrace, makes it clear that the *longing to fall* and the desire for the dark spouse are one, a single perverseness. Peters is not made an angelic representative of instinct and nature even at this critical instant; he remains still a fiend, even in the act of becoming a savior. And the reader is left to wonder what so dark and orgasmic a salvation can possibly mean except the exchange of one death for an even more damnable other. Poe presents us not with the standard resolution of the American's ambiguity toward the life of impulse: an opposition of good savage and evil savage, as in Cooper's confrontation of Pawnee and Sioux, or Mark Twain's contrast of benevolent Negro and malevolent Indian. Though the son of an Upsaroka mother preserves Pym from the menace of the black hordes of Too-Wit ("Seizing a club from one of the savages who has fallen, he dashed out the brains of the three who remained..."), Poe is not finally intent on playing the same symbolic game as Twain in reverse. He is rather portraying a world in which the primitive may save or destroy, but remains always brutal and amoral, from any Christian point of view—diabolic.

Poe espouses, that is to say, the view of instinctual life which is the common property of those writers whom he regards as "men of genius," the view of Brockden Brown and Hawthorne; and he quite consciously rejects the sentimentalizing of the savage which he finds in popularizers like Cooper. Poe is quite at home with what distinctively American strain of the gothic, in which the aristocratic villains of the European tale of terror are replaced by skulking primitives, and the natural rather than the sophisticated is felt as a primal threat. Indeed, Poe's aristocratic pretensions make it impossible for him to adopt such an attitude without the equivocations and soul-searching demanded of such liberal gothicists as the young Brockden Brown. His fictional world needs no good Indians because he believes in none; and try as he will, he cannot keep quite distinct the mutinous black cook, whom he calls a "perfect demon," from the "dusky, fiendish" figure of Dirk Peters. *Theoretically*, the tale of *Gordon Pym* projects through its Negroes the fear of black rebellion and of the white man's perverse lust for the Negro, while symbolizing in the red man an innocent and admirable yearning for the manly violence of the frontier; but in the working out of the plot, the two are confused. Certainly, Pym has prepared himself for the encounter with Peters by reading the journals of Lewis and Clark in his coffin-refuge in the hold; but Peters refuses to become a harmless embodiment of the West, remaining to the end an ogre, his great, bare teeth displayed like fangs.

It is true that the half-breed line-manager offers protection against the shipboard mutineers and the vicious natives of Tsalal; but his sheltering embrace is identified with the mortal hug of the grizzly bear, whose skin he wears to cover his bald pate. The figure of the black man blends ambiguously with that of the slave, while that of the red man blurs into that of the wild beast! The West, at any rate, was always for Poe only half real, a literary experience rather than a part of his life; but the South moved him at the deepest personal level. Insofar as *Gordon Pym* is finally a social document as well as a fantasy, its subject is slavery; and its scene, however disguised, is the section of America[13] which was to destroy itself defending that institution. Poe's novel is surely the first which uses gothicism to express a peculiarly American dilemma identifying the symbolic blackness of terror with the blackness of the Negro and the white guilts he embodies. It is, indeed, to be expected that our first eminent Southern author[14] discover that the proper subject for American gothic is the black man, from whose shadow we have not yet emerged.

Though the movement of *Gordon Pym* seems to bear us away from America, once Nantucket and New Bedford have been left behind, and to carry us through remoter and remoter seas toward the exotic Antarctic, it tends in a region quite unlike the actual polar regions. Heading toward an expected world of ice and snow, Pym finds instead a place of tepid waters and luxuriant growth; seeking a white world, he discovers, beside and within it, a black one. What has gone wrong? It is necessary for Poe to believe in that blessed ignorance which frees forbidden fancies, that Pym's fictional voyage is bearing him toward the polar region, just as it was necessary for him to believe the whole story a delicious hoax; but we, as latter-day readers, need not be the victims of either delusion. For all the carefully worked-up details about penguins, *biche de mer*,[15] gala-pagos tortoises (bait for the audience which was later to subscribe to the *National Geographic*), Poe follows the footsteps not of Captain Cook but of his own first voyage in the arms of his mother, undertaken before his memory began, from new England to the South.[16] In his deepest imagination, any flight from the North bears the voyager not toward but away from the snow—not to the South Pole, but to the American South.

Certainly, it grows not colder, but warmer and warmer, as Pym aboard the last ship to rescue him, the *Jane Gay*, pushes closer and closer to the Pole. "We had now advanced to the southward more than eight degrees farther than any previous navigators. We found... that the temperature of the air, and latterly of water, became milder." Whatever pseudo-scientific explanations Poe may have believed would sustain this improbable notion of a luke-warm Antarctica, certain *symbolic* necessities were of more importance; he is being, in fact, carried back to Ole Virginny[17]—as the color of the natives he meets on the Island of Tsalal (latitude $83^0 20'$, longitude $43^0 5'$W,) clearly indicates. They are brawny, muscular, and jet black, with "thick and woolen hair," "thick and clumsy lips," "these "wretches," whom Pym describes, after they have destroyed all the white men but him and Peters, as "the most wicked, hypocritical, vindictive, blood thirsty, and altogether fiendish race of men upon the face of the globe." Poe very carefully does not ever call them Negroes, though he bestows on them those marks which, in a review of two books[18] on abolition, he listed as the special stigmata by which God distinguished the race that were to become slaves. He "blackened the negro's skin and crisped his hair into wool." At any rate, where an informed reader might have expected some kind of Indian, Poe could only imagine plantation hands in masquerade; and he sets them in a world distinguished not only by blackness and warmth, but by a certain disturbing sexuality quite proper to Southern stereotypes of Negro life. That sexuality can only be expressed obliquely by Poe, who was so squeamish about matters of this kind that the much franker Baudelaire was driven to remark, *"Dans l'oeuvre d'Edgar Poe, il n'y a jamais d'amour."*[19] The phallicism of the island he, therefore, suggests not in human terms but by a reference to the islanders' chief crop, the *biche de mer*—a kind of sea-cucumber of which, Poe informs us, the authorities say that it "renews the exhausted system of the immoderate voluptuary."

The inhabitants of Tsalal are not, of course, the burlesque Negroes, those black "rascals" or "scamps," named pompously "Jupiter" or "Pompey," who lend a minstrel-show note to Poe's lighter tales. Woolly-patted and bow-legged, these characters play the role of mischievous, cowardly, stupid and faithful dependents, good always for a laugh when they say "soldiers" for "shoulders" or "clause" for "cause." No more are the black savages of *Gordon Pym* like the ideal colored servants sketched by Poe in his review of *Slavery in the United States* by J. K. Paulding, the author whose suggestion led to Poe's writing his encoded Southern tale. The "degree of loyal devotion on the part of the slave to which the white man's heart is a stranger," Poe insists, is far "stronger than they would be under like circumstances between individuals of the white race"; and, indeed, such "loyal devotion" ranks high in "the class of feelings by which the heart is made better..." It is precisely such loyalty which the actions of the natives in Poe's novel belie, since it is his hidden doubts on this score which they embody. The dark hordes of Too-Wit project the image of what the Southerner privately fears the Negro may be; just as the idealized body servant of Poe's review projects the image of what the anti-abolitionist publicly claims he is. But the two images are complementary halves of a single view based on wish and terror; the subdued dependent bent to the sick-bed in love and the resentful victim abiding in patience a day of vengeance.[20] It is the darker half, however, which is true to Poe's memories of his boyhood and youth in the Allen household; while the lighter belongs only to certain patriarchal legends, to which he learned to subscribe during his days on *The Southern Literary Messenger*.[21] In the single reference to the Negro in his correspondence, Poe complains to his step-father (the date is 1827): "You suffer me to be subjected to the whim & caprice, not only of your white family, but to the complete authority of the blacks."

At the climax of *Gordon Pym*, Poe dreams himself once more, though a grown man, subject to that nightmare authority; and the book projects his personal resentment and fear, as well as the guilty terror of a whole society in the face of those whom they can never quite believe they have the right to enslave. In Tsalal, blackness is no longer the livery of subjection but a sign of menace; so utterly black, that even the teeth concealed by their pendulous lips are black, the Antarctic savages inhabit a black land in which the vegetation and the animals, water itself are all subdued to the same dismal color. The voyage of Pym has transported him improbably into the black belt, a black belt transformed from the level of sociology to that of myth, in whose midst the reigning Caucasian is overwhelmed by a sense of isolation and peril. Not even the glimmer of white teeth bared in a heartening smile cuts the gloom of this exclusive and excluding dark world, whose ultimate darkness is revealed in that final chasm in which Pym and Peters are trapped after the treacherous destruction of their white shipmates. "We alone had escaped from the tempest of the overwhelming destruction. We were the sole living white men upon the island." At this point, the darkness of "Nigger-town" merges at last into the darkness of the womb which is also a tomb, an intestinal chamber from which there is apparently no way of being born again into a realm of light.

How has Pym arrived here, in this place where whiteness itself is taboo, where even the flicker of a handkerchief, the flash of sunlight on taut sails, a little flour in the bottom of a pan stir terror, and doom the white man who feels at home in a world full of such pale symbols? Pym has sought a polar whiteness and has discovered instead a realm of the domination of black. It was (as Marie Bonaparte and other analytical critics have made clear) his mother whom Poe was pursuing in his disguise as Pym: that lost, pale mother, white with the whiteness of milk and the pallor of disease; and the imaginary voyage is a long regression to childhood. But hostilely guarding the last access to the White Goddess,[22] stands the black killer, Too-Wit. In the ultimate reaches of his boyhood, where he had confidently looked for some image of maternal comfort and security, Poe-Pym finds *both* the white chasm and cascade and the black womb sealed off by black warriors. Surely, the latter fantasies represent memories of the black mammy and the black milk brother,[23] who has sucked at the same black breast.

Writing from the conscious level of his mind and addressing a public largely Southern, Poe dealt with the effect of these, quasimaternal and fraternal bonds sanguinely enough. Those very feelings, he argued, "by which the heart is made better… have their rise in the relation between the infant and his nurse. They are cultivated between him and his fostering brother…. They are fostered by the habit of affording protection and favors to the younger offspring of the same nurse. … But the buried mind of Poe does not believe what the rationalizing intelligence propounds; in dreams (and in the fiction which is close to those dreams), the foster-brother arises to destroy and crush, to block the way to the lost, pale mother who preceded the Negro nurse. And even the good foster-brother, whom Poe split off from his dark imago in Peters, he cannot finally feel as benign; for him the black man and the "blackness of darkness" are one. That they remain one in much distinguished American fiction after his time is probably not due to the direct influence of Poe. He rather prophetically anticipates than initiates a long line of American books, in which certain gothic writers exploit the fear and guilt which the comic Negro of popular art attempts to laugh out of existence.

II

Down through the history of the minstrel show, a black-faced Sambo (smeared with burnt cork, whether Negro or white, into the grotesque semblance of the archetypal nigger) tries to exorcise with high-jinks and ritual jokes the threat of the black rebellion and the sense of guilt which secretly demands it as penance and purge. But our more serious writers return again and again to the theme Melville, for instance, in "Benito Cereno" treating quite explicitly the tragic encounter between certain sentimental and comic stereotypes of the Negro and a historic instance of a slave mutiny. In that story, Captain Amasa Delano fails to recognize the rebellion on a Spanish slave-ship which he encounters, precisely because he is a good American. He is endowed, that is to say, with an "undistrustful good nature" and will not credit "the imputation of malign evil in man." This means in fact that he is quite willing to believe almost any evil of a European aristocrat, like the Don Benito who gives the tale its title; and is prepared to accept the most incredible behavior as the kind of "sullen inefficiency" to be expected of a Latin crew. On the other hand, he is incapable of believing a Negro, particularly a body servant, anything but a "faithful fellow."

It is just this phrase which occurs to Captain Delano as he watches Babo, a black slave who is actually holding his master prisoner, threatening death with the razor he presumably wields to shave him. "'Faithful fellow!' cried Captain Delano, 'Don Benito, I envy you such a friend, slave I cannot call him.'" But Melville will not let it go, adding on his own behalf—in a tone less ironical than one would expect:

> Most negroes are natural valets and hairdressers... There is ... a smooth tact about them in this employment... And above all is the great gift of good-humour... a certain easy cheerfulness... as though God had set the whole negro to some pleasant tune... to this is added the docility arising from the unaspiring contentment of a limited mind, and that susceptibility of bland attachment sometimes inhering in indisputable inferiors... Like most men of a good, blithe heart, Captain Delano took to negroes... just as other men to Newfoundland dogs.

But Babo is, in fact, the leader of a black uprising that has already murdered his master's closest friend and bound his corpse to the prow; and Captain Delano in his unwillingness to imperil his fondness for Negroes, almost kills Don Benito when he makes a last desperate attempt to escape. Still convinced that the true source of moral infection is to be found only in the decaying institutions of Europe, Captain Delano cannot understand why, even after the exposure of Babo, Benito Cereno continues to pine away, seems to long only for death.

Though the fact of slavery, out of which all the violence and deceit aboard the Spanish ship has been bred, remains a part of his own democratic world as well as Don Benito's aristocratic one, Amasa Delano is undismayed. Though only an incident has been dealt with and its deep causes left untouched, he finds in this no cause for despair, but demands that the Spaniard join with him in recognizing a happy ending. "You are saved...," he cries to Don Benito, "You are saved: what has cast such a shadow upon you?" And he will not understand when the Spanish captain answers, "The negro." Indeed, Melville seems to share the bafflement of his American protagonist; a Northerner like Captain Delano, Melville finds the problem of slavery and the Negro a little exotic, a gothic horror in an almost theatrical sense of the word. Before his story is done, at any rate, he lets it lapse back into the language of the written record where he had to look for it in the first instance—quite unlike Poe who found this particular theme at the very center of his own experience.

In this regard, Mark Twain is much more like Poe than Melville. Whatever his conflicting allegiances, he was a Southerner in his roots and origin, who all his life long carried on a family quarrel with the part of the country in which he had long ceased to live. He had enlisted briefly on the side of the Confederacy, though he became finally a convert to the abolitionist cause and wrote in his finest book an attack on slavery;[24] and he could never really disavow the Southern notion of "honor," though he mocked all his life Sir Walter Scott and the mad chivalric codes which the South had derived from Scott's books. The town in which Twain was born and to which his imagination compulsively returned existed on a boundary between South and West; and, indeed, his two youthful careers led him to turn first in one direction then in the other. As a riverboat pilot before the Civil War, he followed the Mississippi down to New Orleans; as a journalist and fortune-hunter after Abolition, he headed across that same river toward Nevada and California. Both worlds lured him, turn and turn about; and in his two most profound books,[25] he faces first one way then the other, but reverses the actual order of his life.

Huckleberry Finn ends with Huck pointed west, ready to light out for the territory in search of a freedom he had deludedly and vainly sought with Jim by going down the Mississippi. Why, critics have asked ever since the book appeared, did Huck not cross the river to the Illinois side, go east to where freedom really existed as a political fact? But the East, though it claimed Twain at last, had no symbolic meaning for him; the motion toward childhood is for him a motion toward the South, down the river. It was, therefore, down to Arkansas that Twain moved the Missouri farm of his mother's sister and her husband, the Great Good Place of his earliest years, which is celebrated in the most moving and lyrical section of the *Autobiography*, and which had appeared earlier as a mythical refuge in *Huckleberry Finn* (1885) and *Tom Sawyer Detective* (1896). Like Poe, Twain thought of the trip home as a voyage south; but like the earlier writer, too, he felt that trip a descent into hell. Though Twain was always consciously more attracted than repelled by the ambivalent Eden of his boyhood, and in his memoirs tends to idealize its terror almost out of existence, his fiction tells quite another story. Huck Finn is able to reject Aunt Sally's utopia out of hand for all the redolence of its good home cooking; and in *Tom Sawyer Detective*, it takes all of Tom's ingenuity to exorcise murder and the threat of madness from the earthly paradise. In neither of these works, however, does Twain make it quite clear what has cast a shadow upon his idyllic world, what particular terror haunts his most nostalgic memories.

Only in *Pudd'nhead Wilson*, his most gothic book and an almost diagrammatic study in black and white, does he reveal that his specter is identical with Poe's and Don Benito's: "The negro." *Pudd'nhead Wilson* begins and ends in the village where *Huckleberry Finn* began and *Tom Sawyer* was played out, on the banks of the same symbolic river and in the same mythical pre-Civil War years. But between the "St. Petersburg" of the earlier books and the "Dawson's Landing" of the later one, there is a terrible difference. Pudd'nhead is represented as a mature and cynical stranger coming into the place at which Twain had never managed before to look from the outside. To his two boy heroes, it is so totally and entirely their world that they know it no more than their own faces. Only the outsider, the estranged adult Twain had become, rather than the unalienated child he remembered himself, offers an opportunity for perspective; and the opening of the novel pans slowly down on the village, its rose-clad houses, its cats, its sleepiness, and its fragrance—all preparing for the off-hand give-away of the sentence beginning, "Dawson's Landing was a slaveholding town…"

Striving to return as a grownup to the limit of a boy's memory, Twain arrives at the fact of slavery, once as imperceptible to him as the town itself. The Civil War is the watershed, in Twain's life, between childhood and manhood, innocence and experience, joy and despair; and this very fact insures that in his time of experience and despair he come to know that his innocence and joy, as well as the life that sustained them, were based on the labor and indignities of slaves. Yet the lost happiness, however based, was real; and Twain, whose dogmatic anti-Christianity can conceive no other paradise cannot leave off returning to it in reminiscence and in art. All the same, he cannot deny the shamefulness of his plight, the pity of being forced to dream a boy's dream of freedom acted out in the world of slavery.

In *Tom Sawyer*, the paradox at the heart of Twain's essential myth is hushed up for nostalgia's sake and in the interests of writing a child's book; in *Huckleberry Finn*, it is present as a constant tension, though camouflaged by the poetry and high spirits of the text; in *Pudd'nhead Wilson*, it falls apart into horror and horseplay. In that novel, Hannibal[26] is rendered from the very start not as a Western but as a Southern town. The river is no longer presented as a just-passed frontier, a defining limit between the realms of civilization and nature, a boundary which America touches and crosses on its way west; it is felt as a passageway into the deep South. "Down the river" is the phrase that gives a kind of musical unity to the work: a guilt-ridden, terrible motif repeated with variations, from the jesting taunt of its heroine, the Negress Roxana, to a fellow slave, "if you b'longed to me I'd sell you down the river fo' you git too fur gone…" to the bleak irony of the novel's final sentence, "The Governor… pardoned Tom at once, and the creditors sold him down the river."

The contrast with *Huckleberry Finn* inevitably suggests itself; for here the direction of the river Twain loved is regarded as pointing *only* into the ultimate Southern horror, the unmitigated terror of conscienceless and brutal slavery. The movement of the plot, the very shape of *Pudd'nhead Wilson* is determined by this symbolic motion toward the Gulf of Mexico—the movement of the Father of Waters[27] toward a confluence with the great maternal sea; though here that symbolic motion represents no longer a dream of the flight to freedom, but only a nightmare of the passage into captivity. And at the center of the motion and the plot, stands the figure of the slave-girl Roxana, precisely the black mammy of Poe's sentimental editorializing, who has held at her breast both her own child and her master's, black and white milk-brothers. Roxana, however, defies all clichés; she is no gross, comfortable, placid source of warmth, all bosom and grin, but a passionate, complex, and beautiful mulatto, a truly living woman distinguished from the wooden images of virtue and bitchery that pass for females in most American novels. She is "black" only by definition, by social convention, though her actual appearance as described by Twain, "majestic... rosy... comely," so baffled the platitude-ridden illustrator of the official edition that he drew in her place a plump and comic Aunt Jemima![28]

Her own child, called Valet de Chambre, or Chambers, has been sired by Cecil Burleigh Essex, a white Virginian gentleman, and hence is even less the woolly-haired, swart, blubber-lipped caricature than she. Indeed he is scarcely distinguishable with his "blue eyes and flaxen curls" from his milk-brother, Thomas a Becket Driscoll, so that Roxana has no trouble switching the two in their cradles when Valet de Chambre is threatened with being sold down the river. Twain makes clear, that is to say, what Poe and Paulding have disingenuously concealed, that there is in the South no absolute distinction of black and white, merely an imaginary line—crossed and recrossed by the white man's lust—that makes one of two physically identical babies "by a fiction of law and custom a negro." Once the "negro" Valet de Chambre has been dressed in a soft muslin robe and the "white" Thomas a Becket Driscoll in a towline shirt, their roles are reversed and each plays the traditional role of his imagined race. The real Tom persists in protecting his "young master" despite the beatings he receives at his hands, and even saves him from drowning. But when, after his rescue, the white fellows of the false Tom tease him by calling his rescuer his "nigger pappy," the false Tom attempts to kill that rescuer. He cannot abide the suggestion that "he had a second birth into life, and that Chambers was the author of his new being," cannot assent to the American archetype embodied in Jim and Huck in *Huckleberry Finn*—and so drives a knife into his savior. No more can he abide being the son of a Negress, and ends by selling his mother down the river.

But it is not only the literally "false" Toms who betray their black mothers and play Cain to their Negro brothers; Twain's protagonists merely make melodramatically evident the fact that every mistreatment of a Negro, the simple continuance of slavery as an institution, is both a betrayal of the breast at which the Southerner who calls himself white has sucked, and of the brother he calls black, who has sucked at that breast beside him. In the mythical denouement of Twain's book, it is suggested that all sons of the South, whether counted in the census as black or white, are symbolically the offspring of black mothers and white fathers, products of a spiritual miscegenation at the very least, which compounds the evil of slavery with an additional evil. The whitest aristocrat has nestled up to a black teat; the dullest slave may have been sired by some pure-blooded F. F. V.[29] blade, discharging his blind lust upon a field wench or a house servant.

The family pattern of *Pudd'nhead Wilson* is opposite to that of *Huckleberry Finn*; for while the former is the portrait of a Southern, which is to say, a patriarchal society, the latter portrays a Western or matriarch alone. In the earlier book, the "sivilization" which Huck finally rejects is a world of mothers, that is, of what Christianity has become among the females who maintain it just behind the advancing frontier. It is a relatively simple-minded world, whose goal is virtue, which is defined as not cursing, stealing, smoking, or lying, but rather keeping clean, wearing shoes, and praying for spiritual gifts. In this world, the male principle is represented, if at all (Tom Sawyer has no father), by outcasts and scoundrels like Huck's unredeemable Pap—or some representative of nature and instinct like the runaway slave, Nigger Jim. In *Pudd'nhead Wilson*, on the other hand, it is the fathers who represent society, who are the defenders of a chivalric code which Twain elsewhere affects to despise, and the descendants of cavaliers. York Leicester Driscoll, Percy Northumberland Driscoll, Pembroke Howard, and Colonel Cecil Burleigh Essex:[30] the names make the point perhaps too obviously. This is a world continuous with that of Renaissance England, a world in which "honor" is the sole code.

The patriarchal world of "honor" is also one of gallantry, of a kind of lustiness associated in Twain's mind with the court of Elizabeth, which for him represented a lost sexual Eden, contrasted (in his privately circulated *1601*) with a debilitated America, where men "copulate not until they be five-and-thirty years of age… and doe it then but once in seven yeeres." Though the men of Dawson's Landing, being Virginians, are potent still, their white women, who languish and retreat and die, are latter-day Americans, almost asexually genteel, so that only the Negress can match the vigor of the fathers with a corresponding fertility and power. Roxy is just such a Negress, and her union with Cecil Burleigh Essex represents not only a sociological but a symbolic truth. If the fathers of the South are Virginia gentlemen, the mothers are Negro girls, casually or callously taken in the parody of love, which is all that is possible when one partner to a sexual union is not even given the status of a person.

Twain's own judgment of sexual relations between black and white, slave and free is not explicitly stated; but there seems no doubt that he regarded the union between Roxy and Essex with a certain degree of horror, regarded it as a kind of fall—evil in itself and a source of doom to all involved. Paired together, *Huckleberry Finn* and *Pudd'nhead Wilson* express both sides of a deep, half-conscious American conviction, which we have already noticed as it was reflected before Twain by Fenimore Cooper. There are two possible relations, two kinds of love between colored and white projected in our fiction, one of which is innocent, one guilty; one of which saves, one damms. The first provides a sentimental relation for the highbrow Western, the second a terrible one for the Southern gothic romance. The innocent relationship can exist only between men, or a man and a boy; the other, suspect and impure, tries to join the disjoined in heterosexual passion, and its end is a catastrophe, a catastrophe symbolized by the "blackness" of the Negro, outward sign of an inward exclusion from grace. For Poe, who accepted slavery as God-given, a divine mystery, this catastrophic fact remains merely a fact not a riddle; but for Melville and Twain, committed to the abolitionist cause, it poses a terrible problem. Why should the Negro be condemned to wear the livery of the guilt which is really the white man's? It is a question which is asked everywhere in the strain of American gothic we have begun to examine; and the answers only compound the ambiguity which prompts them.

At one level, Twain seems willing to accept the tragic position of the Negro as an inexplicable curse, crying out through the mouth of the pseudo-Tom in his moment of bafflement and despair, "What crime did the uncreated first nigger commit that the curse of birth was decreed for him…" And certainly Roxy seems to share her master's assumption that blackness of the skin, the invisible taint of the blood, carries with it an inevitable moral weakness. Her son's malice and cowardice, she is disconcertingly willing to attribute to the quantum of Negro blood which she has bequeathed him. "It's de nigger in you, days what it is," she screams at her son when he has refused to fight a duel: "Thirty-one parts o'

you is white en on'y one part nigger, en dat po' little one part is yo' soul."
Conversely, she has assured him at an earlier moment, after revealing to
him the secret of his birth ("You's a *nigger—bawn* a nigger en a *slave!*"),
that his white father at least had been a great man, who had been honored
with "de bigges' funeral dis town ever seed." "Dey ain't another nigger in
dis town dat's as high-bawn as you is … jes you hold yo' head up as high
as you want to—you has de right…"

This is, of course, a conventional kind of humor; and Twain is after
the laughs which are easy enough to get by portraying one Negro calling
another "nigger" in the proper dialect. But certain ironies proliferate
disturbingly beneath the burlesque; and we are left baffled before the
spectacle of slaves and outcasts accepting, as they insult each other, not
only the offensive epithet "nigger," but all the assumptions implicit in the
epithet. Insofar as Twain asks us to accept certain vaudeville gags as social
history, we find his book and its meanings distasteful, an uncomfortable
reminder of his own human failings; but we cannot help suspecting that
behind the horseplay and grotesque melodrama of his plot, he may be
attempting to translate an account of local prejudice into a fable revealing
man's more universal implication in guilt and doom. If the false Tom is
meant to represent not merely a Negro vainly pretending to be white, but
the fruit of the betrayal and terror and profaned love which join all men,
white and black, in our society, he must be made to embody the seeds of
self-destruction which that relationship contains within it. He must
therefore lie, steal, kill, and boast of his crimes, until he reveals himself
out of hybris as a secret slave.

Though it is Pudd'nhead Wilson, local character, fingerprint expert
and amateur detective, who presumably unmasks the impostor and wins
the town's applause, it is really the false Tom himself who brings on his
own downfall. Twain cannot resist a courtroom denouement, a revelation
and reversal sprung by some self-appointed sleuth at the darkest moment

of a plot. Tom Sawyer, indeed, exists precisely to make such exposures not only in the books called by his name, but even in the one written in Huckleberry Finn's. Most readers will remember (and the reader of *Pudd'nhead Wilson* must to fully savor that book) how at the climax of *Huckleberry Finn*, Tom Sawyer, "his eyes hot, and his nostrils opening and shutting like gills," cries out of Jim: "They hait't no *right* to shut him up... Turn him loose! He ain't no slave; he's as free as any cretur that walks this earth!" "As free as any cretur," the boy hero declares, blithely convinced that freedom is real, realer than the illusion of slavery; and we believe him, putting down that sanguine book.

But a wry joke is already implicit in the phrase, which Twain no more sees than does Tom; and we as readers are not permitted to see it, as long as we remain within the spell of the happy ending. In *Pudd'nhead Wilson*, however, the protagonist, who is obviously Tom himself permitted at long last to grow up, rises to answer his own earlier courtroom cry, in just such a situation as he has always loved: "Valet de Chambre, Negro and slave... make upon the window the finger prints that will hang you!" The double truth is in that instant complete: the seeming slave is free, but the free man is really a slave. It is an odd denouement to a detective story enlivened by touches of farce: this revelation which condemns a hitherto free man to a life of servitude down the river, and leaves his mother sobbing on her knees, "De Lord have mercy on me, po' miserable sinner dat I is!" There is a happy ending this time for no one really except David Wilson (no longer called contemptuously "Pudd'nhead"), if one considers his acceptance by the philistine community really a blessing. To be sure, the same fingerprints which prove the presumed Tom a slave, establish the presumed Chambers as free; but his "curious fate" is equivocal if not actually tragic. Neither black nor white in his self-consciousness, he is excluded by long conditioning from the world of upper-class society, and barred from the "solacing refuge" of the slave kitchens by the fact of his legal whiteness. Had he turned on his foster-brother at the moment of revelation, he could only have yelled what he earlier cried out to his presumed mother, "Yah-yah-yah!... Bofe of us is imitation *white*—dat's what we is..." And what would he have made of Twain's afterthought, one of the final jottings in his journal, "The skin of every human being contains a slave"?

Certainly, Pudd'nhead Wilson, in his exhibitionist courtroom speech, when he rises to announce once more the old scandal that the son has killed his father (Twain somewhat timidly makes them only stepfather and stepson), does not succeed in restoring to the community a sense of its own innocence by establishing the guilt of a single culprit. Yet this, as W. H. Auden[31] convincingly argues, is the archetypal function of the detective story, to which genre *Pudd'nhead Wilson* seems to be long. It is, in fact, an *anti*-detective story, more like *The Brothers Karamazov*[32] than *The Innocence of Father Brown*, its function to expose communal guilt: our moral, bankruptcy, horror and shame, the stupidity of our definition of a Negro, and the hopeless trap of our relations with him. Wilson's disclosure of Roxy's hoax coalesces with Mark Twain's exposure to America of its own secret self. Each of Twain's chapters is headed by a quotation from "Pudd'nhead Wilson's Calendar," a collection of small-town dangerous thoughts; and at the head of the final chapter, under the rubric "Conclusion," he inscribes the following text: "*October 12, The Discovery. It was wonderful to find America, but it would have been more wonderful to miss it.*" It is the most improbable of endings for a detective story, which depends precisely upon its readers' faith in discovery; but it is one appropriate enough for the anti-Western novel at the moment that it becomes anti-American in its revulsion from all clichés of innocent, new frontiers.

The assault upon the Western and its image of America did not, of course, die with Twain. In our time, it is most notably carried forward by

Robert Penn Warren,[33] a poet, critic, and pedagogue as well as a novelist, who has attempted the risky game of presenting to our largest audience the anti-Western in the guise of the Western, the anti-historical romance in the guise of that form itself. In this enterprise, he has followed the example of Twain himself, who pretended to be writing in *Pudd'nhead Wilson* a popular detective story even as he mocked the form; and who in "A Double-Barrelled Detective Story" carried the process even further, specifically parodying the methods of Conan Doyle[34]. It is with historical fiction that Warren prefers to deal, seeing himself perhaps as the researcher (his first book dealt with the life of John Brown[35]) just as Twain sees himself as the sleuth. In *World Enough and Time* (1952), at any rate, Warren attacks directly the myth of the West, using for his purposes the famous Beauchamp case,[36] which had been treated earlier by Simms and Edgar Allan Poe. Warren, however, is not primarily interested in the fable of seduction and revenge, on which we have commented earlier, by shifting the point of interest from the Persecuted Maiden to her avenging lover, whom he calls Jeremiah Beaumont, he converts the tale from a study of the encounter of innocence and lust to a study of the encounter of romanticism and reality. Through all his attempts to substitute for life, or impose on life itself a sentimental dream of life, Beaumont has assumed the existence of a paradisal West, an unfallen Eden to which he can flee when all else fails him. In the end, Warren permits him to escape hanging (changing the facts of the original story for this purpose) and to seek out the wilderness of which he has so long dreamed. But that wilderness he finds to be no more than a festering swamp, in which he is ultimately murdered and his beloved, withered and haggard, commits suicide; and presiding over the travesty of the Great Good Place, no noble and immaculate Natty Bumppo, but a hump-backed monster dying in sensuality and filth: *la grande Bosse*,[37] river pirate and nightmare made flesh, the visible shape of original sin which Beaumont's sentimental version of the West had denied.

In *Brother to Dragons* (1953), a long verse narrative, Warren continues his assault on the theory of original innocence, drafting Thomas Jefferson as a ghostly witness to a particularly brutal and meaningless crime committed by two of his nephews, who slaughter in a meat-house, for trivial reasons, a Negro—acting out ritually the guilt of the white man toward those he has enslaved.

It is not until *Band of Angels* (1955), however, that Warren, a southerner himself and once involved in the Agrarian movement,[38] turns to a full-scale treatment of the subject Twain had broached in *Pudd'nhead Wilson*, the plight of the white Negro. By turning the false Tom into a girl, however, Warren transforms the novel of miscegenation from the masculine murder mystery to the feminine bosom book, the erotic historical romance, creating a hybrid form whose strange pedigree would read: out of Margaret Mitchell by Mark Twain![39] Its fable deals with Amantha Starr, a young woman who discovers on her father's death that she is legally a slave and a Negro—and of her difficulty in deciding what, beneath "the fiction of law and custom," she really is. The problem of identity is not for her as simple as it was for the exposed Valet de Chambre; what his mother confides in him and Pudd'nhead declares in open court, he himself believes. But Amantha does not know what to believe, for she has been sent as a child to an enlightened and pious college, where she has acquired a set of abolitionist clichés as useless to her in understanding the realities of slavery and being a Negro as are the opposite clichés of the Southern slaveholders. Nonetheless, an aura of miscegenation hangs over the series of love affairs which make up the history of Amantha, threatening to dissolve each embrace into a spasm of nausea or to convert it into a rape; yet she will not, she cannot bring herself to say, "I am a Negro!" No more capable of declaring herself white, she chooses to be nothing: an abstract victim without a particular identity. Like the hero of

Ralph Ellison's[40] *The Invisible Man*, she fades from sight because she becomes nothing except her role; but in her case, the invisibility is willed. Her decision justifies her lovers in approaching her with disgust or condescension or pity—anything, that is to say, but love; and it is for that reason that they are destroyed. Only when her white husband comes to realize that he, too, is a victim, she, too, a human ("The skin of every human being contains a slave" and its obverse), is he able to live with her not as a master or a benefactor, but as one weak and suffering being with another; and Amantha is at last free. It is a finally sentimental resolution, a retreat from the tragic blackness toward which Mark Twain had, however falteringly, moved.

To find a writer capable of accepting the darker implications of Twain's gothicism and pressing on to even more terrible resolutions, we must turn back to Warren's immediate master, William Faulkner. Faulkner instinctively begins with the realization, which we have discovered in Twain, that not murder only but miscegenation, too, must preside over the relations of black and white to produce the full gothic shiver. More shocking to the imagination of the South than the fantasy of a white man overwhelmed by a hostile black world is the fear that finally all distinctions will be blurred and black and white no longer exist. On what can the assurance of a God-given right to enslave Negroes or deprive them of rights be based, when no man can say with security who is the real Thomas a Becket Driscool, who some black pretender? Precisely this prevision of total assimilation and chaos is entrusted to the young Canadian Shreve at the end of Faulkner's *Absalom, Absalom!* (1935):

> I think that in time the Jim Bonds are going to conquer the western hemisphere. Of course it won't be quite in our time and of course as they spread toward the poles they will bleach out again like the rabbits and birds do, so they won't show up so sharp against the snow. But it will still be Jim Bond; and so in a few thousand

years, I who regard you will also have sprung from the loins of
African kings.

But Jim Bond in the novel is an idiot, elusive as a ghost, a specter haunting
the ravaged white family whose blood he shares.

In Faulkner's work, the threat of miscegenation is posed not only in
terms of future racial contamination, but also in those of a present sexual
threat. Out of the semi-obscene sub-literature of Southern racists, he
captures and redeems the hysterical vision of the black rapist, the Negro
who, by stealth or force (in Faulkner it is typically by stealth, which is to
say, under the cover of a pseudo white skin), possesses a white woman.
The archetype answers precisely the abolitionist myth of the helpless
Negro servant girl assaulted by her master. Against Roxana, pitifully proud
of her relationship with the gentleman who leaves her pregnant with a
flaxen-haired slave, is set the mother of Joe Christmas in *Light in August*
(1932),[41] trying to convince the doctor who attends her that the man who
had fathered her bastard "was a Mexican. When old Doc Hines could see
in his face the black curse of God Almighty." And against Simon Legree in
Uncle Tom's Cabin, pursuing the terrified and virginal Emmeline, is
balanced (in *Absalom, Absalom!*) the figure of Charles Bon,[42] who has
persuaded a white woman to marry him. A Channing and handsome Negro,
who has "passed" without difficulty, he turns to the somewhat younger
white man, who has adulated him and to whose sister he is engaged,
deliberately evoking the vulgar taunt of the crudest Negro-baiters "I'm the
nigger that's going to sleep with your sister. Unless you stop me, Henry."
And Henry, as he must, though only after long delay, shoots him!

Yet just before Bon speaks the words that doom him, Henry has cried
to him, "You are my brother." Such brotherhood is more than a metaphor
in *Absalom, Absalom!*, more even than the bond of having shared a single
breast that links Twain's Tom to Chambers. In Faulkner's plot, the white
man and the Negro who love and destroy each other are quite literally the

sons of the same father, of Thomas Sutpen, the passionate, damned hero of the action. The younger, white son was born of a timid, genteel, rustic, puritanical creature, married for the sake of the status and respectability she could bestow; the older, black one was the offspring of a Haitian breed, foisted on an ignorant and ambitious young man by her unscrupulous parents. Of that first wife, Sutpen says somewhat critically, "I found that she was not and could never be through no fault of her own adjunctive and incremental to the design which I had in mind, so I provided for her and put her aside." He cannot, however, avoid the miasma of miscegenation by so simple a device as flight; and Sutpen's children, white and black, find themselves locked finally in a terrible triangle, the two brothers more in love with each other than either with the sister (perhaps Bon loves no one, only wants to provoke his proud father into admitting the relationship from which he has fled), and the threat of incest over them all.

This is the final turn of the screw, the ultimate gothic horror which serves both to produce one more shock and to add one more level of symbolic relevance to the action. Not only in Faulkner's plot but in the general life of the South, the man who screams in panic that some blackbuck is about to rape his sister is speaking of one who is, indeed, his brother, and whom secretly he loves. But the event of such love is only guilt and death and a retreat into a dark house, already sacked and gutted in a war fought to maintain the order which had bred the relationship itself. Sutpen and his Negro bride had already mated, already produced a child neither white nor black; and the frustration of a second incestuous match saves nothing. It serves only to prevent the grafting onto the narrow, Protestant provincialism of the rural South of a Catholic and urban grace, nurtured in Creole New Orleans. The adulterated Sutpen line eventuates, not in the sensuous, elegant hybrid that might have been produced out of a mating of Charles Bon and Sutpen's white daughter, but in Jim Bond, mindless child of the offspring of Bon's self-punishing marriage to an ignorant, ugly Negress: "…there was nothing left now, nothing out there now but that idiot boy to lurk around those ashes and those four gutted chimneys and howl until someone came and drove him away. They couldn't catch him and nobody ever seemed to make him go very far away, he just stopped howling for a little while."

Jim Bond (the name which meant "good" corrupted to one which means "slave")[43] is not so much living flesh and blood as the terrible ghost that haunts the mind of such Southerners as Quentin Compson,[44] who has been driven to uncover step by step the mystery of the Sutpens, and who represents the conscience of Faulkner himself. No wonder he grows frantic under his roommate's questioning: "'Now I want you to tell me just one thing more. Why do you hate the South?' 'I dont hate it,' Quentin said, quickly, at once, immediately; 'I dont hate it,' he said. *I dont hate it* he thought, panting in the cold air, the iron New England dark; *I dont. I dont! I dont hate it! I dont hate it!*" These are the final words of the book; but they are followed by a genealogy, in which we read of Quentin Compson that he died in the very year in which he uncovered the secret of the death of Charles Bon, not yet twenty years old: a suicide, we learn in another place.[45] It is the only possible ending to a novel in which the "Southern" as a genre reaches its final form. At the same time that *Absalom, Absalom!* solves the detective-story problem of who killed Charles Bon, it is answering another, profounder question, satisfying the Southerner's need to "know at last why God let us lose the war."[46] The query is as desperate as that posed by Captain Delano: "What has cast such a shadow upon you?" And the answer is the same: "The Negro."

Yet the theme we have been examining does not exhaust the meanings of Faulkner's book. It represents only a single strand in an intricately constructed and immensely complex work, a showpiece of sustained rhetoric, whose total effect makes it at first bewildering, but which, in the long run, proves the most deeply moving of all American gothic fictions. In the history of that genre, *Absalom, Absalom!* is remarkable for having first joined to the theme of slavery and black revenge, which is the essential sociological theme of the American tale of terror, that of incest, which is its essential erotic theme. Poe had already treated the latter subject in his shorter fictions, though in his work it is kept quite separate from the subject of the encounter of Negro and white. In Faulkner's early book, *The Sound and the Fury* (1929), it is thus isolated, too, functioning as fantasy rather than fact, the private horror of a family drama only incidentally connected with larger social problems. So also Faulkner deals by itself with the theme of miscegenation in *Light in August*, throughout which Joe Christmas revenges himself upon the world of women by informing each new girl as he lies beside her in bed, that he is a Negro! Not until *Absalom, Absalom!*, however, does he find a story in which he can project the dual theme of incest and miscegenation, which was the concern of Cooper and Twain and that of Edgar Allan Poe.

III

In Poe the incest theme belongs to the private world of his own tortured psyche rather than the broader arena of social life in the South. Over and over, the writer, who married his scarcely nubile cousin and called her Sis, returns to the theme, particularly in that series of tales involving dark and terrible ladies, which is his most authentic and convincing achievement. The first of these stories is "Berenice" ("Berenice and I were cousins, and we grew up together in my paternal halls…"); and the line continues on through "Eleanora" ("She whom I loved in youth…was the sole daughter of the only sister of my mother long departed") to reach a climax in "The Fall of the House of Usher," in which the doomed beloved is at last identified as the protagonist's sister. Sometimes; as in "Morella" and "Ligeia," the dying succubus-bride is portrayed as not even being kin to her husband; but always she is clearly a dark projection of his psyche, as intimately related to him as his own image in the mirror. And always, too, she bears the stigmata of a tabooed figure: the dark eyes and hair, which mark her as the carrier of madness and death. She tends to become, indeed, the symbol of mortality, the figure of death itself—combining the characteristics of shadow and *anima*, as if intended to signify that the soul of a man and his death are one thing.

The uses of incest in sentimental and gothic fiction are, as we have already noticed, many; and brother-sister incest in particular comes to stand in Romantic symbology for the rebellion against paternal authority, for the spirit of revolution itself. But precisely because of its Oedipal significance (the triangle father-sister-brother is the nineteenth century's expurgated version of the more terrible primal triangle father-mother-son), it projects not only the desire to revolt but also to die; that is to say, beneath the yearning for rebellion lies hidden the wish to be punished for it. In Poe, who deals customarily with problems of impotence rather than of power, the death-wish is always uppermost; and the desire to embrace the sister-bride means for him first of all a yearning to *fall*—a perverse longing to plunge into the destructive embrace of his own image in a dark tarn. The ending of "The Fall of the House of Usher" expresses directly the lust for a union with death which is Poe's ruling passion. Madeline, the sister of Usher, whom he has buried alive, returns from the grave to claim her brother just as he has, almost equally, feared and desired:

> Without those doors there DID stand the lofty and enshrouded figure of the Lady Madeline of Usher: There was blood upon her white robes, and the evidence of some bitter struggle upon every portion of her emaciated frame. For a moment she remained trembling and reeling to and fro upon the threshold, then, with a low moaning cry, fell heavily inward upon the person of her brother, and in her violent and now final death agonies, bore him to the floor as a

corpse…

It is the most horrific of *Liebestods*[47], the ultimate expression of Poe's obsessive dream of being possessed by the dead, raped by a cadaverous sister-beloved, elsewhere projected in the story of Ligeia, who returns from death to take over the body of a second bride. But there is in Poe a complementary desire to possess the dead, to return embrace for embrace, violation for violation. At its mildest and most conventional, this longing is satisfied in fantasies of lovers joined as fellow ghosts beyond the grave or chatting cozily after the cataclysmic destruction of the world. In such tales, the erotic commerce, of the specter is confined to speech, as in "The Colloquy of Monos and Una" or "The Conversations of Eiros and Charmion." Occasionally, however, Poe's necrophilia heroes returns with the bloody teeth of his beloved, or the narrator of "Ulalume," who scarcely knows why he has drifted back to the "dank tarn of Auber." Most frank of all Poe's celebrations of the union with a corpse is confided to the disarmingly sweet verses of "Annabel Lee":

> And so, all the night—tide, I lie down by the side
> Of my darling— my darling—my life and my bride,
> In the sepulchre there by the sea—
> In her tomb by the sounding sea.

The odd syndrome of child-love, necrophilia and incest in Poe is too personal and pathological to shed much light on the general meaning of the latter theme in American literature and life. It is not without interest, however, to reflect that Poe, too, like most of our classic writers, has come to be thought of as a children's classic; and his fantasies—in which adults never copulate in the flesh, only rape each other's minds, at least as long as they are alive—are considered proper selections for classroom anthologies. In any case, he has had little direct influence on later serious American writers, until, perhaps, the time of Vladimir Nabokov[48], in whose *Lolita* the example of Poe is combined so oddly with that of

Gogol.[49] "When gothic incest became a major theme in the mid-nineteenth century, it was embodied not in the figure of Madeline Usher but that of Beatrice Cenci."

The most gothic books of both Hawthorne and Melville are presided over by the mythic face of this lady as painted by Guido Reni[50] and adulated by two generations of American tourists. Over *The Marble Faun* of the one and the *Pierre* of the other, Beatrice Cenci casts a shadow of parricide and incest, suggests an added dimension of horror that Hawthorne at least was too cautious to specify in his own plot. It is important to remember that it was not really the original seventeenth-century painting of her in the Palazzo Barberini[51] to which both Hawthorne and Melville made the obligatory pilgrimage; for both alike were possessed by a literary tradition which had grown up around the portrait, finally making it impossible to see. It was this tradition which persuaded travelers to buy by the thousands those inferior copies of the original, of which Hawthorne has one of his characters remark scornfully, "Everywhere we see oil-paintings, crayon sketches, cameos, engravings, lithographs, pretending to be Beatrice…" Melville himself bought one such engraving—aptly enough, on the same day he saw and was impressed by the relief of Antinotts; of the latter he wrote in his journal "beautiful"; of the Beatrice only "offered a Cenci for $ 4.00. Surprisingly cheap." When he had seen the original, however, he was moved to remark on the "expression of suffering about the mouth" and the "appealing look of innocence." The latter remark reflects apparently Hawthorne's impression, too; at least, in *The Marble Faun*, he makes Hilda call Beatrice "sinless." "Fallen, and yet sinless," she qualifies her comment, "a fallen angel."

In response to the *myth* of the portrait, both American writers vibrated in accord; but about what it looked like they totally disagree. "With blue eyes and fair complexion, the Cenci's hair is golden," Melville writes;

while Hawthorne informs us that from beneath Beatrice's turban "strayed a lock or two… of auburn hair. The eyes were large and brown…" Since each had approached the picture as literature, each reenvisioned it in his own style. For Melville, the incest-stained innocent must be blond in order to make his symbolic point (elsewhere worked out in *Typee* and *Mardi*) that in some women the Fair Maiden[52] and the Dark Lady are disturbingly confused:

> …physically… all is in strict, natural keeping; which, nevertheless, still the more intensifies the suggested anomaly of so *blonde* a being, being double-hooded, as it were by the black crape of the two most horrible crimes… possible to civilized humanity—incest and parricide.

It is, indeed, the blond Lucy of his own *Pierre* who, in that novel, stands before the portrait, which reflects the incest and terror that she has not recognized, not allowed herself to recognize in her closest companions, Isabel and Pierre.

Hawthorne goes even further by suggesting an actual resemblance between his Anglo-Saxon snow maiden and the mysterious portrait, that to him symbolizes not so much the ambiguity of light and dark as the mystery of alienation: "It was the saddest picture ever painted or conceived; it involved an unfathomable depth of sorrow… a sorrow that removed this beautiful girl out of the sphere of humanity, and set her in a far-off region, the remoteness of which… makes us shiver as at a spectre." In Hawthorne, the copy of Guido's Beatrice that plays a part in his own tale, is not the product—as in Melville—of an unknown hand, but has been lovingly painted by the Fair Girl herself, by his dove-like Hilda. Looking into her mirror, she fancies a similarity between her own expression and that of the Beatrice before whom she has sat so long. Hawthorne, however, hastens to make it clear that not her own sin but that of another had frightened Beatrice Cenci "into a remote and inaccessible region; where no sympathy would come," and that it is a similar fate which is shadowed on Hilda's face. Just as the earlier innocent had been crushed by a sense of her father's guilt, Hilda risks being crushed by an awareness of the crime of her friend, the Dark Lady, Miriam. It is Miriam who is involved in a mysterious scandal which binds her to the sinister palace of the Cenci itself, Miriam to whom Hawthorne's mouthpiece, Kenyon, says, "I shudder at the fatality that seems to haunt your footsteps, and throws a shadow of crime about your path, you being guiltless." But what precise crime has cast a shadow upon her, Hawthorne cannot bring himself to tell. It is connected, we know, with the hairy Model who dogs her footsteps, and who is bound to her; it is suggested, by blood as well as a complicity, a man "so evil, so vile, and yet so strangely subtle, as could only be accounted for by the insanity which often develops itself in old, close kept races of men when long unmixed, with newer blood." This suggestion of immemorial inbreeding, joined with the repeated allusions to Miriam's implication in "one of the most dreadful and mysterious events that have occurred within the present century" implies surely the sin of incest; but Hawthorne is at once too genteel and too fond of playful mystification to speak out that dread word. His half-teasing, half-timid reticence is, as a matter of fact, the chief fault of this brilliant, uneven, and finally chaotic book, which never manages to confess the secret theme which haunts it.

Hawthorne had dealt openly with the subject of incest only in "Alice Doane's Appeal," whose basic fable oddly resembles Faulkner's *Absalom, Absalom!* It opens with a murder whose solution involves the exposure of the feelings that bind together in an unnatural triangle a young man, his sister, and a stranger whom he suspects of being her lover, but who proves in the end brother to both: "He was my very counterpart," says Leonard Doane of Walter Broame; and this uncanny resemblance seems to him reason enough for his sister Alice to "inevitably love him… with all the strength of sisterly affection, added to that impure passion which alone engrosses all the heart." Driven half-mad by imaginings which project onto the stranger his own unconfessed desire for his sister, and infuriated further by that stranger's boasts of having conquered her, Leonard kills him. At the moment of death, however, he sees in the face of the man he has murdered "a likeness of my father."

As in Faulkner's novel, the brothers are as culturally unlike as they are physically the same; for just as in the twentieth-century fiction, one has been educated "in the cities of the old world" and one "in this rude wilderness." Cosmopolitan sybarite and rustic stalwart, they represent in their conflict not the struggle of Creole black and Puritan white brother, but the encounter of Old World and New World sons of the same fatherland, loyalist and colonial in a struggle for possession of the body of America. In the end, Hawthorne's fragmentary story threatens to become a parable of the American Revolution—a gothic treatment of the international theme, set back into the period when our national consciousness was in the process, of being forged.

In the final years of his life, Hawthorne tried once more to create a substantial fiction dealing, beneath its spectacular machinery of bloody footsteps, ancestral curses, and lost wills, with the bloody confrontation of England and America. He achieved only a handful of fragmentary manuscripts in which the theme of incest struggles to assert itself, as it must in any fable treating a guilt-ridden fraternal relationship which begins in love and ends in murder.

In light of Hawthorne's life-long obsession with the subject, one is tempted to believe the contention of certain critics (finally unproven) that the incestuous Pierre of Melville's gothic romance is intended to be a portrait of Hawthorne; that the book was Melville's attempt to confess for his alienated friend the secret sin which presumably haunted him through all his years. Melville seems to have believed, at any rate, that he had penetrated the heart of Hawthorne's mystery; for when Hawthorne's son visited him in 1883, Melville told him—so Julian Hawthorne[53] wrote later—"that there was some secret in my father's life which had never been revealed, and which accounted for the gloomy passages in his books." Julian was not much impressed, however, observing dryly, "It was characteristic of him to imagine so; there were many secrets untold in his own career." Whether, indeed, the "secret" revealed in *Pierre* is Melville's or Hawthorne's or neither's matters little; what is important is that it is the major underground concern of American gothicists in general, the erotic relationship proper to that form: brother-sister incest. *Pierre* represents the major attempt in the history of our fiction at making of that theme great art: at redeeming it from the stereotypes into which it had fallen and wresting from it whatever symbolic meaning it had all along contained.

Even in the first chapters of *Pierre*, suggestions of a sickly incestuousness hover over the euphoric rustic scene. The young Pierre not merely flutters about his mother with the excessive gallantries of a courtly lover, tying her ribbon, her shoe-lace, but he addresses her as "Sister Mary"; and she, speaking of the blond Lucy who is to be Pierre's wife, refers to her as a "little sister." There is more than a trace of pride registered in the adjective, for Pierre's mother is securely aware of her sexual superiority to "little" Lucy, reflecting later that beside her son's fiancée she herself seems a quart decanter of port next to a pint decanter of pale sherry! But Pierre is not content just to *play* at incest with his mother, and marry—as an assurance of his fidelity to her—a girl who is clearly no sexual rival. Instead, he turns to a dark, alien, figure, the complete denial of everything in his mother's milky, blue, pink, and gold idyllic world, but a reminder of what his wild father might have been before his marriage. This is a perfidy to the mother of a monstrously complex sort—not at all the anti-paternal gesture which *Geschwisterinzest*[54] generally is, but a kind of homosexuality once removed.

To complicate matters further, Isabel,[55] the swart *anima*-figure who may be his sister, is half-mad and an outcast, so that to espouse her cause can be made to seem moral dedication and an attack on conformity. When Pierre decides finally to run off with Isabel, to pretend to the world that they are man and wife—so that he can at once protect her and not expose his father as a breeder of bastards—he is able to feel himself Christ-like, and his act a more than human self-sacrifice. Melville, however, refuses either him or the reader the privilege of living long with this illusion, pointing out that in attempting to transcend the codes of conventional society, Pierre has risked becoming a scandalous sinner rather than a moral hero. In the end, he is not the Christ or Titan[56] he dreams himself, not even a Memnon or Hamlet, but a latter-day Widow of Ephesus. Like the woman of that legend, who, in dedicating herself to an impossible ideal of fidelity, ended by desecrating the grave of her husband in lust and hanging his body on a public gallows, Pierre invents for himself crimes beyond the ken of ordinary men, a denouement almost as comic as it is terrible.

Even at the moment when he first confides to Isabel his decision to run off with her and accept the world's blame, conscious of his blamelessness, Pierre really knows what he is after. The secret motive of his ostensible sacrifice surges over the lintel of his awareness.

> He held her tremblingly; she bent toward him; his mouth wet her ear; he whispered it... Over the face of Pierre there shot a terrible self-revelation; he imprinted repeated burning kisses upon her; pressed her hand; would not let her sweet and awful passiveness go.

> Then they changed; they coiled together, and entangledly stood mute.

The image of the serpent signals the presence of the serpentine horror of incest, already implicit in the pressure of a damp mouth at the ear; but there is a further fall to come. After Pierre has fled to the city, and has found there only failure and the torments of guilt, he comes to his dark sister to be consoled, to be held in her arms in "the peace of the twilight." But folded into that "sweet and awful passiveness" again, he leaps up in anguish, crying, "If to follow Virtue to her uttermost vista… if by that I take hold on hell, and if the uttermost virtue, after all, prove but a betraying pander to the monstrousest vice,—then close in and crush me, ye stony walls, and into one gulf let all things tumble together!"

It is pseudo-Shakespearean rant, the rhetoric of the cheapest gothic melodrama, a theatrical debasement of the pure Faustian cry of terror, but beneath its superficial falseness, there is at work an insidious attack on the platitudes of Romanticism, which had made of fraternal affection the symbol of an impossible purity. The gothic mode is essentially a form of parody, a way of assailing clichés by exaggerating them to the limit of grotesqueness; and, in *Pierre*, Melville is mocking the banal tender plea, "Let me be a sister to you!" just as in *Absalom, Absalom!*, Faulkner was to mock the banal harsh taunt, "Would you want a nigger to sleep with your sister!" Yet there is rage in Melville, too, anguish at the thought that there cannot be an immaculate love of brother and sister, that this, too, is one of the ambiguities referred to by the subtitle of his novel.[57] Such rage and anguish are customarily present in the gothic, distinguishing it from more smug or simple kinds of satire.

At this point, Pierre begins to rethink the evidence which has convinced him that Isabel was, indeed, his father's illegitimate daughter: her perhaps imagined resemblance to a portrait of his father as a young man, her disordered memories, an initialed handkerchief. "Call me brother no more!" he cries in despair, and the next moment he tries to argue away the concepts of virtue and vice, even as he has argued away their blood relationship. Only the denial of one or the other can save him from confessing his utter damnation, and he scarcely knows which to disavow first. He brushes aside "these two shadows cast from one nothing," and goes on to insist that "these, seems to me are Virtue and Vice… It is all a dream that we dreamed we dream… From nothing proceeds nothing, Isabel! How can one sin in a dream." But when Isabel, content with his dismissal of sin, unconcerned in her passivity, says simply, "Let us sit down, again, my brother," Pierre is driven to repeat his first denial, "I am Pierre." Isabel still unruffled amends her request, "Let us sit down again, Pierre…" and together in the growing dark with no lamp lit, they fade into each other in their fatal embrace.

Just as he sins (or perhaps does not) in the dream which is his life, Pierre also dreams within that dream, and his dream within a dream contains Melville's own reading of his book, a guide to future critics. The most analytic of novelists, Melville insisted always on being the explicator of his own symbols and themes; and incest was for him not a bedrock fact but a symbol, beyond which the reader must go in search of total comprehension, a riddle to be solved. Pierre sees in his dream a mountain shaped like a Promethean man, an outcropping of rock near his ancestral home, which fades into the figure of Enceladus,[58] the mutilated but "deathless son of Terra"; and in turn this "American Enceladus," half-buried and castrated ("Nature…performed an amputation, and left the impotent Titan without one serviceable ball-and-socket above the thigh"), fades into the image of Pierre: "but on the Titan's armless trunk, his own duplicate face and features gleamed upon him with prophetic discomfiture and woe."

When he awakes from "that ideal horror to all his actual grief," Pierre calls upon all his knowledge of myth and legend, hammers away at the riddle like Moses at the rock,[59] until he has made clear to his own and Melville's satisfaction the meaning of his vision:

Old Titan's self was the son of incestuous Coelus and Terra,[60] the son of incestuous Heaven and Earth. And Titan married his mother Terra, another and accumulatively incestuous match. So

Enceladus was both the son and grandson of an incest; and even thus, there had been born from the organic blended heavenliness and earthliness of Pierre, another mixed, uncertain, heaven-aspiring, but still not wholly earth-emancipated mood; which again, by its terrestrial taint held down to its terrestrial mother, generated there the present doubly incestuous Enceladus within him; so that the present mood of Pierre—that reckless sky-assaulting mood of his, was nevertheless on one side the grandson of the sky. For it is according to eternal fitness, that the precipitated Titan should still seek to regain his paternal birthright even by fierce escalade.

It seems almost more an evasion than an explanation; and certainly Melville permits himself to get trapped in the intricacies of his image, becoming as much its victim as its exploiter. What he seems to be saying on the simplest level is that in each individual there is a fundamental conflict of two principles, called variously earth and heaven, nature and spirit, id and super-ego; and that every human action is bred of a marriage of these principles, or of a union between one of them and some previous action bred of an earlier marriage. In Western civilization, these principles are typically identified with the mother and father, and any attempt to allegorize them produces, on the literal level, a story of incest. To become somehow one with the father—even at the risk of seeming to betray the mother or of threatening the sovereignty of the paternal principle itself—this is for Melville the meaning of Enceladus' escalade and of Pierre's elopement.

Whether or not this seems finally satisfactory as an explanation of the fable of Melville's book, it is, perhaps, the only example in our literature of a writer's conscious attempt to know what he is unconsciously meaning when he takes up the subject of incest. At the opposite pole from this is Poe, who was content simply to be possessed by his subjects (when pressed he could always pretend they were parodies or hoaxes, or disown them as "silly"), and whose works, therefore, seem in large part symptoms rather than achievements.

IV

Yet Poe produced, after all, one completely achieved work of art in his writing career，a character who belongs specifically to none of his stories though he is, in part, the creation of all of them—a composite of Julius Rodman, Gordon Pym, William Wilson, Roderick Usher, and all the other pale, tormented failures at aggression, exploration, and love, who are haunted, buried alive, or clasped in the arms of corpses. That character, who is, of course, Edgar Allan Poe (even the middle name is an invention, part of the legend), Poe not only wrote but *lived*—taking cues from Brockden Brown and Byron and Bulwer Lytton; and adding, where necessary, the appropriate lies. He told incompatible stories about his birth, falsified his age, claimed to have gone off to Greece to help in the fight for freedom; and when he died, bequeathed his life-long task of composing a Poe-image to a particularly hostile executor, Rufus Griswold.[61] It was perhaps Poe's last hoax, a perverse joke on himself and his public; for Griswold, as Poe must have foreseen, proceeded to blacken Poe's reputation with all the aplomb of a self-consciously righteous man exposing a scoundrel. To make Poe seem an utterly irresponsible villain, Griswold was not above forging letters or lifting appropriate passages out of popular novels and fitting them into his account. Like Poe himself, that is to say, Griswold approached his subject's life as if it were a work of art.

So also did Baudelaire,[62] that second and unforeseen collaborator in the posthumous rewriting of Poe, who was moved by a passion equal and opposite to Griswold's. In need of a hero, an alter ego, a model for his own version of the *poete maudit*,[63] Baudelaire took up the still plastic image of Poe and made of it that French *symboliste* once-removed, the *Edgairpo*[64] of the Europeans, which to this day baffles visitors from our side of the Atlantic. Baudelaire saw Poe simultaneously as the victim of America and as a second Christ whose cross was alcohol.[65] Speaking from the first view, he says, "Some of the documents which I have seen persuade me that Poe found in the United States a large prison from which all his life he was making desperate efforts to escape"; and from the second, "I say without shame, because I feel that it springs from a profound sense of pity and affection, that I prefer Edgar Poe, drunk, poor, persecuted and a pariah, to a calm and virtuous Goethe or Walter Scott. I should willingly say of him and of a special class of men what the catechism says of our Lord: 'He has suffered much for us!'"

It is easy enough to discount both statements of Baudelaire as examples of a new sentimentality, the sentimentality of the antibourgeois European poet, who tries to put art in the vacant place of God and America and mass society in that of the Devil. Poe was by no means the first or only writer in the United States to find himself at odds with his country. It is, indeed, the typical relationship between Americans and serious native writers of all kinds, even James Fenimore Cooper (who represented to Poe the antithesis of that to which he aspired) having found himself estranged from his fellow citizens, hostile to their way of life. But whatever quarrels Cooper may have had with the American public, he was never alienated from the deepest levels of the American mind. If, at his death, he was being read less and less, still his passing was felt as an occasion for national mourning, and Daniel Webster, the official spokesman of the era, called upon to pronounce his funeral oration. Poe, on the other hand, lay without a tombstone for twenty-six years, and when one was erected, the only notable American present was Walt Whitman. Yet it was not Cooper but Poe who became for the American imagination the eternal prototype of the American Writer. Cooper, who could make a nation's myths, could not himself become such a myth; while Poe, who created no archetypal figure to rival Natty Bumppo, himself became a legend. This is perhaps not quite what Poe meant when he referred in reviewing Cooper to two kinds of literature, in one of which "the books some times live, while the authors usually die"; while in the other, "even when the works perish the man survives"; but it is close enough to it to indicate that dimly he felt the nature of his own mythical role as well as that of the highbrow writer in general.

Poe represents, of course, the artist as outcast or outsider, surrogate for all in himself that the common reader secretly regrets having to reject in the name of morality or success; and as such, he is our own local instance of an almost universal archetype. Just before Poe's day, Byron (to whom Baudelaire compared Poe, calling the latter "*le Byron egare dans le mauvais monde*")[66] had played that mythic role for all of Europe and America, composing his public figure by combining the image of Don Juan with that of the gothic hero-villain, whose ancestry we have traced back to Richardson[67] and Prevost. The most ancient avatar of the alienated artist, however, is Euripides—that is to say, the legendary creature fabricated by Greek commentators and called by that tragedian's name. The pattern is typical in all respects: born of poor and disreputable parents, himself sullen and disagreeable, Euripides is portrayed as returning contempt for contempt, withdrawing to a seaside grotto to be alone with the books he prefers to men; and at the last, it is told, he is torn to pieces by dogs or, preferably, by enraged women,

The final apocryphal anecdote is, of course, drawn from the legend of Orpheus[68], a mythical being with whom the actual historical figure of the poet was hopelessly confused. But what does the Orpheus archetype, of which Poe was the improbable New World avatar, signify? It is intended, apparently, to express the dismay of the popular mind before the kind of poet who is no longer content to represent bardically the traditions of a closed society, but speaks in his own person—invents, as it were, personal consciousness. In such a poet, the community foresees its own imminent fall from the unity and peace of pre-conscious communal life, and they condemn him to death. But the spokesman for the ego is destroyed by representatives of the id—Maenads[69], the devotees of Dionysus, wild beasts—and in his moment of destruction is made divine, becomes one with Dionysus himself. Even at its most primitive level, the myth of the outcast poet does not end with his exclusion and death. He has had to suffer and be despised; yet he is loved, even apotheosized precisely for that suffering and despite.

In the nineteenth century, the alienated artist still functions as a scape-hero, though by this time he knows his own role in advance, collaborates in his life and work with the community who seek to impose the traditional role on him. Perhaps, he is a little too self-conscious of what he is doing, a little too much in love with his own pain and exclusion to ring quite true; but society needs him still. His role has, however, been subtly changed, though the legendary events of his career remain the same; for in the bourgeois world, he comes to stand (and here is the essence once more of what is called Romanticism!) not for the heroic psychic pioneer insisting that where id was ego shall be, but for an advocate of the id against a world imprisoned in its own rigidified ego-ideals. The poet himself plays the role of the Maenad, the celebrant of impulse in a society which honors only practicality, decorum, and common sense. Such a society demands of the poet that he enact in his life the rejected values of heedlessness, disorder, and madness—and also that he permit himself to be abused and rejected for enacting them; that he take upon himself both sin and punishment, and so free the community from the burden of its repressed longings and its secret guilt.

This poor Poe was, for his own good masochistic reasons, only too willing to do; and where he did not quite conform to the necessary pattern, Griswold amended the facts of his life, converting the dandy, the lonely aristocrat of the spirit, the lost Byron of the Western world into a willful, drunkard, a dope addict, a feckless bohemian. Failing to understand the archetypal necessities of the case, certain respectable scholars of our own time have attempted to redeem Poe from his legend—perhaps because their own peace of mind depends on their proving that all the great writers of our past were as sane and orderly as any member of the Kiwanis Club,[70] to which they themselves are likely to belong. One such critic writes, for instance, "One would like, for all time, to destroy fictions that Poe was a drunkard...; he was not a dope fiend...; and he was not a rake. His life was, in fact, one of the dullest any figure of literary importance has lived in the past two hundred years." All of which adds up, apparently, to the finest claim one can make on behalf of the interests of gentility. But Poe did, after all, marry a thirteen-year-old child and watch her die painfully over five years; did at least believe himself the victim of D. T.'s, and yet fling himself into frantic bouts of drinking when faced by sexual problems he could not solve; was at last picked up in the streets of Baltimore[71] senseless, and turned over to a doctor, who wrote: "There is a gentleman, rather the worse for wear, at Ryan's 4th ward polls, who goes under the cognomen of Edgar A. Poe, and who appears in great distress..."; did die, four days later, of alcoholic poisoning. It is not quite as lively a death scene as that attributed by legend to Euripides, but it is surely not the dullest in the past two hundred years. And it haunts us still in the pages of Hart Crane's *The Bridge*, in which the poet fixes once and for all the truth no scholar can really desecrate:

> And when they dragged your retching flesh,
> Your trembling hands that night through Baltimore—
> That last night on the ballot rounds, did you
> Shaking, did you deny the ticket, Poe?

The image of Poe which for over a century has possessed the American mind is that image of failure and impotence so necessary to us in a world of success and power: an image of one who is the victim of society and of himself. But it is more specifically, perhaps essentially, the image of the *poet as drunkard*, the weak-stomached, will-less addict, forever swearing off and forever succumbing again. "For more than ten days I was totally deranged...," Poe writes in a letter. "All was hallucination arising from an attack which I had never before experienced—an attack of mania-a-potu. May heaven grant that it prove a warning to me for the rest of my days... Mania-a-potu; it is the same somewhat unusual work Poe has used in *Gordon Pym* for *delirium tremens*. But D. T.'s are a part of American folklore, like drinking itself the source of an endless stream of uneasy jokes: "Close the windows; they're coming through the door!" The morning-after, the malfunctioning liver, the "shakes"—no jest will finally charm away the shadow which they throw over the idyllic dream of an innocent night at the bar with the boys.

In Poe's life, the fiction of "social drinking" is given the lie; for to him, even the first drink was a plunge toward dissolution, a kind of symbolic suicide. He plays in the American mind to role of an anti-Rip Van Winkle, projecting the fear that after the bust, one does not awake to a new and wifeless world, but continues to sleep the tormented sleep of the damned. If the figure of Poe in Baltimore refuses to be exorcised from the national imagination, it is because Poe's terrible death befell him in a moment of typically American evasion; not only did he fall drunken beside a balloting place (and to be drunk on Election Day is surely the most American of acts!), but his drunkenness was prompted by a flight from women and marriage. No wonder the folk mind never wearies of crying, "Let him die for the act we dream! Let him die the death we secretly desire!" It is in this sense, not Baudelaire's, that America was guilty of Poe's death—as it was guilty afterward of Scott Fitzgerald's and Hart Crane's and Dylan Thomas': those latter-day scape-heroes, who found not only sacrificial ends similar to Poe's but even Griswold's of their own to celebrate them.

The figures Poe created in his work were never as satisfactory, unfortunately, as the figure he composed with his life. Certainly Gordon Pym—though he moves into the first major scene "not a little intoxicated" and early confesses himself a member of the "numerous race of the melancholy"—does not ever come alive as a significant character, much less assume the tragic dimensions attainted by Poe himself. Poe lacks as a writer a *sense of sin*, and therefore cannot raise his characters to the Faustian level which alone dignifies gothic fiction. When he tries to treat in his tales (in the "Duc de l'Omelette," for instance) the Satanic pact, he is embarrassed and seeks refuge in the heavy-handed horseplay he took for humor. The relations of Pym with Peters suggest from time to time the terrible bargain between Faust and Mephisto[72]; but Poe will not permit Peters to become a real Devil, and Pym has obviously no soul to sell. Poe liked to boast that he had transformed the gothic from a "horror of Germany" to a "horror of the soul"; but by "soul" he seems to have meant only what we should call "sensibility." Certainly Pym, who in this respect resembles all of Poe's protagonists, responds even to torment aesthetically rather than morally; and for all his concern with evil, Poe provides only what Wallace Stevens would call an *Esthetique du mal*.[73] If his own life seems to offer a more genuinely metaphysical shudder, this is thanks not to him but to the Puritan conscience of Griswold, which made of him a kind of vulgar Faust for the American market, just as Baudelaire made of him a *Poete maudit* for the French one. If there seem to be even now two Poes, it is because he left a half-finished self that has been completed in one way for the American middlebrow audience, and in quite another for the highbrow French public.

〔注释〕

Chapter I

1. Andre Gide：纪德（1869-1951），法国作家，作品有《蔑视道德的人》（1902）、《伪币犯》（1925）等，1947 年获诺贝尔文学奖。

2. Dashiell Hammet：哈米特（1894-1961），美国侦探小说家。

3. *Iliad*：《伊利亚特》，古希腊荷马史诗，以特洛伊战争为题材。

4. "belle Aude" of the *Chanson de Roland*：《罗兰之歌》中的人物。*Chanson de Roland*：《罗兰之歌》，中世纪法国英雄史诗，描写查理曼大帝罗兰之死。

5. *Beowulf*：《贝奥武夫》，古英语史诗。

6. the baroque：巴罗克风格，指 17 世纪意大利的一种艺术风格，以及受意大利影响的各国类似的风格，一反文艺复兴时期的严肃、含蓄、平衡，倾向于豪华、浮夸。

7. the rococo：洛可可风格，由巴罗克艺术发展而来，最先在法国兴起，18 世纪遍及欧洲，特点是在建筑、文学、绘画、音乐方面过分注重优雅、纤巧和装饰性。

8. English Augustans：指 18 世纪上半叶英国新古典主义文学时期的作家。

9. Cordelia：卡狄莉娅，莎士比亚悲剧《李尔王》中的三公主。下文中 Edgar：埃德加，《李尔王》中人物。二者皆在被父亲误解的情况下仍对父亲忠贞不渝。

10. 18 世纪认为文学创作的目的在于提高人们的精神境界，而莎士比亚的《李尔王》让高尚的人（如李尔王的三女儿 Cordelia）死去，似对世人有不良影响，于是他们修订莎士比亚的剧本，上演新《李尔王》，剧中李尔王及三公主都活了下来。

11. Lovelace 和 Clarissa：英国作家理查逊（Samuel Richardson，1689-1761）的小说《克拉丽莎》（*Clarissa*）中的男女主人公。

12. Don Juan：唐·璜，欧洲文学中的传奇人物，相传生于 14 世纪西班牙的一个显赫家族，一生浪迹天涯，他的名字成为豪华、风流、诱惑的象征。英国浪漫主义诗人拜伦的长诗之一便取名为《唐·璜》。

13. Unrornan：即 anti-novel。

14. *Madame Bovary*：《包法利夫人》，法国作家福楼拜著。*Anna Karenina*：《安娜·卡列尼娜》，俄国作家托尔斯泰著。*Pride and Prejudice*：《傲慢与偏见》，英国女作家奥斯汀著。*Vanity Fair*：《名利场》，英国作家萨克雷著。

15. *The Last of the Mohicans*：《最后一个莫西干人》。1826 年出版，美国作家库珀（Fenimore Cooper, 1789-1851）著。*The Red Badge of Courage*：《红色英勇勋章》，美国作家克兰（Stephen Crane, 1871-1900）著。

16. Rip Van Winkle：出自美国作家华盛顿·欧文的同名故事，是带有荷兰血统的美国人。一日在山中游荡，遇着荷兰装的侏儒，饮其酒而醉，沉睡 20 年。醒后回村，发现世道已变。

17. "Light out for the territory"：引自马克·吐温所著的《哈克贝利·芬历险记》最后一章。

18. Queequeg：印第安人，麦尔维尔《白鲸》中的人物；Chingachgook：库珀《皮袜子故事》中的人物，莫西干人首领；Nigger Jim：马克·吐温《哈克贝利·芬历险记》中的人物，黑人，哈克沿密西西比河而行的同伴。

19. Injun Joe：马克·吐温所著的《汤姆·索耶历险记》中的人物。下文中"Benito Cereno"：麦尔维尔的一部中篇小说。

20. the headless horseman：出自欧文的《睡谷传奇》（"The Legend of Sleepy Hollow"）。

21. the bargain with the Devil：指浮士德与魔鬼立约，将自己的灵魂出卖给魔鬼。

22. Thanatos：塔那托斯，希腊神话中的死神。Eros, 厄洛斯，希腊神话中的爱神，即罗马神话中的丘比特。

23. Blackness ten times blank：出自麦尔维尔对霍桑的《古宅青苔》的评论（"Hawthorne and His Mosses"）。

24. A mercant class in search of dignity：指理查逊的小说，下文中

Tory squirearchy consumed by nostalgia：指司各特小说。托利派地主阶层在 19 世纪的政治、经济地位日趋下降。

25. typical：意为"typological"。

26. Eudora Welty：韦尔蒂（1909），美国作家，主要描写密西西比河郊外的居民生活，下文中 Paul Bowles：包尔斯（1910- ），美国作家和音乐家，John Hawkes：霍克斯（1925- ），美国作家。

27. Baudelaire：波德莱尔（Charles Baudelaire, 1821-1867），法国诗人和文学批评家，主要作品收集在诗集《恶之花》（1857）中。

28. Marquis de Sade（1740-1814），法国作家，作品多描写性变态，"Sadist"一词因其作品而出现。下文中"Monk"Lewis：指刘易斯（Matthew Gregory Lewis, 1775-1818），英国作家，代表作为恐怖小说 *Ambrosio，the Monk*（1795），故称"Monk"Lewis；John Cleland：克莱兰（1709-1789），英国小说家，其作品《范尼山》（*Fanny Hill*）以色情为题材。

29. 指麦尔维尔所著的《白鲸》。

30. 出自马克·吐温的《哈克贝利·芬历险记》。哈克打算搭救黑奴吉姆，但他仿佛听见有声音说，这样做他就要下地狱。哈克经过思想斗争，还是决定救吉姆。这是他下决心时所说的话。

31. P.T.A.：即 Parent Teacher Association，学生家长和教师联谊会。

32. 指马克·吐温写在《哈克贝利·芬历险记》故事开始前的告示："Persons attempting to find a motive in this narrative will be prosecuted ..."

33. *1601*：《一六零一年》，马克·吐温于 1876 年写的随笔，完整的标题为"1601 Conversation, As It Was by the Social Fireside, in the Time of the Tudors"，即想象中伊丽莎白女王同莎士比亚和培根等人关于性关系等问题的谈话。

34. 霍桑于 1842 年与苏菲娅·皮博迪（Sophia Peabody）结婚，时年 38 岁，苏菲娅 31 岁。马克·吐温于 1870 年同生长于上流社会的奥利维亚·兰登（Olivia Langdon）结婚，时年 35 岁，奥利维亚 25 岁。

35. Sturm and Drany：德文，即 Storm and Stress（"狂飙突进"运动），为 18 世纪后半叶随着启蒙运动的发展在德国兴起的一股文学思潮，预示着浪漫主义在德国的到来。

36. Diderot：狄德罗（Denis Diderot 1713-1784），法国思想家、文学家，百科全书派领袖，浪漫主义的先驱，作品有《命运论者雅克》和《拉摩的侄子》等。

37. *Bouleversement*：法文，意为"动荡"、"动乱"。

38. de Sade 一生曾因性变态行为多次下狱，包括巴士底狱。The Bastille：巴士底狱，法国国家监狱，为王权的象征。

39. reductio：拉丁文，意为"the action of bringing back (from exile)"。

40. Rousseau：卢梭（Jean-Jacques Rousseau, 1712-1778），法国 18 世纪思想家、作家，对以后社会思想和文学思想影响甚大。下文中 Saint-Just：（1769-1794），法国革命家，曾与罗伯斯庇尔共建资产阶级政府，是卢梭理论的狂热追随者。

41. Don Juan ... hero：指 1819 年拜伦发表的长诗《唐·璜》。下文中 Shylock：夏洛克，莎士比亚喜剧《威尼斯商人》中的犹太人，高利贷者。

42. Beatrice Cenci：毕阿特丽斯·沉西（1577-1599），罗马人，其父一生为恶，对子女极尽迫害之能事，乃至与女儿发生乱伦关系。Beatrice 与家人图谋杀死亲生父亲，后案发，Beatrice 被处决。雪莱曾以此为题材作诗剧《沉西》（*Cenci*）；意大利画家基多（Guido Reni）也曾据此作画。该画在霍桑的《玉石像》（*The Marble Faun*）中屡被提及。

43. 浪漫主义文学特征之一。

44. 卢梭在一封信中谈到他的创作灵感时说，一天他去万森市（Vincennes）看望受文字狱之苦的好友狄德罗，路上买了一份报纸，上载第戎学院的广告，征集关于"艺术与科学是否改善了法国的风俗"方面的优秀论文。卢梭的头脑突然兴奋，思想澎湃，于是坐在树下，以镇定精神。当他安定下来时，发现衣襟已被泪水湿透。他的论文后来获奖，他的文学与哲学著作生涯自此开始。

45. the Great Mother—cast down by the most patriarchal of all religions：在希腊罗马神话的神谱中，"地母"的位置相当显赫。泰初，地母（Earth）生子"天"（Uranus），"天"与"地"合生子"时间"（Cronos），Cronos 与妹 Rhea（后又名 Cybele）合生宙斯与希腊诸神，Rhea 遂被尊为诸神之母。后来信奉"上帝"（Father）的基督教产生，母神与希腊诸神同遭废黜。the most patriarchal of all religions：指基督教。

46. Lilith：女魔鬼，据亚述传说，总是魂缠风雨交加的荒野，对儿童危险极大，名字意为"夜"。原为亚当之妻，后成为魔王的母亲和妻子。

47. Protestantism：新教，主张革除天主教的礼仪，反对崇拜圣母，不承认"炼狱"，教义严厉，故称"希伯莱化的"（Hebraizing）。

48. Philosoyhes：指法国 18 世纪的一些思想家，如狄德罗、达朗贝、霍尔巴赫、爱尔维修等，他们主张唯物主义，反对神学迷信。

49. Atlantis：古代神话中大西洋里的一个美丽岛屿，那里有一个繁荣强盛的王国，后被海水淹没；Ultima Thula：古希腊人和罗马人对北欧（当时所知世界的最北部）的称谓；Western Isles：大西洋的岛区，在英国苏格兰西北岸外。

50. 指但丁《神曲·地狱篇》第 26 章。

51. Pillars of Hercules：据传说，赫勒克利斯（Hercules）在地中海西方将一座山分为两段，形成直布罗陀海陕。一分为二的两座山头即称为 Pillars of Hercules。

51. 指讲拉丁语族语言、信奉天主教的。

52. The purchase of Louisiana Territory：指美国于 1803 年以一千五百万美元从法国购买北美密西西比河谷（当时属法国）的 2,144,520 平方英里的区域，当时法国和美国分别由拿破仑和杰佛逊当政。

53. Lewis and Clark：指 Meriwether Lewis（1774-1809）和 William Clark（1770-1838），美国开发者，二人一起曾翻越落基山，横跨密苏里，来到美国西部太平洋沿岸。

54. David：大卫（Jacques-Louis David, 1748-1825），法国画家，

法国新古典主义画派的创始人，同情革命；Monticello：杰佛逊总统的庄园，其建筑、设计均为美国古典主义复兴的典范。

55. Houdon：胡敦（Jean-Antoine Houdon，1741-828），法国雕塑家，雕塑艺术中的洛可可派代表人物。

56. the Cincinnatus of the West：Cincinnatus，传说中的罗马英雄，大约出现在前 500 至前 430 年间，在罗马遭到敌人的威胁时，被举为最高领袖。在打败敌人、解救人民危难之后，放弃权力，回乡务农。

57. toga：古罗马人日常服装；下文中 marble brow：指古典主义雕塑。

58. Abe：指林肯（Abraham Lincoln，1809-1865）。

59. *Encyclopedie*：指 1751 至 1776 年狄德罗和达朗贝编辑出版的《百科全书》，它囊括了 18 世纪哲学思想，企图用理智解释世界，反对迷信。

60. Delacroix：德拉克洛瓦（Eugene Delacroix, 1798-1863），法国画家，反对大卫绘画中的古典、正统技法，为浪漫主义画派领袖。

61. Machiavellian：马基维利主义的。马基维利（Niccoli Machiavelli, 1469-1527），佛罗伦萨政治家、理论家，主张只要能使国家富强，可以不择手段，不管是使用恐怖方式还是进行斯骗。Machiavellism：指政治阴谋或不择手段的政治。

Chapter XI

1. The blackness of darkness：出自《新约·犹太书》，坡在其小说《亚琴·戈登·皮姆的故事》（*The Narrative of A. Gordon Pym*）中曾引用，见下文。麦尔维尔在他对霍桑的《古宅青苔》的评论（"Hawthorne and His Mosses"）的评论中也曾引用过该文。

2. Lewis and Clark：见上面 Chapter I 注 53。

3. John Neal：尼尔（1793-1876）；下文中 Simms，西姆斯（William Gilmore Simms, 1806-1870），均为美国作家。

4. Paulding：包尔丁（J. K. Paulding, 1778-1860），美国作家。

5. 相传库柏读一本小说时曾说自己可以写出更好的作品，库柏夫人在旁以言相激，他遂提笔开始创作生涯。

6. Western：西部文学作品。

7. 菲德勒似认为《亚琴·戈登·皮姆的故事》是爱伦·坡本人复杂生活历史及心理状态的再现。详见下文分析。

8. *Cantus firmus*：拉丁语，意为"圣歌旋律"。

9. 指 Daggoo（the Black giant）。

10. poet-sailor＝Poe-Pym。

11. Gehenna：在耶路撒冷附近，原为偶像崇拜之地，后来偶像崇拜被废止，遂成为存放垃圾以及动物与犯人尸体的地方，为防止传染病曾被点火燃烧不止。后人也用以指代地狱。

12. Marie Bonaparte：法国文学评论家，所著《埃德加·坡的生平与著作》（*The Life and Works of Edgar Poe, A Psycho-Analytic Interpretation*, 1949）以心理分析理论分析坡的作品，很有见地，是关于坡的文学评论经典著作之一。

13. the section of America：指美国南部；下文中 that institution 指 slavery。

14. 指爱伦·坡。

15. biche de mer：意为"海参"；下文中 *National Geographic*，即 *National Geographic Magazine*（《全国地理杂志》），美国全国地理学会于 1888 年创办的月刊；Captain Cook：柯克船长（James Cook, 1728-1779），英国航海家和探险家，澳大利亚和新西兰的发现者，曾绕南极冰带航行。

16. 坡出生在波士顿流浪艺人家庭，两岁时其父弃家出走，母亦早逝，1811 年由弗吉尼亚富商约翰·爱伦收养，故在南方长大。

17. Ole Virginny＝Old Virginia。

18. two books：（根据下文）一部为 J·K·包尔丁著《美国的蓄奴制》（*Slaves in the United States*），另一部不详。

19. 法文，意为"在埃德加·坡的心里从未有过爱"。

20. the subdued dependent... vengeance：指坡心目中白人与黑人的爱与恨关系，在坡看来爱是臆想，恨是现实——白人恐惧心理的根源；

dependent 和 victim 皆指黑人。

21. *The Southern Literary Messenger*：1834 至 1864 年间的一种文学杂志，坡曾任该杂志编辑，并撰写文学评论。坡的不少观点就是在这本杂志上公诸于世的。

22. the White Goddess：白色女神，这里指坡的生母。

23. the black mammy and the black milk brother：昔日美国南方风俗，白人孩子随黑人乳母及其子女同食同住，一般至 7 岁，后则分主、仆等级。

24. 指《哈克贝利•芬历险记》。

25. 指《哈克贝利•芬历险记》和《傻瓜威尔逊》（*Pudd'nhead Wilson*），菲德勒认为，前者所描写的是西部的母系社会，后者描写的则是南方的父系社会，而马克•吐温的生活经历是先向南（做为领航员沿密西西比河向南去新奥尔良），后向西（即去内华达和旧金山）开始其创作生涯，故其作品里的西一南顺序和其实际生活中的南一西顺序恰恰相反。

26. Hannibal：位于密苏里州东北部，马克•吐温曾在该地度过童年。

27. Father of Waters：即密西西比河。

28. Aunt Jemima：美国流行的黑人女厨师形象。

29. F. F. V.：First Family of Virginia 的缩写，指贵族或带有贵族派头的。

30. 皆为《傻瓜威尔逊》书中人物。

31. W. H. Auden：奥顿（1907-1973），英国诗人，文学评论家。

32. *The Brothers Karamazov*：《卡拉玛佐夫兄弟》，俄国小说家陀斯妥耶夫斯基著。下文中 *The Innocence of Father Broom*：英国作家切斯特顿（G. K. Chesterton，1874-1936）著。

33. Robert Penn Warren：华伦（1905- ），美国小说家和文学评论家。

34. Conan Doyle：柯南•道尔（1859-1930），英国作家，以福尔摩斯探案故事闻名。

35. John Brown：约翰·布朗（1800-1859），美国废奴运动领袖，曾组织"地下铁路"，帮助黑奴逃离南方，并举行暴动，暴动失败后被处死。

36. Beauchamp Case：亦称 Kentucky Tragedy, S. P. Sharp 曾使 Ann Cook 失身。后来 Ann Cook 与 J. O. Beauchamp 结婚，并使丈夫发誓杀死 Sharp。1825 年，Beauchamp 化装杀死了 Sharp。案发后，Beauchamp 被捕，并被判死列。临刑前 Ann 与 Beauchamp 企图自杀。Ann 刺死自己，Beauchamp 自杀未遂，被处决。西姆斯（W. G. Simms, 1806-1870）和坡以此为题材的作品分别为长篇小说《布尚》（*Beauchamp: or, The Kentucky Tragedy*）和短篇小说 "Politian"。

37. to gande Bosse＝the big hump。

38. Agrarian movement：20 世纪初叶美国西方的一些知识分子欲以南方的生活方式同美国的即工业的生活方式相抗衡的思潮。主要发起者和参加者是拉沙姆（John Crowe Ransom）、戴维森（Donald Davidson）、华伦（Robert Penn Warren）、塔特（Allen Tate）等人。曾出版《逃亡者》（*The Fugitive*）期刊。这些人把独立的农场主视为亚当式的人物，把过去的、美国的南方庄园视为失去的伊甸，把北方的科学视为撒旦，把现代城市视为地狱。他们认为现代主义摧毁了有秩序与有意义的人生的存在条件，提出坚持传统的极端必要性。他们的思想和主张成为"南方文艺复兴"的基本动力。

39. out of Margaret Mitchell by Mark Twain：玛格丽特·米切尔和马克·吐温一起生的（孩子）；指华伦小说中女主人公的处境既像米切尔所著的《飘》（*Gone with the Wind*）中的女主人公郝思嘉（Scarlet O'Hara），又似马克·吐温作品《傻瓜威尔逊》里的瓦勒（Valet de Chambre）。

40. Ralph Ellison：埃利森（1914-1994），美国黑人作家，代表作为《看不见的人》（*Invisible Man*）。

41. *Light in August*：《八月之光》，福克纳的长篇小说。Joe Christmas 为其主人公，Doc Hines 为 Joe 的外祖父。

42. Charles Bon：《押沙龙，押沙龙》人物之一，与其同父异母妹相恋，被同父异母弟亨利（Henry）所杀。

43. Jim Bond：为 Charles Bon 之子，Bon 意为"good"，Bond 意为"slavery"。

44. Quentin Compson：《押沙龙，押沙龙》一书的叙事者之一，在哈佛大学读书，与斯里夫（Shreve）住同屋，该书故事主要以两人谈话方式写出。

45. Quentin 亦出现在福克纳小说《喧嚣与愤怒》(*The Sound and the Fury*)，在该故事中，他因失望和痛苦而自杀。

46. Why God let us lose the war：the war 指美国内战，us 指南方人。福克纳的作品显示出，由于南方文明建立在白人压迫黑人和印第安人的非正义的基础之上，它最后必然灭亡。

47. Liebestods：德文，意为"情死"（death for love）。

48. Vladimir Nabokov：纳博科夫（1899-1977），美籍俄国小说家，其作《洛莉塔》(*Lolita*) 出版于 1955 年。

49. Gogol：果戈里（Nikokay Vasilyevich Gogol, 1809-1852），俄国作家，被称为俄国现实主义之父。

50. this lady ... by Guido Reni：见 Chapter I 注 42。

51. the Palazzo Barberini：巴贝里尼艺术宫，位于罗马，巴贝里尼为古意大利一显赫家族名。

52. Fair Maiden：在美国文学中，指象征社会价值观的女子，常为"blonde"，通常显得疲惫无力，如霍桑的《七个尖角阁的房子》(*The House of the Seven Gables*) 中的 Phoebe 和《玉石雕像》(*The Marble Faun*) 中的 Hilda。Dark Lady 与 Fair Maiden 相对，常为"Brunette"，如《红字》(*The Scarlet Letter*) 中的 Hester Prynne，《玉石雕像》中的 Miriam，她们通常精力旺盛，具有反叛精神。

53. Julian Hawthorne：(1846-1934)，霍桑之子，曾著《霍桑生平》(*Nathaniel Hawthorne and His Life*)，及《霍桑和他的朋友》(*Hawthorne and His Circle*) 等。

54. *Geschwisterinzest*：德文，意为"兄妹或姐弟乱伦"。

55. Isabel：可能是 Pierre 的父亲的私生女。

56. Titan：提坦巨人，希腊神话中乌拉诺斯（Uranus）和地神盖亚（Gaea）的子女，共六男六女。这些巨神受母亲的唆使，推翻乌拉诺斯，拥戴 Titan 之一的克洛诺斯（Kronus）为新王。但克洛诺斯之子宙斯又把父亲推翻，自己在奥林匹斯山称王。巨神们与宙斯顽强争斗，最后被宙斯打败，并被打入塔耳塔罗斯（Tartarus）地狱。下文中，Memnon：门农，荷马之后的神话中特洛伊战争的英雄，提托尼斯（Tithonus）和厄俄斯（Eos）之子，厄提俄皮亚之王。后帮助特洛伊人抵抗希腊人的进攻，在战场上被杀；Widow of Ephesus：见下文。

57. *Pierre* 一书的完整的标题为 *Pierre：or，The Ambiguities*。

58. Enceladus：恩塞拉都斯，希腊神话中提坦巨人之一，曾反叛众神，后被雅典娜压在西西里岛下面。下文中的 Terra：见下面注 60。

59. Mosses at the rock：摩西，《旧约》中古希伯莱人先知。当他率以色列人出埃及后，跋涉于旷野，因缺少水源，众人多有怨言。摩西听从上帝的吩咐，以"先前击打河水的杖"击打"何烈的磐石"，于是水从磐石中流出。参阅《旧约·出埃及记》第 17 章。

60. Coelus and Terra：希拉斯和泰拉，希腊神话中的天神和地神，原为兄妹。

61. Rufus Griswold：格里斯乌德（1815-1857），编辑；作为爱伦·坡的遗稿保管人，无视事实，在坡去世以后，撰稿把坡描写成一个魔鬼式的文人，使坡在很长时间内成为美国文学史上最受误解的作家之一。

62. Baudelaire：波德莱尔（Charles Baudelaire, 1821-1867），法国诗人，坡的崇拜者，花费多年时间翻译坡的著作，使坡在法国和欧洲声名大振。

63. *Poete maudit*：法文，意为"被咒骂的诗人"。

64. Edgairpo：Edgar Poe 的法文写法。

65. 坡一生好酗酒，因酗酒失业，最后因酒醉丧生。

66. Le Byron egare dans le mauvais monde：意为"Byron wandering in a wicked world"。

67. Richardson：理查森（1689-1761），英国小说家，下文中的

Provost：普雷沃斯（1697-1763），法国小说家。

68. Orpheus：俄尔甫斯，希腊神话中的诗人和歌手，善弹奏竖琴，他的演奏能使草木点头、顽石移动、猛兽驯服。后被愤怒的妇女杀死。

69. Maenads：酒神狄俄尼索斯（Dionysus）的女祭司。

70. Kiwanis Club：遍及美国和加拿大的商人与实业家俱乐部。

71. Baltimore：巴尔的摩市，坡于 1849 年 10 月 7 日死于此地。

72. Faust and Mephisto：浮士德和魔鬼；Mephistopheles，《浮士德》中的魔鬼。

73. *Esthetique du mal*：法文，意为"恶的美学"。

Questions For Discussion：

1. Classic American novelists seem to avoid treating "love" directly in their works in the opinion of Leslie Fiedler. Discuss with reference to the major authors and their major works that you know well and define the accuracy of his generalization.

2. Why is the Gothic form most fruitfully used in the best American writers? How did Edgar Allan Poe contribute to its development in American literature along with Melville, Mark Twain and Faulkner (to name just a few)?

3. Fiedler seems to see an asexual-homosexual-relationship alive in some classics of American literature. Do you agree with him?

4. What new light does Fiedler's book throw on your understanding of the American sensibility as is revealed in the best of American fiction?

For Further Reading：

1. Lawrence, D. H. *Studies in Classic American Literature*. New York: Doubleday, 1960.

2. Chase, Richard. *The American Novel and Its Tradition*. New York: Doubleday, 1957.

Richard Chase

〔作者介绍〕

理查德·查斯（Richard Chase，1914-1966），美国文学评论家、英语教授，出生于新英格兰的新罕布什尔州，就读于达特默斯学院和哥伦比亚大学。查斯是第二次世界大战后美国文学评论界的重要人物之一。他同卡津（Alfred Kazin）、菲德勒（Leslie Fiedler）等人一起，把文学评论由新批评阶段推向神话与象征研究及文化传统分析的新阶段。他的最富影响的评论著作是《美国小说及其传统》（*The American Novel and Its Tradition*，1957）等著作。

The American Novel and Its Tradition

〔作品介绍〕

《美国小说及其传统》1957 年由纽约达博蒂公司出版，现已成为美国文学评论经典著作之一。它强调指出，"传奇"（romance）是美国小说创作的明显特征，并对许多美国文学作品的象征及抽象的特点进行了较为全面而深刻的分析。作者在详尽地评论美国小说家布朗（Charles Brockden Brown，1771-1810）、库柏（James Fenimore Cooper, 1789-1851）、霍桑（Nathaniel Hawthorne, 1804-1864）、麦尔维尔（Herman Melville，1819-1891）、马克·吐温（Mark Twain，1835-1910）、亨利·詹姆斯（Henry James，1843-1916）、弗兰克·诺里斯（Frank Norris, 1870-1902）、凯布尔（George Washington Cable，1844-1925）、豪威尔

斯（William Dean Howells，1837-1920）、菲茨杰拉德（F. Scott Fitzgerald, 1896-1940）及福克纳（William Faulkner, 1897-1962）的作品的同时，精辟地论述了美国小说本身的伟大之处及弱点。

查斯认为，"传奇"小说有闹剧性和抒情的特点，它益于探索人的下意识或无意识，有助于抛开道德问题，去表现现实主义有时无法表达的复杂而奥妙的真理。查斯认为，美国"传奇"小说的根源有二：一是表现善与恶的清教主义闹剧，一是由于怀念过去以务农或边疆生活为主的美国传统而产生的田园抒情式情调。古希腊诗人及马洛和狄更斯等英国作家曾熟练运用过的闹剧手法，首先由布朗介绍进美国文学中来；布朗把它用于美国题材及美国背景，因而使之在美国生根。布朗的作品显示出这种技巧在美国文学创作中的广泛用途。查斯认为，库柏的《皮袜子五部曲》（The Leatherstocking Tales）主人公纳蒂·班波坚持西部边疆生活方式，热爱它的粗犷与天真，而对"文明"的腐朽和丑恶则切齿拊心，这是美国文学中田园抒情格调的典型表现。这种对处女地和纯朴生活的追怀情感后来成为美国文学传统的有机组成部分。

查斯指出，"传奇"小说更倾向于采取神话、寓言和有象征性质的艺术表现形式。库柏的小说，如《草原》（The Prairie)借助于过去、文化传统感及主人公的超人力量，赋予人的生活经历以神话般的意义。霍桑的传世之作《红字》（The Scarlet Letter)从形式到内容都集寓言或艺术因素之大成；诚然，霍桑的作品并非纯属寓言性质的作品，这是因为它内含所指不清的象征意义。查斯认为，寓言式作品和象征主义作品间存在着根本区别。前者重点在于说明公认的真理，而后者则意在发现或创造真理。

《美国小说及其传统》还不时旁鹜笔锋，以相当的篇幅论述美国文学研究方面的其他一些重要内容，如"幸运的堕落"、"不可饶恕的罪"、人间的友爱、唯我主义、自我禁锢等。

这里选注的是该书第1章。

An Excerpt from *The American Novel and Its Tradition*

CHAPTER I

THE BROKEN CIRCUIT[1]
A CULTURE OF CONTRADICTIONS

The imagination that has produced much of the best and most characteristic American fiction has been shaped by the contradictions and not by the unities and harmonies of our culture. In a sense this may be true of all literatures of whatever time and place. Nevertheless there are some literatures which take their form and tone from polarities, opposites, and irreconcilables, but are content to rest in and sustain them or to resolve them into unities, if at all, only by special and limited means. The American novel tends to rest in contradictions and among extreme ranges of experience. When it attempts to resolve contradictions, it does so in oblique, morally equivocal ways. As a general rule it does so either in melodramatic actions or in pastoral idylls, although intermixed with both one may find the stirring instabilities of "American humor." These qualities constitute the uniqueness of that branch of the novelistic tradition which has flourished in this country. They help to account for the strong element of "romance" in the American "novel."

By contrast, the English novel has followed a middle way. It is notable for its great practical sanity, its powerful, engrossing composition of wide ranges of experience into a moral centrality and equability of judgment. Oddity, distortion of personality, dislocations of normal life, recklessness of behavior, malignancy of motive—these the English novel has included. Yet the profound poetry of disorder we find in the American novel is missing, with rare exceptions, from the English. Radical maladjustments and contradictions are reported but are seldom of the essence of form in the English novel, and although it is no stranger to suffering and defeat or to triumphant joy either, it gives the impression of absorbing all extremes, all maladjustments and contradictions into a normative view of life. In doing so, it shows itself to derive from the two great influences that stand behind it—classic tragedy[2] and Christianity. The English novel has not, of course, always been strictly speaking tragic or Christian. Often it has been comic, but often, too, in that superior form of comedy which approaches tragedy. Usually it has been realistic or, in the philosophical sense of the word "naturalistic." Yet even its peculiar kind of gross poetic naturalism has preserved something of the two great traditions that formed English literature. The English novel, that is, follows the tendency of tragic art and Christian art, which characteristically move through contradictions to forms of harmony, reconciliation, catharsis, and transfiguration.

Judging by our greatest novels, the American imagination, even when it wishes to assuage and reconcile the contradictions of life, has not been stirred by the possibility of catharsis or incarnation, by the tragic or Christian possibility. It has been stirred, rather, by the aesthetic possibilities of radical forms of alienation, contradiction, and disorder.

The essential difference between the American novel and the English will be strongly pointed up to any reader of F. R. Leavis's[2] *The Great Tradition*. Mr. Leavis's "great tradition" of the novel is really Anglo-American, and it includes not only Jane Austen, George Eliot, Conrad and Henry James but, apparently, in one of its branches Hawthorne and Melville. My assumption in this book is that the American novel is obviously a development from the English tradition. At least it was, down to 1880 or 1890. For at that time our novelists began to turn to French and Russian models and the English influence has decreased steadily ever since. The more extreme imagination of the French and Russian novelists has clearly been more in accord with the purposes of modern American writers than has the English imagination. True, an American reader of Leavis's book will have little trouble in giving a very general assent to his very general proposition about the Anglo-American tradition. Nevertheless, he will also be forced constantly to protest that there is another tradition of which Mr. Leavis does not seem to be aware, a tradition which includes most of the best American novels.

Ultimately, it does not matter much whether one insists that there are really *two* traditions, the English and the American (leaving aside the question of what writers each might be said to comprise) or whether one insists merely that there is a radical divergence within one tradition. All I hold out for is a provisional recognition of the divergence as a necessary step towards understanding and appreciation of both the English and the American novel. The divergence is brought home to an American reader of Leavis's book when, for example, he comes across the brief note allotted to the Brontes. Here is Leavis's comment on Emily Bronte:

> I have said nothing about *Wuthering Heights* because that astonishing work seems to me a kind of sport... she broke completely, and in the most astonishing way, both with the Scott tradition that imposed on the novelist a romantic resolution of his themes, and with the tradition coming down from the eighteenth century that demanded a plane-mirror reflection of the surface of "real" life. Out of her a minor tradition comes, to which belongs, most notably, *The House with the Green Shutters*.[3]

Of course Mr. Leavis is right; in relation to the great tradition of the English novel, *Wuthering Heights* is indeed a sport. But suppose it were discovered that *Wuthering Heights* was written by an American of New England Calvinist or Southern Presbyterian background. The novel would be astonishing and unique no matter who wrote it or where. But if it were an American novel it would not be a sport; it has too close an affinity with too many American novels, and among them some of the best. Like many of the fictions discussed in this book *Wuthering Heights* proceeds from an imagination that is essentially melodramatic, that operates among radical contradictions and renders reality indirectly or poetically, thus breaking, as Mr. Leavis observes, with the traditions that require a surface rendering of real life and a resolution of themes, "romantic" or otherwise.

Those readers who make a dogma out of Leavis's views are thus proprietors of an Anglo-American tradition in which many of the most interesting and original and several of the greatest American novels are sports. *Wieland*[4] is a sport, and so are *The Scarlet Letter* and *The Blithedale Romance, Moby Dick, Pierre,* and *The Confidence Man, Huckleberry Finn, The Red Badge of Courage, McTeague, As I Lay Dying, the Sun Also Rises*—all are eccentric, in their differing ways, to a tradition of which, let us say, *Middlemarch* is a standard representative. Not one of them has any close kinship with the massive, temperate, moralistic rendering of life and thought we associate with Mr. Leavis's "great tradition."

The English novel, one might say, has been a kind of imperial enterprise, an appropriation of reality with the high purpose of bringing order to disorder. By contrast, as Lawrence observed in his *Studies in Classic American Literature*, the American novel had usually seemed content to explore, rather than to appropriate and civilize, the remarkable and in some ways unexampled territories of life in the New World and to reflect its anomalies and dilemmas. It has not wanted to build an imperium but merely to discover a new place and a new state of mind. Explorers see more deeply, darkly, privately and disinterestedly than imperialists, who must perforce be circumspect and prudential. The American novel is more profound and clairvoyant than the English novel, but by the same token it is narrower and more arbitrary, and it tends to carve out of experience brilliant, highly wrought fragments rather than massive unities.

For whatever reason—perhaps the nagging scrupulosity of the Puritan mind has something to do with it—the American novel has, sometimes approached a perfection of art unknown to the English tradition, in which we discover no such highly skilled practitioners as Hawthorne, Stephen Crane, Henry James, or Hemingway. These writers, often overestimated as moralists, seem content to oppose the disorder and rawness of their culture with a scrupulous art-consciousness, with aesthetic forms—which do, of course, often broaden out into moral significance.

In a well known passage Allen Tate[5] refers to the "complexity of feeling" that everyone senses in the American novel and that, as Mr. Tate says, "from Hawthorne down to our own time has baffled our best understanding." The complexity of the American novel has been much exaggerated. With the exception of one or two of James's novels no American fiction has anything like the complexity of character and event of *Our Mutual Friend*,[6] for example. In *The Scarlet Letter* or *Moby Dick* the characters and events have actually a kind of abstracted simplicity about them. In these books character may be deep but it is narrow and predictable. Events take place with a formalized clarity. And certainly it cannot be argued that society and the social life of man are shown to be complex in these fictions.

But of course Tate says "complexity of feeling," and he is right about that. The states of feeling, and the language in which they are caught, are sometimes very intricate in American novels. Yet these musing tides of feeling and language that make such a rich poetry in our fiction often seem to be at variance with the simplified actions and conceptions of life our novels present. The origins of this apparent anomaly must be sought in the contradictions of our culture. Marius Bewley[7] takes up Tate's remark in an essay called "Fenimore Cooper and the Economic Age" and traces this "complexity of feeling" to a "tension" which he finds not only in Cooper but in Hawthorne and James. It is, he thinks, a political tension in its origins, although as embodied in the works of these authors, it assumes many forms. This tension, he says, "was the result of a struggle to close the split in American experience, to discover a unity that—for the artist especially—almost sensibly *was not there.*" What was the nature of the division that supported this conflict? It took on many forms concurrently; it was an opposition between tradition and progress or between the past and the future, between Europe and America, liberalism and reaction, aggressive acquisitive economics and benevolent wealth. These same divisions existed in Europe also, but there they were more ballasted by a denser social medium, a richer sense of the past, a more inhibited sense of material possibilities.

Mr. Bewley's apt discussion of the matter needs to be amended in one fundamental way. The kind of art that stems from a mind primarily moved by the impulse toward aesthetic and cultural unities and thus "struggles to close the split in American experience" as an artist might wish to close it—this kind of art is practiced often, though not always, by Henry James, but less often by Hawthorne and Cooper, and much less often by Faulkner, Melville, and Mark Twain. The fact is that many of the best American novels achieve their very being, their energy and their form, from the perception and acceptance not of unities but of radical disunities.

Like many readers of American literature, Bewley makes the mistake of assuming both that our writers have wanted to reconcile disunities by their art and their intelligence and that this is what they *should* have wanted to do. Behind this assumption is a faulty historical view, as well as a certain overplus of moralism, which neglects to observe that there have been notable bodies of literature, as well as of painting and sculpture, that have proposed and accepted an imaginative world of radical, even irreconcilable contradictions, and that with some important exceptions, the

American novel (by which I mean its most original and characteristic examples) has been one of these bodies of literature.

Surely Cooper (as will be noted later) is not at his best in a novel like *Satanstoe*, which is a "culture-making" novel and in which his mind is moved by an image of aesthetic and political harmony. On the contrary he is at his best in a book like *The Prairie*, where the search for unity is not at the center of the stage and he can accept without anxiety or thought the vivid contradictions of Natty Bumppo and his way of life—those contradictions which, as Balzac saw, made him so original a conception. In this book Cooper is not inspired by an impulse to resolve cultural contradictions half so much as by the sheer romantic exhilaration of escape from culture itself into a world where nature is dire, terrible, and beautiful, where human virtues are personal, alien, and renunciatory, and where contradictions are to be resolved only by death, the ceaseless brooding presence of which endows with an unspeakable beauty every irreconcilable of experience and all the irrationalities of life.

Mr. Bewley is not alone in assuming it to be the destiny of American literature to reconcile disunities rather than to pursue the possibility it has actually pursued—that is, to discover a putative unity *in* disunity or to rest at last among irreconcilables. In *Democracy in America* Tocqueville tried to account for a number of related contradictions in American life. He noted a disparity between ideals and practice, a lack of connection between thought and experience, a tendency of the American mind to oscillate rather wildly between ideas that "are all either extremely minute and clear or extremely general and vague."

Tocqueville sought a genetic explanation for these disparities. He pointed out that in aristocratic societies there was a shared body of inherited habits, attitudes and institutions that stood in a mediating position between the individual and the state. This, he observed, was not true in a democracy, where "each citizen is habitually engaged in the contemplation of a very puny object, namely, himself: If he ever looks higher, he perceives only the immense form of society at large or the still more imposing aspect of mankind... What lies between is a void." Tocqueville believed that this either/or habit of mind also owed much to the sharp distinctions made by Calvinism and its habit of opposing the individual to his God, with a minimum of mythic or ecclesiastical mediation. He found certain advantages in this "democratic" quality of mind, but he warned Americans that it might produce great confusion in philosophy, morals, and politics and a basic instability in literary and cultural values, and that consequently Americans should try to discover democratic equivalents for those traditional habits of mind which in aristocracies had moderated and reconciled extremes in thought and experience.

Tocqueville knew that the dualistic kind of thought of which he spoke was specifically American only in the peculiar quality of its origin and expression. He saw that with the probable exception of England, Europe would characteristically concern itself during the nineteenth century with grand intellectual oppositions, usually more or less of a Hegelian[11] order. But even though the tendency of thought Tocqueville predicated belonged to Western culture generally, one is nevertheless struck by how often American writers conceive of human dilemmas according to his scheme, and how many make aesthetic capital out of what seemed to him a moral and intellectual shortcoming.

In his studies of the classic American writers, D. H. Lawrence presented his version of the contrariety, or, as he said, "duplicity" of the American literary mind by saying that he found in writers like Cooper, Melville, and Hawthorne "a tight mental allegiance to a morality which all their passion goes to destroy," a formulation which describes perfectly the inner contradiction of such products of the American imagination as the story of Natty Bumppo. In general Lawrence was thinking of an inherent conflict between "genteel" spirituality and a pragmatic experientialism which in its lower depths was sheer Dionysian[9] or "Indian" energy and violence. Acute enough to see that the best American artistic achievements had depended in one way or another on this dualism, he seemed ready nevertheless to advocate, on moral grounds, a reconciliation of opposites, such as he thought he discerned in the poems of Whitman. In short, like all the observers of American literature we are citing in these pages, Lawrence was trying to find out what was wrong with it. He is a sympathetic and resourceful reader—one of the best, surely, ever to turn his attention to the American novel. But he thinks that the American novel is sick, and he wants to cure it. Perhaps there is something wrong with it, perhaps it is sick—but a too exclusive preoccupation with the wrongness of the American novel has in some ways disqualified him for seeing what, right or wrong, it *is*.

Finally, there is the division of American culture into "highbrow" and "lowbrow" made by Van Wyck Brooks in 1915 in his *America's Coming of Age*. Brooks's essay is a great piece of writing; it is eloquent, incisive, and witty. But we have lived through enough history now to see its fundamental error—namely, the idea that it is the duty of our writers to heal the split and reconcile the contradictions in our culture by pursuing a middlebrow course. All the evidence shows that wherever American literature has pursued the middle way it has tended by a kind of native fatality not to reconcile but merely to deny or ignore the polarities of our culture. Our middlebrow literature—for example, the novels of Howells[10]—has generally been dull and mediocre. In the face of Brooks's desire to untie the highbrow and the lowbrow on a middle ground, there remains the fact that our best novelists have been not middlebrows, but either highbrows like James, lowbrows like Mark Twain, Frank Norris, Dreiser, and Sherwood Anderson, or combination highbrow-lowbrows like Melville, Faulkner, and Hemingway. Here again American fiction contrasts strongly with English. The English novel at its best is staunchly middlebrow. The cultural conditions within which English literature has evolved have allowed it to become a great middlebrow literature—the only one, it may be, in history.

Let us in all candor admit the limited, the merely instrumental value of the terms used in the last paragraph. They work very well, and are in fact indispensable, in making large cultural formulations. But in applying them to individual authors the terms must be constantly reexamined. We might ask, for example, whether from one point of view both Hawthorne and James performed the unlikely feat of becoming great middlebrow writers. Both of them, at any rate, achieve a kind of contemplative centrality of vision within the confines of which their minds work with great delicacy and equanimity. In so far as they do this, one certainly cannot chide them for shying away from some of the more extreme contradictions, the more drastic forms of alienation, the more violent, earthy, or sordid ranges of experience which engage the minds of Melville and Faulkner, and in fact most of our best writers. Yet to achieve a "contemplative centrality of vision" certainly requires an action of the mind, whereas the word "middlebrow," although suggesting centrality of vision, inevitably suggests, judging by our American literature, a view gained by no other means than passivity and the refusal of experience.

To conclude this brief account of the contradictions which have vivified and excited the American imagination, these contradictions seem traceable to certain historical facts. First, there is the solitary position man has been placed in this country, a position very early enforced by the doctrines of Puritanism and later by frontier conditions and, as Tocqueville skillfully pointed out, by the very institutions of democracy as these evolved in the eighteenth and nineteenth centuries. Second, the Manichaean[11] quality of New England Puritanism, which, as Yvor Winters and others have shown, had so strong an effect on writers like Hawthorne and Melville and entered deeply into the national consciousness. From the historical point of view, this Puritanism was a backsliding in religion as momentous in shaping the imagination as the cultural reversion Cooper studied on the frontier. For, at least as apprehended by the literary imagination, New England Puritanism—with its grand metaphors of election and damnation, its opposition of the kingdom of light and the kingdom of darkness, its eternal and autonomous contraries of good and evil—seems to have recaptured the Manichaean sensibility. The American imagination, like the New England Puritan mind itself, seems less interested in redemption than in the melodrama of the eternal struggle of good and evil, less interested in incarnation and reconciliation than in alienation and disorder. If we may suppose ourselves correct in tracing to this origin the prevalence in American literature of the symbols of light and dark, we may doubtless suppose also that this sensibility has been enhanced by the racial composition of our people and by the Civil War that was fought, if more in legend than in fact, over the Negro.

More obviously, a third source of contradiction lies in the dual allegiance of the American, who in his intellectual culture belongs both to the Old World and the New. These are speculative ideas which I can only hope to make concrete and relevant in the succeeding pages. I would hope to avoid, at the same time, the rather arid procedure that would result from trying to find a contradiction behind every character and episode.

NOVEL VS. ROMANCE

Nothing will be gained by trying to define "novel" and "romance" too closely. One of their chief advantages is that, as literary forms go, they are relatively loose and flexible. But especially in discussing American literature, these terms have to be defined closely enough to distinguish between them, even though the distinction itself may sometimes be meaningless as applied to a given book and even though, following usage, one ordinarily uses the word "novel" to describe a book like Cooper's *The Prairie* which might more accurately be called a "romance" or a "romance-novel."

Doubtless the main difference between the novel and the romance is in the way in which they view reality: The novel renders reality closely and in comprehensive detail. It takes a group of people and sets them going about the business of life. We come to see these people in their real complexity of temperament and motive. They are in explicable relation to nature, to each other, to their social class, to their own past. Character is more important than action and plot, and probably the tragic or comic actions of the narrative will have the primary purpose of enhancing our knowledge of and feeling for an important character, a group of characters, or a way of life. The events that occur will usually be plausible, given the circumstances, and if the novelist includes a violent or sensational occurrence in his plot, he will introduce it only into such scenes as have been (in the words of Percy Lubbock)[12] "already prepared to vouch for it." Historically, as it has often been said, the novel has served the interests and aspirations of an insurgent middle class.

By contrast the romance, following distantly the medieval example, feels free to render reality in less volume and detail. It tends to prefer action to character, and action will be freer in a romance than in a novel, encountering, as it were, less resistance from reality. (This is not always true, as we see in what might be called the static romances of Hawthorne, in which the author uses the allegorical and moral, rather than the dramatic, possibilities of the form.) The romance can flourish without providing much intricacy of relation. The characters, probably rather two-dimensional types, will not be complexly related to each other or to society or to the past. Human beings will on the whole be shown in ideal relation—that is, they will share emotions only after these have become abstract or symbolic. To be sure, characters may become profoundly involved in some way, as in Hawthorne or Melville, but it will be a deep and narrow, an obsessive, involvement. In American romances it will not matter much what class people come from, and where the novelist would arouse our interest in a character by exploring his origin, the romancer will probably do so by enveloping it in mystery. Character itself becomes, then, somewhat abstract and ideal, so much so in some romances that it seems to be merely a function of plot. The plot we may expect to be highly colored. Astonishing events may occur, and these are likely to have a symbolic or ideological, rather than a realistic, plausibility. Being less committed to the immediate rendition of reality than the novel, the romance will more freely veer toward mythic, allegorical, and symbolistic forms.

THE HISTORICAL VIEW

Although some of the best works of American fiction have to be called, for purposes of criticism, romances rather than novels, we would be pursuing a chimera if we tried, except provisionally, to isolate a literary form known as the American prose romance, as distinguished from the European or the American novel. In actuality the romances of our literature, like European prose romances, are literary hybrids, unique only in their peculiar but widely differing amalgamation of novelistic and romance elements. The greatest American fiction has tended toward the romance more often than the greatest European fiction. Still, our fiction is historically a branch of the European tradition of the novel. And it is the better part of valor in the critic to understand our American romances as adaptations of traditional novelistic procedures to new cultural conditions and new aesthetic aspirations. It will not damage our appreciation of the originality and value of *Moby Dick* or *The Blithedale Romance* to say that they both seem to begin as novels but then veer off into the province of romance, in the one case making a supreme triumph, in the other, a somewhat dubious but interesting medley of genres and intentions. Inevitably we look to the writings of James Fenimore Cooper, for it was he who first fully exemplified and formulated the situation of the novelist in the New World. His first book, *Precaution*, was a novel of manners, somewhat in the style of Jane Austen. Considering this a failure, he wrote *The Spy*, a story of the Revolution, in which, following Scott, he put his characters in a borderland (in this case between the American and British armies) where the institutions and manners of society did not obtain. He sketched out in Harvey Birch the semi-legendary hero who would find his full development in Natty Bumppo. As for characterization and realism of presentation, he contented himself with what he called in *Notions of the Americans* "the general picture" and "the delineation of principles"—this being, as he said, all that could be expected of the American writer, given the "poverty of materials"[13] and the uniformity of behavior and public opinion. He introduced an element of melodrama, believing that this might be suitable to scenes set in the American forest, even though we had no mysterious castles, dungeons or monasteries. He introduced also a certain "elevation" of style and a freedom in arranging events and attributing moral qualities to his characters. It is thus apparent that if American conditions had forced Cooper to be content with "the general picture" and "the delineation of principles" this was, if a step away from the novel form proper, a step *toward* the successful mythic qualities of the Leatherstocking Tales. Here was proof of Tocqueville's idea that although the abstractness and generality of the democratic imagination would make unavailable some of the traditional sources of fiction, this abstractness would in itself be a new source of mythic ideality.

In Cooper's books we see what was to be the main drift of American fiction. Responding to various pressures, it would depart markedly from the novelistic tradition. When it did so, it would—with variations that may be observed in such writers as Hawthorne, Melville, Mark Twain, Faulkner, and Hemingway—become either melodrama or pastoral idyll, often both.

Although Cooper gave an indubitably American tone to romance he did so without ceasing to be, in many ways, a disciple of Scott. Another disciple of Scott, and to a lesser extent of Godwin,[14] was Gooper's near contemporary, the South Carolina journalist and romancer William Gilmore Simms.[15] This author is no less convinced than Cooper that romance is the form of fiction called for by American conditions. Historical romance was his particular *forte*, and his *Views and Reviews* (1895) contains an interesting investigation of the materials available to the American romancer. In his prefatory letter to *The Yemassee*, his most popular tale of Indian warfare (first published in 1835), Simms defines the romance as the modern version of epic:

> You will note that I call *The Yemassee* a romance, and not a novel. You will permit me to insist on the distinction... What are the standards of the modern Romance? What is the modern Romance itself? The reply is immediate. The modern romance is the substitute which the people of the present day offer for ancient epic. The form is changed; the matter is very much the same; at all events, it differs much more seriously from the English novel than it does from the epic and the drama, because the difference is one of material, even more than of fabrication. The reader who, reading *Ivanhoe*[16], keeps Richardson and Fielding beside him, will be at fault in every step of his progress. The domestic novel of those writers, confined to the felicitous narration of common and daily occurring events, and the grouping and delineation of character in the ordinary conditions of society, is altogether a different sort of composition; and if, in a strange doggedness or simplicity of spirit such a reader happens to pin his faith to such writers alone circumscribing the boundless

horizon of art to the domestic circle, the Romances of Maturin, Scott, Bulwer, and others of the present day, will be little better than rhapsodical and, intolerable nonsense.

　　When I say that our Romance is the substitute of modern times for the epic or the drama, I do not mean to say that they are exactly the same things, and yet, examined thoroughly... the differences between them are very slight. The differences depend upon the material employed, rather than upon the particular mode in which it is used. The Romance is of loftier origin than the Novel. It approximates the poem. It may be described as an amalgam of the two. It is only with those who are apt to insist upon poetry as verse, and to confound rhyme with poetry, that the resemblance is unapparent. The standards of the Romance... are very much those of the epic. It invests individuals with an absorbing interest— it hurries them rapidly through crowding and exacting events, in a narrow space of time—it requires the same unities of plan, of purpose, and harmony of parts, and it seeks for its adventures among the wild and wonderful. It does not confine itself to what is known, or even what is probable. It grasps at the possible; and, placing a human agent in hitherto untried situations, it exercises ingenuity in extricating him from them, while describing his feelings and his fortunes in the process.

Loosely written as it is, this statement, with its echoes of Aristotle's *Poetics*,[17] remains something of a classic in the history of American criticism, its general purport being one which so many of our prose fictionists have accepted. American fiction has been notable for its poetic quality, which is not the poetry of verse nor yet the domestic or naturalistic poetry of the novel but the poetry of romance. In allying romance to epic Simms was reflecting his own preoccupation with panoramic settings, battles, and heroic deeds; doubtless he had also in mind, vociferous nationalist that he was, the power of epic to mirror the soul of a people. There are many American fictions besides *The Yemassee* which remind us of epics, large and small; Cooper's *Prairie, Moby Dick, The Adventures of Huckleberry Finn*, Faulkner's *As I Lay Dying*, for example. Yet on the whole, American fiction has approximated the poetry of idyll and of melodrama more often than of epic.

Not all of Simms's own romances have the epic quality. *Confession: or the Blind Heart* (1841), *Beauchampe* (1842), and *Charlemont* (1856) are "tales of passion" and have to do with seduction, murder, revenge, and domestic cruelty. They are dark studies in psychology that reflect Godwin and the Gothic tradition at the same time that in their pictures of town life, lawyers, court trials, and local customs they forecast later Southern writers, such as Faulkner and Robert Penn Warren. Simms's stales of passion, however, are fatally marred by the carelessness and crudity with which they are thrown together, and it was in the work of Hawthorne that for the first time the psychological possibilities of romance were realized.

As we see from the prefaces to his longer fictions, particularly *The Marble Faun*, Hawthorne was no less convinced than Cooper and Simms that romance, rather than the novel, was the predestined form of American narrative. In distinguishing between forms, his Preface to *The House of the Seven Gables* makes some of the same points Simms had made:

> When a writer calls his work a romance, it need hardly be observed that he wishes to claim a certain latitude, both as to its fashion and material, which he would not have felt himself entitled to assume, had he professed to be writing a novel. The latter form of composition is presumed to aim at a very minute fidelity, not merely to the possible, but to the probable and ordinary course of man's experience. The former—while, as a work of art, it must rigidly subject itself to laws, and while it sins unpardonably so far as it may swerve aside from the truth of the human heart—has fairly a right to

present that truth under circumstances, to a great extent, of the writer's own choosing or creation. If he **think** fit, also, he may so manage his atmospherical medium as to bring out or mellow the lights, and deepen and enrich the shadows, of the picture. He will be wise, no doubt, to make a very moderate use of the privileges here stated, and especially, to mingle the marvelous rather as a slight, delicate, and evanescent flavor, than as any portion of the actual substance of the dish offered to the public. He can hardly be said, however, to commit a literary crime, even if he **disregard** this caution.

As Hawthorne sees the problem confronting the American author, it consists in the necessity of finding (in the words of the Introduction to *The Scarlet Letter*) "a neutral territory, somewhere between the real world and fairyland, where the Actual and the Imaginary may meet, and each imbue itself with the nature of the other." Romance is, as we see, a kind of "border" fiction, whether the field of action is in the neutral territory between civilization and the wilderness, as in the adventure tales of Cooper and Simms, or whether, as in Hawthorne and later romancers, the field of action is conceived not so much as a place as a state of mind—the borderland of the human mind where the actual and the imaginary intermingle. Romance does not plant itself, like the novel, solidly in the midst of the actual. Nor when it is memorable, does it escape into the purely imaginary.

In saying that no matter what its extravagances romance must not "swerve aside from the truth of the human heart," Hawthorne was in effect announcing the definitive adaptation of romance to America. To keep fiction in touch with the human heart is to give it a universal human significance. But this cannot be done memorably in prose fiction, even in the relatively loose form of the romance, without giving it a local significance. The truth of the heart as pictured in romance may be more generic or archetypal than in the novel; it may be rendered less concretely; but it must still be made to belong to a time and a place. Surely Hawthorne's romances do. In his writings romance was made for the first time to respond to the particular demands of an American imagination and to mirror, in certain limited ways, the American mind. In order to accomplish this Hawthorne had to bring into play his considerable talent for psychology. Cooper was not a psychologist of any subtlety and outside of the striking conception of the stoic inner life of Natty Bumppo, he gave to romance no psychological quality that might not find its close analogue in Scott. Although no one would mistake a fiction of Simms for one of Scott, Simms's originality was circumscribed by his apparent belief, as stated in the quotation above, that American romance would differ from earlier forms only because it had different material rather than a "particular mode" of rendering this material. His claim to originality was severely limited by the crudity and indecision of his literary form and of his psychological insights.

In the writings of Brockden Brown, Cooper, and Simms we have the first difficult steps in the adaptation of English romance to American conditions and needs. Following these pioneers we have had, ever since, two streams of romance in our literary history. The first is the stream that makes the main subject of this book and includes Hawthorne, Melville, James, Mark Twain, Frank Norris, Faulkner, Hemingway, and others who have found that romance offers certain qualities of thought and imagination which the American fiction writer needs but which are outside the province of the novel proper. These are writers who each in his own way have followed Hawthorne both in thinking the imagination of romance necessary and in knowing that it must not "swerve aside from the truth of the human heart."

The other stream of romance, justly condemned by Mark Twain and James, is one which also descends from Scott, and includes John Esten

Cooke's[18] *Surry of Eagle's Nest* (1886), Lew Wallace's *Ben Hur* (1880), Charles Major's *When Knighthood Was In Flower* (1899), and later books like *Gone with the Wind* and the historical tales of Kenneth Roberts. Although these works may have their points, according to the taste of the reader, they are, historically considered, the tag-end of a European tradition that begins in the Middle Ages and has come down into our own literature without responding to the forms of imagination which the actualities of American life have inspired. Romances of this sort are sometimes defended because "they tell a good story"—as opposed to the fictions of, say, Faulkner and Melville, which allegedly don't. People who make this complaint have a real point; yet they put themselves in the position of defending books which have a fatal inner falsity. The fact is that the word "romance" begins to take on its inevitable meaning, for the historically minded American reader, in the writing of Hawthorne. Ever since his use of the word to describe his own fiction, it has appropriately signified the peculiar narrow profundity and rich interplay of lights and darks which one associates with the best American writing. It has also signified, to be sure, that common trait shared by the American romances which are discussed in this book and all other romances whatsoever— namely, the penchant for the marvelous, the sensational, the legendary, and in general the heightened effect. But the critical question is always: To what purpose have these amiable tricks of romance been used? To falsify reality and the human heart or to bring us round to a new, significant and perhaps startling relation to them?

JAMES ON THE NOVEL VS. THE ROMANCE

In the two preceding sections of this chapter, I have tried to formulate preliminary definitions of "romance" and the "novel" and then to look at the matter in a historical perspective. In order to amplify the discussion, in both the abstract and the concrete, it will be of value at this point to return, with the aid of Henry James's prefaces, to the question of definition. In doing so, I shall risk repeating one or two observations which have already been made.

The first four prefaces James wrote for the New York edition of his works set forth, or at least allude to, the main items of his credo as a novelist, and although they are perhaps well known, there may be some advantage in looking them over again before noticing what James had to say directly about the relation of the romance to the novel. The four prefaces are those to *Roderick Hudson, The American, The Portrait of a Lady,* and *The Princess Casamassima.*

We might take as a motto this sentence, from the Preface to *The Princess*: "Experience, as I see it, is our apprehension and our measure of what happens to us as social creatures." Although James himself does not overtly contrast his procedure with that of romance until he comes to the Preface to *The American*, we shall be justified in ourselves making the contrast, since James is obviously seeking to show, among other things, how the imperfections of romance may be avoided. And thus we reflect that, in a romance, "experience" has less to do with human beings as "social creatures" than as individuals. Heroes, villains, victims, legendary types, confronting other individuals or confronting mysterious or otherwise dire forces—this is what we meet in romances. When James tells us that the art of the novel is the "art of representation," the practice of which spreads "round us in a widening, not in a narrow circle," we reflect on the relative paucity of "representation" in the older American romances and their tendency towards a concentrated and narrow profundity. Again we hear that "development" is "of the very essence of the novelist's process," and we recall how in romances characters appear really to be given quantities rather than emerging and changing organisms responding to their circumstances as these themselves develop one out of another. For if characters change, in a romance, let's say as Captain Ahab in *Moby Dick* or the Reverend Dimmesdale in *The Scarlet Letter* change, we are not shown a "development"; we are left rather with an element of mystery, as with Ahab, or a simplified and conventionalized alteration of character, as with Dimmesdale. Similarly, the episodes of romance tend to follow each other without ostensible causation; here too there is likely to be an element, either of mystery or convention. To "treat" a subject, James says, is to "exhibit… relations"; and the novelist "is in the perpetual predicament that the continuity of things is the whole matter, for him, of comedy and tragedy," but in a romance much may be made of unrelatedness, of alienation and discontinuity, for the romancer operates in a universe that is less coherent than that of the novelist.

As for the setting, James says that it is not enough merely to report what it seems to the author to be, in however minute detail. The great thing is to get into the novel not only the setting but somebody's *sense* of the setting. We recall that in *The Scarlet Letter* the setting, although sketchy, is pictorially very beautiful and symbolically *a propos*. But none of the characters has a *sense* of the setting; that is all in the author's mind and hence the setting is never dramatized but remains instead a handsomely tapestried backdrop. In *Moby Dick* the setting is less inert; it becomes, in fact, a kind of "enveloping action." Still only in some of the scenes do we have Ishmael's[19] sense of the setting; during most of the book Ishmael himself is all but banished as a dramatic presence.

The whole question of the "point of command" or "point of view" or "center of intelligence"[20] is too complicated to go into here. Suffice it to say that the allotment of intelligence, the question of what character shall be specially conscious of the meaning of what happens to and around him so that we see events and people more or less through his eyes, thus gaining a sense of dramatic coherence—these questions are less and less pertinent as fiction approaches pure romance. Natty Bumppo need be conscious only of what the Indians are going to do next. Hawthorne's Chillingworth[21] and Melville's Ahab are clairvoyantly conscious, but with a profoundly obsessive distortion of the truth. They are not placed in context in order to give concrete dramatic form to a large part, of what the author sees, as is the "point of command" in a James novel; all we learn from them is how *they* see. And as I shall suggest in speaking of *The Blithedale Romance*, the dyed-in-the-wool romancer like Hawthorne merely proves that you mustn't have a central observer in your story, because if you do you simply point up the faults of romance and admit your incapacity to follow out a fully developed novelistic procedure. In the romance too much depends on mystery and bewilderment to risk a generally receptive intelligence in the midst of things. Too often the effect you are after depends on a universe that is felt to be irrational, contradictory, and melodramatic—whereas the effect of a central intelligence is to produce a sense of verisimilitude and dramatic coherence.

One or two further items from the prefaces may point up the contrast. A character, especially "the fictive hero," as James says, "successfully appeals to us only as an eminent instance, as eminent as we like, for own conscious kind." He must not be "a morbidly special case"—but in romance he may well be. Again, says James, when economy demands the suppression of parts of the possible story they must not be merely "eliminated"; they must be foreshortened, summarized, compressed but nevertheless brought to bear on the whole. But in the looser universe of the romance, we may think "elimination" will be less criminal and unexplained hiatuses and discontinuities may positively contribute to the effect. To take an obvious case, in *Moby Dick* we are content to think the sudden elimination of Bulkington an interesting oddity rather than a novelistic blunder and we gladly draw on the poetic capital Melville makes of it.

As for the moral significance of the novel, James sees a "perfect dependence of the 'moral' sense of a work of art on the amount of felt life concerned in producing it." We must ask, he says, "is it valid, in a word, is it genuine, is it sincere, the result of some direct impression or perception of life." These questions bear less on the romance, one of the assumptions of which is that it need not contain a full amount of felt life, that life may be felt indirectly, through legend, symbol, or allegory. Nor does the romance need the sincerity of the novel; indeed, as Lawrence points out, American romances, especially, tend to make their effect by a deep "duplicity" or ironic indirection.

To come finally to James's specific comments on the question we are considering. In the prefaces he follows his own advice as that had been expressed twenty-odd years earlier in "The Art of Fiction"—he sees no reason, that is, why the practicing writer should distinguish between novel and romance. There are good novels and bad ones, novels that have life and those that haven't—and this, for the novelist, is the only relevant question. The implication is that the novelist will be also the romancer if the "life" he is rendering extends into the realm of the "romantic." But if we are not, except as critics and readers, to distinguish between novel and romance, we still have to distinguish within the novel that may be also a romance, the "romantic" from the "real." And this James essays in his Preface to *The American*. In rereading this early novel James found a large element of romance in the free and easy way in which he had made his semilegendary hero Christopher Newman[22] behave on his European travels. Particularly, James thought, the picture of the Bellegard family was "romantic." James had made them reject Newman as a vulgar manufacturer when actually common sense tells us that "they would positively have jumped at him." And James comments that "the experience here represented is the disconnected and uncontrolled experience—uncontrolled by our general sense of 'the way things happen'— which romance alone more or less successfully palms off on us." At the same time James finds an unexpected pleasure in rereading *The American,* which somewhat compensates for the lapses of verisimilitude. And his description of this pleasure makes a fair definition of the pleasure of romance— "the free play of so much unchallenged instinct... the happiest season of surrender to the invoked muse and the projected fable."

"The disconnected and uncontrolled experience," then, is of the essence of romance, and any adequate definition must proceed from this postulate. First, however one may clear out of the way certain conventional but inadequate descriptions of romance, it is not "a matter indispensably of boats, or of caravans, or, of tigers, or of 'historical characters,' or of ghosts, or of forgers, or of detectives, or of beautiful wicked women, or of pistols and knives"—although one might perhaps be a little readier than James to think that these things might be of service. Yet one follows him assentingly when he decides that the common element in sensational tales is "the facing of danger" and then goes on to say that for most of us the danger represented by caravans and forgers is certainly benign or impotent compared with the "common and covert" dangers we face in our everyday existence, which may "involve the sharpest hazards to life and honor and the highest instant decisions and intrepidities of action."

The "romantic" cannot be defined, either, as "the far and the strange," since, as such, these things are merely unknown, whereas the "romantic" is something we know, although we know it indirectly. Nor is a novel romantic because its hero or heroine is. "It would be impossible to have a more romantic temper than Flaubert's Madame Bovary, yet nothing less resembles a romance than the record of her adventures." Nor can we say the presence of absence of "costume" is a crucial difference, for "where... does costume begin or end."

James then arrives at the following formulation:

The only *general* attribute of projected romance that I can see, the only one that fits all its cases, is the fact of the kind of experience with which it deals—experience liberated, so to speak; experience disengaged, disembrolled, disencumbered, exempt from the conditions that we usually know to attach to it and, if we wish so to put the matter, drag upon it, and operating in a medium which relieves it, in a particular interest, of the inconvenience of a *related*, a measurable state, a state subject to all our vulgar communities.

And James goes on in words that are particularly illustrative of his own art:

The greatest intensity may so be arrived at evidently—when the sacrifice of community, of the "related" sides of situations, has not been too rash. It must to this end not flagrantly betray itself; we must even be kept if possible, for our illusion, from suspecting any sacrifice at all.

In a fully developed art of the novel there is, as James says, a "latent extravagance." In novelists of "largest responding imagination before the human scene," we do not find only the romantic or only reality but a "current… extraordinarily rich and mixed." The great novelist responds to the "need of performing his whole possible revolution, by the law of some rich passion in him for extremes."

To have a rich passion for extremes is to grasp both the real and the romantic. By the "real," James explains, he means "the things we cannot possibly *not* know, sooner or later, in one way or another." By the "romantic" he means "the things that, with all the facilities in the world, all the wealth and all the courage and all the wit and all the adventure, we never *can* directly know; the things that can reach us only through the beautiful circuit and subterfuge of our thought and our desire."

We hear much in these prefaces of the novelist's rich and mixed "current," of the possible "revolution" of his mind among extremes, of the "circuit" of thought and desire. James speaks, too, of the "conversion" that goes on in the mind of the novelist's characters between what happens to them and their *sense* of what happens to them, and of "the link of connection" between a character's "doing" and his "feeling." In other words James thinks that the novel does not find its essential being until it discovers what we may call the circuit of life among extremes or opposites, the circuit of life that passes through the real and the ideal, through the directly known and the mysterious or the indirectly known, through doing and feeling.

Much of the best American fiction does not meet James's specifications. It has not made the circuit James requires of the "largest responding imagination." And the closer it has stuck to the assumptions of romance the more capital it has made, when any capital has been made, exactly by leaving the Jamesian circuits broken. That very great capital can be made in this way James does not acknowledge or know, and hence his own hostility, and that of many of his followers, to the more extreme forms of American fiction—those we associate, for example, with Brockden Brown, Poe, Melville, and Faulkner.

Nevertheless James's theory of the novel, his idea of the circuit of life which allows him to incorporate in his novels so many of the attributes of romance, is the most complete and admirable theory, as at their best James's are the most complete and admirable novels yet produced by an American. And it is against James's theory and often, though certainly not always, his practice that we have to test the achievements of his compatriots. But the danger is that in doing so we should lapse into an easy disapproval of that "rich passion… for extremes" which James praised on his own grounds but which may be seen operating to advantage on other grounds too.

〔注释〕

1．源于詹姆斯（Henry James）的文学评论。作者在本章结尾有详述。

2. F. R. Leavis：利维斯（1895-1978），英国文学评论家，著有《英国诗歌的新义》（1952），《英国诗歌的传统和发展》（1936），《小说家 D. H. 劳伦斯》（1955）等。他的重要著作《伟大的传统》（1948）着重评论了奥斯汀、乔治·艾略特、康拉德和詹姆斯等作家的作品。

3. *The House with the Green Shutters*：《带有绿色百叶窗的房子》，英国作家道格拉斯（George Douglas Brown, 1869-1902）作，出版于 1901 年。

4. *Wieland*：《威兰德》，美国早期小说家布朗（C. B. Brown, 1771-1810）的第一部传奇小说。下文中《白鲸》（*Moby Dick*）、《皮埃尔》《*Pierre*》及《骗子》（*The Confidence Man*）皆为美国作家麦尔维尔的作品。《红色英勇勋章》（*The Red Badge of Courage*）为美国作家克兰（Stephen Crane, 1871-1990）的代表作。《麦克提格》（*McTeague*）为美国小说家诺里斯（Frank Norris，1870-1902）的作品。《当我弥留之际》（*As I Lay Dying*）为美国作家福克纳（William Faulkner, 1897-1962）的作品。《太阳照常升起》（*The Sun Also Rises*）为海明威（Ernest Hemingway, 1899-1961）的作品。《米玛镇》（*Middlemarch*）为英国女作家乔治·艾略特（George Eliot, 1819-1880）的名作。

5. Allen Tate：塔特（即 John Orley, 1899-1879），美国诗人和文学评论家。

6. *Our Mutual Friend*：《我们共同的朋友》，英国作家狄更斯（Charles Dickens, 1812-1870）的小说。

7. Marius Bewley：比尤利（1918-1973），美国文学批评家。

8. Hegelian：这里指黑格尔（G. W. F. Hegel, 1770-1831）的辨证逻辑。黑格尔为德国古典哲学的集大成者。

9. Dionysian：酒神式的，源于狄俄尼索斯（Dionysus）一词。狄俄尼索斯为希腊神话中的酒神，希腊悲剧就是从庆祝酒神的狂欢节中发展成型的。"Dionysian"意为"非理性的、潜意识的、狂乱的",同"Apollonian"相对。下文中"Indian"意为"印第安人的",亦即"原始的、非理性的"。

10. Howells:豪威尔斯(William Dean Howells,1837-1920),美国现实主义作家、文学评论家。

11. Manichacan:摩尼教的。摩尼教(Manichaeism),公元 3 世纪由波斯人摩尼(Mani,约 216-约 276)创立的一种原始宗教,宣扬善恶二元论:以光明与黑暗为善与恶的本原,光明王国与黑暗王国对立,善人死后可获幸福,而恶人则须堕地狱。

12. Percy Lubbock:卢柏克(1879-1965),英国文学批评家,著有《小说的技巧》(*The Craft of Fiction*)。

13. poverty of materials:引自库柏所著的《美国人的观点》(*Notions of the Americans*)一书。美国早期作家如欧文、库柏、霍桑以及稍后的享利·詹姆斯等在他们的作品或文章中均报怨美国历史短暂、文物典籍不足,因而缺乏创作素材。

14. Godwin:葛德文(William Godwin, 1756-1836),英国社会哲学家。

15. William Gilmore Simms:西姆斯(1806-1870),美国小说家,以写作历史体裁而闻名。

16. *Ivanhoe*:《艾凡赫》,英国小说家司各特的一部名著。下文中 Richardson:理查逊(Samuel Richardson, 1689-1761),英国小说家。Fielding:菲尔丁(Henry Fielding, 1707-1754),英国小说家。这两位作家尽管风格迥异,但都以描写现实生活见长。Maturin:马图林(Charles Robert Maturin, 1782-1824),爱尔兰作家,主要写哥特式恐怖故事。Bulwer:布尔沃(Edward George Earle Lytton Bulwer-Lytton, 1808-1873),英国小说家。

17. Aristotle's *Poetics*:亚里士多德的《诗学》,西方美学史上最早的经典著作之一,对后世美学和文艺批评影响极大。

18. John Eston Cook:库克(1830-1886),下文中 Lew Wallace(华莱士,1827-1905),Charles Major(梅杰,1856-1913),以及 Kenneth

Roberts（罗伯茨，1885-1957），皆为美国作家，以写作历史传奇见闻，作品销路很广。*Gone with the Wind*:《飘》，为美国作家米切尔（Margaret Mitchell, 1900-1949）所作。

19. Ishmael：麦尔维尔著《白鲸》的叙事人。

20. 指叙述角度。

21. Chillingworth：霍桑《红字》中的人物。

22. Christopher Newman：詹姆斯著小说《美国人》（*The American*）的主人公。下文中 Bellagard family 出自《美国人》。

Questions For Discussion：

1. Is Chase's thesis tenable that the American novel tends to rest in contradictions which constitute the basic features of American culture? Is the best American novel an acceptance of radical disunities? How does the American novel fit into Mr. Leavis's "great tradition"?

2. What are the differences between the American novel and the English?

3. How is the novel different from romances?

4. What does the term " broken circuit" mean?

For Further Reference：

1. Doren, Carl Van. *The American Novel*. New York：Macmillan, 1945.

2. Klinkowitz, Jerome. *The Practice of Fiction in America：Writers from Hawthorne to the Present*. Ames, Iowa：The Iowa State Univ. Press, 1980.

F. O. Matthiessen

马西森（F. O. Matthiessen，1902-1950），美国著名文学评论家，出生于加利福尼亚州帕萨底纳市，1924 年毕业于耶鲁大学，1925 年在牛津大学学习一年，1927 年在哈佛大学获博士学位。从 1929 年起到他去世，马西森一直在哈佛大学执教，任历史和文学教授。他作为文学评论家，对美国文学史及文学与社会的关系尤感兴趣。他还是一位虔诚的基督教徒和坚定的社会主义者。他的《美国的文艺复兴》（*American Renaissance*, 1941）已成为美国文学评论的经典著作。1950年他自尽卒世，享年 48 岁。马西森的作品总是充满感人的热诚和激情，他是一位具有独特见解的评论家。

American Renaissance: Art and Expression in the Age of Emerson and Whitman

美国现代著名诗人埃兹拉·庞德（Ezra Pound，1885-1972）说过，一种艺术的历史乃是名作的历史。马西森的《美国的文艺复兴：爱默生与惠特曼时代的艺术和表达》依照这一格言，对 19 世纪 70 年代以前，即浪漫主义或新英格兰超验主义时代的主要作家爱默生、梭罗、霍桑、麦尔维尔和惠特曼的主要作品进行了透彻而精辟的分析。马西森旁征博引，把关于这些作家的历史背景和生平方面的研究成果精粹巧妙地运用到自己的评述中，加之他本人的博览贯通和铢积寸累，使他的这部评论著作成为后来者进一步研究这段时期美国文学的必读之书。

马西森认为，他所评介的五位作家的共同之点在于他们"对民主的希望的热诚"。他以 19 世纪中期为焦点，诠解美国小说与诗歌的发展过程。他认为，艺术家对语言的运用最能敏感地体现文化历史，因此他极重视阐释这些作家的文艺理论。他不仅透彻地分析了诸如《白鲸》（*Moby Dick*）、《华尔腾》（*Walden*）及《草叶集》（*Leaves of Grass*）等名著的形式和内容，而且探索了至 20 世纪 40 年代尚被世人忽略的这些作家之间的关系。马西森详述了 19 世纪美国浪漫文学的重要方面，如爱默生的学说及其巨大影响、梭罗的基本思想和特点、霍桑同美国小说的关系及其传统对诸如詹姆斯（Henry James, 1843-1916）和艾略特（T. S. Eliot, 1888-1965）等后代作家的影响，以及惠特曼的诗歌和超验主义及浪漫主义有机整体论的关系等。马西森在论述这些相互关系的基础上探骊得珠，揭示出关于文学基本性质的一些模式和原则。他在谈及霍桑和麦尔维尔等人作品的悲剧观时强调了这些作家对个人与社会、善与恶等根本问题的关注。马西森还涉及爱默生、梭罗和麦尔维尔与英国 17 世纪诗人托马斯·布朗（Thomas Browne, 1605-1682）及约翰·堂恩（John Donne, 1571-1631）等人密切的亲缘关系，从而阐明了现代美国对堂恩所代表的"玄奥诗派"（metaphysical poetry）产生兴趣的文化传统基础。马西森还探索与叙述了惠特曼对柯勒律治（Samuel Taylor Coleridge, 1772-1834）"有机的文体"（the organic style）的运用和发展，从而帮助人们理解现代机能论（modern functionalism）的来龙去脉。

《美国的文艺复兴》一书是作者惨淡经营、笔耕十载而成的巨著，1941 年由牛津大学出版社出版，几十年来已再版多次。全书长达 678 页，共分四章，每章皆可自为一体，作为专著来读。第一章，"从爱默生到梭罗"，主要论述爱默生的思想，其中亦有相当的篇幅说到梭罗。其余三章分别专论霍桑、麦尔维尔和惠特曼的作品内容及风格，文笔细腻，佐证翔实，读来颇有发聋振聩的效果。最后一节以作家的题材

及其对美国民主"神话"的不同态度为线索，对这一时期内主要作家
进行了综合性论述。最后对惠特曼和麦尔维尔时代的神话同詹姆斯·
乔伊斯（James Joyce, 1882-1941）和托马斯·曼（Thomas Mann,
1875-1955）时代的神话，进行了发人深省的比较。

这里选注的是该书的最后一章。

An Excerpt from *American Renaissance: Art and Expression in the Age of Emerson and Whitman*

XII

MAN IN THE OPEN AIR

> "We have had man indoors and under artificial relations—man in war, in love (both the natural, universal elements of human lives)—man in courts, bowers, castles, parlors—man in personal haughtiness and the tussle of war, as in Homer—or the passions, crimes, ambitions, murder, jealousy, love carried to extreme as in Shakespeare. We have been listening to divine, ravishing tales, plots inexpressibly valuable, hitherto (like the Christian religion) to temper and modify his prevalent perhaps natural ferocity and hoggishness—but never before have we had *man in the open air*, his attitude adjusted to the seasons and as one might describe it, adjusted to the sun by day and the stars by night."

—Whitman

1. THE NEED FOR MYTHOLOGY

"We need a theory of interpretation or Mythology."

—Emerson's *Journal* (1835)

Where the age of Emerson may be most like our own is in its discovery of the value of myth. The starting point is in Emerson's "History," the opening essay in his first collection. He believed that history can be recreated only by a man for whom the present is alive. He had reached his initial premise of "the identity of human character in all ages" as a schoolmaster of nineteen. But his example then was the convention alone; "There is as much instruction in the tale of Troy as in the Annals of the French Revolution." In his mature work the emphasis was to be reversed. He was still concerned with "the universal nature which gives worth to particular men and things." But his chief desire was to translate the Then into the Now. In the academic sense, his interest was unhistorical. He was never satisfied with studying process. His belief that "the use of history is to give value to the present hour" was a natural corollary to his conception of time, that when we come to the quality of the moment we drop duration altogether. The opening sentences of *Nature* were a protest against being history-ridden: "Our age is retrospective. It builds the sepulchers of the fathers. It writes biographies, histories, and criticism. The foregoing generations beheld God and nature face to face; we, through their eyes. Why should not we also enjoy an original relation to the universe?"

His essay on "History" was thus compelled by his deepest needs. The compensation of the isolated villager lay in Emerson's assurance that "civil and natural history, the history of art and of literature, must be explained from individual history, or must remain words." His idealism and his individualism, his religion and his politics joined when he said: "I believe in Eternity. I can find Greece, Asia, Italy, Spain and the Islands, — the genius and creative principle of each and of all eras, in my own mind." Yet he had, as always, the counterpoise to his extreme subjectivity. If all public facts were to be individualized, all private facts must be generalized. On the last page of his essay he declared that every history should be written in a wisdom that looks on facts as symbols. And though he gave only the shadowiest indication of an awareness of the intricate forces that had conditioned the activities of men in any epoch, he held fast to his conviction of the artist's responsibility to "employ the symbols in use in his day and nation to convey his enlarged sense to his fellow-men."

We recall that Emerson also found "the cardinal fact" about Thoreau to be that he had learned to regard "the material world as a means and symbol." Thoreau's greater concentration carried him to explicit statement of the connections between symbol and myth. In his affirmation both of the moment and of all time, he often differed from Emerson only in his special philological twist: "The life of a wise man is most of all extemporaneous, for he lives out of an eternity which includes all time." He believed that mythology best expressed that eternal quality, and developed his meaning characteristically when reflecting on the beauty of some trout. He could hardly trust his senses as he stood over them, "that these jewels should have swam away in the Aboljacknagesic[1] water for so long, so many dark ages; —these bright fluviatile flowers, seen of Indians only, made beautiful, the Lord only knows why, to swim there! I could understand better for this, the truth of mythology, the fables of Proteus, and all those beautiful sea-monsters, —how all history, indeed, put to a terrestrial use, is mere history; but put to a celestial, is mythology always."

He made the same distinctions even in less poetic moods. Delighted with the kinship between folktales of widely separated races, he took this for "the most impressive proof of a common humanity." Moreover, he relived the process of myth-making for himself. He believed that "as men lived in Thebes, so do they live in Dunstable[2] today." If mythology was more primitive than history, the nature that had inspired the myths was still flourishing. He could walk out into a world "such as the old prophets and poets," Menu[3], Moses, Homer, Chaucer, walked in. He felt certain that he could establish this identity between past and present, because he had seized upon the living principle of nature. "If I am overflowing with life, am rich in experience for which I lack expression, then nature will be my language full of poetry, —all nature will *fable*, and every natural phenomenon be a myth." When he looked at the result rather than the process, he said: "A fact truly and absolutely stated… acquires a mythologic or universal significance."

Those sentences bring us back to the chief propositions about the organic style. They reassert the fusion between the word and the thing. They suggest again how Grimm[4] and others could arrive at mythology through the study of the origins of language. Emerson knew that "language is fossil poetry." Thoreau could back up the truth with a specific example. In studying a dictionary of the Abenaki[5] tongue, he perceived how language provides an index to the primitive and hence real history of any race. "Let us know what words they had and how they used them, and we can infer almost all the rest." The Indians had left records there of what they had seen and felt and imagined, what they were.

Thoreau's major concern was with what men are. If symbols from the past could give expansion to life, his intense localism kept him aware that most people discern the heroic past only, that they read Plutarch[6] but ignore John Brown. In the short essay on history that he wrote for *The Dial* and used again in his *Week*[7], the leading idea was: "Critical acumen is exerted in vain to uncover the past; the *past* cannot be *presented*; we cannot know what we are not. But one veil hangs over past, present, and future, and it is the province of the historian to find out, not what was, but what is. Where a battle has been fought, you will find nothing but the bones of men and beasts; where a battle is being fought, there are hearts beating…Ancient history has an air of antiquity. It should be more modern."

Thomas Mann[8] has said almost the same things about myth. He has called it the mode of celebrating life whereby the moment becomes infinitely larger than itself, and the individual existence escapes from its narrow bounds and finds sanction and consecration. Writing about "Freud and the Future," he stated that "life in the myth, life, so to speak, in quotation, is a kind of celebration, in that it is a making present of the past, it becomes a religious act; the performance by a celebrant of prescribed procedure; it becomes a feast. For a feast is an anniversary, a renewal of the past in the present." That is akin to Emerson's sense of what he could find in the Now, and celebrate as ecstasy. If the Now is eternal, the role of the prophet, the poet, becomes the same in all incarnations and Emerson becomes Saadi,[9] becomes a representative man.

Mann has found corroboration for his belief wherever he has turned, as did one of his "past masters," Nietzsche. In his essay on Lessing,[10] Mann set out to revitalize the meaning of "classic" by giving it a mythical significance, because "the essence of the myth is recurrence, timelessness, a perpetual present." He has spoken in almost the same terms of why he has been drawn to recreate the legend of Joseph[11]: "At any time，therein lies the mystery... For the mystery is timeless, but the form of timelessness is the now and here. For the essence of life is presentness." Freud has taught him that the infancy of a human being recapitulates the infancy of the race, and that myths are collective dreams: That Whitman arrived instinctively at the first of these truths is shown by the significance he could give to his own adolescent experience in such a poem as "There was a child went forth." Without ever formulating it into a theory, Melville illustrated the second truth in his chapter on "Dreams" in *Mardi*, in his discovery of "all the past and present pouring in me."

The reasons why we have felt again today the need for the reinforcement of myth could take us too far afield into a diagnosis of modern culture. We have inevitable been even more burdened than Emerson's contemporaries by the accretions of another century of the historical method. To Lawrence the merely critical mind had become so desiccating that he could find his renewal only in the realms of the unconscious, and declared that the great myths "now begin to hypnotize us again, our own impulse towards our own scientific way of understanding being almost spent." Twenty years ago Eliot spoke of how *The Golden Bough*[12] has influenced our generation profoundly. "What he discovered in anthropology is what Mann has also found, the reassertion—for an age almost overwhelmed by its sense of historical tendencies—of the basic dramatic patterns in the cyclic death and rebirth of nature and of man. In the primitive and the remote Eliot first regained contact with sources of vitality deeper than his mind. But unlike Lawrence, he was not satisfied with the primitive for its own sake. The problem still remained to integrate its vitality with the complex life of the present. In the year after *The Waste Land*, Eliot wrote a short essay on "*Ulysses*,[13] Order, and Myth": "In using the myth, in manipulating a continuous parallel between contemporaneity and antiquity, Mr. Joyce is pursuing a method which others must pursue after him… It is simply a way of controlling, or ordering, of giving a shape and a significance to the immense panorama of futility and anarchy which is contemporary history."

Even this glimpse of the myth-making faculty of our modern writers reveals a difference from Emerson's discovery of the paradox that "always and never man is the same." Emerson's innocent celebration of our common nature is radically unlike Mann's understanding of the disease latent everywhere in society, of man's corruptibility. Hawthorne is more like Eliot in his sense of the weight of the past, in his discernment of human traits which are constant beneath varying guises, and especially in his discovery of the lasting bond between the ages in man's capacity for suffering. His awareness of "the haunted mind"[14] also points towards our concern with the subconscious. But Hawthorne, alone of the five writers who have been the subject of this volume, did not conceive of his work in any relation to myth. He did not seek for universal analogies, but gained his moral profundity by remaining strictly a provincial and digging where he was. When he spoke of how "all men must descend" into "dark caverns... if they would know anything beneath the surface and illusive pleasures of existence,"[15] he showed where his consciousness of suffering had brought him. He was at the threshold of the descent into myth, he was using almost Mann's words in the "Prelude" to *Joseph and His Brothers*.[16] By the very fact of not consciously intending it, Hawthorne thus furnishes a striking if oblique, example of Emerson's and Thoreau's major reason for valuing myth, the way it reveals the inevitable recurrence of the elemental human patterns.

2. REPRESENTATIVE MEN

What Emerson conceived to be "the symbols in use in his day and nation," which he must use in turn if he was to express the meaning of its life, can be read most clearly in *Representative Men*.[17] Notwithstanding his satisfaction in his New England setting, he repeatedly declared that nature must be humanized, that its beauty "must always seem unreal and mocking, until the landscape has human figures that areas good as itself." His selection of such figures—Plato, Swedenborg, Montaigne, Shakespeare, Napoleon, and Goethe—is by itself ample evidence of his freedom from any restrictions of nationalism. He knew that an American renaissance needed the encouragement of great writers and thinkers. His timelessness took for granted his country's immediate share in the whole cultural heritage.

One inevitable stimulus to the form of this book was Carlyle's *Heroes and Hero-Worship* (1841).[18] But even before that appeared, Emerson had reached his own position that "there is properly no history, only biography," a position that Thoreau, in his confidence, carried to the point of saying, "Biography, too, is liable to the same objection; it should be autobiography." Carlyle's book was more than a stimulus; it provided the assumptions against which Emerson made a quiet but fundamental counterstatement. The difference between the titles is significant. "Great men," said Emerson, "the word is injurious"; and his grounds for objection to Carlyle were both religious and social. The source of his own title was probably Swedenborg, whom he celebrated for daring to take the last and boldest step of genius, to provide a theory of interpretation for the meaning of existence. Emerson quoted triumphant evidence of this from *The Animal Kingdom*:[19] "In our doctrine of Representations and Correspondences we shall treat of both these symbolical and typical resemblances, and of the astonishing things which occur, I will not say in the living body only, but throughout nature, and which correspond so entirely to supreme and spiritual things that one would swear that the physical world was purely symbolical of the spiritual world." Swedenborg's correspondences were in harmonious keeping with Emerson's belief: that what made one man more representative than another was the degree to which he was a receptive channel for the superincumbent spirit. Emerson held Carlyle's greatest blemish to be his inadequate understanding of spirituality. As Henry James, Sr.[20] phrased it: "Moral force was the deity of Carlyle's unscrupulous worship, —the force of unprincipled, irresponsible will." As a result he had glorified the strong men of history, in a sequence that devolved from Odin[21] to Cromwell to Frederick of Prussia, and thus helped prepare the way for our contemporary fatal worship of force. Though Emerson did not phrase himself with James' terseness, he grew to realize the drastic importance of Carlyle's defect.

What Emerson wanted to say was that "no individual was great, except through the general." He could go so far as to speak of the "inflamed individualism" that separated the man of power from the mass of his fellows. But he had not gone far enough to satisfy himself. As soon as he had sent *Representative Men* to press, he regretted that "many afterthoughts, as usual... come just a little too late; and my new book seems to lose all value from their omission. Plainly one is the justice that would have been done to the unexpressed greatness of the common owner and laborer." Thoreau had developed that same strain when writing his essay on Carlyle (1847). Balancing Thoreau's belief that history must be written as though it had happened to the writer was his equally strong conviction that if so written it would not be the history of reigns but of peoples. The trouble even with Carlyle's *French Revolution* was that there were no chapters called "Work for the Month," "State of the Crops and Markets," "Day Labor"—"just to remind the reader that the French peasantry did something beside go without breeches, burn chateaus, get ready knotted cords, and embrace and throttle one another by turns." In consequence of this lack, Carlyle did not speak to "the Man of the Age, come to be called workingman."

Thoreau thus phrased in its simplest form the theory of history that he believed must prevail in America. On the basis of such a theory Parker[22] held Prescott's[23] dramatic pageants to amount to no more than rhetorical *tours de force*, the product of a superficial aristocrat. In Parker's solid if somewhat naive objections we come to the democratic core of New England transcendentalism. For Parker believed that an American historian must write in the interest of mankind, in the spirit of the nineteenth century. He must be occupied with the growth of institutions, not with glamorous spectacles. "He must tell us of the social state of the people, the relation of the cultivator to the soil, the relation of class to class. It is well to know what songs the peasant sung; what prayers he prayed; what food he ate; what tools he wrought with; what tax he paid; how he stood connected with the soil; how he was brought to war; and what weapons armed him for the fight."

Through this view of history Emerson's age found its myth. Whitman joined to the full in the objections to Carlyle. Though he valued the challenge of Carlyle's attack on democracy, and wrote his own *Democratic Vistas* (1871) partly as an answer to *Shooting Niagara* (1867), he believed the worship of heroes to be poisonous. He was sure that "always waiting untold in the souls of the armies of common people, is stuff better than anything that can possibly appear in the leadership of the same." Even when talking about Lincoln he said that "man moves as man, in all the great achievements—man in the great mass." Thoreau did not share Whitman's confidence in mass movements, and said that California was "3,000 miles nearer to hell," since its gold was a touchstone that had betrayed "the rottenness, the baseness of mankind." Yet even Thoreau could respond to the myth of the age when he looked (1851) at a panorama of the Mississippi. He saw in his imagination "the steamboats wooding up, counted the rising cities, gazed on the fresh ruins of Nauvoo… I saw that this was a Rhine stream of a different kind; that… the famous bridges were yet to be thrown over the river; and I felt that *this was the heroic age itself*, though we know it not, for the hero is commonly the simplest and obscurest of men."

Emerson penetrated to the heart of this myth in his conception (1846) of "the central man," the creative source of all vitality. He imagined himself in talk with him, and that the voice of the central man was that of Socrates. "Then the discourse changes, and the man, and we see the face and hear the tones of Shakespeare… A change again, and the countenance of our companion is youthful and beardless, he talks of form and color and the riches of design; it is the face of the painter Raffaelle."[24] Next it is Michel Angelo, then Dante, afterwards Jesus; "And so it appears that these great secular personalities were only expressions of his face chasing each other like the rack of clouds." The Orphic[25] poet who spoke at the end of *Nature* had voiced a kindred parable of the continual renewal of man's heroic energy. Emerson felt that in *Representative Men* he had only managed to suggest this under a few shadowy guises. Looking back at this book a dozen years later, he said that he had sensed when writing it that Jesus was the "Representative Man" whom he ought to sketch, but that he had not felt equal to the task. What he might have tried to present is suggested by a few sentences in his journal several years before (1842): "The history of Christ is the best document of the power of Character which we have. A youth who owed nothing to fortune and who was 'hanged at Tyburn,'[26]—by the pure quality of his nature has shed this epic splendor around the facts of his death which has transfigured every particular into a grand universal symbol for the eyes of all mankind ever since." That is similar to Melville's conception of democratic tragedy, and also to what Hawthorne had perceived in Sodoma's[27] picture of Christ bound to a pillar—the union of suffering and majesty. But it is unlikely that Emerson would have concentrated long on the tragic aspect. Even in his journal he went on to say, "This was a great Defeat; we demand Victory," and to insist on the mind's conquest of Fate.

Where he was at his best in *Representative Men* was in translating Plato into Concord, in giving a portrait of Socrates as a "plain old uncle…with his great ears, an immense talker," "what our country people call an old one." Emerson's concern in this book with man's common nature also gave him an insight into the value of tradition that we would hardly expect from him. Elsewhere, as in "Self-Reliance," he often said, "Where is the master who could have taught Shakespeare?… Every great man is a unique." But here he saw that "the rude warm blood of the living England circulated in the play, as in street-ballads." He went even farther and declared: "What is best written or done by genius in the world, was no man's work, but came by wide social labor, when a thousand wrought like one, sharing the same impulse." Unhappily Emerson, as we have seen, could not make much out of that perception. The "genius of humanity" that he announced to be his real subject could become very amorphous, most devastatingly so in his vague treatment of his modern figures, Napoleon and Goethe. It was no accident that his passage on the different incarnations of "the central man" ended with these sentences, "Then all will subside, and I find myself alone. I dreamed and did not know my dreams."

3. AMERICAN DEMIGODS

Carlyle, who kept urging Emerson to carve an American hero out of the facts of the nineteenth century, drove through (1849) to an imaginative conception of a possible American myth of the frontier: "How beautiful to think of lean tough Yankee settlers, tough as gutta-percha, with most occult unsubdurable fire in their belly, steering over the Western Mountains, to annihilate the jungle, and bring bacon and corn out of it for the Posterity of Adam… There is no Myth of Athene or Herakles equal to this fact."

The circumstances of Thoreau's "heroic age" called out many independent efforts to create a mythology that would express it, conscious and instinctive, exuberantly playful and highly serious. Between them they give the collective portrait that Whitman wanted, the likeness of "man in the open air." Whitman's poetic phrase symbolizes the fact that this age of the rise of the common man was still mainly agrarian. The writers tended to show that even in their looks. All of Emerson's pictures could be those of a village parson. Melville as an old New Yorker still continued to look like a sailor, though not the "rubicund sailor" to whom Whitman seemed akin in Eakins' canvas. Thoreau struck a surprised admirer as being indistinguishable from "a respectable husbandman," and Hawthorne, though in appearance less a man of the country than the others, retained in his language the marks of his ineradicable rusticity.

Since they were still close to the soil, analogies with the great nature myths came naturally to most of them, though their awareness of these as analogies differentiate their creations from those of a primitive age. What Greenough found is relevant to their problem: "Though the country was young, yet the people were old…as Americans we have no childhood, no half-fabulous, legendary wealth, no misty, cloud-enveloped background." This fact may have determined in part why humor has been such a natural expression for our national character. Max Eastman's hypothesis about our particular enjoyment of laughter starts with some of the same facts that Greenough observed. He finds that we believe in being humorous more than most civilized peoples "because we have had the energy and the abounding spirits of a young nation, and yet our childhood fell in a day of skepticism instead of animal faith."

None of our major writers of the mid-century worked primarily in comic modes. Yet even Emerson said, in his essay on "Heroism": "The great will not condescend to take anything seriously; all must be as gay as the song of a canary, though it were the building of cities or the eradication of old and foolish churches." Though Emerson did not know it, the "frolic health" he wanted in our poets was the best description of the mood that produced the tall tale. Thoreau turned, half-humorously, to the possibilities of a new western mythology to take its place beside that of the Greeks: "Who knows what shape the fable of Columbus will at length assume, to be confounded with that of Jason and the expedition of the Argonauts. And Franklin—there may be a line for him in the future classical dictionary, recording what that demigod did, and referring him to some new genealogy, 'Son of—and—.' [31] He aided the Americans to gain their independence, instructed mankind in economy, and drew down lightning from the clouds!"

Melville's gusto enabled him to create modern myths befitting "the honor and glory of whaling": "Any man may kill a snake, but only a Perseus, a St. George,[32] a Coffin, have the heart in them to march boldly up to a whale." And if any Englishman should seriously maintain that St. George's dragon was "a crawling reptile of the land" instead of the great monster of the deep, so much the worse for that hero's legend; Melville's democratic scrutiny was also levelled on the contemporary recipients of the Order of St. George[33]; Let not the knights of the honorable company (none of whom, I venture to say, have ever had to do with a whale like their great patron), let them never eye a Nantucketer[34] with disdain, since even in our woollen frocks and tarred trousers we are much better entitled to St. George's decoration than they."

Melville's chief use of the mock-heroic, unlike the eighteenth century's, was not to satirize. Believing in the potentialities of his age, he wanted to magnify it beyond the scope of the past. He spoke of Hercules as "that antique Crockett"[35] and "Kit Carson." His own accents were at times closer than he probably realized to those of Crockett himself. When Melville wanted to rise to the heights of his theme he shouted, "Give me Vesuvius' crater[36] for an inkstand! Friends, hold my arms!" That might have been the gamecock of the backwoods warming up to proclaim that he was "half-horse, half-alligator, a little touched with the snapping turtle," who could whip his weight in wild-cats—and if any gentleman pleases, for a ten-dollar bill, he may throw in a panther-hug a bear too close for comfort, and eat any man opposed to Jackson.

The created heroes of the tall tales provided a substantial western fact for Carlyle, though not one whose value that prophet could recognize. Nor does Emerson, nor, for that matter, do any of our serious writers appear to have given attention to William Trotter Porter's *Spirit of the Times* (1831-1861).[37] Yet that "Chronicle of the Turf, Agriculture, Field Sports, Literature and the Stage," edited in New York, boasted that its circulation of forty thousand or more went to readers "from Hudson's Bay to the Caribbean," and that its contributions of native oral humor came from men of all sorts, army officers and country gentlemen, lawyers and frontiersmen, all "gifted with good sense and knowledge of the world," fond of whisky and story-telling. The *Boston Times* asserted as early as 1840 that Porter had "done more to develop and foster the humorous genius of his countrymen that any man alive."

Our concern with this material here may be only with the way it fills out the contours of the myth of the common man. The legend of Davy Crockett (1786-1836) shows how the myth-making faculty of the day could start with an actual man and transform him to fabulous proportions. The most extraordinary of the frontier humorists among Porter's contributors was George Washington Harris (1814-1869), the creator of Sut Lovingood.[38] "He brings us closer than any other writer to the indigenous and undiluted resources of the American language, to the tastes of the common man himself. The unprinted stories that legend attributes to Lincoln were probably not very different from those Harris put into the mouth of his mischief-making hero, a tough young frontier Till Eulenspiegel."[39]

Elected to Congress from the canebrake of Tennessee for no better reason than that he was a great bear-hunter, Crockett took himself seriously, but he was really a grotesque frontier joke. When he turned against Jackson for not being loyal enough to what Davy conceived to be the frontier interests, Whig politicians were quick to exploit this opposition. They encouraged him to go around the country making anti-Jackson speeches and let him sit on the same platform with Daniel Webster. The hands of clever journalists are discernible in the sketches of his legendary prowess that now began to appear under his name. Somebody said that he ought to be the next president, and he believed it. He boasted and strutted, and showed to the full his capacity for blatant egotism and resentful meanness. As Parrington[40] has remarked, Davy the politician, whose greatest asset for electioneering was the shrewd instinct when to pay for his constituents' liquor, was a huge figure for comedy; but

Davy the wastrel character, the reckless hunter who slaughtered the resources of the frontier, was "a hard, unlovely fact" typifying a stage of our civilization.

Instead of rising to the presidency, he failed of re-election to Congress. Staggered at first, he soon wrote characteristically, or so at least the legend wove: "As my country no longer requires my services, I have made up my mind to leave it." He determined to say good-bye to Tennessee and follow manifest destiny to the Mexican border. "I have a new row to hoe a long and rough one; but I will go ahead." He added, "I told my constituents they might all go to hell, and I would go to Texas." So he went, to live up to his legend, and was killed at the Alamo. And out of his farce sprang the materials for an American tragedy.

That tragedy was not written, but after Crockett's death the humor and imagination of the Southwest continued to dwell on him and made him into a more universal figure. Crockett Almanacs. illustrated with clumsy woodcuts, appeared all over the country (1835-1856), and their jokes and stories show how much that we have connected with Mark Twain really belonged not to any one man but to the frontier soil. The poetry of folklore also touched Crockett's legend. The bears and buffaloes are made to rejoice at his death "bekos the rifle of Crockett is silent forever." Then he came to life again in even bolder stature. One of the almanacs began his story by picturing him as a baby giant fed by buffalo's milk. Another affirmed that as a boy he had carried home five cubs in his cap. In still another he twisted off the tail of comet. Once he went up Niagara Falls on the back of an alligator: "The alligator walked up the great hill of water as slick as a wild cat up a white oak." Always a wanderer, he became in the end a demigod, a frontier Prometheus.

One January morning it was so all screwen cold that the forest trees were stiff and they couldn't shake, and the very daybreak froze fast as it was tryin' to dawn. The tinder box in my cabin would no more ketch fire than a sunk raft at the bottom of the sea. Well, seein' daylight war[41] so far behind time I thought creation war in a fair way for freezen fast; so, thinks I, I must strike a little fire from my fingers, light my pipe, an' travel out a few leagues, and see about it. Then I brought my knuckles together like two thunderclouds, but the sparks froze up afore I could begin to collect 'em, so out I walked, whistlin' "Fire in the mountains!" "…Well, arter I had walked about twenty miles up the peak o' Daybreak Hill I soon discovered what war the matter. The arith had actually friz fast on her axes, and couldn't turn round; the sun had got jammed between two cakes o' ice under the wheels, an' thar he had been shinin' an' workin' to get loose till he friz fast in his cold sweat. C-r-e-a-t-i-o-n! thought I, this ar the toughest sort of suspension, an' it mustn't be endured. Somethin' must be done, or human creation is done for. It war then so anteluvian an' premature cold that my upper and lower teeth an' tongue war all collapsed together as tight as a friz oyster; but I took afresh twenty-pound bear off my back that I'd picked up on my road, and beat the animal agin the ice till the hot ile began to walk out on him at all sides. I then took an' held him over the airth's axes an' squeezed him till I'd thawed' em loose, poured about a ton on't over the sun's face, give the airth's cog-wheel one kick backward till I got the sun loose—whistled "Push along, keep movin'!" an' in about fifteen seconds the airth gave a grunt, an' began movin'. The sun walked up beautiful, salutin' me with sich a wind o' gratitude that it made me sneeze. I lit my pipe by the blaze o' his top-knot, shouldered my bear, an' walked home, introducin' people to the fresh daylight with a piece of sunrise in my pocket.

The distinctively American thing about such legendary figures, Eastman has maintained, is not their size. "All mythical heroes have been exaggerations, but they have been serious ones. America came too late for that. Her demigods were born in laughter; they are consciously preposterous; they are cockalorum demigods. That is the natively American thing—not that her primitive humor is exaggerative, but that her primitive exaggerations were humorous." That generalization would apply to Paul Bunyan[42] and Pecos Bill and many others. But it does not seem to leave enough room for the deep strain of lyric poetry which runs through that final anonymous transformation of Crockett. And behind the extravagant high spirits of some of our folk heroes, you can occasionally catch a more serious expression. Mike Find (1770? -1823?), "the last of the boatmen," the king of the Ohio River outlaws before the coming of steam, vaunted himself on his prowess with women and whisky. Yet between his fits, of "flyting," he sometimes lapsed into sadness: "What's the use of improvements? Where's the fun, the frolicking, the fighting? Gone! All gone!" A boat song that kept alive his fame is a mournful elegy for a vanished past:

> Hard upon the beech oar
> She moves too slow!
> All the way to Shawneetown
> Long while ago.

Johnny Appleseed was never a boaster at all. In life he had been John Chapman (1775?-1847), a New England Swedenborgian who had conceived it to be his mission to sow fruit trees through the Middle West, and had spent nearly half a century travelling by canoe and on foot, reading aloud from the Bible and leaving orchards behind him. The Indians thought of him as a great medicine man. After his death from pneumonia following a long hard trip to a distant orchard, he became a frontier saint, almost a god of fertility.

...

4. FULL CIRCLE

"Make-belief is an enervating exercise of fancy not to be confused with imaginative growth. The saner and greater mythologies are not fancies; they are the utterance of the whole soul of man and, as such, inexhaustible to meditation. They are no amusement or diversion, to be sought as a relaxation and an escape from the hard realities of life. They are these hard realities in projection, their symbolic recognition, co-ordination and acceptance. Through such mythologies our will is collected, our powers unified, our growth controlled. Through them the infinitely divergent strayings of our being are brought into 'balance or reconciliation.' The 'opposite and discordant qualities' of things in them acquire a form; and such integrity as we possess as 'civilized' men is our inheritance through them. Without his mythologies man is only a cruel animal without a soul—for a soul is a central part of his governing mythology—he is congeries of possibilities without order and without aim."

—Richards,[44] *Coleridge on Imagination*

Thoreau's ability to create myth ran on a deeper level than his amused fancies about Franklin. Those fancies were the instinctive product of his sense of the age's plenitude. He would have liked Mann's description of myth as "the holiday garment," "the recurrent feast which bestrides the tenses and makes the has-been and the to-be present to the popular sense: Thoreau's own superabundant life let him find a river god in a logger on the Penobscot,[45] it let him read in Homer about "such afire-eyed Agamemnon as you may see at town meetings." He was following there one of Emerson's most fruitful leads. The birth of a first son (1836) had given Emerson's life at Concord its final consecration. He felt that he had at last reached the solidity of life's fundamental pattern: "A wife, a babe; a brother, poverty; and a country, which the Greek had, I have." Emerson continued these thoughts in a passage that he later incorporated into "History": "Our Admiration of the Antique is not admiration of the old, but of the natural. We admire the Greek in an American ploughboy often." Thoreau might have said that, but there turned out to be this crucial distinction: there was a great deal of admiration of the antique in Thoreau's practice, in the precision and toughness of language that the Greeks and Romans had taught him to be his goal. Emerson's heart, as Santayana[46] has said, "was fixed on eternal things," his Now was that of the metaphysicians', and—despite his earnest desire that it should be otherwise—had very little relation to an actual present or past. Thoreau possessed more of the past, not through his mind, but as an experienced linguistic discipline. Therefore he inevitably possessed a more concrete present as well.

He re-created a basic myth because he was able to assimilate his conscious analogies into re-enacting what Emerson had perceived but could not put his muscle into, the union of work and culture. As Odell Shepard has discerned, "This man who read his Homer in a hut by a woodland lake" can show us better, perhaps, than any other teacher we have yet had how to coordinate whatever is peculiarly American with the tradition of the ages. "The day after Thoreau had settled by Walden he felt that he had found the very light and atmosphere in which the works of Grecian art were composed, and in which they rest." He was glad on summer nights to sit on the shore of his Ithaca, "a fellow-wanderer and survivor of Ulysses." But the reason why his allusions did not become merely literary, the reason why he accomplished his rare coordination, lies in the way he reacted to his reading. Cato's *De Re Rustica*[48] did not remain quaint for him. He described it thus (1851): "A small treatise or Farmer's Manual of those days, fresh from the field of Roman life, all reeking with and redolent of the life of those days, containing more indirect history than any of the histories of Rome of direct, —all of that time but that time,—*here* is a simple, direct pertinent word addressed to the Romans. And where are *the Romans*?" Thoreau's answer was that the Romans are ordinarily "an ornament of rhetoric," but that "we have here their *New England Farmer* the very manual those Roman farmers read... as fresh as a dripping dish cloth from a Roman kitchen." It was as if he read the letters of Solon Robinson[49] and how much was paid to Joe Farrar "for work done."

Thoreau thus became an actor in the great cyclic drama, but did not give up his New England accent. He had not perceived more than Emerson of the New England character. For Emerson had caught its essence when observing the struggle between "sage and savage" in Ezra Ripley (1834): "These old semi-savages do from the solitude in which they live and their remoteness from artificial society and their inevitable daily comparing man with beast, village with wilderness, their inevitable acquaintance with the outward nature of man, and with his strict dependence on sun and rain and wind and frost, wood, worm, cow and bird, get an education to the Homeric simplicity, which all the libraries of the Reviews and the Commentators in Boston do not countervail." Thoreau had the immeasurable benefit of such thought from the day he listened to *The American Scholar*. He could give it sturdier expression. His words ring with the authority of having experienced both halves of his comparison when he says that Minott[51] tells his long stories with the same satisfaction in the details as Herodotus[52]. In his sympathy with the seasons as well as with the farmers' often grim effort to wrest subsistence from them, Thoreau learned that "the perennial mind" did not die with Cato, "and will not die with Homer." This mind was nothing rarefied; it was an integral part of the functioning of the human organism. What interested Thoreau most in literature was the expression of this mind, the insight it gave into collective existence: "it is the spirit of humanity, that which animates both so-called savages and civilized nations, working through a man, and not the man expressing himself," Thoreau had come to that fundamental understanding while studying the Indians, just as Mann came to it at the close of his essay on Durer,[53] in whose deep humanity he had found "history as myth, history that is ever fresh and ever present. For we are much less individuals than we either hope or fear to be."

Thoreau's accent is no less that of a New Englander for betraying an awareness of both the Romans and the Indians. Living in an age of waning Christianity, he became convinced that there was no important difference between his countrymen's religion and that of the ancient world: "the New Englander is a pagan suckled in a creed outworn." Thoreau's light-hearted worship, of Pan set the tone for his *Week*. But much of his praise of Jupiter in place of Jehovah was designed simply to shock, and some of it is merely frivolous gaining its license from the accepted fact of the Christian background. He struck his most autochthonous vein when he noted the difference between English and American time, how here he could penetrate almost immediately to a savage past. He was not a savage himself, more the villager than the hunter, but he felt in his world no unbridgeable gap between these roles. His sense of closeness to the Indian strengthened his hold on the primitive, and kept him from writing Victorian idylls. He was most nearly an antique Roman when he said: "Superstition has always reigned. It is absurd to think that these farmers dressed in their Sunday clothes, proceeding to church, differ essentially in this respect from the Roman peasantry. They have merely changed the names and number of their gods. Men were as good then as they are now, and loved one another as much—or little."

The source of vigor in Thoreau's New England festival was his knowledge that "the husbandman is always a better Greek than the scholar is prepared to appreciate." The old customs still survive, even while antiquarians grow gray in commemorating their past existence. The farmers crowd to the fair today in obedience to the same ancient law, which Solon[54] or Lycurgus did not enact, as naturally as bees swarm and follow their queen. Thoreau's quality there, as we have found it in *Walden*, is more cultivated than wild. It is more lyric and pastoral than heroic though this, like the question of whether he belonged to the village or to the forest or to the borderline between, is simply a matter of degree. He saw the classical present in his own surroundings just as Sarah Jewett[55] was to do when she envisaged the Bowden family reunion in its procession across the field to the picnic grove as though it was a company of ancient Greeks going to worship the god of the harvests: "We were no more a New England family celebrating its own existence and simple progress; we carried the tokens and inheritance of all such households from which this had descended, and were only the latest of our line." Unlike Thoreau's, Miss Jewett's tone is generally elegiac. Robert Frost has more of Thoreau's dramatic immediacy, but since the forests have now receded, and the cities have encroached on the farms, Frost's scope as a poet of nature has inevitably been contracted to the more purely personal.

The heroic quality is absent from *North of Boston*[56], if by that quality you mean what Thoreau could sense in Whitman, that he was "something a little more than human." Thoreau was not blind to the element of brag, but when he called on Whitman in Brooklyn (1856), he felt at once, "He is apparently the greatest the world has ever seen." It is hardly necessary to dwell on Whitman's creation of myth, since it is so explicit throughout the whole breadth of his work. He looked at the past in a more reckless mood than Thoreau: "As if the beauty and sacredness of the demonstrable must fall behind that of the mythical! As if men do not make their mark out of any times! As if the opening of the western continent by discovery and what has transpired since in North and South American were less than the small theatre of the antique or the aimless sleepwalking of the middle ages!" That was the opening blast of his 1855 preface, though he presently added:

> In the name of the States shall I scorn the antique?
>
> Why these are the children of the antique to justify it.

Whitman set out more deliberately than any of his contemporaries to create the kind of hero whom Emerson had foreshadowed in his varying guises of the Scholar and the Poet. Looking back over his career in his final preface, he said that *Leaves of Grass* had been impelled by his desire to realize his own personality, both physical and spiritual, in the midst of its momentous surroundings, "to exploit that Personality, identified with place and date, in a far more candid and comprehensive sense than any hitherto poem or book." He had said long before, "I have but one central figure, the general human personality typified in myself." He had felt from the time of his first *Leaves* that if his book was to be true to its American origin, it must be "a song of the great pride of man in himself." What saved Whitman from the last extreme of egotism was his insistence on the typical and his boundless store of fellow-feeling. His one quarrel with Thoreau was his "disdain for men (for Tom, Dick, and Harry); inability to appreciate the average." If the poet had discovered himself to be at the creative center of life, with all its potential energies radiating out from him, this discovery was the property of all. Whitman wanted his book to compel "every reader to transpose himself or herself into the central position and become the living fountain." He took his final pleasure in reflecting: "I have imagined a life which should be that of the average man in average circumstances, and still grand, heroic."

His work inevitably assumed cosmic proportions. He said that from the press of his foot to the earth sprang "a hundred affections" that eluded his best efforts to describe them. But the language of his poems does not suggest contact with the soil so much as with the streets of Brooklyn. When he thought of the past, his instinctive analogy was:

> Lads ahold of fire-engines and hook-and-ladder ropes

no less to me than the gods of the antique wars.

When he envisaged his "stock personality" in its most godlike stature, he made it come to life by breaking into slang:

> Earth! you seem to look for something at my hands,
>
> Say, old top-knot, what do you want?

Otherwise his cult of himself as the bearded prophet could lead into pages of solemn straining for effect. The dichotomy that we observed in both his diction and his content expresses itself again in the contrast between Whitman's actual and ideal selves. Tocqueville[57] foresaw his problem when he observed that the poet of democracy, having given up the past, thus ran the risk of losing part of the present in his excessive preoccupation with the future destinies of mankind. Lawrence's distinction between the poetry of the future and the poetry of the present is likewise partly relevant. Lawrence held that the first may possess the crystallized perfection of things to come whereas the second, lacking this, seeks to catch the present in all its confusion, and is "plasmic." Whitman possessed none of the power of thought or form that would have been necessary to give his poems of ideal democracy any perfection, and to keep them from the barrenness of abstraction. He created his lasting image of the common man and the pending action of this Time and Land we swim in when he remained the instinctual being who found no sweeter fat than stuck to his own bones.

He was never conscious of the dichotomy, but he described its consequences in his surprised and hesitant admission as an old man that Thoreau, though not "so precious, tender, a personality" as Emerson, was "one of the native forces" and so possibly "bigger." The heroic stature that Whitman recognized in Thoreau was the result of Thoreau's having lived up to his own dictum that "it is the faculty of the poet to see present things as if... also past and future, as if distant or universally significant." By so doing Thoreau made actual the classical present instead of merely perceiving it like Emerson. Whitman had neither Thoreau's lucidity nor firmness. By cutting himself loose from any past, he often went billowing away into a dream of perfectibility, which tried to make the human literally divine and was hence unreal. But because he was more porous to all kinds of experience, he gave a more comprehensive, if confused, image of his fluid age than Thoreau did.

The cult of perfection was an inevitable concomitant of the romantic cult of the future. The attitude behind both received its most searching contemporary analysis from Hawthorne. He sensed that Emerson's exaltation of the divinity in man had obliterated the distinctions between man and God, between time and eternity. Although no theologian, Hawthorne did not relax his grip on the Christian conception of time. This had been obscured by Thoreau and Whitman no less than by Emerson in their exhilaration over the fullness of the moment. Hawthorne knew that he lived both in time and out of it, that the process of man's history was a deep interaction between eternity and time, an incessant eruption of eternity into time. And he knew the tragic nature of such conflict. In spite of the capacity of man's soul to share immediately in eternal life, his finite and limited nature made it inevitable that nothing perfect could be realized in time. Hawthorne's understanding of human destiny ran counter to all the doctrines of progress. It made him cling fast to the quality of actual existence even though he was aware of its impermanence; it made him insist that "all philosophy that would abstract man from the present is no more than words." It made him, profoundly, conscious that the moments of greatest human import were the moments of moral crisis, for then men and women entered most nearly into the eternal nature even as they were aware of their limitations.

Such a reading of destiny came to Hawthorne through his resistance to what he could not deem otherwise, than transcendental fads. It enabled him to criticize, in *The Blithedale Romance*, one phase of the contemporary myth, the quest for Utopia. However inadequately worked out some of his social criticism may be, there is no questioning the acuity with which he saw the weaknesses of Brook Farm. He could not help feeling that its spirit was essentially that of a picnic, of an escape to a woodland paradise. As he watched the community's competition with the outside market-gardeners, he soon realized that with relation to "society at large, we stood in a position of new hostility, rather than new brotherhood." These views might well have seemed captious to George Ripley's[58], who gave his heart's blood to prove that such experiments could lead the way to a more just organization of society as a whole. Where Hawthorne's criticism runs no risk of being obscurantistic is in his portrait of Hollingsworth,[59] man the reformer. There Hawthorne could make articulate his understanding of what happened when a man failed to distinguish between time and eternity, between his fallibility and his longing for the ideal. Hollingsworth was desperately earnest in his scheme for reforming criminals "through an appeal to their higher instincts," but he had no faint inkling of the complexity of man's nature. He was warped by his single thought, to which he would brook no opposition, and was interested in other people only to the extent that they accepted his plan. He became an incarnation of the terrible egotism that mistakes its own will for the promptings of God.

Emerson had more opportunity to study reformers than Hawthorne, since they were always swarming around him, but he never saw the problem they presented with such deadly lucidity. He found many of them bores, but he was partial to their trust in uplift, and relied on compensation to atone for their want of balance. When Thoreau and Whitman thought of a reformer, they, like Emerson, remembered the heroic affirmation of John Brown, of whom Hawthorne said: "Nobody was ever more justly hanged. He won his martyrdom fairly and took it firmly." But both Whitman and Thoreau could have learned something from the example of Hollingsworth.

Their images of the rising common man are far more compelling than anything Hawthorne conceived through Holgrave[60]. But Whitman's belief in the poet as his own Messiah escaped Hollingsworth's tragedy only by the counterpoise of his generous warmth. And although Thoreau evaded the literal-minded apostles of improvement, his weakest element lay in the impossible perfection he demanded from mankind. ("I love my friends very much, but I find that it is no use to go to see them. I hate them commonly when I am near them.") So far as there was a defect in his valiant self-reliance, it emerged when he turned his back on other men, and sought for truth not in the great and common world but exclusively within himself.

What Hawthorne found through his descent into the caverns of the heart was the general bond of suffering. His discovery gave Melville his only clue through the labyrinth of the age's confusions. He plunged deeper into the blackness than Hawthorne had, and needed more complex images to express his findings. He developed one by likening Ahab's buried life, "his whole awful essence," to the mystic grandeur of an ancient statue far beneath the modern surface of existence. The primitive spoke to Melville with different meanings than it did to Thoreau. He might joke about Hercules as an antique Crockett, but he did not so often think of the presentness of the past as of the pastness of the present, of its illimitable shadowy extensions backward, to the roots of history, to the preconscious and the unknown. "Ten million things were as yet uncovered to Pierre[61]." The old mummy lies buried in cloth on cloth; it takes time to unwrap this Egyptian king. Yet now, forsooth, because Pierre began to see through the first superficiality of the world, he fondly weens he has come to the unlayered substance. But, far as any geologist has yet gone down into the world, it is found to consist of nothing but surface stratified on surface. To its axis, the world being nothing but superinduced superficies. That is akin to Mann's reflection on the bottomless well of the past, on the incertitude of the researcher as he lets down his plummet into unfathomable depths. But the author of *Pierre* did not possess Mann's humanistic patience. He had become identified with his hero's agony: "By vast pains we mine into the pyramid; by horrible gropings we come to the central room; with joy we espy the sarcophagus; but we lift the lid—and no body is there! appallingly vacant as vast is the soul of a man!"

Such a mood could lead only to nihilism. But the passion with which Melville made his demands upon life had given him previously an instinctive awareness of the significance of myth. He had commented in *Moby Dick* on the loss of poetic mythology "in the now egotistical sky." He had sensed the primal vitality of the stories that are preserved in the popular memory, and that help keep alive the hidden strivings of the human spirit by giving them concrete shape. He had sensed too the destructive quality of the enlightened mind if by its criticism it served merely to divorce man from his past by dispelling the reality of the myths, by reducing them to a remote and naive stage of racial development. Though Melville did not articulate his theory of history, he affirmed its values by finding figures of tragic stature on board a whaler, and in Ahab all the majesty of a biblical king. Melville knew that beyond the bright circle of man's educated consciousness lay unsuspected energies that were both magnificent and terrifying. He wanted to rouse his country to its "contemporary grandeur." His detailed recording of the whaling industry sprang from his comprehension that the living facts of ordinary existence were the source of whatever heroic myths Americans could live by. His choice of material was hardly thus deliberate, but by taking the segment of human activity that he knew best, he re-enacted through it the major significances of myth. He had been attracted to whaling as the great adventure of his day, around which had clustered such widely current legends as the one Emerson had reported in his journal (1834) after a trip from New Bedford to Boston: "A seaman, in the coach told the story of an old sperm-whale, which he called a white whale, which was known for many years by the whalemen as Old Tom, and who rushed upon the boats which attacked him, and crushed the boats to small chips in his jaws, the men generally escaping by jumping overboard and being picked up. A vessel was fitted out at New Bedford, he said, to take him. And he was finally taken somewhere off　Payta Head by the Window[62] or the Essex." That was the subject for an adventure story, but the way Melville transformed his version shows the principal function of myth, its symbolizing of "the fundamental truths." In his narrative of whaling Melville could see how this industry typified man's wresting a livelihood from nature and extending his power over the globe by peaceful commerce rather than by war. He could trustingly visualize the whale ship as a means of communication, battering down ancient prejudices, opening doors in the Orient, even, as we have noted, leading the way to the liberation of South America from autocratic domination and to the establishment "of the eternal democracy" there.

But that was scarcely Melville's main theme. The dark half of his mind remembered what effect the white man had left on the South Sea islands; and as he meditated too on the brutal savagery in the conquest of the whale, his imagination stirred to the latent possibilities in the story Emerson had heard. He grasped intuitively the process that Whitehead[63] has described: "We inherit legends, weird, horrible, beautiful, expressing in curious, specialized ways the interweaving of law and capriciousness in the mystery of things. It is the problem of good and evil. Sometimes the law is good and the capriciousness evil; sometimes the law is iron and evil and the capriciousness is merciful and good." Melville could not say directly whether the law was good or evil. He had been born into a world whose traditional religion was in a state of decay, and whose grim Jehovah often struck him as being only the projection of man's inexorable will to power. But as Melville responded to the Christian belief in equality and brotherhood, he poured out his praise to "the great God absolute, the centre and circumference of all democracy."

Melville did not achieve in *Moby Dick* a Paradise Lost or a Faust. The search for the meaning of life that could be symbolized, through the struggle between Ahab and the White Whale was neither so lucid nor so universal. But he did apprehend therein the tragedy of extreme individualism, the disasters of the selfish will, the agony of a spirit so walled within itself that it seemed cut off from any possibility of salvation. Beyond that, his theme of the White Whale was so ambivalent that as he probed into the meaning of good and evil he found their expected values shifting. His symbols were most comprehensive when they enabled him to elicit "what remains primeval in our formalized humanity," when they took such a basic pattern as that of his later discernment of Abraham[64] and Isaac in Captain Vere and Billy. When the Pacific called out the response of his united body and mind, he wrote the enduring signature of his age. He gave full expression to its abundance, to its energetic desire to master history by repossessing all the resources of the hidden past in a tuneless and heroic present. But he did not avoid the darkness in that past, the perpetual suffering in the heart of man, the broken arc of his career which inevitably ends in death. He thus fulfilled what Coleridge held to be the major function of the artist—he brought "the whole soul of man into activity."

〔注释〕

1. Aboljacknagesic：系作者杜撰，意为"令人陶醉的"。
2. Dunstable：邓斯特布尔，位于伦敦西北。
3. Menu：古印度贤人之一。

4. Grimm：指格林兄弟（Jacob Ludwig Carl Grimm，1785-1864；Wilhelm Carl Grimm, 1786-1859），日尔曼语言学的奠基者，曾通过研究印欧语系诸言的关系，试图发现统一的神话。

5. benaki：阿布纳基印地安人，从前居住在美国缅因州。

6. Plutarch：普鲁塔克（约 46-119），古希腊传记家，著有《希腊、罗马名人传》。下文中 John Brown：约翰·布朗（1800-1859），梭罗的同代人，美国废奴运动领袖，曾组织黑奴暴动，后被处决。

7. *Week*：指梭罗的 *A Week on the Concord and Merrimack Rivers*（1847 年）。

8. Thomas Mann：托马斯·曼（1878-1955），德国伟大的小说家，曾获诺贝尔文学奖。

9. Saadi：萨迪（约 1213-1292），波斯诗人，著有《果园》和《蔷薇园》。

10. Lessing：莱辛（Gotthold Ephraim Lessing, 1729-1781），德国戏剧作家和批评家。托马斯·曼关于莱辛的论文载于他的论文集《高贵的精神》（1945）。

11. Joseph：约瑟，《圣经》中人物。约瑟被其兄弟卖给埃及人为奴，历经磨难，成为埃及的大臣；后来他的兄弟和以色列部族荒年觅食逃往埃及，方得以幸存。

12. *The Golden Bough*;《金枝》，苏格兰人类学家弗雷泽（Sir James Frazer, 1854-1941）著。

13. *Ulysses*：指小说《尤利西斯》，爱尔兰小说家乔伊斯（James Joyce，1882-1941）著。

14. 出自霍桑的随笔 "The Haunted Mind"。

15. 引自霍桑的 *The Marble Faun*。

16. *Joseph and His Brothers*：《约瑟夫和他的弟兄们》，托马斯·曼所著的四部曲长篇小说，1933 年出版。

17. *Representative Men*：《人杰》，爱默生的名著之一。

18. Carlyle：卡莱尔（Thomas Carlyle，1795-1881），苏格兰散文作家、历史学家、哲学家，著述甚丰，下文所指他的设想，即"The History

of the world is but the Biography of great men"。参阅《英雄与英雄崇拜》第1讲。

19. *The Animal Kingdom*：指 Swedenborg 的 *The Economy of the Animal Kingdom* (1846)。

20. Henry James, Sr.：老詹姆斯（1811-1882），美国哲学家、作家，美国小说家亨利·詹姆斯之父。

21. Odin：北方神话的主神，造物者，卡莱尔称之为"Hero as Divinity"。下文中 Cromwell：克伦威尔（Oliver Cromwell，1599-1658），英国资产阶级革命时国会军领袖，推翻斯图亚特王朝，后称护国公。Frederick of Prussia：指弗雷德里克二世（1712-1796），普鲁士国王，其统治较开明，对普鲁士的发展起了一定作用。

22. Parker：帕克（Theodore Parker, 1810-1860），美国学者、教士。

23. Prescott：普雷斯科特（William Hickling Prescott, 1796-1859），美国历史学家。

24. Raffaelle：亦写为 Raphael, 拉斐尔（Sanziol Raphael, 1483-1520），意大利画家。下文中 Michel Angelo，亦写为 Michelangelo，指米开朗基罗（Buonarrotti Michelangelo，1475-1564），意大利雕刻家、画家、建筑家、诗人。

25. Orphic：源于希腊神话中理想的琴手和诗人 Orpheus，他崇拜酒神。Orphic 延伸意"mystic"。The Orphic poet：理想的诗人。在这里指爱默生。

26. Tyburn：在伦敦市区，过去常在该地处决犯人。

27. Sodoma：即 Giovanni Antonio Bazzi（1477-1549），意大利画家。文中所指的画曾在霍桑的 *The Marble Faun* 中屡被提及。

28. Eakins：伊金斯（Thomas Eakins,1844-1916），美国画家，擅长肖像画。

29. Greenough：格里诺（Horatio Greenough, 1805-1852），美国雕塑家。

30. Max Eastman：伊斯门（1883-1969），美国作家。

31. "Son of—and—"："某人与某人之子"；希腊神话中介绍神或

人的身世时惯用的格式。

32. St. George：圣乔治，英国的"Patron Saint"，据传他曾杀死过一条龙。有学者认为此传说同佩尔修斯（Perseus）传说有关。下文中 Coffin：麦尔维尔小说《白鲸》中的人物。

33. The Order of St. George：圣乔治勋章。

34. Nantucketer：Nantucket 人。Nantucket 位于马萨诸塞州东南，一度为捕鲸业中心。

35. Crockett：指 David（Davy）Crockett（1786-1836），曾任美国国会议员，反对杰克逊，其事迹为报界大事渲染。下文中 Kit Carson：卡森（1809-1868），著名边地人，向导，不少边地故事都与他有关。

36. Vesuvius crater：维苏威火山口。维苏威火山位于那不勒斯海湾以西，公元 79 年爆发时曾摧毁庞贝市。

37. William Trotter Porter：波特（1809-1858），曾创办《时代精神》（*Spirit of the Times*）杂志（1831-1861）。

38. Sut Lovingood：哈里斯所著的《苏特的故事》（*Sut Lovingood Yarns*）一书。

39. Till Hulenspiegel：中世纪一文学人物，哈里斯的人物苏特与之相似。

40. Parrington：指帕灵顿（Vernon Louis Parrington, 1871-1929），美国学者，思想史家、文学史家。

41. war= was; 下文中 freezen = frozen; afore=before; arter =after; airth =earth; friz= frozen; thar＝there; at=are（应为 is）；agin＝against; ile=oil; sich＝such。

42. Paul Bunyan：五大湖与太平洋西北部伐木工人中流传的故事中的主人公，身高力大。下文中 Pecos Bill：西南部故事中的巨人英雄。

43. John Henry：一些黑人歌谣和幽默故事（Tall Tale）中的主人公。

44. Richards：理查兹（I. A. Richards, 1893-1979），英国文学批评家。

45. The Penobscot：缅因州中部一河流。

46. Santayana：桑塔亚那（George Santayana, 1863-1952），哲学家、诗人，生于西班牙，1872 年赴美，但保留西班牙国籍。

47. 指梭罗。

48. Cato：加图（Marcus Porcius Cato, 234-149 BC），古罗马政治家。*De Re Rustica*：《农事论》。

49. Solon Robinson：鲁宾逊（1803 1880），印第安那州政治、舆论、贸易方面的领袖人物。

50. Ezra Ripley：里普利（1751-1841），新英格兰一牧师。爱默生在一篇纪念文章中曾提到他。

51. Minott：英国 14 世纪一些关于战争的诗歌的作者。

52. Herodotus：约纪元前 484-430 至 420 年。古希腊历史学家，被称为"历史学之父"。

53. Durer：丢勒（Albrecht Durer，1471-1528），德国画家。

54. Solon：梭伦（约纪元前 630-约 560），古希腊雅典政治家、诗人。下文中 Lycurgus：（约纪元前 390-324），古希腊演说家和金融家。

55. Sarah Jewett：朱厄特（1849-1909），美国小说家。下文中"the Bowden family reunion"出自米厄特代表作《尖尖的枞树之乡》（*The Country of Pointed Firs*, 1896）。

56. *North of Boston*：弗罗斯特的诗集。

57. Tocqueville：指 Clerel de Tocquevllle（1805-1859），法国作家、政治家，著有《美国的民主》等。

58. George Ripley：里普利（1802-1880），美国宗教思想家、作家、改革家，曾建立乌托邦布鲁克农庄。

59. Hollingsworth：霍桑《福谷传奇》（*The Blithedale Romance*）中的人物。

60. Holgrave：霍桑《七个尖角阁的房子》（*The House of the Seven Gables*）中的人物。

61. Pierre：皮埃尔，麦尔维尔所著的《皮埃尔》（*Pierre*）的主人公。

62. the Window：船名；下文中 Essex 亦为船名。

63. Whitehead：怀特黑德（Alfred North Whitehead, 1861-1947），英国数学家、哲学家。

64. Abraham：亚伯拉罕, Isaac：以撒，均为《旧约》中人物。下文中 Captain Vere and Billy：麦尔维尔小说《比利·巴德》（*Billy Budd*）中的人物。

Questions For Discussion：

1. What was it that made Emerson and his contemporaries feel the acute need of a mythology?

2. What is the difference in emphasis between Emerson's representative man and Thomas Carlyle's hero? What does he mean by "genius of humanity"?

3. The American experience, one important aspect of which was the frontiers continually pushed further west, constitutes the basis of American folklore. Discuss the growth of American folklore with reference to relevant literary works.

4. How did the major writers of the age of American Renaissance help in their own ways toward representing the spirit of their times?

5. To what extent did these writers succeed in developing an original relationship to the world in which they lived?

For Further Reference：

1. Foerster, Norman. *American Criticism: A Study in Literary Theory from Poe to the Present*. New York: 1928.

2. Foerster, Norman. *The Humanities and the Common Man*. New York: 1946.

3. Feidelson, Charles Jr., and Paul Brodtkorb, eds. *Interpretations of American Literature*. New York: 1959.

Charles Feidelson

查尔斯·菲德尔森（Charles Feidelson，1919- ），美国文学评论家。早年就读于耶鲁大学，后为耶鲁大学英文教授。《美国文学中的象征主义》（*Symbolism and American Literature*，1953）是他最著名的文学评论专著。

Symbolism and American Literature

〔作品介绍〕

《美国文学中的象征主义》一书是研究美国文学，特别是 19 世纪浪漫主义时期美国文学的经典文学评论专著，1953 年由芝加哥大学出版社出版。作者在《序言》中明确表示，这一时期几位著名作家——霍桑、麦尔维尔、惠特曼、爱默生及埃德加·爱伦·坡的共同点不是 F. O. 马西森在其《美国的文艺复兴》一书中所说的对民主前景的热诚，而是他们对象征主义手法的兴趣和运用。

菲德尔森认为，美国文学中的象征主义是 17 世纪及 18 世纪美国文明史发展的必然产物。他在对霍桑、惠特曼、麦尔维尔及坡等作家进行重点分析后指出，象征主义是 19 世纪中期美国文学创作的动力之一。它是这些作家进行创作的指导原则，既是技巧，又是内容。菲德尔森还用一整章（第二章）的篇幅追溯了象征主义的发展过程。他指出，象征主义是现代文学的显著特征之一。象征主义力求在二元论的前提之外寻觅重使表面分裂的世界趋于统一的可能性；象征主义媒介使物我合而为一。菲德尔森追溯了 19 世纪美国文学中象征主义的渊源。他指出，美国清教主义传统决定了美国清教徒自从踏上北美大陆以后便逐渐形成的象征主义的观察世界的独特方式。另外，美国文学中的象征主义也在不同程度上受到国外思想如拉莫斯、笛卡尔、洛克、康德、休姆等哲学家的思想的影响。

　　本书详细地论述了爱默生和麦尔维尔两位作家的作品中的象征主义思想及手法。作者认为他们代表着美国象征主义运动的两个极端，而其他的主要作家则簇集在他们的周围——梭罗与惠特曼尾随在爱默生之后，霍桑和坡则离他较远。爱默生堪称为美国象征主义运动的理论家，他的"辩证"认识方法解决了二元论问题。他的名作《论自然》是运用象征主义的典型作品。麦尔维尔是自觉的艺术家。他的作品是他的"一切事物里都隐藏着某种含义"的思想的体现。菲德尔森对麦尔维尔的重要作品《白鲸》等书的研究令人信服地说明了这一点。

　　这里选注的是该书第三章。

An Excerpt from *Symbolism and American Literature*

III. AN AMERICAN TRADITION

What could become of such a child of the seventeenth and eighteenth centuries, when he should wake up to find himself required to play the game of the twentieth?

The Education of Henry Adams[1]

John Winthrop records in his journal that in the midst of a sermon before the synod at Cambridge a snake appeared behind the pulpit and was killed by one of the elders. Winthrop's comment, with its queer leap from fact as fact to fact as meaning, embodies a kind of symbolic perception that pervaded the life of the American Puritans:

> This being so remarkable, and nothing falling out but by divine providence, it is out of doubt, the Lord discovered somewhat of his mind in it. The serpent is the devil; the synod, the representative of the churches of Christ in New England. The devil had formerly and lately attempted their disturbance and dissolution; but their faith in the seed of the woman[2] overcame him and crushed his head.

What John Winthrop felt in the Cambridge meeting-house was neither a historical event nor an allegorical fancy but an experience that united the objectivity of history with the meaningfulness of Scripture. The deviltry of the serpent was as present as its scales; to name the creature as a serpent was to imbue it with the quality of Satan. The destruction of the serpent was a symbolic act grounded in biblical speech and in the heroic dreams of the New England theocracy. A similar passage occurs in the diary of Samuel Sewall[3], Cotton Mather was visiting Sewall's house during a hailstorm and "had just been mentioning that more Ministers Houses than others proportionably had been smitten with Lightening, enquiring what the meaning of God should be in it." A moment later the hail had broken the windows; Mather "told God He had broken the brittle part of our house, and prayed that we might be ready for the time when our Clay-Tabernacles[4] should be broken." Within, not superadded to such happenings was a constitutive language; the devil-serpent and the body-house took shape and were experienced as radical metaphors made by God. As Joshua Moody[5] stated, the practical activities of life were capable of being transmuted, "spiritualized," by being conceived under the aspect of scriptural usage: "All our Relations and Conditions, as well as Imployments, are... improved to our Hands by the spirit of god in his Word... From the King upon the Throne to the Hewer of wood and drawer of water, the Lord is in his word teaching us by such familiar and known

Metaphors taken from those Callings that we are versed in."

The symbols themselves were meager, for the mental economy of the Puritans gave little scope for aesthetic realization of the natural world. These men narrowed "the meaning of God" to the meanings of a crabbed schoolmaster. Yet the symbolizing process was constantly at work in their minds. For them, the word "wilderness" inherently united the forty years of the ancient Hebrews[6] with the trials of the New England forest. "When they wandered in the deserte wilderness out of the way, and found no citie to dwell in, both hungrie, and thirstie, their sowle was overwhelmed in them." Here for a moment Bradford is not merely narrating the facts of Plymouth history; he is invoking an image which colored that history as it was actually experienced. And the symbol took on another aspect in the words of Thomas Shepard: "Wee cannot see but the rule of Christ to his Apostles and Saints, and the practise of Gods Saints in all ages, may allow us this liberty as well as others, to fly into the Wilderness from the face of the Dragon." When Edward Johnson[7] urges all who long for the destruction of Antichrist to "pray continually with that valiant worthy Joshua[8] that the Sun may stand still in Gibeon, and the Moone in the vally of Aijalon," persons and places like Joshua, "Gibeon," and "Aijalon" are drawn out of the realm of biblical history and become parts of a living language through which he perceives the world. Johnson has a vision of Christ as an oriental monarch, in which the terms of kingship permeate the conception of God, and a complete fusion, based on the language of Scripture, takes place:

> See, there's their glorious King Christ one [on] that white Horse, whose hoofes like flint cast not only sparkes, but flames of fire in his pathes. Behold his Crown beset with Carbunkles, wherein the names of his whole Army are written. Can there be ever night in his Presence, whose eyes are ten thousand times higher [brighter] than the Sun? Behold his swiftness, all you that have said, where is

the promise of his comming?[9]

In the everyday life of New England images like the "Holy commonwealth" and the "Wars of the Lord" converted human activity into a symbolic drama. New England was "the place where the Lord will create a new Heaven, and a new Earth in, New Churches, and a new Commonwealth together." The unfolding drama was at once human and divine; physical life was simultaneously spiritual. Every passage of life, enmeshed in the vast context of God's plan, possessed a delegated meaning. Under the aspect of the Holy Commonwealth, the crude huts and muddy streets were transmogrified into a focal symbol of God's emerging idea: "Wee are as a City set upon an hill, in the open view of all the earth, the eyes of the world are upon us." As the colonies became more worldly, and the gap between practical life and its symbolic aura widened, the ministers insisted the more strongly that New England was an emblem of God's thought, not a commercial enterprise:

> 'Tis possible that our Lord Jesus Christ carried some thousands of Reformers into the retirements of an American desert, on purpose that... He might there, to them first, and then by them, give a specimen of many good things, which He would have His Churches elsewhere aspire and arise unto; and *this* being done, he knows not whether there be not *all* done, that New England was planted for; and whether the Plantation may not, soon after this, come to nothing. [10]

Just as the Heavenly City was implicit in the Colonial villages, the conflict of good and evil in New England was an epitome of the war of Heaven and Hell, not merely in the sense of representing it but as an organic part of it, a true synecdoche. The Old Testament battles were at one with the slaughter of the Indians, the rooting-out of heresy, and the execution of witches. In Edward Johnson's *Wonder-working Providence* King Christ sends out his heralds to enlist soldiers:

For the Armies of the great Jehovah are at hand. See you not his Enemies stretched out on tiptoe, proudly daring on their thresholds, a certaine signe of their sudden overthrow? be not daunted at your small number, for every common Souldier in Christs Campe shall be as David,[11] who slew the great Goliah, and his Davids shall be as the Angels of the Lord, who slew 158,000 in the Assyrian Army.

Satan was present in the Indians, "their quarrell being as ancient as Adams time, propagated from that old enmity betweene the Seede of the Woman, and the Seed of the Serpent, who was the grand signor of this war in hand"; and it seemed to some of the soldiers, quite literally, that the Indians' bodies were impervious to swords because the devil was in them. The Wars of the Lord, which included all the "manifold afflictions and disturbances of the churches in New England," were radically metaphoric, a mode of perception that united past and present, idea and material fact, in the objectively given. Satan, the age-old Enemy, was an embodied idea. In the days of Moses,[12] says Cotton Mather, wildernesses "were counted very much an habitation of devils"; indeed, he adds emphatically, they "really were what they were counted." And Moses lived on in the diabolic wilderness, for "the Christians who were driven into the American desert, which is now call'd New England, have to their sorrow seen Azazel[13] dwelling and raging there in very tragical instances."

The wearisome reiteration of "providences" in the Puritan writings is actually a record of symbolic experience that never attained formal literary structure. The commissioning of a history of Massachusetts Bay in order "to take due notice of all occurrances & passages of Gods providence towards the people of this jurisdiction since their first arrivall in these parts" reflected a popular mind that could grasp events only in terms of a totality, the mind of God, presupposed by every occurrence. Memoirs were cast so as to reveal God's intention at every juncture. A favorable wind was God's answer to prayer, the death of a profane young man was "a spetiall worke of Gods providence," and the triumph of the Pilgrims over hardship was an example to the indifferent world. Cotton Mather gathered such "significant" events by the score, and in 694 the president and fellows of Harvard College proposed a systematic collection:

> The things to be esteemed *memorable*, are especially all *unusual accidents*, in the heaven, or earth, or water; all wonderful *deliverances* of the distressed; mercies to the godly; *judgments* on the wicked; and more glorious fulfilment of either the *promises* or the *threatenings* in the Scriptures of truth; with *apparitions*, *possessions*, *inchantments*, and all extraordinary things wherein the existence and agency of the *invisible world* is more sensibly demonstrated. [14]

Trivial and grotesque as the individual "providences" and mechanical compilations often appear, in them a powerful imaginative capacity was haltingly exercised. Behind the "providences," and referred to in each, was Providence, the eternal "concurrence" of God sustaining the order of things and giving to divine and human acts a perpetual unison. In government, for instance, "there are not two several and distinct actings, one of God, another of the People; but in one and the same action, God, by the Peoples suffrages, makes such an one Governour, or Magistrate, and not another." By "special providences" God gave a particular direction to the process of natural events, thereby creating an effective sign of one of his ever present purposes. And miracles, in which God interrupted the natural order, were like exclamations in the divine discourse, eruptions of the force, which motivated all things: "He can stop the Sun in its course, and cause it to withdraw its shining; He can give check to the Fire, that it shall not burn; & to the hungry Lions, that they shall not devour." The "reading" of events was the inadequate form taken by a basically symbolic vision; the Puritans saw the world as instinct with meaning by reason of

God's concurrence and susceptible of interpretation by reason of God's salient acts.

They did not understand the gift. The fusion of serpent and devil, Hebrew and New Englander, Christ and king, which followed from their basic apprehension of a world permeated with God's ideas, seldom entered their literature as functional metaphors with a symbolic structure. Instead, their practice was to "open" a figure, to render it illustrative or decorative by analytic presentation. When Edward Johnson set out to portray Anne Hutchinson as Sisera[15], he proceeded by logical steps:

> And now to follow our first simile of a Souldier, the Lord Christ having safely landed many a valiant souldier of his on these Westerne shores, drawes hither also the common enemies to Reformation, both in Doctrine and Discipline; But it was for like end, as the Lord sometime drew Sisera the Captaine of Jabins's army to the River Kishon[16] for their destruction, onely herein was a wide difference; there Sisera was delivered into the hands of a Woman, and here Sisera was a woman; their weapons and warre was carnall, these spirituall; there Jabin was but a man, here Jabin was the common enemy of man's salvation.

Johnson produced the bare hones of a metaphysical conceit, a paraphrase of a complex figure that never came into actual existence. The same kind of logical analysis vitiates the elaborate similes of Anne Bradstreet's[17] *Meditations*; when she tries to present Christ with the saints and angels as the sun surrounded by stars, the passage reads like an exposition of some other writer's poem on the subject.

In the best Puritan writings the images are frankly illustrative, and sometimes, all unawares, they quicken into symbols as idea and illustration coalesce. The attempt to follow an opposite method to imitate directly in literary form the metaphoric experience of every day resulted only in the crude mannerisms of Cotton Mather. The historian of the Wars of the Lord, for whom broken windows were the appointed sign of the destruction of our "Clay Tabernacles," awkwardly built his tales around double meanings and outright puns. He approaches the subject of Roger Williams obliquely through the figure of a windmill:

> In the year 1659, a certain Windmill in the Low Countries 18, whirling round with extraordinary violence, by reason of the violent storm then blowing; the stone at length by its *rapid motion* became so intensely hot, as to fire the mill, from whence the flames, being dispersed by the high winds, did set a whole town on *fire*. But I can tell my reader that, about twenty years before this, there was a whole country in America like to be set on *fire* by the *rapid motion* of a windmill, in the head of one particular man. Know, then, that about the year 1630, arrived here one Mr. Roger Williams;... being a preacher that had less *light* than *fire* in him...

Even beyond the nervous italics, there are double-entendres; the Low Countries were the gathering place of sectaries and swept by winds of doctrine. In Mather's account of Anne Hutchinson a "special providence" is played upon in a similar style. The "testimony of heaven" is translated into deliberate word-play and a labored pun:

> While these things were managing, there happened some very surprising *prodigies*, which were lookt upon as testimonies from Heaven, against the ways of those greater prodigies, the sectaries. The *erroneous gentlewoman* herself, convicted of holding about thirty monstrous opinions, growing big with child, and at length coming to her time of travail, was delivered of about *thirty* monstrous births at once; whereof some were bigger, some were lesser; of several figures; few of any perfect, none of any *humane* shape. This was a thing generally then asserted and believed; whereas, by some that were eye-witnesses, it is affirmed that these were no more *monstrous births*, than what it is frequent for women,

labouring with false *conceptions*, to produce.

The crudity of Mather's attempt to duplicate in literary form the overlapping structure of experience which he knew outside of literature reflects a fundamental limitation in the Puritan views of knowledge and language. A properly symbolic method was denied the Puritan writer by his assumptions on method in general. Aquinas[19] held that things have multiple meaning and that language is at one with the symbolic structure of reality. The Puritans made a drastic break with this Catholic tradition. For Samuel Willard[20] the only realistic form of language was logical, and logic was the way in which men necessarily apprehended the world:

> It is impossible for us to know or understand things, but by some rule of reason or other. *Reason is nothing else but the manner of a Being, whereby it is acted upon our Understanding.* We know nothing of God but by putting some Logical Notion upon him. *All things are conveyed to us in a Logical way*, and bear some stamp of reason upon them, or else we should know nothing of them.[21]

Although the Puritan mind easily united Palestine and Massachusetts into a fluid realm where God's ideas were enacted, theory was all against the cultivation of this practice, and the New Englanders were governed by theory as no people before or since. According to their theory, the truth of Scripture was not aesthetic but propositional understanding consisted in analytic interpretation:

> *A Scripture consequence is a Trueth evidently & necessarily arising out of a proposition, held forth therein in express termes*; So that, if the doctrine conteined in the proposition held forth in express termes be true, then is the doctrine conteined therein by consequence, also true... The greatest part of Scripture-trueth is revealed in Scripture-consequences. Yea many fundamentall trueths are not held forth in express termes, but by manifest consequence.[22]

If the real structure of language and reality was purely logical, aesthetic form was merely an ornament. The Puritan clergy possessed a sort of universal *vade mecum* in the philosophy of Peter Ramus, a sixteenth-century French logician and rhetorician, whose works were transmitted to them in a multitude of summaries and commentaries. Whereas Scholastic philosophy[23] had given rhetoric virtually an equal status with logic in the scheme of things, thus providing a sanction for symbolism as a form of knowledge, Ramus treated rhetoric as decoration added to and presupposing a logical framework:

> This is the true distinction between Dialectic and Rhetoric. For even if the oration be most illustrious or most ample, subtlety of invention in thinking the arguments, of truth in enunciation, of consequence in syllogism, and of order in method, is entirely, I say, a matter of dialectic and logic. But ornament and elocution in trope and figure, and pronunciation in voice and gesture is entirely a matter of rhetoric and completely pertaining to it, even if the disputation itself be mostly philosophical.[24]

Since "trope and figure" were merely embroidery on the logical doctrine, interpretation was a simple process of reduction. A rhetorical expression was equated with some univocal logical paraphrase. The method was to find a grammatical bridge between the figure and its logical equivalent:

> *All Rhetorical expressions must be reduced to the Grammatical sense, and accordingly interpreted.* Types and figures must be allowed to the Scriptures as well as to other writings, else God had not spoken in our mode, and this way is not too obscure, but to illustrate, and also to move the affections, but still we must reduce it to the Intention: Rhetorick, is but an Ornament of Speech, and must therefore be brought to the Grammar of it.[25]

This ornamentalism effectually destroyed the Puritan sense of artistic coherence. To the New England mind the poetry of the Psalms was extrinsic and separable from the meaning conveyed, as Richard Mather[26] declared in his Preface to the *Bay Psalm Book*. Thomas Hoker[27] assumed a radical distinction between the "quaintnesse of language," which serves only "to please the nicenesse of mens palates," and "the substance and solidity of the frame..., which pleaseth the builder." The meaning could not inhere in the poetry, or the substance in the rhetoric; the Ramistic scheme offered no ground for a functional symbolism.

The Puritan revolt from Catholicism was not only doctrinal but methodological: from one point of view it was part and parcel of the vast movement which established the scientific technique of modern thought. Whitehead[28] has shown how the habit of picturing nature in atomistic form grew upon the modern consciousness. The scientific method devised in "the Century of Genius" prescribed a world made up of objects with "simple location" in space and time, objects lacking "any essential reference... to other regions of space and to other durations of time." But these objects, Whitehead points out, were devised by "high abstraction"; they are "the products of logical discernment" supervening upon the world as it is concretely experienced. In concrete reality we apprehend no "mere multiplicity of points" ordered mechanically but rather an organic whole in which "each part is something from the standpoint of every other part, and also from the same standpoint every other part is something in relation to it." Poetry since the seventeenth century has very often been an attempt either to accept the world of simple location as a kind of *pis aller* or to displace the narrowly logical habits of mind which created that vision of nature.

Calvinistic Protestantism,[29] as Whitehead says, was the theological counterpart of the contemporary science. It too imposed upon the world the pattern of a simplistic logic, which issued in "the mechanism of God" just as scientific method issued in "the mechanism of matter." Like the scientific theory of knowledge and the scientific metaphysics, it had the effect of invalidating the organic structure of poetry and nullifying the organic world of experience that poetry claims to render. The logical methodology which the Puritans derived from Ramus mapped out a world of discrete entities—"arguments"—each with its simple location in the conceptual scheme. Anything—a substance, a quality, an action, a relation—was an "argument," and the ten Aristotelian categories[30] were lost in this sweeping concept. Every discipline could be schematized by a succession dichotomies so as to distinguish and put in their places the arguments of which it was composed. The syllogism was of minor importance beside this technique of dichotomizing. In some respects, as will presently appear, the Ramistic logic was more than a mechanically divisive system; but its practical effect was to convert the universe into an assemblage of logical counters, a mechanical framework of causes and effects, "subjects" and "adjuncts," whose "either-or" relationship was dramatized by the elementary principle of dichotomy. The Aristotelians against whom Ramus contended were inclined to be nominalistic, but the Ramistic logicians made their boast that the "places" of their skeletal outlines were the "places" of reality. By his revision of the Aristotelian logic—at once a bold extension of logical method and a drastic leveling—Ramus created a world which in its utter simplicity was the more plainly a "high abstraction."

Medieval Catholicism was sufficiently devoted to logic but inherited and cultivated another mode of thought as well. The Jewish theologians of Alexandria, caught between Greek philosophy and the Mosaic law, had rescued themselves by an ingenious method of biblical interpretation: The ancient words, they decided, must contain a multiplicity of meaning: "As a hammer divides fire into many sparks, so every verse of Scripture has many explanations." Rules of "allegorical" interpretation were gradually formulated. According to the "fourfold interpretation" invented by the early Fathers[31] and accepted thereafter, the four levels of meaning in the language of the Bible ("literal," "moral," "allegorical," and "anagogical") were all equally true and mutually supplementary. The principle of "multiplex intelligentia," although it became an artificial formula in the course of time, was actually a recognition of symbolic thinking, for it originated in an effort to use the figures of the Bible as vehicles for a variety of ideas, and it persisted as a means of unifying the complex intellectual heritage of Christianity. "Multiplex intelligentia" was no freak of words but coincident with the nature of things. Aquinas held that interpretations "are not multiplied because one word signifies several things, but because the things signified by the words can be themselves types of other things." All the interpretations grew out of the "literal" meaning, the simple designation of an object; reality had a symbolic structure, in which everything referred beyond itself. The theory bore fruit in the *Divine Comedy*, the meaning of which, Dante explained, "is not of one kind only; rather the work may be described as 'polysemous,' that is, having several meanings." The meanings all converge into the literal one, "that sense in the expression of which the others are all included, and without which it would be impossible, and irrational to give attention to the other meanings." The "poetriae," the medieval literary handbooks, treated figurative language as ornamental circumlocution and afforded no basis for symbolism, but theology fostered the capacity to think and feel in figures, so that the medieval mind "moved as frequently from symbol to symbol as from fact to fact."

The Puritans gingerly preserved this Catholic tradition as the science of "typology," a system of correspondences between the Old Testament and the New. Adam and David were types of Christ, and the deliverances from Egypt and Babylon "shadowed forth" the deliverance of the Church from the Antichrist. These relationships were real, designed and instituted by God like sacraments. They were expressly distinguished from merely illustrative similes and metaphors. Yet precisely in this distinction appears the characteristic narrowness of Puritan thought. The Puritan typologist was afraid of the types, or rather of the symbolic thinking necessary to perceive them, and he consigned many figures of the Bible, and all outside it, to an "arbitrary" status. Gone were the habits of mind that produced the *Divine Comedy* out of a sense of multiple meaning inherent in real things. Although such images as "the Wars of the Lord" and "the Holy Commonwealth" were an effort to carry typology one step further, from the New Testament into the New World, a measure of the forces working to constrain the Puritan imagination is given by this warning:

> Men must not indulge their own Fancies, as the Popish Writers use to do, with their Allegorical Senses, as they call them; except we have some Scripture ground for it. It is not safe to make anything a Type merely upon our own fancies and imaginations; it is Gods Prerogative to make Types.[32]

The obvious difficulty that one might well mistake an individual fancy for a divinely appointed type (both are "similitudes," and the rules given to discover the "Scripture ground" are hardly conclusive) did not affect the principle. The types belonged in a special and jealously guarded category; figures in general, unless plainly illustrative or decorative, became dangerous subjective fancies emulating the types. As to the particular types of Scripture, there might remain some slight difference of opinion, but "typical" thinking in literature was beyond the pale.

The intellectual stance of the conscious artist in American literature has been determined very largely by problems inherent in the method of the Puritans. The isolation of the American artist in society, so often lamented, is actually parallel to the furtive and unacknowledged role of artistic method in the American mind; both factors began in the seventeenth century with the establishment of Puritan philosophy and of a society that tried to live by it. Hence the crudity or conventionality of a great part of American literature from 1620 through the third quarter of the nineteenth century may be attributed no more surely to frontier conditions, provinciality, and industrialism than to inherited mental habits which proscribed a functional artistic form. And the symbolism of Emerson, Thoreau, Melville, Hawthorne, and Whitman was an attempt to hew out such a form in defiance of intellectual methods that denied its validity.

The effect of Puritanism, however, was not simply repressive. The early Colonial writers, in their limited fashion, did perpetuate the medieval symbolist tradition. The purpose of Mather's *Magnalia* was to bring to bear "innumerable Antiquities, *Jewish, Chaldee, Arabian, Grecian, and Roman*… with a *sweet light* reflected from them on the word, which is our *light*." In daily life the Puritans customarily evaded their rhetorical theory, and in them, as Emerson said, "the whole Jewish history became flesh and blood." What the Puritan mind bequeathed to American writing, from the standpoint of literary method, was a special and extreme case of the modern literary situation: a conflict between the symbolic mode of perception, of which our very language is a record, and a world of sheer abstractions certified as "real." The divided consciousness which Whitehead sees beginning in England, in the seventeenth and eighteenth centuries under the impact of physical science, and coming into the open in romantic and Victorian literature, had an even deeper foundation in America, for here it began with Puritan rationalism.

The rationalism itself was not wholly rational. The highly wrought logic of the "Covenants" had a symbolic pattern which bound together the theoretically distinct Covenant of Grace, Church Covenant, and Civil Covenant. These three bargains with God were the gigantic shadow cast by the new society of commercial contracts and constitutional government; more particularly, they reflect the conventicles and small group agreements under which the New England colonies were founded. The earthly covenant, such as marriage or the relation of master and servant, frequently offered by the theologian as an example of spiritual contract, "must in fact have been exemplar," and the Covenant idea gained its real cogency not from rational argument but from the way in which its various levels shed light on each other. This symbolic reference, which gave a kind of organic unity to the entire scheme, is the more striking in that the Covenant idea per se was a repudiation of the organic society and imputed a mechanical quality to the relationship between man and God. Puritan method was actually at odds with itself. Ramus and his followers gave an ontological status to a highly simplified version of the logic of classes; his "arguments," linked only by the concepts of formal logic, and his technique of dichotomizing every whole into radically distinct parts, evince, in the most thoroughgoing fashion the effort of the modern mind to picture an atomic world. But it was possible to found upon this system a doctrine of mutually subservient disciplines, the universal organ on known as "technologia":

> All the Arts are nothing else but the beams and rays of the Wisdom of the *first Being* in the Creatures, shining, and reflecting thence, upon the glass of man's understanding; and as from *Him* they come, so to him they tend; the circle of Arts is a *Deo ad Deum*[33]. Hence there is an affinity and kindred of Arts … which is according to the reference and subordination of their particular ends, to the utmost and last end; One makes use of another, one serves to another, till they all reach and return to Him, as Rivers to the Sea, whence they flow.

The God who sanctioned technologia was not the supreme Mechanic but rather a mind whose organic unity was reflected in nature and potentially in the mind of man.

From its beginning the logic of Ramus was avowedly "dialectic," a process of right thinking as well as an external description of thought. The claim was made with the utmost seriousness. The Puritan obsession with "method" was not simply a love of logical form but more fundamentally an intense concern with thought, language, and reality: Like the originators of "multiplex intelligentia," who evolved a philosophy of language at the turning point of the classic and Christian eras, the Protestant reformers in their revolt from Catholic modes of thought were thrown back on the nature of words. The language of the Bible was authority; since the Bible had been variously misinterpreted, it was necessary to know how this language worked; and, since truth was subject to controversy, one must be able to use language according to its nature. The Puritan ministers spent their lives immersed in the meaning of words. They were quick to grasp the value of any nuance and to turn it to their own purposes:

> Bernard, upon that clause in the Canticles[34] ["O thou fairest among women!"], has this ingenious gloss: *Pulchram, non omnimode quidem, sed pulchram inter mulieres eam docet; videlicet cum distinctione, quatenus ex hoc amylius reprimatur, et sciat quid desit sibi* ["Fair, not in an absolute sense, but fair among women; implying a distinction, in order that his praise may have due qualification, and that she may apprehend her deficiencies"]. Thus, I do not say, that the Churches of New England are the most regular that can be; yet I do say, and am sure, that they are very like unto those that were in the first ages of Christianity. [35]

Although, in his hostility to Catholic methods and in the manner of his age, the Ramist assumed that language is essentially logical and that "al things," as Willard said, "are conveyed to us in a Logical way," his very concern with language as the *way things are conveyed* gave a peculiar quality to his logic. Puritan rationalism, unlike the scientific world view that supplanted it and to which it is in some ways cognate, predicated an indivisible unity of thought, word, and thing. The Ramistic "argument" did not "refer to" an external thing, nor did it "signify" a subjective idea. "Had Ramists known the terms, they would have allowed no distinction between the idea and the '*ding-an sich*,'[36] or at any rate very little." The argument was the thing, or the name of the thing, or the mental conception of the thing all at once." The Puritans were not troubled by modern epistemological difficulties. Willard's faith in logical language depended upon his belief that "knowledge is made by an assimilation between the Knower, and the thing known," that "the object known must be (some way) in the faculty knowing," and that the word is part of a unit which is knowledge.

Dialectic is a logic that moves in the realm of symbolism, where there are no things or ideas apart from the language that makes them, and the criterion of truth is coherence, not correspondence to external fact. The very them "argument," for which there is no modern equivalent, expresses this conception. Arguments were "invented" by the mind in the sense that they became present to it, just as the eye perceived colors, and no other demonstration was necessary to prove them true. Laid side by side, arguments built up axioms, which were similarly validated: "The light of nature... reveals itself in the observer, and a natural assent follows when an arrangement of this kind is perceived." Similarly, a complete discourse was constructed by the juxtaposition of axioms containing within themselves an evident connection and order. Although arguments and axioms were the terms and propositions of discursive thinking, at once the instruments and products of abstraction, another force was operating on this logic. While the argument was basically anatomistic logical entity, prior to all combinations into which it entered and remaining unaltered by them, at the same time it was inherently relational, as is shown by Ramus' definition: "An argument is whatever is affected to the arguing of something else." The axiom was simply a proposition, but the Ramists pointedly minimized the process of inference (the syllogism was a means of checking, not the essence of method) and depended on juxtaposition to reveal a pattern in thoughts and things. Working to modify the mechanistic tendency to which any logic is prone, and of which the Puritan method had more than its share, was a sense of organic unity—not only between the mind and objects but also, growing out of that, among all things in the given world. The arguments were "glued together," said Alexander Richardson, in the nature of things,[37] and each axiom, according to Nathaniel Ward,[38] contained some tincture of the whole of God's truth:

> The least Truth of Gods Kingdome, doth in its place, uphold the whole kingdome of his Truths; Take away the least *vericulum*[39] out of the world, and it unworlds all, potentially, and may unravell the whole texture actually, if it be not conserved by an Arme of extraordinary power.

It was not merely a desire to popularize, therefore, which led Ramus to illustrate his method by quotations from poets and orators. As dialectic, his logic was germane to the organic forms of aesthetic experience and partially modified by them. Nor did the vogue of Ramus among the seventeenth-century poets, which has recently been explored, result only from a common desire to make poetry logical. On the contrary, his method was accessible to the poetic mind because it was also inclined to poeticize logic and thus, however flimsily, to bridge the gap between abstract and concrete thinking. The American Puritans fastened upon another, more obvious aspect of the system; its apparent elimination of aesthetic form from the structure of reality. But a quasi-aesthetic, dialectical strain belonged to the method, little as they were aware of it. It crops up again in Emerson, both as theory and as practice, and Emerson consciously relates it to the theory and practice of symbolism.

Meanwhile, the Puritans, who longed for a stable, timeless order, found that dialectic has its own momentum, which cannot be halted arbitrarily. Emerson was prepared to accept the incompleteness of any logical statement; he saw that every proposition aims at an absoluteness which its very nature precludes, since "we cannot strongly state one fact without seeming to belie some other." But his seventeenth-century ancestors thought they had captured the whole of reality in the texture of a rational language, and they were doomed to pay for their mistake. They were plagued by controversies over the meaning of words; their vocabulary concealed logical oppositions that could only jar against each other and draw apart. Since word, thought, and thing were one, the controversialist could appeal only to immediate apprehension by the "natural light" of reason and try to convince by demonstrating a necessary meaning. To gain acceptance became increasingly difficult. At the trial of Anne Hutchinson a quarrel arose over the relation of the Holy Ghost to the believer. In desperation, "it was earnestly desired, that the word person might be forborn, being a term of human invention, and tending to doubtful disputation in this case." The same sort of difficulty persisted, the lady and her judges differing over the meaning of a "rule." John Cotton summed up the whole controversy as a dispute "about magnifying the grace of God; one party seeking to advance the grace of God within us, and the other to advance the grace of God towards us (meaning by the one justification, and by the other sanctification)." The latent tensions of Puritanism, lacking any vehicle for symbolic unity, emerged in equivocation on terms like "person," "rule," "within us," and "towards us." Moreover, the terms were continually being spirited away into a new context that utterly changed their sense. The arbitrary God who had bound himself by "covenant" was at once a medieval seigneur and a modern businessman with a contract. The balance of this conception was hard to maintain by logic alone; if the arbitrary God was bound by law, it might seen logical to consider the law more important, than God. In the eighteenth century, when a society of contract had largely replaced the medieval society of status, the Calvinistic balance was lost, and the doctrine that laws were good because God made them verged easily into the quite opposite belief that God made them because they were good. The shift was already taking place in the logical exercises of mid-seventeenth-century divines:

> It is his [God's] will and good pleasure to make all laws that are moral to be first good in themselves for all men, before he will impose them upon all men. And hence it is a weakness for any to affirm, that a moral law is not such a law which is therefore commanded because it is good, because (say they) it is not the goodness of the thing, but the sovereign will of God, which makes all things good; for it is the sovereign will of God (as is proved) to make every moral law good, and therefore to command it, rather than to make it good by a mere commanding of it.[41]

There are not many steps between this bit of reasoning and the completely secularized opinion of Benjamin Franklin:

> Revelation had indeed no weight with me, as such; but I entertain'd an opinion that, though certain actions might not be bad because they were forbidden by it, or good because it commanded them, yet probably these actions might be forbidden *because* they were bad for us, or commanded *because* they were beneficial to us, in their own natures, all the circumstances, of things considered.[42]

The logical marches and countermarches of the New England theologians, in their effort to stabilize a dissolving system, were farther and farther removed from experience. Language was tortured until "regeneration became merely an 'X,' which filled a gap in a theological structure; a mere postulate in an ideology." When Nathanael Emmons[43] defined visible saints as "those who appear to profess real holiness," he precipitated endless discussions in which all the permutations of "appear," "profess," and "real" were paraded like speculative geometries that no one could live by. It was as though, betrayed by the logical method of their fathers, the later Calvinists had no recourse save to further increasingly mechanical juggling of terms. At length, the Unitarians dissolved the Trinity itself by uncompromising logic. According to Andrews Norton:

When it is affirmed that "the Father is God, and the Son is God, and the Holy Ghost is God, and yet there are not three Gods, but one God," no words can more clearly convey any meaning, than those propositions express the meaning, that there are three existences of whom the attributes of God may be predicated, and yet that there is only one existence of whom the attributes of God may be predicated. But this is not an incomprehensible mystery; it is plain non sense.[44]

Norton had completely lost the capacity for symbolic thinking. Whereas the original Puritans had retained a vital symbolism in everyday experience and even, however unconsciously, in the structure of their system, meaning for their descendants was either rational or nonexistent. Norton recognized "the intrinsic ambiguity of language"—indeed, he devoted many pages to the subject—but he insisted that interpretation must "distinguish among possible meanings, the actual meaning" of a passage. Just as the doctrines of Calvinism gravitated into eighteenth-century benevolence, the old rational method drifted into the rationalism of deists and infidels. There is not much to choose, as far as habits of thought are concerned, between Norton and the *philosophe* Thomas Jefferson, to whom "the Trinitarian arithmetic, that three are one, and one is three," was an "incomprehensible jargon," or the infidel Thomas Paine,[45] whose attack on "the Christian system of arithmetic, that three are one, and one is three," was only part of a general assault on the whole of Christian symbolism.

In this harsh intellectual climate, brought on by the Puritans' commitment to a dialectic which they did not fully understand, men like Emerson were born. They proposed to rescue the intellect by showing that controversy grew out of the nature of logical language. The supplanting of one creed by another, they declared, was the normal course of dialectic; through the jostling of formulas wider generalizations became possible; and the full substance of theology could never be rendered in creeds at all, but only in complex symbols. Running counter to the Calvinistic orthodoxy of New England was a strain of liberalism, stemming ultimately from Luther's doctrine of the priesthood of all believers. Roger Williams set up his colony as a haven for all varieties of belief; he regarded his own creed as provisional and called himself a "seeker." The conventional Puritans condemned Williams not only for heresy but for obvious illogicality:

> How all Religions should enjoy their liberty, Justice its due regularity, Civill cohabitation morall honesty, in one and the same Jurisdiction, is beyond the Artique of my comprehension. If the whole conclave of Hell can so compromise, *exadverse*, and *diametriall contradictions*, as to compolitize such a multi-monstrous maufrey of heteroclytes and quicquidlibets quietly; I trust I may say with all humble reverence, they can doe more then the *Senate* of Heaven.[46]

Actually, Williams had accepted the inevitability of logical opposition and moved on to another principle. The proliferation of dialectic—each proposition generating its opposite—had become a resource of thought for the "seeker." A century and a half later, after infinite logical acumen had failed to check the disintegration of Calvinism, Channing[47] proclaimed that the mind needs to entertain contradictory ideas in order to encompass the truth:

> God's sovereignty is limitless; still man has rights. God's power is irresistible; still man is free. One God we entirely depend; yet we can and do act from ourselves, and determine our own characters. These antagonist ideas, if so they may be called, are equally true, and neither can be spared. It will not do for an impassioned or an abject piety to wink one class of them out of sight. In a healthy mind they live together...

Out of the view that mutually exclusive ideas may be equally true and necessary came Emerson's defiance of system and Horace Bushnell's[48] assertion that he was ready to accept as many creeds as fell in this way. For both, the answer to Puritan logic-chopping was the method of liberalism. And, for both, the ultimate expression of the liberal mind was the symbolic "language of paradox."

The history of New England theology had demonstrated what the better instinct of the New Englanders themselves had said all along—that a language to live in could not be made in the image of mathematics but must articulate the organic processes of human activity and experience. Horace Bushnell defined his main problem as "how to get a language, and where"—the question posed for American literature by the Puritan obsession with "method" and emphasized by the decline and fall of Calvinism. His answer, that language is made by giving oneself to words, not calculating upon them, was equally implicit in the tradition. Ramus had created a dialectic rather than a pure logic because he held that "not art in itself, but the exercise and practice of it, makes the artisan." The abstract and descriptive terms of theory became concrete as functions in the process of knowledge; apart from the substance of concrete experience, they were mere instrumental signs. Richard Sibbes, an English Puritan, brought out the point even more explicitly when he warned that "religion is not a matter of word, nor stands upon words, as wood consists of Trees... but religion is a matter of power, it makes a man able." The being of religion did not consist in dogma, which could only refer to it. The "art" (or theory) must enter into the "trade" (or activity), the words into the things they designated: "A Trade is not learned by words, but by experience; and a man hath learned a Trade, not when he can talk of it, but when he can work according to his Trade." The Puritans were aware that two very different kinds of knowledge are possible, and in the midst of their concerted effort to formulate the world in doctrines they clung to the active perception that is prior to all logical statement:

There is great odds betwixt the knowledge of a Traveller, that in his own person hath taken a view of many Coasts... and by Experience hath been an Eye-witness... and another that sits by his fire side, and happily reads the story of these in a Book, or views the proportion of these in a Map, the odds is great, and the difference of their knowledge more than a little... The like difference is therein the right discerning of sin... The one sees the History of sin, the other the Nature of it; the one knows the relation of sin: it is mapped out, and recorded; the other the poyson, as by experience he hath found and proved it. [49]

Jonathan Edwards was the most notable exponent of knowledge by experience. Although his "real sense of the excellency of God" seemed to him a "divine and supernatural light," as distinct from imagination and inspiration as from doctrines and propositions, he set it off in this way in order to save his theology from the charge of mere subjective willfulness, and his over-all aim was to validate the language of direct perception. Theology aside, Edwards anticipated the symbolic consciousness of Emerson. He shared Emerson's conviction that "the spontaneous or intuitive principle" is superior to "the arithmetical or logical":

There is a difference between having an opinion; that God is holy and gracious, and having a sense of the loveliness and beauty of that holiness and grace. There is a difference between having a rational judgment that honey is sweet, and having a sense of its sweetness... There is a wide difference between mere speculative rational judging any thing to be excellent, and having a sense of its sweetness and beauty. The former rests only in the head, speculation only is concerned in it, but the heart is concerned in the latter. [50]

In "sense" were united the opposites that "judgment" had distinguished God's power and his love, logical extremes on which the most diverse sects had been founded and which were turning, points of Puritan controversy, were combined by Edwards in his intuition of "the glorious majesty and grace of God":

> I seemed to see them both in a sweet conjunction; majesty and meekness joined together; it was a sweet, and gentle, and holy majesty; and also a majestic meekness; and awful sweetness; a high, and great, and holy gentleness.[51]

The language of Scripture, Edwards discovered, was not propositional at all, but a functional rhetoric:

> The design of the Spirit of God does not seem to be to represent God's ultimate end as manifold, but as one. For though it be signified by various names, yet they appear not to be names of different things, but various names involving each other in their meaning; either different names of the same thing, or names of several parts of one whole, or of the same whole viewed in various lights, or in its different respects and relations. [52]

And finally, at his most daring, Edwards maintained that nature as well as the Bible is radically figurative. Within "those metaphors and similes, which to an unphilosophical person do seem so uncouth," were real affinities, for "there is really… an analogy or consent between the beauty of the skies, tress, fields, flowers, etc., and spiritual excellencies."

The "images or shadows of divine things" that Edwards collected in a notebook throughout his life were an attempt, as Perry Miller has shown, to find a ground for religious perception without denying the Newtonian universe. [53] Edwards rehabilitated the old typology in a new context. He wished as earnestly as the most cautious of his predecessors to avoid mistaking mere personal fancy for a divinely appointed figure (his reason for this was even more compelling than theirs, since the objectivity of religion could not be established by subjective inventions). Yet at the same time he knew that the types must no longer be confined to Scripture and would have to be extended into Nature, the empirical world of eighteenth-century science, if religion were not to become an isolated mental habit. What he needed was a medium where valid ideas and the data of sense would be inseparable. To this end, he accepted the new principles[54] that all knowledge is derived from experience but proceeded to modify Locke's theory of knowledge out of all recognition. "As Edwards read the new sensationalism, far from setting up a dualism of subject and object, it fused them in the moment of perception. The thing could then appear as concept and the concept as thing." For Edwards, real types existed in the realm of "experience":

> Seeing the perfect idea of a thing, is, to all intents and purposes, the same as seeing the thing. It is not only equivalent to seeing it, but it is seeing of it; for there is no other seeing but having an idea. Now, by seeing a perfect idea, so far as we see it, we have it.[55]

But this is only to say that Edwards was a philosophical symbolist. There can be no "doubt whether John Locke would have been altogether happy over his American disciple." The case is not essentially, as Miller would suggest, that of a man who used the philosophy of science to substantiate the philosophy of religion; rather, Edwards was trying to affirm the basic premises of symbolism, which were part of his intellectual tradition, in contemporary terms. His epistemology did not derive from Locke in any fundamental way; he reinterpreted Locke in the light of his epistemology. If he anticipated a post-Kantian like Emerson, as is certainly true, it was because he brought to the sense-world of empiricism a symbolist tradition that Emerson was to rediscover after empiricism had worked itself out. Edwards and Emerson used an old philosophy to reorient the new philosophy. After all, the issue had been defined long before and did not come as an utter novelty, since Puritan method, which embodied the groundwork of symbolism, had equally embodied and illustrated the ways of modern science.

Alexis de Toqueville in 1831 foresaw the coming vogue of pantheism in America:

> If there is a philosophical system which teaches that all things material and immaterial, visible and invisible, which the world contains are to be considered only as the several parts of an immense Being, who alone remains eternal amid the continual change and ceaseless transformation of all that constitutes him, we may readily infer that such a system, although it destroys the individuality of man, or rather because it destroys that individuality, will have secret charms for men living in democracies.[56]

The American principle of human equality, which Tocqueville regarded as the essence of democracy, could lead in two opposite directions. While each individual was independent of all others in the land of the social contract, at the same time he was only a unit in the level mass and secretly yearned to be submerged in humanity. Tocqueville extended this pattern from politics to habits of thought and language. On the one hand, "nothing is more repugnant to the human mind in an age of equality than the idea of subjection to forms. Men living at such times are impatient of figures; to their eyes, symbols appear to be puerile artifices used to conceal or to set off truths that should more naturally be bared to the light of day." Tocqueville reported that he knew no country in which Christianity was emptier of "forms, figures, and observances" than in the United States. Yet, on the other hand, the democratic mind had a passion for generalization, which corresponded to the feeling that individuals differ little from each other, and the American language was marked by "continual use of generic terms or abstract expressions."

Tocqueville was studying *homo americanus* as modern man in his native habitat, and he traced "the philosophical method of the Americans" back to the modern rationalist tradition of "private judgment." In the atomism of society, and the repudiation of intellectual forms, in majority rule and the love of generalization, America was the embodiment of ideas that began with the Protestant reformers in the sixteenth century and with Descartes[57] and Bacon in the seventeenth. Tocqueville did not see, however, that the doubleness of American thought was more than an outcome of this rationalist tradition and actually pointed toward a revolt against it. The destruction of individuality by pantheism followed a different method from the subordination of persons to majority opinion and the grouping of ideas under abstract concepts. Pantheism, as Tocqueville's own description intimates, would substitute processes for the individual entities of eighteenth century logic and politics; the "parts" would be related to the "immense Being" not as members to class but as functions to existence. Although, because of the prevalent individualism, symbolic forms were strikingly absent from American thought, abstract generalization was not the only means of unifying the American world. Side by side with the generic terms of American speech, Tocqueville found unusual ambiguity. One writer after another, by "giving an unwonted meaning to an expression already in use," built up an indeterminate vocabulary: American authors seemed almost never "to dwell upon a single thought" but rather "to aim at a group of ideas."

The issue (though Tocqueville could hardly have been expected to view it in this light) was not only between the extremes of individualism and conformity, the part and the whole, but also between two ways of conceiving individuals and forms, things and their relations. The two worlds over which the Puritans hovered came into open conflict in the early nineteenth century, when the abstract method of modern thought, on which the Puritans unconsciously depended, had completely entered into the texture of American life. Emerson was separated from his conservative critics by more than differences of opinion; as Margaret Fullers[58] said, his mind worked differently from theirs:

> They were accustomed to an artificial method whose scaffolding could easily be retraced and desired an obvious

sequence of logical inferences. They insisted there was nothing in what they had heard, because they could not give a clear account of its course and purport. They did not see that Pinder's odes might be very well arranged for their own purpose, and yet not bear translating into the methods of Mr. Locke.

The new movement in American philosophy which was beginning about the time of Tocqueville's visit sprang up as a renewed awareness of the functions of language; it was not so much doctrinal as methodological. Emerson and his fellows contended that man was involved in society, ideas in the whole of truth, things in nature, and the mind in its objects, far more profoundly than the methods of Mr. Locke had suggested. The real form of the world was not logical, and the real use of language was not as an artificial framework. Instead, language should inhere in experience and render the fluidity of experience:

So Speech represents the flowing essence as sensitive, transitive; the word signifying what we make it at the moment of using, but needing life's rounded experiences to unfold its manifold senses and shades of meaning. Definitions, however precise, fail to translate the sense. They confine in defining...[59]

The conventional American mind could only interpret such remarks in terms of its own Lockian nominalism: "Transcendentalism," Noah Porters[60] declared, was "rather unbelief than disbelief. Subtle, refining, symbolizing all living truths and real facts into inert and powerless myth." Yet to say, as Alcott did, that "the world is but the symbol of mind, and speech a mythology woven of both," was not to reduce truth and fact to a barren subjectivity but to give all the shapes of language an objectivity that men like Porter never thought possible. "Transcendentalism" in this sense could not be escaped even by writers like Melville, Hawthorne, and Poe, who were hostile to its superficial features. As a method, the new philosophy extended beyond the provincial clique which was labeled "transcendentalist" and which stated the theory most fully; for it arose as a function of American life and thought and, more generally, as a function of the modern world.

Even the orthodox rationalist was forced to admit that the issues of the day were on an utterly different plane from the interminable New England controversies of the past. "Certain it is," Francis Bowen[61] wrote in 1837, "that a revolution in taste and opinion is going on among our literary men, and that philosophical writing is assuming a phase entirely new." The conservatives blamed it all on alien ideas, primarily German idealism and French eclecticism, and reaffirmed their faith in "the mode of philosophizing which has for several generations prevailed among our British ancestors." But actually the new philosophy was thoroughly native, though not in sense that cuts it off from contemporary thinking. Superficially, it is true, the mid-nineteenth-century intellectual revolution in America was a version of European romanticism and post-Kantian idealism, spiced with the local religious tradition and with Platonic, Neo-Platonic, oriental, and Swedenborgian[62] ideas. Doubtless every speculation of the American "transcendentalists" could be paralleled from Fichte[63] or Schelling or Hegel, from Coleridge or Wordsworth or Carlyle, not to mention the remoter analogues. The movement was proudly dependent on the "usage" of its own day: "The very time sees for us, thinks for us; it is a microscope such as philosophy never had. Insight is for us which was never for any." Yet Emerson is here defining a subtler relationship than imitation, and to put the case in terms of mere "influence" is to miss the point. The American mind fell easily into this usage, and the American writer was an agent of a world-wide process, which was as much his as another's: "Above his will and out of his sight he is necessitated by the air he breathes and the idea on which he and his contemporaries live and toil, to share the manner of his times, without knowing what that manner is." The American shared the manner of his times because his whole history was a modern instance; the intellectual situation of nineteenth-century America was a kind of epitome of modern intellectual conditions. Although Emerson and his colleagues were often simply imitative of romantic and idealistic cliches, their distinction was to have grasped a basic issue of modern thought, in which idealism and romanticism were only an episode. "The movement," Orestes Brownson[64] emphatically declared, "is really of American origin, and the prominent actors in it were carried away by it before ever they formed any acquaintance with French or German metaphysics; and their attachment to the literatures of France and Germany is the effect of their connexion with the movement; not the cause."

The basic cause lay in a peculiarity of the whole American tradition and not least in the very "mode of philosophizing" which the orthodox defended. Though the method of Emerson and Alcott seemed and was a violent departure from eighteenth-century rationalism, the American brand of rationalism had set the stage for their advent by its own distinctively methodological cast. In 1715 Samuel Johnson, the future president of King's College, gave up Ramistic logic and was "wholly changed to the New Learning," to the philosophy of Descartes and Locke, the natural science of Bolye[65] and Newton. The suddenness of his conversion, which he noted dramatically at the end of his uncompleted "Tech-nologia," indicates his real motive. Johnson, though in a way a genuinely speculative man, had no notion of the potential problems raised by the modern philosophy he accepted. He was concerned with systematizing, not with metaphysics, and the first use to which he put the new learning was to revise his Ramistic "Encyclopedia" into another "system of travails of the humane intellect." Jonathan Edwards, who came upon Locke a few years later, found much more in empiricism than a new logic, but in his case too the Puritan obsession with logical method was perpetuated long after the Lockian "why of ideas" had replaced the dialectic of Ramus:

One reason why, at first, before I knew other Logick, I used to be mightily pleased with the study of the Old Logick, was because it was very pleasant to see my thoughts, that before lay in my mind jumbled without any distinction, ranged into order and distributed into classes and subdivisions, so that I could tell where they all belonged, and run them up to their general heads.[66]

The secularization of Calvinism, which proceeded throughout the eighteenth century, was made possible by this continuity between the old method and the new and by the unsuspecting fashion in which the Lockian approach was assimilated. In turn, the major figures of the American Enlightenment were completely indifferent to the philosophic matrix from which their thoughts emerged; Jefferson's "self-evident" truths were a means of achieving "certainty without metaphysics." By 1800 the philosophy taught in American colleges was almost entirely Lockian, and the political, social, and economic life of the New World was an embodiment of the New Learning; for Tocqueville, in the 1830's, the United States was the country "where the precepts of Descartes are... best applied." Yet Descartes and Locke and all they stood for had been adopted chiefly as a method, both in theory and in practice; their basic assumptions, their historical derivation, and their skeptical potentialities were largely ignored.

This uncritical commitment to an abstract methodology had both positive and negative results. The uniformity of American character and opinion, which Tocqueville noted as a paradoxical counterpart to the democratic faith in "private judgment," was intensified by the lack of philosophic perspective in America. Since everyone thought in the same way, without asking why, everyone was inclined to think much the same things. Religious controversy, rich in method and poor in substance, became a conventional game. Here is the way a writer in 1839 described the New England habit of mind:

The theology of this school has always been, in a high degree, metaphysical; but the metaphysics is of a Hyperborean sort, exceedingly cold and fruitless. In the conduct of a feeble or even an ordinary mind, the wire-drawing processes of New England theologizing become jejune and revolting. Taught to consider mere ratiocination as the grand, and almost sole function of the human mind, the schoolboy, the youth, and the professor, pen in hand, go on day after day, in spinning out a thread of attenuated reasoning, often ingenious, and sometimes legitimately deduced, but in a majority of instances a concatenation of unimportant propositions.[67]

Yet if the dominant strain of American thought, from one point of view, was a method without context and often without content, it was able, by virtue of that very fact, to become extraordinarily flexible. Unitarianism, the end product of New England controversy, found freedom in the exercise of uninhibited reason. The liberalizing effect of the Unitarian movement, as Parrington[68] says, came about, as much "because of" as "in spite of its eighteenth-century nurture," for the Unitarians depended so completely on a kind of autonomous rational inquiry that they deprived rationalism of any doctrinal basis:

They had no creed, and no system of philosophy on which a creed could be, by common çonsent, built. Rather were they open inquirers, who asked questions and waited for rational answers, having no definite apprehension of the issue to which their investigations tended, but with room enough within the accepted theology to satisfy them, and work enough on the prevailing doctrines to keep them employed. Under these circumstances, they honestly but incautiously professed a principle broader than they were able to stand by, and avowed the absolute freedom of the human mind as their characteristic faith; instead of a creed, the right to judge all creeds; instead of a system, authority to try every system by rules of evidence.[69]

The negative outcome of American rationality was conventional orthodoxy and empty verbalism; its positive result was a consciousness of method that freed the spirit from dogma. The Unitarians reasserted private judgment in a special sense: they emphasized the act of inquiry. Their children went further and emphasized the act of experience in all its multiplicity. When the older generation protested against their "mania of tolerance and many-sidedness," the reply was easy: "You must plead guilty for some part of my vagaries. You bade me be a Seeker." There is one continuous movement from the Puritan era through the new learning of Locke to the new philosophy of Emerson. As Brownson declared in his disillusionment, "Protestantism ends in Transcendentalism." While the native rational method was being transmuted under its own momentum, a still newer new learning—German idealism—finally arrived in the United States. The blindfold was suddenly lifted from American philosophy, and there stood revealed a coherent intellectual trend of modern times which included as an integral part the long-cherished "Mr. Locke." Kantian idealism had a unique impact in America because it called attention to issues that had previously been neglected, though implicit in the very language being used. In this sense the future of the 1830's and 1840's was not a mere provincial imitation of European transcendentalism. It was an attempt to give body to the problems of modern philosophy. To that end the New England revolutionary fed upon all the scraps of literature and speculation that came his way. Sampson Reed's[70] "Observations on the Growth of the Mind" (Boston, 1826) had "the aspect of a revelation" to Emerson, and one revelation followed another; Coleridge's *Aids to Reflection* and *The Friend*, edited by James Marsh[71] of Vermont (Burlington, 1829 and 1831); Carlyle's early *Edinburgh Review* articles, which were being published about the same time; Victor Cousin's "Introduction to the History of Philosophy," translated by H. G. Linburg and published at Boston in 1832. When the excited young liberals "rushed into life, certain that the next half century was to see a complete moral revolution in the world," they were partisans not so much of a particular philosophy as of Philosophy itself, and in this respect, as Francis Bowen remarked at the time, the American situation was very different from that in England, where "the taste for metaphysical speculations" had virtually disappeared.

From Descartes to the post-Kantians, technical philosophy had had a skeleton in the closet. The abstractive intellect, whether rationalistic, empirical, or idealist, produced a world neatly divided into the two mutually exclusive categories of mind and matter. But "in between," as Whitehead has said, "there lie the concepts of life, organism, function, instantaneous reality, interaction, order of nature, which collectively form the Achilles' heel of the whole system." The characteristically modern "problem of knowledge," the attempt to rejoin what Descartes put asunder, has been the oblique admission that a richer world exists than abstract reason dreams of. The suppressed reality asserted itself in a roundabout way as the question of how knowledge is possible. "Knowledge was not a problem for the ruling philosophy of the Middle Ages; that the whole world which man's mind seeks to understand is intelligible to it was explicitly taken for granted." Man, according to Ramus, who in this respect was sufficiently medieval, "has naturally within him the power to know all things." But Descartes explicitly proposed a method of doubt, since "only those objects should engage our attention, to the sure and indubitable knowledge of which our mental powers seem to be adequate." His "two ultimate classes of real things,"[73] which could not be united except externally, raised the extraordinary issue of how he could be certain of anything.

Similarly, Locke found it imperative "to examine our own abilities, and see what objects our understandings were, or were not fitted to deal with," because he assumed that "observation" had two distinct fields, being "employed either, about external sensible objects, or about the internal operations of our minds perceived and reflected on by ourselves." Locke does not name "the difficulties that rose on every side" as he and his friends sat in his chamber; but his way of resolving them—by a critique of knowledge—was the result of a particular difficulty, which was doubtless at the bottom of those he consciously felt. The Cartesian dualism made the world safe for science by creating separate repositories, called "matter" and "mind," for the scientifically relevant and irrelevant, yet at the same time made it hard to see how even the scientific object could be known. Empirical theory held that the given materials of knowledge are atomistic sensations, passively received and variously combined by the intellect, so that the fullness of subjective life becomes unreal, and, in Hume's[74] words, the "creative power of the mind amounts to no more than the faculty of compounding, transposing, augmenting, or diminishing the materials afforded us by the senses and experience." But the creative power of the mind had its revenge when Hume proved that even the mathematical world of extension, figure, and motion had no claim to objectivity:

> It is a question of fact, whether the perceptions of the senses be produced by external objects, resembling them: how shall this question be determined? By experience surely, as all other questions of a like nature. But here experience is, and must be entirely silent. The mind has never anything present to it but the perceptions, and cannot possibly reach any experience of their connexion with objects. The supposition of such a connexion is, therefore, without any foundation in reasoning.

Hume simultaneously gave away his methodology (the true source of his difficulty) and tried to avoid the question of method by declaring that the relation of mind to objects is "a question of fact." Kant's new principle, "that the objects must conform to our mode of cognition," brought the vital question of method into prominence by explicitly reversing Hume's approach. Kant maintains, moreover, that "the primary datum of knowledge is... the single whole of experience." He is aware that "thoughts without contents are empty, intuitions without concepts are blind... By their union only can knowledge be produced." Yet he sees "no reason for confounding the share which belongs to each in the production of knowledge." Although Kant, by making the mind active instead of passive, brought out in high relief the equivocal position of his forerunners, he himself was committed to a similar equivocation: As James Gibson[75] puts it, "the Kantian theory is dominated throughout by the antithesis between the abstract universal as an object of conceptual thought and a mere manifold of sense impressions; and between these two, as thus opposed, only an artificial, and external union is possible." Kant began under the old dispensation with a general picture of two elements, "that which we receive through impressions, and ... that which our own faculty of knowledge... supplies from itself"; he ended with the conviction that "in the world of sense, however far we may carry our investigation, we can never have anything before us but mere phenomena...; the transcendental object remaining unknown to us." It has never been sufficiently emphasized by historians of American "transcendentalism" that the movement was generally regarded by its exponents as a revaluation of empirical philosophy. "Now the young are oppressed by their instructors," Emerson declared. "Bacon or Locke saw and thought, and inspired by their thinking a generation, and now all must be pinned to their thinking, which a year after was already too narrow for them." Placed in a wider context, Locke seems ingnorant of "the meaning of ideas," and "Hume's abstractions are not deep or wise." The founders of the "Transcendental Club,"[76] although their positive aims were so vague that they were not even sure how or why they got their name, were sure of one thing: "What we strongly felt was dissatisfaction with the reigning sensuous philosophy, dating from Locke, on which our Unitarian theology was based." Such men viewed their situation in an almost melodramatic manner. Their obsession with the evils of empiricism became a popular joke. They pictured mankind as prisoners of an outworn creed and spoke with "distrust and dread" of Locke's "iron hand":

> The notion, that the human soul is but a capacity, more or less extensive, for the reception of impressions to be made upon it by surrounding objects through the external senses, seems to be the darkest, the most deathlike predicament in which humanity could be entrammelled... The worst result of this error is its very general diffusion. The notion and the language of it pervades [sic] all ranks... We may appeal to the current language employed in everyday life, through the mouth and through the pen, for proof to what an extent this depressing idea prevails of man being passive to surrounding objects.[77]

It was this sense of crisis that enabled the American mind to seize upon the basic problem rather than the results of modern philosophy. Although the absolute reign of Locke had been, as James Marsh said, a "peculiar misfortune" of the United States, it created a situation in which Kant's reversal of approach would have a remarkable poignancy. In America it was startling news that "since the time of Descartes," through Locke, Berkeley,[78] and Hume to Kant and his followers, there had been a continuous problem and that this issue had been "before all a question of the human mind itself":

> Can I know? Can I know that I know? What is it, psychologically considered, to know? What is it to know that I know? How do I know? How do I know that I know? These are the problems, and problems very nearly peculiar to modern times.[79]

Ancient philosophy, Brownson informs us, was seldom concerned with such questions, "and the scholastic philosophy, never." The American intellectual turned to Kantian idealism not as the answer to what now seemed "the fundamental problem of human science" but as its "strongest expression." German thought was most patently what the whole modern tradition had been— "not a *ratio essendi* but a *ratio cognoscendi*"[80]—and the premises of Locke, which had remained unexamined for so long, must now be seen in the perspective of Kant's criticism. In 1803 Locke's Essay, according to Samuel Miller, established "an era in the history of metaphysical science," while Kant was obscure and probably inconsistent. By 1848 J. B. Stalloel[81] could assert that "'the Critique of Pure Reason,' though it nowise contains the sought-for axiom of the philosophy of the present, is nevertheless the cabalistic formula that has conjured it up."

The revolt from Locke reinforced the American awareness of method by affording a perspective where the language of empiricism became only a partial language. In history, it was now apparent, system was opposed to system, and one merged into another, so that no method was absolute, though method was the key to it all. At the same time, the concept of method was deepened by the new perspective of history and became something more than the free-floating rationalism of the Unitarians. The clash of Locke and Kant betrayed a basic problem of approach, and one that was still unsettled. In this light the significance of Kant was his own shift of emphasis from dogma to methodology. The American "transcendentalists" dallied with transcendental doctrine but hardly understood it in sufficient detail to become disciples; what they singled out was "the transcendental grammar of the intellect," the Kantian emphasis on form and method. The earliest American historian of modern idealism, James Murdock, noted that Kent's first *Critique* "is not properly a system of philosophical knowledge" but "rather an introduction to sound philosophizing." Men like Theodore Parker and Frederick Hedge[82] echoed the distinction. Parker "found most help in the works of Immanuel Kant," but not in Kant's conclusions: "He... gave me the true method, and put me on the right road." Hedge attributed the flourishing science and literature of Germany not to the current idealistic theories, which were disappointing, but "to the faculty which that philosophy has imparted of seizing on the spirit of every question, and determining at once the point of view from which each subject should be regarded, —in one word, to the transcendental method."

To take German idealism in this way was to follow the same path as Coleridge, whose aim, as James Marsh pointed out, was "not so much to teach a speculative system of doctrines built upon established premises... as to turn the mind continually back upon the premises themselves." By explicitly putting the question of the "conformity" between subject and object, idealism focused attention on the farming process and led to Emerson's feeling that "the state of the world at any one time [is] directly dependent on the intellectual classification then existing in the minds of men." And, for Emerson, Kant was the philosopher of "intellectual classification":

> The Idealism of the present day acquired the name of Transcendental from the use of that term by Immanuel Kant, ...who replied to the skeptical philosophy of Locke, which insisted that there was nothing in the intellect which was not previously in the experience of the senses, by showing that there was a very important class of ideas or imperative forms, which did not come by experience, but through which experience was acquired; these were intuitions of the mind itself; and he denominated them Transcendental forms.[83]

But what was the premise, the classifying form, of idealism? Emerson's faithful, though simplified, version of the Kantian scheme is chiefly important for the issue it leaves open. Forms do not "come by" experience; are they then imposed upon it externally? What is the locus of form? It

was essentially this question that had secretly badgered the seventeenth-
and eighteenth-century epistemologists. Kant had corrected the method of
his predecessors, but he had not given up the first and most devastating
principle of their approach. After all, he fell back on a form that made
form itself problematic; he "left reason standing in the face of the schism
between subject and object, with the dread conviction that the two were
irreconcilable." A true method must somehow escape this dilemma:

> Spiritualism and materialism both have their foundation in our
> nature, and both will exist and exert their influence. Shall they exist
> as antagonist principles? Is the bosom of Humanity to be eternally
> torn by these two contending factions?... Here then is the mission of
> the present. We are to reconcile spirit and matter... Nothing else
> remains for us to do. Stand still me cannot. To go back is equally
> impossible.[84]

Behind George Ripley's rhetoric (which was instigated by Brownson) was
the feeling stated more formally by Stallo: "The whole theory of two
independent factors of existence, Mind and Matter, Force and Inertia, is an
absurdity." Since "between the radically hostile there can be no peace," the
new point of departure would be the conception of interdependence. For
Brownson, "the subject and the object are both given simultaneously in
one and the same thought or act." Different systems, from this standpoint,
are different forms of the integral reality, different relations between the
two elements simultaneously given in all thinking. This was to make the
most of the notion of "form" implicit in the Kantian idea of "conformity."
Instead of absolute substances, one dealt with "modes of philosophizing"
and "orders of thought." While the contemporary psychology texts
invariably laid down the proposition that "all existence, as far as human
knowledge extends, is either material, or immaterial; corporeal, or
spiritual," in Emerson's rephrasing these alternatives become "two modes
of thinking," which, since they are both natural, are possibly reconcilable:

> As thinkers, mankind have ever divided into two sects, Materialists and Idealists; the first class founding on experience, the second on consciousness; the first class beginning to think from the data of the senses, the second class perceive that the senses are not final, and say, the senses gave us representations of things, but what are the things themselves, they cannot tell.[85]

The transformation of dualism into ways of thinking, which were often (in imitation of Coleridge) traced back to Plato and Aristotle, became one of the mannerisms of the time. Here was the conclusion of Alcott's lifelong quest for the "nexus" of mind and matter: "Nature and spirit are inseparable, and are best studied as a unit... The idealist's point of view is the obverse of the naturalist's."

The orthodox opposition, intrenched in its Lockian dogmatism, tried to denounce "the latest form of infidelity" as a doctrinal heresy and was thoroughly bewildered by the real innovation of the movement, the basic shift of standpoint involved. Under the pressure of the conflict between idealism and empiricism, and in an effort to get beyond it, Emerson and others had developed the concept of dialectic. The locus of form was the universe of discourse; the solution to the inherited problem of method was to assume a realm where method and content were one. And dialectic tended in the direction of symbolism. By extending his principle to all points of view, Alcott was able to picture a "spherical" truth and a language constantly expanding in "manifold senses and shades of meaning" as it took on various aspects of the whole. The hostile critics noted that the new school made "little reference... to the distinction between matter and spirit." Its aim was to avoid the distinction by returning to a mode of knowledge prior to that separation of the knower from the known which Emerson called "the Fall of Man." To the prelapsarian mind, according to James Marsh, "all things were real." But, as reason supervened upon direct perception, the religious and poetic consciousness could at best attain only "a kind of mental vacillation between the subjective idea, and the objective reality of the thing believed." The disjunction that logical procedures necessarily make had dissolved the complete realism of the primitive mind, and the intrinsic duality of logic had been translated by modern philosophy into a metaphysical principle. Although Emerson said that this whole development was "very unhappy, but too late to be helped," he and his contemporaries were trying to rescue themselves. The central question, as they saw it, was no longer the external relation between subject and object but rather the internal transmutation of thoroughly realistic forms:

Unless… [the mind] have the higher power of divesting itself of all that is peculiar in its acquired forms of thought, and in those conceptions by which it takes cognizance of the objects of its knowledge, of clothing itself anew in the forms of thought peculiar to another people, and of so adopting their conceptions for its own, as to, contemplate the world around them under the same relations with them, the man can never participate in their emotions, nor breathe the spirit of their poetry.[86]

The meaning of "knowledge" had been changed from objective certainty to organic experience:

We no longer think of a truth as being laid up in a mind for which it has no affinity, and by which it is perhaps never to be used; but the latent affections, as they expand under proper culture, absolutely require the truth to receive them, and its first use is the very nutriment it affords.[87]

To the conservative mind, Emerson's "Divinity School Address" seemed not only profane but absurdly illogical: "He tells us that religious sentiment is myrrh, and storax, and chlorine, and rosemary; that the time is coming when the law of gravitation and purity of heart will be seen to be identical." This, perhaps, was poetry, yet a poetry that would not remain safely fanciful and that claimed some odd revelation out of its very extravagance. But to the school of Emerson it was clear that poetic forms bring together terms "which taken literally... would give nonsense, or at least bad sense." The habit of organic apprehension was a denial of rational method: the stuff of knowledge was a "fact of consciousness," not a fact. Organic activity issued in organic forms—"not mere *forms continent* of life, but forms which are *formed life*"—and the transmutation of form was potentially hostile to logical distinctions. Logic, from this standpoint, was a kind of slide rule for the immature. When the mind met nature immediately in the act of knowledge, rational structure was superfluous:

> Syllogistic reasoning will be superseded by something higher and better. It amounts to nothing but the discernment and expression of the particulars which go to comprise something more general; and, as the human mind permits things to assume a proper arrangement from their own inherent power of attraction, it is no longer necessary to bind them together with syllogisms.[88]

The conscious aim of these men was to attain a language without particulars. Those who "regard each object in its individual capacity, as a separate, independent existence," are crippled by their own method; one must consider "the relation it bears to other objects, or to some indwelling principle of which it is the exponent." The transmutation of form is possible because the true coherence of divergent formulas is not that "of a merely logical arrangement, but of a natural development, and a growth." The age was beginning to perceive, according to W. H. Channing, "that through all varieties of creeds, through the thousand-fold forms of mythology and theology, through the systems of philosophers and the visions of poets, has spoken more or less audibly one Eternal Word." The new philosophy in America was an attempt to speak in consonance with that self-realizing language. Beneath "the discordant jargon of ten thousand dialects," as Reed said, it postulated "a language not of words, but of things," by which was meant a speech so devoid of artificiality that, while manifesting the mind, it would "lose itself in nature."

〔注释〕

1. Henry Adams：亚当斯（1838-1918），美国历史学家、小说家。《亨利·亚当斯的成长》是他以第三人称写作的自传性回忆录，表达出作者对西方文化衰落的深刻认识，是他的传世之作。引文取自该书第1章；"a child"为亚当斯自谓之语。

2. the woman：指夏娃。

3. Samuel Sewall：西沃尔（1652-1730），美洲殖民地时期马萨诸塞州首席法官，曾参加1692年的巫师审判。

4. our Clay-Tabernacles：意为"我们的身体"。

5. Joshua Moody：穆迪（1633-1679），北美拓殖初期普利茅斯殖民区的牧师。

6. 据《旧约·出埃及记》第16章，古希伯莱人在摩西率领下逃离埃及，在进入迦南以前在旷野漫游40余年。

7. Edward Johnson：爱德华·约翰逊（1598-1672），美国殖民地时期史书编纂家。

8. Joshua：约书亚，《圣经》中摩西卒世以后的以色列人领袖。他曾率军于基遍（Gibeon）城下大败迦南联军。在夜幕降临时，他郑重祷告说；"日头啊，你要停在基遍，月亮啊，你要止在亚雅伦谷[Aijalon]！"太阳和月亮果然停在天上不动，直到以色列人完全消灭残敌。参阅《圣经·约书亚书》10：12-13。

9. 引自爱德华·约翰逊所著的《新英格兰锡安救世主创造奇迹的神力》（*The Wonder-working Providence of Sion's Saviour in New England*）一书。

10. 引自科顿·马瑟所著的《基督在美洲的丕迹》（*Magnalia Christi Americana*）一书。

11. David：大卫（公元前 11 世纪-前 962 年），古以色列第二代国王。大卫杀非利士人歌利亚一事，见《圣经·撒母耳记上》第 17 章。

12. Moses：摩西，公元前 13 世纪希伯莱人的领袖，犹太教中最伟大的先知和导师，曾领希伯莱人离开埃及，摆脱奴役。

13. Azazel：阿撒泻勒，犹太教传说中的一个邪灵，象征污秽，被后世称为堕落的天使。

14. 引自《基督在美洲的丕迹》。

15. Sisera：西塞拉，《圣经》中的迦南将军，曾指挥亚宾（Jabin）的军队与德巴拉和巴拉的军队作战，战败后被杀。Jabin：亚宾，哈佐尔国王，曾以武力统治以色列人 20 多年，后被德巴拉的军队打败。

16. the River Kishon：基伸河，今西亚的穆长塔河。

17. Anne Bradstreet：布莱兹特里特（1612-1672），美国女诗人。*Meditations*：《沉思录》。

18. the Low Countries：指北海沿岸国家荷兰、比利时、卢森堡等。

19. Aquinas：即 St. Thomas Aquinas（阿奎纳，1226-1274），意大利神学家，中世纪欧洲经院哲学家。

20. Samuel Willard：威拉德（1639-1707），北美殖民地牧师。

21. 引自威拉德所著的《完整的神圣实体》（*A Complete Body of Divinity*, 1726）一书。

22. 引自约翰·诺顿（John Norton，1606-1663）所著的《新英格兰为当代的亵渎行为而悲伤》（*The Heart of New England Bent at the Blasphemies of the Present Generation*，1659）。

23. Scholastic philosophy：经院哲学，欧洲中世纪基督教会的官方哲学。它是以哲学形式论证基督教教义的思想工具，被称为"神学的侍女"。

24. 引自《彼得·拉莫斯文集》（1572）。

25. 引自威拉德的《完整的神圣实体》。

26. Richard Mather：理查德·马瑟（1596 -1669），北美殖民地第

一代牧师,《海湾赞歌集》(*Bay Psalm Book*)作者之一。

27. Thomas Hooker:胡克(1586-1647),北美殖民地牧师。

28. Whitehead:怀特海德(Alfred North Whitehead, 1861-1947),英国数学家、哲学家;下文引自其所著的《科学与现代世界》(*Science and the Modern World*, 1933)。

29. Calvinistic Protestantism:加尔文清教主义,源于6世纪法国宗教改革家加尔文(John Calvin,1509-1564)的神学理论,其教派为清教的一支。它主张原罪说、命定说,宣称《圣经》是信仰的唯一源泉。

30. The ten Aristotelian categories:见亚里斯多德所著的《物类》(*The Categories*),所讲的十类为:substance, quantity, quality, relation, place, time, position, state, action, affection。

31. The early Fathers:指基督教兴起后最初6个世纪的主要神学家。

32. 引自塞缪尔·马瑟(Samuel Mather)的《旧约中心的形象或象征》(*The Figures or Types of the Old Testament*, 1705)。

33. *Deo ad Deum*:拉丁语,意为"神中之神"。

34. The Canticles:《雅歌》,《圣经》的一卷。括号中的引文引自《雅歌》1:8。

35. 引自《基督在美洲的丕迹》。

36. ding-an-sich:德语,意为"物自体"。

37. 引自亚历山大·理查森(Alexander Richardson)所著的《逻辑学家的老师》(*The Logician's School-Master*,1657)。

38. Nathaniel Ward:沃德(1578-1652),北美殖民区清教牧师。

39. vericulum:拉丁语,意为"基本真理"。

40. a society of contract:取自卢梭的《社会契约论》(*le contract scoirl*)。18世纪人类宇宙观发生巨大变化,原先世人认为崇拜上帝的最佳方式是为人行善,而卢梭的"人本性是美好和快活的"论点是对基督教原罪说的直接评击。

41. 引自托马斯·谢波德《文集》第3卷。

42. 引自本杰明·富兰克林的《自传》。

43. Nathanael Emmons：爱莫思（1745-1840），美国公理会牧师，保守派理论家。

44. 引自安德鲁斯·诺顿所著的《论不信仰三位一体论者的原因》（*A Statement of Reasons for Not Believing the Doctrine of Trinitarians*, 1856）。

45. Thomas Paine：潘恩（1737-1809），思想家、革命家、作家，生于英国，曾参加美国独立战争和法国革命，他的作品，如《常识》、《人权论》、《理性的时代》等对欧美革命影响很大。

46. 引自纳撒尼尔·沃德所著的《单纯的鞋匠》。

47. W. E. Channing：昌宁（1780-1842），美国思想家，新英格兰超验主义的先驱，对爱默生等人影响较大，下面引文出自其《前言》（"Introductory Remarks"，1841）。

48. Horace Bushnell；布什奈尔（1802-1876），美国神学家。

49.引自托马斯·胡克著《赎罪的用途》（*The Application of Redemption*, 1659）。

50. 引自乔纳森·爱德华兹著《神圣不凡的光》（"A Divine and Supernatural Light"）。

51. 引自乔纳森·爱德华兹著自传。

52. 引自爱德华兹著《论上帝造世的目的》（"Dissertation Concerning the End for which God Created the World"）。

53. the Newtonian Universe：即 "Mechanical Universe"，认为宇宙如机械般运转。17 世纪末牛顿发表《自然科学的数学原理》（*Philosophiae Naturalis Principia Mathmatica*），对世人的宇宙观产生深刻影响，自神论（deism）及其他新思想遂产生，认为宇宙是上帝所创造的，但它依照自身的自然规律，宛如钟表般运转。

54. the new principle：即洛克（John Locke, 1632-1704）的认识论——知识源于经验和感官。

55. 引自爱德华兹的《神圣事物的形影》（*Images and Shadows of Divine Things*）。

56. 引自托克维尔（Alexis de Tocqueville）著《美国的民主》（*Democracy in America*, 1835-1840）。

57. Descartes：笛卡尔（Rene Descartes, 1596-1650），法国哲学家、数学家。下文中 Bacon：培根（Francis Bacon, 1561-1626），英国经验论哲学家。

58. Margaret Fuller：福勒（1810-1850），美国女评论家、文学家，19 世纪新英格兰超验主义者。下面引文出自《玛格丽特·福勒作品集》（*The Writings of Margaret Fuller*, 1941）。Pindar: 品达（公元前 518-438），古希腊诗人，所作的颂歌是公元前 5 世纪希腊合唱抒情诗歌的高峰。

59. 引自阿尔科特（A. B. Alcott, 1799-1888）著《言论集》（*Tablets*, 1868）。

60. Noah Porter：波特（1811-1892），美国教育家，哲学家和辞典编纂家。

61. Francis Bowen：博文（1811-1890），美国哲学家。

62. Swedenborgian：斯维登堡的。斯维登堡（Emanuel Swedenborg, 1688-1772），瑞典著名科学家、神秘主义者、哲学家和神学家。他认为上帝是不可描述的，因为它本身既是实体又是形式，但上帝的本质可从他的爱和智慧这两种品质上得到理解。他对爱默生等一些美国作家影响很深。

63. Fichte：费希特（Immanuel Hermann von Fichte, 1786-1879），德国哲学家，对 19 世纪美国思想界颇有影响。Schelling: 谢林（Frederich Willhelm von Schelling, 1775-1854），德国哲学家，德国古典哲学的主要代表之一，对 19 世纪美国思想家颇有影响。

64. Orestes Brownson：布朗逊（1803-1876），美国作家，编辑。

65. Boyle：波伊尔（Robert Boyle, 1627-1691），英国物理学家及化学家。

66. 引自乔纳森·爱德华兹《文集》第 1 卷。

67. 引自 J. W. 亚历山大和 A. B. 托德著《超验主义》（"Transcendentalism"）。

68. Parrington：帕灵顿（V. L. Parrington，1871-1929），美国历史

学家，著有《美国思想的主流》，影响颇大。

69. 引自 O. B. 弗罗辛厄姆的《新英格兰超验主义史》（*Transcendentalism in New England: A History*, 1876）。

70. Sampson Reed：里德（1800-1880），波士顿商人，斯维登堡学说的宣扬者，其著作对爱默生影响较大。

71. James Marsh：马什（1794-1842），美国学者、牧师。

72. Victor Cousin：库辛（1792-1869），法国哲学家、教育改革家和历史学家，具有系统的折衷主义思想。

73. 指物质与思想（matter and mind）。

74. David Hume：休漠（1711-1776），英国哲学家，不可知论的代表。他认为客观事物是否存在，人们无法得知，他主张感觉是"唯一的存在"，是一切知识的来源。下文引自他的《人类理智及道德原理研究》（*Enquries Concerning Human Understanding and Concerning the Principles of Morals*）。

75. James Gibson：吉布森（17001752），美国作家。

76. The founders of the "Transcendental club"：指 1836 年左右新英格兰改革家、思想家爱默生、昌宁、阿尔科特及玛格丽特·福勒等人。他们不定期集会，讨论哲学与神学等问题，世人称之为"超验主义俱乐部"。当时颇含贬义。

77. 引自查尔斯·莱恩所著的《A.布朗森·阿尔科特的著作》，载于《日轨》杂志（1842-1843）。

78. Berkeley：伯克利（George Berkelay, 1685-1753），爱尔兰主教、哲学家。

79. 引自布朗森（Orestes Brownson）《文集》第 1 卷。

80. *ratio essendi*：拉丁语，意为"据此某物存在"; *ratio cognoscendi*："据此某物被已知存在"。

81. J. B. Stallo：斯塔罗（1822-1900），德国出生的美籍相学家、法学家、哲学家。

82. Frederick Hedge：赫奇（1805-1890），美国牧师、作家。

83. 引自爱默生《文集》第 1 卷。

84. 引自乔治·里普利所著的《布朗森的著述》，载于《日轨》杂志（1840-1841）。

85. 引自爱默生《文集》第 1 卷。

86. 引自詹姆斯·马什所著的《希伯莱诗歌精神》译本的《前言》。

87. 引自里德所著的《论意识发展》。

88. 同上。

Questions For Discussion：

1. Define what Charles Feidelson terms "American Tradition." What is the major feature of the American Puritan mode of perception? To what extent has this mode of perception influenced American writers in their literary endeavors?

2. How is the evolution of an indigenous American tradition of literary symbolism rooted in the intellectual history of the West?

3. Discuss the continuity of ideas from the early Puritan theologians through Jonathan Edwards to Emerson, and the religious and philosophical inevitability of the evolution of the Puritan mode of perception and expression as exemplified in American literary works.

For Further Reading：

1. Miller, Perry. *Errand into the Wilderness*. Cambridge, MA：Harvard Univ. Press, 1956.

2. Feidelson, Charles Jr., and Paul Brodtkorb, Jr. eds. *Interpretations of American Literature*. New York: Oxford Univ. Press, 1959.

3. Nye, Russell B., and Norman S. Grabo, eds. *American Thought and Writing: the Colonial Period*. Boston, 1965.

南开英美文学精品教材

美国文学批评名著精读

（下）

The Scholar's Library for the Study of American Literature

常耀信　主编

南开大学出版社
天　津

前　言

　　美国文学评论的发展，至 20 世纪 70 年代，大体经历了三个重要阶段。自 19 世纪 40 年代爱默生的《论诗人》始至 90 年代威廉·狄恩·豪威尔斯的《批评与散文》止的半个世纪，是美国独立文学和文化的炼铸成形时期，是美国作家和评论家为美国独立文学的发展而鸣锣呐喊的时期。第二阶段从 19 世纪末始至 20 世纪 30 年代末止，这是美国文学评论气氛活跃、论争热烈、具有决定意义的阶段。除了 T. S. 艾略特、埃德蒙·威尔逊、艾伦·塔特等"新批评"的声音之外，还有一些不同凡响的声音——凡·威克·布鲁克斯、H·L·门肯以及伦道夫·伯恩等人对美国文学"业已成年"的断言。这是美国文学评论家以全新的目光看待本国文学独特的伟大之处的时代。如果说在这以前，人们习惯于以剖析欧洲和英国文学的思想和方法看待美国文学，因而结论总不外乎"不够伟大"、"不能同欧洲作家的鸿篇巨制相提并论"的话，那么，在这一阶段中，美国评论家已开始从美国的国情出发认识本国文学，认识到美国文学经过近三百年的演变，已于 1901 年至 1920 年间达到"成年"。这一论断开创了美国文学评论的新纪元；它标志着美国文学评论界重新评估美国文学的开端。

　　第三阶段可从 20 世纪 40 年代初 F·O·马西森的《美国的文艺复兴》和艾尔弗雷德·卡津的《在本国土地上》两部文学评论巨著的发表为始。这是一个"重新发现"美国文学的阶段。美国文学评论界一扫过去追随欧洲文学评论的气氛，把精力集中到从本国的文化历史实际出发剖析美国文学上面。如果二三十年代的论断尚需佐证，40 年代后的文学评论则从空泛的议论跃进到从作品的具体实际出发，寻觅出赏析美国文学的理论的阶段。美国文学评论界"重新发现"美国文学的激情在五六十年代升至其"沸腾点"，评论巨著迭相面世，每部新书都立论新颖，给人以一新耳目、发聩振聋的印象，真可谓群芳竞艳，让人目不暇接，读者对评论的兴趣有时竟超过对文学作品本身的兴致。倘然美国文学在 20 世纪前 20 年已趋成年，那么美国文学评论作为文学的一个有机组成部分，在五六十年代业已成年，并以自己的独特风格和欧洲文学评论比肩齐名。这一时期的评论重点在于美国早期文学，即 19 世纪美国文学的主要作家及作品，兼及 20 世纪二三十年代的杰出作家与作品。

20 世纪 70 年代以后，美国文学评论又有了长足发展。在继续探索早期美国文学的内在模式的同时，对 20 世纪以来，即现代和当代文学的评论数目剧增。新一代评论家又独辟蹊径，从不同的角度赏析现当代文学，进一步巩固了美国文学与文学评论在世界文坛上不可小觑的地位。今天美国文学在世界上几乎处于首屈一指的地位，大有取代英国文学的来头，这和美国文学评论界多年来不懈的杰出努力是有密切关系的。

多年来，美国文学评论的突出特点是它的多样性和独创性。正如美国现代诗人华莱士·史蒂文斯的一首诗所说，看山乌鸟的方式可有十三种之多，美国文学评论界自始至今所提出的研究美国文学的理论也是各式各样的。事实上，美国文学评论的基本特点在于它的"多元化"；但是透过这些纷然杂陈的观点，人们可以看到评论家都在努力寻觅一种"合成"理论，以诠释几位作家或某一时期内作家的创作活动，使之具有令人信服的理性基础。他们从美国历史或文化发展的角度去赏析本国文学，每人提出的理论都有合理之处。各种理论的总和便使读者有可能在较可靠的基础上看到美国文学的全貌。而且，他们是"百花齐放、百家争鸣"，各抒己见，不落窠臼，不肯"吃别人嚼过的馍"，有时某些评论家很有"语不惊人死不休"的气势。有人评论说，阅读过去的文学评论，特别是 20 世纪五六十年代的文学评论，其趣味不亚于阅读他们所评论的文学作品。编者本人就很有这种体会。

因此，把这些理论的精粹编选出来以飨读者是非常必要的。

正是出于这种意图，编者编写了《美国文学评论名著精读》，作为大学本科高年级及硕士和博士研究生的美国文学评论课教科书和必备的参考书。由于侧重点不在于反映美国文学评论的历史颠末，因而它的内容主要不是前面所讲的第一阶段和第二阶段，而是第三阶段，即美国文学评论业已成熟的阶段内的各种评论观点。本书共分上、下两册，辑录了美国评论家（除 D·H·劳伦斯外）对早期美国文学的各种评论，收集了评论界关于现当代美国文学的各种颇富影响的评论。所选注的文章皆出自美国学术界所公认的美国文学研究经典著作，都具有一定的经典性，不拘泥于概念的纷争，不玄秘艰涩，兼具科学性与知识性，对美国文学名家和名著进行生动、透辟的分析，视角多变，说理简洁，文字极流畅，在文学评论史上极有可能成为"里程碑"式的作品。它们的出版时间多为 20 世纪五六十年代，但也有相当数量的作品出现在 20 世纪的初年乃至三四十年代（尤其是包括在附件部分的作品）。他们的作者都无疑是美国文学评论界的佼佼者。他们的作品都具有一定的普遍意义及永久性。因而，这些评论文章应是美国文学研究者——本科生、研究生以及社会读者——所必读的"学者文库"中所包括的评论著作。这些作品应有助于增强美国文学学习者和研究者的底蕴和铺垫，应成为美国文学教学与研究工作者的学术基础的中心组成部分。

《美国文学评论名著精读》共选入 23 位著名评论家的专著或专论。每篇选文均由作者介绍、作品介绍、文章节选、注释、讨论题及参考书五部分组成，以利于美国文学的教学。编者相信，本书对美国文学的教学与学术研究工作将有很大的裨益。在美国文学的教学一线工作的教师们，会从本文选中汲取必要的资料，以充实教学的广度和深度，取得更好的教学效果。

在本书的编写过程中，王蕴茹教授在查核资料、对照原文以及通读全文方面，做出了可观的努力和贡献。

尽管编者做了最大努力，书里错讹之处一定仍然不少，敬请各位专家、学者、读者等拨冗不吝指教。

常耀信

2006 年 7 月于南开

Table of Contents

Daniel Hoffman

〔作者介绍〕

　　丹尼尔·霍夫曼（Daniel Hoffman，1923- ），美国诗人、文学评论家。他出生在纽约，就读于哥伦比亚大学，获博士学位。曾在斯沃思莫尔大学和哥伦比亚大学任教，做过印第安纳大学文学院研究员，曾任法国第戎一大学客座教授。1972 年任美国诗人协会主席，1973年任美国国会图书馆诗歌顾问。自 1966 年起为宾夕法尼亚大学英语教授、"驻校诗人"。他曾于 1964 年获哥伦比亚大学魁奇奖章和费城文学协会文学奖。

　　霍夫曼迄今已出版六本诗集，其中包括《三十条鲸鱼》（*An Armada of Thirty Whales*）、《一个小故事》（*A Little Geste*）、《令人满意的城市》（*The City of Satisfactions*）及《我到厄尔巴岛前天下无敌》（*Able Was I Ere I Saw Elba*）等。作为诗人，霍夫曼技巧精湛，文笔典雅，其作品常有出人意外的效果。

　　霍夫曼是出色的文学评论家，他的文学评论和他的诗歌一样，表现出对神话及其影响的浓厚兴趣和独到见解。他的主要文学评论著作有：《保尔·班扬》（*Paul Bunyan*）、《最后一名边疆神人》（*The Last of the Frontier Demigods*）、《斯蒂芬·克兰的诗》（*The Poetry of Stephen Crane*）、《野蛮的知识：叶芝、格雷夫斯及米尔诗歌里的神话》（*Barbarous Knowledge; Myth in the Poetry of Yeats，Graves，and Muir*）、《美国小说的形式与寓言》（*Form and Fable in American Fiction*）以及《坡》（*Poe Poe Poe Poe Poe Poe Poe*）。20 世纪 70 年代末，霍夫曼主编了《美国当代文学》（*Harvard Guide to Contemporary American Writing*）。他还编选了斯蒂芬·克兰和罗伯特·弗罗斯特的诗歌选集。

Form and Fable in American Fiction

〔作品介绍〕

　　《美国小说的形式与寓言》是研究民间传说与神话对早期美国文学的影响的一部经典性文学批评著作，1965 年在纽约出版。它探讨的范围既包括曾深刻影响过早期美国小说家欧文、霍桑、麦尔维尔、马克·吐温的题材，也涉及这些作家独特的写作风格。

　　全书共由四部分及一篇"后记"组成。第一部分"寓言与现实"属概论，它阐述了作者关于神话与寓言对美国小说家的影响的观点。霍夫曼认为，早期美国小说的素材和灵感的源泉为民间传说、神话、礼仪及巫术等，因此领悟民间传说与神话在小说中的体现会加深对作品的欣赏和理解。虽然民间口头传说几乎尽人皆知，但是在事实上，对作家的创作发挥影响的传说题材是屈指可数的。这可以从欧文、霍桑、麦尔维尔及马克·吐温的作品里看出来。早期美国小说属于"传奇"（romance）类，其特点是回避"现实"，表现出作者不愿正视社会现实问题，在创作过程中多借助于狂想、感情及闹剧形式的倾向。

　　霍夫曼对几位早期小说家的十部短篇及长篇作品进行了深刻分析。这些作品包括欧文的《睡谷传奇》（"The Legend of Sleepy Hollow"），霍桑的短篇小说《村里的大伯》（"The Village Uncle"）、《我的族人莫里诺少校》（"My Kinsman, Major Molineux"）、《五月柱》（"The Maypole of Merry Mount"）、《好小伙子布朗》（"Young Goodman Brown"）、《红字》（*The Scarlet Letter*）、《七个尖角阁的房子》（*The House of the Seven Gables*）、《福谷传奇》（*The Blithedale Romance*）、麦尔维尔的《白鲸》（*Moby Dick*）及《骗子》（*The Confidence Man*）和马克·吐温的《哈克贝利·芬历险记》（*The Adventures of Huckleberry Finn*）。霍夫曼推究事理，力求钩深致远，不仅寻究这些作品从民间传说与神

话中吸取题材的情况，而且考查它们的文学形式和所取题材的内在关系。他把"民间传说"、地区性传奇故事、巫术与奇闻轶事、北方乡巴佬和骗子、民间故事同欧洲的"神话"（诸如神的死而复生等）相提并论，把地区性或历史性的事实同古代的典型同样看待，把民众文化同西方文学传统并重，不分厚薄，这就把美国小说置于神话的框架里，而赋予它以新的丰富的内涵。霍夫曼认为，美国小说因凭借寓言、哥特文体、民间传说和神话等的力量而独具魅力。

　　这里选注的是该书第一章第三节。

An Excerpt from *Form and Fable in American Fiction*

The American Hero: His Masquerade

> "Something further may follow of this Masquerade."
>
> —Melville, *The Confidence Man*

ONE

　　"What then is the American, this new man?" asked Crevecoeur[1] in1782, posing at the birth of the Republic the question of national identity which our writers have never since ceased trying to answer. Even from the earliest settlement the conviction loomed large that human nature itself was changed by being transplanted to new circumstances. The Puritans had felt as a divine visitation the call to leave the Old World for the New and found under God's will a new Zion[2] in the wilderness. By the middle of the eighteenth century the thoughts of emigration and the untamed land continued to sway men's minds. We have noted in the paradisal symbolism of the frontier that the wilderness becomes the fecund Garden of tall-tale fame. Melville would envisage the West as inhabited by "the White Steed of the Prairies... A most imperial and archangelical apparition of that unfallen western world, which to the eyes of the old trappers and hunters revived the glories of those primeval times when Adam walked majestic as a god, bluff-browed and fearless." Characteristically, Melville mythicized into more heroic dimensions a conviction of popular culture. The Englightenment version of the "bluff-browed and fearless" American settler was indeed unfallen and Adamic, but not quite as majestic or godlike as Melville proposes. This we can see in Crevecoeur's answer to his own question, "What then is the American, this new man?"

> He is an American, who, leaving behind him all his ancient prejudices and manners, receives new ones from the new mode of life he has embraced, the new government he obeys, and the new rank he holds... The American is a new man, who acts on new principles; he must therefore entertain new ideas, and form new opinions. From involuntary idleness, servile dependence, penury, and useless labour, he has passed to toils of a very different nature, rewarded by ample subsistence.
>
> —This is an American.

The character of this new man soon clearly revealed itself. At first there was the miraculous rebirth of the British serf as a freeholder in the New World; the career of one such serf, Andrew the Hebridean, was appended to the third of Crevecoeur's *Letters from an American Farmer*. But one need not be born a serf on the isle of Barra[3] to be reborn in the American colonies. That rebirth and metamorphosis are the bywords of American life is among the lessons in Benjamin Franklin's *Autobiography*. That work and Crevecoeur's [work] are the earliest and most influential examples of the new American character in literature. As yet the lineaments of that character are "colonial," the products rather of general political and social institutions than of the special culture of a particular region. Such localization was the next step in the development of popular concepts of character. Along the northeastern seaboard a well-defined type, the Yankee, developed early in folklore and, by the 1830's, appears in unpopular culture to have displaced the undifferentiated American of the Franklin and Crevecoeur variety. A parallel development along the frontier brought the character of the Backwoodsman into folktales, almanacs, popular fiction, theatricals, and, in the person of Davy Crockett,[3] into national political prominence. Metamorphosis, adaptability, and indomitable self-mastery are the qualities these three types of the hero share. Whether actual men or fictitious characters, these heroes insist upon the constancy of the self behind their changing masks. Yet, as the more reflective minds of Hawthorne, Melville, and Twain used these popular stereotypes in their fiction, the question of identity could not so casually be laid to rest. Crevecoeur's question, what is the American, becomes for their characters, Who am I? Which of my masks is Me?

Andrew the Hebridean, however, felt no such ambiguity about *his* identity.

> All I wish to delineate [Crevecoeur writes] is, the progressive steps of a poor man, advancing from indigence to ease from oppression to freedom; from obscurity and contumely to some degree of consequence— not by virtue of any freaks of fortune, but by the gradual operation of sobriety, honesty, and emigration.

To succeed, Andrew must cast off his ancient heritage as though it were a chrysalis. Only then can the real man within come forth in all his human power, sustained by the laws; for "we are the most perfect society now existing in the world." Arriving in Philadelphia, Andrew is befriended by the benevolent American Farmer who assures him that "Your future success will depend entirely upon your own conduct; if you are a sober man... laborious, and honest, there is no fear that you will do well." No less than twelve times do these adjectives, the apices of bourgeois virtue, come together in Crevecoeur's discourse on Andrew. It is true that the Hebridean does not know how to handle a hoe or an axe, and that his wife must be apprenticed in a friendly kitchen to learn the rudiments of pioneer housekeeping. These skills being soon acquired, Crevecoeur and a friend stake Andrew to a hundred acres of land. The ever benevolent farmer invites the neighborhood to a frolic; amid the convivial folk festival of houseraising a new American is born:

> When the work was finished the company made the woods resound with the noise of their three cheers, and the honest wishes they formed for Andrew's prosperity. Thus from the first day he had landed, Andrew marched towards this important event: this memorable day made the sun shine on that land on which he was to sow wheat and other grain ... Soon after, further settlements were made on that road, and Andrew, instead of being the last man towards the wilderness, found himself in a few years in the middle of a numerous society. He helped others as generously as others had helped him ... he was made overseer of the road, and served on two petty juries, performing as a citizen all the duties required of him.

The combination of his own sobriety, industry, and honesty with "our customs, which indeed are those of nature" and our laws, which derive "from the original genius and strong desire of the people," leads ineluctably toward the triumphant transformation of Andrew. By Crevecoeur's time, deistic optimism[4] had for many colonists quite replaced the earlier Puritan emphasis on original sin. Man, in accordance with the new philosophy of the age, is inherently good, and America, being free from the inherited evils and injustices of Europe, offers him the unprecedented opportunity to be reborn to a brighter destiny. Although neither Crevecoeur nor his age held credence in such superstitions as witchcraft or wonders, surely this transformation of a peasant into a free American is as miraculous an instance of shape-lifting as anything reported at Salem.[5] The power of transformation, of self-transformation, is no longer seen as malevolent. It partakes of the same beneficent energy that populates the forests and the farmyards with prodigious plenitude of game and fecundity of crops. Already the American character is defined as the exercise of metamorphic power.

Crevecoeur's ingenuous account of Andrew is the prototype of the Horatio Alger story.[6] It is the new fairy tale of the new man on the new continent. He begins life in Europe, in the stage of subjection to which history has condemned him. But by emigrating to the New World, he begins to feel the effects of a sort of resurrection; hitherto he had not lived but simply vegetated; he now feels himself a man, because he is treated as such. His symbolic gesture is to discover his own humanity in a land where all men hold the highest and equal rank of citizens.

In time the American hero developed a more sophisticated character. The next representative hero adapted himself to almost all of the human possibilities of thought and action in his time. Benjamin Franklin begins his dizzying progress in much the same vein that Crevecoeur had begun Andrew's adventures:

> Having emerged from the poverty and obscurity in which I was born and bred, to a state of affluence and some degree of reputation in the world, and having gone so far through life with a considerable share of felicity, the conducing means I made use of, which with the blessing of God so well succeeded, my posterity may like to know, as they may find some of them suitable to their own situations, and therefore fit to be imitated.[8]

It is worth recalling that Franklin formed the plan of his life upon his reading of Cotton Mather's *Essays To Do Good*. Although the didacticism of his purpose perpetuates the Puritan emphasis on studying the example of a holy life, his goal is not holiness. It is success. The simple bourgeois formula of honesty, sobriety, and industry which brought about Andrew's resurrection is elaborated in Franklin's famous table of virtues, as well as in a hundred examples drawn from his own life. One cannot gainsay D. H. Lawrence's mockery of Benjamin for his denial that "The soul of man is a dark vast forest, with wildlife in it: Think of Benjamin fencing it off!... He made himself a list of virtues, which he trotted inside, like a gray nag in a paddock." [9] This charge, or at least its spirit, was anticipated by Melville. As one who dived deep into the recesses of the self, he could not help but find Franklin's character a shallow show of outward versatility lacking inner conviction. Thoreau was more in tune with the popular culture of the time when he wrote, "Franklin—there may be a line for him in the future classical dictionary, recording what that demigod did, and referring him to some new genealogy. Son of—and—. He aided the Americans to gain their independence, instructed mankind in economy, and drew down lightning from the clouds." [10] It was his role as rebel rather than as conciliator, and his hard-headed virtues and practical approach to the mastery of life which made the hero of the *Autobiography* seem a prototypical figure among his countrymen. Quite consistent with these qualities was his rationalistic derision of the superstitions of Puritan times in his bagatelle, "A Witch Trial at Mount Holly."

In the midst of so much that is admirable in Franklin's career, what seems to have most appealed to the popular mind were the ingredients of a stock figure, half wily savant, half homely philosopher. The emergent Yankee trickster was already limned in Ben's burning his light later than his rival's, pushing a wheelbarrow down Main Street to promote his own reputation for industry, rising in the world by the heft of his own cunning till at last he dines with kings. Allied with this emphasis on the too-clever side of Ben is the popular confusion of Franklin himself with Poor Richard, his fictitious gaffer who paved *The Way to Wealth* [11] with proverbs. "Love your neighbor; yet don't pull down your hedge"; "Write with the learned, pronounce with the vulgar"; "Fish and visitors stink after three days"; "If you would be wealthy, think of saying as well as getting." These apothegms of bourgeois caution could, like his tricky maneuvers to get ahead, be regarded as somewhat incompatible with the other Franklin of popular tradition—the wise statesman, the original scientist, the patriarchal patriot. Mark Twain, in a sketch at Franklin's expense, complained that "His maxims were full of animosity toward boys. Nowadays a boy cannot follow out a single natural instinct without tumbling over some of those everlasting aphorisms and hearing from Franklin on the spot." Franklin, pretending industriousness, might say "Procrastination is the thief of time," but Mark Twain knows better: "In order to get a chance to fly his kite on Sunday he used to hang a key on the string and let on to be fishing for lightning."

He was always proud of telling how he entered Philadelphia for the first time, with nothing in the world but two shillings in his pocket and four rolls of bread under his arm. But really, when you come to examine it critically, it was nothing. Anybody could have done it.[12]

In a trenchant satirical sketch of Franklin, Melville presents the sententious, calculating sage at Passy,[13] in whom "The diplomatist and the shepherd are blended; a union not without warrant; the apostolic serpent and dove." This portrait, in *Israel Potter*,[14] is perhaps as shrewd an assessment of Franklin's virtues and as striking an indictment of his faults as the narrator of the *Autobiography* has ever received. Melville ranks him with Jacob in the Bible, and Hobbes,[15] as "labyrinth-minded, but plain-spoken Broad-brims... keen observers of the main chance; prudent courtiers; practical Magians in linsey-woolsey." The dualism of his personality, the contrast between his humble beginnings and the worldly, sophisticated, and cunning old soothsayer Israel Potter meets in Paris, makes Franklin suspect:

Having carefully weighed the world, Franklin could act any

part in it. By nature turned to knowledge, his mind was often grave, but never serious. At times he had seriousness—extreme seriousness—for others, but never for himself… This philosophical levity of tranquility, so to speak, is shown in his easy variety of pursuits. Printer, postmaster, almanac maker, essayist, chemist, orator, tinker, statesman, humorist, philosopher, parlour man, political-economist, professor of housewifery, ambassador, projector, maxim-monger, herb-doctor, wit; Jack of all trades, master of each and mastered by none—the type and genius of his land. Franklin was everything but a poet.[16]

In his protean and hydra-headed versatility the metamorphic Franklin seemed a moral chameleon. Who and what is he, ultimately, underneath all, these rebirths and resurrections? Franklin's own character exhibited in its most highly developed form that versatility which frontier conditions and a limited population made necessary in a new country. De Tocqueville had noticed the premium placed in America on the Jack-of-all-trades, at the expense of the master-craftsman who was useless beyond his one specialty. If this prized versatility did not long outlast the division of labor brought about by post-bellum industrialization, it was characteristic of American life in the early twentieth century. This was true on every level of society, from the farmer-mechanic-peddler to the likes of George Washington and Thomas Jefferson, both of whom were quondam philosophers, scientists, architects, statesmen, politicians, and farmers. That the plebeian Franklin should have been the most successful citizen of this universe suggests the remarkable degree of social and intellectual mobility possible even before the establishment of the Republic.

Franklin's philosophy was too self-confident for us to view his life as a search for values, although he so viewed his early years. He soon enough found the set of values—respectability and probity in business, an accommodating deism in religion, a faith of serving God through service to man in public life—which he followed throughout the rest of his long career. His intellectual energy was equaled only by his curiosity, and his theoretical interests never far outran his pragmatism in applying new concepts. No sooner had he discovered the electric nature of lightning than he patented a lightning-rod! Here was Yankee science at its birth, in which intuitive hunches lead to the discovery of great principles, and those discoveries to immediate applications.

But if Franklin had no doubt about his own identity, we cannot say the same for every young man who emulated him by trying half a dozen careers. Washington Irving and Walt Whitman taught school and edited newspapers and entered politics before discovering their essential selves. Melville of course was teacher, clerk, sailor, whaler, captive of cannibals, and Polynesian beachcomber until he found by the accident of writing his adventures that literature was his true career. Mark Twain started out as cub pilot, miner, and itinerant journalist, before making the literary strike that uncovered his richest ore. What a man does determines in the long run what he is. These writers did not know who they were until they found their right vocations. Yet their writings are populated with American characters who, true to the expansive spirit of the age, move from one identity to another with neither effort, preparation, nor reflection. At the same time, however, the problem of identity, of discovering the essential self, has been a particularly acute one in American literature. With so many selves to choose from, anyone who does have deeper commitments to the life of the spirit than Melville detected in Ben Franklin must discover which of his own masks is made of the flesh and skin of the face that wears it.

The metamorphic variety of American life and the impetus it gave toward self-determined transformation is thus made spectacularly apparent in Ben Franklin's career. Franklin, with his universality, fairly represents the nascent American character. In popular culture and our early literature, however, native characters did not have Franklin's easy movement through all the conditions of life. They began as local characters whose idiosyncrasies were typical of their regions. From the first the colonies had been differentiated by their several creeds, methods of settlement, and systems of government. These differences, to which was added the greatest difference of all—that between the life of the settled seaboard and the harsh existence of the frontier—are already visible in the earliest depictions of indigenous character. As befits a national literature in its primitive beginnings, these earliest depictions often appear in theatricals. They were, in fact, ritualistic portraits in which the several identities of the American were enacted and revealed. Whether as Yankee peddler or Kentucky boatman, metamorphosis, on a humbler level than Franklin's yet just as self-determined and as optimistic, was at the core of their nature.

TWO

One evening in Boston, in 1838, a crowd in a theatre gasped with awe and terror as Dan Marble, the famous Yankee actor, deliberately leaped over Niagara Falls—from the very roof of the theatre, seventy feet above the stage—to reappear, ebulliently, in a pool of foam. The piece of which this leap was the climax was *Sam Patch; or, The Daring Yankee*. Many in the audience had already seen, or would soon see, the renowned James Hackett, another actor, in his famous impersonation of Nimrod Wildfire, "The Lion of the West." This remarkable hero of *The Kentuckian; or, A Trip to New York*, in his buckskin and powder-horn, characteristically admonished an English fop.

> If you think to get rid of me without exchanging a shot, you
> might as well try to scull a potash kettle up the falls of Niagara with
> a crowbar for an oar.

Defying the falls of the Niagara, as Carlyle observed at about this time, was a proverbial expression of the American Spirit. And so were the two rodomontade braggarts on the stage. The Yankee and the Frontiersman had come out of the country village and the virgin timber, shouting their boasts, revelling in their own rusticity. These two plays were but selected instances in a flood of stage pieces, journalistic sketches, almanac characters, humorous collections, folk-told yarns, ballads, doggerel verses, and songs which limned their collective portraits in the early nineteenth century. Not only did they body forth the types already long familiar to the popular mind; their adventures, as sung, written, read, and enacted in crude though symbolic gestures, exemplified the attitudes toward character and destiny of the popular culture whose creatures they became.

The impulse which launched these rustic heroes on their impudent careers reverberated too in the aphoristic profundity of a voice much more couth than theirs. While Nimrod Wildfire and Sam Patch cavorted on their respective stages, in a nearby lecture hall another crowd leaned forward in hushed attention to a seer's[17] admonishment:

> There is a time in every man's education. When he arrives at the conviction that envy is ignorance; that imitation is suicide; that he must take himself for better or for worse as his portion... The power which resides in him is new in nature and none but he knows what that is which he can do, nor does he know until he has tried...

> Whoso would be a man must be a nonconformist... No law can be sacred to me but that of my own nature. Good and bad are but names very readily transferable to that or this; the only right is what is after my constitution, the only wrong what is against it.

The evening's lecture was "Self-Reliance"; the lecturer, an accomplished impersonator who, on other nights, would be billed as "The Hero," "The Poet," "The Philosopher," "The American Scholar," "The Man of the World," "The Reformer," "The Transcendentalist." A decade later he would be characterized in Lowell's "A Fable for Critics" as

A Greek head on right Yankee shoulders, whose Range

Has Olympus for one pole, for t' other, the Exchange.

These lines on Emerson, from the pen which in that same year (1848) immortalized the Yankee type in the homely guise of Hosea Biglow,[18] suggest the kinship of the Sage of Concord[19] with the rude and rustic stereotype of regional popular character. The same contradictions that Lowell finds in Emerson he sees in the Yankee at large— "A strange hybrid, indeed, did circumstance beget, here in the New World, upon the old Puritan stock, and the earth never before saw such mystic-practicalism, such niggard geniality, such calculating-fanaticism, such cast-iron enthusiasm, such sour-faced humor, such close-fisted generosity."[20]

Emerson's transcendental counsel has its affinities with the self-assertive folk spirit of both the Yankee and the Kentuckian. Half mystical though his vision of the world might be, in his attempts to ground the perception of the spirit in the experience of the senses he even leaned toward the folk vocabulary of the time. Yet these affinities with popular culture in Emerson's essays were but fragmentary, compared with the effect the popular stereotypes of character would have on the fiction of his contemporaries, Hawthorne and Melville, and after them, Mark Twain.

What were these images? How did they evolve?

The origin of the very name *Yankee* is a mystery, a secular mystery. *The Dictionary of American English* discovers the term to be no older than the French and Indian War, when it was apparently the cognomen of certain regiments from Connecticut. In any case, we owe to the British redcoats of the Revolution the distinctive sobriquet, for it was they who used it to deride their homespun foes. If we knew who first coined the term we might also be able to know the original author of the song, "Yankee Doodle." This catchy fife tune soon enough passed into folk provenience. Its verses recapitulated the adventures of a nascent folk hero—the young man from the provinces who comes to town to enlist in the Continentals and make his way in the world. In the decades after the Revolution this high-stepping, wide-eyed man underwent some interesting transmogrifications and enjoyed some adventures as yet unsuspected by the Down East seamen, merchants, and farmers who rallied to Paul Revere's[21] harried cry. "Yankee Doodle" became a stock property of the Yankee drama which emerged just after the Revolution—the rustic Jonathans, Jedediahs, and Ichabods of a score of plays announced their independence as they whistled, sang or recited the famous song. Even before the song got into plays—the Yankee first walks onstage as the rustic servant Jonathan in Royall Tyler's[22] famous comedy, *The Contrast* (1787)—it had inspired many a stanza depicting rustic life in original poems which took their rhythm and refrain from its well-nigh universal popularity. Among the most popular of these was a broadside written in 1795 by Thomas Green Fessenden,[23] "Jonathan's Courtship," known also as "The Country Lovers":

A merry tale will I rehearse,
As ever you did hear, sir,
How Jonathan set out so fierce
To see his dearest dear, sir.

Yankee doodle, keep it up,
Yankee doodle dandy,
Mind the musick—mind the step,
And with the girls be handy...

"Miss Sal, I's going to say, as how
"We'll spark it here tonight,
"I kind of love you, Sal, I vow,
"And Mother said I might."
　　　　Yankee doodle &o...

> "Are you the lad who went to town,
>
> "Put on your streaked *trowses,*
>
> "Then vow'd you could not see the town,
>
> "There were so many houses?"
>
> Yankee doodle &o….

Here was Jonathan Jolthead, rustic swain: circumlocutious, head abulge with gossip and afire with witchcraft superstition, bashful, tongue-tied, and afraid for his life of sparking. A more amusing picture of a farm boy's discomfiture in romance was hot rhymed again for half a century, until Lowell wrote "The Courtin."[24] Fessenden's broadside was at once reprinted, anthologized, and republished in his *Original Poems* (London, 1805; Philadelphia, 1806). Its comic portrayal of the New England rustic represents the first stage in the emergence of the Yankee as a character type.

The second stage is his appearance in plays. The earliest stage Yankees, like Jonathan in *The Contrast*, were usually bumpkin servants on their first trip to town; but soon the Yankee end-man became the center of the show. By the 1820's such character actors as Dan Marble and Yankee Hill were commissioning plays in which to exhibit their mastery of the stereotyped comic character. To the original qualities of rusticity, boastfulness, inquisitiveness, and independence, played off against the mores of a more highly polished urban society, the Yankee as hero added a bracing bravery, downright honesty, and upstanding moral certitude. These sterling qualities were often exhibited in plots of treacle which involved the attempt of a villain to seduce or abduct the heroine—dastardly knavery foiled by the indomitable Jonathan. In Richard M. Dorson's detailed study of these early plays at least eleven examples of stock Yankee characters appear before 1819. Since these all conform to a single type rather than exhibit individual characteristics, Dorson concludes that "it is more probable that a permanent Yankee folk type existed apart from [Tyler's] dramatic imagination and was adopted, and not created, by the playwrights." The facts that the playwrights sometimes used the Yankee traits as a disguise for other characters and that these plays have repeated references to the Yankee as "an original," "a perfect-natural," "a real live Yankee," indicate the "existence of a mythical Yankee who was properly the property of the folk." Further evidence is the "tendency to give individual examples of the genus a common name, Jonathan." Tyler's play stated the theme which most of the later stage Yankees repeated: the contrast between the polished manners of the English dandy (aped by his obsequious butler), who proves to be both a villain and a fraud, and the dashing honesty and manliness of the American swain, aided by his oafish, naive, and bungling Yankee servant, Jonathan, who has a heart of gold beneath a comically unsophisticated exterior.

On stage the Yankee had been the country clown in the city. A smart Down East editor, Seba Smith[25] of Portland, hit upon the notion of rusticating the now-familiar Yankee character, and exhibiting him against the background of his native village. Happily, Smith was able to elaborate this conception, having an unusual ear for the cadences and vocabulary of actual New England country speech and a sense of humor which delighted in comic portraiture as well as in political satire. Once Jonathan is recast as Major Jack Downing of Downingville, Away Down East in the State of Maine, he suddenly ceases to be the oafish victim of his own unfamiliarity with the decorum of the city. The Yankee as countryman reverses the role. He now plays a version of Pastoral, in which he possesses the limitless wisdom of his mother wit. It is the complexities of an overweening sophistication, both social and political, which get the short end of the axe handle when measured against his horse sense, honesty, and shrewdness in appraising human motives. Smith could take advantage, in the Major Jack Downing papers, of the satirical possibilities offered him by a character both naive and clairvoyant. Thus Major Downing, as a political commentator, acts on the presumption that in a democracy the common citizen can address the head of the State (he writes directly to General Jackson), since the Government cares as much about each of the people as the people care about the Government. His native village is named for his grandfather, a doddering gaffer who detains every passerby with his endless account of the "fatigue of Burgwine."[26] The old soldier's discursive garrulity, first published in 1833, would not be matched in print until Mark Twain wrote down "His Grandfather's Old Ram' in *Roughing It*" (1871). The Major's grandfather was not only a Revolutionary soldier, but also a pioneer. It is curious how his settling as far Down East as he could go prefigures the western treks of so many later veterans and folk heroes. When Major Downing first appears, then, he is seen in the settlement his own family had founded and lived in for three generations. This roots him to a place in a way that most Yankee characters are not rooted in popular lore; at the same time Downing Ville prefigures the Jalaam[27] of Lowell's *Biglow Papers*, the Poganuc and Oldtown[28] of Mrs. Stowe's novels, the Deep Haven of Miss Jewett's[29] stories, the Tilbury Town of Robinson's[30] poems, and so represents a large forward step in the development of New England's regional literature.

On the 18th of January, 1830, readers of the Portland, Maine *Daily Courier* first made the acquaintance of Jack Downing. In a letter to his cousin Ephraim Downing, "up in Downingville," Jack declared as how he had come to Portland to "sell my load of axe handles, and mother's cheese, and cousin Nabby's bundle of footings." While in town he has been to a meeting, and to the museum, and to both Legislaters, the one they call the House, and the one they call the Sinnet. Of course this village boy is the yokel of Yankee joke lore, who doesn't get the point at all of the political wrangling he sees. But as a matter of fact the parliamentary wranglers look pretty venal and stupid when measured against his clear notions of how a democratic legislature ought to conduct itself. This simple pattern of using the good life of the bumpkin village to measure the devious city takes full advantage of the nostalgia for a golden age of simplicity. The rural village appears constantly in American literature, oratory, and thought of as an almost contemporary symbol of the Golden Age. Associated with this concept are several other equally seminal notions: Rousseau's ideal of the Noble Natural Man, Crevecoeur's idealization of the farmer, Jefferson's of the artisan and farmer class; and the opposite but complementary conceptions about the city as the place of evil. The usual pattern of one numerous genre of the American novel is to move an innocent character from his country home into the temptations and evils of city life. This pattern conforms not only to that found in the "young man from the province" class of novels, but also to the movement of populations in the American nineteenth and twentieth centuries.

With the Rural Village as the locus of a paradisal symbolism in folklore and popular culture, we may well expect to find secular analogues to the Fall.[31] Seba Smith achieved a delicate balance in Jack Downing between innocence and knowledge; his Major—his whole village of Downing Ville—has a knowledge which does not cost them their Down East paradise because it is instinctual knowledge, not the hard, mean knowledge gained by experience. Their innate good natures and their birthright of Yankee wisdom make such characters as Major Downing inviolable against chicanery. (The stage Yankee, too, had been a towering pine tree of natural goodness and virtue.) But when the Yankee character is uprooted from the stabilizing influences of village life, and, in accordance with the mercantile temper of the times, takes to the roads with a pack of notions, clocks, and nutmegs, the moral quality of our delight in the folk character is perceptibly altered. President Timothy Dwight of Yale College, "whose experience with the peddlers of Connecticut must have been extensive," inveighed against their effect upon mercantile morality in New England:

Men, who begin life with bargaining for small wares, will almost invariably become sharpers. The commanding aim of every such man will soon be to make a good bargain; and he will speedily consider every gainful bargain as a good one. The tricks of fraud will assume, in his mind, the same place, which commercial skill and an honourable system of dealing hold in the mind of a merchant. Often employed in disputes, he becomes noisy, pertinacious, and impudent... I believe this unfortunate employment to have had an unhappy influence on both the morals and manners of the people.[32]

Doubtless there were honest peddlers, but nobody told stories about *them*. In folk anecdote and jokelore the itinerant Yankee peddler came into focus. The sketches featured his pack of notions and his sharp bargaining ways. They told of the Connecticut peddler who tried to sell brooms to the merchants of Providence. (This one was recorded in 1852, three decades after President Dwight's jeremiad.) Having no luck, at last he found a dealer who "would put his goods at cost price, for the sake of trading." After long negotiations they agreed to terms: payment for the brooms to be half in cash and half in goods. The brooms unloaded and cash payment made, the merchant asked, "Now what will you have for the remainder of your bill?"

The peddler scratched his head...walked the floor, whistled, drummed with his fingers on the head of a barrel. By and by, his reply came—slowly and deliberately.

"You, Providence fellers are cute, you sell at cost... and make money. I don't see how 'tis done. Now I don't know about your goods, barrin' one article, and, if I take anything else, I may be cheated. So, seein' as t'won't make any odds with you, I guess I'll take brooms. I know them like a book, and can swear to what you paid for 'em."

Note that this sharp deal was driven because both merchant and peddler pitted wits for the sake of trading. There were countless stories of similar shrewdness.

The heroes of folklore and of popular culture inevitably display those qualities of character which their celebrants admire. Since the recorded anecdotes of the nineteenth century contain so many yarns of this type, we may well ask ourselves what indeed is the significance of the popularity of the Yankee peddler as a roguish picaro. In an interesting discussion of the relation between mythical concepts and personal identity, Jerome S. Bruner remarks on two basic mythic plots:

> the plot of innocence and the plot of cleverness—the former being a kind of Arcadian ideal, requiring the eschewal of complexity and awareness, the latter requiring the cultivation of competence and awareness, the latter requiring the cultivation of competence almost to the point of guile. The happy childhood, the good man as the child of God, the simple plowman, the Rousseauian ideal of natural nobility—these are the creatures of the plot of innocence. At the other extreme there are Penelope, the suitors, and Odysseus… New versions arise to reflect the ritual and practice of each era—the modifications of the happiness of innocence and the satisfaction of competence.[33]

For early nineteenth-century America, the Yankee villager is one expression of the myth of innocence, the Yankee peddler of the myth of competence. But our native trickster hero has of course sold his soul for knowledge[34]—not that he ever thinks about his soul in the crafty jokelore that preserves the shards from which his *Odyssey* might have been written. Even in the most ambitious attempts to give the peddler a name, a face, a personality, he remains rather the shifty, sparring, crafty side of a man than does he become a personality nearly as well-rounded as Major Downing.

It was a Nove Scotian judge named Thomas Chandler Haliburton[35] who took up Seba Smith's idea of a series of satirical newspaper sketches about a single regional character, and substituted for the village yokel of Downing Ville a master of shifts and disguises in the itinerant profession. By 1837 Haliburton had published in book form his first collection, *The Clockmaker, or the Sayings and Doings of Samuel Slick*. His Sam Slick is admirable, as tricksters are without being exactly *likeable*. He peddles his clocks and opinions up and down New England, Canada, the West, and even visits England and the Continent in a series of books that spanned the next twenty years. Fencing wits with whoever crosses his path, he assumes changes of costume (Easterner's broadcloth or Westerner's legging), temperament, or opinion as the occasion warranted. Like the Connecticut broom peddler, he trades just for the sake of trading; he goes the broom peddler one better, trading not for profit but for pure pride:

> I met a man this morning, said the clockmaker, from Halifax, a real conceited lookin' critter as you een a most ever seed, all shines and didos. He looked as if he had picked up his airs arter some officer of the regulars had worn 'em and cast 'em off…
>
> Well, says he to me, with the air of a man that chucks a cent into a beggar's hat, a fine day this sir. Do you actily think so said I? and I gave it the real Connecticut drawl. Why, said he, quite short, if I didn't think so, I wouldn't say so. Well says I, I don't know, but if I did think so, I wouldn't say so. Well says I, Don't know, but if I did think so, I guess I wouldn't say so. Why not? says he—Because, I espect, says I, any fool could see that as well as me; and then I stared at him, as much as to say, now if you like that are swap, I am ready to trade with you again as soon as you like.[36]

Now the yokel comes out on top against the city slicker, a further reversal of the earlier Yankee role.

By the Civil War the Yankee stereotype had divided in the popular mind, as journalists and dramatists spawned two varieties of Yankee creatures to catch the public fancy. His shrewd, narrow-nosed commercialism and self-seeking aspects, joined to his impervious egotism and colossal self-satisfaction, made for a caricature of the already proverbial type. Sam Slick was the most popular expression of this side of the Yankee—albeit Lowell accused him of being a slander against the regional character. To the South, in Alabama, another rogue's adventures were laughingly devoured in the newspapers where Johnson J. Hooper[37] first published his *Adventures of Simon Suggs* (reprinted in book form, 1845). Hooper's hero, whose motto proclaimed "it is good to be shifty in a new country," is the most fully developed American picaro before Melville's *The Confidence Man*. In this introductory passage his creator allows us a glimpse behind the comic mask Simon usually wore:

> The shifty Captain Suggs is a miracle of shrewdness. He possesses in an eminent degree, that tact which enables man to detect *the soft spots* in his fellow, and to assimilate himself to whatever company he may fall in with. Besides, he has a quick, ready wit, which has extricated him from many an unpleasant predicament, and which makes him whenever he chooses to be so—and that is always—very companionable. In short, nature gave the Captain the precise intellectual outfit most to be desired by a man of his propensities. She sent him into the world a sort of he-Pallas, ready to cope with his kind from infancy, in all the art by which men "*get along*" in the world; if she made him in respect to his moral conformation, a beast of prey, she did not refine the cruelty by denying him the fangs and the claws.[38]

One instance of his avarice and shifty deception is already familiar in Mark Twain's borrowing from "Simon Suggs Attends a Camp Meeting" for his description of the spiritual and literal piracy of the King in *Huckleberry Finn* (chap. 20).

Yet the native picaro had admirable qualities too—his enterprise, his adaptability, and his peddler's mission (whatever the motive) of bringing the comforts of civilization to every cabin on the farthest frontier. In the 1840's a folk hero embodying these qualities appeared. First in cabins and farms along the Muskingum valley, then in the pages of Henry Howe's[39] *Historical Collections of Ohio*, and eventually in the folklore and fiction of the entire country. The adventures of Johnny Appleseed[40] grew even more miraculously than did the orchards he had planted. Paddling down the Ohio to Marietta at the mouth of the Muskingum, then up that stream to its tributaries, John Chapman set out apple seeds to make ready the earth for populations yet unborn. He also left behind him foods, which he split into sections and passed out to lonely settlers on one trip, circulating the fragments from cabin to cabin on his return. Beloved by the Indians, he was immune to their ferocities during the War of 1812; in fact he saved many settlers from their vengeance. He befriended the animals; if he saw one abused by its master he would buy it and give it away to a more humane pioneer. Johnny Appleseed spoke frequently with angels.

It does not matter that a painstaking biography of John Chapman shows him to have been a Yankee trader after all. Born in Leominster, Massachusetts, in 1774, he appeared, during his travels in Ohio, to be as representative a Yankee type in his "mystic practicalism" as any friend of Hosea Biglow in Jalaam. First, his mysticism. Robert Price has shown how theologically sophisticated was this early disciple of Swedenborg and how important his role in spreading the doctrine of the New Jerusalem on the unpromisingly hard terrain of the Ohio frontier. He even offered to trade some of his land to the New Church in return for shipments of Swedenborg's tracts, which he would disseminate on his journeys. This offer points to the conclusion that Johnny Appleseed was no "pauper philanthropist"—actually he owned hundreds of acres of choice Ohio land and based his seemingly eccentric life on a sound principle of economics. "The one unique thing about John's seedling tree business…was his scheme for moving it with the frontier."[41] These facts, which Price spent years tracking down, were obliterated by the popular image of Johnny Appleseed, as it was embellished and romanticized in succeeding decades. To become this humble image of the Hero as Civilizer, Sam Slick had to cast off all his characteristics but his garments and his peripatetic ways. Gone are the shiftiness, the cunning, the insidious sophistry, the trade for the sake of trading. To bring religion and reading to the trappers and woodsmen in their lonely cabins, to enrich the hillsides with orchards for the sake of mankind yet to come, this peddler all but denies his Yankee lineage.

Yankee self-assertion—the impulse of self-definition through symbolic action—appears most dramatically in the figure of Sam Patch. Like Johnny Appleseed Patch was an actual person, a textile worker in Pawtucket, Rhode Island, who attracted local attention by plunging, feet first, from the roof of a shed into the river beneath. Spurred on to seek fortune and national fame by spectacular leaps, Sam Patch abandoned his loom for a grand tour of waterfalls. Heralded by handbills proclaiming his motto, "Some things may be done as well as others," he climbed to flimsy platforms and plunged into the swirling froth. Sam conquered the great Niagara, but the Falls of Genesee[42] at last proved his undoing. Attempting his feat after one too many drinks of whiskey, he lost his poise about twenty feet from the water and landed sideways. As often happens, a mysterious death may catapult a poseur into legendary fame. Sam's body didn't come to the surface for six months. By then it was far too late to prove that he was dead. He had jumped through the bowels of the world and turned up alive in the south seas. He was also knocking about the American West, as alleged by many travellers. While some might scoff, none could deny that he had been on the stage of many a theatre. As Nature imitates Art, [43] so men are tempted to assume the role of the heroes in their myths: Dan Marble leaped from the height of the theatre into a trap in the floor, behind the pool of water, where a bedspring padded with shavings cushioned his fall. Even more significant than professional theatricals, however, the jumping mania affected audiences. Clerks jumped counters, farmers jumped fences, boys and old folks vied in "doing" Sam Patch.

Here was a natural subject for celebration by these very clerks and farmers. Sam's common origin, his braggadocio, and senseless defiance of danger—not to mention his showmanship—objectified in one symbolic act the qualities of self-assertive independence, rebellion against convention and authority, and, above all, self-reliance no matter what the stakes or the odds. These attributes had long been rooted in the American grain, in the Yankee character, and the boys and oldsters jumping fences to "do" Sam Patch were in a sense performing a ritual by which they asserted that for them, too, "Some things may be done as well as others." Those things included plunging from the security of seaboard cities into the unfathomed perils of the wilderness.

THREE

The settlers of the West developed images of their indigenous traits too. In the period before the Civil War the prototypical frontiersman, like his Yankee counterpart, provided a multiple image. At first, as Backwoodsman, he is a type of the natural man, inherently superior to civilized decadence, his egalitarian good fellowship not quite disguised by his shaggy exterior and helliferocious manner of speech. Backwoods brawlers must have formed an unofficial fraternity throughout the sparsely settled districts of the young Republic, for early travelers' journals report countless instances of their ear-chewing, cheek-ripping, eye-gouging battles. Augustus Baldwin Longstreet[44] gives vivid descriptions of such fights, and of a lone plowboy's rehearsal of one, in his *Georgia Scenes,*

Characters, Incidents, &o. in the first Half Century of the Republic, a work which in 1835 marks the inception of a Frontier literature comparable to the Yankee regional writings discussed above. But Longtreet's "The Fight" and "Georgia Theatrics" were no exaggeration of the real thing; if elaborated with tall talk and, touched with fantasy, they were yet based on life.

The frontiersman, it is well to remember, was not always a Westerner, but he was usually farther west than the seaboard Yankee. In the early days of the republic the frontier was often just a few miles inshore or a few hundred yards from the inland village or town. In her study, "The Rise of Theatricals," Constance Rourke[45] identifies the first frontiersman intended for the American stage as "A minor character called Raccoon or Coony in the early comic opera *The Disappointment* [who] seems to have been a frontiersman, but the piece was never performed... though it was twice printed, in 1787 and 1796, and so must have had some sort of circulation." By a curious coincidence Royal Tyler's Jonathan emerged on the stage at the same time (1787), and our two principal character types have been in tandem almost ever since. In her tantalizingly unspecific way Miss Rourke adds that "With his braggadocio and half-Indian way he was pictured in a few stories of the War of 1812." Just which stories, whether drama or fiction, she does not say, but she does remark that "Cockalorum... the lively typical figure with his... gaudy hunting costume was not to emerge noticeably in the theater until 1822, when he appeared with a rush—to music, gusty music, a song," The Hunters of Kentucky, which celebrated those backwoods Kentuckians, "half horse, half alligator," who had helped Jackson win the Battle of New Orleans.[46]

The frontiersman's earliest full-dress appearance in fiction is, surprisingly, in a famous sketch by our first gentleman of polished letters. Brom Bones,[47] in Washington Irving's "The Legend of Sleepy Hollow," demonstrates already in 1819 that the Dutch rowdies of the upper Hudson

Valley were frontiersmen of the same stamp as the Ohio riverboatmen and Missouri trappers. Lacking the stories of the War of 1812 mentioned by Rourke, however, it would seem that the first frontiersman actually to appear in a stage play is the character Opossum in Alphonso Wetmore's three-act farce, *The Pedlar*, "Written for the St. Louis Thespians, By Whom It Was Performed with Great Applause" in early 1821. In the final curtain speech Opossum reveals the original on whom his character was doubtless based: "If you'll let me live single, till after the dog days, Mike Fink[48] and I wilt go and catch a Barr, and we'll have a barbecue, for wedding supper, anyhow."[49] In earlier speeches Opossum reproduces the boisterous brag of the backwoods bully :

> *I'm half sea horse & half sea serpent.* Did you ever see my coon dog, stranger? (*Whistles.*) Which eye shall I take out, Mary?… I'll tell you, stranger, my name is Opossum—I'm a "wild-cat"—I've got the swiftest horse, the sharpest shooting rifle, and the prettiest sister—so if you offer to wrestle with her again, you must run faster than the yankee peddler did, or my coon dog will tree you.

There is, inevitably, a "yankee peddler" in the piece:

> *Nutmeg*: Hallo the house! I suppose the old cogger is not up yet. He little thinks the greatest genius in the universe, now stands before his door, ready to cheat him out of half he is worth. (*Window opens, old Praire puts his head and the muzzle of a rifle out.*)
>
> *Old Prairie:* Who the devil are you, Mr. Impudence?
>
> *Nutmeg:* A travelling merchant, sir—all the way over the mountains, from the town of New Haven, with a cart load of very useful, very desirable and very pretty notions: such as, tin cups and nutmegs, candlesticks and onion seeds, wooden clocks, flax seed and lanterns, Japanned coffee pots, and tea saucers, together with a variety of cordage and other dry goods.

By the end of Act I, Nutmeg has sold a lantern to every member of Old

Prairie's household and has cheated the sailor Harry Emigrant in a horse-swap.

Contrasted to his shrewdness with its smack of the counting house is the energetic activism of the frontiersman. A drunken boatman enters, singing:

> *Boatman*: Quarter less twain. (*Opossum rises, and advances*.)
>
> *Opossum*: Who are you, stranger?
> *Boatman*: A steamboat, damn your eyes.
> *Opossum*: Then I'm a Missouri snag—I'm into you.
> *Boatman*: I'm full of chain pumps—come on—I'm a five horse team.
> *Opossum*: Then I'll blaze your leader. (*Strikes him in the face…*)
> *Boatman*: No gouging?
> *Opossum*: And no ear biting…

It is obvious that these three characters, who so closely resemble the Yankee peddlers and ring-tailed roarers of the Jacksonian newspaper sketches a decade later, are based on the already widely known stock figures of oral tradition. Yet *The Pedlar* is not lacking in literary derivations. As Scott C. Osborn's preface to the recent reprint observes, Wetmore's piece is "A crude mixture of melodrama, farce, low comedy, Restoration comedy, and intrigue play…" *The Pedlar* is "derivative almost throughout," based entirely on stock devices—"disguises, mistaken identities, assignations, the fortuitous discovery of a long-lost son and a will, the eloping couples." The characters too are dramatic conventions: the female wit, the clever servant, the discomfited father, the old man in love with a young girl; "Pecanne is a Lydia Languish, Opossum a Tony Lumpkin, Harry Emigrant an imitation of salty-spoken sailors from Wycherly[50] on." Two scenes are adapted from *She Stoops To Conquer*,[51] while "Nutmeg's lament for the loss of his wares is a burlesque of Wolsey's[52] farewell to his greatness." The playwright who combined dependence upon all of these eighteenth-century staples with realistic observations of frontier life and the adaptation of native stereotypes from oral tradition was a Connecticut-born soldier, merchant, lawyer, publisher, and sometime author. Osborn concludes that "*The Pedlar* has no literary value," and that its only merit "lies in its Western characters and local color." Part of its historical value, however, is to remind us of the complexity of the literary matrix into which characters, themes, and settings from folklore were introduced. Even so crude a production as *The Pedlar* (the only play by a man who was after all a literary amateur) demonstrates the cultural background—richly cosmopolitan, by folk standards—of the earliest drama on the American frontier.

The Pedlar illustrates one of the knottiest problems involved in understanding the absorption of folk materials into literature. The transformation to which folklore is necessarily subjected by the literary imagination complicates its identification. Even when the author retells verbatim stories from oral tradition, he is never a folk redactor. The literary context in which he places such tales is itself a change worked upon them. He may enclose the folk motifs in a more elaborate literary structure or contrast them to a different frame of reference than would a folk raconteur telling the same story. Further, he may extend and develop germinal plots or characters. One of the most important functions of folk materials in literature is to offer contrasts to the materials drawn from traditions other than the folk. The interplay of native folklore and European literary traditions is one of the important sources of tension in much American writing. Mark Twain, for instance, made Tom Sawyer a repository of chivalric notions from *Don Quixote* and Sir Walter Scott, while Huck Finn, with his protean disguises, superstitions, innocence, and closeness to nature, is a figure embodying many themes, traits, and motifs of American folklore.

Wetmore's frontiersman had alluded to Mike Fink, the original on whom his own braggart prowess was modelled, almost a decade before Fink himself became the hero of a cult of popular literature which lasted into the 1880's. Walter Blair and Franklin Meine, who reconstructed Fink's biography and reprinted the literature about him, find considerable evidence that in the decade of the 1820's Mike Fink had already become a hero of oral folklore. [53] Like Sam Patch and Johnny Appleseed, Mike was at first just a real man, born in Fort Pitt (Pittsburgh) around 1770 when that rowdy and endangered settlement comprised twenty cabins. Life there hardened the men and boys who lived it, and Mike, a settler…, became a prodigy of physical strength, appetites, and endurance. He was soon a super marksman and a famous hunter.

Mike was bred as an Indian fighter. He had an appetite for that business, which was his first career. Later, when Pittsburgh had grown and the Indians retreated, he became a keelboatman. When the steamboats encroached on the keel- and flat-boats he went west of the rivers and began his third career as a trapper. In each of his manifestations he retreated from society to preserve his own savage nature from change. During his lifetime Fink was the hero and scourge of towns along the Ohio and the Mississippi. In time he became the archetype of his breed. "He was in fact a Mississippi river-god, one of those minor deities whom men create in their own image and magnify to magnify themselves," Miss Rourke claims for him.[54] Whether fact or legend, the stories told about him typified popular attitudes toward the men who first rid the wilderness of Indians and split the silence of the waters with their boat horns and ballads of Shawnee town.

Who could have foretold that the first scribe to record the rough saga of this shaggy boatman would be a contributor to a satin-bound ladies' annual? True, *The Western Souvenir, A Christmas and New Year's Gift for*

1829, was published in Cincinnati, and its editor, James Hall, declared independence from Eastern originals, saying, "It is written and published in the Western country… and is chiefly confined to subjects connected with the history and character of the country which gives it birth." Although Hall, a leading early writer of the Ohio Valley, wrote much of the contents, his work was overshadowed by "The Last of the Boatmen," contributed by Morgan Neville.[55] This author had actually known Mike Fink during his own Pittsburgh boyhood. Just as Longstreet in *Georgia Scenes* and Hooper, in *Adventures of Simon Suggs* would describe the outrageous barbarity and guile of frontiersmen from the viewpoint of an observer from a higher culture, so did Neville present his uncouth Achilles as a picturesque specimen of an already vanishing phase of Western life. Unlike the later writers from the South, Neville does not abandon his own hifalutin style to reproduce the barbaric yawp of his subject. He tells of meeting Mike, while on a riverboat, and witnessing Mike's feat of shooting a tin cup from his brother's head—the William Tell[56] motif in buckskins; recounts Mike's prowess at killing an Indian; alludes to "a thousand legends [that] illustrate the fearlessness of his character"; and reports that his hero died when, performing his tin cup shoot, he aimed too low, and a friend of the victim, "suspecting foul play, shot Mike through the heart before he had time to reload his rifle."

In addition to these simple motifs Nevill contributes a picturesque description of his hero and a set of ennobling comparisons:

> With a figure cast in a mold that added much of the symmetry of an Apollo to the limbs of a Hercules, he possessed gigantic strength … At the court of Charlemagne he might have been a Roland; [57] with the Crusaders he would have been the favorite of the Knight of the Lion-heart;[58] and in our revolution, he would have ranked with the Morgans and Putnams of the day. He was the hero of a hundred fights, and the leader in a thousand daring

adventures… Wherever he was an enemy, like his great prototype, Rob Roy,[59] he levied the contribution of Black Mail for the use of his boat … On the Ohio, he was known among his companions by the appellation of the "Snapping Turtle"; and on the Mississippi, he was called "The Snag."

Within the next two decades Fink's adventures were retold and elaborated in such repositories of Western local color as the Cincinnati *Western Monthly Review*, the St. Louis *Reveille*, and the nationally admired *Spirit of the Times*; the authors were such then-prominent litterateurs of the West as Timothy Flint, Thomas Bangs Thorpe, John S. Robb, and Emerson Bennett. Briefer, more vigorous sketches than theirs appeared in the Davy Crockett Almanacs for 1837, 1839, and 1850-53. None of these writings is in itself of first quality, but taken together they form a strong sub literary tradition which defines the anarchic frontiersman's character with a clarity that helps us understand the significance of the type in the writings of Melville and Twain.

The Mike Fink sketches present an unwitting mixture of sentimentality and barbarism. When looking for a fight, Mike Fink announces himself in Emerson Bennett's version of the ring-tailed roarer's brag:

> Hurray for me, you scapegoats! I'm a land-screamer—I'm a watchdog—I'm a snapping truckle—I can lick five times my own weight in wildcats. I can use up Injuns by the cord. I can swallow niggers whole, raw, or cooked. I can out-lick, out-dance, out-jump, out-dive, out-drink, out-holler, and out-lick any white thing in the shape o' human that's put foot within two thousand miles o' the big Massassip…

John S. Robb improved upon the original tale of Mike's marksmanship. He has Mike take up the taunt, "Why, you couldn't hit the hinder part of that nigger's heel up thar on the bluff," "'thout damagin' the bone."

Dead-eyey Fink fired in jest; when the local magistrate tried to arrest him for the prank, Mike quipped, "I want you to pay me for trimmin' the heel of one of your town niggers! I've just altered his breed, and arter this his posterity kin warr the neatest kind of a boot!" To cure "a woman who passed for his wife" of winking at another man, Mike made her lie down in a bed of leaves which he then set afire: He kept her there till her hair blazed; this was quite a joke.

Thomas Bangs Thorpe, the author of "The Big Bear of Arkansas," wrote of Mike in "The Disgraced Scalp Lock" (1842). His Fink gives a brave Indian the mortal insult of plucking a feather from his headdress; he pursues Mike a thousand miles down the river but Fink's rifle cheats the Indian of a deserved revenge. Mike's philosophy is dualistic in this sophisticated adventure story: on the one hand he gives us the ruthless wilderness code which Uncle Ben, in Arthur Miller's *Death of a Salesman*, will preach in mid-twentieth-century; "I was never particular about what's called a fair fight … It's nature that the big fish should eat the little ones." But speaking in a different voice, Thorpe's Mike transcends his time in this lament:

> What's the use of improvements? When did cutting down trees make deer more plenty? Who ever found wild buffalo or a brave Indian in a city? Where' the fun, the frolicking, the fighting? Gone! Gone! The rifle won't make a man a living now—he must turn nigger and work.

The woodsman who makes possible the coming of civilization cries out in nostalgia and bitterness against the things he has wrought. Mike Fink, the retrograde bully and roustabout, is here made to mouth the ambivalent feelings of a more polite public regarding the destruction of the wilderness Eden—in which his cruelties were never called to account—by the outcome of civilization, law, and restraint.

However savage such men as Mike Fink were in fact, their

unknowing roles as harbingers of civilization justified an idealization of the frontiersman's character:

> Though held in sort a barbarian, the backwoodsman would seem to America what Alexander was to Asia—captain in the vanguard of conquering civilization. Whatever the nation's growing opulence or power, does it not lackey his heels? Pathfinder, provider of security to those who come after him, for himself he asks nothing but hardship. Worthy to be compared with Moses in Exodus, or the Emperor Julian in Gaul,[60] who on foot, and bare-browed, at the head of covered or mounted legions, marched so through the elements, day after day. The tide of emigration let it roll as it will, never overwhelms the backwoodsman into itself; he rides upon advance, as the Polynesian upon the comb of the spray.

This is Melville, eulogizing the frontiersman in *The Confidence Man* (1857). Melville's woodsman is not Mike Fink but another Ohio Valley character first drawn by James Hall,[61] who had published Neville's sketch of Fink in 1829. Three years later Hall, in his *Legends of the West*, outlined the career of one Colonel Moredock, a monomaniacal Indian hater. Although Moredock's passion invests his character with a tragic dignity lacking in Fink, it is noteworthy that Melville's treatment of the woodsman, whom he presents ideally and then in the grimness of his barbarous fixation, parallels the dualistic popular conceptions of frontier character.

A decade after *The Pedlar* appeared, the poets William Cullen Bryant and Fitz-Greene Hallecke[62] served, with Prosper Wetmore, as judges of a contest offering a three hundred dollar prize for "an original comedy whereof an American should be the leading character." The winner was James Kirke Paulding[63] with his farce, *The Lion of the West*. The play was produced the following year (1831), but in the course of its theatrical history it was twice rewritten—the second time, for its London run in 1833,

similar sketch fourteen years earlier in *Letters from the South* about a battle between a bateaux-man and a Wagoner; and second, the much superior version from his play was lifted by the author of *The Sketches and Eccentricities of Col. David Crockett of West Tennessee* (1833), who changed little beside the name of the candidate in the next election. This however, was fair enough, since Paulding had modelled Nimrod Wildfire on Davy Crockett in the first place. When, according to one observer, "at Crockett's request Hackett gave the play in Washington," and came on stage in the character of Wildfire, he bowed first to the audience and then to Crockett. The redoubtable Davy returned the compliment to the amusement and gratification of the spectators.[65]

The pattern of humor in *The Lion of the West* devolves upon the contrast between Nimrod Wildfire and one Mrs. Wollope, an English lady bearing an unmistakable resemblance to the author of the recently published *Domestic Manners of the Americans*. Arriving in America, she remarks,

> At length I've reached the scene of my experiment. To ameliorate the barbarism of manners in America has been the ruling wish of my life ... the plan I have concerted is founded, I conceive, on a true knowledge of the national character. The root of all the evils of this country is familiarity—where every one is equal, every one is familiar; and this is linked with another barbarism—the women here like those of Turkey are treated as domestic slaves. Now my system is to raise my own sex to its proper dignity, to give them the command and so refine the men.

It is curious to see how this sententious and self-righteous Englishwoman (as Paulding depicts her) offers, as the butt of the satire, two opinions which other American authors would find in the native grain. James Fenimore Cooper and Herman Melville (in *The Confidence Man*) would have no quarrel with her suspicion of the evils of egalitarian dogma; while

Hawthorne, in *The Blithedale Romance* and Henry James in *The Bostonians* would show the passion for feminist agitation to be, as James observes in his notebook, "the most salient and peculiar point in our social life." As a dramatic work *The Lion of the West* is slap dash; its humor is rudimentary, its situations stock, and Paulding's opinions pretty chauvinistic. The comedy runs along these lines:

> *Caesar*: Gemman at de bar send you his card.
>
> *Mrs. Wollope*: His card—the king of clubs? (*Turns it over and reads*) Colonel Wildfire. Is he a gentleman?
>
> *Caesar*: Don't know, marm—said he was a horse. (*Exit*)
>
> *Mrs. Wollope*: A horse! Oh, of the horse—a cavalry officer—the very thing I wished to see. Now for a specimen of an American gentleman.

Wildfire enters, brings forward two chairs, sits in one and puts his feet on the other. Mrs. Wollope inquires where he is from:

> *Wildfire*: Old Kaintuck's the spot. There the world's made upon a large scale.
>
> *Mrs. Wollope*: A region of superior cultivation—in what branch of science do its gentlemen excel?
>
> *Wildfire*: Why, madam, of all the fellers either side the Alleghany hills, I myself can jump higher—squat lower—dive deeper—stay longer under and come out drier.

A moment later he tells her the yarn of the hat floating in the swamp—when he lifted it with his whip, "a feller sung out from under it, Hallo stranger, who told you to knock my hat off? ... I'm doing beautifully—got one of the best horses under me that ever burrowed—claws like a mole." "This," says Mrs. Wollope, "shall be the first well authenticated anecdote in my perusal." If the Englishwoman is an overbearing snob, the backwoodsman is likewise a caricature, although of course a kindly one. His integrity as one of Nature's noblemen makes a manly contrast to the cowardice of another character, a fraudulent English lord. The Flower of the Forest always shows his virtues best when played off against the decadence and the moral decay which our popular mythology viewed as the inevitable burdens of complex social organization and of the aristocratic past.

The figure of Nimrod Wildfire in Paulding's play lends support to Mody Boatright's contention that "tall talk ... is a notification of the repudiation of the values of the outsiders, that is, of gentility... The frontier braggart assumed the role expected of him; but in exaggerating it to comic epic proportions, he satirized it."[66] The difficulty with this argument is that on occasion the satire becomes the thing itself. This we may observe in the case of Davy Crockett, the real-life original of Paulding's Nimrod Wildfire.

FOUR

Colonel Crockett has but lately died another death. For almost a century, only folklorists studying the heroes of nineteenth-century telltales or historians interpreting the Age of Jackson concerned themselves with the life and supposed writings of David Crockett or with the fragmentary yarns and apocryphal legends which became attached to his name. The resurrection of Davy Crockett as a temporary hero of contemporary culture is a sociological phenomenon of great interest. Why should this all-but-forgotten congressman from the canebrakes, this picturesque bear-killing, yarn-spinning, hard-drinking Indian fighter with no qualification for public life other than his gregarious manner and ready tongue, suddenly become a national infatuation whose fame was celebrated in every medium of mass communication, whose name endorsed a hundred and one products in the market place?

In considering Crockett's recent resurrection it is well to remember that he had had two earlier careers as a figure in the popular imagination. The first corresponds more or less to the events of his own lifetime, as they are recounted in his "autobiography." This is the Crockett whom V. L. Parrington attacks in *Main Currents of American Thought*—the ignoramus who buys his constituents drinks to win their votes, the wise-cracking hick whose folksy jokes distract the crowd from the serious speeches of his better-qualified opponents. This is the Crockett who boasts that "at the age of fifteen, I did not know the first letter in the book," and that when appointed a magistrate he could scarcely sign his name but "relied on natural born sense, and not on law to guide me; for I had never read a page of a law book in all my life."[67] The popular appeal of this Crockett is easy to assess, even though the book to which a friend more literate than he signed his name (*A Narrative of the Life of David Crockett...* [1834]) is one of the most pedestrian and circumstantial of American biographies. Crockett's amanuensis (the evidence compiled by James A. Shackford[68] indicates that he was Thomas Chilton) was not an able writer. Only in the accounts of the Colonel's electioneering does his style approach the vividness of a well-told yarn; this, despite the opportunities many Indian fights and bear hunts afforded him to draw the long bow. Despite its flatness, however, this life of Crockett had popular appeal because his career confirmed a stereotyped pattern of American life. It tells "how I worked along to rise from a canebrake to my present station in life," and gives jocular intimations that a seat in Congress is only a way-station on the road to the White House. This is not merely a success story, a rags-to-riches fable; it is an incarnation of the democratic dogma at its lowest level. The Crockett of *A Narrative* professes to love his parents, to share his meat with the hungry, to be a brave fighter and a skilled hunter, to stand on his principles against even President Jackson; but what makes him a success is none of these virtues. It is his ability to feel out the meanest level of approach in dealing with his constituents, to conceal from them his ignorance of the matters on which he will have to deliberate, and to undercut his opponents in stumping the district. The appeal of Crockett as politician is dangerous and demagogic. As Randall Jarrell[69] has remarked in quite another connection, "When you defeat me in an election simply because you were, as I was not, born and bred in a log cabin, it is only a question of time until you are beaten by someone whom the pigs brought up out in the yard."

But Crockett as politician fades from the popular memory even during his own lifetime and the outlines of the second phase of his renown begin to emerge. Now in *Colonel Crockett's Exploits and Adventures in Texas* (1836) the magnetism of Crockett the frontiersman already attracts incident and anecdote from free-floating comic tradition, both oral and journalistic, and his adventures verge on the fabulous. The climax of course is the apocryphal account of his heroic death at the Alamo. Thereafter, as Constance Rourke observes in "her biography of Crockett, " the popular imagination took license to make of Crockett what it would. The best indication of what his second image became is found in the anecdotes from the Crockett almanacs collected in Richard M. Dodson's *Davy Crockett: American Comic Legend.* Here is a genre of popular literature—the yarn—scarcely removed from oral tradition; the best of these almanac stories derive their rhetorical structure, their vividly animistic imagery, and their compelling combination of the humorous, the grotesque, the heroic, and the horrible from the art of the folk raconteur. Here we find Crockett supernaturally hideous, Crockett entering the animal world; Crockett displaying Jovian and Promethean prowess, Crockett screaming his brag, Crockett snapping fire and lightning from his knuckles, Crockett climbing Niagara, Crockett saving the earth from extinction with a kick and a daub of bear-oil when the sun freezes fast on axis.

The diction of these fantasies is as remarkable as their situations; the yarns abound in such prodigies of the language as "tetotatious," "exfluncate," "absquatualte," "slantindicular." Where the Crockett of the autobiographies congratulated himself on his own illiteracy, these etymological sideshows are obviously parodies of the Latinate vocabulary and rhetorical fustian of the high oratorical style of the time. To have invented or understood the point of such words as these, one would have to be capable of comprehending Mr. Henry Clay,[70] and perhaps of declining Latin nouns oneself.

"Popular declamation of the '30's and '40's has often been considered as bombast when it should be taken as comic mythology," Miss Rourke observes.[71] This mythology, like every other, must embody widely shared convictions about man's place in the universe. When Crockett appears as a virtual demigod he does indeed represent communal values colored by folk fantasy. He symbolizes man's uneasy relation to nature on the frontier. His aggressions against bears and his command of lightning and waterspouts are surely imaginative reactions to peril. If this second Crockett is mythological, the myth is that man can easily conquer nature and control it. In the most Promethean of his exploits—his rescuing the world from icy darkness by freeing the earth and sun from the frozen machinery of the universe—his reward is not the vulture and the rock, but this:

> The sun walked up beautiful, salutin' me with sich a wind o' gratitude that it made me sneeze. It lit my pipe by the light o' his top-knot, shouldered my bear, an' walked home, introductin' people to the fresh daylight with a piece of sunrise in my pocket.

There is not even the recognition of tragic possibility, much less of tragic fate, in these ebullient assertions of man's superhuman powers. The frontiersman knew tragedy enough in the life he lived and the deaths he died, but his folktales and popular writings transformed the materials of tragic life into either melodrama or farce. The folk imagination dealt with such realities as death and decomposition by affirming their existence in terms so outrageously revolting as to deny the mere realities themselves their due in human felling.

It is apparent that this phase of Crockett's fame corresponds to a passing phase of American history. With the settlement of the frontier, the supplanting of the clearing by the village, the dominance of industry over a handcraft and agrarian economy, and especially the accelerating effects of the Civil War upon social change, the fantasies of Crockett from the ante-bellum frontier faded from the popular mind. Except in Texas, where the Alamo and its traditions have always been revered, Crockett was all but forgotten.

Why, then, was Davy Crockett revived on a nation-wide scale in the 1950's? Did his most recent image draw on either the demagogy of his first popular appearance of the folk fantasy of the second? It is obvious that the third Crockett is an artifact not of folklore but of contemporary popular culture. There was no current oral tradition of folktales to be tapped by the authors of television and radio scripts, comic strips, juvenile storybooks, songs, and jingles. Both the historical Crockett and the almanac folk hero had been so long dead that the new Crockett could be made—would have to be made—to fit contemporary needs and to dramatize contemporary concepts of character.

We can relate the Crockett fad to the increasing antiquarian interest in certain folkloristic materials from the American past. Stanley Hyman,[72] among others, had commented on the growing vogue for "the folksy" in the theatre, the dance, painting, and other arts. The art forms of popular culture are among the most potent of "technicways" (to use Howard Odum's term), ready at a moment's notice to create new images to satiate the hungers of the popular imagination. The manufactured heroes of mass media thus fulfill an important function in maintaining the stability of certain values in contemporary society. One such value is the illusion of continuity with the historical past. As many observers have remarked, the need for cultural roots seems to be proportionately greater as the rate of social change increases. The disruptive effects on the sense of personal identity of rapid technological change, the high rate of social and spatial mobility, and the insecurities inevitable in a culture where status is (or is thought to be) achieved rather than ascribed—all these factors make attractive the common sharing of references to the national past. This complex of factors applies to the appeal of Dave Crockett even though the majority of the American population is descended from forebears who came to this country after Crockett had died. But since the vision of the national past shared in popular culture is created and presented by the technic ways, what is shared is the past that the present desires, not the actual traditions (folkways) of the past as it really was.

Again, if we consider Crockett with the other heroes of juvenile popular culture, we observe that the fantasies they offer of escape from the present are conceived in terms of two contrary simplifications of life. One—the category to which Crockett belongs—presents an idealized past in which technology and science are absent; the other looks forward to a future still more technological and scientific than the present. The alternation between these two juvenile utopias has, I suspect, been going on for quite a time. One would need precise information on the respective reigns of such figures as Tom Swift, Tom Mix, Buck Rogers, the Lone Ranger, and Superman, as well as Davy Crockett. Underlying the variations of these heroes' fantasy-worlds there is of course a basic pattern of similarity. They all not only invite their audiences to escape into the remoteness of the Vanished American West or of the Supercity of the Future; they also reinforce certain values in the world from which they offer escape. The morality of their fantasy-worlds is absolute—no gradations of innocence or guilt. Consequently their decisiveness is never hedged about by such deterrents to immediate action as the complex circumstances of actual life usually and painfully provide. The security they offer is that of absolute rightness combined with force. This is obviously a dangerous simplification, but an attractive one. Crockett, whose motto, as everyone knows, was *"Be sure you're right, then Go Ahead!"* fits well into this pattern of superconfident, self-righteous individualism.

While alternation between the Western Folk Hero and the Future Spaceman (or perhaps their simultaneous appeal) seems to characterize popular culture, we may wonder why the recent version of the Westerner was not the usual cowboy but a long-forgotten backwoods politician. Surely the identity of the heroes of juvenile popular culture bears some relation to the preoccupations of the adult world. Is there some possible connection between the rise of the resurrected Crockett and the going-ahead of Senator McCarthy?[73] Although some observers felt that the Crockett boom ended because the hero had been "oversold" and his youthful public simply tired of him, it may not be irrelevant to note that Crockett faded from the airwaves a little after McCarthyism ceased to be the most sensational feature of the political scene.

Among the literary manifestations of the recent Crockett fad were two reprintings of his supposed autobiographies. Both run together the three narratives of 1834, 1835, and 1836 without indicating where one ends and the other begins, and they make many unacknowledged deletions from Hamlin Garland's already condensed text. For instance in the new editions we find the following passage:

> I let the people know as early as then, that I wouldn't take a collar around my neck.

(Citadel edition, p. 130; Signet edition, p. 87)

In the Garland edition this passage occurs on page 111, Chapter XIII of *A Narrative of the Life of David Crockett* .. . (1834) and reads:

> I let people know as early as then, that I wouldn't take a collar around my neck with the letters engraved on it,
>
> MY DOG.
>
> Andrew Jackson

Why is the legend on Davy's collar inadmissible now? Because Andy Jackson too is a hero of consequence who stands in the popular mind for the same values imputed to Crockett: coonskin democracy, the triumph of the common man. Crockett's opposition to Jackson's western land policy no longer interests us. In the pantheon of our popular culture we cannot have such a repudiation of one hero by another who represents the same values, for how then could we affirm those values? Accordingly, the new editions of Crockett's life do not make much sense, for the embarrassing fact of his opposition to Jackson is so intrinsic to the political part of the text that it cannot be eliminated by an editor's shears.

Half a century ago Frank Norris[74] in an eloquent polemic declaimed:

> The plain truth of the matter is that we have neglected our epic … no contemporaneous poet or chronicler thought it worth his while to sing the song or tell the tale of the West because literature in the day when the West was being won was a cult indulged in by certain well-bred gentlemen in New England who looked eastward to the Old World, to the legends of England and Norway and Germany and Italy for their inspiration, and left the great, strong, honest, fearless, resolute deeds of their own contemporaries to be defamed and defaced by the nameless hacks of the "yellow back" libraries…
>
> And the Alamo![75]…the very histories slight the deed… Yet Thetmopylae[76] was less glorious, and in comparison with that siege the investment of Troy was mere wanton riot… Young men are taught to consider the "Iliad," with its butcheries, its glorification of

inordinate selfishness and vanity, as a classic. Achilles, murderer, egoist, ruffian and liar, is a hero. But the name of Bowie, the name of the man who gave his life to his flag at the Alamo, is perpetuated only in the designation of a knife. Crockett is the hero only of a "funny story" about a sagacious coon.[77]

We can no longer blame the gentility of Eastern writers for our failure to have created an epic of the Alamo or to have supplanted Achilles with Colonel Crockett. Although the age of epic literature would seem of belong since over, such a literate may yet come from the winning of the West. It will first require our recognition as a national culture that Prometheus chained to the rock is not only myth but reality, while the image of Davy Crockett striding over the hills, exempt from sacrifice for the piece of sunlight in his pocket, is our nation's self-defeating dream.

FIVE

The American folk hero is startlingly different from most of the great heroes of myths or of Marchen.[78] Unlike them, the American has no parents. He has no past, no patrimony, no siblings, no family, and no life cycle, because he never marries or has children. He seldom dies. If death does overtake him, it proves to be merely a stage in his transformation, to still another identity. No one has cursed his birth or set him afloat on the sea; neither was he suckled by a beast nor rescued by a cowherd from the fierce elements to which a tyrannous father had condemned him. Although he may wear many disguises, it cannot be usually said that he returns incognito to his homeland, rids his country of scourges, and is recognized as the throne's true heir. The pattern of action of the hero tale, as outlined by Lord Raglan[85] in *The Hero*, does not fit very well the adventures of our plebeian peddlers, brawlers, and emergent capitalists. Nor can we apply to them with much confidence Otto Rank's[80] view that myths of the hero are created "by means of retrograde childhood fantasies" in which the Oedipal "family romance of neurotics" become universalized as the life histories of mythical heroes.[81]　Our folk heroes have no family romances. Among our group of heroes only the careers of Franklin and Crockett begin to approach the fullness of the human lifecycle in their respective autobiographies: In popular culture we have seen how Franklin is reduced to the get-ahead Poor Richard while Crockett becomes the go-ahead woodsman whose varied exploits in guile, hunting, and conquest of nature are entirely discontinuous, a collection of motifs rather than a coherent story. Other men who became folk heroes—Fink, Patch, Johnny Appleseed—left behind a still more fragmentary basis for their reputations. Each lived in the minds of his celebrants and emulators as an instance of metamorphosis culmination in a single dramatic gesture. From Andrew the Hebridean onward, that gesture was the annunciation of their own destinies as self-made men, their abandoning an old self for rebirth in a new. But after Andrew the old self that was let die was not that of a European peasant; it was simply an earlier incarnation of a character whose essence was not radically altered by his assumption of successive roles.

The American folk hero appears as a generic expression of the youthful culture which produced him. His characteristic virtues are the qualities of youth: indomitable self-confidence, and a courage in his adaptation to the world which proves almost a heroic denial that tragedy can be possible for *him*. But from another perspective the virtues of youth are the defects of immaturity. In his easy progress from one role to another without ever being compelled to accept the full commitment of spirit to any, the ever-popular image of the American folk hero exists on a psychological plane comparable to that of adolescent or pre-adolescent fantasy. In every culture the concept of maturity implies a full commitment to fixed values; until modern times these values were sacred. Their fixity had been established by supernatural powers, and the passage from childhood to maturity was marked by initiatory rites in which the sacred knowledge that came to the present from the beginning of time was passed on to the initiate. To be worthy of this knowledge the child in him had to die; his soul had to seek its sources in the power that created the world; and he had then to be reborn into his responsibilities and his grace. Before the submission to his immutable pattern, however, the child-spirit can envisage any or all fulfillments of the potentialities of its psychic energies. In the American folk hero the transformations are metamorphoses without being rebirths. The concentration of psychic energy necessary for spiritual commitment and spiritual change is not apparent in either the bourgeois get-ahead values of Ben Franklin-Poor Richard or in the sly or boisterous go-ahead values of Sam Slick-Davey Crockett. Only in the person of the American Literatus Walt Whitman does the power of self-determined metamorphosis approach the transcendent heroism of those myths of the Old World from which all our folk images attempted to liberate us. Fox only in Whitman is the assertion of selfhood made with such all-encompassing passion as to become in itself an escape from selfhood. The "self" Walt sings is, as Richard Chase observes,[82] a metaphor with the power of myth, linking the ego to the entire world of apprehended sense and transforming all that it encompasses into "a knit of identity."

Identity, as de Tocqueville foresaw, would prove an elusive and prepossessive concern for an egalitarian society. The American temperament has always favored activism over meditation; the typical self-discovery of the American character has been conceived as an immersion in experience, rather than as contemplative withdrawal. It is as though the more reality one's experiences could encompass or be touched by, the nearer one could come to self-definition. Consequently, the metamorphic pattern of American life and of the American folk hero's career sets its exemplars in linear motion through as many conditions of "reality" as possible. These metamorphoses, as we have seen, are only outwardly comparable to the rebirths achieved by initiatory rites in cultures or institutions of sacred orientation. Their function, nonetheless, is a ritualistic one: not a *rite de passage*[83] but a ritual of intensification, in which the powers of the self are affirmed, reinforced, and glorified by each demonstration of their successful use. These powers prove the self spiritually indomitable and adaptable to the wildest vicissitudes of fortune or nature. The historical and folk examples we have traced prove not only these considerable positive powers, but also the limitations of the American notion of selfhood. The self-determinative hero turns out to have as his goals a set of concepts more characteristic of the culture of the early American republic than of human history at large. His character is aggressive, competitive, and shrewd. He seeks mastery over nature. With respect to society, he seeks to demonstrate superiority over other individuals but ordinarily does he recognize society as an organic structure, in which power can be exercised for extra-personal ends.

Since the exposition of character is both an aim and method of fiction, what could American authors make of the fragmentary folk sagas which outlined the folk concepts of heroic personality? These sketches could be taken uncritically, accepted in the same spirit of resilience in which they were offered by the popular mind. Hawthorne's peddler Dominiucs Pike, his Holgrave in *The House of the Seven Gables*, Melville's Ishmael, and Twain's Huck Finn, all reflect both the metamorphoses and the self-reliance of the folk models we have examined. But these authors could use the same folk concepts to create characters whose qualities they viewed with the gravest reservations. Often these characters, critically examined by their authors, are presented in situations which define their fates as representative of the national destiny. Hawthorne's Robin in "My Kinsman, Major Molinedux," Melville's Captain Delano in "Benito Cereno", his Ahab and the whole cast of *The Confidence Man*, Twain's

Duke and Dauphin, all project elements of the American folk hero into situations with which his spiritual immaturity and his lack of human depth make him inadequate to deal. Further, the literary enlargement of the native folk heroes is often drawn against a contrasting set of heroic values, those of the world-mythical heroes whose fates and powers are so different from their own. Thus Hawthorne contrasts his Yankee Robin against the ancient ritualistic figure of the Dying King; Ishmael presents himself as a Yankee, both bumpkin dupe and trickster; while Ahab, though in part a frontiersman—an "Arkansas duelist"—also subsumes the attributes of a Slayer of the Beast (Perseus, St. George), a shaman, and a Christ. Huck Finn, as I have mentioned, represents the triumphantly moral American imagination in contrast to the decadent European chivalric romanticism of Tom Sawyer. The patterns seem as capable of variation as the imaginations of their authors could make them. The depiction of native character, whether sympathetic or critical, and tensions between them and representatives of the older heroic traditions in world mythology, contribute much to the sense of largeness, of archetypal representativeness, which we find in the American prose romance. This represtetitiveness is certainly not the function of surface realism. It inheres in the romance because the characters themselves are so often modeled on half-legendary archetypes projected fragmentarily by the folk imagination.

〔注释〕

1. Crevecoeur：赫克托·圣约翰·戴·克里夫古尔（Hector St. John de Crevecoeur, 1735-1813），游记作家和社会历史学家。他的名著为《来自一个美国农夫的信》（*Letters from an American Farmer*）。

2. Zion：锡安，意为圣城，出自《圣经》。

3. the isle of Barra：巴拉岛，苏格兰外赫布底里群岛中的一个岛，Andrew the Hebridean 的出生地。

4. Davy Crockett：克罗克特（1786-1836），美国边地开拓者、政治家、传奇式人物。

5. deistic optimism：18 世纪启蒙时代流行的自然神论，认为上帝造世之后不再参与世事，让世界依自然规律运行；认为人本性善良而自由。这些都和悲观的原罪说不同。

6. Salem：塞勒姆镇，位于马萨诸塞州，1692 年此地发生逐巫案（The Witchcraft Trial）。美国作家霍桑的名作《七个尖角阁的房子》便以此事为背景。

7. the Horatio Alger story：阿尔杰（Horatio Alger, 1834-1899），美国儿童文学作家，以描述富兰克林式"成功的故事"而著称。

8. 引自富兰克林的《自传》开首文学部分。

9. 引自劳伦斯的《美国经典文学作品研究》第 2 章。

10. 转引自 F. O. 马西森（F. O. Matthiessen, 1902-1950）所著《美国文艺复兴》（*American Renaissance*, 1941）英文原著第 636 页。

11. 1733 年，富兰克林开始出版《理查德历书》（*Poor Richard's Almanac*），延续达 25 年之久；其中的格言、警句等，被富兰克林择优选入他的《致富之路》（*The Way to Wealth*, 1744）一书中。

12. 引自《晚期的富兰克林》，载于《新旧随笔：马克·吐温作品集》，纽约 1917 年版，第 23 卷，第 188-192 页。

13. Passy：巴黎一区，位于塞纳河左岸。

14. *Israel Potter*：麦尔维尔的讽刺作品。

15. Hobbes：霍布斯（Thomas Hobbes, 1588-1679），英国哲学家，著有《列维坦》等。

16. 引自麦尔维尔的 *Israel Potter*。

17. 指爱默生。

18. Hosea Biglow：毕格罗，美国诗人、文艺评论家罗维尔（James Russell Lowell, 1819-1891）所著《毕格罗文集》（*Biglow Papers*）中一人物。

19. The Sage of Concord：康科德的圣人，指爱默生。

20. 引自《毕格罗文集》第 1 部序言。

21. Paul Revere：里维亚（1735-1818），美国革命时期的民间英雄。1775 年 4 月 18 日夜，他骑马将英军即将入侵的消息通报给波士顿居民。

22. Royall Tyler：泰勒（1757-1826），美国律师、教师和剧作家。美国第一部喜剧《对比》（*The Contrast*）的作者。

23. Thomas Green Fessenden：费森登（1771-1837），美国诗人、作家，以其诗《乔纳森的求婚》（"Jonathan's Courtship"）而出名。

24. "The Courtin"：罗维尔所著《毕格罗文集》中最著名的一首诗，共 24 诗节。

25. Seba Smith：塞巴·史密斯（1792-1868），美国幽默文学作家、编辑。

26. Burgwine：意为勃艮第（Burgundy）酒。

27. Jalaam：罗维尔所著《毕格罗文集》中毕格罗先生的故乡。

28. Poganuc 和 Oldtown 皆为斯托夫人作品中的地名。

29. Miss Jewetti：朱厄特（Sarah Orne Jewett, 1849-1909），美国乡土文学女作家，Deep Haven 是她所著的 *Deephaven* 小说和札记集中臆想的一个缅因州村庄。

30. Robinson：罗宾逊（Edwin Arlington Robinson, 1869-1935），美国诗人，Tilbury Town 是罗宾逊诗作里臆想的一个村镇名。

31. the Fall：《圣经》中的用语，指亚当和夏娃偷吃智慧果被驱逐出伊甸园一事，亦即人类的堕落。

32. 引自《新英格兰及纽约游记》（*Travels in Near-England and New York*），吉特利支（G. L. Kitredge）在其《老农夫和他的历书》（*The CU Farmer and His Almanack*）（剑桥 1904 年版）中转引，第 145 页。

33. 引自《神话与个性气》，刊于《代达罗斯》1959 年春季号，第 353-354 页。

34. sold his soul for knowledge：暗引浮士德（Faust）的故事；浮士德为欧洲中世纪传说中的人物，为了得到知识，他把自己的灵魂出卖给魔鬼。

35. Haliburton：哈利波通（Thomas Chandler Haliburton，1796-1865），加拿大幽默作家。他刻画的最著名的人物为 Sam Slick。

36. 引自哈利波通所著《为哈利法克斯刀片配制的扬基佬刀柄》（"A Yan-kee Handle for a Halifax Blade"），载于《钟匠》（*The Clockmaker*），费城 1837 年版，第 101-102 页。

37. Johnson J. Hooper：胡波尔（1815-1862），美国南方幽默作家。

38. 引自《西蒙·萨克斯上尉历险记》（*Adventures of Captain Simon Suggs*），费城 1845 年版，第 12-13 页。

39. Henry Howe：豪（1816-1893），美国历史学家。

40. Johnny Appleseed：美国拓荒者、果园主查普曼（John Chapman，1774-1845）的绰号。他向中西部提供了大量苹果树苗，从而促进了拓荒事业的发展。

41. 引自罗伯特·普来斯（Robert Price）的《苹果佬约翰：其人和其传说》（*Johnny Appleseed: Man and Myth*），布鲁明顿 1954 年版，第 38 页。

42. the Falls of Genesee：杰纳西瀑布，美国杰纳西河大部分在纽约州境内，它在罗彻斯特峡谷内有三处瀑布。

43. Nature imitates Art：引自 19 世纪英国唯美主义者王尔德（Oscar Wilde, 1854-1900）所著《谎话的衰退》（"The Decay of Lying"）。王尔德认为，艺术高于生活，自然（nature）必须模仿艺术方有意义。

44. Longstreet：朗斯特利（Augustus Baldwin Longstreet, 1790-1870），美国法学家、教育家、作家。

45. Constance Rourke：鲁尔克（1885-1941），美国历史学家，研究美国文化和民族特色的先驱。

46. 引自鲁尔克所著《美国文化之根》（*The Roots of American Culture*），纽约 1942 年版，第 125-126 页。

47. Brom Bones：华盛顿·欧文的小说《睡谷传奇》中的人物。

48. Fink：芬克（1770-1823），美国拓荒者，传奇式人物。

49. 引自爱尔冯诺·韦特莫尔的《商贩》（*The Pedlar*），圣路易斯

1821 年版，第 34 页。

50. Wycherly：威彻利（William Wycherly, 1640-1716），英国王政复辟时期的剧作家，作品有有淫邪情调。

51. *She Stoops To Conquer*:《屈身求爱》，英国作家哥尔斯密（Oliver Goldsmith, 1730-1774）的一部著名剧作。

52. Wolsley：Thomas Wolsley，17 世纪红衣主教，一位传记作家曾为他做传，描写他的沉浮。

53. 引自《半马半鳄鱼：麦克•芬克传说的发展》（*Half Horse Half Alligator: The Growth of the Mike Fink Legend*），芝加哥 1956 年版，第 43-55 页及 260 页。

54. 引自《美国幽默》（*American Humor*）第 54 页。

55. Morgan Neville：纳维尔（1786-1839），美国作家。

56. William Tell：威廉•退尔，瑞士传奇人物，生活于 13 世纪末、14 世纪前半叶，曾因蔑视奥地利当局而被迫向放在儿子头上的苹果射箭。德国著名作家席勒曾著《威廉•退尔》一剧，于是退尔成为世界闻名人物。

57. Charlemagne：查理曼，或称查理曼大帝。公元 768 至 814 年为法兰克国王。下文中罗兰（Roland）是查理曼王朝中的一位骑士，法兰西史诗《罗兰之歌》中所歌颂的主人公。

58. Lion-heart：指狮心王查理一世（Richard the Lion Heart）。

59. Rob Roy：罗布•罗依，司各特的小说《罗布•罗依》中的主人公。

60. Emperor Julian：尤里安皇帝（95331/332-363），罗马皇帝，曾率军前往高卢，击败阿勒曼尼人和法兰克人，将他们从高卢赶走。

61. James Hall：霍尔（1793-1868），美国作家。

62. William Cullen Bryant：布莱恩特（1794-1878），美国诗人。Fitz-Greene Halleck：哈勒克（1790-1867），美国诗人。

63. James Kirke Paulding：波尔丁（1779-1860），美国作家、政治家。

64. William Bayle Bernard：伯纳德（1807-1875），美国剧作家，

1819 年移居英国。

65. 引自提德维尔（Tidwell）的《西部之狮》序言（"Introduction to *The Lion of the West*"）第 8 页。

66. 引自《美国边区的民间笑声》（*Folk Laughter on the American Frontier*）第 22 页。

67. 引自哈姆林·加兰（Hamlin Garland, 1860-1940，美国作家）所编的《大卫·克罗克特自传》（*The Autobiography of David Crockett*），纽约 1923 年版，第 369 页。

68. 引自《大卫·克罗克特：其人和其传说》（*David Crockett, the Man and the Legend*），1956 年版，第 89-90 页。

69. Randall Jarrell：杰雷尔（1914-1965），美国诗人、小说家、评论家。

70. Henry Clay：克雷（1775-1852），美国政治家。

71. 引自《美国幽默》，第 64 页。

72. Stanley Hyman：海曼（1919-1970），美国评论家。

73. Senator McCarthy：麦卡锡（Joseph Raymond McCarthy, 1909-1957），美国共和党参议员。20 世纪 50 年代曾发起过臭名昭著的反共运动。1954 年受到美国参议院指控。

74. Frank Norris：诺里斯（1870-1902），美国小说家。

75. Alamo：阿拉莫，美国得克萨斯州圣安东尼奥市内一历史纪念地。1835 年在得克萨斯革命中，200 名得克萨斯志愿军与 4 000 名墨西哥军队于此展开激战，后全部阵亡。

76. Thermopylae：希腊东部一山隘。公元前 480 年，300 名斯巴达士兵在利尔纳达斯的率领下于此阻击入侵的波斯军队，后全部阵亡。下文中的 Troy 指古代特洛伊战争，Iliad 指荷马史诗《伊利亚特》。

77. 引自弗兰克·诺里斯所著《论作者身份》（"Essays on Authorship"），收在《全集》（*Complete Works*）（纽约 1903 年版）第 4 卷中，第 280-281 页。

78. Marchen：德语，意为"故事"，尤指童话及民间故事。

79. Lord Ragland：拉格伦男爵（1788-1855），英国陆军元帅。

80. Otto Rank：兰克（1885-1939），奥地利心理学家。他把精神分析学理论扩展到传奇、神话、艺术和创造力的研究方面。

81. 引自《英雄出生之神话》（*The Myth of the Birth of the Hero*），纽约 1959 年版，第 69、84 页。

82. 引自《再论惠特曼》（*Walt Whitman Reconsidered*），纽约 1955 年版。Richard Chase：美国当代著名文学评论家。

83. *rite de passage*：法语，意为"帮助个人压制冲动而改变其生理和社会特征的宗教仪式"。

Questions For Discussion：

1. How did Crevecoeur manage to begin writing the new fairy tale of the newman on the new continent? Define the nature of the tale and the qualities of the man. How did a stock figure evolve out of the life of people like Franklin?

2. The popular stereotypes of character had an enormous effect on the American fiction, especially nineteenth-century American fiction. Discuss.

3. How did the prototypical western frontiersman develop his multiple images which would in due time become part of the American fable?

4. What significance is there in the resurrection of nineteenth-century tall-tale heroes like David Crockett?

5. What is the difference between the American folk hero and the heroes of myths?

For Further Reference:

1. Walter Blair, *Naive American Humor*. San Francisco, 1960.

2. B. A. Botkin, *A Treasury of American Folklore*. New York, 1944.

Van Wyck Brooks

〔作者介绍〕

　　凡·威克·布鲁克斯（Van Wyck Brooks, 1886-1963），美国文学史家、散文作家。生于新泽西州，毕业于哈佛大学。一生著述丰富，在评述美国文化与文学方面颇有建树。他在他的第一部作品《清教徒之酒》（*The Wine of the Puritans*, 1909）中开始批评美国的清教传统。在《美国的成长》（*America's Coming of Age*, 1915）一书中，他提出美国社会生活中存在的两极倾向，对后来的文化和文学评论很有影响。他的著作在 20 世纪 30 年代以后日渐闻名，但观点日趋保守，主要有《马克·吐温的考验》（*The Ordeal of Mark Twain*, 1920）等。

America's Coming of Age

〔作品介绍〕

　　《美国的成长》（*America's Coming of Age*）一书 1915 年由纽约 B. W. 韦伯斯克公司出版，是作者评论美国文化传统和美国文学状貌的重要著作之一。

　　在这部书中，布鲁克斯强调分析了美国人思想中存在的两种截然不同的倾向和伏流，以及它们在社会生活和文学创作中所产生的不良后果。他指出，美国清教主义传统在美国文化和文学中占主导地位，它具有明显的两重性，即笃信上帝和讲求实际，同时蕴含着精神与金钱这两种互不相容的因素。这种两重性在爱德华兹和富兰克林这两位思想家的思想中充分体现出来。爱德华兹认为上帝无所不在、无所不容，世间一切都是精神的体现，因而追求一种在精神上与上帝融为一体的理想主义，这种理想主义导致了美国文化传统中的不切实际性质。爱德华兹的思想成为 19 世纪美国爱默生（Emerson）先验主义（Transcendentalism）的先导。另一方面，美国清教徒务实以奉上帝的思想在富兰克林的思想体系中形成一种哲学，导致了美国社会生活中讲求实际的特点。于是，幻想的理想主义与赤裸裸的金钱关系在美国文化中形成一种僵持局面，美国社会、文化和文学出现了"高档"（high-brow）和"低档"（low-brow），而青年人则饱受挟制之苦：他们在学校里接受的理想主义教育到了讲求实际的社会中却处处碰壁，理想于是演变成失望和愤世嫉俗。布鲁克斯将美国文化的这种缺点归咎于世俗化的清教徒所奉行的过分放纵自我的个人主义。在布鲁克斯看来，自我完善是生活的目标，但它只有在一个"包罗万象的、有机的人性社会"中才能真正实现。他潜心研究了在美国社会中不能实现自我完善的原因，认为美国和理想的社会相比，仍处于"达尔文时期"：左右人们言行的是坚持己见而并非自我完善，国民意识的指导方针是物质财富的积累而不是寻求自身的发展与成熟。把精神与金钱分割开的清教主义两重性，使现代美国文化也相应地分裂为"阳春白雪"与"下里巴人"两种，对文学创作产生不良影响。"阳春白雪"派游离于社会之外，而"下里巴人"派又和社会过分亲近，生出一种世俗化的商业气息。布鲁克斯认为，过去的美国文学已和现实完全脱节。他指出，倘然世人决心积财致富，过去的文学家如梭罗、爱默生、坡、霍桑等人，谁也不能说服他们改变主意，这是因为人们不再理睬这些文学家，而社会上的真正"英雄"是"受到神启的百万富翁"。布鲁克斯在书中对不少作家进行了精辟的分析。

《美国的成长》一书共分五章，这里选注的是该书的第一章的部分章节。

An Excerpt from *America's Coming of Age*

II

They ["high brow" and "low brow"] always have divided American life between them; and to understand them one has to go back to the beginning of things—for without doubt the Puritan Theocracy is the all-influential fact in the history of the American mind. It was the Puritan conception of the Deity as not alone all-determining but precisely responsible for the practical affairs of the race, as constitution, in fact, the State itself, which precluded in advance any central bond, any responsibility, any common feeling in American affairs and which justified the unlimited centrifugal expediency which has always marked American life. And the same instinct that made against centrality in government made against centrality in thought, against common standards of any kind. The imminent eternal issues the Puritans felt so keenly, the equally imminent practical issues they experienced so monotonously threw almost no light on one another; there was no middle ground between to mitigate, combine, or harmonize them.

So it is that from the beginning we find two main currents in the American mind running side by side but rarely mingling—a current of overtones and a current of undertones—and both equally unsocial: on the one hand, the current of Transcendentalism, originating in the piety of the Puritans, becoming a philosophy in Jonathan Edwards,[1] passing through Emerson, producing the fastidious refinement and aloofness of the chief American writers, and, as the coherent ideals and beliefs of Transcendentalism gradually faded out, resulting in the final unreality of most contemporary American culture; and on the other hand the current of catchpenny opportunism, originating in the practical shifts of　Puritan life, becoming a philosophy in Franklin,[2] passing through the American humorists, and resulting　in the atmosphere of contemporary business life.

Thus the literature of the seventeenth century in America is composed in equal parts, one may fairly say, of piety and advertisement; and the revered chronicles of New England had the double effect of proving how many pilgrim souls had been elected to salvation and of populating with hopeful immigrants a land where heaven had proved so indulgent.

For three generations the prevailing American character was compact in one type, the man of action who was also the man of God. Not until the eighteenth century did the rift appear and with it the essential distinction between "Highbrow" and "Lowbrow." It appeared in the two philosophers, Jonathan Edwards and Benjamin Franklin, who share the eighteenth century between them. In their amazing purity of type and in the apparent incompatibility, of their aims they determined the American character as a racial fact, and after them the Revolution became inevitable. Channing, Lincoln, Emerson, Whitman, Grant, Webster, Garrison, Edison, Mr. Rockefeller, Mrs. Eddy[3] are all, in one way or another, permutations, and combinations of these two grand progenitors of the American character.

Strange that at the very outset two men should have arisen so aptly side by side and fixed the poles of our national life! For no one has evermore fully and typically than Jonathan Edwards displayed the infinite inflexibility of the upper levels of the American mind, nor any one more typically than Franklin the infinite flexibility of its lower levels.

The intellect of Jonathan Edwards was like the Matterhorn,[4] steep, icy, and pinnacled. At its base were green slopes and singing valleys filled with all sorts of little tender wild-flowers—for he was the most lovable of men; but as soon as the ground began to rise in good earnest all this verdurous life came to an abrupt end: not one green or living thing could subsist in that frozen soil, on those pale heights. It was the solitude of logic that led him to see in destiny only a wrathful tyrant and a viper's trail in the mischievous ways of little boys and girls.

I confess to an old-time and so to speak aboriginal affection for this man, so gently solicitous to make up in his daily walk and conversation for the ferocious impulsions of that brain of his. He was even the most romantic of men, as I thought once, and I well remember that immense old musty book of his theology, covered with mildew, with its desert of tiny print, which I carried out with me into the fields and read, in the intervals of birdnesting, under the hedgerows and along the borders of the wood: the sun fell for the first time on those clammy old pages and the pallid thoughts that lay in them, and the field-sparrows all about were twittering in a language which, to tell the truth, was no more unintelligible to me. But everything that springs from solitude shines by a light of its own, and Manfred among the Alps was not more lonely than this rapt scholar in his parsonage among the Indians.[5]

There are, however, solitudes and solitudes. Great poets and fruitful thinkers live apart themselves, perhaps, but they have society and the ways of men in their blood. They recollect in tranquillity, as it were, gestate, live again, and reveal the last significance of active generations rich in human stuff, in experience, in emotion, in common reason. Nothing like this existed in the background of Jonathan Edwards, no profound and complex race-life. Intellect in him, isolated and not responsible to the other faculties, went on its way unchecked; and he was able to spin those inept sublimities of his by subtracting from his mind every trace of experience, every touch of human nature as it really was among his innocent country-folk.

Notoriously, of course, our great Dr. Franklin simplified existence in precisely the opposite way; for the opposite of unmitigated theory is unmitigated practice. Who can deny that in *Poor Richard* the "Lowbrow" point of view for the first time took definite shape, stayed itself with axioms, and found a sanction in the idea of "policy"? It emerges there full-fledged, in its classical form, a two-dimensional wisdom, a wisdom shorn of overtones, the most accommodating wisdom in the world.

Were ever two views of life more incompatible than these? What indeed could Poor Richard have in common with an Angry God?[6]

...

III

"Our people," said Emerson, "have their intellectual culture from one country and their duties from another." In how many spheres that phrase can be applied! Desiccated culture at one end and stark utility at the other have created a deadlock in the American mind, and all our life drifts chaotically between the two extremes. Consider, for example, our use of the English language. Literary English in England is naturally a living speech, which occupies the middle of the field and expresses the flesh and blood of an evolving race. Literary English with us is a tradition, just as Anglo-Saxon law with us is a tradition. They persist not as the normal expressions of a race, the essential fibre of which is permanently Anglo-Saxon, but through prestige and precedent and the will and habit of a dominating class largely out of touch with a national fabric unconsciously taking form "out of school." No wonder that our literary style is "pure," that our literary tradition, our tradition especially in oratory and political prose, retains the spirit of the eighteenth century. But at what a cost! At the cost of expressing a popular life which bubbles with energy and spreads and grows and slips away ever more and more from the control of tested ideas, a popular life "with the lid off," which demands an intellectual outlet and finds one in slang, journalism, and unmannerly fiction.

After seventy years Carlyle's well-known appeal to Emerson still applies to the spirit of American culture: "For the rest, I have to object still (what you will call objecting against the Law of Nature) that we find you a speaker indeed, but as it were a *Soliloquazer* on the eternal mountain-tops only, in vast solitudes where men and their affairs lie all hushed in a very dim remoteness; and only the *man* and the stars and the earth are visible—whom, so fine a fellow seems he, we could perpetually punch into, and say, "Why won't you come and help us then? We have terrible need of one man like you down among us! It is cold and vacant up there; nothing paintable but rainbows and emotions; come down and you shall do life-pictures, passions, facts…"

And what a comment on the same utterance that at this very moment an amiable New Englander should have been painting in Parson Wilbur[7] and Hosea Biglow; respectively, unconscious of any tragic symbolism of things to come, the unbridgeable chasm between literate and illiterate America! Morally, no doubt, in Jaalam, they understood one another and got along very well, as Yankees will. But in Chicago?

〔注释〕

1. Jonathan Edwards：爱德华兹（1703-1758），美国清教主义神学家和哲学家，19 世纪美国超验主义的先驱。

2. Franklin：富兰克林（Benjamin Franklin, 1706-1790），美国政治家、著作家和发明家。他出身贫贱，但自强不息，艰苦创业，终于积财致富，成为美国和世界名人。

3. Channing：昌宁，19 世纪美国作家，主张美国文学独立。Garrison：加里森（William Lloyd Garrison, 1805-1879），美国废奴主义者。Mrs. Eddy：艾娣（1821-1910），美国基督教科学派的创立人。

4. the Matterhorn：马特合恩峰，阿尔卑斯山系最著名的山峰（4 478

米）。

5. Manfred：曼弗雷德为拜伦同名诗剧的主人公。他拒绝同魔鬼订约，成为完全独立于社会和外界力量的人，他的孤独是必然的。

6. an Angry God：爱德华兹笃信上帝，认为人的不规和罪孽会使上帝发怒。这是他一次布道中用的一个词语。

7. Parson Wilbur：威尔伯，《毕格罗诗集》中的理想主义人物。Jaalam：《毕格罗诗集》中的一个地名。

Questions For Discussion：

1. What exactly do "highbrow" and "lowbrow" mean? How do they characterize the American cultural tradition?

2. It is now generally accepted that American Puritanism is a two-faceted heritage, with Jonathan Edwards representing its idealistic, emotional aspect and Benjamin Franklin its practical, commonsensical aspect. Discuss the relevance of the notion to the American literature.

For Further Reference：

1. Spiller, Robert. *The Cycle of American Literature: An Essay in Historical Criticism.* New York: Macmillan, 1955.

2. Miller, Perry, ed. *Major Writings of America.* New York: Harcourt, Brace, and World, Inc., 1962. Vol. I.

3. Nye, Russell B., and Grabo, Norman S., eds. *American Thought and Writing: The Colonial Period.* Boston: Houghton Mifflin, 1965.

Frederick John Hoffman

〔作者介绍〕

　　弗雷德里克·约翰·霍夫曼（Frederick John Hoffman, 1909-1967），美国著名文学评论家。曾就学于斯坦福大学和明尼苏达大学。他一生致力于美国现代文学的研究，成果斐然。其主要著作有：《弗洛伊德主义与文学头脑》(*Freudianism and the Literary Mind，* 1945)、《二十年代：战后十年的美国文学》(*The Twenties: American Writing in the Postwar Decade,* 1949)、《美国现代小说》(*The Modern Novel in America,* 1951)、《格特鲁德·斯坦》(*Gertrude Stein,* 1961)、《塞缪尔·贝克特：自我的语言》(*Samuel Beckett: The Language of Self, 1962*)、《南方小说的艺术》(*The Art of Southern Fiction,* 1967) 和《想象的新开端：神学与文学》(*Imagination's New Beginning: Theology and Literature, 1967*)。

The Twenties: American Writing in the Postwar Decade

〔作品介绍〕

　　波谲云诡的 20 世纪 20 年代一直是众多的历史学家、社会学家和文学评论家津津乐道的话题。对这一时期的评价也一直莫衷一是。深恶痛绝者有之，趋之若鹜者有之，人人又都固执己见，以偏概全，导致在理解该时代方面出现种种谬误和歪曲。霍夫曼的《20 年代：战后十年的美国文学》就是针对这种情况而写的。它旨在匡正对这一年代的歪曲与误解，还历史以本来面目。他认为对 20 年代的研究不能搞流水账式的大事记，这样会失之毛皮；更不能像某些人那样逐臭争腥，陶醉于对当时放荡生活方式的描写，这样会流于庸俗。他提出要从文学作品中发现当时社会的世态人情，从文学角度观察当时的生活。

本书共分 8 章，依次探讨了 20 年代的社会精神状貌，第一次世界大战所造成的后果，年轻一代的心态，新旧两派在传统问题上的论战，文学形式与内容的创新，对科学与宗教的态度，对中产阶级的批判，最后以对 20 年代的反思归结全书。每章篇末都附有对某篇精选作品的分析，以此来进一步说明和总结该章所讨论的问题，有画龙点睛之效。

作者指出，20 年代的主旋律是对旧文化、旧道德和旧文学的不满与反叛。青年一代不再俯首听命于老一辈的意志。他们开始怀疑、腹诽，以至于攻评所有的陈规陋习，企图用全新的思想和全新的文化取而代之。霍夫曼研究了第一次世界大战在人们（特别是青年知识分子）心中留下的创伤，再现了年轻一代在新旧交替的世界中的苦闷、仿徨和迷惘困惑；详尽地介绍了以保罗•摩尔为代表的人文主义者和以兰色姆为代表的农业主义者与激进派在传统问题上锋芒毕露的论战；并以欣赏的口吻，用大量的篇幅，介绍了先锋派（avant-garde）文学家在文学形式与内容上林林总总的创新，阐释了诸如意象主义、达达主义和超现实主义的发轫及其主旨，精辟入里地分析了海明威、奥尼尔等美国作家写作风格的形成及其特色。

信仰危机和对工业化的恐惧是 20 年代的又一特色。当机器的轰鸣把人从虔诚的梦中惊醒过来之后，人们发现上帝不见了，四周是一片荒原。霍夫曼记录了当时人们无所适从的心态，描述了知识分子从惶恐到无可奈何地接受这一现实的过程。

中产阶级"摇头派"（即评论家门肯所谓的 booboisie）一直是富有创造力的美国知识分子的靶子。中产阶级代表旧秩序、旧文化、旧的伦理道德规范和旧的文学趣味，他们满足于现状，对新思想恐惧万分。霍夫曼以整整一章的篇幅叙述了以门肯为首的知识分子对中产阶级展开的全面进攻及其历史意义。

本书最后一章综述了十多年来人们对 20 年代的各种看法（1929

年经济危机爆发标志着 20 年代的终结，霍人曼是在 1945 年之后开笔写此书的）。其中包括过来人（如菲兹杰拉德）的忏悔和后来者的钦羡以及指责。霍夫曼在结束此章时指出，虽然 20 年代有许多偏差，然而它对新文化和新道德的确立作出了不可估量的贡献。

　　正如作者再三强调的，此书的主旨在于最大限度地提供关于 20 年代的资料。全书材料翔实，记录忠实，组织精心，是了解和研究美国现代文学的必读书。

　　此处所选为该书的第一章第一节及第六章第一节。

An Excerpt from *The Twenties: American Writing in the Postwar Decade*

I　The Temper of the 1920s

1. THE OLD GANG[1]　AND THE MEW

　　The postwar decade in America has probably been given more varieties of distorted perspective than any other comparable time in our history. It seems to invite excesses of sentimentally, nostalgia, or moral censure.

　　One way of getting close to an accurate picture of the 1920s is to examine certain documents peculiar to the time. They are not necessarily true, or free from distortion, in themselves, and may even be gross exaggerations of the truth; but their prejudices sometimes indicate a common disposition，help us to realize the decade in at least one of its aspects and to appreciate some of its peculiarities of mind and spirit. There were many documents of this kind, though none so rich in suggestions as the symposium magisterially entitled *Civilization in the United States*, edited by Harold Stearns,[2] one of the decade's literary vagabonds.

On July 4, 1921, Stearns finished his preface to this volume; taking with him the manuscript of his own still uncompleted contribution, he sailed for Paris, to escape the monster he had helped to create and to serve as an example to his readers. In its own way the book, which appeared early in 1922, was a historical landmark of the post-World War I years, a curious document of disaffection, pointing to and reiterating the failure of culture, entertainment, family life, religion—of everything but science, and even it scored only a partial success in the survey of American life and institutions.

It was scarcely a surprise to those who knew the work of the contributor—among them, H. L. Mencken,[3] Stearns himself, Van Wyck Brooks, and George Jean Nathan. Nor was it an outcry of pained youth, rebelling against an older generation. The average age of the thirty-three contributors was almost thirty-six; the oldest was fifty-seven, the youngest twenty-seven. It is not unreasonable to think of them as a middle generation encouraging a younger to reject its heritage and to look to other lands and other cultures.

The incriminating details appear with monotonous regularity on page after page of the symposium: the city is an index of our material success and our spiritual failure (Mumford[4]); on every hand we can observe "the incurable cowardice and venality of the normal American politician" (Mencken), the press is corrupt and controlled by advertisers, and the public accepts uncritically what the newspaper provide (John Macy); in the American university the general student becomes a "specialist in the obvious" (R. M. Lovett); our cultural interests and activities have been turned over to the almost exclusive custody of women and the only hopeful sign in "The Intellectual Life" is the disrespect the younger people have for their elders (Stearns); in such a setting the literary life will inevitably be "a very weak and sickly plant" and talents will scarcely find nourishment in such a soil (Brooks); in our business life we no longer have an ethic; "business morality" is a term without meaning. Business is neither moral nor immoral. It represents "man's acquisitive instinct acting outside of humanistic motives" (Garet Garrett); finally in his family life, the American husband, overcome by mother worship, "becomes everything in his business and nothing in his home, with an ultimate neurotic breakdown or a belated plunge into promiscuity. The wife, on her part, either becomes hysterical or falls a victim of religious reformatory charlatanism" (Alfred Kuttner).

Very few of the essays discovered any means to mitigate or to vary the indictment. Stearns commented in his Preface on the underlying unity of the opinions expressed. This was especially surprising, he said, "in view both of the fact that every contributor has full liberty of opinion and that the personalities and points of view finding expression in the essays are all highly individualistic." He could only suggest that the contributors had independently come to their conclusions because these were the only conclusions available to an impartial board of review.

With such guides as this to a world fashioned and made intolerable by the prewar generation, the men and women who took over in the postwar decade could have had little confidence in either the precepts or the conveniences of their country. A pattern of rejection was soon established, abundantly supported by an accumulation of prejudices and views. However distorted and exaggerated, it followed rather closely the lines of a threefold criticism of the prewar generation and of the civilization it had made; there was, first, a failure of communication; second, a failure of social meaning and value; and third, a failure of morality. These failures—in each case crucial because they touched closely the dominating emotional and aesthetic needs of the younger generation—while not caused by the war, were revealed by the events of the war. Faith in the older generation, not unmixed with criticism of its enormities, persisted through what Van Wyck Brooks has called "the confident years" (1885-

1915); but when the war had ended, this generation discovered that it had lost most of its influence.

Long before, especially in the second half of the nineteenth century, many Americans had felt uncomfortably inferior in their attainments of mind and had quite naturally assumed the need to search in Europe (if the chance occurred) for a cultural "finish"; they either went themselves to Europe or had their agents send as much of Europe to them as they could afford. They apologized for their own country on the grounds that it had no time to develop a culture; or that culture was after all only a secondary matter, to be added later; or that they possessed a high degree of moral probity, which they might trade to Europe for its art.

This recognition of cultural immaturity was only one aspect of American self-criticism. As for the moral failure, they were aware of that too, but never quite so sharply as was the generation that sought its way out in the 1920s. Criticism of public venality and corruption, never so strong as in the days when Edward Bellamy,[5] Mark Twain, and Robert Herrick   attended to it, was, however, generally softened by the hope that men of good will would eventually change all that; that man, who is naturally good, has also a natural inclination to improve his status. The naive utopian zeal of Bellamy's novels was not unique. The extreme form of naturalistic theory, of course, defined man as hopelessly depraved, invariably doomed, incapable of the least effort to dignify his brief stay on this earth. But even the darkest and the gloomiest of the naturalists had accesses of optimism and tenderness; the naturalist thesis[6] almost never triumphed entirely. And while the naturalists wrote in partial or total commitment to that thesis, parallel with their writings were the findings of the muckraking journalists and novelists.[7] In a very reassuring way all of them shared the "veritist" confidence of Hamlin Garland[8] and the serene assurance of William Dean Howells. The myth of improvement held them all in the years leading up to World War I; and even the most intransigent

American of them all, Ezra Pound, spoke of the hope, perhaps of the imminence, of a Risorgimento,[9] an awakening, as he described it in 1912 (in *Patria Mia*), that "will make the Italian Re-naissance look like tempest in a teapot."

Pound, looking across the ocean at the America he had first left four years before, appreciated his country's tremendous energy but failed to find in it a "guiding sense," a "discrimination in applying the force." That "the force" was there everyone who had looked at the country, whether with sympathy or indignation, agreed, whatever his interpretation; and that the means existed to redirect it was seldom denied. For some this meant a change of government; for others a defeat of taboos and the restoration of "healthy common sense" to social and family life; for a few, the sharpening of instruments of communication, a move toward greater precision and "classicism" and away from the vague, meaningless deception of the romantic point of view.

Before 1915 the liberal, the dissident, the progressive member of society hoped for a moral, intellectual, and aesthetic resurgence: literature could bring about a better society, and a better society would help establish a better literature—or so men like Upton Sinclair felt. Sinclair's *The Jungle* (1906)[10] was itself a testimony to the reasonableness of the hope. These hopes, which were not only indefinite but subject of frequent abuse and disappointment, were all but abandoned at the end of World War I. Socialism seemed a lost cause, at least for the moment. It had never really held out more than a slender hope, kept alive by the wishful thinking of a number of men and women of good will. Their thought was largely a continuation of an earlier socialism and they felt little need to hasten the process of social change, though Emma Goldman[11] wished the time of change were near, and sometimes thought it was; and her friend Alexander Berkman had thought to perform a Caesarean operation upon the old world. In 1919 both Miss Goldman and Berkman sailed, with more than two hundred other undesirable citizens, on the *S.S. Buford*, as punishment for their hopes. Event had discouraged most radicals from hoping for a change in social values and had forced the extremists over seas or underground.

For those who contributed to *Civilization in the United States* there was no longer any basis of a reasonable hope, and in the volume there is no program or pattern of constructive suggestion. Though Carl Van Doren[12] (*Nation*, February 22, 1922) saw in it a "guiding confidence" in the worth of the intellectual, and George Santayana (*Dial*, June 1922) thought the presence of thirty such spirits was scarcely evidence that civilization was lacking in the United States, the document was nonetheless a grim and melancholy index of failure in almost every field of human activity and expression.

In many respects this failure may best be defined as a loss of precision in the communication of basic ideas—in the university and in education in general; in the morality of public life; in the arts themselves. Ezra Pound spoke in 1912 of this crisis in communication:

> When a young man in America, having the instincts and interiors of a poet, begins to write he finds no one to say to him: "Put down exactly what you feel and mean! Say it as briefly as possible and avoid all sham of ornament. Learn what technical excellence you can from a direct study of the masters, and pay no attention to the suggestions of anyone who has not himself produced notable work in poetry."

This was what Pound repeated to the young men and women who even then were coming from America to hear him say it. And, indeed, Pound was to go on, in London, and later in Paris and Rapallo,[13] guiding young poets and prose writers alike, as no one else had been able or willing to do. Harriet Monroe, who had many reasons to respect, admire, and hate Pound, said in her autobiography that America, in letting him go to Europe, lost a great teacher. But that part of America which wanted to learn followed him to Europe—and there, with his aid and that of Gertrude Stein and Ford Madox Ford[14] helped to inaugurate twentieth-century literature.

Meanwhile, in Pound's view, for one, the Old Gang was doing its best to keep that literature from coming alive. Writing to Margaret Anderson[15] in January 1918, Pound said, apropos of his failure to find any worth while writing in his own country, "There appears to be nothing in America between professor and Kreymborg and Bodenheim.[16] ...Anemia of guts on one side and anemia of education on the other." Though Pound appreciated what Whitman had done, he felt that the "barbaricyawp"[17] was not enough—"we can't stop with the 'yawp.' We have no longer any excuse for not taking up the complete art." In his "Pact"[18] with Walt Whitman (1915), he acknowledged that Whitman had helped to make the break from the past ("It was you that broke the new wood"), but wanted now to go on to the task of refining the language and making it more precise ("Now is a time for the carving"). He had found nothing but timidity in writers and critics, and intimidating, dogmatic force on the part of those who might have made an artist's life tolerable.

Pound was very conscious of his role in Europe, which was neither to restore Europe nor efficiently to admire its cathedrals (like Christopher Newman of Henry James's *The American*), but to encourage the "helpless few in y country,/O remnant enslaved!"[19]—those other Americans who felt intimidated or stifled in Davenport or Philadelphia or Crawfordsville. "The Rest" states melodramatically what many of Pound's contemporaries felt:

> *Artists broken against her,*
> *Astray, lost in the villages,*
> *Mistrusted, spoken-against,*
> *Lovers of beauty, starved,*
> *Thwarted with systems,*

Helpless against the control;—

And he begged those who could not adjust themselves to the success pattern of American business to take heart:

You who can not wear yourselves out.

By persisting to successes,

You who can only speak,

Who can not steel yourselves into reiteration…

He might serve as their example; he had, after all, come through:

I have weathered the storm,

I have beaten out my exile.

The failure in communication had long before disturbed Howells, who himself had almost failed of precise honesty and courage. Many of the writers whom Howells sponsored[20] did seem aware of the need to smash the barriers to honest expression; but, despite their earnest study and dedication, they were too often careless of their art, not clear about its necessary limits and decorum. They would not have appreciated Pound's call for precision, for they thought themselves precise enough. Frank Norris, Stephen Crane, Jack London, and Theodore Dreiser suffered from one or another imprecision in style, form, or vision. While they had conquered timidity and arrogance in one way, they had failed to master them in another; and their work, for all its thrilling newness and audacity, was scarcely the ideal attack on the Old Gang and its hold on American cultural life.

One thing they had early succeeded in doing: they had again and again pointed to the contradictions in social values and to the hypocrisies underlying the preaching and practice of democracy. The social and moral criticism of the 1920s was largely concerned with the failure of society to provide breathing space for its independent spirits. The "flight from democracy" was described in dozens of minor novels, from Floyd Dell's *Moon-Calf* to Ben Hecht's *Erik Dorn*; it was provided with a rationale in scores of books and magazines, which emphasized the absurdities as well as the dangers of a leveling society.

In the *Dial* (1918) and the *Freeman*[21] (1920 and 1921), Harold Stearns published a group of essays, subsequently gathered under the title *America and the Young Intellectual* (1921), which was, for its time at least, a crucial statement of the failure of social definition of which the generation of the 1920s accused the Old Gang. The danger, as Stearns saw it, was that the young men, seeing with what fear and hostility and distinction was treated, would themselves "subscribe to the conventions and traditions." The "reforming zeal" of the years 1885-1915 had not sufficed to reduce his danger; such zeal was too often of a piece with the large-scale effort to make everyone alike in mind and mariner. Nor could they hope to escape through false sophistication, which denied the problem and debased the arts, so that these became mere ornaments of a futile life.

This range of argument, while it gave Stearns' contemporaries immense gratification, was scarcely the equivalent of Pound's criticism of democracy. In fact, Pound so severely judged the evidences of democratic practice that what he proposed seemed at times not to be democracy at all. He had a sharp sense of urgency in his criticism that was all but absent from the documentation found every month in Mencken's *American Mercury*. Pound was not simply or solely interested in the ludicrous. He was not just comfortably amused by human foibles but sincerely and honestly concerned about the democratic social position—about the efforts to deceive its citizens to mold them falsely, to teach them mediocrity as a virtue and thus deny them the chance to prove themselves worthy of something better. "'Tis of my country that I would endite," he wrote in "L'Homme Moyen Sensuel," not to prove himself the wiser, but "In hope to set some misconceptions right." Radway, the model democratic Christian of the poem, has learned early to respect and obey his tutors; and his mind is formed by

> *These heavy weights, these dodgers and these preachers,*
> *Crusaders, lecturers and secret lechers,*
> *Who wrought about his "soul" their stale infection.*

From them he finds a guide to proper manners, though the first-rate artists of his country have had to seek their recognition abroad. At the same time Radway is stimulated by what he reads in the daily press; "So he 'faced life' with rather mixed intentions," But in his country all must be alike (at least in public) until the day will come

> *…when man*
> *Will long only to be a social function*
> *And even Zeus' wild lightning fear to strike*
> *Lest it should fail to treat all men alike.*

Having enjoyed his pleasures secretly, Radway atones by joining "an organization for the suppression of sin," and notes how profitable it is to be known, publicly as a crusader against vice:

> *For as Ben Franklin said with such urbanity;*
> *"Nothing will pay thee, friend, like Christianity."*

This is the portrait of "I'homme moyen sensuel": taught by inferior editors and preachers to loathe the improper life, he seeks out his private opportunities while announcing publicly his vigorous Christian virtue, "as a business asset pure and simple."

The deception and hypocrisy that America's artists saw in their society endangered democracy, which, as Whitman had often said, ought to protect the individual as well as further the cause of the mass. Whether because of inherent weaknesses in democracy or because men had long since strayed from its principles, by the end of World War I the air was full of criticism, cavil, and denunciation.

The failure of the Old Gang to please the young gave rise to another form of criticism, directed against a moral failure—which is to say, a failure to achieve and to permit others to achieve a normal, healthy life. As men and women worked toward a definition of the American type, they had also to search in America's past for its history. From November 1916 to October 1917 *The Seven Arts*[23] severely but hopefully pursued its researches into present definitions and past cause. One of its associate editors, Van Wyck Brooks, had in 1915 published the first of his examinations of the moral imbalance of the American man. In *America's Coming of Age* pointed to a most unfortunate division in American cultural life, the two irreconcilable opposites of its character, which had led to the worst forms of cultural depression and illness; idealism (an impractical idealism fostered by Emerson) and "catchpenny opportunism... originating in the practical shifts of Puritan life, becoming a philosophy in Franklin, passing through the American humorists, and resulting in the atmosphere of our contemporary business life."

An entire (and often a quick) survey of the American past served only to enforce the conviction that the Puritan, who had dominated history and was now fully in command of American life, was responsible for an intolerable situation. What Brooks wrote in *Letters and Leads, Ship* (1918) was echoed in a score of other places: the new generation of writers "find themselves born into a race that has drained away all its spiritual resources in the struggle to survive and that continues to struggle in the midst of plenty because life itself no longer possesses any meaning."

This conviction all but dominated American criticism throughout the 1920s. The American was an industrial giant, an emotional dwarf; having repressed his love of life (that is, his emotional predisposition to things, animals, fellow creatures), he came through with ingenious inventions, processes, methods; he built bigger, better, and faster locomotives, and was experimenting with automobiles and playing with airplanes; but the nearer India seemed, the more difficult the passage to it became.[24]

The phenomenon of America's industrial wealth and its spiritual poverty was the subject of one of the most exhaustive examinations in the history of modern criticism. Europeans often inordinately admired the giant and were puzzled to see so many Americans fleeing from him. Americans, closer to a knowledge of the sacrifices needed to make him so enormous, insisted on pointing to the devastating division in the moral economy caused by his growth. Ezra Pound spoke of the "Fordian" tendency[25] in American life:

> This is admirable as far as it goes, but Ford's world is the world of the hired man. Ford himself is the hired men raised to the thousandth degree, a titanic but by no means gargantuan figure, a revolutionist to such a degree that the bickering of impotent reds concerning him is almost comic… But where does this get us? For everything above comfortable brute existence there is a vacuum. (*Nation*, April 18, 1928)

Both the past history and the present condition of the American industrialist were thoroughly examined and accounted for before the decade began. The most important documents in the research were Randolph Bourne's[43] "The Puritans Will to Power" (1917), H. L. Mencken's "Puritanism as a Literary Force" (1917), and Waldo Frank's *Our America* (1919). This last was a "command performance" to explain America to the France and presumably also to Americans in Europe. Two members of the French High Commission, in America to observe their allies, asked Frank to write the book, "Not because I was an authority… Merely because it seemed reasonable to these cultural envoys to spice the mass of American conformist utterance abroad with a statement that could not even remotely be suspected of an official stamp." What Frank wrote was an extreme expression of the *Seven Arts'* point of view regarding the moral failure of the Old Gang, and he added to the stereotype of the person responsible for that failure. The Puritan, in this account, forced himself to repress vital ranges of feeling, emotion, desire; or he was forced by the circumstances of a raw, new, dangerous, and exploitable continent to "do violence upon himself."

Whole departments of his psychic life must be repressed. Categories of desire must be inhibited. Reaches of consciousness must be lopped off. Old, half-forgotten intuitions must be called our from the buried depths of his mind, and made the governors of his life.

In view of these necessities, the Puritan-pioneer had successfully eliminated pleasures, in favor of things and technical processes. By the time there were more than enough of "things" to go around he had lost his capacity to feel life as a whole, and his spiritual energy flowed in only one direction, "that of utilitarian ethics." So the Puritan in history had created not only giants but monsters; a genius of invention and method, he was a lost child in a maze of ill considered and unanswered regarding "the full life." Desire repressed, as every editor of the *Seven Arts* knew, must somehow be satisfied; in this case it "sickened and shriveled and grew perverse. It sought expression in neurotic art obversely sensual religions, in sadistic interference with Desire in others... But it *went on*. For it is life." For the ordinary man. "l'homme moyen sensuel," this public repression of desire led to "the hypocrisy of the American who goes to church on Sunday and bleeds his brother on Monday, who leads a sexually vicious life and insists on 'pure' books, draped statues, and streets cleared of prostitutes, who preaches liberty and democracy and free speech and supports the subtlest oligarchy of modern times."

What could a young man do? Exposed to this criticism, how could he hope to preserve himself, to keep his selfness pure? The documents provided by Stearn, Brooks, Frank, Mencken, and others coincided with the opening of new opportunities of escape, for the most part parents were still financially solvent. The young man could go to Paris; or he could try, in isolated refuges, to set up a life of his own, become an artist, and live the bohemian life, whatever that may have meant. Whether he went to Paris or stayed in Greenwich Village,[26] his criticism on the Old Gang persisted, even though he grudgingly accepted and quickly spent the checks sent to him by his elders in Cleveland or Omaha or Dubuque.[27]

The young generation of the 1920s had two boards of advisers: those represented in Stearns' volume, and those who dedicated their efforts to refining and sharpening the arts. The first group did not unanimously advise Paris as a cure for Dubuque. In fact, it very often condemned the young for fleeing its problems and wasting its talents—though Stearns himself could hardly wait for his boat to sail. The second group not only advised Paris but considered it indispensable as "the laboratory of the spirit," and they were better qualified to answer the question, "What can a young man do?" in a way the young man could appreciate. Above all else, the activities of the young man (born in 1900, in Europe at the age of seventeen or eighteen, twice removed from his American heritage through college and war) were literary activities, sponsored and encouraged by the conviction that of all forms of activity the literary was least pitiful or ludicrous. He was taken in neither by his commercial fathers nor by the boisterous anti-Americanism of the Mencken Boyd-Nathan *Mercury*, but was impressed by the intransigence of Pound, the taste of Gertrude Stein, and the intelligence of Ford Madox Ford.

The 1920s were a time least likely to produce substantial support among intellectuals for any sound, rational, and logical program. Prewar stability and convention were condemned because all evidences of stability seemed illusory and artificial. The very lively and active interest in science was perhaps the decade's most substantial contribution to modern civilization. Yet in this case as well, achievement became a symbol of disorder and a source of disenchantment. Pragmatism and liberalism were important preoccupations among the enlightened elders of the decade. But, together with their radical poor relation, Marxism, these relied too much upon a clear view of society as progressing in a straight line toward a perfection both of means and ends; and this view the young intellectuals refused to accept. Recent history had failed to support such an assurance.

Perhaps the most striking quality of the postwar intellectual was his attitude of refusal—refusal of the comfortable platitudes of the middleclass, refusal of the desperate assurances of liberal tacticians, and finally refusal of the suggestion that the war had provided an opportunity for renewing tradition, reviving it, or changing it without destroying it. This negative attitude was confined for the most part to the decade: it did not survive the debacle of October 1929;[28] nor could it continue once the middle class, the source of its financial support and the object of its derision, had temporarily lost its hold upon public confidence. But while it lasted there was widespread and free experimenting with social and aesthetic forms. The 1920s were marked by a disrespect for tradition and an eager wish to try out any new suggestions regarding the nature of man—his personal beliefs, convictions, or way to salvation.

VI Science and the "Precious Object"

1. THE PROBLEM

Of the hundreds of books and essays published in the 1920s on the matter of science and its gifts to man, two stand out as especially pertinent: Bertrand Russell's [29] "A Free Man's Worship" (1918) and Joseph Wood Krutch's[30] *The Modern Temper* (1929). The first emphasized the challenge offered by a scientific reading of the modern world; the second spoke with almost unrelieved pessimism of a generation's loss of belief and illusion.

The "dilemma of modern youth," said Krutch, as he surveyed the postwar decade, was a consequence of our no longer being able to sustain either an unreasoning faith or a rational doubt. "Unlike their grandfathers, those who are its victims do not and never expect to believe in God; but unlike their spiritual fathers, the philosophers and scientists of the nineteenth century, they have begun to doubt that rationality and knowledge have any promised land into which they may be led." In the past man was supported by myth and illusion, but he has now been relieved of them. "His teleological concepts molded [his world] into a form which he could appreciate and he gave to it moral laws which would make it meaningful, but step by step the outlines of nature have thrust themselves upon him, and for the dream which he made is substituted a reality devoid of any pattern which he can understand."

For the most part, science has been responsible for this sharp division between feeling and thought: "Try as he may, the two halves of his soul can hardly be made to coalesce, and he cannot either feel as his intelligence tells him that he should feel or think as his emotions would have him think, and thus he is reduced to mocking his torn and divided soul." Man is capable of an apparently endless extension of his intelligence, but he is not happy in the knowledge. This is the prevailing mood. So long as man accepts it and acts in terms of it, he will be incapable of belief in anything that his intellect is forced to reject.

With this apparently hopeless division in mind, Krutch examined several of the "illusions" men are forced to reject. Humanism, he said, offers no solution of the dilemma, for its confident assumptions are also disproved by the scientist, or they are hard to accept. Perhaps, if we cannot accept formulations of value by non-scientific minds, we can work with confidence in the laboratory of the scientist? We have long since been disabused of this hope; though scientific knowledge has greatly increased, "Science has always promised two things not necessarily related—an increase first in our powers, second in our happiness or wisdom, and we have come to realize that it is the first and less important of the two promises which it has kept most abundantly." We have discovered that faith does not come from knowledge, that knowledge is more likely to destroy faith or to make its exercise all but impossible. "We are disillusioned with the laboratory not because we have lost faith in the truth of its findings, but because we have lost faith in the power of those findings to help us as generally as we had once hoped they might help."

Krutch next considered the hope that love may prove a substantial source of happiness. The idea of sex as possessing somehow a key to happiness and stability, the idea put forward by the advocates of free, uninhibited love, has failed of its obligation, chiefly because the modern attitude has led only to "a certain lessened sense of the importance of the passions that are thus freely indulged; and, if love has come to be less often a sin, it has come also to be less often a supreme privilege." This fact is brought home to us in the novels of Aldous Huxley,[31] Ernest Hemingway, and others, for whom "love is at times a sort of obscene joke." The mysteries of sex once removed, we are wearied by the monotonies of boudoir and barn loft: "the world is no longer well lost for love."

As for literature, Krutch maintained that it was no longer possible to write genuine tragedy. Great tragedy requires a certain naive faith in the nobility of man and in the genuineness of his suffering, a willingness to suspend current fashions in disbelief and to entertain the illusion that man can act heroically. An educated society cannot give itself to such play-acting; it has "neither fairy tales to assure it that all is always right in the end nor tragedies to make it believe that it rises superior in soul to the outward calamities which befall it." The drama we call tragedy is a depressing reiteration of man's helplessness in a hostile universe. The only kind of tragedy we are temperamentally disposed to tolerate, it produces in the audience "a sense of depression which is the exact opposite of that elation generated when the spirit of a Shakespeare rises joyously superior to the outward casualties which he recounts." The "tragic fallacy" is no longer possible: the illusion that makes great tragedy effective in an age willing to believe in it. "Our cosmos may be farcical or it may be pathetic, but it has not the dignity of tragedy and we cannot accept it as such."

Aesthetic principles cannot give society the stability it needs "because, though the human mind may be made to work in accordance with them, external nature will not, and the ultimate dilemma may be stated thus: the proposition that life is a science is intellectually indefensible; the proposition that life is an art is pragmatically impossible." Similarly, the hope for certitude in a world of maneuverable fact is futile, for this world has been purchased at a sacrifice of other certainties it is now incapable of bringing back. It is true that recent developments in science have suggested a release from the tyranny of materialism, but the scientists have as yet not agreed upon what inferences may be drawn for metaphysics and religion from these new interpretations of the physical universe. The work of the physicists has been too well done to be easily undone; it is doubtful that we may ever return to a belief in what has been so effectively refuted.

Krutch ended his book on a note of resignation but of no comfort. We shall have to make "such peace with [our world] as we may." There is a melancholy satisfaction in having knowingly made our choice and accepted our fate: "we know at least that we have discovered the trick which has been played on us and that whatever else we may be we are no dupes." That we were no longer dupes Bertrand Russell would have agreed. He advised a kind of despairing courage in view of our awareness of an indifferent universe. In his writings on ethics, politics, and government he suggested that the intelligence is its own means of advance in a world indifferent to human wishes. There is a kind of courage that prevents suicide, but on this side of suicide there are infinite variations of human resourcefulness. Man may make of himself what he wishes, either as an individual or in cooperation with his fellows, but he had better not expect any support from the prophets of a beneficent God, for the idea of a world order that smiles on man's desires is an illusion.

Russell's essay, "A Free Man's Worship," first published in *Mysticism and Logic* (1918), remained for many intellectuals a challenging statement of the only attitude it seemed possible for modern man to assume. Science has given us a description of a meaningless world, Russell said, a world in which belief is not possible. Man must recognize that he is of no importance in such a world; unless he realizes his insignificance, he will not adjust himself intelligently to the world. The dispiriting facts of that world, revealed by science, must be faced and accepted:

> That Man is the product of causes which had no prevision of the end they were achieving; that his origin, his growth, his hopes and fears, his loves and his beliefs, are but the outcome of accidental collocations of atoms; that no fire, no heroism, no intensity of thought and feelings, can preserve an individual life beyond the grave; that all the labors of the ages, all the devotion, all the inspiration, all the noonday brightness of human genius, are destined to extinction in the vast death of the solar system, and that the whole temple of man's achievement must inevitably be buried beneath the debris of a universe in ruins—all these things, if not quite beyond dispute, are yet so nearly certain, that no philosophy which rejects them can hope to stand. Only within the scaffolding of these truths, only on the firm foundation of unyielding despair, can the soul's habitation henceforth be safely built.

Not only the conviction of this passage attracted the writers of the 1920's, but its rhetoric, a rhetoric of prayer, whose rhythms were all but guaranteed to persuade the reader of its wisdom and its earnestness. The essay became a naturalist prayer; it appealed to the gloomy, self-conscious vision of a universe indifferent to human endeavor. But Russell followed this announcement of a purposeless universe by an appeal to the intelligence of men to reject the advocates of Power and Force, who, he claimed, have failed to maintain their ideals against a hostile universe. "In this lies Man's true freedom: in determination to worship only the God created by our own love of the good, to respect only the heaven which inspires the insight of our best moments." Though we must often submit "to the tyranny of outside forces," we can remain free "in thought, in aspiration," if we will keep ever before us "the vision of the good."

It is not that good will alter in any way the nature of our world, but that we may make either a heaven or a hell out of our lives, and ought to choose the way that will best utilize our intelligence, with least harm to ourselves. We must endure the insults offered our intelligence by a hostile universe and find a certain glory in preserving liberty for our time and for ourselves. "Brief and powerless is Man's life," Russell concluded, "on him and all his race the slow, sure doom falls pitiless and dark." Man can preserve his dignity and strength only if he is fully aware of the indifference of "omnipotent matter":

> …disdaining the coward terrors of the slave of Fate, to worship at the shine that his own hands have built; undismayed by the empire of chance, to preserve a mind free from the wanton tyranny that rules his outward life; proudly defiant of the irresistible forces that tolerate, for a moment, his knowledge and his condemnation, to sustain alone, a weary but unyielding Atlas, the world that his own ideals have fashioned despite the trampling march of un-conscious power.

In many other essays Russell showed a lively interest in the actual physical and intellectual problems of a world dominated by a scientific point of view; he was interested chiefly in the effects of science upon the industrial and economic worlds. The technical achievements of science, he said in "Cause of the Present Chaos" (1923), are responsible for both industrialism and nationalism; and, though science is non-political, it controls all political occurrences. "It is science, ultimately, that makes our age different, for good or evil, from the ages that have gone before. And science, whatever harm it may cause by the way, is capable of bringing mankind ultimately into a far happier condition than ally that has been known in the past."

In the little volume *What I Believe* (1925), in Dutton's Today and Tomorrow Series,[32] Russell weighed the value of religion and science. The notions of good and evil, he said, are made of man's own wishes and of their clash with society. The danger lies in their having been read into nature, as somehow antedating and governing human acts. "Optimism and pessimism, as cosmic philosophies, show the same naive humanism: the great world, so far as we know it from the philosophy of nature, is neither good nor bad, and is not concerned to make us either happy or unhappy. All such philosophies spring from self-importance, and are best corrected by a little astronomy." Religion has erred by inspiring fear in men, fear of death especially, though all fear is bad and works great harm when it is used as a religious sanction for human acts. The man with a "scientific outlook on life" will not be frightened by either the Scriptures or the Church. "He will not be content to say" such-and-such an act is sinful, and that ends the matter. "He will inquire whether it does any harm, or whether, on the contrary, the belief that it is sinful does harm."

The exercise of intelligence in such matters will help to cut away from our way of life the superstitious and harmful notions of sexual decorum, for example, and will replace them with the two motivating forces of "a good life"—love and knowledge. Specific knowledge of facts is a good deterrent to excessive and irrational behavior. "All moral rules must be tested by examining whether they tend to realize ends that we desire." Russell assumed intelligence as an indispensable accompaniment of desire, for without intelligence we are led to one excess or another, and ultimately the exhaustion of all hope. The fetish of sin is a superstition which has held on to man's habits with a strange tenacity. It can inflict on man "preventable suffering," and Russell described a cradle-to-grave portrait of its effects. "In all stages of education the influence of superstition is disastrous." It prevents the child from learning the normal facts necessary to his intelligent living, and worse, suggests that such facts as have to do with the sex life are sinful. "Moral rules ought not to be such as to make instinctive happiness impossible."

According to Russell, science has both a quantitative and a qualitative gift to make to modern civilization. In the matter of techniques, its quantative gift has already been bestowed to the point of abuse. Man does not possess enough inner stability to take intelligent advantage of it. If he had adequate resources for the intelligent control of this gift, it would never be used to excess. But, as Russell remarked in another Today and Tomorrow essay, *Icarus* (1924), "The sudden change produced by science has upset the balance between our instincts and our circumstances, but in directions not sufficiently noticed. Over-eating is not a serious danger, but over-fighting is."

The real danger is that man, freed of the moral superstitions of the past, which have at least theoretically been disproved, will no longer wish to control his life and will give in to his passions in frightening and destructive measure. If man controls himself, he can use the quantitative gift of science to fullest advantage; if he will not, then science is a danger multiplied a thousand times by techniques. "And so we come back to the old dilemma: only kindliness can save the world, and even if we knew how to produce kindliness we should not do so unless we were already kindly. Failing that, it seems that the solution which the Houyhnhnms adopted toward the Yahoos,[33] namely extermination, is the only one; apparently the Yahoos are bent on applying it to each other."

The history of science between the dates of Russell's essay and

Krutch's book is full of surprises and quick changes in point of view. During the decade important changes in modern physics were anticipated in Einstein's *Theory of Relativity* (1920) and they also had some effect on the philosophical views presented in Whitehead's[34] *Science and the Modern World* (1925). The work of the American pragmatist, John Dewey,[35] proceeded apace with every new development in science, and it formed the very basis of the liberal theory in politics, economics, and morality: for Dewey's examination of all three in terms of consequences, in the light of a psychology of act and a metaphysic of fact, provided a thorough summary of liberal hope for "intelligence in the modern world." Of all the intellectuals of the decade the men most enthusiastic about science were the Communists; they reasoned that the practical results of science held promise for any organization of the body politic and might (*vide* Russia) be most successfully produced, distributed, and used in a Communist state. They were the optimists of the scientific world and were accordingly scornful of the cynics, the doubters, and the escapists. In the opinion of the Communists, all thinking was escapist that did not contribute positively to the hastening of the "new world" or to its liberal stocking of goods.

The persons whom they called pessimists, doubters, and escapists—in short, a considerable body of writers and artists who were convinced neither of the disastrous menace of science nor of its bright promise—regarded with suspicious reserve the achievements of science and its method. In a world that offered the promise of abundance for all, they held firmly to the view that somehow science had failed to gain its objectives. To begin with, they doubted the validity of a method that so cleverly excluded the concrete details of individual experience and sought only for a norm of experience, a manageable commonalty in things and events. They refused to believe that scientific language was accurate, or at least they could not agree with the suggestion of Max Eastman[36] (*The*

Literary Mind, 1931) that poetic language, being inaccurate, had lost its real function and should be banished from serious consideration.

They were, of course, not easily swayed by liberal pragmatic visions of a world happily adjusted and smoothly run by a community of reasonable men. Some of them followed the fashion of sophisticated despair, indulged in the luxury of futility, often to great excess. But the more substantial of them (like John Crowe Ransom,[37] Allen Tate, Pound, and Eliot) worked with precision and confidence on the formulation of a group of aesthetic principles, which had for the most part been neglected in the history of American literature. These were concerned with questions of the precise nature and meaning of literature, its language, its form, and its extent. They availed themselves of whatever suggestions science and philosophy might offer; in consequence, they helped to establish a complex body of criticism, quite without parallel in the previous history of American culture. They were influenced by science in some form or other, but this influence worked chiefly through a medium of opposition—that is, the suggestions science offered were assimilated in an unscientific way and used for unscientific ends.

There were many attempts in the 1920s to establish a "scientific ethic"—that is, a point of view based on intelligence, as Russell had described the term. One would be too naively optimistic to believe that the extraordinary advances could be matched by a corresponding refinement of the intelligence applied to their uses. From the pens of prominent scientists of the day came detailed suggestions for this practical achievement in morality. One of the first requirements was that the theological concept of sin be discarded. In the opinion of both Russell and B. S. Haldane,[38] the religious sanctions against sin had become un-healthful, because they prevented men from doing what they could do for the advancement of their own happiness. This was a plea not for license but for a wider application of intelligence.

These men said in effect that all the skills required for the perfection of man's state on this earth are available, and that man needs only to use a small share of the scientist's intelligence. Haldane, in speaking of the deterrent effects of religions upon progress in morality, said in 1924 that the only kind of religion scientists could accept was one that "will frankly admit that its mythology and morals are provisional." Kirtley F. Mather[39] (*New Republic*, September 9, 1925) admitted that modern science was destructive to faith in a God "whose chief mode of demonstrating his presence is by the breaking of natural laws" and to the childish belief that mankind would some day be saved by "some extraterrestrial force aided only by the prayers of the elect." But there is another kind of religion, one "based on facts and experiences, a religion developed by rigidly scientific methods of thought." Mather believed that the scientist should have the responsibility of establishing and promoting such a religion. Though the scientist is usually indifferent to moral evaluations, when "his attention is called to illogical moral implications or erroneous spiritual by-products with which his truths are cloaked by others, surely he should be expected to point what he considers the correct deductions to be."

This was the modern scientist's contributions to ethics. The suggestions of Mather, Haldane, Russell, and others added up to an appeal for an intelligence that would check the abuses of both fundamentalist morality and industrialism, establish a kind of moral discrimination that had never before been the property of more than a very small minority, and reinterpret basic desires in terms of the capacity of science reasonably to satisfy them.

One of the more interesting of the effects of science upon the thought of the twenties was the modernist view of religion. In its extensive application to all liberal thought, it had a bearing upon most of the reformation of religious ideas; and it acted with vigor and confidence in the interests of establishing its principles among the laymen who assumed important positions in the modernist church.

Herbert Croly, editor of the *New Republic* from the year of its founding to 1930, strongly advocated an intelligent revision of religious attitudes. In the issue of June 9, 1920, he spoke of "a new body of authoritative knowledge which would bind humanity together and save it from falling a victim to its prepossessions, aberrations, and distempers." Science had thus far failed to provide such an authority. In fact, "Its achievements have only intensified that moral chaos, of which the war with its barren victory, its peace without appeasement, and the ominous Bolshevist menace, are different but closely connected expressions." If science could only inspire man with, its power of organization and its intelligence, then the effective reconciliation of science and religion would take place and "human nature would unfold itself with unprecedented momentum."

Such a reconciliation must proceed along lines laid down by Croly in another essay (*New Republic*, January 27, 1926): "Scientific inquiry must posit the existence of a world which the human mind is capable, after a fashion, of understanding. The religious life must posit the existence of a world in a fashion, get themselves realized." The experimental method of science must be applied to the phenomenon of human consciousness—each person, in other words, needs to examine himself with the same kind of discriminating and analytic thoroughness as the experimental scientist uses in his researches. This form of self-analysis is impossible in traditional religions; the paraphernalia of religious ceremony and ritual, Croly maintained, "are devices for preventing the immature from straying rather than positive clues to the true way."

Other suggestions for the scientific renovation of human nature included one from William Pepperell Montague, professor of philosophy at Columbia University. In "The Promethean Challenge to Religion" (*New Republic*, August 6, 1924), Montague portrayed a desirable new religion.

In its streamlined temple "there would be the welcome and luminous absence of sacrosanct authority. Such dogmas as remained, and there would be many, would be transformed into hypotheses. The most fantastic theory of the supernatural, if held as a hypothesis, is honorable, and belief in it is honest and to be expected." The ethic accompanying this religion would resemble it in having discarded the bugaboo of authority, "and with it the great clutter of prohibitions and taboos—rules taken as ends in themselves rather than as means to happiness." We need above all to abandon authority and asceticism; if we can do this, human ethics will for the first time in history be brought into "active partnership with human sciences." This Promethean adventure will succeed in preserving "the old supernatural hope for God and immortality," but it will also be united with an equally pressing demand for the use of creative intelligence.

What Montague's suggestion amounts to is a request that God be allowed in the modern temple on probation, that His attributes and the terms of belief in Him be accepted as hypotheses, presumably hypotheses that might never be pressed for evidence nor embarrassed by the need of verification; unless, of course, the immortality of the soul and the existence of a supernatural being can eventually be proved as "highly probable" through some extension either of science or of religion as yet not proposed.

These were the questions raised because of the position of science in the 1920s: what moral disposition to take with respect to its achievements; how to discriminate between the very effective strategies of its method and the not altogether satisfactory consequences of its applications to human affairs; what to do, either to restore to the human vision the illusions driven out by it, or to reinterpret religious schemata to make them acceptable to a scientific view. They were problems not peculiar to the decade; they had existed for many decades, and they would persist (and become aggravated) in the years to follow. But in no comparable period of time were there such extremes of view among those who tried to solve them.

〔注释〕

1. The Old Gang：指保守派文学评论家。

2. Harold Stearns：哈洛德·斯特恩斯（1891-1941），美国评论家。

3. H. L. Mencken：门肯（1880-1956），文学评论家、编辑、记者。1924 年同乔治·让·纳桑（George Jean Nathan，1882-1958，戏剧评论家）合办《美国信使》（*American Mercury*）杂志。

4. Mumford：刘易斯·芒福德（Lewis Mumford），文学评论家。下文中 John Macy、R. M. Lovett 及 Garet Garrett 等人为文学评论家、作家。

5. Edward Bellamy：爱德华·贝拉米（1850-1898），作家，乌托邦社会主义者。著有《向后看：2000 年~ 1887 年》（*Looking Backward: 2000-1887*）等书。下文中 Robert Herrick：罗伯特·赫里克（1868-1938），小说家。著有《自由的福音》（*The Gospel of Freedom*）等多部现实主义小说。他的小说抨击金钱的丑恶，歌颂美国西部恬静淡泊的生活。

6. Naturalist thesis：自然主义观点。主要来源于法国作家左拉所倡导的法国自然主义。认为人完全为环境与遗传因素所制约，不能主宰自己的命运。

7. the muckraking journalists and novelists：揭发黑幕的记者和小说家，指一批在第一次世界大战以前从事社会改革、揭露美国社会黑暗的记者、作家和改革派人士，其中以辛克莱（Upton Sinclair, 1878-1968）等人的影响为最大。

8. the "veritist" confidence of Hamlin Garland：写真主义（veritism）为作家加兰首先提出，是一种有节制的自然主义，它主张在描写外部世界黑暗和丑恶的同时添上几笔乐观的色彩。

9. Risorgimento：意大利语，意为"复兴"、"复活"。下文中 *Patria Mia*：《我的祖国》，是庞德在 1912 年为伦敦《新时代》（*The New Age*）撰写的一系列文章，1950 年结集出版。

10. *The Jungle*：《屠场》，辛克莱所著长篇小说。

11. Goldman and Berkman：爱玛·戈尔德曼（1869-1940），立陶宛无政府主义者。1885 年移居美国。1889 年与另一无政府主义者亚历山大·伯克曼（Alexander Berkman）相识。1919 年他们与其他 200 余名激进分子被送上布福德号船，驱逐出境。

12. Carl Van Doren：卡尔·凡·道伦（1885-1950），《民族》（*Nation*）纽约周刊杂志编辑（1919-1922）。下文中 George Santayana：乔治·桑塔亚那（1863-1952），西班牙裔美国人。著名诗人、评论家、哲学家、教育家。*Dial*：《日轨》杂志，文学评论月刊。20 世纪 20 年代成为替现代派鸣锣开道的先锋刊物。

13. Rapallo：意大利西北部一濒海城市。庞德于 1924 年起到第二次大战结束一直在此定居。20 世纪 50 年代又返回此地，直至去世。

14. Ford Madox Ford：福特·马多克斯·福特（1873-1939），英国小说家、评论家、诗人。

15. Margaret Anderson：玛格丽特·安德森（1886- 1973），曾任著名的《小评论》（*The Little Review*，1914-1929）杂志的编辑，为新文学推波助澜。

16. Kreymborg and Bodenheim：指阿尔弗雷德·雷姆堡（Alfred Kreymborg, 1883-1966），诗人、评论家。马克斯韦尔·博登海姆（Maxwell Bodenheim, 1893-1954），小说家、诗人。

17. "barbaric yawp"：引自惠特曼诗。

18. "Pact"：《协约》，庞德于 1915 年发表的一首诗。原名 "A Pact"，它表明了庞德对惠特曼较全面的理解和评价。以下本段括号中的引文皆出于该诗。

19. 引自庞德的诗《休息》（"The Rest"）。下文引语亦出自此诗。

20. the writers whom Howells sponsored：豪威尔斯提携起的作家，指克兰、诺里斯及德莱塞等自然主义作家。

21. *Freeman*：《自由人》杂志，1920 年创刊。

22. "L'Homme Moyen Sensuel"：《庸人》，庞德名诗；下文中的 Radway 是其中的主人公。

23. *The Seven Arts*：《七艺》文艺评论杂志（1916-1917）。

24. but the nearer India... became：此句化用惠特曼名诗《到印度去》（*The Passage to India*）中的句子。

25. "Fordian" tendency：亨利·福特（1863-1947），美国汽车制造商，大规模流水作业生产汽车的首创者。他是机械文明的一个代表。

26. Greenwich Village：格林威治村。位于纽约市曼哈顿区西南端。从 1910 年起成为文学艺术团体活动中心，生活放荡不羁的艺术家的聚集地。

27. Cleveland or Omaha or Dubuque：分别为美国工商业中心。Cleveland 是田纳西州东南部的一个城市，Omaha 是美国主要的铁路枢纽、商业中心，Dubuque 是爱荷华州东北部一城市，工业较发达。

28. the debacle of October 1929：指 1929 年 10 月华尔街股票市场的猛跌。这是 20 世纪 30 年代经济大萧条的开始。

29. Bertrand Russell：伯特兰·罗素（1872-1970），英国哲学家、数学家、社会改革家。主要著作有《神秘主义与逻辑》（*Mysticism and Logic*, 1918）和《西方哲学史》（*History of Western Philosophy*, 1946）。他的论文《自由人的信仰》（"A Free Man's Worship"）收在他的《神秘主义与逻辑》一书中。他于 1950 年荣膺诺贝尔文学奖。

30. Joseph Wood Krutch：约瑟夫·伍德·克鲁奇（1893-1970，评论家。《现代的趋势》（*The Modern Temper*，1927）是他的一部文学心理学研究论著。

31. Aldous Huxley：奥尔德斯·赫胥黎（1894-1963），英国小说家、剧作家、杂文作家。

32. Dutton's Today and Tomorrow Series：达顿公司出版的《今天与未来》丛书。

33. the Houyhnhnms...the Yahoos：乔纳桑·斯威夫特的小说《格列佛游记》智马国中的两类居民：智马（Houyhnhnms）和耶胡（Yahoos）。

智马生活在一种宗法式的公社中，虽为畜类但正直、善良。耶胡虽有人形，却生性贪婪、凶残、淫荡，常见利忘义，自相残杀。这是作者对"人不如兽"的人类最尖刻的讽刺。

34. Whitehead：阿尔弗雷德·诺斯·怀特海德（Alfred North Whitehead, 1861-1949），英国数学家、哲学家。在数学、逻辑和科学学方面皆有建树。

35. John Dewey：约翰·杜威（1859-1952），美国哲学家、实用主义者。杜威哲学之最大目的就是怎样使人有创造的思想力。

36. Max Eastman：马克斯·伊斯曼（1883-1969），文学批评家、诗人。与约翰·里德（John Reed, 1889-1920）同为马克思主义文学批评小组成员。曾参与编辑左翼刊物《群众》（*The Masses*）和《解放者》（*The Liberator*）。

37. 兰生（John Crowe Ransom）及下文中提到的作家皆为新批评派的创始人或支持者。

38. J. B. S. Haldane：约翰·伯登·桑德森·霍尔丹（John Burdon Sanderson Haldane, 1892-1964），英国生物学家。

39. Kirtley F. Mather：克特利·F·麦瑟，美国地质学家。

Questions For Discussion：

1. The postwar decade in America was one of disaffection. What made the world of the prewar generation intolerable to the postwar generation of men and women? Discuss with reference to the relevant works of H. L. Mencken and Van Wyck Brooks.

2. Do you agree to the statement that the failure of the United States in all fields of activity can be, in many respects, defined as a loss of precision in the communication of basic ideas?

3. How do you think the dichotomy of the American nation, its industrial wealth and its spiritual poverty, helped to fashion the temper of the 1920s?

4. What was the "dilemma of modern youth"? How was science

instrumental in producing that dilemma?

5. Define Bertrand Russell's "despairing courage." What are the dispiriting facts of life that modern man must face and accept?

6. Was science responsible in any way for the loss of belief and hope of the postwar generation? Was it the problem then?

For Further Reference:

1. Edmund Wilson. *The Shores of Light: A Literary chronicle of the Twenties and Thirties.* New York: Farrar, Straus and Young, 1952.

2. Warren French, ed. *The Twenties: Fiction, Poetry, Drama.* Deland, Florida: Everett/Edwards, Inc., 1975.

3. Milton Plesur, ed. *Intellectual Alienation in the 1920s.* Lexington: D.C. Heath and Company, 1970.

Richard Bridgman

〔作者介绍〕

理查德·布里奇曼（Richard Bridgman, 1927- ），美国文学评论家、学者。他出生在俄亥俄州，1960 年在加利福尼亚大学获博士学位。

布里奇曼悉心从事美国文学研究。他的学术著作包括：《格特鲁德·斯坦分析》（*Gertrude Stein in Pieces*, 1971）、《神秘的梭罗》（*Dark Thoreau*, 1982）及《美国的口语化风格》（*The Colloquial Style in America*, 1966）等。

The Colloquial Style in America

〔作品介绍〕

《美国的口语化风格》是研究美国文学口语化风格形成和发展的经典性评论著作。它深入探讨了这种民族文学风格赖以产生的社会及历史背景，分析了亨利·詹姆斯、马克·吐温、格特鲁德·斯坦、舍伍德·安德森、林·拉德纳和海明威等作家对美国口语化风格形成的贡献，从而勾勒出这一风格生成的全貌。

《美国的口语化风格》共包括《序言》和正文六章。《序言》简括地回顾了口语化风格形成和发展所经历的曲折道路，提出美国小说风格在 1825 至 1925 年间发生了深刻变化，用字愈益具体化，句法更趋简单；这种变化首先在方言作品和小说对话中明显表现出来，至 19 世纪末，作家更明确意识到口语化风格的技巧特点，这些后来逐步发展为成熟的口语风格。第一章通过大量例证综述了美国口语化风格的基本特点，诸如拟声、强调某些词语、重复、解释、事物和行动的罗列、押头韵、并列结构及并连词的使用等等。

第二章论述了在 19 世纪，美国浪漫的个人主义、民族主义的自豪感以及实际需要促进了口语化风格的发展。最初，口语化风格先在方言作家的作品中出现，但多数美国作家尚不熟悉日常语言的幽微特点。他们开始努力在作品中再现美国方言，注意美国本土语言的节奏，它的细节和整体效果。于是在文学作品中出现了方言和"标准语"并列的现象，前者表现出本身不可否认的活力，两者开始相互融合，一种新的风格开始形成。到内战以后，文学作品中的方言经历了一种微妙的变化。在铸造美国文学语言的过程中，19 世纪的作家都做出了自己的贡献。霍桑的对话是叙述故事和安排情节的工具。库柏的对话表现出语言的多样化（虽然运用时尚欠精巧）。麦尔维尔力图使不同人物说出不同的语言。豪威尔斯是探讨中产阶级语言的先驱。

第三章《亨利・詹姆斯和马克・吐温》，详述了这两位风格迥异的作家对美国文学口语化风格所做出的贡献。詹姆斯要表现的是抽象的精神状态，他借用口语的风格，通过重复、夸张、强调、提炼等手段，再现口语的典型的语言模式，这些模式极有助于口语化散文风格的形成。马克・吐温所表现的主要是具体事物和行动。他的语言直接来源于生活中的口语。对他来说，在字与物、象征与象征物之间存在着直接的关系。他的理想是"毫无雕饰地讲出来"。他的风格奠定了美国文学口语化的基础。他用字简短，句法简单，表达效果直接、具体、清晰。虽然詹姆斯和马克・吐温的观点和文风都不相同，但两人在写作形式上有不少共同特点，如在重复、插话、强调单字及声音模式等方面，在处理对话及在叙述文字中部分或全部地借用口语的特点等方面，他们都推进了口语化风格的形成。

第四章论述了自马克・吐温的《哈克贝利・芬历险记》出版以后至 20 世纪 20 年代，包括马克・吐温在内的美国作家在发展口语化风格方面所经历的曲折道路。在《哈克贝利・芬历险记》发表后四分之一个世纪里，口语化风格没有出现明显的进展。这一方面是因为公众未能认真对待马克·吐温，另一方面也是因为作品语言的特殊性，主要作家当中不少人未能从其风格中得到教益。这本书虽受到公众的欢迎，但其风格的革命性没有得到普遍的承认。诸如乔治·艾德及斯蒂芬·克兰等人多以《汤姆·索耶历险记》或《密西西比河上的生活》等书的风格为张本。马克·吐温本人也在继承《哈克贝利·芬历险记》的文风方面遇到困难，他的故事《汤姆·索耶在国外》、《侦探汤姆·索耶》等都未能成功地再现哈克的声音。林·拉德纳用二十年时间观察和再现美国下层人民的语言特点，虽有成绩，但并未形成一种独特的风格。舍伍德·安德森可能是继马克·吐温之后第一位把口语作为表现现实的严肃文学手段的作家，在遣词用字、句法、艺术效果方面都发展了口语风格，对海明威颇有影响；但他未能克服文风上的单调、不协调等弱点。

本书用一整章的篇幅谈及格特鲁德·斯坦在发展美国文学口语化风格方面所做的尝试。斯坦曾在威廉·詹姆斯指导下学习心理学，之后开始作为亨利·詹姆斯的文学弟子进行创作。她的作品注意表现心理状态，人的思想通过谈话得以表达；经常使用重复手法。她保留了口语风格中的一些用字和标点特点，在作品中使词语趋于简单化，以强调重复字词的效果；有时人物行动和传统的主题都似消失，字词本身的效果得到加强，它们的排列产生一种抽象意味。斯坦以此来强调口语的基本结构。她的文字的简单和毫无修饰表现了口语风格的片断性、重点突出以及重复等特征，在重复手法的运用和加强字词之间的抽象关系方面，她把亨利·詹姆斯和海明威的文学创作尝试联结起来，熔为一炉。

最后一章论述了海明威在铸造美国文学口语化风格方面做出的杰出贡献。1916 年海明威开始文学创作时，美国口语在小说中的地位依然没有确定，马克·吐温和亨利·詹姆斯这两条脉络依然没有得到联结，口语风格亦没有形成。海明威熟悉和喜欢中西部方言，这又和他到巴黎后的丰富的记者经历相结合，对形成他的独特文风起到重要作用。他受益于安德森、斯坦和庞德的指教，也从康拉德、克兰、乔伊斯等人的作品中学到不少东西。他悉心研究文学形式及风格，最终理解了《哈克贝利·芬历险记》的重要性。他的尝试产生了重要的结果：一种独立于具体叙事者的精妙的文体，即成熟的口语风格，终于形成，并对美国文学创作产生了深远影响。这种文体语言、句法、节奏都较简明，效果生动、清新，内涵丰富，奠定了稳定的口语风格的基础。至此，自 19 世纪以来几代作家的努力终于结出丰硕果实。

《美国的口语化风格》一书总结和分析了美国文学风格的发展过程，堪称文学风格研究领域中的开拓性者作。

这里选注的是该书《序言》及第一章。

An Excerpt from *The Colloquial Style in America*

Introduction

Little has been written about national prose style, for there are legitimate doubts that such an entity exists. A few pioneering explorations of American literature have located important image-rivers flowing through its style. References to gardens, to heroic innocence, and to darkness appear insistently enough in nineteenth-century American writing of all kinds to be regarded as transcending the preoccupations of any single writer. They constitute a part of the general literary response to national experience, that is, they form part of the national stylistic landscape.[1] Beyond these studies of images, however, and short of linguistics, only offhand generalizations have been advanced about an American way of using language. Such generalizations commonly superimpose political assumptions upon the literary medium, finding it, for example, "democratic"—hence, obviously, "direct," "hardy," and "casual." The usefulness of such descriptions, which as Richard Ohmann points out "name without explaining,"[2] is easily dismissed; yet, their persistent appearance indicates that readers of American literature feel, even though they cannot substantiate their intuition, that this literature possesses certain distinctive stylistic features. The present study attempts to discover the source of those feelings.

My initial assumption is so broad as hardly to admit dispute: that a change has indeed taken place in American prose style in the last century and a half. Even in the absence of absolute proof (which in stylistic matters is unthinkable) most readers would agree, I should think, that the prose of Erskine Caldwell[3], John Steinbeck, William Saroyan, and J. P. Marquand more closely resembles the prose of Ernest Hemingway than that of Nathaniel Hawthorne. Conversely, the prose of George Lippard,[4] Maria Susanna Cummins, Augusta Evans, Susan Warner, and William Ware has more affinities with Hawthorne than it has with writers in the current century. The very look of Hawthorne's page differs from Hemingway's. Its characteristic form is block like with dense and tangled interiors, while Hemingway crosses his page with thin lines and chips of language, clean and well-lighted. Can there be any doubt to whom each of the following two sentences belong?

> Beyond that darksome verge, the firelight glimmered on the stately trunks and almost black foliage of pines, intermixed with the lighter verdure of sapling oaks, maples, and poplars, while here and there lay the gigantic corpses of dead trees, decaying on the leaf-strewn soil.

> We walked on the road between the thick trunks of the old beeches and the sunlight came through the leaves in light patches on the grass.

If we add similar quotations from lesser writers in both centuries, the difficulty of attribution does not appreciably increase:

> She bent down on the velvet moss, while the green leaves of the shrubbery encircling her on every side, and the thick branches of trees, meeting overhead in a canopy of verdure, made the place

seem like a fairy bower of some olden story.

On one side of the road was forest, healthy-looking pine and elm, dark trunks looking almost black against the pale, milky-green of the new foliage.[5]

Now I would agree that for some purposes style cannot be discussed apart from the context in which it operates. Hawthorne's desire to create a sinister impression for the specific story "Ethan Brand" helped to determine the diction he selected: But style is both initiated by the artist and imposed upon him, so that when Hawthorne chose "darksome verge" and "gigantic corpses" to construct an atmosphere of fatality, he drew upon a vocabulary no longer available to Hemingway. Quite aside from his peculiar training and cast of experience, the writer bears the impress of a communal past and he walks through a shared present, which partially overrides individual volition. This study tries to keep both the social and the personal sources of style in mind, that is, to determine what probes and what solutions were virtually forced upon the writer by his time and to give an account of what the writer deliberately contributed to help bring about this general stylistic change.

If one accepts provisionally the existence of a change in American prose style, then the next pertinent question is, when did it begin? Recently the date 1884 has been advanced from several quarters, most succinctly by Ernest Hemingway: "All modern American literature comes from one book by Mark Twain called *Huckleberry Finn*."[6] As early as 1913 H. L. Mencken was championing Mark Twain: "I believe that he was the true father of our national literature, the first genuinely American artist of the blood royal."[7] Later, William Faulkner agreed, saying: "In my opinion, Mark Twain was the first truly American writer, and all of us since are his heirs, we descended from him."[8]

This critical admiration had not extended to Mark Twain's work as a whole, nor to his literary theories (such as they were), nor to his practical criticisms. One book alone has drawn the praise. Whatever the merits of Mark Twain's other writing, and whatever the weaknesses of *Huckleberry Finn*, everyone—literary hacks, artists, and critics—agrees that the style of this single book has had a major effect on the development of American prose. Herman Wouk, for example, recently proposed that Mark Twain "established at a stroke the colloquial style which has swept American literature, and indeed spilled over into world literature."[9] T. S. Eliot placed Mark Twain with Dryden and Swift as one of those writers who have discovered a new way of writing, valid not only for themselves, but for others.[10] Lionel Trilling felt that "as for the style of the book, it is not less than definitive in American literature. The prose of *Huckleberry Finn* established for written prose the virtues of American colloquial speech."[11] Most enthusiastic of all has been Bernard DeVoto's assertion, "In a single step it made a literary medium of the American language; the liberating effect on American writing could hardly be overstated."[12]

DeVoto's claim is an attractive one, but does not seem to me historically justified. I believe we have come to accept a false view of the ease with which writers profited by Mark Twain's example. The stylistic possibilities suggested by *Huckleberry Finn* were ignored, misunderstood, cynically exploited, and finally developed (with painful slowness) into durable form. Moreover, one cannot overlook the importance for style of several nationalistic impulses which initiated the idea of a colloquial prose long before Mark Twain's book appeared.

The literary relations of colonial America and the mother country are familiar enough. Seventeenth-century Americans drew sustenance directly from English sources, many of them having been born and educated there. Any differences in the standard styles of the mother country and of the colonies are attributable to the special conditions imposed by the American wilderness and the special preoccupations of the colonists. English examples determined changes in colonial style, as in the eighteenth century when American magazines pirated Augustan poems from their British counterparts and editors encouraged imitations of Waller,[13] Dryden and Pope. The major American figures maintained the continuity of the English tradition. As Stuart P. Sherman pointed out, "We can distinguish the styles of Franklin, John Adams, and Webster from one another, but not, with any assurance, from that of some British contemporary."[14] Similarly, of early nineteenth-century novelistic style, Leo Marx has commented: "If we ask what is different about German writing, we know very well the first answer to expect; it is written in German. But the language of Cooper is not all that different from that of Scott, and with Cooper's generation the boundary between British and American literature remains uncertain."[15] Only after the achievement of political independence did any significant movement toward the creation of an indigenous literature appear in the United States.

The first surge toward literary independence concentrated more upon content than upon form. Critical battles were joined, for instance, over whether Niagara Falls possessed the intrinsic dignity of Westminster Abbey. Although on some peripheral formal matters, spelling in particular, critics had mixed opinions, the arbiters of taste generally agreed that the crudities of American common speech were to be barred from any decent writer's style. Vulgarity in writing had to be fenced in with quotation marks, or clearly labeled as comic and therefore not to be taken seriously.

Still, a need was felt for a new style in the United States. The theoretical motive for it was to achieve a literary independence commensurate with the political independence already won. So Neah Webster proposed in 1789: "We have… the fairest opportunity of establishing a national language… in North America, that ever presented itself to mankind. Now is the time to begin the plan."[16] The literature of the New World was to reflect its republican ideals. Practically, the pressure for a new style came from the already existing components of that new style in popular speech. Americans shared, especially on the frontier, basic experiences that required a vocabulary not precisely equivalent to that considered standard in England. "It is remarkable," said Captain. Marryat in 1839, "how very debased the language has become in a short period in America... They have a dictionary containing many thousands of words which, with us, are either obsolete, or are provincialisms, or are words necessarily invented by the Americans."[17] The sense of regional uniqueness extended far enough in the early 1800's to produce a *Kentucky English Grammar*. It was not altogether a joke for Sam Slick to comment, "I never seed an Englishman yet that spoke good English."[18]

The linguistic situation in the United States was historically unique. Romantic, nationalistic, and practical pressures impelled American writers to evolve a new means of expression out of the casual discourse of the nation. There, if anywhere, "American" was to be heard. Not that the American language was a new language, distinct from English. Compared to the gross differences which existed between French when it was first being adapted for serious literary use and the Latin from which it was derived, the distinctions between American informal speech and standard literary English were subtle. There was a spoken language in the United States with a natural way of using it (American), and there was a literary language with an accepted way of using it (English). In many respects these overlapped, and yet they were far from identical.

Making a literary vehicle out of the spoken language was more easily conceived than executed. Logically, it seemed to require the sorting out of native elements already present in the standard literary style, and then their reblending with other elements hitherto excluded from the printed page. But how was one to assemble an indigenous vocabulary? And what would it sound like in operation? The most obvious answer was to transfer the speech of an American (whatever that was) to the printed page, the chief consideration being verisimilitude. At first, the writer's ear had to furnish the evidence against which he could check and improve his mimetic powers. Only after various regional and social dialects had been learned and dialogue had been sufficiently refined were enough conventions available to permit stylization. This process of establishing a literary imitation of colloquial speech and then polishing it resembles the gradual stylistic refinement of language in the English Renaissance theater, a recent study of which, after describing the primitive heartiness of the early theater's popular style, designated the problem facing the next generation of playwrights: "To assimilate this raw speech into an organized style that would lend itself to more complex uses without, in the process, losing its vitality and its close kinship with the spoken word."[19]

The fundamental question for all those working with the vernacular was how to eliminate the taint of vulgarity and of humor that normally accompanied popular speech. Taking a long view of the nineteenth century for a moment, one can trace the vernacular's increasing acceptance in the familiar descriptive terms "prose humor," "local color," and "realism." They signal the progressive flooding of the literary world with a common speech that for more and more reader is accepted as a literary norm. What was enjoyed with condescending amusement before the Civil War was encouraged after the war for its vivacious authenticity, then later as the literary manifestation of a militant attitude toward life.

Mark Twain's use of a boy as narrator in Huckleberry Finn provided American writers one important entry to the language and homely particulars of American life. In that story we hear no condescending adult voice by which Huck can be judged insufficient. His idiom is the standard. And because Huck is a boy, not only is his language natural to him, but his attitude toward the world of particulars around him is one of unremitting interest. His quiet concentration upon all that surrounds him invests the commonplace world with dignity, seriousness, and an unforeseen beauty that radiates through the very words he uses. An adult is tainted with stylistic original sin—double vision, awareness of tradition, vanity. Huck's style is prelapsarian in its innocence and single-minded directness. That is its excellence, but its limitation too, for although Huck saw deeply, his was a narrow vision. After the example of *Huckleberry Finn* writers had to learn how to overcome the limits of his restricting viewpoint.

As others have since, Mark Twain met the problem by avoiding it. In his subsequent work he either imitated *Huckleberry Finn* or he regressed to a mixed style where, like his admirers Stephen Crane and George Ade,[20] he deliberately encouraged incongruities for their easy irony. Somewhat later Ring Lardner[21] found a provisional solution. By using an illiterate ballplayer as his narrator, he managed to extend the range of experience of the vernacular voice, yet conserve its linguistic naiveté. The handicaps of this approach, however, were all too evident. Sherwood Anderson tried yet another track, making simplicity in language a doctrinal virtue. But despite an abundance of faith, he lacked the technical control that could protect him from writing simplistic parodies of himself. All in all, the thoroughly puzzled American writers could not disentangle a stable idiom from the vernacular. Merely to recognize the importance of Mark Twain's contribution was not to understand how to adapt his example to the uses of a general American prose style. Although *Huckleberry Finn* was in the sky, the day remained cloudy.

By the last quarter of the century, technical improvements in the management of both dialect and standard dialogue necessitated the move toward stylization, toward a distinctive and cohesive mode of writing. Since perfect accuracy of reproduction in dialect was neither possible nor artistically desirable, at a certain point of sophistication the dialect writer was obliged to change his goal: rather than verisimilitude, he sought to achieve verbal artfulness. His attention shifted from the world "out there" to the prose surface. In order to free colloquial constituents from their naturalistic bondage, the writer had to form new literary conventions, an uncertain process with many a retreat and no clear success. Henry James produced work of special pertinence for solving the stalemate in which the realists like Mark Twain found themselves. He wished to give the impression in his narrative prose of a mind at work, to reveal the slow progress and convoluted recapitulations of thought. Having already produced a form of dialogue that for all its external simplicity bore a heavy psychological burden, James set to work some of the techniques he had developed for dialogue to produce a stylized version of the mind talking. The results sufficiently intrigued him that for a time he exaggerated them to see what further possibilities they might afford his prose style. Radical punctuation, fragmented expressions, and odd verbalisms resulted. James's practice supplied answers which Mark Twain's camp of vernacularists needed, the medium of transmission being Gertrude Stein.

With her abstract exercises in writing, Gertrude Stein drew the basic features of colloquial language out into the open, magnifying and underlining them. Although it was not precisely her intention, she offered colloquial language as free as possible of a subject matter, thus concentrating the attention of the student of style upon pure manner. The instruction provided by both her precepts and her copious examples helped Ernest Hemingway create a definitive style based upon the American colloquial tradition. In his first years as a writer we can watch him experimenting with the narrator whose presence ostensibly legitimizes the presence of the colloquial mode. He later concealed and sometimes withdrew the narrator, but at the same time he tinkered with his prose so that, whether the narrator were present or not, it retained its colloquial base.

On the basis of this summary then and in spite of genuine reservations about the possibility of discussing a national prose style, I believe one can still affirm the following propositions with some confidence:

1) American prose style changed significantly between 1825 and 1925.

2) On the whole the change was toward greater concreteness of diction and simplicity in syntax.

3) The change was initiated primarily in dialect pieces and in fictional dialogue.

4) Toward the end of the century writers became increasingly conscious of the techniques of colloquial writing.

5) These techniques were then stylized to accentuate the following characteristics of colloquial style:

 a) stress on the individual verbal unit,

 b) a resulting fragmentation of syntax, and

 c) the use of repetition to bind and unify.

  If one asks once more, how Hemingway's prose and the prose of the twentieth century differ from that of Hawthorne and his century, the briefest answer would argue the greater verbal simplicity of the modern style. Long words are eliminated or infrequently used, and then as deliberate contrasts. The sentences themselves are shorter. What was hinged and stapled by semicolons in the earlier prose is broken up into a series of declarative sentences in the later. Fewer details are provided, and those offered are precise and concrete. References to a cultural and historical past are stripped away, and the haze of emotive words is dispelled. Primary colors are accented. The immediate material world claims all the reader's attention. The result is a sharp, hard focus. Hemingway's prose is not the ultimate prose by any means, but its lean, artful sufficiency based upon a vernacular diction and a colloquial manner had to be achieved before it could effloresce into more intricate structures.

  Since this study traces a movement in colloquial prose that

progressively simplifies and concentrates verbal expression, it may occur to the reader that some Southern writers have employed an oral style that is fundamentally expansive and opulent in nature. Although Southern writing can be as laconic as other American colloquial prose, it also indulges in that public oratory we habitually associate with the Southern politician, and which we often hear in the prose of Thomas Wolfe [22] and William Faulkner, of Robert Penn Warren and William Styron, and even, ironically, of James Baldwin. Such prose, which is not embarrassed by the oratorical flourish, can be accommodated to the historical process which this study describes, for the oratorical mode shares the characteristics of the colloquial. Its exclamations, repetitions, uncertain backings and fillings, accumulations of synonyms, and rhetorical emphases all originate in the extemporaneousness of speech, the spontaneous jetting of language that maintains its equilibrium by constant movement forward rather than by a poised interrelationship among stable elements.

Except for this last point concerning Southern writing, the propositions advanced in this introduction are elaborated and documented in detail in the chapters to follow. I hope I have offered enough evidence in them to convince the reader until he has had an opportunity to test my conclusions for himself, but not so much as to oppress him. Abuse of the reader being the cardinal sin of stylistic studies, I have tried to alleviate such distress by liberal use of italics and small capitals in order to emphasize significant points in extended quotations. One other procedural note: inasmuch as fiction writers were more open to new techniques than were the essayists committed to maintaining genteel standards in the American monthlies, my stylistic examples are drawn almost exclusively from fictional prose. Also, since colloquial language must initially issue from a specific speaker or he practiced in dialogue, fiction provided a medium for speech that expository prose of the nineteenth century rarely could. This is not, however, to deny an analogous easing of expository style in the period under investigation.

ONE

Parts of Speech

"Gradually the written language says something and says it differently than the spoken language."

Everybody's Autobiography

I

Speech and writing enjoy an intimate and not altogether separable relationship, but the two forms of verbalization do differ importantly in their physical performance and reception. When one speaks, the listeners hear the words almost as soon as they are uttered. It makes a stylistic difference that words pass more quickly from mind to sound to ear than they do from mind to paper to eye. The extra time required to transcribe sound symbols in visual form can be annoying, especially when the words are flowing rapidly, but it also provides intervals of indeterminate length for making verbal decisions, a luxury not readily available to the speaker. The writer is more conscious of his words than the speaker. Not only can he alter his vocabulary and syntax in his head as he proceeds, but once the word is written, he can change it, move it about upon the page, or strike it out.

There are, to be sure, written speeches, and these may be marked by a high degree of artifice. If the speaker has prepared his speech in advance, he may then read it to the audience from the text, or he may deliver it from memory. But unless the speaker is the most dogged writer imaginable, his speech will differ somewhat from normal written prose. The speaker experienced in the special problems of the platform will acknowledge that his audience is absorbing his message by ear. For modern literate man this activity is more difficult than reading, since listeners are unlikely to visualize words as they listen to a speech, whereas readers frequently not only see the words, but also hear them as they read. This means that because two senses are concentrated on the words, reading is a fuller process than listening. The visual appearance of the word and its sound make their impact simultaneously. The listener, however, absorbs the speech only by ear, and, even if his visual attention is fixed upon the speaker, he may be distracted. For this reason, the experienced speaker will simplify his syntax and repeat or restate key ideas as an aid to comprehension. When Mark Twain prepared a reading from *Huckleberry Finn*, he added italics to guide his verbal emphases and he repeated phrases. One portion originally read: "That was so—I couldn't get around that, no way. That was where it pinched." In his prompt copy Mark Twain changed it to: "That was so—yes, it was so—I couldn't get around *that,* no way. *That* was where it *pinched.*"[23]

The speaker may also insert rhetorical questions, deliberate pauses, even apparent lapses of memory, all to make his speech sound dramatic and "alive." Moreover, the speaker may depart from the written form of his speech through spontaneous interpolations. If the speaker has memorized his speech, he may substitute one phrase for another during his delivery, or he may change the order of his syntax as he speaks, not always consciously. And, whether he reads from a prepared text or delivers a memorized speech, he may add comments as his memory is jogged into some pew perception, or in response to the audience's reactions. When this happens, if the interpolation is of any length, the rhythm of his delivery will normally change noticeably. Everyone knows the experience of watching a speaker look up from his manuscript, begin to grope for words, and finally express himself rather loosely. The rhythm and often the diction of the extemporaneous speech changes. That change in rhythm is as noticeable as a shift in gear. This particular gear, which normally serves to get one around town, is called the colloquial. Because this term and its companion, the vernacular, are critical ones for the revision of literary norms that has occurred in America, they merit some special attention. As a fact of usage, vernacular, normally appears as a noun and *colloquial* as an adjective—a helpful distinction to begin with. The vernacular is the substance, the verbal clay to be shaped. One way in which that clay is shaped in speech and in writing is designated colloquial. The colloquial manner determines what the words will look and sound like in context and what they can do.

Beyond such basic statements, these two terms resist definition. The vernacular is difficult to distinguish from standard English once one acknowledges that it is more than the difference between "an old dog" and "a venerable canine." When, in Cooper's *The Prairie*, Obed Batt identifies Paul Hover as "a collector of the *apes*, or bee," then asks, "Do I use the vernacular now,—am I understood?" (ch. 11), he is not lapsing into vulgarity, but moving from the specialized jargon of the scientist into the daylight of ordinary discourse. Moreover, vernacular changes with the company. The informal vocabulary used by the educated man in his profession is blended with new words when he goes to a hardware store or a cocktail party. One does not descend to the vernacular so much as one moves laterally across different phases of it. Any word used with sufficient frequency as to become generally familiar gains access to the vernacular insofar as the vernacular is defined as a nation's common fund of language.

But other connotations adhering to the vernacular obscure its identity. For example, a recent and widely disseminated definition of the vernacular reads as follows:

English vernacular formerly referred to the native, spoken language—as opposed to the literary languages of Latin or Norman French. It now usually means Non-standard and perhaps Informal English, the native homely, spoken language as contrasted with Formal or literary English, usually with the implication that the vernacular has more vitality and force.[24]

Such a definition shows how sociological assumptions are imposed upon language. The idiom marked by formality and appearing in print is "standard." However, the definition continues, it is usually thought to be less forceful than the vernacular. For the vernacular to be regarded as possessing more force and vitality than standard English is perhaps a triumph of democratic sentiment but it is no great advance over the opposite nineteenth-century assumption that the lower strata of society made animal noises（that is, spoke the vernacular）while the upper, educated classes emitted angelic harmonies (standard English). If one attempts to particularize the general description of the vernacular offered by this modern definition, one may find it difficult to imagine a "native homely, spoken language," for such a description reflects nostalgia for a rural simplicity no longer, if ever, available. While the definition is emotionally accurate, it is practically useless.

The vernacular, like "normal" and "standard," is finally an abstract compound whose elements cannot be directly identified. But even though the vernacular never literally exists on any given page, its influence as a conception is still powerful. Its magnetism draws the writer in a general direction. Men live by their beliefs, however removed from substantive reality those beliefs may actually be. Belief in the reality of heaven will alter one's behavior just as the belief that one's language should be "the natural, instantaneous coinage of our thought"[25] will alter one's prose.

In the nineteenth century, standard diction was distinguished qualitatively, not quantitatively. It represented a euphemistic ideal rather than a national norm. But that decorous ideal was no more standard in the sense of being widely and regularly used than any other jargon or dialect. It, like the others, constituted but a portion of the English language as a whole, with the special distinction of being certified by those then in power. Power does determine standards though, and for this reason the vernacular as it appeared in early nineteenth-century literature did have some identifiable characteristics. Because its spokesmen were invariably of the lower class, used regional dialects, made frequent grammatical blunders, and were largely preoccupied with country matters involving violence and cloacal humor, it appeared that the vernacular was essentially a vulgar medium.

But the national mood altered over the century, and the alteration caused a redefinition of "standard." The change is not completed yet, as the famous dispute over the permissiveness of *Webster's Third New International Dictionary* may remind us. For the aristocratic temperament, standard is prescriptive; at its worst, it represents a dialect that has succeeded, guarded against interlopers by intricate passwords. The democratic inclination, however, is to make standard descriptive; the standard is statistically determined, as it were, for its features are understood to be the mass norm. "A nation's language is a very large matter," said Mark Twain. "It is not simply a manner of speech obtaining among the educated handful; the manner obtaining among the vast uneducated multitude must be considered also." If the vernacular is not regarded as inevitably vulgar, but merely as ordinary, then it is clear that as the nineteenth century wore on, ordinary language became increasingly identified with an ever-broadening middleclass. As the speech of that class was reproduced with greater fidelity, the basic identity of the vernacular as it appeared in literature changed. During the transition from prose humor to local-color writing, such raw objects and activities as privies, decaying corpses, dog fights, kicking, butting, and gouging were gradually replaced by more acceptable yet homely details of everyday life. The American writer tapped a diction which was neither evasively decorous nor violently coarse, yet one which was familiar to him and to his readers. So even as serious literature was absorbing the vernacular, the nature of the vernacular itself was undergoing a change. And whereas in the nineteenth century a very real distinction could be made between the vernacular and standard diction as they were used in prose, in the twentieth century the vernacular had virtually become standard.

While the *idea* of the vernacular was of the very greatest importance in the evolution of American prose style, the mercurial indeterminacy of its actual existence lessens its usefulness as an identifying feature of that style. The crucial determinant is not which word is used so much as how it is used. The disposition of words has already been identified as colloquial, but how in fact shall that disposition be recognized? The answer most ready at hand is to define the colloquial mode as any prose written as if it were spoken by someone. To this, one must add that the presence of a narrator is no guarantee that the result will be colloquial, just as, conversely, the basic features of colloquial writing may appear even without an announced narrator. Those colloquial features are derived from the psychology of speech; and of speech itself it can be said that it turns often and rarely observes neat sequences of thought. Having been submitted by the operating mind to only the hastiest preliminary organization, talk moves through a series of discursive units observing a logic of its own. The speaker digresses to chase a will-o'-the-wisp into the thickets of private association, or is distracted from what he took to be his main line of thought by the challenges of his listener. Dead spots occur in talk which have no purpose other than to sustain the rhythm and hold the floor while the speaker locates the next set of ideas. Improvisation requires on-the-spot adjustment to increase its effectiveness. All of these result in the rhetorical maneuvering which constitutes the colloquial situation. Such maneuvers eventually find their way into prose, where some are swiftly discarded while others are seized upon and stylized. The characteristics that ultimately identify the colloquial style—stress, fragmentation, and repetition—are not in themselves unique to it. But in aggregate and in heavy concentrations, they do signal a major and identifiable style. Because of the importance of these colloquial features, their sources and the nature of their occurrence need to be examined in greater detail.

II

Several observers have noted that modern American prose appears to give unusual prominence to single elements within its sentences. Harold Whitehall, expanding his sense of the difference between American and British English, wrote:

> In the most typical American writing, sentences seem to be constructs in which the key words function as isolated counters of expression... [while] in British English, individual words, even the key words, seem to be far more submerged into the larger syntactical units of expression. The sense hovers over the whole phrase or sentence, not over the word ...[27]

Malcolm Cowley also described the colloquial American style as composed of sentences which focused on a key word. That word, he thought, gained its conspicuous position by appearing repeatedly in a context of flat assertions made with simple, monosyllabic words.[28] More recently, Northrop Frye has distinguished three basic rhythms of verbal expression: that of verse with a regularly recurring pattern of speech; that of prose based upon the unit of the sentence; and that of ordinary speech, which he regards as centered upon a short phrase which contains the essential idea or word upon which the speaker is concentrating. The surrounding verbal sounds, he believes "are largely rhythmic filler."[29] Frye,

Whitehall, and Cowley all agree that there is a certain style of verbal communication, especially associated with North America (although Frye is establishing universal categories), which emphasizes single words or phrases at the expense of the larger verbal structure. The jewel is displayed against a plain, featureless background; the pearl is located in the formless viscosity of the oyster. What accounts for this colloquial propensity for outlining and elevating single words?

Some vernacular words had always drawn more than normal attention to themselves, as words, often abetted by the writer's attitude toward their informality. When writers first began to introduce questionable diction into their prose, they quarantined it with quotation marks, or put it in italics to emphasize its alien identity, or introduced it with a phrase that designated its origin and dissociated the writer from intimacy with it. John Neal, whom one twentieth-century critic has called "the first in America to be natural in his diction,"[30] prided himself on the colloquial vigor of his language: In a series of articles he wrote during 1824 and 1825 for *Blackwood's Magazine* on the subject of American writers, Neal remarked: "We have continued, as we began— using *low* words, unless they were wholly beneath us, whenever the subject required it; whenever they were more suitable, expressive, or vigorous, than *high* words."[31] But as late as 1869, in his autobiography, *Wandering Recollections*, Neal still formally set off his colloquial expressions:

> He had written, or made, as he termed it, an article for the "North-American Review."
>
> I had to put up with a "glittering generality" as we politicians would call it. When a boy, I was always a bungler, not being sure of hitting a barn-door —I might say of fetching a two-story house.
>
> Most of us tried our hand at what our secretary called ex-trumpery speaking.
>
> I came to be talked about as rather an ugly customer. [32]

The writer's attitude toward his vernacular material can give it the double prominence that anything reaches which，in addition to being odd，is declared, odd. Neal's behavior is altogether typical of many writers who were attracted to the vernacular yet unwilling to commit themselves wholly to it. Whether rhetorical or typographical，procedures such as Neal employed in 1834 caged the vernacular and，by caging it，drew attention to it：

> With this, the hunter "squared himself, and sot his triggers," fully determined either to hunt the disputed game, or be vanquished in combat.[33]

Deep-seated social attitudes are reflected in this use of quotation marks with the vernacular. Certain words, like certain clothes, schools, and professions, are proper for the educated and others are not. On a reduced scale, such quarantining of the vernacular resembles the humorist's frequent use of a frame of standard English to enclose vernacular stories. The presence of a literate narrator to introduce the vernacular speaker permitted the reader to enjoy colorful informality, yet be assured that the hierarchy of social values still stood, that the vulgar was still under control.

On such occasions, the robust candor of the vernacular threatened the legitimacy of standard literary English. For example, when George, the educated narrator who normally introduces Sut Lovingood's tales, has translated a passage of Sut's "English," Sut bursts out: "Now why the devil can't I 'splain myself like yu? I ladles out my words at random, like a calf kickin at yaller-jackids; yu jis' rolls 'em out to the pint, like a feller a-layin bricks—every one fits. How is it that bricks fits so clost enyhow; Rocks won't ni du hit."[34] Even as Sut expresses his exasperation with the clumsiness of his diction, he is exposing standard prose to criticism. Rocks make up the vernacular world—hard, individual, rough, heavy, intractable. Bricks are a product of an organized social world. That is why they fit so well. They are manufactured, artificial, uniform, and capable of being manipulated without difficulty. And when a rock appeared in a brick wall, even if it was not formally set off, its very incongruity drew the reader's attention to it. Vernacular life offered details simply alien to standard prose, whether from the diction of steamboating, bear-hunting, or courting, or such idiomatic expressions as "I'm married folks," or the metaphorical comparison, "green as a jimson weed." Even as the power of the printed obscene word attests, the mind is arrested by the appearance of a word it has not seen before, however familiar it may otherwise be. In an extreme way, the shock of four-letter words suggests the power of the vernacular term encountered for the first time in a normal context.

Misspellings also emphasized individual words by so disguising them that, even if the words were not newly encountered, they were encountered for the first time looking as they did. The motives for misspelling varied, and as we shall see in the following chapter, it makes a difference whether the writer's goal was accuracy or buffoonery. Sometimes the word is spelled phonetically by a semi-literate writer, *fite, enuf, jist* or *jest,* and *strate.*[35] At other times the malformation is not an error in spelling, but reproduces a dialect pronunciation, although sometimes one cannot distinguish naive phonetic literalness from scientific accuracy, since the spellings *larn, fellers*, and *sartain* [36] could result from ignorance or a wish to represent the sounds. Barbarisms are also spelled "correctly" in the sense that their rendering accurately represents usage: *onst* (once), *seed* (seen), *hearn* (heard). Such errors resemble those misspellings where the actual construction of a word is mistaken. Sometimes in these cases plain distortion takes place—*norate* for *narrate*; sometimes folk etymology is at work—*cowcumbers* for *cucumbers*; sometimes malapropisms occur in which the known word is inadvertently substituted for another: "Tha found him requitted of murder, but tha found him gilty of salt an batter."[37] Finally, there are occasional instances of the kind of revelation associated with the portmanteau economy of the language of *Finnegans Wake*.[38] So Huck Finn describes one of the subjects taught by the duke and the king as "yellocution" (ch. 31).[39]

These vernacular tricks with language arouse various responses in the reader; superiority, amusement, curiosity, the pleasure of mimetic recognition. The point, however, is that the reader's mind is more than normally engaged by the actual structure of the vernacular word, and, depending upon the nature of the disguise it is given, the adjustment necessary to translate it may be quite complicated. *Norate* is no word, *cowcumber* is a partially familiar one, *salt an batter* are familiar words in the wrong context, and *yellocution* is at once no word and a neologism superior to the proper one. The effort to understand in each of these instances accentuates the word itself.

In the more rudimentary stages of vernacular writing, the disguised word is not only misspelled, but italicized as well so that none may miss the joke. When an ailing woman is told by her doctor that she must be cupped on the sternum, she shrieks, "What I … you cup me on de *starn!*"[40] A rural matron reassures a traveler spending the night in her home that he may undress without trepidation; "You can un*kiver* now, stranger; I'm *married folks.* you ain't afeard o' *me*, I reckon!"[41] An appeal for a drink of whiskey is rendered: "Colonel, let us have some of your *byled* corn."[42] In short, comic punch lines contain punch words and the blow is always a vernacular one.

If one major preoccupation of those using the vernacular was to render the words as they actually sounded, another was to determine what those words meant. This again focused attention on the single word. Sometimes this was done quite baldly, as when Cooper in *The Prairie* refers to "the brown and party-colored livery of the fall," then footnotes it: "The Americans call the autumn the 'fall' from the fall of the leaf" (ch. 8). As late as 1887 in *Zury* Joseph Kirkland[43] was doggedly defining his vernacular terms:

> "Chuck-holes" is the expressive Western name for the short, sharp depressions which use makes in unworked country roads.

> The "prairie flowers" (blue gentian) gave to the whole award a tinge of pale azure.

> "Puncheons" or "slabs" are the side-cuts from logs squared for sawing.

Overt definition also frequently occurs in the narrative itself when opposed points of view come into conflict. With at least an upper and a lower linguistic world recognized in the United States, a good deal of inter-translation was necessary. Sometimes the genteel narrator served as the interpreter, either furnishing a paraphrase of the vernacular, or actually defining the troublesome word. Sut Lovingood's heavy dialect required frequent explanation. George was his sympathetic but sometimes puzzled interlocutor:

> "What have you been doing, Sut?"

> "Helpin to salt ole Missis Yardley down."

> "What do you mean by that?"

> "Fix in her fur rotten cumfurtably, kiverin her up wif sile, to keep the buzzards frum cheatin the wurms."

> "Oh, you have been helping to bury a woman."[44]

Only after Sut has provided several ugly versions of his activity can George understand and translate his idiom into acceptable decency. Sometimes the translation proceeds in the other direction, from standard down to coarse. Sut, for example, tells of a young blacksmith so smitten with love "he splotch'd his whiskers wif foam," whereupon he is asked:

> "What was the matter with this Mr. Mastin? I cannot understand you, Mr. Lovingood; had he hydrophobia? —"

> "What du yu mean by high-dry-foby? —"

> "A madness produced by being bit by some rabid animal—"

"Yas, hoss, he hed high-dry-fob? *orful*, an' Mary Mckildrin...hed gin him the complaint."[45]

The one occasion when George, the representative of normality, lapses into a sentimental idiom occurs, appropriately enough, when he begins to recount a youthful escapade. Hypnotized by nostalgia, George soon reflects: "'Tis strange how faithfully memory paints the path and places belonging to our boyhood-happy, ragged, thoughtless boyhood." Sut knows that George's memory is anything but faithful, so as George muses on about "the Bluff with its triple echo... the Dardis lot, and its forbidden grapes ... the old church and its graveyard," all stock ingredients of sentimental fiction, Sut exclaims, "Oh, komplikated durnashun! That hain't hit... Yu's drunk, ur yure ashamed to tell hit."[46]

The actual incident in George's "happy, ragged, thoughtless boyhood" involved terror, violence, and a repellent conclusion in which young George splashes through an uncovered privy hole. Sut being familiar with the incident calls for a drink. "Arter I'se spunged my froat, I'll talk hit all off in English, an' yu jis watch an' see ef I say 'echo,' ur 'grapes,' ur 'graveyard' onst."[47] Again, a specific dictional critique brings an uncustomary stress to bear upon individual words.

The interchanges between Sut and George involve gross alternatives. Their misunderstandings and disputes over diction were a staple of comic writing so long as dialects existed in the United States. But as the nineteenth century progressed, this same process of criticism and redefinition began to take place within the arena of the norm. Henry James dramatizes innumerable clashes over words and the tone in which they are used:

"I don't like the way you say that," she declared.

"It's too imperious."

"I beg your pardon if I say it wrong. The main point's to give you an idea of my meaning."[48]

The linguistic issue here is no longer the crude one of decorum facing vulgarity. Now the most familiar of words come under scrutiny. One's words stand for one's experience, as one's experience changes, the words one uses become crucial.

>"Did you ever hear anything so quaint?"

>"So 'quaint,' my dear?"

As standards and the certainties that bolster them disintegrate, the meaning of words becomes less certain. The lengthy fencing matches between Henry James's men and women represent their attempts to define themselves and their companions by defining what they say.

>"You're old enough, dear Miss Miller, to be talked about."

>Daisy wondered to extravagance. "Talked about? What do you mean?"

The defining impulse, which concentrates upon the word, is integral with the stylistic shift toward the colloquial.

Definition, whether explicitly carried out or accomplished by translation or by the confrontation of two conflicting meanings for a single term, is but another way for words to achieve abnormal prominence. Still another occurs in lists of things. Lists define by proximity, by implicitly comparing similarities and contrasting differences. Lists, possessing little visible organization, are common in American vernacular writing. The natural sequence of objects as they are found in life or in the unconscious associative processes of the mind of the narrator determine the order in which the items of the list will be named.

Sut Lovingood describes the contents of an overturned cupboard,

>Pickil crocks, preserves jars, vinegar jugs, seed bags, yarb bunches, paragorick bottils, aig baskits, an' delf war—all mix'd dam permiskusly…"[49]

Lacking awareness of any principle of imposed order, Sut lists things as they appear—"dam permiskusly." But what then constitutes the special interest of each item in such a list? I can discern three answers, each peculiar to the vernacular tradition. First, the things in themselves are colorful and unfamiliar to conventional literature. Second, the distorted spelling forces extra attention on the word to decipher and to hear it. To object that the added attention required is so minimal as to be meaningless is, I think, to underestimate the sensitivity of man as a reading mechanism. Like the other irregularities common to the colloquial situation, such as italics, incomplete phrases, alliteration, repetition, word play, each misspelling makes an impression on the mind. The third distinctive feature of the list is its artful juxtaposition of things for humorous effect. Humor—and emphasis—can be achieved by placing the dandy in a frontier setting. So here Sut's list is principally composed of receptacles for foods and medicines, but he ends with Delftware smashed together with the more homely containers—crocks, jars, jugs, bags, bottles and baskets—to make a pottery version of the prim schoolmarm suddenly thrown into the crude violence of the far West.

At the end of the century Mr. Dooley[50] contributed another list that interests us in the same way as does Sut's list. Its terms, odd, misspelled and ironically juxtaposed, lead to a satiric climax:

> An' th' inventions—th' steam-injine an' th' bicycle an' th' flyin' machine an' th' nickel-in-th'-slot machine an' th' Croker machine an' th' sody fountain an'-crownin' wur-ruk iv our civilization—th' cash raygisther.[51]

The atomizing effect of such a list is increased because the conjunctions serve not only as connectors but also as buffers. In the Dooley example, the reiterated "an' th'" separates the items visually as well as aurally. The conjunctions establish an exclusive territory for each noun. The effect is that of a line of people on a darkened stage, each in turn being caught by a spotlight. Or, reading such a list resembles watching a long freight train pass by, the items being the cars, the conjunctions the couplings. Each item is independent, yet joined to the whole. The conjunctions are also unifiers in their unobtrusive and monotonous way. As the separate cars roll by, an underlying rhythmic beat is felt. The variety of a list is notable, yet there is a basic regularity to it which can be worked by the skilled writer, In the following sentence from *Huckleberry Finn* Mark Twain repeats "I took" three times, then discards "I," in the next unit, and finally discards "took" to move into a crescendo of physical items:

> I *took* all the coffee and sugar there was, and all the ammunition; I *took* the wadding; I *took* the bucket and gourd; *took* a dipper and a tin cup, and my old saw and two blankets, and the skillet and the coffee-pot. (ch. 7, italics added)

In lists of physical objects, and in sentences like this where the verbs are muted, things are displayed in themselves. They do nothing; they are merely available for inspection as objects at rest. Such static displays also heighten the importance of the individual word.

The compound sentence characteristic of colloquial prose is basically a list—a list of actions. The vernacular speaker offers those actions in an unsubordinated series, just as he does physical objects. He seems to display only the crudest awareness of how the actions are related, not because of stupidity, but because he literally recounts the events in the order in which they occurred. This focuses attention upon the single unit of action as it is caught and isolated between commas and conjunctions. One can observe the increased technical proficiency with which the compound sentence is managed by beginning with the irregular extravagance of an 1843 dialect story, then moving to the fluent simplicity of *Huckleberry Finn* in the 1880's and finally to the deliberately angular rhythm of Hemingway sentence written in the 1930's. First, "Mike Hooter's Bar Story":

> Torectly I see Ike take down the ole shooter, AND kinder kersamine [examine] the lock, AN' when he done that, he laid her on

his shoulder, AND shook his fist at the bar, AND walked towards home, AN' the bar he shuk his fist, AN' went into the cane brake, AND then I cum off.[52]

Then Huck Finn:

> I went out in the woods AND cooked a supper, AND I had about made up my mind I would stay there all night when I heard a *plunkety-plunk, plunkety-plunk,* AND says to myself, horses coming, AND next I hear people's voices. (ch. 8, capitals added)

And finally, a Hemingway drifter speaks:

> I could see her floating plain AND I hit the glass twice with the wrench hard AND I heard the noise clink in my ears BUT it wouldn't break AND I had to come up. [53]

Such compound sentences originate naturally in the psychology of the colloquial situation. Because the speaker lacks the time to distribute the events in synthetic categories, he produces a linear sequence, moving from event to event, observing democratic equality in the arrangement of his clauses. The most repeated phrase in *Huckleberry Finn* is "by-and-by" which is no more than a vernacular alternative to "and then…" Actions enumerated but barely related constitute the basic sentence of the colloquial style.

The enumeration of events is but the last of the many ways we have discovered, in which the psychology of speech separates and emphasizes the single word and phrase. The word may be deformed for dialectal accuracy. It may represent an instance of word-play, a malapropism or a pun. The word may be drawn from unfamiliar jargon, or it may be coined for the occasion. It may be italicized, repeated, defined, discussed, or argued about. Moreover, the colloquial prose surface is fragmented by the cut-and-thrust of dialogue, by the rhetorical emphases of one speaker, and by the groping hesitancy of another. And, as the stylization of colloquial prose continued, its ground was cleared of the underbrush off qualification.

The subject-verb-object relationship was made as direct as possible, and then, with the burden on each word heavier than ever before, each word took on an added importance, but even as individual words achieved increased independence, the basic unifying elements among them also emerged into prominence.

III

The propensity of colloquial prose to fragment is compensated for by its innate repetitiveness. It is true that instances of repetition occur in all writing, but not to the degree that they do in colloquial prose. The colloquial writer will retain, and at the pitch of stylization even cultivate, repetition. It begins in the simplest possible way, with single letters and syllables—"aquaking and shaking"[54]—and extends on up through full independent clauses— "She loved to fish. She loved to fish with Nick." The repetitions are visual and semantic as well as aural. Their source often appears to be below the level of consciousness, although in the later stages of colloquial writing, heightened technical awareness diminishes the incidence of inadvertent repetition.

Repetition often turns up when the action is crucial, or where the whiter-speaker is in some way thoroughly engaged. With the mind diverted, one combination of letters summons up a similar combination. Extemporaneous speakers such as the revivalist[55] depend upon the repetition of phrases to hold the audience, but they themselves become mesmerized by the rhythms of their speech. "Oh, come to the mourners' bench! come, black with sin! (*amen!*) come, sick and sore! (*amen!*) come, lame and halt, and blind! (*amen!*) come, pore and needy, sunk in shame! (*a-a-men!*)" (*HF*: ch. 20). Here meaning plays a distinctly secondary role to patterned noise.

Any kind of distraction or mutiny of the intellectual monitor may increase verbal echoes. A journalist keeping a day-to-day account of the deliberations of the U. S. Senate describes "Cordell Hull's very hush-hush huddle."[56] The stupor of fatigue and narcotics in which Norman Mailer [57] testifies he revised *The Deer Park* may be responsible for such phrases as "men lacquered with liquor" and a "painful jail of jealousy." Or, to take a quite different example, Beatrix Potter's[58] first story of Peter Rabbit displays unmistakable sound associations not present in her other work, probably because she improvised the original story in a letter to a child. So, the onomatopoetic sound of a hoe determines the verb that follows: "the noise of a hoe—SCR-R-RITCH, SCRATCH, SCRATCH, SCRITCH. Peter SCUTTERED underneath the bushes." When Peter emerges, his vantage point calls up the next verb: "He came out, and climbed upon a WHEELBARROW, and PEEPED over." The improvisation, haste, and distraction evidenced in these quotations constitute an integral part of the colloquial situation.

We can never determine absolutely what the author's state of awareness was at the time of composition, but the distinction between conscious and unconscious sound association can be demonstrated in three passages from Harriet Beecher Stow's[59] "The Minister's Wooing." When Mrs. Stowe writes,

> They fussed and fuzzled and wuzzled till they'd drinked up all
> the tea in the teapot,

one is confident that she deliberately encouraged the alliteration for the reader's amusement. But in a second sentence marked by a high incidence of the letter "P," one cannot be as certain with any confidence how conscious the alliteration was:

> Hudly...showed 'em her pantries, and her cakes, and herpies,
> and tiepuddin's, and took 'em all over the house; and they went
> peekin' and poking...

Finally, when Mrs. Stowe catalogues some flowers to lend color rather than humor to her story, the syllable "-ar" dominates her list. But it seems improbable that she deliberately assembled the unobtrusive internal rhymes:

> Hudly planted marigolds and larkspurs, pinks and carnations ... and trained up mornin's glories and scarlet runners round the windows.

The repeated syllable either emanates from the unconscious or represents a case of sheer coincidence.

Fits of alliteration and other sound repetitions and associations may be brought on then when the writer is more preoccupied with the imagined experience than with the surface of his prose. This is no more than to say that instances of repetition arise more often in speech than in writing, and more often in colloquial writing than in other prose. The writer may be excited, he may be pleasurably relaxed, he may be writing in a hurry, but the result will be an increase in sound associations. Henry Nash Smith has pointed out that "when Mark Twain is working up a rhetorical effect, he resorts to conspicuous alliteration ('winding rivers, and weary wastes')."[60] Mark Twain alliterates not only when he himself is straining for an effect, but also when circumstances strain his character Huck Finn. When the crowd disinters Peter Willks, Huck's tension heightens the alliteration, the rhyme, and the repetition of whole words:

> So they *dug* and *dug* like everything; and it got awful *dark*, and the rain *started,* and the wind *swished* and *swushed* along, and the lightning came *brisker* and *brisker*...At last they got out the coffin and begun to un*screw* the lid, and then such another *cro*wding and *sho*uldering and *sho*ving as there was, to *scroo*ge in and get a *s*ight, you never see... (ch. 29, italics added)

Rhetorical control for the colloquial writer begins in repetition and controlled variation. Even as he jettisons conventional arrangements for his prose, he begins to build new ones in his own medium. The listing of food at a Tennessee frolic is threaded through with the sound "uh."

> The SUPPER is made UP by the fellers; every one, fetches SUMTHIN; SUM A lick of meal, SUM A middlin of bacon, SUM A hen, SUM A POSSUM, SUM A PUNKIN, SUM A grab of taters, or a, pocket of peas, or dried apples, an SUM only fetches a good appetite and a skin chock FULL of particular deviltry.

The effect is one of casually managed variety. The serpentine sentence, made up like this one of a series of separate images, each of which emerges to take on a peculiar brilliance, the whole unified by the droning regularity of the narrator's tone and supplemented by the alliterative rhythm, is common to the colloquial.

> Well, the eyes KEP COMIN' CLOSER and CLOSER, and gettin BIGGER and BRIGHTER, and the fust thing I know'd ther was a whole grist of 'em all follerin' right after the fust ones, and DODGIN' up and DOWN in the DARK like they was so many DANCIN' DEVILS.[62]

Even when the repetition is not exact, one word conjures up a compatible partner. Threaded through out *Huckleberry Finn* are such phrases as

> squirming and scrouging
> moaning and mourning
> sobbing and swabbing
> fretted and sweated
> thinking, and wrinkling
> warmed up and went warbling and warbling
> chipping in a little Scripture (chs. 21, 23 , 25, 31, 31, 29 , 28)

Mark Twain's sensibility responded with unusual acuteness to the stimuli of sounds, especially in this book. These minute repetitions and a thousand others constitute the musical murmur of Huck's voice. From time to time it breaks into overt but diversified repetition. The form of dug and dug

and

　　　　　　　brisker and brisker

is varied by the comma in

　　　　　　　he drank, and drank;

and by the italics in

　　　　　　　and begged and *begged*

and

　　　　　　　well, go on, *go* on;

and it lengthens into

　　　　　　　and listened, and listened, and listened

as well as

　　　　　　　always moving back, and back; and back

and

　　　　　　　told me to say it *again*, say it *again*, say it *again*!

　　　　　　　(chs. 24, 29, 25; 27, 40, 21, 28)

　　As some of these quotations suggest, the eye makes associations, too. In the phrase, "It STOOD on her BACKSTOOP, minus a HOOP,"[63] one passes from the "stoo-" in *stood* to its visual repetition in *stoop*; then on to the aural repetition of "-oop" in *hoop*. In *Huckleberry Finn* the "oh" sound is mixed with the "ow" look;

　　　　…besides some TOW. I TOTED up a LOAD, and went back and set
　　　　down on the BOW of the skiffS to rest. (ch. 6, capitals added)

　　Nor need the associations literally repeat. They may only approximate the original. Consider these three sentences from *Huckleberry Finn*:

　　　　It was all grass clear to the canoe; so I hadn't left a track. I
　　　　followed around to see. I stood on the bank and looked out over the
　　　　river. All safe. (ch.7)

Can there be any doubt that "all grass" produced "all safe"? Or when Huck sees a canoe "riding high like a duck," does not that observation of aquatic wild life give rise to the figure of speech with which he describes his next action?— "I shot head first off the bank, like a frog" (ch. 7).

The associations may reveal a pictorial or semantic connection as well as a visual or aural one. The vision of a log calls up the idiom "fit to split" when Mike Hooter[64] finds himself in a state of high amusement; "I never see ennything so funny in all my life! There was I layin' down behind er log, fit to split..." A newspaper reviewer of the novel *Candy* observed that although it had "sold like hotcakes," any public discussion of its subject necessarily called for "fudging."[65] Another reviewer of a biography of Lord Alfred Douglas fittingly enough referred to a "pugnacity, marked by the Queensberry rules."[66]

The level at which such associations are created may often be below what we would deem conscious; so in fact may be their reception. But the point is that all of these various repetitions and associations go to make up the unity of form in colloquial prose. They join company with the frequent occurrence of coordinating conjunctions, which Walt Whitman sometimes brought to the fore in his verse.

I believe in those wing'd purposes,
And acknowledge red, yellow, white, playing within me,
And consider green and violet and the tufted crown intentional,
And do not call the tortoise unworthy because she is not something else,
And the jay in the woods never studied the gamut, yet trills pretty well to me,
And the look of the bay mare shames silliness out of me.[67]

Compare this with a sentence from *Huckleberry Finn*, similarly arranged:

Then she got to talking about her husband,
And about her relations up the river,
And her relations down the river,

And about how much better off they used to was,

And how they didn't know but they'd made a mistake coming to our town, instead of letting well alone—

And so on and so on,

Till I was afeard I had made a mistake coming to her to find out what was going on in the town;

But by-and-by she dropped onto pap and the murder,

And then I was pretty willing to let her clatter right along. (ch. 11)

These coordinating conjunctions furnish the beat for long colloquial sentences. The sense may wander, the meaning may cloud over, and clarification may never come (since cloudiness is the truest vision of the moment), but underneath it all pulsates that monotonous, barely noticeable rhythm of the conjunctions, sufficiently dependable to sustain equilibrium and to provide the confidence and comfort that go with it.

The resemblance between Whitman and the colloquial prose writer is no more coincidental than the frequent references to the poetic quality of modern America prose. When the distractions of the abnormal, the clownish, and the awkward handling of the colloquial manner were eliminated, what remained was a highly rhythmic prose with frequent internal rhyme and alliteration making concentrated statements with concrete images. In the first flush of colloquial stylization, the following sentence from Hemingway's "My Old Man" was the rule rather than the exception:

"He won't win," George says, very low, leaning over and buttoning the bottoms of his breeches. [68]

Colloquial writers had to become aware of the repetition inherent in their prose and of what use they might make of it. In the process of stylizing the colloquial traits learned in dialogue, American writers seized on repetition to restore a coherence threatened by that fragmentation which was in turn produced by the stress of individual words and phrases.

The way of fragmentation led toward incoherence, the way of repetition toward verse. Discretion and practice were needed to reach a prose compromise. But before studying the negotiations that achieved that compromise, I should like first to consider the historical motives for cultivating the colloquial voice and its early routes into literature.

〔注释〕

1. 这里所提到的著作包括亨利·纳什·史密斯所著《处女地》（坎布里奇哈佛大学出版社，1950 年出版）、R·W·B·刘易斯所著《美国的亚当》（芝加哥市芝加哥大学出版社，1955 年出版）及哈利·利文所著《悲剧观的威力》（纽约克诺普夫出版社，1958 年出版）。

2. 引自纽约哥伦比亚大学 1959 年出版的哈罗德·C·马丁所编《散文小说的风格》中的《散文小说风格分析序》第 14 页。Richard Ohmann：奥赫曼，文学评论家。

3. Erskine Caldwell：考德威尔（1903-1987），美国小说家。下文中的萨罗扬（William Saroyan, 1908-1981）及马昆德（J. P. Marquand, 1893-1960）均为美国小说家。

4. George Lippard：利帕德（1822-1854），美国作家。下文中柯明斯（Maria Susanna Cummins, 1827-1866）、埃文斯（Augusta Evans, 1835-1909）、沃纳（Susan Warner, 1819-1885）及韦尔（William Ware, 1797-1852）皆为美国作家。

5. 此处引文第 1 段出自 1850 年版《伊桑·布兰德》（霍桑所著短篇小说），第 2 段出自 1925 年版《太阳照常升起》（海明威所著小说），第 3 段出自乔治·利帕德所著《贵格城》（1844 年出版），第 4 段出自欧文·肖所著《小狮子》（1948 年出版）。

6. 引自《非洲的青山》（纽约查尔斯·斯克里伯纳之子公司，1935 年出版）。这段引语接下来说："你如读它，你就须在黑人吉姆被从孩子们那里偷出处停住。这是真正的结尾。其余部分都是骗人的。可是，这是我们有过的最好的书。以前没有过，后来也没有过这样好的书。"当然，黑人吉姆不是从"孩子们"那里，而只是从哈克那里被偷走的。

7. 引自菲利普·拉夫所编《美国的文学》（纽约子午书局，1957年出版）中《信条》一文第 300-301 页。

8. 引自罗伯特·A·杰里夫所编《福克纳在长野》（东京研究社出版社，1956 年出版）第 88 页。

9. 引自旧金山《史记》（1956.8 .5）中《这个世界》部分第 20 页《美国的声音是马克·吐温的声音》。Herman Wouk：沃克（1915-　），美国小说家、剧作家。

10. 引自《华盛顿大学研究新系列丛书——语言与文学》1956 年第 23 期第 16 页《美国文学与美国语言》。

11. 引自纽约莱因哈特公司 1948 年版《哈克贝利·芬历险记》第 16 页《引言》。Lionel Trilling：特里林（1905-1975），文学评论家。

12. 引自纽约瓦伊金公司 1946 年版《马克·吐温袖珍读本》第 28 页。Bernard DeVoto：德维托（1897-1955），编辑、文学评论家。

13. Waller：沃勒（Emund Waller, 1606-1687），英国诗人。下文中屈莱顿（John Dryden, 1631-1700）及蒲伯（Alexander Pope, 1688-1744）皆为英国诗人。

14. 引自《观点》（纽约查尔斯·斯克里伯纳之子公司，1924 年出版）中《美国的文体》一文。Stuart P. Sherman：舍尔曼，文学评论家，新人文主义者。

15. 引自约瑟夫·丁·奎亚特和道丽·特比所编《美国文化研究》（明尼亚波利斯明尼苏达大学，1960 年出版）第 109 页《美国文学中的方言传统》一文。Leo Marx：马科斯（1919-　），文学评论家。

16. 引自波士顿 1789 年出版的《英语论文集》第 36 页。

17. 转引自米特福德·M·马修斯所著《美国英语的发端》（芝加哥市芝加哥大学出版社，1931 年、1963 年出版）第 131 页。Captain Marryat：马里亚特（Frederick Marryat, 1792-1848），英国皇家海军上校，作家。

18. 引自托马斯·钱德勒·哈里伯顿所著《哈里伯顿法官的扬基佬故事集》（费城，1844 年出版）第 2 卷第 8 页。Sam Slick 为一篇故事中的人物。

19. 引自乔纳斯·巴里什所著《本·琼生与散文喜剧的语言》（坎布里奇哈佛大学出版社，1960 年出版）第 19 页。

20. George Ade：艾德（1866-1944），美国剧作家。

21. Ring Lardner：拉德纳（1885-1933），美国作家。

22. Thomas Wolfe：沃尔夫（1900-1938），美国小说家。下文中 Robert Penn Warren：沃伦（1905 1988），美国小说家、诗人、评论家；William Styron：史泰伦（1925- ），美国小说家；James Baldwin：鲍德温（1924- ），美国小说家。

23. 引自亨利·纳什·史密斯编辑并为之作序的《哈克贝利·芬历险记》（波士顿霍顿·米夫林公司，1958 年出版）第 261 页。

24. 引自波特·G·佩林所著《作家英语指南和索引》（芝加哥司各特—福里斯曼公司 1959 年出版第 3 版）第 756 页。

25. 引自 F·L·帕蒂编辑、约翰·尼尔所著《美国作家：为〈布莱克伍德〉杂志撰稿集》（达勒姆市杜克大学 1937 年出版）第 186 页。John Near：尼尔（1793-1876），美国文学评论家。

26. 引自纽约 1896 年版《汤姆·索耶在国外及其他故事集》第 370 页《关于美国语言》一文。

27. 引自《肯尼庸评论》（1946 年冬）第 8 期第 159-160 页《语言爱国者》。Harold Whitehall：怀特霍尔，文学评论家。

28. 引自 1945 年 7 月 15 日《纽约时报书评》第 3 页、第 14 页。Malcolm Cowley：（1898- ），美国著名文学评论家。

29. 引自《有修养的评论家》（布鲁明顿印第安纳大学出版社 1963 年出版第 21 页。Northrop Frye：弗赖伊（1912- ），文学评论家。

30-31：引自《美国作家》第 185-186 页。

32. 上面 4 段引文引自《忙碌一生的散乱回忆：一部自传》（波士顿罗伯茨兄弟公司，1869 年出版）一书第 235, 261, 315, 44, 71 页。

33. 引自詹姆斯·霍尔所著《机智与幽默百科全书》（威廉·E·伯

顿编，纽约 1858、1870 年出版）中《彼得·费瑟顿》一文第 111 页。

34. 引自乔治·华盛顿·哈里斯所著《苏特·拉文古德》（纽约，1867 年出版）中《亚德勒夫人的棉被》第 134 页。George 及 Sut Lovingood 皆为书中的人物。'splain＝explain; yaller-jackids ＝yellow jackets，yu jis'＝you just; to the pint＝to the point; feller＝fellow; clost ＝close; ni du hit= not do it.

35. fite＝fight; enuf=enough; jist or jest=just; strate=straight.

36. larn＝learn; sartain=certain.

37. 此处几例引自威廉·T·波特编辑的《肯塔基季赛及其他故事集》（费城，1846 年出版）第 182,174, 46 页。

38. *Finnegans Wake*：《芬尼根觉醒》，是爱尔兰作家乔伊斯（James Joyce, 1882-1941）的小说。

39. yellocution=elocution.

40. 此段引自《肯塔基季赛及其他故事集》第 186 页。de sfaru=the stern，意为"臀部"。

41. 引自《肯塔基季赛及其他故事集》第 59 页。unkiver=uncover，意为"undress"。

42. 引自《肯塔基季赛及其他故事集》第 14 页。

43. Joseph Kirkland：柯克兰（1830-1894），美国小说家。*Jury*：《朱里》柯克兰的代表作。下文中 3 段引自该书第二卷第 10，第 21 页。

44. 引自《苏特·拉文古德》第 134 页。ole=old; fur=for; cumfurtably=comfortably; kiverin＝covering; wif sile=with silt，wurms ＝worms.

45. 引自《苏特·拉文古德》第 231 页。yas=yes; hors=horse; arful=awful; gin＝given.

46. komplikated durnashun＝complicated damnation; hain't hit＝ isn't it; ur=or.

47. 引自《苏特·拉文古德》第 115-116 页。arter = after; froat= throat; ef=if; onst＝once.

48. 此段及以下两段引自亨利·詹姆斯所著《小说选集》（纽约杜

顿公司 1953 年版，里昂·伊德尔做序）一书中《苔瑟·米勒》一篇第 44, 40, 48 页。

49. 引自《苏特·拉文古德》第 92 页。ayarb=herb; aig=egg; delf war=delft-ware；dam＝damned；permiskusly＝promiscuously.

50. Mr. Dooley：美国作家邓恩（Finley Peter Dunne, 1867-1936）所著系列书中的主人公。

51. 引自邓恩所著《论维多利亚时代》，见瓦尔特·布莱尔所著《美国本土幽默》（旧金山钱德勒出版社，1960 年出版）第 461 页。wur-ruk = warrant; iv = of; raygister=register.

52. 引自詹姆斯·霍尔所著《机智与幽默百科全书》第 220 页。Torectly=Directly.

53. 引自《海明威短篇小说集》（纽约 1938 年版）中《暴风雨后》一篇第 472 页。

54. 引自《哈克贝利·芬历险记》第 13 章。下文引自《海明威短篇小说集》第 206 页。

55. the revivalist：指哈克等遇到的牧师。

56. 引自艾伦·德鲁里所著《参议院日志：1943-1945》（纽约，1963 年出版）第 119 页。Cordell Hull：哈尔（1871-1955），美国政治家，1933 至 1944 年间任国务卿。

57. Norman Mailer：梅勒（1923- ），美国小说家。*The Deer Park*：《鹿园》，梅勒的小说；下文引语引自该书（纽约 1955 年版）第 4 页和第 257 页。

58. Beatrix Potter：波特（1866-1943），英国儿童文学作家。Peter Rabbit：老兔彼得，波特塑造的一个故事主人公。下文引自《老兔彼得的故事》（纽约，1904 年版）第 48、49 页。

59. Harriet Beecher Stowe：斯托夫人（1811-1896），美国作家。下文引自詹姆斯·巴尔所编《美国的幽默》（纽约，1894 年出版）第 63, 69 页。

60. 引自《马克·吐温：一个作家的成长》（哈佛大学出版社，1962

年出版）第 17 页。Henry Nash Smith：亨利•纳什•史密斯（1906-1986），文学评论家、历史学家。

61. 引自《狄克•哈兰的田纳西州聚会》，载于《肯塔基季赛及其他故事集》第 83 页。sumthin＝something.

62.引自《机智和幽默百科全书》第 243 页。kep=kept; fust=first, follerin'=follwing.

63. 引自《美国的幽默》第 128 页。

64. Mike Hooter：詹姆斯•霍尔所著《迈克•胡特的酒吧故事》中的故事叙述者，见《机智和幽默百科全书》第 219 页。

65. 引自唐纳德•斯坦利所著《性的革命》，载于旧金山《检查者》（1964 年 6 月 28 日）第 15 页。

66. 见理查德•艾尔曼所著《在阿尔弗雷德勋爵的阵营里》，载于 1964 年 4 月 30 日《纽约书评》第 7 页。The Queensberry rules：或曰 the Marquis of Queensberry rules，是在昆斯伯里侯爵道格拉斯主持下制定的拳击规则。

67. 见惠特曼所著《自我之歌》第 13 节。

68. 见《海明威短篇小说集》第 295 页。

Questions For Discussion:

1. What are the basic propositions that Bridgman's book tries to affirm?

2. Define the vernacular in terms of the changes which its nature went through over the last century and a half.

3. What are the essential features of colloquial prose?

4. How has vernacular writing evolved in America?

For Further Reference:

1. Fenton, Charles. *The Apprenticeship of Ernest Hemingway*. New York：Farrar, Straus & Young, 1958.

2. Philip Young, *Ernest Hemingway*. New York：Rinehart &. Co., 1952.

3. Carlos Baker, *Hemingway, The Writer as Artist*. Princeton: Princeton Univ. Press, 1956.

Daniel Aaron

〔作者介绍〕

　　丹尼尔·艾伦（Daniel Aaron, 1912- ），美国学者。1933 年毕业于密西根大学，1943 年获哈佛大学博士学位。自 1975 年起在哈佛大学任教迄今。艾伦是美国现代语言协会、美国学协会及美国历史协会成员，1967 至 1968 年曾任美国学协会副会长，1971 至 1973 年曾任该协会会长。他的研究领域是文学和历史。

　　艾伦的著作甚丰。他的主要作品有《乐观者》（*Men of Good Hope*, 1959）、《爱默生现代文选》（*Ralph Waldo Emerson: A Modern Anthology*, 1959）、《左翼作家》（*Writers on the Left*, 1961）、《美利坚合众国史》（*The United States: A History of the Republic*, 1963；与人合作）、《未写过的战争：美国作家与内战》（*The Unwritten War: American Writers and the Civil War*, 1973）；他还编辑过《保罗·艾尔默·莫尔论文集》（*Paul Elmer More's Shelbourne Essays*, 1963），与人合编过《艰难的时代：二十世纪三十年代社会思想录》（*The Strenuous Decade: A Social and Intellectual Record of the 1930s*, 1973）等书。

Writers on the Left

〔作品介绍〕

　　《左翼作家》1961 年在纽约出版，是 20 世纪 50 年代美国"麦卡锡时代"结束之后出版的探讨美国左翼作家活动及其历史背景的重要著作之一。

《左翼作家》主要论述 1912 年至 20 世纪 40 年代初"文学中的共产主义运动"。作者认为，美国作家一向有"反抗精神"，20 世纪初的几十年，尤其是 30 年代美国左翼作家的活动，正是这种反抗精神的表现之一。该书具体地回顾了这些作家对共产主义思想所持的拥护态度，叙述了 20 世纪前 40 年间影响作家思想倾向的主要问题和事件。40 年代之后的美国文坛风向发生剧变，左翼文学已不再是美国文化生活的主流，故该书对此所用笔墨极淡。

《左翼作家》详细描述了两类作家的思想和创作情况：一类是曾加入共产党的作家，此类数目很小；另一类曾是共产党的"同路人"，曾同情共产党的目标，为其报刊撰稿，或参与它组织的机构或活动。后者是左翼文学的主力，是自由派或激进派，表现出文学中共产主义思想或苏俄的主要影响。他们受到当时激进主义的左右，愤怒地反对他们认为是残酷和愚蠢的现行社会制度。作者力求回答的问题包括：为什么艺术家和知识分子在那一阶段思想发生变异，为什么他们当中许多用心很好、思想敏感而富有天赋的人离开他们所属的阶层或阶级转而信仰共产主义或支持共产主义行动，以及为什么许多人在"运动"中只停留片刻，最后又分离出去等。

《左翼作家》力求把这些激进文学作家的活动放到美国文化史的框架内加以分析和认识。作者访向了当事人——右派、左派和中间派，把他们的经历写成历史事件记录，以此披露出"运动"的各个侧面及其成员的思想发展趋势。该书虽涉及了许多作家，但重点突出，强调记述了一些具有代表性的作家和批评家。例如，在第三部分《清醒与退出》中，虽然许多作家的活动状况可以作为佐证，但是作者却只重点评述了六位文学家的态度。

全书共含三部分十八章。第一部分《反抗的模式》，着重回顾十月革命以后美国文坛向左倾斜的历史，追述了美国文学界对苏俄形象的热烈反应及社会主义运动对作家的影响。第二部分《共产主义的吸引力》，叙述了 30 年代的美国文学史，突出描绘了 30 年代大萧条时期美国作家进一步向左转的历史状貌。作家对社会现状不满，对苏联的欣欣向荣表示欣赏，政治和社会问题成为作家创作的主要内容。这一部分记叙了许多作家和文学工作者的矛盾心理和思想变化过程，描述了第一次作家大会的历史实况。第三部分，如上所说，记录了六位文学家具有代表性的思想变化过程。

《左翼作家》具有宝贵的史料价值。它突破禁区，首次透露出许多鲜为人知的历史细节，解答了关于美国文化与文学史上常被人轻描淡写的一个历史阶段的疑难。在某种意义上讲，它恢复了这段历史的本来面貌。它对阅读和理解两次世界大战之间二十余年内的美国文学具有不可或缺的指导作用。

这里所选的是三个部分的引言部分。

An Excerpt from *Writers on the Left*

PART ONE   Patterns of Rebellion

American literature, for all of its affirmative spirit, is the most searching and unabashed criticism of our national limitations that exists, the product of one hundred and fifty years of quarreling between the writer and his society. The social criticism of writers, both the open and the veiled kind, has usually sprung from an extreme sensitiveness to the disparity between ideals and practices, but it has also reflected the hostility of the artist to a world that slights his needs and holds his values in contempt.

The American writer, of course, has shared many of the convictions of his audience and, like the members of other minority groups, has shown signs of self-hatred and guilt for his failure to measure up to the national ideal. Reared in a society honoring action rather than contemplation, a society distrusting any effort, intellectual or physical, that served no obviously useful purpose, the writer was sometimes hard-pressed to justify his occupation. He had not only to reckon with the indifference of the average man, engrossed in the problems of everyday living; he had also to face the clerical and religious bias against the unsanctified imagination.

Hence the nineteenth-century American writer sermonized in his poetry and fiction. Lest his public condemn him as frivolous if not subversive, he presented himself in the role of secular priest and often chose literary forms (the religious treatise, the humorous dialogue, the educational essay, the political tract, among others) best suited for inspiration and instruction as well as for entertainment.

From its beginnings, American literature has been hortatory and didactic, a literature of "exposure," of the first person; and although the moral tone becomes less obvious and persistent after the mid-nineteenth century, it never disappears. The didactic note sounds not only in the angry "protest" novels that have periodically aroused a lethargic public since the days of *Uncle Tom's Cabin*, but also in the less evangelical and more truly dangerous novels like *Huckleberry Finn* where the moral burden is masked in genial humor.

Paradoxically, the American writer's running quarrel with his society, his natural inclination to admonish and to castigate in the guise of entertainment, may have Sprung as much or more from his identity with that society as from his alienation: He has never been easy during his rebellious moods, never able to divorce himself from the cowards, scoundrels, and vulgarians he attacks. Indeed, the very intensity with which insurgent generations of rebels have assaulted the unkillable beliefs of the bourgeoisie suggests an attachment to their enemy the rebels themselves have hardly been aware of. Made bitter by rejection, and despising a milieu so uncongenial for the creative artist, the aberrant or misfit writer still yearns to be reabsorbed into his society, to speak for it, to celebrate it. And the history of rebellious literary generations, which is in one sense the history of the writer in America, is a record of ambivalence, of divided loyalties, of uneasy revolt.

These revolts seem to have occurred periodically from the early nineteenth century to the present, and although each displays unique features, a recurring pattern seeing to run through them all.

In act one which might be called the preparatory stage, the new generation of writers comes of age. Usually the beneficiaries of a culture that has nourished and educated them, they are often precious and censorious, impatient of traditional literary or aesthetic conventions, and frequently unaware or neglectful of the accomplishments (and blunders) of their predecessors. That is why some critics have seen the history of American letters as a succession of new starts, as "momentary efforts by solitary writers or by intellectual groups to differentiate themselves and to set a new current in motion, with the inevitable petering out, and the necessity of a fresh start over again." That is why we have a "new generation of writers every five years" and why American literary movements, unlike those abroad, seem to move back and forth without ever incorporating what has already been accomplished.

Each new generation has its prophet, sometimes more than one, who articulates its aspirations and directs the assault against the Philistines.[1] The period of preparation is usually marked by the pursuit and discovery of a philosophical system, sometimes of a domestic but more often of a foreign origin, to sanction the movement American intellectuals, like American technicians, have always been great borrowers; Europe has traditionally provided the theory, America the application. Molded by American conditions and preoccupied by American problems, the artist or intellectual "reaches out for the results of an older and more complex culture ... reworks them and refashions them to suit his own needs, and... perturbs and enriches the life of America."[2] Coleridge, Carlyle, Fourier, Taine, Spencer, Tolstoy, Nietzsche, Freud, Shaw, and Marx are only a few of the European prophets who have been domesticated and sometimes vulgarized to serve American intellectual purposes.

Act two, the flood tide of the movement, is customarily heralded by a manifesto of some kind. Then what begins as philosophical criticism soon turns into social criticism, from the false ideas of the dominant class to its false and ridiculous practices. In sermons, essays, poems, and plays, in fully realized works of art and in thinly concealed tracts, the artist conveys his vision of society. Sometimes he remains a party of one; sometimes he is associated with other literary or quasi-literary alliances. Usually in each literary period, economic or social events or "causes" break through the artist's isolation: economic depressions; Negro slavery; the plight of labor, the urban poor, the farmer; trials and miscarriages of justice; corruption and graft; civil-rights issues; foreign revolutions; imperialism and wars. For short periods, the engaged writer takes a stand on public issues.

In act three, the movement declines, for literary radicalism never seems to be sustained over a long period, and the writer is gradually absorbed again into the society he has rejected. The aftermath of his revolt is sometimes tragic, sometimes pathetic or ludicrous. Often the disenthralled writer becomes embittered or ashamed after his adventure in nonconformity, or he becomes tried as his idealism flags and the prison-house of the world closes upon him.

But even as the old revolution is expiring, a new one is flickering into life and a new generation, equally brash, confident, or angry will announce itself with the customary flourish.

The history of American literary communism is the story of one more turn in the cycle of revolt. Like the earlier experiments in rebellion, it has its ancestors and founders, its foreign prophets, its manifestoes, its saints and renegades. It also begins in joy and ends in disenchantment. And growing amidst its monuments and ruins are the shoots of the rebellions to come.

PART TWO   The Appeal of Communism

In his epilogue to *Exile's Return*,[3] Malcolm Cowley described the joyless desperate New Year's Eve parties that ushered in the Depression decade. One of his friends, after a night of party-going, "found himself in a storage sub-cellar joint in Harlem. The room was smoky and sweaty and ill-ventilated, all the lights were tinted green or red, and, as the smoke drifted across them, nothing had its own shape or color; the cellar was likely somebody's crazy vision of Hell; it was as if he was caught there and condemned to live in a perpetual nightmare. Out of this Tartarus,[4] this capitalist nightmare, his friend stumbled into the harsh, cold, ugly, but clear light of a new day and a new era.

Cowley did not say that he and his friends were "reborn" in the religious sense, but their change in attitude, their exhilarating insights, their resolving of plaguy contradictions, followed the classical formula of the conversion experience. For one thing, it meant the end of romantic dichotomies: art and life, intellectual and Philistine, poetry and science, contemplation and action, literature and propaganda. The collapsing world and the new faith made such distinctions impertinent. Now Cowley emended a humanistic art that would transform the rapidly changing world into myth without neglecting "the splendor and decay of capitalism and the growing self-awareness of the proletariat." No longer could the artist hold aloof from the class struggle. To do so involved the risk of "blinding and benumbing" himself. Embracing the cause of the workers might cut him off from his culture and his class; yet an alliance with the untutored and the dispossessed would put an end "to the desperate feeling of solitude and uniqueness that has been oppressing artists for the last two centuries."[5] He had come in the words, William James used to describe Tolstoy's conversion, "to the settled conviction ... that his trouble had not been with life in general, not with the common life of common men, but with the life of the upper, intellectual, artistic classes, the life which he had personally always led, the cerebral life, the life of conventionality, artificiality, and personal ambition. He had been living wrongly and must change."[6] Cowley predicated "great days ahead for artists" if they survived the struggle, kept "their honesty and vision," and learned "to measure themselves by the stature of their times."[7]

Conservatives interpreted the literary turn to the Left as a new fad or as a conversion to "the Gospel of St. Marx."[8] Radicals attributed the politicizing of the writer to economic necessity. Neither was wholly wrong, although each simplified the process. Personal inadequacy, the need to conform, the disease of careerism also drew writers into the radical movement. But the radical impulse before and after 1930 sprang from the motives that had prompted good men in all ages to denounce, in Hawthorne's words, "the false and cruel principles on which human society has always been based." The elation and hope that stirred Cowley and his friends did not outlast the decade. They learned, like the narrator of *The Blithedale Romance*,[9] "the most awful truth in Bunyan's book:[10]— from the very gate of heaven is a by-way to the pit!" Yet after they had resigned from the Party of Hope, they might also have said with Hawthorne's disenchanted poet and would-be Utopian, "Whatever else I may repent of, therefore let it be reckoned neither among my sins nor follies that I once had faith and force enough to form generous hopes of the world's destiny."[11]

It is not hard to understand why many writers who were once fascinated by Soviet Communism but who ultimately became disenchanted should now feel the need to divulge the "baser drives" that made the "Soviet myth" so appealing and to play down the objective reasons for their temporary aberration. The apostate must confess his delinquencies if he sincerely wishes to be readmitted into the American Establishment, and many liberal intellectuals felt obliged to seek absolution, to explain to the world and to themselves why they had been deluded into excusing the deceptions and cruelties of a false faith.

Unquestionably, a number of them entered the movement for less high-minded reasons than they supposed. No man, as Jonathan Edwards knew, is immune to "the labyrinthine deceits of the human heart." Yet who in retrospect can deny that the situation at home and abroad during the thirties justified a critical appraisal of the social and the political order? Who can question the sincerity and magnanimity of those hundreds of artists and intellectuals who took upon themselves the task of saving mankind from poverty and war? Communism's appeal can never be understood if it is considered merely an escape for the sick, the frustrated, and the incompetent or a movement of fools and knaves. Not the "aberrations of individuals" drew men to Communism in the 1930's, but the "aberrations of society."[12]

The Great Depression, with its hunger marches, its Hoovervilles,[13] its demoralized farmers, its nomads and park sleepers, its angry workers, its joyless, youth and bankrupt entrepreneurs was not the projection of sick personalities. The writers who wrote about bread lines, for whom evictions were "an everyday occurrence" and the furniture of the dispossessed "a common sight in the streets," and who described in novels, poems, and plays the economic and moral breakdown of middle-class families did not get their instructions from Moscow. As might be expected, they dramatized their private difficulties and expressed, often with more passion than felicity, their feelings of outrage at what they saw with their own eyes.

Other writers before them had made literary capital out of the sordidness and violence in American life. Stephen Crane's sketches of human misery, Frank Norris's unclinical studies in degeneration, Upton Sinclair's stomach-turning descriptions of the Chicago stockyards, and Jack London's catastrophic visions of revolution had already documented some of the unsmiling realities. This was the first time, however, an entire literary generation explored so relentlessly those areas hitherto ignored by the majority of their predecessors. After 1929 it was hardly necessary for the social writer to work up his subject matter in libraries; history collaborated with his designs, and every day's newspapers furnished him with a thousand themes.

For this, as Edward Newhouse explained in his novel *You Can't Sleep Here* (1934), was not the "lost generation," but the "crisis generation," disburdened of some of the moral problems that had obsessed their elders but just as troubled and guilty as the generation of Hemingway and Faulkner. It consisted of the young people who had to live with their parents because they "had never been absorbed into industry or the professions," of recent college and high-school graduates who knew with painful certainty that the economy had no place for most of them.

Whether the writer chose for his subject the lives the "Bottom Dogs," the adventures of young Irish delinquents, the "Neon Wilderness" of Chicago's North Side Poles, the Negro slum dwellers, the poor East Side Jews, Georgia "crackers," California fruit pickers, toilers on the Detroit assembly lines, Gastonia's textile workers, decaying Southern families, rebellious farmers, department-store wage slaves, or "boxcar" hoboes, it was the Depression itself, impersonal and ubiquitous, that gave meaning to their specific documentations. If much of the so-called "proletarian" writing violated almost every literary canon and if to many it positively recked with the Depression, the best of it managed to objectify the social forces as they operated in the lives of real people.

In contrast to the dreary scenes of capitalism in decline, Russia during the early thirties seemed a hive of happy industry—not only to its well-wishers, but also to a large number of unideological observers. Confronted with what appeared to be a social and economic breakdown in their own country, a good many Americans were powerfully affected by the well-publicized achievements of the U.S.S.R., where history "was acting like a fellow-traveler." They contrasted the unemployment, the labor violence, the social disorders, the widespread despair in the United States with the energy and hopefulness of the Soviets. "The contrast," wrote Arthur Koestler, "between the downward trend of capitalism and the simultaneous steep rise of planned Soviet economy was so striking and obvious that it led to the equally obvious conclusion: They are the future—we, the past."[14]

Joshua Kunitz found it impossible to communicate his deep feelings of joy and excitement in beholding busy bustling Moscow in the summer of 1930. The hardships persisted, the food shortages, the dearth of consumer goods, but at least there was no unemployment, and the people were heroic. Five years later, he could scarcely find words to describe the miraculous transformation that had occurred between his first and last visits:

> The entire trip has been one continuous gasp of wonderment. The excellent shops, splendid window displays, asphalted streets, cars, trucks, buses, glittering new trams and trolley buses-noise, movement, snappy traffic cops, innumerable parks of culture and rest—young trees, flowers all along the main streets in all cities I visited—cars, ties, felt hats, European clothes, dance halls, cafes, new schools, new sanitaria and the universal spirit of song, joy and creative effort—these all one must see and experience really to believe.
>
> The Moscow subway is not an isolated phenomenon; it is merely a superb symbol of the beautification of life that is proceeding at an inconceivable rate allover the USSR. The Soviet peoples are reaping the results of their superhuman labor and great initial sacrifices in industrializing and collectivizing the country.
>
> And this is just beginning.[15]

Other friendly visitors to the Soviet Union, as well as Kunitz himself, were by no means oblivious of the blights and blemishes in the Socialist Eden. Waldo Frank, for example, worried a little about "intellectual absolutism" in Russia, but he went on to say, "perhaps the want of flabby relativism which goes by the name of liberalism in the West and which is so often nothing but a want of conviction, is not an unmixed evil."[16] So far as he was concerned, the West was culturally finished, and many "friends" of the U.S.S.R., enraptured by the poetry of Soviet statistics and depressed by the inability of the American Government to cope with the crisis at home, were ready to agree that the future might belong to the "greasy muzhiks" and their canny leaders.

In America, the government turned its troops against the Washington bonus marchers. Had three thousand bourgeois marchers descended on the Kremlin, Malcolm Cowley wrote in 1933, "They would be efficiently suppressed (not executed; the day of mass executions has passed in Russia). What would happen if 3,000 proletarians marched on the Kremlin? They wouldn't do so, because the Soviets are their own government. But if they ever did march, the government would yield to them, or cease to be communist."

Just as the Russian worker entered joyously into the mighty schemes of the new socialist commonwealth, so the Russian writers, the literary "shock troops," were also pictured as eager participants in the task of socialist reconstruction. Unlike their unemployed and unhonored equivalents in America, they were valued by the state and closely tied to their vast readership. Faced with the bewildering changes in daily life, they found, according to Kunitz, the newspaper incomparably more fascinating than the fairy story. They discovered the poetry of fact, the magic of collective farms and tractor factories. It was not enough for them to reflect life; they had to mold it as well.

Amidst these "cultural crusaders in the service of the Revolution,"

American writers sometimes felt a little apologetic, a little humiliated to be introduced as mere students of literature. So Isidor Schneider felt when, he "admitted shamefacedly" to a machinist in a Moscow park "that I was a writer." As Americans, they could not share the intoxication that came with the knowledge that one was a part of a gigantic idealistic enterprise. Commenting on the literary life of Moscow in 1935, Matthew Josephson described it as "the *ville lumiere* which was Paris," a center of activity, creation, and joy. The exiles who crowded the city joined with people instead of "festering idly" as foreigners. Although Josephson regretted the excessive attention to reportage, the unremitting revolutionary tempo which allowed no place for a "genial disinterested and prophetic vision," he felt the excitement of the great projects in which all the Russian writers were involved. He noted, too, how comfortably they lived.

To many American writers, then—the eminent and the obscure—Russia in the thirties was both a reproach to America and a hope of the world. Its totalitarian features were not ignored, its curtailing of civil and intellectual liberties regretted, but its gains and its ultimate goals appeared to overbalance its failures. Were it not for its enemies, waiting for a chance to destroy it, the Russian leaders would not have had to devote the bulk of their country's resources to national defense or to limit personal freedom. Even so, according to Upton Sinclair, who sent his revolutionary greetings to the U.S.S.R. in 1937, the Russians had followed the advice of Emerson and hitched their wagon to a star.[17] They had solved the problem of national minorities, raised a degraded peasantry "from superstition and drunkenness," introduced modern machinery, ended racial discrimination, and established a workers' government. Finally, and perhaps most important for a large number of American intellectuals after 1932, they had assumed the leadership in the world struggle against the menacing power of international fascism.

Before Hitler seized power in January 1933, the American

Communist Party, following the lead of the Comintern, had made no effort to mobilize all antifascist opinion in the United States. Not until late March did the *Daily Worker* call for "A United Front to fight Fascism." Meanwhile, Joseph Freeman,[18] on his own authority, wrote a manifesto against the Nazis in *The New Masses*, and on March 3, a number of writers and journalists were invited by the editors to send in their protests against German fascism.

The statements from Newton Arvin, Roger N. Baldwin, Heywood Broun, Lewis Corey (Fraina); Waldo Fran, Michael Gold, Horace Gregory, Granville Hicks, Sidney Hook, Horace M. Kallen, Scott Nearing, James Rorty, Isidor Schnieider, and Edwin Seaver, while differing in emphasis, agreed on fundamental points: 1) Hitlerism was a brutish doctrine, "pitilessly hostile to every impulse of the intellectual or the creative life"; 2) the Nazis represented the last murderous impulse of a dying capitalism; 3) the victory of National Socialism in Germany would encourage and strengthen America's native fascists; 4)the Nazi threat compelled a "grim rallying together of all progressive groups throughout the world"; 5)the American intellectuals had to politicize themselves and to take the lead in setting up "an anti-Fascist front of intellectual workers in America."

Until the Nazi-Soviet pact in 1939, hatred of world fascism brought writers and intellectuals into the Left orbit who otherwise might never have affiliated with the movement. The New Deal was at least beginning to grapple with the problems of the Depression; undoubtedly the Roosevelt administration won over a good many incipient radicals. Even those who were not prepared to junk capitalist democracy, however, unhesitatingly supported any antifascist organization no matter what group or party was sponsoring it. Their antifascism was subsequently judged in some quarters as "premature," but throughout the thirties, fascism and Nazism were hardly phantom movements. There is no need to ask why so many writers, prompted by the age-old vision of the just society, should have believed their joint resistance to Hitlerism was at once moral and practical.

The revulsion inspired by the Nazis in American liberals and radicals antedated the revelations of Belsen and Auschwitz;[19] to them, Hitler was a forerunner of a "new and bloody 'dark ages.'" The reports, official and unofficial, flowing out of Germany after his triumph, the stories of pogroms and book burnings and concentration camps, enforced the image of the Third Reich as a medieval hell. It is impossible to understand why so many writers and artists flocked into the movement unless one can begin to sense the violent loathing, rage, and fear provoked by the Nazis. Any group, in or out of the United States, that condoned or aided fascism took on its gruesome aspect, whether it was the Ku Klux Klan, the Black Legion, or the Croix de Feu,[20] any group persecuted by the Naizs, whether Communist or Socialist or Catholic or Jewish, met with approbation. The majority of writers during the thirties agreed with Mike Gold's assertion: "Every antifascist is needed in this united front. There must be no base factional quarrels."

The culmination of antifascist sentiment among the American writers came at the point when many of them had become skeptical of Stalin's grandfatherly mask and disturbed by some of the party tactics. The event that aroused them more powerfully than any other episode during the entire violent decade and which distracted them from the Moscow trials his managers had already begun to stage, was the Spanish Civil War and the armed intervention of Germany and Italy.

We shall see later how the party benefited from this sentiment and why some of the volunteers who literally crawled on their hands and knees to cross the border into Spain became disillusioned. It is enough to say now that between 1936 and 1939, an overwhelming majority of the American intelligentsia—artists, teachers, writers, men and women of all the professions—regarded the Spanish war as "a testing ground for war with fascism in general." The writers and artists who spoke for the Spanish Loyalists, who raised money for medical aid, or who smuggled themselves into Spain as volunteers were not consciously furthering party interests, nor was there anything ulterior or sinister in their devotion to the Spanish peasantry. The issues appeared clear-cut, the cause of Spain was the cause of democracy and morality. Sectarian bickerings seemed contemptible in the light of such awesome events, and for more than a few, the nobility of the Spaniards engendered a comparable nobility in themselves. The writers beguiled by "the colossal attraction" of Bolshevism's "ultimate vision" did not consider their acceptance of Marxism as a departure from traditional progressive values. They conceived of it, rather, in Arthur Koestler's words, "as the logical extension of the progressive humanistic trend … the continuation and fulfillment of the great Judeo-Christian tradition—a new fresh branch on the tree of Europe's progress through Renaissance and Reformation, through the French Revolution and the Liberalism of the nineteenth century, toward the Socialist millennium." If the rebel's quarrel with society had neurotic roots, as Koestler profoundly believes, he observes nonetheless "that in the presence of revolting injustice the only honorable attitude is revolt." The perversion of noble ideals that marks the end of most revolutions signifies both human fallibility and the melancholy truism "that a polluted society pollutes even its revolutionary offspring."

The writers subsequently, identified with the Communist Party, either as converts or as sympathizers, made up a most diverse group and one not easy to classify. A few were dedicated socialists, spiritually thirsting for community. For them the party was the beneficent agency through which the good society would be inaugurated and mankind released from its long bondage, and they felt strengthened as writers, less weak and vulnerable and useless, when they gave themselves to the revolutionary cause. It was not a decision lightly taken, as Meridel Le Sueur described it:

It is difficult because you are stepping into a dark chaotic passional world of another class, the proletariat, which is still perhaps unconscious of itself, like a great body sleeping, stirring, strange and outside the calculated, expedient world of the bourgeoisie. It is hard road to leave pour own class and you cannot leave it by pieces or parts; it is a birth and you have to be born whole out of it. In a complete new body, none of the old ideology is any good in it. The creative artist will create no new forms of art or literature for the new hour out of that darkness unless he is willing to go all the way, with full belief, into that darkness.[21]

For others, agreement with Communist interpretations and solutions involved no such trauma or rapture. Communism appealed to them because it seemed a science as well as an ethic, because it explained and foretold as well as inspired, and because it had become incarnate in a dynamic country directed by a hardheaded elite. Contemptuous of their own "politicians" and impatient with the government's failure to cope with the Depression at home or to recognize the menace of fascism abroad, American intellectuals uncritically accepted the Bolshevik self-portrait. Soviet propaganda pictured a society where unemployment and racial discrimination had been permanently abolished, where artists and writers were honored and made use of, a country resolutely opposed to imperialistic ventures and staunchly antifascist.

In America, tirades against the "Reds" by reactionaries and Right Wing crackpots, the frenetic anti-Communist editorials in the Hearst newspapers, seemed to confirm the party's cartoon image of its enemies and amounted almost to an endorsement. According to Isidor Schneider, the Communist Party had "ideas and a program, unlike the intellectually-dead 'regular' parties, which concealed their programs." "That is why," he wrote, "although numerically at any given moment the Communists may be vastly outnumbered by sporadic and amorphous movements like the Townsend Plan[22] and Coughlin's League for Social Justice, Communists make the strongest and most enduring impression; why the hatred of the bourgeoisie is concentrated against them; why unorganized elements within the masses turn to 'red' organizations in spite of the bitter propaganda against them; and, finally, why there is so great curiosity about them." No other party, he might have added, sponsored such an array of cultural and political organizations, bookshops, theatrical companies, dance groups, and films, or such well-publicized and carefully staged mass meetings. "The Communist calendar," Orrick Johns discovered after he had joined the party, was "as full of dates as *festas* in Italy, all of which must be prepared for and exploited in one way or another: the anniversary of Marx, of Lenin, of the Sacco-Vanzetti execution, of May Day, of the October Revolution and so on." The tens of thousands who attended mass meetings in the San Francisco Civic Auditorium to hear Dreiser speak on behalf of Tom Mooney[23] never suspected the weeks of preparation that preceded it. Although jointly sponsored by trade-unionists, socialists, anarchists, and liberals, the "moves of the hostile colleagues were anticipated at 'fraction' meetings, and district meetings. The best way to work with this opposition was worked out, and speakers were planted to deal with the controversial points. As a result the Communists usually carried the argument."

The comments of neither Schneider, nor Johns, however, begin to make clear why the party attracted the relatively small number of writers who became bona fide members in the 1930s. Nor does the published and unpublished testimony of converts really give the literary historian much to go on. Retrospective explanations many be illuminating, but not completely trustworthy. With some writers, the reading of a book initiated the impulse: Malraux's *Man's Fate*,[24] Lenin's *The State and Revolution*, John Strachey's *The Coming Struggle for Power,* and Lincoln Steffens's *Autobiography* each demanded in its own way that the reader make a choice for or against humanity. Others were drawn into the movement by their friends or because a solicitous editor of *The Masses* had invited them to contribute to the magazine, or because they had visited the U.S.S.R., or because they wanted the chance to mingle with real proletarians.

It was also reassuring to feel that one belonged to an international movement whose ultimate triumph no temporary setbacks could avert, that one was working for mankind. At the same time, the party might solve racial, sexual, social, or economic anxieties as well as satisfy spiritual yearnings. The dances in Webster Hall,[25] the unit socials, benefits, picnics, and forums guaranteed that no good Bolshevik need be lonely.

Yet for the majority of writers who were associated in some way or another with the movement, it was the times, not the party, that made them radicals. The party attracted them because it alone seemed to have a correct diagnosis of America's social sickness and a remedy for it. The overwhelming majority never joined the party, but they put on "red shirts" as an emblem of revolt, as a way of showing their repudiation of the "stuffed shirts."[26] Few were ready to make the sacrifices demanded by the party in the early thirties, but the issues that preoccupied the party during the first half of the thirties—the plight of the hungry and the evicted, the exploitation of the Negro, the miseries of the unemployed, the persecutions in Germany, the struggles of labor—became their preoccupations. For a short time, American writers wrote novels, poems, plays, criticism, and reports that dealt rudely and sometimes powerfully with the most pressing issues of American life.

In the thirties ended in disenchantment, and if passionate men with passionate convictions sometimes deceived others and more often were self-deceived, in no other decade did writers take their social roles more devotionally. As in all periods of great revivals, whether religious or political, the majority of the converts lapsed into their old ways, unable to maintain the enthusiasm that momentarily overcame them. Only a few held on to the vision after its earthly prophets had been discredited.

PART THREE　Disenchantment and Withdrawal

Can the serious writer ever reconcile his art with activist politics, and continue to write while serving in the ranks of a revolutionary party or any party?

Most American writers did not have to face that question. Before 1935 the American Communist leaders showed little interest in writers; after 1935 the party preferred to concentrate on the popular literary figures whose sympathy, even if qualified, they could explore for publicity purposes. At no time, however, were writers completely trusted. They constantly threatened to kick over the traces and become an embarrassment; and the "big names"—Dreiser, Sinclair, Steinbeck, Hemingway, MacLeish, Wolfe—were the most uncertain and unreliable of all. The writers who worked more closely with the party rarely did so with the uncritical enthusiasm of the "Jimmy Higgins's." As one former party member, a well-known woman[27] observed, they refused to shut up or to take discipline. They wanted to rewrite the petitions they were asked to sign. She herself concluded, after trying to write a novel from the party point of view, that she was handicapped by being a writer and a Communist; this one could not be good at both.

Yet these writers did not leave the movement because they were dictated to. Very few of them were hauled over the coals and forced to recant. Rather, it seems to have been boredom that repelled them and killed their zeal: the rituals of meetings where nothing of importance was discussed, the discovery that one's comrades, among the leaders and the rank and file, were ignorant or vulgarly ambitious or unpleasant. Thus, in 1928 a disgruntled radical wrote to a friend:

One of the bitternesses of human relations is that one gets

inspiration and passes it on only to another. Once I got it from Floyd Dell and Max Eastman, people that now seem to me to have such feet of clay, and from two or three women you don't know—now I get it from people mostly dead, Stendhal and Proust, and Joyce. In the mess of cynicism, of hackwork, of lies and prostitution that so quickly come to surround the kernel of truth, one forgets sometimes the rewards for choosing a way of life that originates at least in honesty.

It occurred to this man as it must have occurred to many radicals before and since; that the artist's problems remained no matter what the society: "the truth is that it is not we who are out of joint, but the time as well. I read Blake last night at the library, and have no illusions that the world will ever seem a happy place to certain kinds of people,—his problems, his panics were so like mine, and so, I suppose, were King Akhnaton's sculptor's[28] if one only knew."

The depth and intenseness of a writer's disillusionment, of course, depended upon the motives that first drew him into the movement, the length of time he stayed in, and the extent of his involvement. The radicals of the twenties had embraced Communism when it offered no prestige, no tangible rewards. The latecomers, although they may have turned left for the same reasons as the pioneers— "experience of social injustice or degradation; a sense of insecurity bred by slumps and social crises; and the craving for a great ideal or purpose, or for a reliable intellectual guide through the shaky labyrinth of modern society"—were less likely to have experienced the full emotional impact of "the great Idea."

This was especially true, in all likelihood, for the majority of fellow-traveling liberals whose rejection of bourgeois society and capitalism was less thoroughgoing than they had imagined and who, perhaps unconsciously, yearned to be reabsorbed into the America they had denounced. Never having broken with their class, they could slip back into their old ways and old thoughts without having to make any serious readjustment; but to a Joseph Freeman, a Granville Hicks, a Richard Wright, if not to a Howard Fast, the retreat from Communism was not so deftly managed.[29]

Why did some remain in the party even though they harbored doubts and resentments? "There is the powerful drug of habit," Joseph Freeman has pointed out. "But there is also loyalty—to an idea, a party, individuals. Unlike periods of relative social peace, a revolutionary situation fuses political and private life into one burning, existence inspired by a common goal which is also your personal goal. And your fellow Christians, Jacobins or Communists are also—and with that as an indispensable basis—your personal friends. The cumulative revolutionary tradition is not only one of liberty and quality, but of *fraternity*. Besides, outside the fold there is no salvation. To leave is to be dammed by your former comrades and friends, —and your own conscience."

A number of writers renounced their allegiance to the party only after the alternative, the condoning of policies and practices that violated the very principles the party allegedly stood for, became impossible. There was a time or an occasion for each, a "last straw" situation, an "ideological boiling point," after which the writer renounced his allegiance. The final act of rejection was usually preceded by an extended period of uncertainty during which he stifled his doubts, extenuated or irrationalized away unpleasant facts, or simply refused to contemplate them. To the anarchists and the social revolutionaries of the October Revolution, disaffection might have started with the Soviets' bloody suppression of the sailor rebels at the Kronstadt naval base in 1921.[30] Alexander Berkman[31] broke with the Bolsheviks over the handling of that insurrection, and a series of succeeding "Kronstadts," as Louis Fischer called them, provided occasions for other disillusioned Communists and sympathizers to separate themselves once and for all from the Great Cause.

Whether the particular issues happened to be momentous ones, like the expulsion of the anti-Stalin opposition in 1927 and the exile and deporting of Trotsky, the forced collectivization of the peasants which began in 1929, the mass treason trials of 1936-38, Stalin's savage persecution of his own nationals who had been sent to aid the Spanish Loyalists, or the Nazi-Soviet pact of 1939, or whether the "Kronstadts" were of lesser consequence, like the suicide of Trotsky's daughter in 1933, or the Madison Square Garden riot in 1934,[32] the consequences were the same. In anger or sorrow, or sometimes with a sense of relief, the writer quietly slipped away from the party or noisily took his leave. Some waited to be thrown out for intellectual deviations, refusing at the last moment to yield or to recant.

The careers of many writers episodes in this story of disenchantment, but I have narrowed the number to six. Two, Joseph Freeman and Granville Hicks, had been at one time or another members of the Communist Party. Two, Max Eastman and V. F. Calverton, had been for many years critical but unfaltering supporters of the Communist regime in Russia, and two, Malcolm Cowley and John Dos Passos, could be described each in his own way as passionate fellow travelers. None broke at time, and each had his special grievances. Their collective political experience between 1920 and 1940 provides a record of the meanness and nobility of the radical cause, "Innocence and infamy, spiritual depravity and fair repute."

〔注释〕

1. the Philistines：庸人，尤指不懂文学艺术的人。作者在原注中说，他所指的"庸人"包括爱默生时代的"通达者"、镀金时代的"财阀"、20 世纪初叶的"清教徒"、20 年代的"中产阶级人物"、30 年代马克思主义所称的"资产阶级"、50 年代的中产阶级以及当代的"古板守旧派"。

2. 引自派利·米勒所著《超验主义者文选》（马萨诸塞州坎布里奇市，1950 年版）第 10 页。

3. Exile's Return：《流浪者返乡》，写成于 1934 年，主要描写"迷惘的一代"所生活的时代状貌。

4. Tartarus：地狱，取自希腊罗马神话。

5. 引自《流浪者返乡》第 293, 299 页。

6. 引自威廉·詹姆斯所著《宗教经历种种》（现代图书馆版）第 181 页。

7. 引自《流浪者返乡》第 300, 302, 203 页。

8. "the Gospel of St. Marx"：指马克思主义，表现出保守派的讽刺口吻。

9. *The Blithedale Romance*：《福谷传奇》，霍桑著，1852 年出版。

10. Bunyan's book：指英国作家班扬（John Bunyan, 1628-1688）所著的《天路历程》（*Pilgrim's Progress*）。

11. 上面 3 段引语分别引自霍桑著《福谷传奇》（诺顿图书馆 1958 年版）第 46, 247, 38-39 页。

12. 引自约翰·盖茨所著的《一个美国共产党人的故事》（纽约，1958 年版）第 13 页。

13. Hoovervilles：20 世纪 30 年代大萧条时建立在垃圾堆边或城区荒地上的临时性建筑，供流浪者、无家可归者等居住。

14. 引自亚瑟·考斯特勒所著《空中之箭》（纽约，1952 年版）第 27 页。

15. 引自《新大众》1935 年 9 月第 16 期第 21 页。

16. 引自瓦尔多·法兰克发表在 1933 年 1 月《新共和国杂志》第 73 期上的文章。

17. 爱默生名言，意为"追求高尚的事物"。

18. Joseph Freeman：弗里曼（1897-1965），美国左翼作家、编辑。

19. Belsen and Auschwitz：贝尔森及奥斯威辛，德国法西斯两大集中营与灭绝营，前者位于德国，后者位于波兰。

20. the Ku Klux Klan，the Black Legion，or the Croix de Feu：三 K 党、黑党及火十字党。

21. 引自梅里德尔・洛苏尔所著的《局外迷》（载于《新大众》1935 年 2 月第 14 期）。

22. the Townsend Plan：汤森德计划，由美国社会改革家汤森德（Francis Everett Townsend, 1867-1960）提出。1933 年大萧条最严重时期，汤森德提出"老年退休金计划"，虽遭国会否决，但很得人心，促进了后来社会安全法的通过。下文中 Coughlin's League for Social Justice，指美国天主教电台司铎库格林（Charles Edward Coughlin, ?-1879）通过电台做弥撒所拥有的虔诚听众，他在所创办的《社会正义》杂志中激烈攻击共产主义、华尔街和犹太人。

23. Tom Mooney：穆尼（1882-1942），美国社会主义工会的组织者及活动家。1916 年旧金山发生一起爆炸案，穆尼被受审判刑，引起公众抗议。

24. Malraux's *Man's Fate*：马尔罗（Andre Malraux，1901-1976），法国著名小说家，他所著的《人类的命运》1933 年面世，获龚古尔奖，下文中 John Strachey：约翰・斯特雷奇（1901-1963），英国社会主义作家和工党政治家，所著《即将到来的争夺权力的斗争》发表于 1932 年；Lincoln Steffens：林肯・斯蒂芬斯（1866-1936），美国新闻记者、演说家、政治哲学家，20 世纪初"揭发黑幕运动"重要成员之一，所著《自传》发表于 1931 年，获极大成功。

25. Webster Hall：韦伯斯特宫，位于纽约市，曾是美国共产党活动中心之一。

26. the "stuffed shirts"：有钱人。

27. 作者在原注中表示不肯透露其姓名。

28. King Akhnaton：阿肯那顿国王，公元前 1397 至 1362 年间埃及国王，沉缅于艺术，因而使埃及失去了它的光辉的帝国。

29. Granvllle Hicks：希克斯（1901-1982），美国文学批评家；下

文中 Richard Wright：赖特（1908-1960）；Howard Fast：法斯特
（1914-2003），著名黑人小说家。三人都曾有左倾倾向，法斯特 1942
年加入美国共产党，1957 年宣布退出。

30. the sailor rebels at the Kronstadt naval base in 1921：1921 年喀琅
施塔得海军基地水兵叛乱，被苏维埃政权镇压。

31. Alexander Berkman：伯克曼（1870-1936），美国无政府主义者，
生于俄国，幼时移民至美国。20 世纪 30 年代后期因对布尔什维克失
望而在法国自杀。下文中 Louis Fischer：费舍尔（1896-1970），美国
作家，主要著作有《苏联与世界事务》（1930）、《俄国的机器与人》
（1933）、《圣雄甘地》（1950）及《斯大林》（1952）等。

32. Madison Square Garden：麦迪逊花园广场，纽约市室内运动场，
文中所提"骚乱"发生在 1934 年 2 月，社会党人与共产党人在这里举
行的集会上发生激烈冲突。

Questions For Discussion:

1. What does *Writers on the Left* mainly propose to deal with? What
does "writers on the left" essentially mean?

2. Why did many writers turn Left in the first decades of the 20th
century and then leave "the movement"? How authentic do you think the
author's accounts actually are?

3. One important point which the book discusses concerns the
relationship between art and politics. Can the serious writer ever reconcile
his art and activist politics? Discuss.

For Further Reference:

1. May, H. F. *The End o f American Innocence; The First Years of
Our Own Time, 1912-1917*. New York：1959.

2. Wilson, Edmund. *The Shores of Light*. New York: 1952.

3. Bell, Daniel. *The End of Ideology*. Glencoe, Illinois: 1960.

Alfred Kazin

〔作者介绍〕

艾尔弗雷德·卡津（Alfred Kazin, 1915- ），当代美国著名文学评论家。他生于 1915 年，1930 年大学毕业，1935 年在哥伦比亚大学获硕士学位。此后他做过一些杂志的编辑，并先后在多处大学执教。他曾多次获得各种学术奖和荣誉称号。

卡津毕生从事美国文学研究，著述甚丰，被公认为美国评论界有影响的评论家。对卡津来说，小说似乎比诗歌及戏剧更令人感兴趣。他的两部力作《在本国土地上：论现代美国散文文学》（*On Native Grounds: An Interpretation of Modern American Prose Literature*, 1942）与《人生光明之书：美国小说家——从海明威到梅勒》（*Bright Book of Life: American Novelists and Story Tellers from Hemingway to Mailer*, 1970-1971）都是关于现当代美国小说家的论述。卡津还著有论文集《最内部的一页》（*The Inmost Leaf: A Collection of Essays*, 1955）和《当代人》（*Contemporaries*, 1962）。他还写了《城市中的一个行人》（*A Walker in the City*, 1951）、《从三十年代起步》（*Starting Out in the 30's*, 1965）与《纽约犹太人》（*New York Jew*, 1978）等三部自传体作品。

On Native Grounds

〔作品介绍〕

《在本国土地上》出版于 1942 年。该书深入详尽地探讨了 1890

至 1940 年间美国文学的发展情况，被公认为美国文学研究的经典著作之一。

此书分三部分，计十六章。第一部分题为"寻求现实"（"The Search for Reality ［1890-1917］"），追述从豪威尔斯至第一次世界大战结束这一时期内美国文学的发展。卡津指出，这一时期的主要特点表现为现实主义文学的发展。反映工业社会现实的美国现代小说发端于豪威尔斯。1891 年底豪威尔斯从波士顿迁居纽约，这一行动具有重要的象征意义，它标志着现实主义文学的起步。豪威尔斯主张小说要反映现实，反对传统的浪漫传奇，这对当时哈姆林·加兰、斯蒂芬·克兰、弗兰克·诺里斯等年轻的自然主义作家产生了重大影响。这些新秀对社会现实黑暗面的揭露比豪威尔斯更加直率大胆，同时他们的作品也流露出一种悲观情绪。在这一部分中，卡津还分析了西奥多·德莱塞与伊迪丝·沃顿两位作家，并论述了 20 世纪初叶兴起的"社会进步运动"和"揭发黑幕运动"。

本书第二部分题为"大解放"（"The Great Liberation ［1918-1921］"），详尽叙述了第一次世界大战之后十年间美国文学的状况。残酷的战争及其后果，促使许多美国人对他们旧有的价值观念进行全面反思，战后美国文学也因此呈现出新的特色。舍伍德·安德森与辛克莱·刘易斯的"新的现实主义"与豪威尔斯、德莱塞及诺里斯等战前的现实主义或自然主义相比具有不同特点。战后文学作品中的反叛精神，不再是惊涛骇浪式的；作家把眼光投向人们的日常经历，挖掘生活、表现生活。在现实主义的主流下，还有一股文学支流，这些作家的创作弥漫着一种唯美的、颓废的和追求享乐的情绪。卡津将这些作家如卡贝尔和卡尔·范维克顿（Carl Van Vechten）等称之为"唯美派"（Exquisites），并辟专章评介。卡津还评析了薇拉·凯瑟与爱伦·格拉斯哥两位女作家及新人文主义等文学批评流派。当然，卡津倾注笔墨最多的，还是"迷惘的一代"。这些年轻作家在战火硝烟中步入人生，暴力与死亡震撼着他们的心灵，摧毁了他们自幼所接受的那些传统价值观念。他们与旧梦决裂，却又一时找寻不到新的理想。这种精神上的空虚和迷惘以及对新价值观的追求，使他们成为文学史上崭新的一代，并对后继者产生了深远影响。菲茨杰拉德的小说乃至他本人的一生，都是 20 年代这一特殊时期的生动体现。卡明斯的小说《巨大的房间》猛烈抨击一切虚伪的传统和摧残人性的权威。海明威的硬汉形象颇有拜伦式英雄的气概：孤独、绝望然而又英勇顽强地与命运搏斗。多斯·帕索斯怀着迷惘的心情把目光投向了整个社会，其作品在"迷惘的一代"与 30 年代社会小说之间，具有承前启后的作用。

卡津称 30 年代的美国文学为"危机文学"，这也是该书第三部分的题目（"The Literature of Crisis [1930-1940]"）。这一部分描述了经济危机爆发后十年间美国文学的发展状貌。卡津认为，这一时期内出现了"自然主义的复兴"。他介绍了这一时期成名的作家，如奥哈拉及斯坦贝克等，分析了他们的创作风格和局限性。卡津还对 30 年代涌现的各种文学批评思潮进行了评介，对当时的马克思主义文学观点颇有微词。威廉·福克纳是这部分中重点分析的作家。

卡津坚持自己的文学批评方法。他反对当时流行的纯社会学式和新批评式的研究，认为两者从不同方面割裂了文学与社会的关系。在他看来，文学源于社会，但并非社会的创造；文学批评既不是单纯的政治武器，也不是纯粹的学术考据。《在本国土地上》一书自始至终地贯穿了卡津这一观点，它在研究文学现象时，考虑到社会背景、历史发展、作家经历和作品本身的内容风格等诸多因素，从而得出精辟独到的见解。它旁征博引，侃侃而谈，语言流畅，是了解和研究美国文学不可多得的一部好书。

这里选注的是该书第 12 章和第 15 章的一部分。

An Excerpt from *On Native Grounds*

CHAPTER 12　Into the Thirties: All the Lost Generations

"What do you think happens to people who aren't artists? What do you think people who aren't artists become?"

"I feel they don't become; I feel nothing happens to them; I feel negation becomes of them."

—E. E. Cummings, Introduction to *The Enormous Room*

"All right we are two nations."

—John Dos Passos, *U.S.A.*

When Paul Elmer More denounced one of John Dos Passos's early novels, *Manhattan Transfer*, as "an explosion in a cesspool," he was yielding to his familiar rage against the whole trend of realism and naturalism in America rather than expressing a judgment on Dos Passos. Yet as the tradition of that realism, so uniformly abominable to More and his fellows, passed on to the younger writers of Dos Passos's own generation, it became clear that it was not uniform at all, and that with these writers, for whom life and literature had begun with the war, a fateful new influence had entered American writing.

In 1920 and 1921 their first novels, *This Side of Paradise*[1] and *Three Soldiers*, had been among the leading testaments of contemporary revolt and had come in with the stream of new novels like *Winesburg*, *Main Street*, *Jurgen* and *My Antonia*. The Hemingway character dominated the imagination of the twenties as easily as the Mencken irreverence, and the "flapper generation" which found its historian in Scott Fitzgerald was the most obvious of postwar phenomena. But where the writers of the "middle generation," like Lewis and Anderson, Cabell and Mencken, had been released by the new current of freedom after the war, had been given opportunities and themes in the postwar scene, the young writers who had been through the war made it and its aftermath their very substance. Born in the middle nineties, when modern American writing was just beginning to emerge as a positive force, they arrived on the scene just at the moment of triumph; and they seemed from the first not merely the concentration of all that the modern revolution had brought to America, but its climax.

Standing at the center of the whole modern literary experience in America, writers like Fitzgerald, Hemingway, and Dos Passos were significantly the evangels of what had been most tragically felt in the American war experience. They were "the sad young men,"[3] the very disillusioned and brilliant young men, "the beautiful and the damned," and counterparts of all those other sad and brilliant young men in Europe, Aldous Huxley and Louis Aragon,[4] to Ernst Toller and Wilfred Owen, who wrote out of the bitterness of a shattered Europe and the palpable demoralization of Western society. Between Hemingway and Sherwood Anderson, between Fitzgerald and Sinclair Lewis, there was as wide and deep a gulf as there had been between Stephen Crane and Howells. And it was in that gulf, something more for these young writers than the familiar disassociation of the American generations, that they lived and wrote—proud and stricken in the consciousness of their difference from their predecessors, from all those who had not shared their intimacy with disaster, from all those who spoke out of an innocence the young writers no longer knew, or through a style that seemed to them conventional.

It was the war, of course, that had made that difference primarily, even for a writer like Scott Fitzgerald, who had not been abroad to the war at all, and had written the first of the lost-generation novels, *This Side of Paradise*, under army lanterns at an officers' training camp. The war had dislodged them from their homes and the old restraints, given them an unexpected and disillusioning education, and left them entirely rootless. They were—in the slogan Gertrude Stein gave to Hemingway—the lost generation, the branded victims, the generation that had been uprooted and betrayed, a generation cast, as one of them wrote, "into the dark maw of violence." Life had begun with war for them and would forever after be shadowed by violence and death. *"The only place where you could see life and death, i. e., violent death now that the wars were over, was in the bull ring and I wanted very much to go to Spain where I could study it."* But it was not only the war that had at once isolated them and given them their prominence; it was also their sense of an artistic mission. Alone in their disenchantment and famous for it, they were at the same time the appointed heirs of modernism, the new American pilgrims of art, closer to James Joyce than to Mencken, and more familiar with Gertrude Stein's revelations than with Warren G. Harding's[5] blunders. It was their enforced education in the international community of war and art, their impatience with an art that did not express *them*, that separated them so persistently from the older writers who had become famous in the twenties with them. They had leaped at one bound from the Midwestern world of their childhood[6] into the world of Caporetto, of Dada, of Picasso and Gertrude Stein, and their detachment from the native traditions now became their own first tradition.

Mencken and Lewis and Cabell spoke for them in the sense that they spoke for all young people after the war, but in the greater sense they did not speak for them at all. What had Hemingway, the Hemingway who, it is said, had been left for dead on the Italian front and was now dreaming away in Verlaine's old room in Paris of a new style, to learn from the older writers save Sherwood Anderson's honest simplicity? What had Scott Fitzgerald, the golden boy of the twenties who moved through them like a disenchanted child, to learn from the complacent satirists of a society that he at once enjoyed more lustily and held more cheaply than they? What had the very sensitive and romantic and conscientious Dos Passos to learn from writers who could mock everything save the essential cruelty and indignity of the industrial culture he hated? In its own mind the lost generation was not merely lost in the world; it was lost from all the other generations in America. It was a fateful loss and perhaps a willing loss, no tragedy for them there; but it was part of the general sense of loss, the conviction by which they wrote (and experienced the world, as with different senses), which gave them so epic a self-consciousness. Lost and forever writing the history of their loss, they became specialists in anguish; and as they sentimentalized themselves, so they were easily sentimentalized. "It was given to Hawthorne to dramatize the human soul," John Peale Bishop[7] once wrote. "In our time Hemingway wrote the drama of its disappearance." No other literary generation could have commented on itself with such careless grandeur. Had Hemingway really recorded the disappearance of the human soul "in our time"? Had Dos Passos's America, so symmetrical a series of hell pits, as much correspondence to America as his inclusive ambition promised? No, but what was so significant about these writers from the first was that they were able to convince others that in writing the story of their generation, they were in some sense describing the situation of contemporary humanity. It was the positiveness of their disinheritance, the very glitter of their disillusionment, the surface perfection of a disbelief that was like the texture of Hemingway's novels, that made them so magnetic an influence, in manners as well as in literature. They had a special charm—the Byronic charm, the charm of the specially damned; they had seized the contemporary moment and made it their own; and as they stood among the ruins, calling the ruins the world, they seemed so authoritative in their dispossession, seemed to bring so much craft to its elucidation, that it was easy to believe that all the roads really had led up to them—that a Hemingway could record "the disappearance of the human soul in our time."

Indeed, it was even easy to believe that they were not merely a group of brilliantly talented young writers enjoying a special prominence, but major voices, major artists.

2

Beyond this point, of course, these writers differed very strikingly.

Hemingway and Dos Passos were as essentially unlike each other as two contemporaries sharing in a common situation can ever be. Fitzgerald, who never underwent the European apprenticeship that the others did, always stood rather apart from them, though he was the historian of his generation, and for a long time its most famous symbol. For Fitzgerald never had to create a lost-generation legend or apply it to literature—the exile, the pilgrimage to Gertrude Stein, the bullfighters at the extremity of the world, the carefully molded style, the carefully molded disgust. The legend actually was his life, as he was its most native voice and signal victim; and his own career was one of its great stories, perhaps its central story. From the first he lived in and for the world of his youth, the glittering and heartbroken postwar world from which his career was so indistinguishable. Living by it he became for many not so much the profoundly gifted, tragic, and erratic writer that he was, a writer in some ways inherently more interesting than any other in his generation, but a marvelous, disappointed, and disappointing child— "a kind of king of our American youth" who had long since lost his kingdom and was staggering in a void. He became too much a legend in himself, too easily a fragment of history rather than a contributor to it. And when he died in his early forties, the "snuffed-out candle," dead in that Hollywood that was his last extremity, with even one of his greatest books, *The Last Tycoon*, unfinished like his life, glittering with promise like his life, he served the legend in death as he had served it by his whole life. *Eheu fugaces!*[8] Scott Fitzgerald was dead; the twenties were really over; the waste and folly had gone with him.

It was almost impossible, of course, not to discount Fitzgerald in some such spirit, for he was as much a part of the twenties as Calvin Coolidge,[9] and like Coolidge, represented something in the twenties almost too graphically. He had announced the lost generation with *This Side of Paradise* in 1920, or at least the home guard of the international rebellion of postwar youth, and the restiveness of youth at home found an apostle in him, since he was the younger generation's first authentic novelist. Flippant, ironic, chastely sentimental, he spoke for all those who felt, as one youth wrote in 1920, that "the old generation had certainly pretty well ruined this world before passing it on to us. They give us this thing, knocked to pieces, leaky, red-hot, threatening to blow up; and then they are surprised that we don't accept it with the same attitude of pretty, decorous enthusiasm with which they received it, way back in the eighties." As the flapper supplanted the suffragette, the cake-eater the earnest young uplifter of 1913,[10] Fitzgerald came in with the modernism that flew in on short skirts, puffed audaciously at its cigarette, evinced a frantic interest in sport and sex, in drinking prohibited liquor, and in defying the ancient traditions. In 1920 he was not so much a novelist as a new generation speaking; but it did not matter. He sounded all the fashionable new lamentations; he gave the inchoate protest of his generation a slogan, a character, a definitive tone. Like Rudolph Valentino,[11] he became one of the supreme personalities of the new day; and when his dashingly handsome hero, Amory Blaine, having survived Princeton, the war, and one tempestuous love affair, stood out at the end of the novel as a man who had conquered all the illusions and was now waiting on a lonely road to be conquered in turn, it seemed as if a generation ambitious for a sense of tragedy had really found a tragic hero.

Like Alfred de Musset's Rolla,[12] Fitzgerald might now have said: *Jesuis venu trop tard dans un monde trop vieux pour moil*[13]—and he did, in all the variants of undergraduate solemnity and bright wisdom. With its flip and elaborately self-conscious prose, *This Side of Paradise* was a record of the younger generation's victory over all the illusions. The war, Amory Blaine confesses, had no great effect on him.

> …but it certainly ruined the old backgrounds. Sort of killed individualism out of our whole generation… I'm not sure it didn't

kill it out of the whole world. Oh, Lord, what a pleasure it used to be to dream I might be a really great dictator or writer or religious or political leader—and now even a Leonardo da Vinci or Lorenzo de Medici couldn't be a real old-fashioned bolt in the world.

Knocking loudly and portentously at the locked doors of convention, Fitzgerald had already become the voice of "all the sad young men." With a sly flourish, he announced that "none of the Victorian mothers—and most of the mothers were Victorian—had any idea how casually their daughters were accustomed to be kissed." Mothers swooned and legislators orated; Fitzgerald continued to report the existence of such depravity and cynicism as they had never dreamed of. The shock was delivered; Fitzgerald became part of the postwar atmosphere of shock. But thought it was inconsequential enough, *This Side of Paradise* had a taste of the poignance that was to flood all Fitzgerald's other books. To tell all was now the fashion; flaming youth was lighting up behind every barn; but of what use was it? Behind the trivial irony of Fitzgerald's novel, its heroic pose, its grandiose dramatizations (Amory was alone—he had escaped from a small enclosure into a great labyrinth. He was where Goethe was when he began "Faust"; he was where Conrad was when he wrote "Almay's Folly") lay a terrible fear of the contemporary world, a world young men had never made. Freedom had come, but only as a medium of expression; while some of the young men licked their war wounds, others sought certainty. We *want* to believe, but we can't. The problem was there for all men to ponder, and for "the beautiful and the damned" to suffer. But how did one learn to believe? What was there to believe in?

Fitzgerald never found the answer, yet he did not mock those who had. In those first years he did not seek answers; perhaps he never did. As Glenway Wescott said in his tribute at the end, he "always suffered from an extreme environmental sense." He commented on the world, swam in it as self-contentedly as the new rich, and understood it sagely—when he wanted to; he had no innerness. His senses always opened outward to the world, and the world was full of Long Island[14] Sundays. This was what he knew and was steeped in, the procession and glitter that he loved without the statement of love, and he had the touch for it—the light yet jeweled style, careless and knowing and affable; the easiness that was never facility; the holiday lights, the holiday splendor, the twenties in their golden bowl, whose crack he knew so well. He was innocent without living in innocence and delighted in the external forms and colors without being taken in by them; but he was pre-eminently a part of the world his mind was always disowning. The extravagance and carnival of the times had laid a charm on him, and he caught the carnival of the world of his youth, and its welling inaudible sadness, as no one else did—the world of Japanese lanterns and tea dances, the hot summer afternoons in *The Great Gatsby*, the dazzle and sudden violence, the colored Easter eggs whose tints got, into his prose, the blare of the saxophones "while a hundred pairs of golden and silver slippers shuffled the shining dust. At the gray tea hour there were always rooms that throbbed incessantly with this low, sweet fever, while fresh faces drifted here and there like rose petals blown by the sad horns around the floor."

Inevitably, there was a persistent tension in Fitzgerald between what his mind knew and what his spirit adhered to; between his disillusionment and his irrevocable respect for the power and the glory of the world he described. "Let me tell you about the very rich," he wrote in *All the Sad Young Men*.

They are different from you and me. They possess and enjoy early, and it does something to them, makes them soft where we are hard, and cynical where we are trustful, in a way that, unless you were born rich, it is very difficult to understand. They think, deep in their hearts, that they are better than we are because we had to discover the compensations and refuges of life for ourselves … They are different.

He was fascinated by that difference, where a writer like Hergesheimer[15] merely imitated it; none of the others in his generation felt the fascination of the American success story as did Fitzgerald, or made so much of it. ("The rich are not as we are," he once said to Hemingway. "No." Hemingway replied. "They have more money.")This was the stuff of life to him, the American achievement he could recognize, and hate a little, and be forever absorbed by. And from Amory Blaine's education to Monroe Stahr's[16] Hollywood in *The Last Tycoon*, Fitzgerald's world did radiate the Carfier jewel glints of the twenties—the diamond mountain, in "The Diamond as Big as the Ritz," Anson Hunter in "The Rich Boy," Jay Gatsby's mansion and dream, the preschool princelings who swagger through so many of his stories, the luxurious self-waste of the last expatriates in *Tender Is the Night*, and finally Monroe Stahr, the Hollywood king, "who had looked on all the kingdoms, with the kind of eyes that can stare straight into the sun."

Fitzgerald did not worship riches or the rich; he merely lived in their golden eye. They were "different"; they were what the writer who lived forever in the world of his youth really knew; and they became for him what war became for Hemingway, or the anarchy of modern society for Dos Passos—the pattern of human existence, the artist's medium of understanding. His people were kings; they were imperious even in their desolation. They were always the last of their line, always damned, always the death-seekers (there are no second generations in Fitzgerald).Yet they were glamorous to the end, as the futilitarians in *Tender Is the Night* and Monroe Stahr were iridescent with death. For Fitzgerald always saw life as glamour, even though he could pierce that glamour to write one of the most moving of American tragedies in *The Great Gatsby*. Something of a child always, with a child's sudden and unexpected wisdom, he could play with the subtle agonies of the leisure class as with a brilliant toy; and the glamour always remained there, even when it was touched with death. In one sense, as a magazine writer once put it, his books were "prose movies," and nothing was more characteristic of his mind than his final obsession with Hollywood. In the same way much of his writing always hovered on the verge of fantasy and shimmered with all the colors of the world. Just as the world swam through his senses without being defined by him, so he could catch all its lights and tones in his prismatic style without having to understand them too consciously. What saved his style from extravagance was Fitzgerald's special grace, his pride in his craft; but it was the style of a man profoundly absorbed in the romance of glamour, the style of a craftsman for whom life was a fairy world to the end.

To understand this absorption on Fitzgerald's part is to understand the achievement of *The Great Gatsby*, the work by which his name will always live. In most of his other works he merely gave shallow reports on the pleasures and self-doubts of his class, glittered with its glitter. He tended to think of his art as a well-oiled machine, and he trusted to luck. Rather like Stephen Crane, whom he so much resembled in spirit, the only thing he could be sure of was his special gift, his way of transfusing everything with words, the consciousness of craft; and like Crane he made it serve for knowledge. But like Crane in another respect, he was one of those writers who make their work out of a conflict that would paralyze others—out of their tragic moodiness, their troubled, intuitive, and curiously half-conscious penetration of the things before them. And it is this moodiness at the pitch of genius that lights up *The Great Gatsby*. For Fitzgerald was supremely a part of the world he there described, weary of it, but not removed from it, and his achievement was of a kind possible only to one who so belonged to it. No revolutionary writer could have written it, or even hinted at its inexpressible poignance; no one, perhaps, who was even too consciously skeptical of the wealth and power Jay Gatsby thought would make him happy. But for Fitzgerald the tragedy unfolded there, the tragedy that has become for so many one of the great revelations of what it has meant to be an American at all, was possible only because it was so profound a burst of self-understanding.

To have approached Gatsby from the outside would have meant a sacrifice of Gatsby himself—a knowledge of everything in Gatsby's world save Gatsby. But the tragedy here is pure confession, a supplication complete in the human note it strikes. Fitzgerald could sound the depths of Gatsby's life because he himself could not conceive any other. Out of his own weariness and fascination with damnation he caught Gatsby's damnation, caught it as only someone so profoundly attentive to Gatsby's dream could have pierced to the self-lie behind it. The book has no real scale; it does not rest on any commanding vision, nor is it in any sense a major tragedy. But it is a great flooding moment, a moment's intimation and penetration; and as Gatsby's disillusion becomes felt at the end it strikes like a chime through the mind. It was as if Fitzgerald, the playboy moving with increasing despair through this tinsel world of Gatsby's, had reached that perfect moment, before the break of darkness and death, when the mind does really and absolutely know itself—a moment when only those who have lived by Gatsby's great illusion, lived by the tinsel and the glamour, can feel the terrible force of self-betrayal. This was the playboy's rare apotheosis, and one all the more moving precisely because all of Gatsby's life was summed up in it, precisely because his decline and death gave a meaning to his life that it had not in itself possessed.

Here was the chagrin, the waste of the American success story in the twenties: here, in a story that was a moment's revelation. Yet think, Fitzgerald seems to say to us, of how little Gatsby wanted at bottom—not to understand society, but to ape it; not to compel the world, but to live in it. His own dream of wealth meant nothing in itself; he merely wanted to buy back the happiness he had lost—Daisy, now the rich man's wife—when he had gone away to war. So the great Gatsby house at West Egg glittered with all the lights of the twenties, and there were always parties, and always Gatsby's supplicating hand, reaching out to make out of glamour what he had lost by the cruelty of chance. "Gatsby believed in the green light, the orgiastic future that year by year recedes before us. It eluded us then, but that's no matter—tomorrow we will run faster, stretch out our arms farther... And one fine morning—" So the great Gatsby house, Gatsby having failed in his dream, now went out with all its lights, save for that last unexpected and uninvited guest whom Nick heard at the closed Gatsby door one night, the guest "who had been away at the ends of the earth and didn't know that the party was over." And now there was only the wry memory of Gatsby's dream, left in that boyhood schedule of September 12, 1906, with its promise of industry and self-develop— "Rise from bed... Study electricity... work... Practice elocution and how to attain it... Read one improving book or magazine per week." So all the lights of Fitzgerald's golden time went out with Jay Gatsby—Gatsby, the flower of the republic, the bootlegger who made the American dream his own, and died by it. "So we beat on, boats against the current, borne back ceaselessly into the past."

Gatsby's was Fitzgerald's apotheosis, too. As the haunting promise of *The Last Tycoon* testifies, he did not lose his skill; there is a grim poetic power in his unraveling of Monroe Stahr greater in itself than anything else in his work. But something in Fitzgerald died concurrently with the dying of his world. His fairy world decomposed slowly, lingeringly; and he lived with its glitter, paler and paler, to the end. Writing what he himself called "the novel of deterioration" in *Tender Is the Night*, he kept to the glow, the almost hereditary grace, that was so natural for him. But he lavished it upon a world of pure emptiness there; he was working away in the pure mathematics of sensation. The subtlety of his last books was a fever glow, a neurotic subtlety. He had always to return to the ancient dream of youth and power, the kings who always died in his work but were kings nevertheless—the dominating men, the ornate men, the imperials in whose light he lived because they were the romantic magnifications of the world of his youth. And reading that painful confession of his own collapse, the essay smuggled away in *Esquire*[17] which he called "The Crack-Up," one felt how fantastic it was, as Glenway Westcott put it in his tender tribute to Fitzgerald, "that a man who is dying or at least done with living—one who has had practically all that the world affords, fame and prosperity, work and play, love and friendship, and lost practically all—should still think seriously of so much fiddledeedee of boyhood." But Fitzgerald was a boy, the most startlingly gifted and self-destructive of all the lost boys, to the end. There is an intense brooding wisdom, all Fitzgerald's keen sense of craft raised and burnished to new power, in *The Last Tycoon* that is unforgettable. To see how he could manipulate the emergence of Stahr's power and sadness, the scene of the airplane flight from New York to Hollywood and the moment when the earthquake trembled in Hollywood, is to appreciate how much closer Fitzgerald could come than most modern American novelists to fulfillment, of a kind. But what is Monroe Stahr—the Hollywood producer "who had looked on all the kingdoms," who died so slowly and glitteringly all through the book as Fitzgerald did in life—but the last, the most feverishly concentrated of Fitzgerald's fairy world characters in that Hollywood that was the final expression of the only world Fitzgerald ever knew? Fitzgerald could penetrate Hollywood superbly; he could turn his gift with the easiest possible dexterity on anything he touched. But he did not touch very much. With all his skill (it is odd to think that where he was once too easily passed off as the desperate Punch of his generation, he may now be rated as a master craftsman in a day worshipful of craftsmanship), Fitzgerald's world is a little one, a superior boy's world—precocious in its wisdom, precocious in its tragedy, but the fitful glaring world of Jay Gatsby's dream, and of Jay Gatsby's failure, to the end.

3

After Fitzgerald, much of the story of his lost generation is the story of the war he never saw, the craftsmanship which became so great an ideal for his generation, and the blistering new world of the thirties and early forties in which he died.

In 1922, two years after F. Scott Fitzgerald had first propounded the idea of the lost generation in *This Side of Paradise*, a young artist and poet, Edward Estlin Cummings, published the record of this unique war experience in a narrative entitled *The Enormous Room*. It was not the first of the American war novels—John Dos Passos, like Cummings a Harvard graduate and a volunteer in the Norton-Harjes Ambulance Serivce,[18] had already published *One Man's Initiation* in 1920 and the better-known *Three Soldiers* in 1921—but it showed a new kind of sensibility, as *This Side of Paradise* had announced a generation. Unlike Fitzgerald, Cummings had seen the war at first hand, and his book was something more than Fitzgerald's defense of a generation that "had grown up to find all Gods dead, all wars fought, all faiths in men shaken." *The Enormous Room* was one of those works that break so completely with one tradition that they mechanically inaugurate another. The book seemed to be an exercise in violence; it rumbled with an indignation that was as livid as the experience it described. Its language, more radical in spirit than the buck-sergeant profanity of *What Price Glory?*,[19] was less obvious, and suggested a philosophy of war compounded equally of resignation, hatred for all authority, and an almost abstract cynicism. America had possessed no Barbusse[20] or Sassoon[21] or Wilfred Owen during the war; the irreverence of its war literature, like its bitter reaction against the war spirit, came much later. Cummings's harsh book was thus almost the very first to express for America the emotions of those artists, writers, students, and middle-class intellectuals who were to constitute the post-mortem war generation, and whose war experience was to transform their conception of life and art.

Cummings's war experience had not been typical. Serving as a volunteer in the gentlemanly Norton-Harjes Ambulance Service, he had been arrested by French military police because of some indiscreet letters written by his friend Slater Brown. Jaded with the war spirit, he gave flippant answers at his hearing and was shipped off to a foul and barn-like "preliminary" prison in the south of France, where he spent months in the company of international spies and suspects, thieves, eccentric vagrants from every corner in Europe, prostitutes, and profiteers. The enormous room was his theater of war he fought no battles, followed the progress of the war through rumor, and spent most of his time trying to keep sane, to get a little food, and to escape. Yet huddled together with the flotsam of war, living on the grudging patronage of a government too busy with routine to be kind, and too suspicious of its prisoners to be fair, Cummings experienced the indignity, the brutality, and the mechanical cruelties of war as a personal disaster. He lived the war through on a lower level, where the slogans seemed farcical, the reality more oppressive, and the great movements of the armies almost unreal. The enormous room concentrated the war. Living on dirty mattresses, humbled by a succession of punishments and insults, deprived of freedom though not confined to "jail," thrown together without common loyalties or even a common purpose, its inmates consciously parodied the war ideals and the war mind. They lived in a perpetual state of mutiny, but there was nothing to protest except life and the French state, no one outrage on which to fix their indignation save the general outrageousness of existence. The enormous room, by its very remoteness from war, mirrored and intensified its inherent meaninglessness; it became a maze in which men clawed each other to escape or to keep their reason. And the central theme of their imprisonment was chaos.

The enormous room was a cell-like sliver torn from life, and its character, as Cummings saw it, was sheer monstrousness. It was a world so profoundly irrational that anger was wasted on it. It was so atrocious that it was comic; it mingled a perverse horror with hysterical exaltation. It was like a surrealist vision of the universe, for it seemed to caricature the conventional dimensions and emotions with such a contempt for order that the very effort to express its horror ended in jollity. *C'est de la blague.*[22] "Who is Marshal Foch?"[23] the Dadaists used to ask in 1921. "Who is Woodrow Wilson? What is war? Don't know, don't know, don't know." War, Cummings proclaimed in this spirit, was the history of decomposition. It was reflected in the tubercular German girl, interned for the greater protection of the French Republic, who was choking to death in solitary. It was the tragic life of Jean Le Negre,[24] the great dumb beast playing with war as a child plays with blocks. It was the living corpses on their mattresses, the gamblers whispering of European stakes, the lechery and the gossip.

> The doors opened with an uncanny bang and in the bang stood a fragile minute queer figure, remotely suggesting an old man. The chief characteristic of the apparition was a certain disagreeable nudity which resulted from its complete lack of all the accepted appurtenances and prerogatives of old age. Its little stooping body, helpless and brittle, bore with extraordinary difficulty a head of absurd largeness, yet which moved on the fleshless neck with a horrible agility. Dull eyes sat in the clean-shaven wrinkles of a face neatly hopeless. At the knees a pair of hands hung, infantile in their smallness. In the loose mouth a tiny cigarette had perched and was solemnly smoking itself.

The enormous room was a Black Bourse[25] of all the war emotions.

To describe this procession of horrors Cummings needed a prose that was as nervously mobile as jazz, as portentously formal as a document, and as crisp and precise as his own poetry. He developed a style as far removed from declamation as possible, but one that parodied the pompous undertones of declamation, a style that took its pace and weight and diction from the unspoken resources of war cynicism. The essential character of this prose was its self-conscious originality. In a world nerve-lacerated by the prevailing sense of defeat, riddled with pretensions and platitudes that were grisly in their unconscious irony, it offered none of the conventional courtesy that a young writer can tender to standard rhetoric. It was a rebellious prose, defiantly new, and contemptuous of conventional patterns. And though it scattered its effects carelessly, the motive behind it was austere: Cummings's great desire was for a prose that should be, beyond everything else, completely and inexorably true; a prose that would express, as Hemingway later said in a celebrated statement, of his own purpose, "the truth about his own feelings at the moment when they exist." It was to be a prose as ruthless, as impolite, as sharp, as consciously and even elaborately bitter, as the world it described. It was to be a prose so contemptuous of conventional standards that no one could doubt its purpose or the depth of the experience behind it.

Cummings's prose was not the hard and deliberately plain prose which Hemingway and later Dos Passos established as their own. Like theirs, it was a prose of inverted lyricism, but more frankly emotional and self-assertive. What he had rejected in his novel was the tonelessness, the machinelike pattern of conventional writing, its implicit submission to the objective world and lack of personal force. With the same passionate individualism that he was soon to bring to his poetry—an individualism not unrelated, as some critics have observed, to the Emersonian and New England tradition that has always been so strong in Cummings—he sought to impose a new conception of reality. Like so many in his generation, he had returned to an elemental writing, as writers often do in periods of social crisis; but his "simplicity" was a form of grotesquerie and not, like

Wordsworth's realism or Whitman's, a serene faith that his fellow men would approve a democratic language and purpose. As Cummings saw it, the world was composed of brutal sensations and endured only by a fiercely desperate courage and love; it was so anarchical that all attempts to impose order were motivated by either ignorance or chicanery. What remained to the artist, who was always the special victim of this world, was the pride of individual self-knowledge and the skill that went beyond all the revolutionary and sentimental illusions of a possible fraternity among men and gave all its devotion to the integrity of art.

A paralled code of fatalism developed in Ernest Hemingway's hands into the freshest and most deliberate art of the day. What Cummings had suggested in his embittered war autobiography was that the postwar individual, first as soldier and citizen, now as artist, was the special butt of the universe. As Wyndham Lewis[26] wrote later of the typical Hemingway hero, he was the man "things are done to." To Hemingway life became supremely the task of preserving oneself by preserving and refining one's art. Art was the ultimate, as it was perhaps the only, defense. In a society that served only to prey upon the individual, endurance was possible only by retaining one's identity and thus proclaiming one's valor. Writing was not a recreation, it was a way of life; it was born of desperation and enmity and took its insights from a militant suffering. Yet it could exist only as it purified itself; it had meaning only as it served to tell the truth. A writer succeeded by proving himself superior to circumstance; his significance as an artist lay in his honesty, his courage, and the will to endure. Hemingway's vision of life, as John Peale Bishop put it, was thus one of perpetual annihilation. "Since the will can do nothing against circumstance, choice is precluded; those things are good which the senses report good; and beyond their brief record there is only the remorseless devaluation of nature."

The remarkable thing about Hemingway from the first was that he did not grow up to this rigid sense of tragedy, or would not admit that he had. The background of his first stories, *In Our Time,* was the last frontier of his Michigan boyhood, a mountainous region of forests and lakes against which he appeared as the inquisitive but tight-lipped youth—hard, curt, and already a little sad. With its carefully cultivated brutality and austerity, the sullen boy in *In Our Time* revealed a mind fixed in its groove. These stories of his youth, set against the superb evocation of war monotony and horror, elaborately contrived to give the violence of the Michigan woods and the violence of war an equal value in the reader's mind, summarized Hemingway's education. Their significance lay in the number of things the young Hemingway had already taken for granted; they were a youth's stricken responses to a brutal environment, and the responses seemed to become all. Just as the war in *A Farewell to Arms* was to seem less important than the sensations it provoked, so the landscape of *In Our Time* had meaning only as the youth had learned from it. For Hemingway in his early twenties, the criticism of society had gone so deep that life seemed an abstraction; it was something one discounted by instinct and distrusted by habit. It was a sequence of violent actions and mechanical impulses: the brutality of men in the Michigan woods, the Indian husband who cut his throat after watching his wife undergo a Caesarian with a jackknife, adolescent loneliness and exaltation, a punch-drunk boxer on the road. And always below that level of native memories, interspersed with passing sketches of gangsters and bullfights, lay the war.

> Nick sat against the wall of the church where they had dragged him to be clear of machine-gun fire in the street. Both legs stuck out awkwardly. He had been hit in the spine. His face was sweaty and dirty. The sun shone on his face. The day was very hot... Two Austrian dead lay in the rubble in the shade of the house. Up the street were other dead... Nick turned his head carefully and looked at Rinaldi. "Senta Rinaldi. Senta. You and me we've made a

separate peace."

The glazed face of the Hemingway hero, which in its various phases was to become, like Al Capone's,[27] the face of a decade and to appear on a succession of soldiers, bullfighters, explorers, gangsters, and unhappy revolutionaries, emerged slowly but definitively in *In Our Time*. The hero's first reaction was surprise, to be followed immediately by stupor; life, like the war, is in its first phase heavy, graceless, sullen; the theme is sounded in the rape of Liz Coates by the hired man.[28] Then the war became comic, a series of incongruities. Everybody was drunk. The whole battery was drunk going along the road in the dark... The lieutenant kept riding his horse out into the fields and saying to him: "I'm drunk, I tell you, mon vieux. Oh, I am so soused." ...It was funny going along that road. "Then the whole affair became merely sordid, a huddle of refugees in the mud, the empty and perpetual flow of rain, a woman bearing her child on the road." It rained all through the evacuation. By the sheer accumulation of horrors, the final phase was reached, and the end was a deceptive callousness.

> We were in a garden at Mons. Young Buckley came in with his patrol from across the river. The first German I saw climbed up over the garden wall. We waited till he got one leg over and then potted him. He had so much equipment on and looked awfully surprised and fell down into the garden. Then three more came over further down the wail. We shot them. They all came just like that.

Hemingway's own values were stated explicitly in the story called "Soldier's Home," where he wrote that "Krebs acquired the nausea in regard to experience that is the result of untruth or exaggeration." The Hemingway archetype had begun by contrasting life and war, devaluating one in terms of the other. Now life became only another manifestation of war; the Hemingway world is in a state of perpetual war. The soldier gives way to the bullfighter, the slacker to the tired revolutionary, the greed of war is identified with the corruption and violence of sport. Nothing remains but the individual's fierce unassailable pride in his pride, the will to go on, the need to write without "untruth or exaggeration." As a soldier, he had preserved his sanity by rebelling quietly and alone; he had made the separate peace. Mutiny was the last refuge of the individual caught in the trap of war; chronic mutiny now remains the safeguard of the individual in that state of implicit belligerence between wars that the world calls peace. The epos of death has become life's fundamental narrative; the new hero is the matador in Chapter XII of *In Our Time*. "When he started to kill it was all in the same rush. The bull looking at him straight in front, hating. He drew out the sword from the folds of the muleta and sighted with the same movement and called to the bull, Toro! Toro! and the bull charged and Villata charged and just for a moment they became one." The casual grace of the bullfighter, which at its best is an esthetic passion, is all and even that grace may become pitiful, as in the saga of the aging matador in "The Undefeated." For the rest, defeat and corruption and exhaustion lie everywhere: marriage in "Cross-Country Snow," sport in "My Old Man" ("Seems like when they get started they don't leave a guy nothing"), the gangrene of Fascism in "Che Ti Dice la Patria?" The climax of that first exercise in disillusion is reached in the terse and bitter narrative called "The Revolutionist," the story of the young boy who had been tortured by the Whites in Budapest when the Soviet collapsed, and who found Italy in 1919 beautiful. "In spite of Hungary, he believed altogether in the world revolution."

"But how is the movement going in Italy?" he asked.

"Very badly," I said.

"But it will go better," he said. "You have everything here. It is the one country that every one is sure of. It will be the starting point of everything."

4

When Hemingway published those first stories in 1925, he was twenty-seven years old, and the rising star—"the surest future there," Lincoln Steffens recalled in his autobiography—in the American literary colony in Paris. Unlike most of the writers in the "lost generation," he had not gone to a university; after completing a round of private schools he had gone to work, still in his teens, for the *Kansas City Star*, a paper famous for its literary reporters. He had driven an ambulance on the Italian front before America entered the war, been wounded gloriously enough to receive the Croce di Guerra, and after 1921 had traveled extensively as a foreign correspondent. "In writing for a newspaper," he reported seventeen years later in the rambling prose of *Death in the Afternoon*, "you told what happened, and with one trick or another, you communicated the emotion aided by the element of timeliness which gives a certain emotion to any account of something that has happened on that day. But the real thing, the sequence of motion and fact which made the emotion and which would be as valid in a year or ten years or, with luck and if you stated it purely enough, always, was beyond me and I was working very hard to get it."

Hemingway's intense search for "the real thing" had already singled him out in Paris before he published *In Our Time*. In those early years, guided by his interest in poetry and his experiences as a reporter of the European debacle, he seemed to be feeling his way toward a new prose, a prose that would be not only absolutely true to the events reported and to the accent of common speech, but would demand of itself an original evocativeness and plasticity. What he wanted, as he said later in *Death in the Afternoon*, was a prose more intensely precise than conventional prose, and hence capable of effects not yet achieved. He wanted to see "how far prose can be carried if anyone is serous enough and has luck. There is a fourth and fifth dimension that can be gotten... It is much more difficult than poetry. It is prose that has never been written. But it can be written without tricks and without cheating. With nothing that will go bad afterwards." Yet what he was aiming at in one sense, F. O. Matthiessen has pointed out, was the perfect yet poetic naturalness of a Thoreau. Hemingway's surface affiliations as a prose craftsman were with his first teachers, Gertrude Stein and Sherwood Anderson, who taught him the requisite simplicity and fidelity and—Gertrude Stein more than Anderson—an ear for the natural rhythms of speech. But his deeper associations went beyond them, beyond even the Flaubertian tradition of discipline and *le mot juste*.[29] He did not want to write "artistic prose," and Gertrude Stein and Anderson, equally joined in their hatred of display and their search for an inner truth in prose, had certainly taught him not to. But he wanted not merely to tell "the truth about his own feelings at the moment when they exist"; he wanted to aim at that luminous and imaginative truth which a writer like Thoreau, on the strength of a muscular integrity and passion for nature very like his own, had created out of a monumental fidelity to the details of life as he saw them. What he wanted was that sense of grace, that "sequence motion and fact" held at unwavering pitch, that could convey, as nothing else could, the secret fluid symbolism in the facts touched and record.

It was this that separated him essentially from Gertrude Stein and Anderson. Anderson was not fundamentally interested in *writing*; Gertrude Stein, who could help everyone in the world but herself, was interested in nothing else. The Hemingway legend, which Hemingway himself fostered in the twenties, encouraged the belief that he was only a pure nihilist and coldly assimilative, even brutish in imagination. But nothing could have been more false. He brought a major art to a minor vision of life, and it is as important to measure the vision as it is to appreciate the art. But his seeming naivete was really an exemplary straightforwardness and a remarkable capacity for learning from every possible source. As a practicing artist he had the ability to assimilate the lessons of others so brilliantly that he seemed to impart a definitive modern emotion to everything he touched. He learned so brilliantly, indeed, that the extent of his borrowing has often been exaggerated. What is significant in Hemingway's literary education is not that he learned prose rhythm from the Gertrude Stein of *Three Lives*, the uses of simplicity from Sherwood Anderson, the sense of discipline from Ezra Pound and the cosmopolitan literary ateliers of postwar Paris, but that they gave him the authority to be himself. Despite his indebtedness to Mark Twain's *Huckleberry Finn*—the greatest book in all American writing for him—he had no basic relation to any prewar culture. Byron learned from Pope, but Hemingway learned to write in a literary environment that could not remember 1913. Even the literary revolution that found its appointed heir in him, an avant-garde forever posing under its Picasso, and talking modernism with a Midwestern accent, could not long claim him. Once Hemingway had learned the principles and tricks of his art, made a literary personality out of the Midwestern athlete, soldier, and foreign correspondent, created a new hero for the times in the romantically disillusioned postwar dandy, he went his own way in his search for "the real thing."

It was in his unceasing quest of a conscious perfection through style that Hemingway proclaimed his distinction. To tell what had happened, as he wrote later, one used "one trick or another," dialogue being the supreme trick. But "the real thing," the pulse of his art, was to Hemingway from the first that perfect blending of fact into symbol, that perfect conversion of natural rhythm into an evocation of the necessary emotion, that would fuse the various phases of contemporary existence—love, war, sport—and give them a collective grace. And it was here that style and experience came together for him. Man endured the cruelty and terror of life only by the sufferance of his senses and his occasional enjoyment of them; but in that sufferance and enjoyment, if only he could convey them perfectly, lay the artist's special triumph. He could rise above the dull submissive sense of outrage which most men felt in the face of events. By giving a new dimension to the description of natural fact, he could gain a refuge from that confusion which was half the terror of living. What this meant was brilliantly illustrated in the association of the worlds of peace and war in *In Our Time*; the theme of universal loneliness in the midst of war that was sounded in the very first paragraph of *A Farewell to Arms* and attained its classic expression in the retreat at Caporetto, where the flowing river, the long grumbling line of soldiers, the officers who are being shot together by the carabinieri, seem to melt together in the darkness; the extraordinary scene in *The Sun Also Rises* where Robert Cohn, sitting with Jake and his friends at the bullfight, is humiliated a moment before the steer is gored in the ring. In each case the animal in man has found its parallel and key in some event around it; the emotion has become the fact.

If "the real thing" could not always be won, or retained after it had been won, there were other forms of grace—the pleasures of drinking and making love, the stabbing matador dancing nervously before his bull, the piercing cry of the hunt, the passionate awareness of nature that would allow a man to write a sentence like "In shooting quail you must not get between them, or when they flush they will come pouring at you, some rising steep, some skimming by your ears, whirring into a size you have never seen them in the air as they pass." If art was an expression of fortitude, fortitude at its best had the quality of art. Beyond fortitude, which even in *For Whom the Bell Tolls* is the pride of a professional integrity and skill, there was the sense of nature paralyzed, nature frozen into loneliness or terror. No nature writer in all American literature save Thoreau has had Hemingway's sensitiveness to color, to climate to the knowledge of physical energy under heat or cold, that knowledge of the body thinking and moving through a landscape that Edmund Wilson,[30] in another connection, has called Hemingway's "barometric accuracy." That accuracy was the joy of the huntsman and the artist; beyond that and its corresponding gratifications, Hemingway seemed to attach no value to anything else. There were only absolute values or absolute degradations.

The very intensity of Hemingway's "nihilism" in his first stories and novels proved, however, that his need for an ideal expression in art was the mark of a passionate romanticist who had been profoundly disappointed. The anguish of his characters was too dramatic, too flawless; it was too transparent an inversion. The symbols Hemingway employed to convey his sense of the world's futility and horror were always more significant than the characters who personified them, and they so often seemed personified emotions that the emotions became all. The gallery of expatriates in *The Sun Also Rises* were always subsidiary to the theme their lives enforced; the lovers in *Farewell to Arms* were, as Edmund Wilson has said, the abstractions of a lyric emotion. Hemingway had created a world of his own more brilliant than life, but he was not writing about people living in a real world; he was dealing in absolute values again, driving his characters between the two poles of an absolute exaltation and an absolute frustration, invoking the specter of their damnation.

After that, *Death in the Afternoon* and the Hemingway legend. There had always been a Hemingway legend, and with good reason; like Byron, he was in part the creation of his own reputation. But the legend became ominous and even cheap only when Hemingway chose to treat it as a guide to personal conduct and belief; when, in truth, he became not only one of his own characters but his own hero. After *Death in the Afternoon*, Hemingway's work became an expression of the legend, where the legend had once been a measure of the world's response to his work. The sense of shock, the stricken malaise of his first stories, were now transformed into a long and cynical rhetoric. "Madame, all our words from loose using have lost their edge," Hemingway tells the Old Lady in *Death in the Afternoon*;

and proves it by his own example. "Have you no remedy then?" she asks. "Madame, there is no remedy for anything in life." The pose pretentious in one scene becomes merely gluttonous in another. The high jinks of the wastrels in *The Sun Also Rises* had suggested a tragic self-knowledge, an affirmation of life as they saw it; Hemingway's own tone was now giggle and a little frantic. "So far, about morals I know only that what is moral is what you feel good after and what is immoral is what you feel bad after." It was on a plane with the famous parody of Marx in "The Gambler, The Nun, and the Radio":

> Religion is the opium of the people... Yes, and music is the opium of the people... And now economics is the opium of the people; along with patriotism the opium of the people in Italy and Germany. What about sexual intercourse; was that an opium of the people? Of some of the people. Of some of the best of the people. But drink was a sovereign opium of the people, oh, an excellent opium. Although some prefer the radio, another opium of the people... Along with these went gambling, an opium of the people if there ever was one... Ambition was another, an opium of the people, along with a belief in any new form of government.

As the years went by, one grew accustomed to Hemingway standing like Tarzan against a backdrop Nature; or, as the tedious sportsman of *Green Hills of Africa*, grinning over the innumerable beasts he had slain, while the famous style became more mechanical, the sentences more invertebrate, the philosophy more self conscious, the headshaking over a circumscribed eternity more painful. Most of the lost generation had already departed to other spheres of interest; Hemingway seemed to have taken up a last refuge behind the clothing advertisements in *Esquire*, writing essays in which he mixed his fishing reports with querulous pronouncements on style and the good life. Then, eight years after the publication of *A Farewell to Arms*, when the Hemingway legend had already lost its luster with the disappearance of the world that had encouraged that legend with emulation and empty flattery, Hemingway wrote *To Have and Have Not*. It was a frantically written novel, revealing a new tension and uncertainty in Hemingway; but for all its melodrama, it was not cheap, and it was strange to note that it was the first novel he had written about America. The dry crackle of the boozed cosmopolitans eating their hearts out in unison, the perpetual shift of scene to Malaga or Pairs or the African jungle, seemed to have been left behind him. The America of *To Have and Have Not* was Key West, like the Paris of 1925 an outpost of a culture and its symbol. It was by Key West that Hemingway had come home, and it was Key West; apparently, that became a working symbol of America for him, a cross-section: the noisy, shabby, deeply moving rancor and tumult of all those human wrecks, the fishermen and the Cuban revolutionaries, the veterans and the alcoholics, the gilt-edged snobs and the hungry natives, the great white stretch of beach promising everything and leading nowhere.

The Hemingway of *To Have and Have Not* was not a "new" Hemingway; he was an angry and confused writer who had been too profoundly disturbed by the social and economic crisis to be indifferent, but could find no clue in his education by which to understand it. Inevitably, he lapsed into melodrama and sick violence. To the Hemingway who had gained his conception of life from the First World War only to crash into the Second by way of international panic and the Spanish Civil War, mass suffering had always been a backdrop against which the Hemingway hero persisted by dint of his Byronic pride, his sense of grace. But this new crisis had to be endured with something more than artistic fortitude; every generation was caught up in it, every phase of contemporary culture and manners was transformed by it, as even his beloved Spain was being devastated by it. It was like Hemingway, of course, to pick for his new hero in the thirties the pirate of *To Have and*

Have Not and the international secret agent of *The Fifth Column*: the two men left in the era from Black Friday to Munich who could remain casual about annihilation! He was reaching for something in these two productions that he could not identify satisfactorily or project with confidence, and it was inevitable that both Hairy Morgan and Philip[31] should represent a tormented individualism passionately eager for human fellowship and contemptuous of it. The Hemingway hero was now a composite exaggeration of all the Hemingway heroes, yet nothing in himself. He was the *Esquire* fisherman and an OGPU[32] agent in Spain who found that he had to choose between the Spanish Republic and a Vassar girl; he was a murdering gangster who killed only because Hemingway wanted to kill something at the moment, and a sentimental sophisticate who, when he heard the militia sing "*Bandera Rossa*" downstairs in the shell-battered Hotel Florida, cried: "The best people I ever knew died for that song." Yet Philip in *The Fifth Column* was not one of the best people; he was Jake Barnes[33] making up for his impotence by murdering Fascists, and the Fascists were as unreal as the sick wisdom he and the perennial Lady Brett mumbled at each other in the midst of a civil war that was shaking Western society.

　　Whatever it was Hemingway tried to reach, however, he found in some measure in Spain; and he found it first in an extraordinary little story, "Old Man at the Bridge," that he cabled from Barcelona in April, 1938. "It will take many plays and novels to present the nobility and dignity of the cause of the Spanish people," he wrote in his preface to *The Fifth Column*, "and the best ones will be written after the war is over." "Old Man at the Bridge" was more than an introduction to the retrospective wisdom of *For Whom the Bell Tolls*; it was a record of the better things Hemingway had learned in Spain, an intimation of a Hemingway who had found the thwarted ideal clear and radiant again through the martyrdom of the Spanish masses. In the retreat of the Loyalist forces a Spanish officer encounters the last refugee from San Carlos, an old man who has been taking care of eight pigeons, two goats, and a cat, but has been separated from them and from his own people by the advancing Fascist armies, "And you have no family?" the Loyalist officer asks. "No," replies the old man, "only the animals I stated. The cat, of course, will be all right. A cat can look out for itself, but I cannot think what will become of the others." "What politics have you?" the officer asks. "I am without politics," replies the old man. "I am seventy-six years old. I have come twelve kilometers now and I think now I can go no further."

It was in something of this spirit that Hemingway wrote *For Whom the Bell Tolls*, the work of a profound romanticist who had at last come to terms with the ideal, and who had torn down the old charnel house with such ardor that his portrait of the Spanish war was less a study of the Spanish people than a study in epic courage and compassion. The idealism that had always been so frozen in inversion, so gnawing and self-mocking, had now become an unabashed lyricism that enveloped the love of Robert Jordan and Maria, the strength of Pilar, the courage and devotion of the guerrillas, the richness and wit of Spanish speech, in a hymn of fellowship. "All mankind is of one Author, and is one volume… No man is an Island, entire of itself." Nothing could have been more purely romantic than the love story of Robert and Maria, and no love story ever seemed so appropriate an expression of a writer's confidence in life and his overwhelming joy in it. Hemingway had apparently gained a new respect for humanity in Spain, an appreciation of the collectivity that binds all men together; and in the spirit of the Catholic devotion by John Donne which gave him his title,[34] it seemed as if his long quest for an intense unity, the pure absolute fortitude and grace, had become a joyous unison of action and battle and love.

Yet *For Whom the Bell Tolls* is among the least of Hemingway's works. Its leading characters are totally unreal; as a record of the human and social drama that was the Spanish Civil War, it is florid and never very deep. And if one compares this work of his ambitious conversion, with its eloquence, its calculation, and its romantic inflation, with the extraordinarily brilliant story of this late period, "The Snows of Kilimanjaro," it is clear that the attempted affirmation of life in the novel, while passionate enough, is moving only in itself, while the concentrated study of waste and death in the story is perfectly dramatic, perfectly Hemingway's own. Hemingway's world is a world of death still, even in *For Whom the Bell Tolls*; and the great things in it, like the battle scenes or the pillage of the Fascist town, flow with a carefully contrived violence and brutality from him. But the Spanish war is essentially only Robert Jordan's education—"It's part of one's education. It will be quite an education when it's finished." The Hemingway "I" is still the center of existence, as only he could alternate between the war and Maria in the sleeping-bag so easily; as only he could seem less a man entering into the experience of others than the familiarly dammed, familiarly self-absorbed lost-generation Byron playing a part beside them. Yes, and the Hemingway hero is still "the man things are done to"—the war is something happening to Robert Jordan—still the brilliant young man counting the costs of his own life among the ruins. *For Whom the Bell Tolls* is thus an unsatisfactory novel, certainly unsatisfactory for Hemingway, because it is a strained and involuntary application of his essentially anarchical individualism, his brilliant half-vision of life, to a new world of war and struggle too big for Hemingway's sense of scale anode that can make that half-vision seem significantly sentimental.

The will is there, the reaching hope; nothing could be more false than the familiar superstition that Hemingway wanted to go round and round in the old nihilist circle. But as Robert Jordan lived and fought the war so curiously alone, so he dies alone, waiting for the enemy to come—the Hemingway guerrilla dying a separate death as once he made a separate peace, the last of the Hemingway heroes enjoying the final abnegation, and now the least impressive. That separate death and abnegation were all there before, and they were very good before. Good when the hunter was alone in the hills, the matador before his bull, the quail skimming through the air. Good when Gertrude Stein could teach a young man fresh from war to write perfect sentences, and the triumph of art was equal to the negation of life. Good when the world could seem like a Hemingway novel; and the "I" was the emblem of all the disillusionment and fierce pride in a world so brilliant in its sickness; and the sentences were so perfect, spanning the darkness. It did not matter then that the art could be so fresh and brilliant, the life below its superb texture so arid and dark. For Hemingway's is one of the great half-triumphs of literature; he proved himself the triumphal modern artist come to America, and within his range and means, one of the most interesting creators in the history of the American imagination. But if it did not matter then, it matters now—not because what is supremely good in Hemingway is in any way perishable, but because his work is a stationary half-triumph, because there is no real continuity in him, nothing of the essential greatness of spirit which his own artistic success has always called for. It matters now that Hemingway's influence has in itself become a matter of history. It will always matter, particularly to those who appreciate what he brought to American writing, and who, with that distinction in mind, can realize that Hemingway's is a tactile contemporary American success; who can realize, with respect and sympathy, that it is a triumph in and of a narrow, local, and violent world—and never superior to it.

5

Technically and even morally Hemingway was to have a profound influence on the writing of the thirties. As a stylist and craftsman his example was magnetic on younger men who came after him; as the progenitor of the new and distinctively American cult of violence, he stands out as the greatest single influence on the hard-boiled novel of the thirties, and certainly affected the social and left-wing fiction of the period more than some of its writers could easily admit. No one save Dreiser in an earlier period had anything like Hemingway's dominance over modern American fiction, yet even Dreiser meant largely an example of courage and frankness during the struggle for realism, not a standard of craftsmanship and a persuasive conception of life, like Hemingway's. Hemingway is the bronze god of the whole contemporary literary experience in American. Yet in a sense he marks an end as clearly as he once marked a beginning. If we consider how the whole lost-generation conception of art and society reached its climax in him, and how much that conception was the brilliant and narrow concentration of the individualism and alienation from society felt by the artist in the twenties, it is clear that Hemingway's stubbornly atomic view of life is the highest expression of the postwar sequence, not a bridge to the future. Despite his will and formal conversion to "the interests of humanity," the "I" and society do not meet imaginatively for him. The writing that came after him in the thirties had only the surface of his brilliance, when it had that at all; but by its absorption in the larger concerns of society, its conviction that no man is alone today, it reveals a departure from Hemingway as much as its toughness reveals his association with it.

CHAPTER 15　The Rhetoric and the Agony

　　"The terror of which I write is not of Germany, but of the soul."
　　　　　　　　　　　　　　　　　　　　—Edgar Allan Poe

On the surface much of the prose literature of the thirties was an attempt to study and to meet the crisis on a literal plane of social realism. But there were great secret depths in it, depths of individual terror and sensibility; and in those depths strange new sea-monsters lived.

When William Faulkner published a first novel in 1926 entitled *Soldiers' Pay*, no one could possibly have known that the ghost of the Gothic novel had appeared to record a new and portentously macabre view of contemporary dissolution. Cheerfully slapdash in its structure and rather poignantly overwritten, *Soldiers' Pay* was no more than what it appeared to be—a weary epilogue of the peace to the already familiar lost-generation autobiography of the war; a turgid and roughly composed story of postwar disillusionment by a Southern gentleman who had an obvious taste for romantic rhetoric and plainly betrayed a neatly inverted romantic view of life. What distinguished it from almost all the other lost-generation novels, however, was the extraordinary verbal resources which its author exhibited with such pretentious and melancholy defiance. It was the work of a poet who was not sure that he wanted to write poetry and of a novelist whose use of the novel was at once irritably contemptuous and frantically bold. Yet the confused and opaque bitterness of the book also hinted mysteriously at a disillusionment that was somehow more elusive and profound than the fashionable arbitrary disgust with war standards and a war would. *Soldiers' Pay* was the work of a writer who was so regional that he was almost parochial; and he had tasted the ultimate bitterness of the war at home, in that South which was forever after to provide him with an image of existence and a concept of tragedy. Unlike his international-minded contemporaries—Hemingway, Cummings, Dos Passos—Faulkner was the creature of a tradition and completely, if restively, submissive to it. Born into a distinguished Mississippi family that had once played an important role in state politics, he had lived in Oxford—the seat of the state university—from early childhood, been educated at the university, and had returned to the town (the "Jefferson"[35] of his future sagas) after his experiences in the Canadian and British Air Forces. He had worked in a bookstore in New York and written descriptive sketches for newspapers while living with Sherwood Anderson in New Orleans; but his life was in Oxford, where he wrote pastoral verse, recovered from a war wound, and worked at odd jobs as a carpenter, a roof-painter and a postmaster at the university. He was a Southerner, but hardly a Southern university intellectual, and his associations and interests were not overtly esthetic. He might write novels, like his great-grandfather, Colonel William Faulkner, author of the popular romance *The White Rose of Memphis*; he even published a book of his pastoral verse in 1924 and sold most of the copies to a local bookstore at ten cents each; but he was not a writer in the sense that Hemingway, Cummings, Fitzgerald, Dos Passos, and so many writers of his generation were.

Superficially and publicly Faulkner did not, in those early days, appear to be consciously "literary." He liked to write, as he liked to drink beer with the boys after an afternoon painting roofs; but he wrote too fluently to think too much about it, and he practiced his writing with the same apparent fatalism with which he worked at hard-laboring jobs and was soon, when *Sanctuary* had been rejected by the New York publishers, to support himself by shoveling coal in a power plan. He was an impoverished Southern gentleman who had run away to war as a boy, been wounded and matured in it, and had returned to seek his place in the only tradition he had ever known. The bitterness of being a Sartoris[36] (the Southern aristocrat *manqué*) in a Snopes world, the world of the small, mean traders and expropriators and ambitious poor whites) was very real, and became one of the foundations of his thought; but he could project it idly, as it seemed, only because his disenchantment was a vague and expansive moodiness. Despite the terror-stricken atmosphere that was to fill his novels, and an almost ferocious misanthropy, Faulkner was essentially a boyish mind for all his complexity, a mind humorous in the broad country fashion, and given to lazy improvisations; and a certain slyness, an indirectly comic view of life, at once racy and tormented and ambiguous, appeared in his work from the first. His sophistication was secret and violent. He had returned from the war, as Warren Beck has commented, "with an enlarged perspective which discerned the decadence of his native region while still holding to his associations with it," and this, along with the shock of his war experiences, was the source of the tension in his work which was ever after to show itself as nervous power. But his bitterness with the South was only one phase of a generally romantic and even self-complacent pessimism, and one which life in the South, enclosing him on all sides, illustrated in dramatic and fertile symbolism.

It was long ago realized that Faulkner was anything but a "Southern realist," that silly tag applicable to George W. Cable[37] and Thomas Wolfe alike; but his relationship to the South, even his conception of that relationship in his novels, has never been understood. In any other age Faulkner would have been one of the world's great romantic novelists, as in one sense he still is. But his ability to invest his every observation of Southern life and manners with epic opulence and profligate rhetoric and Poe-like terror concealed the fact that he had no primary and design-like conception of the South; that his admiration and acceptance and disgust operated together in his mind. He was at once a fallen aristocrat and a fantasist; a quasi-philosophical critic of the South's degradation and a native son in whom its antics and institutions excited a lazily humorous disgust that was often indistinguishable from cynical acquiescence. He admired the South, loathed it, wept for it, enjoyed it, lived in it; but he could not imagine an order of experience fundamentally different from it. If he thought of it as the jungle in *Sanctuary*, it could also become the gracious manor house in *Sartoris*, the seat of the gracious feudal mind in *The Unvanquished*. If it as a neighborhood full of racy farmers and sly village yokels in *The Hamlet*, it was also the cesspool of *As I Lay Dying*;

the futile, corrupt, festering village world of *Soldiers' Pay* and *The Sound and the Fury*; the maniacal traditionalism, epic in scale, of *Absalom, Absalom!* If the South was a repository of a great frustrated tradition and Channing memories, it was also—as he proved almost too well to be convincing—a symbol of all the hatred and terror in the world. In Faulkner's mind the association was instinctive and violent; life was the South, and what he saw and remembered or was told of it exhausted the imaginative range and depth of the human mind for him. Like a Homeric battlefield, it was not only the center of the world's stage, the polar symbol, but the very periphery of existence, that barrier of the imagination beyond which life could not be said to exist at all.

It was because he was so completely bound up in this tradition and yet hardly subject to it that Faulkner's extraordinary intensity, the superabundance of which has often seemed profligate and mechanical, was turned directly upon the South in a hot and confused fury. In one sense, of course, his love and hatred for his native region were so inextricably fused that his passion became the struggle of the will against itself, the interlocked anguish and complacence and joy with which a man may hate the earth he stands on, yet hate himself most for his enmity. But another expression of his divided will, even the suspension of will which went so far to explain his luxurious incoherence and euphuism, his need of a facile magnificence in rhetoric, was a driving and really fantastic vitality of mind, a virtuosity and ready inventiveness unsurpassed in modern American writing. As a thinker, as a participant in the communal myth of the South's tradition and decline, Faulkner was curiously dull, furiously commonplace, and often meaningless, suggesting some ambiguous irresponsibility and exasperated sullenness of mind, some distant atrophy or indifference. Technically he soon proved himself almost inordinately subtle and ambitious, the one modern American novelist whose devotion to form has earned him a place among even the great experimentalists in modern poetry. Yet this remarkable imaginative energy, so lividly and almost painfully impressed upon all his work, did not spring from a conscious and procreative criticism of society or conduct or tradition, from some absolute knowledge; it was the expression of that psychic tension in Faulkner which Sherwood Anderson had observed when they were living together in New Orleans; and which, as his almost monstrous overwriting proves, was a psychological tic, a need to invest everything he wrote with a wild, exhilarated, and disproportionate intensity—an intensity that was brilliant and devastatingly inclusive in its energy, but seemed to come from nowhere.

The problem that faces every student of Faulkner's writing is its lack of a center, the gap between his power and its source; that curious abstract magnificence (not only a magnificence of verbal resources alone) which holds his books together, yet seems to arise from debasement or perplexity or a calculating terror. It is the gap between the deliberation of his effects, the intensity of his every conception, and the besetting and depressing looseness, the almost sick passivity, of his basic meaning and purpose. No writer, least of all a novelist so remarkably inventive and robust of imagination, works in problems of pure technique alone; and though it is possible to see in his books as Conrad Aiken[38] has shown, the marks of a writer devoted to elaboration and wizardry of form, who has deliberately sought to delay and obscure his readers so that the work may have a final and devastating effect, Faulkner's "persistent offering of obstacles, a calculated system of screens and obtrusions, of confusions and ambiguous interpolations and delays," seems to spring from an obscure and profligate confusion, a manifest absence of purpose, rather than from an elaborate but coherent aim.

For while Faulkner has brought back into the modern American novel a density of perception and elaboration of means unparalleled since Henry James, his passion for form has not been, like James's, the tortuous expression of an unusual and subtle point of view; it has been a register of too many points of view, and in its way a substitute for one. It is precisely because his technical energy and what must be called a tonal suggestiveness are so profound, precisely because Faulkner's rhetoric is so portentous, that it has been possible to read every point of view into his work and to prove them all. To a certain type of social or moralist critic, his work seems at once the product of some ineffable decadence and a reluctant commentary upon it. To certain sympathetic Southern readers, such as George M. O'Donnell, Faulkner has even seemed a traditional moralist, not to say a belated neo-Humanist, devoted to the "Southern social-economic-ethical tradition which [he] possesses naturally as a part of his sensibility." To many critics and graduate students (no novelist has ever been so rich in citations), he has even seemed a new and distinctive philosophical voice in the novel. For Faulkner's fluency, even his remarkable fecundity, has been such that it is almost impossible not to take his improvisations for a social philosophy, his turgidity for complexity, and even his passivity for a wise and reflective detachment. It is not strange that he has appeared to be all things to all men, and often simultaneously—a leading exponent of the cult of violence and a subtle philosophical force in the novel; a calculating terrorist and (as in *Sartoris*); a slick-magazine sentimentalist of the gladiola South; the most meticulous and misanthropic historian of the South's degeneration and a country-store humorist; an Edgar Allan Poe undecided whether to play Bret Harte[39] or Oswald Spengler. He has been all things to himself. Like Tolstoy at Yasnaya Polyana,[40] he has in one sense been a provincial fastening upon universality, a provincial whose roots are so deep that the very depth and intensity of his immersion have made for a submarine cosmopolitanism of the spirit. His imagination is of itself so extraordinarily rich and uncontrolled, his conscious conceptions so few and indifferent, that he has been able to create an irony of a higher order than he himself shares. For his imagination is not merely creative in the familiar sense; it is devastatingly brilliant, and at the same time impure; it is a kind of higher ventriloquism, a capriciousness at once almost too self-conscious in its trickery and inventiveness, yet not conscious enough, not even direct or responsible enough, in its scope and deliberation.

"I want you to tell me just one thing more," the young Canadian, Shreve McCannon, says to Quentin Compson[41] in *Absalom, Absalom!* "Why do you hate the South?" "I don't hate it," Quentin said quickly, at once, immediately; "I dont hate it," he said. *I dont hate it*, he thought, panting in the cold air, the iron New England dark; *I dont, I dont! I dont hate it! I dont hate it!* By identifying all life with the South, by giving himself so completely to it, Faulkner showed why he could see all things in it and at the same time draw no clear design from it. His absorption was too complete; it was almost a form of abnegation. Accepting the South, hating it, memorializing it, losing himself in it, Faulkner was forced into a series of improvisations; and his need for pyrotechnics and a swollen Elizabethanism of rhetoric, his delight in difficulty and random inventiveness, became the expression of his need to impose some external intensity, an almost synthetic unity upon his novels. The nerve-jangled harshness and self-conscious grandeur of his work show only one elaboration of that inner confusion, that compulsion to brood always at polar extremes. More significant has been his need to present almost all his characters at the unwavering pitch of absolute desperation and damnation, to expand everything to a size larger than life and ambiguously more tragic, to represent everything—every life, every thought, every action—as something unutterably lost and doomed.

There is a pillar of darkness that moves between the Faulkner characters and the world—blotting out the sun, blotting out our simple and confident knowledge of their qualities and relations to each other, blotting out their normality. But if this darkness is in one sense the equivalent atmosphere of Faulkner's misanthropy and bitterness, it is also a mechanism, a stage apparatus, that provides an artificial medium within which his people move, and it suggests some secret and harried compensation for his failure. For what one always feels in even Faulkner's greatest moments is not a lack or falsity of achievement; it is a power almost grotesque in its lack of relation to the situation or character; it is a greatness moving in void. From this point of view the mechanical damnation of his characters is not a valid projection of some conception of damnation which must include everything that draws breath in the South; it is a simple lack of flexibility, some cardinal stiffness or agony of imagination. It is significant to note that while Faulkner's ability to create character has always been superb, his characters are not so much a succession of individuals freshly, directly visualized and created, as molds into which the same fantastic qualities have been poured. They live, they live copiously and brilliantly; but they live by the violence with which Faulkner sustains them, by the sullen, screaming intensity which he breathes into them (often with all of Faulkner's own gestures, fury, and raging confusion of pronouns), by the atmospheric terror, that encloses them, They live because they are incredibilities in action, because they have been scoured by death before they reach the grave, so that one sees them always, in the posture of some fantastic relinquishment and irrevocable agony, the body taut and the soul quivering with death. And if they seem forever to be watching and waiting in their own stupor, to be accumulated sensations rather than people having sensations, to be even the same extreme sensations (the doctor in *The Wild Palms*, Quentin Compson and old Mr. Coldfield in *Absalom, Absalom!*, young Bayard in *The Unvanquished*, the young teacher in *The Hamlet*, Joe Christmas and almost everyone else in *Light in August*), is it not because they are personifications rather than human beings, and is it not their astounding capacity for unhappiness and perdition, a confession of some final awkwardness in Faulkner—his need to write and think in monotones?

Nervously alive, his characters are fundamentally not alive at all, not acting out individual parts, but seem rather to be pure fantastic aggregates. They are multiform qualities acting out, participating in that general myth of Faulkner's creation, the jungle South, and it is significant that the darkness in which they live, the darkness through which they must always be grasped and pieced together, makes them appear curiously distant refractions of refractions. In the end we seem always to be reading the same story, following through the familiar formula of damnation, conscious of the same mysterious submission—extraordinarily abject—to perdition. Yet though the energy that drives them along is torrential, we do not see *them* intensely; we see everything under *conditions* of intensity. It is precisely because Faulkner's characters are charged with a vitality not their own that his is able to do everything with them except make us believe instinctively and absolutely in them. And it is precisely because Faulkner does not know too much about them himself, does not believe in them with sufficient consciousness of purpose, that he is forced into those leaping improvisations of language and incident, that nervous magnificence, which invests everything with epic grandeur that is suspiciously grandiose, that plots and strains and leaves us all too often with the mere fact of tumultuous exaggeration.

"It is with fiction as with religion," Herman Melville wrote in *The Confidence Man*, "it should present another world, and yet one to which we feel the tie." Even at its best, as in the portrait of old Mr. Coldfield in *Absalom, Absalom!*, Faulkner's extraordinary nervous achievement seems rooted in something purely arbitrary, not to say synthetic. Old Mr. Coldfield had barricaded himself *against* the Civil War, had locked himself up and stolidly starved to death because he disapproved of the idea of waste—"of wearing out and eating up and shooting away material in any cause whatsoever." The scene, the image created, is magnificently original, but it is grotesque. Faulkner carries it off with his usual high exhilarated energy, but while it is "convincing" on its own terms, it is an improvisation of pure fantasy and basically unreal. So with the lyrical record of the love of the idiot Snopes[42] in *The Hamlet* for his neighbor's cow. The long dithyramb is clever mimicry and wry, gleeful sentimentality, an idealization that is mostly parody; yet though the mood is sustained almost too well, it is a caricature that mocks itself, a tour de force so calculating that it is corrupt. So with the extraordinary last scene in *The Sound and the Fury,* Faulkner's greatest achievement, the famous—and more than a little cheap—coffin scene in *As I Lay Dying*, the whole scheme of Sanctuary (admittedly a deliberate shocker), the flight of the Negro slaves in *The Unvanquished* when the Confederate armies are broken, the flood scene in *The Wild Palms*. There is always in Faulkner some final obsessive exaggeration, some half-careless, half-cynical grotesquerie, that spoils. And even when he opens upon a scene of complete sincerity and power as in *Light in August*, with its unforgettable image of Lena Grove, pregnant, walking from Alabama to Mississippi, shoes in her hand, looking for her lover, everything is soon engulfed in boiling rhetoric and the impossible plot. Yet though Faulkner's overwriting is usually a striving for total effect, for a kind of over-all intensity that springs from the abundance and confusion of his extraordinary resources, he can caricature his best efforts by some unwilling inflection, as in the scene in *The Hamlet* (admittedly a scene of high comedy) where Mrs. Varner, vexed with her errant daughter and puritanical son, rages: "I'll fix him. I'll fix both of them. Turning up pregnant and yelling and cursing here in the house when I am trying to take a nap!" Not always unwillingly, of course; the fantastic duel between Charles and Henry in *Absalom, Absalom!* at the most critical juncture of the Civil War (love conquers all!), lie so much else in Faulkner, suggests an element of protruding bad taste, often mere carelessness or indifference extending itself into vulgarity. And it suggests what almost every reader of Faulkner must feel at one time or another, his inability to choose between Dostoevsky and Hollywood Boulevard.[43]

In the end one must always return to Faulkner's language and his conception of style, for his every character and observation are lost in the spool of his rhetoric, and no more than they can he ever wind himself free. That rhetoric—perhaps the most elaborate, intermittently incoherent and ungrammatical, thunderous, polyphonic rhetoric in all American writing— explains why he always plays as great a role in his novels as any of his characters to the point of acting out their characters in himself; why he has so often appeared to be a Laocoon writhing in all the outrageous confusions of the ineffable; why he has been able, correlating the South with every imagined principle and criticism of existence, writing in many styles, to project every possible point of view, every shade or extremity of character, and to persuade us of none. In one sense, of course, Faulkner has sought to express the inexpressible, to attain that which is basically incoherent in the novel and analogous only to the most intense mysticism in poetry, where sensations contract and expand like tropical flowers. Yet his novels are not poetry or even "poetic"; they are linked together by a sensational lyricism, itself forever in extremis and gasping for breath, that, as Yeats said of rhetoric, "is an attempt of the will to do the work of the imagination." For what one sees always in Faulkner's mountainous rhetoric, with its fantastic pseudo-classical epithets and invertebrate grandeur, its merely verbal intensity and inherent motor violence, is the effort of a writer to impose himself upon that which he cannot create simply and evocatively. It is the articulation of confusion rather than an evasion of it; a force passing for directed energy. With all its occasional felicity and stabbing appropriateness of phrase, Faulkner's style is a discursive fog, and it is not strange—so clever and ready is his style, the advantage taken over confusion itself—that his extremities should seem intimations of grandeur and the darkness within which his characters move in an atmosphere of genuine tragedy.

"By April," we read of the idiot Snopes's infatuation with the cow in *The Hamlet*, "it was the actual thin depthless suspension of false dawn itself, in which he could already see and know himself to be an entity solid and cohered in visibility instead of the uncohered all sentience of fluid and nerve-springing terror alone and terribly free in the primal sightless inimicality." Or Varner's[44] trip to Ab Snopes's[45] farm:

> When he passed beyond the house he saw it—the narrow high frame like an epicene gallows, two big absolutely static young women beside it, who even in that first glance postulated that immobile dreamy solidarity of statuary (this only emphasized by the fact that they both seemed to be talking at once and to some listener—or perhaps just circumambience—at a considerable distance and neither listening to the other at all) even though one of them had hold of the well-rope, her arms extended at full reach, her body bent for the down pull like a figure in a charade, a carved piece symbolizing some terrific physical effort which had died with its inception, though a moment later the pulley began again its rusty plaint.

The point made, the evocation sought, have passed into endless convoluted variations; and even the incredibility of the scene (who was it saw "that immobile dreamy solidarity of statuary"—a mean backwoods trader like Jody Varner?) seems less fantastic than the mechanical elaboration of the image. Faulkner's perpetual need for some verbal splendor a merely illustrative richness, always, suggests some self-fascinated energy, not the moving intensity of a writer who throws the weight of his body into each word; and it is not strange that his most magnificent effect should so often seem pointless. So in *The Sound and the Fury* Quentin Compson ruminates on a classmate sculling on the

Charles River alone:

> Gerlad would be sort of grand too, pulling in lonely state across the noon, rowing himself right out of noon, up the long bright air like an apotheosis, mounting into a drowsing infinity where only he and the gull, the one terrifically motionless, the other in a steady and measured pull and recovery that partook of inertia itself, the world punily beneath their shadows on the sun.

Jody Varner, taking his sister Eula to school, "had a vision of himself transporting not only across the village's horizon but across the embracing proscenium of the entire inhabited world like the sun itself, a kaleidoscopic convolution of mammalian ellipses." Or Faulkner will begin with one of those perfect and tangential perceptions that light up his books, that perfect talent for incidental perception, and crush it to death, as when Flem Snopes's[46] metallic bow-tie becomes a tiny viciously depthless cryptically balanced splash like an enigmatic punctuation symbol against the expanse of white shirt which gave him Jody Varner's look of ceremonial heterodoxy raised to its tenth power and which postulated to those who had been present on that day that quality of outrageous overstatement of physical displacement which the sound of his father's stiff foot made on the gallery of the store that afternoon in the spring.

Yet why must everything in Faulkner's novels be raised to its tenth power? Why must the idiot Snopes's love agony become "starspawn and hieroglyph, the fierce white dying rose, then gradual and invincible speeding up to and into slack-flood's coronal of nympholept noon"? Why must Rosa Coldfield's[47] hatred of men become "that fond dear constant violation of privacy, that stultification of the burgeoning and incorrigible I which is the mead and due of all mammalian meat, become not mistress, not beloved, but more than even love. I became all polymath love's androgynous advocate"? Why is it that the Faulkner country must always appear as "a shadowy miasmic region," "amoral evil's undeviating absolute," a "quicksand of nightmare," "the seething and anonymous miasmal mass which in all the years of time has taught itself no boon of death"? For the same reason, as it must appear, that despite his extraordinary talents no writer has ever seemed so ambitious and so purposeless, so over-whelming in imaginative energy and so thwarted in his application of it. A fanatic, as Santayana once said, is a man who redoubles his effort when he has lost sight of his aim; and even if it be admitted that Faulkner's effort has been to express the inexpressible, to write the history of the unconscious, to convey some final and terrifying conception of a South that seems always to exist below water, the impression one always carries away from his novels is of some fantastic exertion of will, of that exaggeration which springs from a need to raise everything in Yoknapatawpha County, Mississippi, to its tenth (or its hundredth) power because there is not sufficient belief, or power, or ease in his conception of Yoknapatawpha County, or the South, or human existence in general.

It is not strange, then that his scene should always be some swamp of the spirit, or that his subject should always be murder, rape, prostitution, incest, arson, idiocy (with an occasional interpolation of broad country humor almost as violent as his tragedies); or that the country of his mind should be a Mississippi county larger than life, but not visibly related to it. Faulkner's obsession has been agony, as his art has been the voice of that agony—the agony of a culture, his culture; but it has been even more the agony of his relation to that culture, the tormenting disproportion between his immersion in the South and his flinging, tumultuous efforts to project it. It has been the agony inherent in any effort to transcend some basic confusion by force of will alone. Faulkner's corned, tobacco-drooling phantoms are not the constituents of a representative American epic, protagonists in a great modern tragedy; they are the tonal expression of Faulkner's own torment, the walking phantasmagoria, sensation beating against sensation, of his perpetual tension. No writer ever made so much of his failure; in no writer of his stature is the suggestion of some cardinal failure so ambiguous and yet so penetrating.

2

From another point of view, however, Faulkner's example has a significant historic interest. He represents, as almost everyone has felt, the perpetuation of seemingly inveterate Southern romanticism, the tradition of the weird tale and the grotesque, the florid Southern chevalier defying the heavens by sheer force of rhetoric; but he stands also as a forerunner, and along with Thomas Wolfe and a writer like Henry Miller,[48] as a prime example of a new school of sensibility in the contemporary American novel. Few writers, certainly, have ever exploited so many of the devices of naturalism and remained so basically different in kind from naturalism; and it is curious but significant that Faulkner, one of the patron saints of the cult of violence, a writer who has presented younger novelists with a veritable patrimony of brutality and calculated terrorism and the technique of shock, should actually represent a rejection of naturalism—even of the conventional scheme of realism—that is as marked in contemporary American writing as the passionate social consciousness and materialism of so many left-wing and hard-boiled novelists.

For the violence of Faulkner's novels is, at bottom, not the violent expression of a criticism of society, but the struggles of a sensibility at war with itself, just as the emotionalism of Thomas Wolfe's novels suggests the efforts of a sensibility to comprehend itself, and Henry Miller's the sense of outrage inflicted by society upon the individual soul. The frantic ubiquitous "I" in their books, its manifold agony and susceptibility to rhetoric, marks something more than the explicit rejection of the characteristic mechanisms of realism found in the formalism and preciosity of distinguished craftsmen like Elizabeth Madox Roberts,[49] Kay Boyle, and Katherine Anne Porter. It marks the rise of a school of agony, of romantic sensibility, that is perhaps unconscious in its negation of realism. This "school" is not in any sense a school at all; it does not even stem from a common tradition, save as Henry Miller has acknowledged his debt to Whitman, and Wolfe continually betrayed his; save as Faulkner insistently recalls a whole gallery of American romanticists from Poe through Melville to Ambrose Bierce.[50] Few writers have ever seemed so different in intelligence, or clashed so irreconcilably on so many vital points; yet for all their presumabel lack even of common sympathy, Faulkner and Wolfe particularly represent a tormented individualism in the contemporary novel, a self-centered romanticism, a vitality expressing itself in and through rhetoric, that is one of the most significant phenomena in the moral history of contemporary literature.

Different as Wolfe and Faulkner are, the common note one hears in them is one of pure terror. They represent, like the surrealists, like the anxious and moving search for spiritual integrity in so much contemporary poetry, the loneliness of the individual sensibility in a period of un-paralleled dissolution and insecurity; and they represent even more vividly a reaction against a literature of surface realism that merely records the facts of that dissolution: Like Melville's Captain Ahab, they could both say, "that inscrutable thing is chiefly what I hate," for their violence is the expression of their obsession with the evil that lurks under the surface of contemporary society and thought. In that sense they may be said to represent the subterranean life of the spirit in a society too pressed to preserve, much less to foster, an extreme type of sensibility. Yet what so many have felt even in so cultist and avant-garde a writer as Henry Miller, his essential commonness of spirit—"a naturally genial American," as Philip Rahv said, "who has been through hell"—is in a sense true of Faulkner, for all of his technical virtuosity, and of Wolfe, an ego-centered boy. All these writers seem remote from average men only because of the intensity of their self-exploration; but it is just their capacity for expressing all the fever and exacerbation and gnawing humiliation of average men today that identifies them. They are not great religious spirits or mystics or poets, examples of the inviolate private intelligence that fashions an arbitrary and purely individual conception of existence and compels others to believe in it. Nor are they—not even Faulkner, for all his legerdemain—technicians of the novel, great craftsmen who attempt to mold the novel into a new form of inquiry. They are materialists flying in the face of contemporary materialism; and it is always the agony of common life—the commonness raised "to the tenth power"—that identifies and torments them, for their sensibility is the expression of their reaction against the indignity and violation suffered by men like them. Like D. H. Lawrence, they could say, and with equal ardor: The only thing unbearable is the degradation, the prostitution of the living mysteries in us. Let man only approach his own self with a deep respect, even reverence for all that the creative soul, the "God-mystery" within us, puts forth. But it is of degradation, not of the God-mystery, that they speak. There is no religion in these writers; there is only the religious intensity brought to the understanding of men's alienation from each other today.

It is their rhetoric, a mountainous verbal splendor, that holds these writers together; and it is a very American rhetoric. Just as Trollope said of Hawthorne's weird tales that he believed them to be not manufactured in the Gothic tradition, "but something indigenous, something inescapably there," so it is impossible not to feel in Faulkner and Wolfe and Miller an indiscriminate vitality, a pride in their fresh and overflowing power, that goes back to Whitman, to Melville, to the creators of the great mass-myths of Davy Crockett and Paul Bunyan[51], Johnny Appleseed and Mike Fink. In Faulkner and Wolfe the extravagant and ornamental tradition of Southern rhetoric is manifest, but like Henry Miller (and is there anything more

American than the picture of this last endmost violent of the expatriates, hating America and all its deeds in torrential profanity, yet worshiping Whitman in the slums of Paris?), they are all big men in the colloquial tradition of American demigods—living big, writing big, exuding a power somehow more than their own, a national power in which they share. Colossal even in their extreme neuroticism, they retain all the epic force that went into the making of the great legends of American power and the American promise. Just so did Wolfe burn himself out trying to bring all the rivers, sights, sounds, pleasures, torments, books in America within the compass of the one long novel he wrote all his life. Just so did he express his final contempt, in *You Can't Go Home Again,* for "the world's fool-bigotry, fool-ignorance, fool-cowardice, fool-faddism, fool-mockery, fool-stylism, and fool-hatred for anyone who was not corrupted, beaten, and a fool." Just so has Faulkner invested his every observation of Southern life and manners with epic grandeur, epic hints and portents, Aeschylean darkness and primeval rage. Just so has Henry Miller seen in the contemporary crisis the intimations of an absolute doom, a world dying in pandemonium, "the earth moving out of its orbit," and written with significant exhilaration, in *Tropic of Cancer,* that

> Art consists in going the full length…The task which the artist implicitly set himself is to overthrow existing values, to make of the chaos about him an order which is his own, to sow strife and ferment so that by the emotional release those who are dead may be restored to life.

The significance of these writers thus lies in the subject of their energy. They ate the epic recorders of demoralization and collapse, specialists in doom, as Whitman was the first great voice of American nationality, or Mark Twain of the frontier legends, or Melville of the exuberant myth-making prowess of the imaginative mind in America. In *Tropic of Cancer* Henry Miller wrote:

It may be that we are doomed, that there is no hope for us; *any of us*; but if that is so then let us set up, a last agonizing, blood-curdling howl, a screech of defiance, a war-whoop! Away with lamentations! Away with elegies and dirges! Away with biographies and histories, and libraries and museums! Let the dead bury the dead. Let us living ones dance about the rim of the crater, a last expiring dance. But a dance!

Miller's extremism, however, gives itself away by the sheer exhilaration of his own energy, just as Faulkner's monotonal despair has always seemed the ironic negation of his extraordinary imaginative vitality, and Wolfe's Herculean boyishness always the expression of some uncontrolled power expending itself on every object in view. There is a native strength in all these writers, a comic exaggeration, that always makes a theme of its own prodigality. And it is precisely because their resources are so overwhelming, and so uncontrolled, precisely because their vitality is tumultuous and self-fascinated and desperate, that they embody a perpetual *mal du siecle*,[52] a furious sickness and rage. It is as if the long and deep estrangement of the modern American writer from his society—the inveterate air of crisis which he bears within it—had reached a climax, found some extreme symbol in them. Seeing their unhappiness, or the unhappiness of their relations with the world, in gargantuan terms, they have made epics and historical chronicles and quasi-philosophical systems out of that conflict; but the theme has always been the individual, their own individualism, and their strength, the intensity—majestic and all-inclusive in its rhetoric—possible only to a type of sensibility that hears the reverberation of the world's collapse in the fever ecstasies and desperations of its own isolation. That isolation, expressing itself in many different forms and rhythms and themes, is the central thing in Faulkner, and it tells the story, directly and lividly, of Thomas Wolfe.

〔注释〕

Chapter 12

1. *This Side of Paradise*：《人间天堂》，菲茨杰拉德（F. Scott Fitzgerald）所著，1920 年出版。下文中 *Three Soldiers*：《三个士兵》，约翰·多斯·帕索斯所写的战争小说，1921 年出版。*Winesburg*：即 *Winesburg，Ohio*《小城畸人》，舍伍德·安德森（Sherwood Anderson）的一部短篇小说集，1919 年出版。*Main Street*：《大街》，辛克莱·刘易斯（Sinclair Lewis）所著，1920 年出版。*Jurgen*：《朱尔根》，卡贝尔（James Branch Cabell）的小说，1919 年出版。*My Antonia*：《我的安东尼亚》，女作家薇拉·凯瑟（Willa Cather）所著，1918 年出版。

2. "flapper generation"：源于菲茨杰拉德的小说《轻佻女郎与哲学家》（*Flappers and Philosophers*），书中描绘了一战后美国年轻一代狂歌痛饮、尽情取乐的生活。

3. "the sad young men"：出自菲茨杰拉德所著《所有的痛苦的年轻人》（*All the Sad Young Men*，1926）。下文中 "the beautiful and the damned"：出自菲茨杰拉德所著《漂亮的冤家》（*The Beautiful and the Damned*，1922）。

4. Louis Aragon：路易·阿拉贡（1897-1982），法国文学家，早年曾参与"达达主义"和超现实主义运动，后逐渐转入现实主义，并在思想上倾向社会主义，一生有许多创作。下文中 Ernst Toller：厄恩斯特·托勒尔（1893-1939），德国表现主义剧作家、诗人。他也是 20 世纪 20 年代德国著名的左翼政治活动家。Wilfred Owen：威尔弗雷德·欧文（1893-1918），英国诗人，诗歌多描写战争的残酷，于一战结束前夕阵亡，死后其诗作陆续出版。

5. Warren G. Harding：哈定（1865-1923），美国第 29 届总统。

6. 20 世纪 20 年代成名的许多作家都来自中西部诸州，如海明威（伊利诺州）、麦克尔蒙（Robert McAlmon，1895-1956，堪萨斯州）、凯瑟林·安·波特（Katherine Anne Porter，1890-1980，得克萨斯州）、韦斯科特（Glenway Wescott，1901-1987，威斯康星州）、卡洛琳·戈登（Caroline Gordon, 1895-1981，田纳西州）等，而且多数作品内容也是关于中西部小城和乡村生活的。下文中 Caporetto：指第一次世界大战中的卡波雷托战役。1917 年 10 月，德奥军队在奥意边境地带对意大利发动总攻，意军损失惨重，全线溃退。海明威在他的《永别了，武器》（*A Farewell to Arms*, 1929）中对此战役有生动的描述。Dada："达达主义"，20 世纪初在欧洲兴起的文学艺术思潮，它反对一切传统的审美观和价值观。"达达主义"后来与超现实主义合流，并成为超现实主义的思想基础。Picasso：西班牙大画家、立体派创始人毕加索（1881-1973），在 20 世纪初叶以艺术革新而闻名。

7. John Peale Bishop：约翰·皮尔·毕肖普（1892-1944），美国诗人，作品有诗集《绿色的果子》（*Green Fruit*, 1917）等。

8. Eheu fugaces!：法语，意为 "Alas，the transient things!"

9. Calvin Coolidge：柯立芝（1872-1933），美国第 30 届总统。

10. 此外指第一次世界大战前后美国社会风气的变化，例如战后美国年轻女郎（flappers）着短裙，留短发，吸烟醉酒狂舞，旧传统和道德规范受到挑战，趋于瓦解。"prohibited liquor"：禁酒，美国于 1920 年通过禁酒令，至 1933 年方正式取消。不少人通过私自酿造和贩运禁酒大发横财。

11. Rudolph Valentino：瓦伦蒂诺（1895-1926），美国好莱坞明星。20 世纪 20 年代他的影片风靡全美，许多妇女将其推崇为"伟大的情人"。下文中 Amory Blaine：艾默里·布莱恩，菲茨杰拉德的成名作《人间天堂》（*This Side of Paradise*）的主人公。

12. Alfred de Musset：缪塞（1810-1857），法国诗人及剧作家。Rolla：罗拉，缪塞的长叙事诗《罗拉》（*Rolla*）中的主人公。

13. 法语，意为 "I've come too late to the world which is too old for me."

14. Long Island，长岛，纽约市东南一座繁华的岛屿，《大人物盖茨比》（*The Great Gatsby*）即以此为地点展开故事。

15. Hergesheimer：约瑟夫·赫杰什码（1880-1954），美国作家，著名作品之一为《野桔子》。

16. Monroe Stahr：菲茨杰拉德未竟之作《最后的巨头》（*The Last Tycoon*）中的主人公，一家电影制片厂的老板。下文中 Cartier：以法国航海家卡蒂埃（1491-1557）命名的宝石。

17. *Esquire*：《老爷》，美国一家月刊。

18. the Norton-Harjes Ambulance Service：第一次世界大战期间美国在法国战场上的救护车队，当时有不少年轻人，包括哈佛大学和耶鲁大学的毕业生参加该队，其中一些人后来成为作家。

19. *What Price Glory?*：《荣誉值几个钱?》，安德森（Maxwell Anderson，1888-1959）与斯达林斯（Laurence Stallings,1894-1968）合写的一出反战喜剧，1924 年上演。该剧描写了一对老兵痞子——弗莱格上尉和他拆不散的老对头奎尔特上士大战中在巴黎一家酒馆经历的一场闹剧。

20. Barbusse：巴比塞（1873-1935），法国文学家，法国共产党员，著有描写第一次世界大战的小说《火线》（*Le Fen*）等。

21. Sassoon：萨松（1886-1967），英国诗人，以其激烈的反战诗歌而闻名。

22. *Cest de la blague*：法语，意为 “This is but a joke.”

23. Marshal Poch：福煦元帅（1851-1921），第一次世界大战中法军主要将领之一。

24. Jean Le Negre：卡明斯所著《巨大的房间》中一人物，黑人。

25. the Black Bourse：黑市。

26. Wyndham Lewis：温德姆·刘易斯（1884-1957），英国作家与画家，作品带有强烈的现代派色彩。

27. Al Capone：卡彭（1899-1947），美国有名的歹徒，20 世纪 20 年代为芝加哥犯罪集团首领。

28. 参阅海明威所著短篇小说《在密西根州》（“Up in Michigan”）。

29. 法国现实主义大师福楼拜（Flaubert, 1821-1880）讲求用字精确，认为对作家来说不存在什么同义词，他必找到 “le seul motjuste”（法语，意为 “the only right word”）。

30. Edmund Wilson：埃德蒙·威尔逊（1895-1972），美国作家、

评论家。

31. Harry Morgan and Philip：分别为 *To Have and Have Not* 和 *The Fifth Column* 中之主人公。

32. OGPU：1925 至 1933 年间苏联的特务组织。

33. Jake Barnes 和 Lady Bret 为《太阳照常升起》中的主要人物。

34. 参阅堂恩所著《沉思十七》("Meditation XVII")。海明威《丧钟为谁而鸣》(*For Whom the Bell Tolls*) 一书之书名出自《沉思十七》，其中有 "Any man's death diminishes me because I am involved in mankind, and therefore never send to know for whom the bell tolls, it tolls for thee" 等句。上文中 Robert Jordon, Maria 和 Pilar 均为《丧钟为谁而鸣》中的人物。

Chapter 15

35. Jefferson：杰佛逊镇，福克纳以家乡为原型虚构的小镇，是他的著名的"约克那帕塔法县"(Yoknapatawpha) 县府所在地。福克纳小说几乎都以这一地区为背景，有"约克那帕塔法世系"之称。

36. Sartoris：萨托利斯，福克纳虚构的一个家族，人物众多，形形色色。在《萨托利斯》(*Sartaris*,1929)，与《未被征服的》(*The Unvanquished*，1938) 两部作品中，这个家族居主角地位。下文中 Snopes：斯诺普斯，为福克纳小说世界中另一重要家族，他在三部曲《村子》(*The Hamlet*，1940)、《小镇》(*The Town*，1957) 及《大宅》(*The Mansion*，1959) 中描写这个家族的兴衰。

37. George Washington Cable：乔治·华盛顿·卡布尔 (1844-1925)，美国小说家，出生于弗吉尼亚州，作品有浓郁的南部地方色彩。

38. Conrad Aiken：康拉德·艾肯 (1889-1973)，美国作家、评论家。

39. Bret Hart：哈特 (1836-1902)，美国作家。他的作品具有浓烈的乡土色彩，善于描绘当时西部的边疆生活，著有短篇小说集《喧腾露营地的拉克》(*The Luck of Roaring Camp*，1868) 等。下文中 Oswald Spengler：施本格勒 (1880-1936)，德国哲学家，著有《西方的没落》

（*The Decline of the West*, 1926-1928），认为西方文明已度过创造阶段，进入反思和物质享受阶段，而未来注定要走向衰亡。

40. Tolstoy：托尔斯泰（1829-1910），俄国著名作家。Yasnaya Polyana：雅斯纳亚·波利亚纳，是托尔斯泰的家乡，在莫斯科以南160公里。

41. Shreve McCannon says to Quentin Compson：二者皆为小说《押沙龙，押沙龙!》（*Absalom, Absalom!*）中人物，其中昆丁（Quentin）是小说主人公，托马斯·萨特潘（Thomas Sutpen）的朋友康普森将军（General Compson）的孙子，为故事的主要叙述者。昆丁也是描写康普森家族败落经过的《喧嚣与愤怒》（*The Sound and the Fury*）一书中的重要人物之一。下面所引对话见《押沙龙，押沙龙!》的结尾。

42. the idiot Snopes：《村子》中人物，名 Ike，是斯诺普斯家族中一个白痴，爱上了邻家的母牛。

43. Hollywood Boulevard：20世纪40年代，福克纳迫于生计，曾一度为好莱坞撰写电影剧本。

44. Varner：即威尔·瓦纳，《村子》中人物，原为当地经济巨头，后被斯诺普斯族挤垮。

45. Ab Snopes：艾伯·斯诺普斯，《村子》中人物，斯诺普斯家族第一代，曾是瓦纳家的佃农。

46. Flem Snopes：弗莱姆·斯诺普斯，《村子》等书中人物，该家族第二代。他野心勃勃，贪婪成性，由一个佃农的儿子发迹成为当地显赫人物，后被亲戚所杀。

47. Rosa Coldfield：罗莎·寇德菲尔德，《押沙龙，押沙龙!》中人物，老寇菲尔德之女，托马斯·萨特潘之妻妹。萨特潘丧妻后曾与之订婚，后因萨特潘欲行不轨，罗莎离开了他。

48. Henry Miller：亨利·米勒（1891-1980），美国小说家，20世纪30年代旅居巴黎，作品大多为自传性，带有强烈的个人主义思想色调，追求个性自由。由于他的小说中色情较多，在英美等国一度被禁。

49. Elizabeth Madox Roberts：伊丽莎白·马多克斯·罗伯茨（1886-1941），美国女作家，著有不少以故乡肯塔基州为背景的小说，以反映地方风情和语言见长。下文中 Kay Boyle：凯·傅伊尔（1903-1992），美国女作家，曾移居法国，著有许多小说和诗歌。Katherine Anne Porter：凯瑟琳·安妮·波特（1890-1980），美国著名的南方女作家，擅长写短篇小说，著有长篇《愚人船》（*Ship of Fools*, 1962）。

50. Ambrose Bierce：安布罗斯·比尔斯（1842-1914），美国记者、作家。短篇小说集《士兵和平民的故事》（*Tales of Soldiers and Civilians*, 1891）等可称其作品中的上乘之作，颇有爱伦·坡的风格。

51. Paul Bunyan：保尔·班扬，伐木巨人，美国边疆开拓的神话人物。他的故事不仅在民间广为流传，而且出现在文学作品中。

52. *mal du siecle*：法语，意为 "sickness of the century"。

Questions For Discussion：

1. Define "the Lost Generation." Why does Kazin say that Fitzgerald's life was "a lost-generation legend"? Discuss the importance of Fitzgerald in American literature.

2. Comment upon Hemingway's theme, style, and the typical Hemingway hero who appears and reappears in his fictional world. Discuss Hemingway's values with reference to his major works, and define his tragic vision.

3. Discuss William Faulkner's relationship to the South and his conception of it in his novels. What is his contribution to the modern American novel? Analyze the "pillar of darkness" which reigns supreme in his fictional Yoknapatawpha, and comment upon the enormous technical energy that goes into its creation.

4. Do you agree that, from a historical point of view, Faulkner is the greatest novelist of the twentieth century?

For Further Reference：

1. Alfred Kazin. *Bright Book of Life: American Novelists and*

Storytellers from Hemingway to Mailer. Boston: 1971.

2. Warren French, ed. *The Twenties: Fiction, Poetry, Drama*. Deland, Florida: 1975.

3. Louis D. Rubin and Robert D. Jacobs, eds. *Southern Renaissance: The Literature of Modern South*. Baltimore: 1953.

Charles Burt Harris

〔作者介绍〕

　　查尔斯·伯尔特·哈里斯（Charles Burt Harris，1940- ），美国文学评论家，美国现代语言协会、中西部现代语言协会、大学英语学会、大学教授协会等学术组织的成员，多年来从事 20 世纪美国文学，尤其是当代美国小说的研究，迄今已出版《当代美国荒诞派小说家》(*Contemporary American Novelists of the Absurd*, 1971)、《激情与技巧：约翰·巴斯的小说》(*Passionate Virtuosity: The Fiction of John Barth*)等专著以及一些专论文章。

Contemporary American Novelists of the Absurd

〔作品介绍〕

　　《当代美国荒诞派小说家》是论述 20 世纪 60 年代美国荒诞派小说家的一部专著，1971 年由美国纽黑文学院和大学出版社出版。

　　本书共分六章。第一章讨论了"荒诞美学"问题。它集中探讨了荒诞派小说产生的社会、思想及文化背景，追溯了荒诞派小说在美国的发展过程，分析了荒诞派小说的独特的创作技巧。作者认为，60 年代小说家生活在一个混乱和毫无意义的荒诞世界里，人们似已习惯于它的荒诞，因而变得无动于衷。敏感的作家认识到，沿用传统的创作方法已不足以表现这个世界的面目和本质，不足以唤起人们的充分注意。他们感到，他们必须使用一种全新的表现方法。他们对传统小说进行滑稽性模仿，嘲笑传统的文学观点如文学为现实、赋予现实以秩序和美学形式的观点，运用表现在情节、性格塑造及语言方面的"荒诞的技巧"，表达他们对荒诞世界的认识。这种形式与内容的融合是美国小说发展中一项重要的革新。

作者着重分析了代表这一派别的四位小说家——约瑟夫·海勒（Joseph Heller, 1923- ）、小库尔特·冯尼格特（Kurt Vonnegut, Jr., 1922- ）、托马斯·品钦（Thomas Pynchon, 1937- ）及约翰·巴思（John Barth, 1923- ），他们的主要作品多发表在 60 年代，是当代美国文坛出现的最重要的荒诞小说。对四位作家的评析在书中所占篇幅大体相同，每人各占一章。由于他们的表现手法有不少共同之处，作者在每章中只着重阐述该章里作家的主要特点。例如在讨论海勒的《第二十二条军规》（Catch-22）时，对小说家的模仿手法、语言及结构进行了透彻分析，详细说明了这些手法对表现作品的荒诞主题所发挥的作用。《第二十二条军规》运用模仿的方式，它的语言本身的荒诞特点，它的否定逻辑秩序的结构，都是美国小说创作中的革新表现，它的出版标志着"荒诞的十年"的开端。

冯尼格特的小说经历了从讽刺到荒诞、从早期的抗议到《第五号屠宰场》的泰然隐忍的发展过程。随着他对荒诞认识的加深，他在刻画"二维式人物"等方面的技巧革新也大大加强。他对世界的荒诞本质的深刻认识并未使他变得空虚、愤世嫉俗或绝望，他能正视生活的荒诞，同时又能保留对人类命运的关切以及他的幽默感。笑可以医治生活的痛苦和失望。在品钦的作品里，现代科学，特别是现代物理学中"熵"的原理（即宇宙能量分布逐渐趋向相同的原理）和量子论（认为一切事物都包含有不确定性的理论），对他表现荒诞的主题有不可小觑的影响。他的名作《V.》（V.）便是醒目的例子，"V"有着多种含义。巴思虽然接受"小说已死"的思想，但是他把这种观点反映到自己的素材和创作手段中，创作出具有非凡活力的小说。他巧妙地运用模仿和闹剧，把语言、情节和形式融为一种表现他的荒诞认识的象征，从而保证小说的生命力的延续。作者认为，这几位作家通过自己的创作表明了自己卓越的艺术才能。

本书最后一章讨论了"坎普"（Camp）艺术和流行艺术同荒诞小说的关系。荒诞派小说家从"坎普"和流行艺术形式中看到另外一种否定传统小说概念的可能性。通过采用这两种艺术形式，荒诞派小说家否定和摈弃那种假定本身可以"发现"世界的意义和秩序的小说。因此，他们采用"非严肃"的形式以达到严肃的目的。在这一章里，作者还讨论了包括唐纳德•巴塞尔米（Donald Barthelme）在内的年轻作家所写的一些荒诞小说。

作者指出，荒诞派小说并不局限于美国，阿根廷小说家博尔赫斯（Jorge Luis Borges）和美籍俄国作家纳波科夫（Vladimir Nabokov）都在自己作品中突出地表现出"荒诞"态度和手法。作者还指出，本书虽集中分析 60 年代前后的小说，但是运用荒诞技巧表现荒诞主题的个别作品在 60 年代以前便已出现，如韦斯特（Nathanael West）的小说；韦斯特在许多方面堪称荒诞派之父。但最终，60 年代是荒诞派小说大量出现的年代，是评论界首次意识到小说领域内这一新发展的重要意义的年代，是荒诞派技巧风靡的年代。因此，60 年代是"荒诞的十年"。

这里选注的是该书第一章《荒诞美学》。

An Excerpt from *Contemporary American Novelists of the Absurd*

I The Aesthetics of Absurdity

The absurdist vision may be defined as the belief that we are trapped in a meaningless universe and that neither God nor man, theology nor philosophy, can make sense of the human condition. The expression of this vision in literature is hardly confined to the twentieth century. Yet never before has the notion of absurdity found corroboration in so many extra—literary areas. The "new" logic, with its acceptance of the illogical, and modern science, with its denial of causality and its concept of entropy,[1] elevate chaos to the level of scientific fact. Recent sociological tracts argue convincingly that we are a lonely crowd of organization men, growing up absurd. Modern existential philosophy warns that we face a loss of self in a fragmented world of technology that reduces man to the operational and functional. Each of these theories seems to lend support to what certain writers have believed for a long time, that ours is a disintegrating world without a unifying principle, without meaning, without purpose; an absurd universe.

Even the workaday citizen, non-conversant with such "philosophical" or "technical" matters, is not unaware that ours is an age of distress. In the last decade alone he has witnessed from the comfort of his own living room televised film clips of combat in Viet Nam, the actual slaying of a presidential assassin (repeated in slow motion!), a racial riot in Watts, and a "police riot" in Chicago.[2] A streamlined news media has kept him in touch with such extreme and volatile personalities as Timothy Leary and H. L. Hunt, George Lincoln Rockwell and Malcolm X, Spiro Agnew and George Wallace, Mayor Daley and Abbie Hoffman.[3] Indeed, the term modern itself—in Irving Howe's definition— "as it refers to both history and literature, signifies extreme situations and radical solutions. It summons images of war and revolution, experiment and disaster, apocalypse and skepticism; images of rebellion, disenchantment, and nothingness."[4]

The contemporary American novelist who chooses absurdity as his theme must treat that theme in an age when Nietzsche's agonizing cry that "God is dead!" can be found scrawled upon the graffiti-covered walls of public lavatories, and when the vocabulary of existential anxiety, like the vocabulary of Freudian psychology, has become part of undergraduate cant. He must, in short, write in an age when absurdity, because it is taken for granted, is no longer taken seriously.

Philip Roth comments on this dilemma in an article entitled "Writing

American Fiction." After describing at great length the gruesome yet comic details surrounding a Chicago murder, Roth concludes:

> And what is the moral of so long a story? Simply this: that the American writer in the middle of the twentieth century has his hands full in trying to understand, and then describe, and then make *credible* much of the American reality. It stupefies, it sickens, it infuriates, and finally it is even a kind of embarrassment to one's own meager imagination. The actuality is continually outdoing our talents, and the culture tosses up figures almost dally that are the envy of any novelist.[5]

Burton Feldman joins Roth in believing the contemporary novelist's imagination has not kept pace with an absurd age. Their "humor isn't audacious enough for a world like ours," he complains of the so-called black humor novelists. "The ordinary reader will find that he can trump the nihilism or apocalypse of these novels in a twinkling… Such reader can only be agreed with if he concludes that the world is surely worse than Black Humor is telling him."[6]

In fact, fantasy, which long seemed the exclusive province of art, everyday intrudes itself into the world of reality. There exists, says Bruce Jay Friedman in his introduction to Black Humor, "a fading line between fantasy and reality, a very fading line." To write comic fantasy today, he suggests, all one need do is report, journalistically, the current scene. Sounding a lot like Roth and Feldman, Friedman complains that the novelist's role as social satirist has been unconsciously usurped by the news media:

> The journalist who, in 1964, must cover the ecumenical debate on whether the Jews, on the one hand, are still to be known as Christ-killers, or, on the other hand, are to be let off the hook, is certainly today's satirist. The novelist-satirist, with no real territory to roam, has had to discover new land, invent anew currency, a new

set of filters, has had to sail into darker waters somewhere out beyond satire…[7]

John Aldridge agrees upon the necessity for discovering "a new set of filters." "The task of the novelist in a time like ours," he writes, "can no longer be confined to a simple exploration of the social appearances and surfaces, but must be expanded and deepened to take into account the chaotic multiplicity of meaning, which now confronts us both above and beneath the surfaces." Yet, Aldridge continues, "to deal effectively with the mass complications and ambiguities… to say nothing of the present amorphous state of American society, a writer would ideally need the artistic equipment of an Orwell, a Kafka, Camus, Celine, or Dostoevsky."[8] What has been called "realistic portraiture"[9]—and this includes stream-of-consciousness novels, which constitute a kind of psychic realism—is a method no longer viable in our modern age. In other words, if contemporary novelists are to portray absurdity effectively in a world which already accepts absurdity as a basic premise, an everyday fact, they must find new ways to present their vision.

Recent American novelists of the absurd have responded to this challenge. Verifying this assumption are the repeated attempts of certain critics in the past decade to subsume the novels of the sixties under some general critical heading. "Black Humor," "black comedy," "affluent terrorism," "Epicurean comedy," "the psychic novel," "the novel of disintegration"—all of these have been recently offered as congeneric tagnames. Such an effort by critics suggests that something innovative, perhaps even a new movement in American literature, is indeed afoot. Now a concern with absurdity is not, as students of American literature are aware, new to the American novel. The novels of Melville, the later Twain, West, Hemingway and the early Faulkner, not to mention those novels of the fifties discussed by Ihab Hassan and Richard Lehan in their excellent examinations of the existential novel in America,[10] all reflect a belief that the world is disjointed, purposeless, absurd. New to the novels of the sixties, however, is the particular treatment of absurdist themes. It is to that interesting subject that we must now turn.

An analogue to recent developments in the American novel may be found in the Theater of the Absurd in France. The basic distinction between the Existential theater of Sartrel[11] and Camus and the Theater of the Absurd—that of Beckett, Ionesco, and Genet[12]—is, as Martin Esslin contends, that the former presents absurdity in a "form of highly lucid, and logically constructed reasoning," whereas the latter "strives to express its sense of the senselessness of the human condition and the inadequacy of the rational approach by the open abandonment of rational devices and discursive thought."[13] As we shall see, the absurdist novel of the sixties in America is rarely so total in its commitment to absurdity as are the French plays nor does it completely abandon the use of "rational devices." But its basic distinction from the novels preceding it—which also often maintain absurdist themes—is that the absurdist novel of the sixties, like the French Theater of the Absurd, seeks new ways to integrate subject matter and form.

This is not to say that the novelists covered in this study form part of a self-conscious school or movement. The differences between John Barth and Thomas Pynchon or Joseph Heller and Kurt Vonnegut, Jr., are obvious to most readers. Each of these novelists takes a distinctive approach to both subject matter and form. Yet it is also clear that they share certain innovative characteristics. What is new about these novelists, as Richard Kostelanetz has noted, is their fusion of an "absurd base," or subject matter, with an "absurd surface," or form.[14] Such a fusion, for reasons to be discussed later, is seldom maintained throughout the entirety of any single absurdist novel, and its use is more extensive in some novels than in others. But in almost every novel published by these writers after 1960, the vision of an absurd world not only constitutes the novel's theme but is reflected as well by incident, characterization, and language.

It must be stressed that what I have in mind here is not merely that form reflects content. Such unity forms an organic part of most successful novels. But with one or two exceptions—Melville's *The Confidence Man* and the novels of Nathanael West come to mind—never before in an American novel has the concept of absurdity been actually revealed through form.

My point can be explained by reference to Hemingway's *The Sun Also Rises*. The purposelessness and lack of meaning in the hollow lives of the characters in that novel is certainly emphasized by the novel's circular structure. "Nothing leads anywhere in the book," writes Philip Young, "and that is perhaps the real point of it. The action comes full circle—imitates, that is, the sun of the title, which also rises, only to hasten to the place where it arose...."[15] Similarly, as Young also points out, the language of Hemingway's novel reflects its theme: "the economy and narrow focus of the prose controls the little that can be absolutely mastered. The prose is tense because the atmosphere in which the struggle for control takes place is tense, and the tension in the style expresses that fact."[16] Nonetheless, even though Hemingway's use of form does help define his absurdist vision, the form is not itself absurd. The incidents are credible, not fantastic, and the description is realistic. The use of language, though distinctive, is unobtrusive. In other words, Hemingway made use of "rational devices and discursive thought" in his novel. In the absurdist novels of the sixties, on the other hand, the ultimate absurdity of life is suggested by a series of preposterous and ridiculous events, by characters who—although described with apparent gravity—are distorted, exaggerated and caricatured, and by language which makes use of, to use Eugene McNamara's list, "lexical distortions, meaningless puns, and insistent repetition of empty words, clichés, exaggeration, and deliberately misplaced particulars, and juxtaposed incongruous details." In other words, absurdity in these novels is revealed primarily through the device of comic exaggeration—in a word, burlesque.

Some of the reasons for—and uses of—burlesque in the contemporary novel have been discussed by John Barth in his article, "The Literature of Exhaustion." Barth refers to Jorge Luis Borges's idea that as far as fictional forms are concerned, "literary history... has pretty well exhausted the possibilities of novelty." Consequently, Barth continues, "for one to attempt to add overtly to the sum of 'original' literature by even so much as a conventional short story, not to mention a novel, would be too presumptuous, too naive; literature has been done long since."[18] The serious writer who accepts this point of view faces a creative *cul de sac* and might cease writing altogether. Such a silence, says Barth, would itself be "fairly meaningful" and is perhaps the direction now being taken by Beckett, whom Barth considers a "technically up-to-date artist." The silence of Beckett would then stand as a metaphor of sorts for the "silence *Molloy* speaks of, of which the universe is made."[19]

The charge that art forms are exhausted began as early as the Renaissance. Such charges are repeatedly disproved, however, and artistic conventions are constantly replaced by breakthroughs unimagined by prior generations of artists. Yet Barth's essay is not a dirge sung over the bier of narrative literature. Rather, it offers a suggestion for a new and original direction that the novel might take. Barth's most significant thought is that, instead of silence, the novelist can continue to employ the "exhausted" forms of the past, but he must employ them ironically. If Beethoven's Sixth[20] were composed today, for instance, it would be an embarrassment unless, as Barth maintains, it were "done with ironic intent by a composer quite aware of where we've been and where we are." In this case, the work would make an "ironic comment... on the genre and history of the art..." Even though the form would still be identical to the original, the effect, the ultimate meaning, and therefore the work itself, would be new and different. By consciously imitating a form the possibilities of which are seemingly exhausted and employing it against itself, the composer could produce "new Human work."

Burlesque allows American novelists of the absurd to reject traditional forms and styles while at the same time continuing to use these forms and styles. Consequently, they seldom employ what Lesile Fiedler calls "the fallacy of imitative form" by attempting to reproduce absurdity through an "anti-style." In a way, such "imitation" is what is happening in the French Theater of the Absurd and the *nouveau roman*, both of which may be seen as attempts to reproduce that absurdity felt by the artists to lie just beneath the surface of existence. American novelists of the absurd, on the other hand, while they sometimes exaggerate "reality," seldom feel the need to distort it beyond recognition. In fact, they usually don't imitate "life" at all, but other novels, other forms, other styles. Yet their imitation, because ironic, transcends mere mimesis and becomes a comment upon the artificiality not only of art, but of life as it is usually lived, of mass society, and of all things which prevent the realization that life is absurd. This is what Barth is talking about when he says, "A different way to come to terms with the discrepancy between art and the Real Thing is to *affirm* the artificial element in art (you can't get rid of it anyway), and make the artifice part of your point..."[21] The artifice is of course emphasized by exaggeration: the plots are often a little too elaborately structured and involve a few too many coincidences; the incidents are often fantastic, far beyond the pale of verisimilitude; the language is often florid, comically pyrotechnic. At the same time, when the burlesque is temporarily suspended, what often emerges is beautifully rendered prose; prose, it might be added, that is grammatical, conventionally punctuated and written in sentences that, though highly elaborate, are conventionally structured—a lack of linguistic iconoclasm rare to the American novel since James. Gifted stylists, these novelists can skillfully manipulate the conventions of prose. If they choose instead to burlesque these conventions it is because they believe them appropriate to times less complex than ours. Their use of burlesque, then, allows the novelists of the absurd to utilize all the traditional conventions of characterization, language, and plot while at the same time expressing their distrust of these and similar conventions. Thus they are able, in Barth's words, to "[throw] out the bath water without for a moment losing the baby."[22]

In their ironic use of traditional forms and styles, the contemporary novelists of the absurd often turn to parody[23], a salient characteristic of many of their novels. Barth's *The Sot-Weed Factor*, for example, has been called a mock-epic, a parody of the picaresque novel, and is certainly a burlesque of the historical and biographical novel; his *Giles Goat-Boy* can be read as a parody of the Bible. Heller's *Catch-22* and James Purdy's *Malcolm* have been called American Romance parodies. Malcolm and Donald Barthelme's *Snow White* parody the fairy tale, and several of Vonnegut's novels, especially *Sirens of Titan* and *Slaughterhouse-Five,* may be viewed as parodies of science fiction and Utopian fantasy. Thomas Berger's *Little Big Man* mocks the Western. *Giles Goat-Boy* and Vonnegut's *Mother·Night* masquerade as other works which have been "discovered" or "edited" by the novelist and then "presented" to the reader. Moreover, Barth parodies the complete text of *Oedipus Rex* in *Giles Goat-Boy*, and Pynchon parodies at length a Jacobean tragedy in *The Crying of Lot-49*. Barth's *The Sot-Weed Factor* and Vonnegut's *The Sirens of Titan* contain parodies of historical documents, and parodies of poems and modern song lyrics are sprinkled throughout the novels by these writers.

Now parody and burlesque hardly represent innovations in the novel. Indeed these devices were among the first used by novelists, as such famous parodies as *Shamela* and *Joseph Andrews* attest.[24] Contemporary novelists of the absurd have discovered new ways to use these traditional devices, however. Burlesque in their novels is not only directed toward the external world but, as Robert Buckeye points out, often becomes "reflexive in nature... It is an irony toward the novelist as author, the value of art, the possibility of language."[25] What the contemporary novelists of the absurd wish both to ridicule and place in proper perspective is literature itself—or at least the traditional view of literature.

Literature in general, and the novel in particular, has traditionally been seen as a way of ordering reality. The novelist takes something not aesthetic, life, and gives it shape, form, congruity. Even if his theme is the incongruity of an absurd universe—as in the novels of Hemingway or Camus—his treatment of this theme involves a coherent structure; that is, he orders his materials in an "artistic" way. It is true that the traditional aim of novelists is to make their artistic creation appear to belief, yet—because they artistically shape reality—what is ultimately presented is something unlike reality, or at least unlike reality as it is conceived of in the twentieth century. The reflexive use of burlesque and parody, on the other hand, provides contemporary absurdist novelists a method for rejecting literary pretensions to comprehend and order reality or any part of reality. Thus these writers burlesque not only life but the very vehicle they employ to examine life. This ridicule is by no means confined to literature but is also directed toward history (especially in *The Sot-Weed Factor, V., The Crying of Lot-49* and *Little Big Man*), religion (especially in *Cat's Cradle, The Sirens of Titan,* and *Giles Goat-Boy*) and philosophy (especially Barth's novels), all of which try to impose some direction or order or meaning upon existence.

Life, these novelists believe, resists any impositions of order because its realities are multiple. Any attempt to order these multiple meanings, unless done ironically, results in a falsification of reality. This view of a multiple reality reflects the influence of Einsteinian relativity and quantum physics. The Quantum Theory,[26] as defined by Richard Kostelanetz, maintains that "experience that is discontinuous defies precise definition—its direction is indeterminate; and phenomena that have a semblance of meaning turn out, upon closer inspection, to suggest a multiplicity of answers."[27] Symbols for this multiplicity abound in the contemporary absurdist novels. The multiple V's in Pynchon's *V.*, the multiple identities of Fausto in that same novel, of Henry Burlingame in Barth's *The Sot-Weed Factor,* and of Harold Bray in *Giles Goat-Boy*, the doubt cast upon whether or not characters like Doc Daneeka in Heller's *Catch-22*, Malcolm in Purdy's *Malcolm*, and Jacob Horner in Barth's *The End of the Road* even have identities—each of these suggests that truth is not ambiguous, but multiple; that it is not merely elusive, but, as quantum physics tells us, by its very existence uncertain.

In a world such as this, in which there is no reality but only realities, "what better way to represent it," asks Buckeye, "than [by] parody, to present a reality that is questioned by another…"[28] Parody not only ridicules the pretensions of literature (or history or philosophy or religion) to understand life but rejects as well the view of an ordered universe reflected in the art form being parodied. Moreover, by turning art back upon itself, by confronting what Barth calls "an intellectual dead end and employing it against itself," the novelist achieves a viable art form, its "newness" lying paradoxically in its very "oldness."

Not only traditional forms, but fictional characters as well, are burlesqued in the contemporary novel of the absurd. Both Eugene McNamara and Leslie Fiedler have commented on the resemblance of figures in recent absurdist novels to comic strip characters.[29] Not only their "occasional obviousness and thinness of texture,"[30] but their very names—Dr. Hilarius, Chief White Halfoat, and Billy Pilgrim, for example—suggest the types of names given cartoon figures—Daddy Warbucks, Jughead, Flat-top, etc. As in comic strips, the names often suggest specific attitudes or ideas. Dr. Hilarius is an inept psychiatrist in

The Crying of Lot-49. Billy Pilgrim makes extraterrestrial pilgrimages in Vonnegut's *Slaughterhouse-Five*. *Giles Goat-Boy* contains a scientist named Eierkopf (egg-head) and the overseer of a gigantic furnace room named Maurice Stoker. Scatology abounds: Heller gives us a Lieutenant Schelsskopf, and Pynchon creates a Scheissvogel (in *V.*). Mike Fallopian is a character in *The Crying of Lot-49*, and Harry Pena is a virile fisherman in *God Bless You, Mr. Rosewater*. Even when these names don't directly suggest an attitude, they are comic and obviously not "realistic." In *The Sot-Weed Factor*, Ebeneezer Cook meets an Indian chief named Kebataughtas-sapooekskumoughmass. Pynchon's novels offer characters like Stanley Koteks, Diocletian Blobb, and Genghis Cohen (*The Crying of Lot-49*) and Benny Profane, Bloody Chiclitz, and Winsome, Charisma, and Fu (*V.*). In *God Bless You, Mr. Rosewater*, Vonnegut portrays a sixty-eight-year-old virgin named Diana Moon Glampers, and in *Cat's Cradle* he names a doctor after an organ stop, Dr. Vox Humana. One of Barth's Indians is called Drakepecker.

Contemporary novelists of the absurd did not invent two-dimensional characters or comic names. But they use these devices for new reasons. The use of two-dimensional characters affords these writers one way to emphasize the artificiality of art, which, as we have seen, is one of their aims. Their use of caricature also indicates their rejection of the assumption underlying realistic characterization that human beings can be accurately formulated. As aspects of a protean reality, human beings remain as illusive and as problematic as the absurd universe they occupy. By oversimplifying their characters, in an exaggerated way, contemporary novelists of the absurd suggest the complexity of human nature by indirection.

Another effect of the use of two-dimensional, "comic strip" characters is that normal processes of life and death, not to mention of pain and sorrow, are temporarily suspended. Aesthetically detached and objective, we can only laugh when a cartoon coyote is tricked into falling down a canyon by a cartoon roadrunner. Similarly, we remain detached from the often flat, two-dimensional, and unreal characters in the contemporary absurdist novels. Our disengagement, in fact, explains much of the so-called black humor of these novels. Often we find ourselves laughing at the various cruel and violent events that fill their pages.

What separates these works from usual comic novels is that we are not allowed to maintain the objectivity which permits emotional distance. Realistic incidents frequently intrude upon the fantastic and grotesque. We may be able to laugh at the various attempts made upon Yossarian's life by Nately's whore in Heller's *Catch-22*, and we may giggle at the numerous collisions with inanimate objects encountered by Benny Profane, in Pynchon's *V.*. But we can only be shocked and appalled at the death of Snowden in *Catch-22*, described by Heller in gory detail, and at the graphic description of Esther Harvitz's "nose-job" in *V.*. These passages are as realistic as any found in those novels Paul Levine classifies as "neo-realistic."[31] Indeed, violent and grotesque events such as these are often presented in a calm, precise, and logical prose style. Rather than reflect absurdity, such treatment seems in conflict with the absurdity being presented.

The combination of fantastic events with realistic presentation results in reader disorientation. The reader is faced with a situation comparable to that of Chief Bromden's in Ken Kesey's absurdist *One Flew Over the Cuckoo's Nest*. Bromden sees the world as being "like a cartoon world, where the figures are flat and outlined in black, jerking through some kind of goofy story that might be real funny if it weren't for the cartoon figures being real guys…"[32] Accustomed to the mimetic tradition in the novel, the reader—upon first confronting the fantastic and cartoonlike surface of these absurdist novels—must adjust his expectations. However, as Eugene McNamara points out, "once the reader has adjusted his imagination to the demand of tran[s] ferrial[*sic*] comic strip or cartoon attitudes to the medium of fiction, he is upset again by a return to amore serious traditional attitude."[33] Confusion results, but it is calculated confusion, for the novelist is attempting to evoke in the reader some response to the idea of absurdity. It is as if the novelist is saying, "You may have adjusted to your own absurd world, but it will be more difficult to adjust to the absurdity in the world of my novel." The desired result is similar to the purpose attributed by Esslin to the French Theater of the Absurd.

Human beings [he writes], who in their daily lives confront a world that has split up into a series of disconnected fragments and lost its purpose, but who are no longer aware of this state of affairs and its disintegrating effect on their personalities, are brought face to face with a heightened representation of this schizophrenic universe... And this, in turn, results in the liberating effect of anxieties overcome by being formulated. This is the nature of all the gallows humor and the *humor noir* of world literature, of which the Theatre of the Absurd is the latest example.[34]

The burlesque of plot, characterization and language, which includes the combination of realistic and fantastic modes, is designed, as we have seen, to evoke in the reader a response to the absurd. Although the reader lives in an absurd universe and may even accept its absurdity, his acceptance is academic. He has become inured to absurdity. To present this absurdity in traditionally naturalistic terms only would affect the reader little if at all. But by an ironic exploitation of traditional forms as well as by skillful manipulation of burlesque and naturalistic modes, the novelist achieves a form that is both original and efficacious.

So even though contemporary absurdist novelists mock literature, they have some faith in its efficacy. As Robert Scholes points out, however, theirs is not the faith of the traditional satirist, who hopes to reform society through ridicule and invective, nor of the traditional writer of comedy, who hopes to better mankind by exposing folly and wickedness, although many traditional satiric and comic techniques do appear in their novels.[35] Moreover, although the problems and conflicts of tragedy often appear in these novels, the novelists lack the traditional faith of the tragedian, who believes that though man may fall, the absolute, an ordered universe, lies beyond destruction. "In the final instance," writes Jan Kott, "tragedy is an appraisal of human fate, a measure of the absolute."[36] In the twentieth century, however, no belief in absolutes exists; not only is man out of joint, but so is his universe. Instead of tragedy, therefore, we have the grotesque.

In the world of the grotesque [writes Kott], downfall cannot be justified by, or blamed on, the absolute. The absolute is not endowed with any ultimate reasons; it is stronger, and that is all. *The absolute is absurd…* Various kinds of impersonal and hostile mechanisms have taken the place of God, Nature, and History, found in the old tragedy. The notion of absurd mechanism is probably the last metaphysical concept remaining in modern grotesque. But this absurd mechanism is not transcendental any more in relation to … mankind.[37]

Comedy inheres in the grotesque, for "the absence of tragedy in a tragic world," Kott quotes Maurice Regnault as saying, "gives birth to comedy."[38] But tragic and comic hope for reform, as well as tragedy's possibility of catharsis, are missing. The comedy of the grotesque is, according to Ionesco, "more conducive to despair than the tragic. The comic offers no way out."[39] Accordingly, the contemporary novelist of the absurd seeks no reform of a world probably beyond remedy and certainly beyond comprehension. He is not concerned, as Scholes phrases it, "with what to do about life but with how to *take* it."[40] The absurdity of the human condition, if faced squarely, can be viewed as a cosmic joke. Thus, while the novelist of the absurd emphasizes the blackness of modern existence, the response he seeks is neither stoic resignation nor Camusian scorn, but laughter. In this aim he is at one with French dramatists of the absurd, who believe that "the dignity of man lies in his ability to face reality in all its senselessness; to accept it freely, without fear, without illusions—and to laugh at it."[41]

Before concluding this discussion of the aesthetics of absurdity, a word needs to be said about the quality of the absurd vision shared by these novelists. Paul Hurley has maintained that the basic difference between French and American dramatists of the absurd is the incapability of the latter to commit themselves totally to absurdity. While they may believe that society is absurd, American dramatists like Kopit and Albee cannot, it seems, "surrender themselves to a belief that *life* is absurd."[42] Although they give lip-service to absurdity, they inevitably relent in the name of human and social progress. To a degree, what Professor Hurley says of the American dramatists of the absurd holds true for American novelists of the absurd. Their "No! In thunder," while invariably evident in the form of their novels, is often mitigated by a seemingly irresistible affirmation which is sometimes stated flatly by the novelist.

This affirmation should not be confused with the kind of affirmation found in works of existentialism. Contemporary novelists of the absurd begin with the same basic premise as the existentialists—the world is absurd. But they are post-existential in their view of man, generally lacking the existentialist's faith in the human character. From Nietzsche to Camus, existentialists have agreed that, since no God exists to rely on, man must rely upon himself. Nietzsche's faith in the individual human being reached such Romantic proportions that he could envision a Superman.[43] Even Sisyphus, who had his perpetual rock to roll up that mountain, could surmount his absurd circumstances, deriving meaning from his struggle. "One must imagine Sisyphus happy," Camus concludes his famous tract. [44] And Sartre insists that existentialism is a humanism. To the contemporary novelists of the absurd, on the other hand, man is far too puny and helpless for self-reliance.

But a temporary analgesic for existential pain does exist. Love, contemporary absurdist novelists say with Matthew Arnold, while it cannot eradicate the slings and arrows of an outrageously ravaged universe, offers some consolation to those who suffer them. The essence of existence is unquestionably *nada*, but some solace is discoverable in the clean well-lighted places of the human heart. [45] In this respect, these novelists appear unwilling or unable to remain completely true to the vision that life is meaningless. Or at least they do not insist that despair represents the only possible human response to life's absurdity.

The novelist should have the right to his own vision, and the critic's task—or so it seems to me—should not be to question the validity of that vision but to determine whether or not its presentation is artistically successful. When the novel's affirmative vision clashes with its negative, or absurd, vision, the result is not aesthetically pleasing. The writer tries to hold two contradictory views simultaneously: the world, he seems to say, is both meaningful and meaningless. Because his vision of absurdity is so intense, we find ourselves asking the same question asked by Philip Roth:

> If the world is as crooked and as unreal as … it is becoming, day by day; if one feels less and less power in the face of this unreality, day by day; if the inevitable end is destruction, if not of all life, then of much that is valuable and civilized in life—then why in God's name is the writer pleased? [46]

In other words, the writer's affirmative vision strikes us as insincere or at least as contradictory; it seems imposed upon the narrative, forced into the novel's fabric.

At their best, however, these novelists are able to have it both ways.

In these instances, the novelist refrains from overt moralization or preachment, allowing the form of his novel to act as his surrogate. The incidents themselves, plus the ways in which the novelist manages his language and other artifices of style, allow the twin themes, absurdity and the need for human love, to grow organically from the novel. When this happens, there is no contradiction, and the novel's affirmation is not obtrusive. In cases like this, these novelists succeed in blending both nihilism and the belief that love can be efficacious into an organic whole which does not jar our aesthetic sensibilities. While their belief that certain human relationships can achieve a small degree of meaning alloys an otherwise absurdist vision, it need not, as evidenced by the best of these novels, mar the artistic achievement of the contemporary American novelists of the absurd. In the following pages I hope to demonstrate the ways in which an absurdist vision forms the central element in the novels of Heller, Vonnegut, Pynchon, and Barth; and how these writers have sometimes failed, but more often succeeded, in presenting that vision.

〔注释〕

1. entropy："熵"，热力学函数。它表明宇宙向混乱和同一性运动的倾向。现代物理学认为，宇宙永远处于趋向一致的运动中，能量（或热量）的分布逐渐变得均衡起来。当宇宙达到完全均衡状态时，它就会消亡。这一理论对美国现当代文学创作颇有影响，品钦（Thomas Pynchon）的短篇小说《熵》，便是例征。

2. 指肯尼迪总统遇刺、洛杉矶附近瓦茨地区黑人暴动及芝加哥的警察骚乱，都发生在 20 世纪 60 年代。

3. 美国当代社会、政治生活中几个领域内的富有代表性的人物，如黑人领袖、副总统、保守的总统候选人等。

4. 原注：引自《马萨诸塞评论》1967 年夏季刊第 505-506 页中保罗·莱文所著《非温和地带：当代美国小说的气候》。另外参阅豪所著《现代派文学》（纽约，1967）一书的《导言》以及他的《群体社会与后现代派小说》(刊于《党派评论》1959 年夏第 26 期第 420-436 页》。Irving Howe：欧文·豪，美国文学评论家。

5. 原注：《评论》杂志 1961 年 3 月第 21 期第 224 页。

6. 原注：《黑色幽默剖析》，载于马库斯·克莱恩所编《第二次世界大战以后的美国小说》(纽约,1969 年版,第 225 页)。Burton Feldman：伯顿·费尔德曼，美国文学评论家。

7. 原注：Bruce Jay Friedman：布鲁斯·杰伊·费里德曼，美国文学评论家。

8. 原注：《扼杀与创造的时代：危机中的当代小说》(纽约，1966 年版，第 145 页。John Aldridge：约翰·阿尔德里奇，美国文学评论家。an Orwell, a Kafka, Camus, Celine：奥维尔（George Orwell，1903-1950，英国小说家），卡夫卡（Franz Kafka，1883-1924，奥地利小说家），加缪（Albert Camus, 1913-1960），法国作家，塞利纳（Louis Ferdinand Celine,1894-1961），法国作家。

9. 原注：豪所著《群体社会与后现代派小说》第 429 页。

10. Ihab Hassan 及 Richard Lehan 皆为美国当代著名文学评论家。

11. Sartre：萨特（Jean-Paul Sartre, 1905-1980），法国哲学家、散文家、剧作家、小说家，存在主义的倡导者。

12. Beckett, Ionesco, and Genet：贝克特（Samuel Becket, 1906-1989, 爱尔兰小说家、剧作家），尤内斯库（Eugene Ionesco, 1912-1994, 法国剧作家），热内（Jean Genet，1910-1986，法国小说家、剧作家）。

13. 原注：《荒诞派戏剧》(纽约，1967 年版）第 1920 页。Martin Esslin：马丁·艾思林，文学评论家。

14. 原注：《要说的是，没有什么可说的》，载于《纽约时报书评》(1965 年 6 月 6 日）第 28 页。Richard Kostelanetz：理查德·科斯特兰内茨，文学评论家。

15. 原注：《厄内斯特·海明威》(明尼亚波利斯，1965 年）修订版第 13 页。Philip Young：菲利浦·扬格，文学评论家。

16. 同上，第 38 页。

17. 原注：《当代美国文学的荒诞风格》，载于《人文协会简报》1968 年春第 19 期第 44-45 页。Eugene McNamara：尤金·麦克纳马拉，文学评论家。

18. 原注：《大西洋》刊物 1967 年 8 月第 220 期第 33 页。

19. 原注：……有趣的是，贝克特的最新作品，一出题为《呼吸》的剧作，长仅 30 秒钟，根本没有对话和人物。关于对"沉默文学"的深刻研探，参阅伊哈布·哈桑所著《沉默文学：亨利·米勒和塞缪尔·贝克特》（纽约，1967 年版）。

20. Beethoven's Sixth：贝多芬的《第六（田园）交响曲》。

21. 原注：《巴思：一次采访》第 6 页。上文中 the Real Thing：意即"现实"，援用美国小说家詹姆斯（Henry James）的短篇小说 "The Real Thing"，故大写。

22. 原注：《枯竭的文学》第 31 页。

23. parody：对严肃作品的滑稽性模仿，经常保持原作形式，但改变其严肃内容，从而产生嘲笑原作特点的效果。这种模仿必须有原作为底本。parody 和 burlesque 虽皆为滑稽性模仿，但稍有不同。burlesque 和原作只保持大体相似，可自成一独立作品，它可能把严肃题材写成荒谬可笑，也可能把琐屑题材写成极其重要。

24. *Shamela* and *Joseph Andrews*：《沙米拉》出版于 1741 年，可能是亨利·菲尔丁（Henry Fielding, 1707-1754）所写，模仿嘲笑理查森（Samuel Richardson，1689-1761）1740 年发表的书信体小说《帕米拉》（*Pamela*），描述女仆帕米拉·安德鲁被男主人追求的故事。菲尔丁在其小说《约瑟夫·安德鲁》的开首，描写了帕米拉·安德鲁之兄、男仆约瑟夫·安德鲁被女主人追求的故事，从而通过作品模仿嘲笑了理查森。

25. 原注：《心理小说剖析》第 37 页。

26. The Quantum Theory：量子论，认为一切事物，包括人的知识，都包含有一定的不确定性。

27. 原注：《要说的是，没有什么可说的》第 28 页。

28. 原注：《心理小说的剖析》第 37 页。

29. 原注：《当代美国文学的荒诞风格》第 45 页；莱斯利·菲德勒所著《消失的美国人的归来》（纽约，1968 年版）第 184 页。

30. 原注：菲德勒，同上。

31. 原注：《非温和地带》第 514-519 页。莱文视为"新现实主义"的小说包括威廉·巴勒斯的《裸露的午餐》、约翰·里奇的《夜城》、小赫伯特·赛尔比的《到布鲁克林的最后出口》以及杜鲁门·卡波特的《在冷血中》。莱文给新现实主义的定义是"试图用客观的照相机镜头拍摄现代生活的非现实性"。

32. 原注：《飞越杜鹃巢》，1962 年出版，第 34 页。

33. 原注：《当代美国文学的荒诞风格》第 45 页。

34. 原注：阿尔德里奇对新闻风格的评论在这里很中肯。"（小说家）通过新闻体既能表现素材而又不必对它表态或判断它的意义……如果所选事件忽然失去重要性，或读者因了解事件太多而不再做出反应，那么，作者便被置于一种他的天才无法自拔的窘境里。"引自《第二次世界大战后的美国小说》一书中《寻觅价值》一文。

35. 原注：《虚构者》第 41 页。

36. 原注：《我们的同代人莎士比亚》（伯尔斯洛·塔伯尔斯基译，纽约州加登城，1964 年版）第 92 页。Jan Kott：简·科特，文学评论家。

37. 原注：科特文，第 92-93 页。

38. 原注：同上，第 91 页。

39. 原注：转引自艾思林文，第 133 页。

40. 原注：《虚构者》第 43 页。

41. 原注：艾思林文，第 316 页。

42. 原注：《法国和美国：荒诞的模式》（载于《大学英语》1965 年 5 月第 26 期第 635 页）。Kopit and Albee：科比特（Arthur L. Kopit, 1937- ）和阿尔比（Edward Albee, 1928- ），均为美国剧作家。Paul Hurley：保尔·赫尔利，文学评论家。

43. Nietzsche's Superman：关于尼采的"超人"思想，详见罗素所著《西方哲学史》（纽约，1945 年版）第 25 章。

44. "One...tract"：文中的 Sisyphus 指西叙福斯，希腊神话人物，狡滑的柯林斯国王，死后在地狱被罚推巨石上山，到山顶后巨石便滚落下去，他必须从头推起，如此反复不停。His famous tract：指加缪的哲学随笔《西叙福斯的神话》（1992），加缪在文中分析了当代的虚无主义和"虚诞"感。

45. in the clean ... heart：参阅海明威所著的短篇小说《一个清洁、灯光明亮的地方》（"A Clean, Well-lighted Place"）。"nada" 一词亦出自该篇小说，西班牙语，意即"乌有"、"虚无"。

46. 原注：《创作美国小说》第 231 页。

Questions For Discussion：

1. What are the major features of the world in which the novelists of the 1960s lived and wrote?

2. Why is it necessary for the novelists of the absurd to burlesque and parody? What is the difference between burlesque and parody?

3. Why do the novelists of the absurd write to create a deliberate confusion in the reader?

4. What is the difference between the novelist of the absurd and the satirist and the existentialist?

5. Summarize, in a few sentences, the aesthetics of the absurd. With regard to the quality of the absurd vision, what is the difference between the French dramatists of the absurd and the American dramatists and novelists of the absurd?

For Further Reference：

1. David D. Galloway. *The Absurd Hero in American Fiction.* Austin: Univ. of Texas Press, 1966.

2. Jonathan Baumbach. *The Landscape of Nightmare: Studies in the Contemporary American Novel*. New York: New York Univ. Press, 1965.

3. Douglas M. Davis, ed. *The World of Black Humor*. New York: E.P. Dutton, 1967.

APPENDICES

Kenneth Burke

Psychology and Form

[1925]

It is not until the fourth scene of the first act that Hamlet confronts the ghost of his father. As soon as the situation has been made clear, the audience has been, consciously or unconsciously, waiting for this ghost to appear, while in the fourth scene this moment has been definitely promised. For earlier in the play Hamlet had arranged to come to the platform at night with Horatio to meet the ghost, and it is now night, he is with Horatio and Marcellus, and they are standing on the platform. Hamlet asks Horatio the hour.

> Hor. I think it lacks of twelve.
> Mar. No, it is struck.
> Hor. Indeed? I heard it not: then it draws near the season
>   Wherein the spirit held his wont to walk:

Promptly hereafter there is a sound off-stage. "A flourish of trumpets, and ordnance shot off within." Hamlet's friends have established the hour as twelve. It is time for the ghost. Sounds off-stage, and of course it is not the ghost. It is, rather, the sound of the king's carousal, for the king "keeps wassail." A tricky and useful detail. We have been waiting for a ghost, and get startlingly, a blare of trumpets. And, once the trumpets are silent, we feel how desolate are these three men waiting for a ghost, on a bare "platform," fell it by this sudden juxtaposition of an imagined scene of lights and merriment. But the trumpets announcing a carousal have suggested a subject of conversation. In the darkness Hamlet discusses the excessive drinking of his countrymen. He points out that it tends to harm their reputation abroad, since, he argues, this one showy vice makes their virtues "in the general censure take corruption."

And for this reason, although he himself is a native of this place, he does not approve of the custom. Indeed, there in the gloom he is talking very intelligently on these matters, and Horatio answers, "Look, my Lord, it comes." All this time we had been waiting for a ghost, and it comes at the one moment which was not pointing towards it. This ghost, so assiduously prepared for, is yet a surprise. And now that the ghost has come, we are waiting for something further. Program: a speech from Hamlet. Hamlet must confront the ghost. Here again Shakespeare can feed well upon the use of contrast for his effects. Hamlet has just been talking in a sober, rather argumentative manner—but now the flood-gates are unloosed:

Angels and ministers of grace defend us!

Be thou a spirit of hearth or goblin damn'd,

Bring with thee airs from heaven or blasts from hell...

and the transition from the matter-of-fact to the grandiose, the full-throated and full-voweled, is a second burst of trumpets, perhaps more effective than the first, since it is the rich fulfillment of a promise. Yet this satisfaction in turn becomes an allurement, an itch for further developments. At first desiring solely to see Hamlet confront the ghost, we now want Hamlet to learn from the ghost the details of the murder—which are, however, with shrewdness and husbandry, reserved for "Scene V—Another part of the Platform."

I have gone into this scene at some length, since it illustrates so perfectly the relationship between psychology and form, and so aptly indicates how the one is to be defined in terms of the other. That is, the psychology here is not the psychology of the *hero*, but the psychology of the *audience*. And by that distinction, form would be the psychology of the audience. Or, seen from another angle, form is the creation of an appetite in the mind of the auditor, and the adequate satisfying of the appetite. This satisfaction—so complicated is the human mechanism—at times involves a temporary set of frustrations, but in the end these frustrations prove to be simply a more involved kind of satisfaction, and furthermore serve to make the satisfaction of fulfillment more intense. If, in a work of art, the poet says something, let us say, about a meeting, writes in such a way that we desire to observe that meeting, and then, if he places that meeting before us—that is form. While obviously, that is also the psychology of the audience, since it involves desires and their appeasements.

The seeming breach between form and subject-matter, between technique and psychology, which has taken place in the last century is the result, it seems to me, of scientific criteria being unconsciously introduced into matters of purely esthetic judgment. The flourishing of science has been so vigorous that we have not yet had time to make a spiritual readjustment adequate to the changes in our resources of material and knowledge. There are disorders of the social system which are caused solely by our undigested wealth (the basic disorder being, perhaps, the phenomenon of overproduction; to remedy this, instead of having all workers employed on half time, we have half working fulltime and the other half idle, so that whereas overproduction could be the greatest reward of applied science, it has been, up to now, the most menacing condition our modern civilization has had to face). It would be absurd to suppose that such social disorders would not be paralleled by disorders of culture and taste, especially since science is so pronouncedly a spiritual factor. So that we are, owing to the sudden wealth science has thrown upon us, all *nouveaux-riches* in matters of culture, and most poignantly in that field where lack of native firmness is most readily exposed, in matters of esthetic judgment.

One of the most striking derangements of taste which science has temporarily thrown upon us involves the understanding of psychology in art. Psychology has become a body of information (which is precisely what psychology in science should be, or must be). And similarly, in art, we tend to look for psychology as the purveying of information. Thus, a contemporary writer has objected to Joyce's *Ulysses* on the ground that there are more psychoanalytic data available in Freud. (How much more drastically he might, by the same system, have destroyed Homer's *Odyssey*!) To his objection it was answered that one might, similarly, denounce Cezanne's trees in favor of state forestry bulletins. Yet are not Cezanne's landscapes themselves tainted with the psychology of information? Has he not, by perception, *pointed out* how one object lies against another, *indicated* what takes place between two colors (which is the psychology of science, and is less successful in the medium of art than in that of science, since in at such processes are at best implicit, whereas in science they are so readily made explicit)? Is Cezanne not, to that extent, a state forestry bulletin, except that he tells what goes on in the eye instead of on the tree? And do not the true values of his work lie elsewhere—and precisely in what I distinguish as the psychology of form?

Thus, the great influx of information has led the artist also to lay his emphasis on the giving of information—with the result that art tends more and more to substitute the psychology of the hero (the subject) forth psychology of the audience. Under such an attitude, when form is preserved it is preserved as an annex, a luxury, or, as some feel, a downright affectation. It remains, though sluggish, like the human appendix, for occasional demands are still made upon it; but its true vigor is gone, since it is no longer organically required. Proposition: The hypertrophy of the psychology of information is accompanied by the corresponding atrophy of the psychology of form.

In information, the matter is intrinsically interesting. And by intrinsically interesting I do not necessarily mean intrinsically valuable, as witness the intrinsic interest of backyard gossip or the most casual newspaper items. In art, at least the art of the great ages (Aeschylus, Shakespeare, Racine), the matter is interesting by means of an extrinsic use, a function. Consider, for instance, the speech of Mark Anotony, the "Brutus is an honorable man." Imagine in the same place a very competently developed thesis on human conduct, with statistics, intelligence tests, definitions; imagine it as the finest thing of the sort ever written, and as really being at the roots of an understanding of Brutus. Obviously, the play would simply stop until Anotony had finished. For in the case of Anotony's speech, the value lies in the fact that his words are shaping the future of the audience's desires, of the desires of the Roman populace, but the desires of the pit. This is the psychology of form as distinguished from the psychology of information.

The distinction is, of course, absolutely true only in its nonexistent extremes. Hamlet's advice to the players, for instance, has little of the quality which distinguishes Anotony's speech. It is, rather, intrinsically interesting, although one could very easily prove how the play would benefit by some such delay at this point, and that anything which made this delay possible without violating the consistency of the subject would have, in this, its formal justification. It would, furthermore, be absurd to rule intrinsic interest out of literature. I wish simply to have it restored to its properly minor position, seen as merely one out of many possible elements of style. Goethe's prose, often poorly imagined or neutral in its line-for-line texture, especially in the treatment of romantic episode—perhaps he felt that the romantic episode in itself was enough?—is strengthened into a style possessing affirmative virtues by his rich use of aphorism. But this is, after all, but one of many possible facets of appeal.

In some places, notably in *Wilhelm Meisters Lehrjahre* when Wilhelm's friends disclose the documents they have been collecting about his life unbeknown to him, the aphorisms are almost rousing in their efficacy, since they involve the story: But as a rule the appeal of aphorism is intrinsic: that is, it satisfies without being functionally related to the context. Also, to return to the matter of Hamlet, it must be observed that the style in this passage is no mere "information-giving" style; in its alacrity, its development, it really makes this one fragment into a kind of miniature plot.

One reason why music can stand repetition so much more sturdily than correspondingly good prose is because music, of all the arts, is by its nature least suited to the psychology of information, and has remained closer to the psychology of form. Here form cannot atrophy. Every dissonant chord cries for its solution, and whether the musician resolves or refuses to resolve this dissonance into the chord which the body cries for, he is dealing in human appetites. Correspondingly good prose, however, more prone to the temptations of pure information, cannot so much bear repetition since the esthetic value of information is lost once that information is imparted. If one returns to such a work again it is purely because, in the chaos of modern life, he has been able to forget it. With a desire, on the other hand, its recovery is as agreeable as its discovery. One can memorize the dialogue between Hamlet and Guildenstern, where Hamlet gives Guildenstern the pipe to play on. For, once the speech is known, its repetition adds a new element to compensate for the loss of novelty. We cannot take a recurrent pleasure in the new (in information) but we can in the natural (in form). Already, at the moment when Hamlet is holding out the pipe to Guildenstern and asking him to play upon it, we "gloat over" Hamlet's triumphal descent upon Guildenstern, when, after Guildenstern has, under increasing embarrassment, protested three times that he cannot play the instrument, Hamlet launches the retort for which all this was preparation:

> Why, look you now, how unworthy a thing you make of me. You would play upon me, you would seem to know my stops; you would pluck out the heart of my mystery; you would sound me from my lowest note to the top of my compass; and there is much music, excellent voice, in this little organ, yet cannot you make it speak. Sblood, do you think I am easier to be played on than a pipe? Call me what instrument you will, though you can fret me, you cannot play upon me.

In the opening lines we hear the promise of the close, and thus feel the emotional curve even more keenly than at first reading. Whereas in most modern art this element is underemphasized. It gives us the gossip of a plot, a plot which too often has for its value the mere fact that we do not know its outcome.

Music, then fitted less than any other art for imparting information, deals minutely in frustrations and fulfillments of desire, and for that reason more often gives us those curves of emotion which, because they are natural, can bear repetition without loss. It is for this reason that music, like folk tales, is most capable of lulling us to sleep. A lullaby is a melody which comes quickly to rest, where the obstacles are easily overcome—and this is precisely the parallel to those waking dreams of struggle and conquest which (especially during childhood) we permit ourselves when falling asleep or when trying to induce sleep. Folk tales are just such waking dreams. Thus it is right that art should be called a "waking dream." The only difficulty with this definition (indicated by Charles Baudouin in his *Psychoanalysis and Aesthetics*, a very valuable study of Verhaeren) is that today we understand it to mean art as a waking dream for the artist. Modern criticism and psychoanalysis in particular, is too prone to define the essence of art in terms of the artist's weaknesses. It is, rather, the audience which dreams, while the artist oversees the conditions which determine this dream. He is the manipulator of blood, brains, heart, and bowels which, while we sleep, dictate the mold of our desires. This is, of course, the real meaning of artistic felicity—an exaltation at the correctness of the procedure, so that we enjoy the steady march of doom in a Racinian tragedy with exactly the same equipment as that which produces our delight with Benedick's "Peace! I'll stop your mouth. (*Kisses her*)" which terminates the imbroglio of *Much Ado About Nothing*.

The methods of maintaining interest which are most natural to the psychology of information (as it is applied to works of pure art) are surprise and suspense. The method most natural to the psychology of form is eloquence. For this reason the great ages of Aeschylus, Shakespeare, and Racine, dealing as they did with material which was more or less a matter of common knowledge so that the broad outlines of the plot were known in advance (while it is the broad outlines which are usually exploited to secure surprise and suspense), developed formal excellence, or eloquence, as the basis of appeal in their work.

Not that there is any difference in kind between the classic method of the method of the cheapest contemporary melodrama. The drama, more than any other form, must never lose sight of its audience: here the failure to satisfy the proper requirements is most disastrous. And since certain contemporary work is successful, it follows that rudimentary laws of composition are being complied with. The distinction is one of intensity rather than of kind. The contemporary audience hears the lines of a play or novel with the same equipment as it brings to reading the lines of its daily paper. It is content to have facts placed before it in some more or less adequate sequence. Eloquence is the minimizing of this interest in fact, *per se*, so that the "more or less adequate sequence" of their presentation must be relied on to a much greater extent. Thus, those elements of surprise and suspense are subtilized, carried down into the writing of a line or a sentence, until in all its smallest details the work bristles with disclosures, contrasts, restatements with a difference, ellipses, images, aphorism, volume, sound-values, in short all that complex wealth of minutiae which in their line-for-line aspect we call style and in their broader outlines we call form.

As a striking instance of a modern play with potentialities in which the intensity of eloquence is missing, I might cite a recent success, Capek's *R.U.R.* Here, in a melodrama which was often astonishing in the rightness of its technical procedure, when the author was finished he had written nothing but the scenario for a play by Shakespeare. It was a play in which the author produced time and again the opportunity, the demand, for eloquence, only to move on. (At other times, the most successful moments, he utilized the modern discovery of silence, writing moments wherein words could not possibly serve but to detract from the effect; this we might call the "flowering" of information.) The Adam and Eve scene of the last act, a "commission" which the Shakespeare of the comedies would have loved to fill, was in the verbal barrenness of Capek's play something shameless to the point of blushing. The Robot, turned human, prompted by the dawn of love to see his first sunrise, or hear the first bird-call, and forced merely to say, "Oh, see the sunrise," or, "Hear the pretty birds"—here one could do nothing but wring his hands at the absence of that esthetic mold which produced the over slung "speeches" of *Romeo and Juliet.*

Suspense is the concern over the possible outcome of some specific detail of plot rather than for general qualities. Thus, "Will A marry B or C?" is suspense. In *Macbeth*, the turn from the murder scene to the porter scene is a much less literal channel of development. Here the presence of one quality calls forth the demand for another, rather than one tangible incident of plot awaking an interest in some other possible tangible incident of plot. To illustrate more fully, if an author managed over a certain number of his pages to produce a feeling of sultriness, or oppression, in the reader, this would unconsciously awaken in the reader the desire for a cold, fresh north wind—and thus some aspect of a north wind would be effective if called forth by some aspect of stuffiness. A good example of this is to be found in a contemporary poem, T. S. Eliot's *The Waste Land*, where the vulgar, oppressively trivial conversation in the public house calls forth in the poet a memory of a line from Shakespeare. These slobs in a public house, after a desolately low-visioned conversation, are now forced by closing time to leave the saloon. They say good-night. And suddenly the poet, feeling his release, drops into another good-night, a good-night with *desinvolture*, a good-night out of what was, within the conditions of the poem at least, a graceful and irrecoverable past.

> "Well that Sunday Albert was home, they had a hot gammon,
> And they asked me in to dinner, to get the beauty of it hot."
> [at this point the bartender interrupts; it is closing time]
> "Goonight Bill. Goonight Lou. Goonight May. Goonight. Ta ta.
> Goonight. Goonight. Good-night, ladies, good-night, sweet ladies,
>   good-night, good-night."

There is much more to be said on these lines, which I have shortened somewhat in quotation to make my issue clearer. But I simply wish to point out here that this transition is a bold juxtaposition of one quality created by another, an association in ideas which, if not logical, is nevertheless emotionally natural. In the case of Macbeth, similarly, it would be absurd to say that the audience, after the murder scene, wants a porter scene. But the audience does want the quality which this porter particularizes. The dramatist might, conceivably, have introduced some entirely different character or event in this place, provided only that the event produced the same quality of relationship and contrast (grotesque seriousness followed by grotesque buffoonery). One of the most beautiful and satisfactory "forms" of this sort is to be fund in Baudelaire's "Femmes

Dammees," where the poet, after describing the business of a Lesbian seduction, turns to the full oratory of his apostrophe:

> *Descendez, descendez, lamentables victimes,*
>
> *Descendez le chemin de l'enfer eternal...*

while the stylistic efficacy of this transition contains a richness which transcends all moral (or unmoral) sophistication: the efficacy of appropriateness, of exactly the natural curve in treatment. Here is morality even for the godless, since it is a morality of art, being justified, if for no other reason, by its paralleling of that staleness, that disquieting loss of purpose, which must have followed the procedure of the two characters, the *femmes dammees* themselves, a remorse which, perhaps only physical in its origin, nevertheless becomes psychic.

But to return, we have made three terms synonymous: form, psychology, and eloquence. And eloquence thereby becomes the essence of art, while pity, tragedy, sweetness, humor, in short all the emotions which we experience in life proper, as non-artists, are simply the material on which eloquence may feed. The arousing of pity, for instance, is not the central purpose of art, although it may be an adjunct of artistic effectiveness. One can feel pity much more keenly at the sight of some actual misfortune—and it would be a great mistake to see art merely as weak representation of some actual experience. That artist today are content to write under such an esthetic accounts in part for the inferior position which art holds in the community. Art, at least in the great periods when it has flowered, was the conversion, or transcendence, of emotion into eloquence, and was thus a factor added to life. I am reminded of St. Augustine's caricature of the theatre: that whereas we do not dare to wish people unhappy, we do want to feel sorry for them, and therefore turn to plays so that we can feel sorry although no real misery is involved. One might apply the parallel interpretation to the modern delight in happy endings, and say that we turn to art to indulge our humanitarianism in well-wishing which we do not permit ourselves towards our actual neighbors. Surely the catharsis of art is more complicated than this, and more reputable.

Eloquence itself, as I hope to have established in the instance from *Hamlet* which I have analyzed, is no mere plaster added to a framework of more stable qualities. Eloquence is simply the end of art, and is thus its essence. Even the poorest is eloquent, but in a poor way, with less intensity, until this aspect is obscured by others fattening upon its leanness. Eloquence is not showiness; it is, rather, the result of that desire in the artist to make a work perfect by adapting it in every minute detail to the racial appetites.

The distinction between the psychology of information and the psychology of form involves a definition of esthetic truth. It is here precisely, to combat the deflection which the strength of science has caused to our tastes, that we must examine the essential breach between scientific and artistic truth. Truth in art is not the discovery of facts, not an addition to human knowledge in the scientific sense of the word. It is, rather, the exercise of human propriety, the formulation of symbols which rigidify our sense of poise and rhythm. Artistic truth is the externalization of taste. I sometimes wonder, for instance, whether the "artificial" speech of John Lyly might perhaps be "truer" than the revelations of Dostoevsky. Certainly at its best, in its feeling for a statement which returns upon itself, which attempts the systole to a diastole, it could be much truer than Dostoevsky. And if it is not, it fails not through a mistake of Lyly's esthetic, but because Lyly was a man poor in character whereas Dostoevsky was rich and complex. When Swift, making the women of Brobdingnag enormous, deduces from this discrepancy between their size and Gulliver's that Gulliver could sit astride their nipples, he has written something which is esthetically true, which is, if I may be pardoned, profoundly "proper," as correct in its Euclidean deduction as any corollary in geometry. Given the companions of Ulysses in the cave of Polyphemus, it is true that they would escape clinging to the bellies of the herd let out to pasture. St. Ambrose, detailing the habits of God's creatures, and drawing from them moral maxims for the good of mankind, St. Ambrose in his limping natural history rich in scientific inaccuracies that are at the very heart of emotional rightness, St. Ambrose writes "Of night-birds, especially the nightingale which hatches her eggs by song; of the owl, the bat, and the cock at cock-crow; in what these may apply to the guidance of our habits," and in the sheer rightness of that program there is the truth of art. In introducing this talk of night-birds, after many pages devoted to other of God's creatures, he says:

> What now! While we have been talking, you will notice how the birds of night have already started fluttering about you, and, in this same fact of warning us to leave off with our discussion, suggest thereby a further topic—

and this seems to me to contain the best wisdom of which the human frame is capable, an address, a discourse, which can make our material life seem blatant almost to the point of despair. And when the cock, crows, and the thief abandons his traps, and the sun lights up, and we are in every way called back to God by the well-meaning admonition of this bird, here the very blindnesses of religion become the deepest truths of art.

From *Counter-Statement* by Kenneth Burke, pp. 38-56. Copyright, 1931. Reprinted by permission of Harcourt, Brace and Company, Inc., and the author. Originally published in *The Dial*, Vol. LXXIX (July,1925), pp. 34-46.

Newton Arvin

Individualism and the American Writer

[1931]

"The artist, it cannot be too clearly understood," says Arthur Symons in his book on the symbolist movement, "has no more part in society than amok in domestic life." The dogma of literary individualism has never been phrased more simply or more grotesquely; and, as Mr. Symons belongs to a generation now pretty completely superseded, it is no longer fashionable to say the thing in just these terms, or to appeal to such authority as his for support. But the spirit behind his epigram is a spirit that still operates not only in British but in American letters. Even sentimental estheticism, though the cut of its clothes is no longer in the mode of the nineties, has by no means disappeared; and, on a less fatuous level, the doctrine of irresponsibility—in more forms than one, of course—is virtually the prevailing gospel. The breach between our writers and our society could hardly be wider, one gets a measure of it by trying to imagine a contemporary poet or novelist of distinction occupying the kind of official post—an ambassadorship, a professorship, the editorship of a prosperous magazine or newspaper—which, fifty and sixty years ago, was one of the natural rewards of literary celebrity. This sort of thing is now a joke, and a stale joke at that. Yet there is intrinsically nothing funny in the conception of a writer's role in society as responsble to the point of officialdom; and many things are more unlikely than that we shall return to it in the course of events. Meanwhile, and for excellent reasons, the literary life in America is the scene of a sweeping separatism; the typical American writer is as tightly shut up in his own domain, and as jealous of his prerogatives, as one of the Free Cities of the late Middle Ages. Is this in the very nature of things, or is it a passing circumstance?

To ask such a question is to go, at once, below or beyond the purely literary terrain. It is to pose the whole problem of individuality and its life history. But it is to pose the problem in a form to which writers neither as writers nor as human beings can afford to be indifferent. There is really no more acute, no more concrete, no more pressingly personal a problem, at the moment, than this. Is our familiar individualism, our conception of ourselves as "simple, separate persons," equivalent any longer to the achievement of a sound individuality? "Trust thyself": does every heart still vibrate to that "iron string"? Specifically, can American writers hope to develop fully as individuals while divorcing themselves not only from society as a whole but from any class or group within society? With what group or class, indeed, *can* they ally themselves? Is the alternative to literary individualism the surrender to a merely political movement, or, worse still, to some form of repressive standardization? Are there now no supra-personal purposes with which a writer can affiliate himself?

Our answers to such questions will be really satisfactory only if, in giving them, we are able to look back upon the road we have come on. For the story of American letters is the story of the blossoming, the fruition, and the corruption of exactly the individualism that is now on trial. It is far from being a new thing: it is a many times more than twice-told tale. In its origins it was a fruitful principle because it corresponded to a historical reality, to a historical reality that is now part of our past. In short, American writers have always belonged to the middle class, and not only in the literal sense of being born in it: they have belonged to the middle class spiritually, and their self-reliance, their self-expression, their self-consciousness have expressed the sociological individualism of their class heritage. It is no accident that, emblematically at least, at the very gateway of American literature should stand two autobiographies: no accident that Jonathan Edwards should have written his "Personal Narrative" or Franklin the story of his life. Nothing was more natural than that Edwards and Franklin should have taken themselves as subjects; between them, they span the whole reach, upward and downward, of the individualist principle; they are the sacred and profane extremes of one spirit—Edwards, with his Calvinistic particularism, his intense introspectiveness, his spiritual egoism; Franklin, with his complete system of self-help, his enlightened careerism, his pragmatic worship of frugality and diligence. Neither man can be imagined in a precapitalist order. Only one essential note in our national chorus remained to be struck, and that was the secessionist note of the frontier; when Fenimore Cooper created the character of Leatherstocking, the embodiment of backwoods resourcefulness, independence, and idiosyncracy, the ensemble was complete.

Complete, that is, psychologically. In a literary sense, American individualism was not to reach its apogee until the generation which filled in the twenty or thirty years before the Civil War. These years witnessed, from a cultural point of view, the historic culmination of the principle of self-reliance: during these years that principle, because it rationalized the true needs of society, had a genuine spiritual authority. It was a period, in short, when our special form of individualism could really be reconciled with the deeper-lying claims of individuality; when a man could achieve distinction as a person without going much beyond the limits of self-reliance. This is, of course, what accounts for the literary pre-eminence, in the age, of Emerson ("Accept your genius and say what you think"), of Thoreau ("I would rather sit on a pumpkin and have it all to myself than be crowded on a velvet cushion"), and of Whitman ("I will effuse egotism"). In these three men our individualism, on its brighter side, attained its classic meridian. There was of course, even then, a darker side; there were men for whom the gospel of self-help—or the habit of estrangement, which is a form it may always take—proved to be the path toward confusion, morbidity, and a kind of impotence; and Poe, Hawthorne, and Melville, men of the richest endowments, paid a tragic price for sitting on pumpkins and effusing egotism. Their careers suggest that the principle, from the artist's point of view, sat best a precarious one; and that its spiritual fruitfulness is exhausted almost before it is realized.

The sequel of the Civil War demonstrated the exhaustion at least of its youthful energies. The triumph of economic irresponsibility, in the feverish burgeoning of big business after the war, coincided with the corruption of individualism as a cultural motive. Two things happened: on the one hand, the writers of secondary talents watered down and deodorized the old contumacy until it became reconcilable with the mildest heresies and even with a conformity in which neither self-reliance nor self-expression had breathing-space; on the other hand, the writers of genius, incapable of such surrender, went still farther along the path taken by Poe, Hawthorne, and Melville. To turn from Emerson to G. W. Curtis, from Thoreau to John Muir, from Whitman to Burroughs, is to turn, as if in a single life-span, from Moses to Zedekiah. The contrast is instructive enough, yet it is less eloquent than the spectacle offered by the higher careers of Henry James, Mark Twain, and Henry Adams. Hawthorne's theme of estrangement, the Ishmaelite theme that obsessed Melville, were driven by Henry James to a formulation still more extreme; and expatriation, the frankest form of desertion, became both his literary munition and his personal fate. With Mark Twain the Fenimore Cooper wheel came full circle: the old, heroic anarchism of the backwoods is travestied, in its decay, by Mark Twain's vacillation between a servile conformity and the puerile philosophy of self-interest outlined in "What Is Man?" ("From his cradle to his grave a man never does a single thing which has any *first and foremost* object but one—to secure peace of mind, spiritual comfort *for himself.*") For Mark Twain the outcome was, not Emerson's and Whitman's "fatalistic optimism," but an equally fatalistic pessimism and Henry Adams, who had a truer sense of the limits of self-interest, but whose social impotence and personal isolation were still more thoroughgoing, stands very close to Mark Twain as our first consistent preacher of futility.

II

By the turn of the century the old class basis of American literature was rapidly entering upon the cycle of erosion, subsidence, and re-emergence. It was still true that American writers belonged personally to the middle classes, but the old bond between literary expression and the middle-class philosophy had been broken once for all; and henceforth there seemed to be only the choice between a loyalism that was the negation of individuality and a repudiation that too generally left its heresiarchs high and dry. For a fresh alignment of a positive sort the time was not yet ripe; and by the second decade of the century we found ourselves in the midst of an individualistic revolt which superficially seemed to appeal to the authority of Emerson, Thoreau, and Whitman, but which, unlike theirs, was radically personal and anti-social. It had been anticipated, a few years before, by the Nietzschean egoism of Jack London and the antinomianism of Dreiser; and it was to mingle the elements of misanthropy, transcendentalism, anarchism, and high aspiration in bewildering proportions. The new individualism ran the whole gamut from the Menckenian-Cabellian praise of aristocracy to Anderson's primitivism and O'Neill's romantic affirmations, from Lewis' exposure of the standardized bourgeois to Van Wyck Brooks' subtle studies in frustration.

In the perspective of history, the high colors in which this generation dealt will doubtless show like the hues in the clouds that surround a setting sun. It was the last chapter of one volume, not the first of a new one; and of this essential belatedness the patriarchal gravity, the chilly sagacity of such poets as Robinson and Frost are but convenient measures.

The vitality of that movement was naturally still shorter-lived than the "Emersonian June" itself had been. The hopeless sterility of a pure individualism at this moment in history could hardly be more dramatically demonstrated than by the collapse of the Menckenian boom in our own "reconstruction" after the war. The men who led it, of course, still survive, but they have subsided either into silence or into a bewilderment that masks itself variously; and their juniors, for the most part, have drawn the moral from their experience in either one of two disastrous but natural ways. One group, the heirs of Poe, Hawthorne, and Melville, have retreated, in their despair of finding solid ground on which to build a personal life, to an explicit philosophy of negation; and pitched here and there on the sands of the Waste Land one descries the tents, black as Tamburlaine's on the third day of a siege, of Jeffers and MacLeish, of Krutch and Aiken, of Hemingway and Faulkner. The other group, less honest emotionally, but intellectually more impressive, has taken refuge from the high winds of individualism in the shelter of some archaic code, religious, authoritarian, or sociological: humanism, neo-Thomism, Alexandrianism, royalism, or agrarianism. Both the negativists and the authoritarians betray all the symptoms of corruption: both shine with the phosphorescence of decay; but the latter have at least the logic that goes with positive loyalties.

For the necessary answers to the questions we began with are be-coming arrive. For the moment the important thing is that American criticism should define its position; in the midst of so much confusion, so much wasted effort, so much hesitation, this will itself be an advance.

From *The Nation,* Vol. CXXXIII (October 14, 1931), pp. 391-393. Reprinted by permission of the author and editors.

Edmund Wilson

Marxism and Literature

[1937]

Let us begin with Marx and Engels. What was the role assigned to literature and art in the system of Dialectical Materialism? This role was much less cut-and-dried than is nowadays often supposed. Marx and Engels conceived the forms of human society in any given country and epoch as growing out of the methods of production which prevailed at that place and time; and out of the relations involved in the social forms arose a "superstructure" of higher activities such as politics, law, religion, philosophy, literature and art. These activities were not, as is sometimes assumed, wholly explicable in terms of economics. They showed the mold, in ways direct or indirect, of the social configuration below them, but each was working to get away from its roots in the social classes and to constitute a professional group, with its own discipline and its own standards of value, which cut across class lines. These departments "all react upon one another and upon the economic base. It is not the case that the economic situation is the sole active cause and everything else only a passive effect. But there is a reciprocal interaction within a fundamental economic necessity, which in the last instance always asserts itself" (Engels to Hans Starkenburg, January 25, 1894). So that the art of a great artistic period may reach a point of vitality and vision where it can influence the life of the period down to its very economic foundations. Simply, it must cease to flourish with the social, system which made it possible by providing the artist with training and leisure, even though the artist himself may have been working for the destruction of that system.

Marx and Engels, unlike sore of their followers, never attempted to furnish social-economic formulas by which the validity of works of art might be tested. They had grown up in the sunset of Goethe before the great age of German literature was over, and they had both set out in their youth to be poets; they responded to imaginative work, first of all, on its artistic merits. They could ridicule a trashy writer like Eugene Sue for what they regarded as his *petit bourgeois* remedies for the miseries of contemporary society (*The Holy Family*); they could become bitter about Ferdinand Freiligrath, who had deserted the Communist League and turned nationalist in 1870 (Marx to Engels, August 22, 1870). And Marx could even make similar jibes at Heine when he thought that the latter had stooped to truckling to the authorities or when he read the expressions of piety in his will (Marx to Engels, December 21, 1866 and May 8, 1856). But Marx's daughter tells us that her father loved Heine as much as his work and was very indulgent of his political shortcomings. He used to say that the poets were originals, who must be allowed to go their own way, and that one shouldn't apply to them the same standards as to ordinary people: It was not characteristic of Marx and Engels to judge literature—that is, literature of power and distinction—in terms of its purely political tendencies. In fact, Engels always warned the socialist novelists against the dangers of *Tendenz-Literatur* (Engels to Minna Kautsky, November 26, 1885; and to Margaret Harkness, April 1888). In writing to Minna Kautsky about one of her novels, he tells her that the personalities of her hero and heroine have been dissolved in the principles they represent. "You evidently," he says, "felt the need of publicly taking sides in the book, of proclaiming your opinions of the world... But I believe that the tendency should arise from the situation and the action themselves without being explicitly formulated, and that the poet is not under the obligation to furnish the reader with a ready-made historical solution for the future of the conflict which he describes." When Ferdinand Lassalle sent Marx and Engels his poetic tragedy, *Franz von Sickingen*, and invited them to criticize it, Marx replied that, "setting aside any purely critical attitude toward the work," it had on a first reading affected him powerfully—characteristically adding that upon persons of a more emotional nature it would doubtless produce an even stronger effect; and Engels wrote that he had read it twice and had been moved by it so profoundly that he had been obliged to lay it aside in order to arrive at any critical perspective. It was only after pulling themselves together and making some purely literary observations that they were able to proceed to discuss, from their special historical point of view, the period with which the drama dealt and to show how Lassalle's own political position had led him to mistake the role of his hero. Aeschylus Marx loved for his grandeur and for the defiance of Zeus by Prometheus; Goethe they both immensely admired: Engels wrote of him as a "colossal" and "universal" genius whose career had been marred by an admixture in his character of the philistine and the courtier (*German Socialism in Verse and Prose*); Shakespeare Marx knew by heart and was extremely fond of quoting, but never—despite the long, learned and ridiculous essays which have appeared irk the Soviet magazine, *International Literature*—attempted to draw from his plays any general social moral. So far, indeed, was Marx from having worked out a systematic explanation of the relation of art to social arrangements that he could assert, apropos of Greek art, in his *Introduction to the Critique of Political Economy*, that "certain periods of highest development of art stand in no direct connection with the general development of society, nor with the material basis and the skeleton structure of its organization."

With Marx and Engels there is not yet any tendency to specialize art as a "weapon." They were both too much under the influence of the ideal of the many-sided man of the Renaissance, or the "complete" man, who, like Leonardo, had been painter, mathematician and engineer, or, like Machiavelli, poet, historian and strategist, before the division of labor had had the effect of splitting up human nature and limiting everyone to some single function (Engels' preface to his *Dialectic and Nature*). But with Lenin we come to a Marxist who is specialized himself as an organizer and fighter. Like most Russians, Lenin was sensitive to music; but Gorky tells us that on one occasion, after listening to Beethoven's Appassionato Sonata and exclaiming that he "would like to listen to it everyday: it is marvelous superhuman music—I always think with pride...what marvelous things human beings can do," he screwed up his eyes and smiled sadly and added: "But I can't listen to music too often. It affects your nerves, makes you want to say stupid, nice things, and stroke the heads of people who could create such beauty while living in this vile hell. And now you mustn't stroke anyone's head—you might get your hand bitten off." Yet he was fond of fiction, poetry and the theater, and by no means doctrinaire in his tastes. Krupskaya tells how, on a visit to a Youth Commune, he asked the young people, "What do you read? Do you read Pushkin?" "Oh, no!" someone blurted out. "He was a bourgeois. Mayakovsky for us." Ilyitch smiled. "I think Pushkin is better." Gorky says that one day he found Lenin with *War and Peace* lying on the table: "Yes, Tolstoy. I wanted to read over the scene of the hunt, then remembered that I had to write a comrade. Absolutely no time for reading." Smiling and screwing up his eyes, he stretched himself deliciously in his armchair and, lowering his voice, added quickly, "What a colossus, eh? What a marvelously developed brain! Here's an artist for you, sir. And do you know something still more amazing? You couldn't find a genuine *muzhik* in literature till this count came upon the scene." In his very acute essays on Tolstoy, he deals with him much as Engels deals with Goethe—with tremendous admiration for Tolstoy's genius, but with an analysis of his non-resistance and mysticism in terms not, it is interesting to note, of the psychology of the landed nobility, but of the patriarchal peasantry with whom Tolstoy had identified himself. And Lenin's attitude toward Gorky was much like that of Marx toward Heine. He suggests in one of his letters that Gorky would be helpful as a journalist on the side of the Bolsheviks, but adds that he mustn't be bothered if he is busy writing a book.

Trotsky is a literary man as Lenin never was, and he published in 1924 a most remarkable little study called *Literature and Revolution*. In this book he tried to illuminate the problems which were arising for Russian writers with the new society of the Revolution. And he was obliged to come to grips with a question with which Marx and Engels had not been much concerned—the question of what Mr. James T. Farrell in his book, *A Note on Literary Criticism*, one of the few sensible recent writings on this subject, calls "the carryover value" of literature. Marx had assumed the value of Shakespeare and the Greeks and more or less left it at that. But what, the writers in Russia were now asking, was to be the value of the literature and art of the ages of barbarism and oppression in the dawn of socialist freedom? What in particular was to be the status of the culture of that bourgeois society from which socialism had just emerged and of which it still bore the unforgotten scars? Would there be a new proletarian literature, with new language, new style, new form, to give expression to the emotions and ideas of the new proletarian dictatorship? There had been in Russia a group called the Proletcult, which aimed at monopolizing the control of Soviet literature; but Lenin had discouraged and opposed it, insisting that proletarian culture was not something which could be produced synthetically and by official dictation of policy, but only by natural evolution as a "development of those reserves of knowledge which society worked for under the oppression of capitalism, of the landlords, of the officials." Now, in *Literature and*

Revolution, Trotsky asserted that "such terms as 'proletarian literature' and 'proletarian culture' are dangerous, because they erroneously compress the culture of the future into the narrow limits of the present day." In a position to observe from his Marxist point of view the effects on a national literature of the dispossession of a dominant class, he was able to see the unexpected ways in which the presentments of life of the novelists, the feelings and images of the poets, the standards themselves of the critics, were turning out to be determined by their attitudes toward the social-economic crisis. But he did not believe in a proletarian culture which would displace the bourgeois one. The bourgeois literature of the French Revolution had ripened under the old regime; but the illiterate proletariat and peasantry of Russia had had no chance to produce a culture, nor would there be time for them to do so in he future, because the proletarian dictatorship was not to last: it was to be only a transition phase and to lead the way to "a culture which is above classes ad which will be the first truly human culture." In the meantime, the new socialist literature would grow directly out of that which had already been produced during the domination of the bourgeoisie. Communism, Trotsky said, had as yet no artistic culture; it had only a political culture.

All this seems to us reasonable enough. But, reasonable and cultured as Trotsky is, ready as he is to admit that "one cannot always go by the principles of Marxism in deciding whether to accept or reject a work of art," that such a work "should be judged in the first place by its own law—that is, by the law of art," there is none the less in the whole situation something which is alien to us. We are not accustomed, in our quarter of the world, either to having the government attempt to control literature and art or to having literary and artistic movements tyro identify themselves with the government. Yet Russia, since the Revolution, has had a whole series of cultural groups which have attempted to dominate literature either with or without the authority of the government; and

Trotsky himself, in his official position, even in combating these tendencies, cannot avoid passing censure and pinning ribbons. Sympathizers with the Soviet regime used to assume that this state of affairs was inseparable from the realization of socialism: that its evils would be easily outgrown and that in any case it was a great thing to have the government take so lively an interest in culture. I believe that this view was mistaken. Under the Tsar, imaginative literature in Russia played a role which was probably different from any role it had ever played in the life of any other nation. Political and social criticism, pursued and driven underground by the censorship, was forced to incorporate itself in the dramatic imagery of fiction. This was certainly one of the principal reasons for the greatness during the nineteenth century of the Russian theater and novel, for the mastery by the Russian writers—from Pushkin's time to Tolstoy's—of the art of implication. In the fifties and sixties, the stories of Turgenev, which seem mild enough to us today, were capable of exciting the mast passionate controversies—and even, in the case of *A Sportsman's Sketches*, causing the dismissal of the censor who had passed it—because each was regarded as a political message. Ever since the Revolution, literature and politics in Russia have remained inextricable. But after the Revolution the intelligentsia themselves were in power; and it became plain that in the altered situation the identification of literature with politics was liable to terrible abuses. Lenin and Trotsky, Lunacharsky and Gorky, worked sincerely to keep literature free; but they had at the same time, from the years of Tsardom, a keen sense of the possibility of art as an instrument of propaganda. Lenin took a special interest in the moving pictures from the propaganda point of view; and the first Soviet films, by Eisenstein and Pudovkin, were masterpieces of implication, as the old novels and plays had been. But Lenin died; Trotsky was exiled; Lunacharsky died. The administration of Stalin, unliterary and uncultivated himself, slipped into depending more and more on literature as a means of manipulating a people of whom, before the Revolution, 70 or 80 per cent had been illiterate and who could hardly be expected to be critical of what they read. Gorky seems to have exerted what influence he could in the direction of liberalism: to him was due, no doubt, the liquidation of RAPP, the latest device for the monopoly of culture, and the opening of the Soviet canon to the best contemporary foreign writing and the classics. But though this made possible more freedom of form and a wider range of reading, it could not, under the dictatorship of Stalin, either stimulate or release a living literature, where no political opposition was possible, there was possible no political criticism; and in Russia political questions involve vitally the fate of society. What reality can there be for the Russians, the most socially-minded writers on earth, in a freedom purely "esthetic"? Even the fine melodramatic themes of the post-revolutionary cinema and theater, with their real emotion and moral conviction, have been replaced by simple trash not very far removed from Hollywood, or by dramatized exemplifications of the latest "directive" of Stalin which open the night after the speech that has announced the directive. The recent damning of the music of Shostakovich on the ground that the commissars were unable to hum it seems a withdrawal from the liberal position. And it is probable that the death of Gorky, as well as the imprisonment of Bukharin and Radek, have removed the last brakes from a precipitate descent, in the artistic as well as the political field, into a nightmare of informing and repression, The practice of deliberate falsification of social and political history which began at the time of the Stalin-Trotsky crisis and which has now attained proportions so fantastic that the government does not seem to hesitate to pass the sponge ever month or so over everything that the people have previously been told and to present them with a new and contradictory version of their history, their duty, and the characters and careers of their leaders—this practice cannot fail in the end to corrupt every department of intellectual life, till the serious, the humane, the clear-seeing must simply, if they can, remain silent.

Thus Marxism in Russia for the moment has run itself into a blind alley—or rather, it has been put down a well. The Soviets seem hardly at the present time to have retained even the Marxist political culture, even in its cruder forms—so that we are relieved from the authority of Russia as we are deprived of her inspiration. To what conclusions shall we come, then at this time of day about Marxism and literature—basing our views not even necessarily upon texts from the Marxist Fathers, but upon ordinary commonsense? Well, first of all, that we can go even further than Trotsky in one of the dicta I have quoted above and declare that Marxism by itself can tell us nothing whatever about the goodness or badness of a work of art. A man may be an excellent Marxist, but if he lacks imagination and taste he will be unable to make the choice between a good and an inferior book both of which are ideologically unexceptionable. What Marxism can do, however, is throw a great deal of light on the origins and social significance of works of art. The study of literature in its relation to society is as old as Herder—and even Vico. Coleridge had flashes of insight into the connection between literary and social phenomena, as when he saw the Greek state in the Greek sentence and the individualism of the English in the short separate statements of Chaucer's Prologue. But the great bourgeois master of this kind of criticism was Taine, with his race and *moument* and *milieu*; yet Taine, for all his scientific professions, responded artistically to literary art, and responded so vividly that his summings-up of writers and re-creations of periods sometimes rival or surpass their subjects. Marx and Engels further deepened this study of literature in relation to its social background by demonstrating for the first time inescapably the importance of economic systems. But if Marx and Engels and Lenin and Trotsky are worth listening to on the subject of books, it is not merely because they created

Marxism, but also because they were capable of literary appreciation.

Yet the man who tries to apply Marxist principles without real understanding of literature is liable to go horribly wrong. For one thing, it is usually true in works of the highest order that the purport is not a simple message, but a complex vision of things, which itself is not explicit but implicit; and the reader who does not grasp them artistically, but is merely looking for simple social morals, is certain to be hopelessly confused. Especially will he be confused if the author *does* draw an explicit moral which is the opposite of or has nothing to do with his real purport. Friedrich Engels, in the letter to Margaret Harkness already referred to above, in warning her that the more the novelist allows his political ideas to "remain hidden, the better it is for the work of art," says that Balzac, with his reactionary opinions, is worth a thousand of Zola, with all his democratic ones. (Balzac was one of the great literary admirations of both Engels and Marx, the latter of whom had planned to write a book on him). Engels points out that Balzac himself was, or believed himself to be, a legitimist engaged in deploring the decline of high society; but that actually "his irony is never more bitter, his satire never more trenchant, than when he is showing us these aristocrats … for whom he felt so profound a sympathy," and that "the only men of whom he speaks with undissimulated admiration are his most determined political adversaries, the republican heroes of the Cloitre-Saint-Merri, the men who at that Period (1830-1836) truly represented the popular masses." Nor doe it matter necessarily in a work of art whether the characters are shown engaged in a conflict which illustrates the larger conflicts of society or in one which from that point of view is trivial. In art—it is quite obvious in music, but it is also true in literature—a sort of law of moral interchangeability prevails; we may transpose the actions and the sentiments that move us into terms of whatever we do or are ourselves. Real genius of moral insight is motor which will start any engine. When

Proust, in his wonderful chapter on the death of the novelist Bergotte, speaks of those moral obligations which impose themselves in spite of everything and which seem to come through to humanity from some source outside its wretched self (obligations "invisible only to fools—and are they really to them?"), he is describing a kind of duty which he felt only in connection with the literary work which he performed in his dark and fetid room; yet he speaks for every moral, esthetic or intellectual passion which holds the expediencies of the world in contempt. And the hero of Thornton Wilder's *Heaven's My Destination*, the traveling salesman who tries to save souls in the smoking car and writes Bible texts on hotel blotters, is something more than a symptom of Thornton Wilder's religious tendencies: he is the type of all saints who begin absurdly; and Wilder's story would be as true of the socialist Upton Sinclair as of the Christian George Brush. Nor does it necessarily matter, for the moral effect of a work of literature, whether the forces of bravery or virtue with which we identify ourselves are victorious or vanquished in the end. In Hemingway's story *The Undefeated*, the old bullfighter who figures as the hero is actually humiliated and killed, but his courage has itself been a victory. It is true, as I. Kashkin, the Soviet critic, has said, that Hemingway has written much about decadence, but in order to write tellingly about death you have to have the principle of life, and those that have it will make it felt in spite of everything.

The Leftist critic with no literary competence is always trying to measure works of literature by tests which have no validity in that field. And one of his favorite occupations is giving specific directions and working out diagrams for the construction of ideal Marxist books. Such formulas are of course perfectly futile. The rules observed in any given school of art become apparent, not before but after, the actual works of art have been produced. As we were reminded by Burton. Rascoe at the time of the Humanist controversy, the esthetic laws involved in Greek tragedy were not formulated by Aristotle until at least half a century after Euripides and Sophocles were dead. And the behavior of the Marxist critics has been precisely like that of the Humanists. The Humanists knew down to the last comma what they wanted a work of literature tube, but they never—with the possible exception, when pressed, of *The Bridge* of Sara Luis Rey, about which they had, however, hesitations—were able to find any contemporary work which fitted their specifications. The Marxists did just the same thing. In an article called "The Crisis in Criticism" in the *New Masses* of February 1933, Granville Hicks drew up a list of requirements which the ideal Marxist work of literature must meet. The primary function of such a work , he asserted, must be to "lead the proletarian reader to recognize his role in the class struggle"—and it must therefore (1) "directly or indirectly show the effects of the class struggle"; (2) "the author must be able to make the reader fell that he is participating in the lives described"; and, finally, (3) the author's point of view must "be that of the vanguard of the proletariat; he should be, or should try to make himself, a member of the proletariat." This formula, he says, "gives us … a standard by which to recognize the perfect Marxian novel"—and adds "no novel as yet written perfectly conforms to our demands." But the doctrine of "socialist realism" promulgated at the Soviet Writers' Congress of August 1934 was only an attempt on a larger scale to legislate masterpieces into existence—a kind of attempt which always indicates sterility on the part of those who engage in it, and which always actually works, if it has any effect at all, to legislate existing good literature *out of* existence and to discourage the production of any more. The prescribes for the literature of the future usually cherish some great figure of the past whom they regard as having fulfilled their conditions and whom they are always bringing forward to demonstrate the inferiority of the literature of the present. As there has never existed a great writer who really had anything in common with these critics' conception of literature, they are obliged to provide imaginary versions of what their ideal great writers are like. The Humanists had Sophocles and Shakespeare; the socialist realists had Tolstoy. Yet it ascertain that if Tolstoy had had to live up to the objectives and prohibitions which the socialist realists proposed he could never have written a chapter, and that if Babbitt and More had been able to enforce against Shakespeare their moral and esthetic injunctions he would never have written a line. The misrepresentation of Sophocles, which has involved even a tampering with his text in the interests not merely of Humanism but of academic classicism in general, has been one of the scandalous absurdities of scholarship. The Communist critical movement in America, which had for its chief spokesman Mr. Hicks, tended to identify their ideal with the work of John Dos Passos. In order to make this possible, it was necessary to invent an imaginary Dos Passos. This ideal Dos Passos was a Communist, who wrote stories about the proletariat, at a time when the real Dos Passos was engaged in bringing out a long novel about the effects of the capitalist system on the American middle-class and had announced himself—in the *New Republic* in 1930—politically a "middle-class liberal." The ideal Dos Passos was something like Gorky without the mustache—Gorky, in the meantime, having himself ungone some transmogrification at the hands of Soviet publicity—and this myth was maintained until the Communist critics were finally compelled to repudiate it, not because they had acquired new light on Dos Passos, the novelist and dramatist, but because of his attitude toward events in Russia.

The object of these formulas for the future, as may be seen from the above quotations from Mr. Hicks, is to make of art an effective instrument in the class struggle. And we must deal with the dogma that "art is a weapon." It is true that art may be a weapon; but in the case of some of the greatest works of art, some of those which have the longest carry-over value, it is difficult to see that any important part of this value is due to their direct functioning as weapons. The *Divine Comedy*, in its political aspect, is a weapon for Henry of Luxemburg, whom Dante—with his medieval internationalism and his lack of sympathy for the nationalistic instincts which were impelling the Italians of his time to getaway from their Austrian emperors—was so passionately eager to impose on his countrymen. Today we may say with Carducci that we would as soon see the crown of his "good Frederick" rolling in Olona vale: "Jove perishes; the poet's hymn remains." And, though Shakespeare's *Henry IV* and *Henry V* are weapons for Elizabethan imperialism, their real center is not Prince Hat but Falstaff; and Falstaff is the father of *Hamlet* and of all Shakespeare's tragic heroes, who, if they illustrate any social moral—the moral, perhaps, that Renaissance princes, supreme in their little worlds, may go to pieces in all kinds of terrible ways for lack of a larger social organism to restrain them—do so evidently without Shakespeare's being aware of it. If these works may be spoken of as weapons at all, they are weapons in the more general struggle of modern European man emerging from the Middle Ages and striving to understand his world and himself—a function for which "weapon" is hardly the right word. The truth is that there is short-range and long-range literature. Long-range literature attempts to sum up wide areas and long periods of human experience, or to extract from them general laws; short-range literature preaches and pamphleteers with the view to an immediate effect. A good deal of the recent confusion of our writers in the Leftist camp has been due to their not understanding, or being unable to make up their minds, whether they are aiming at long-range or short-range writing.

This brings us to the question of what sort of periods are most favorable for works of art. One finds an assumption on the Left that revolutionary or pre-revolutionary periods are apt to produce new and vital forms of literature. This, of course, is very far from the truth in the case of periods of actual revolution. The more highly developed forms of literature require leisure and a certain amount of stability; and during a period of revolution the writer is usually deprived of both. The literature of the French Revolution consisted of the orations of Danton, the journalism of Camille Desmoulins and the few political poems that Andre Chancier had a chance to write before he was guillotine. The literature of the Russian Revolution was the political writing of Lenin and Trotsky, and Alexander Blok's poem, *The Twelve*, almost the last fruit of his genius before it was nipped by the wind of the storm. As for pre-revolutionary periods in which the new forces are fermenting, they *may* be great periods for literature—as the eighteenth century was in France and the nineteenth century in Russia (though here there was a decadence after 1905). But the conditions that make possible the masterpieces are apparently not produced by the impending revolutions, but by the phenomenon of literary technique, already highly developed, in the hands of a writer who has had the support of long-enduring institutions. He may reflect an age of transition, but it will not necessarily be true that his face is set squarely in the direction of the future. The germs of the Renaissance rein Dante and the longing for a better world in Virgil, but neither Dante nor Virgil can in any real sense be described as a revolutionary writer: they sum up or write elegies for ages that are passing. The social organisms that give structure to their thought—the Roman Empire and the Catholic Church—are already showing signs of decay. It is impossible, therefore, to identify the highest creative work in art with the most active moments of creative social change. The writer who is seriously intent on producing long-range works of literature should, from the point of view of his own special personal interests, thank his stars if there is no violent revolution going on in his own country in his time. He may disapprove of the society he is writing about, but if it were disrupted by an actual upheaval he would probably not be able to write.

But what about "proletarian literature" as an accompaniment of the social revolution? In the earlier days of the Communist regime in Russia, one used to hear about Russian authors who, in the effort to eliminate from their writings any vestige of the bourgeois point of view, had reduced their vocabulary and syntax to what they regarded as an ABC of essentials—with the result of becoming more unintelligible to the proletarian audience at whom they were aiming than if they had been Symbolist poets. (Indeed, the futurist poet Mayakovsky has since that time become a part of the Soviet canon.) Later on, as I have said, Soviet culture followed the road that Trotsky recommended: it began building again on the classics and on the bourgeois culture of other countries and on able revolutionary Russian writers who had learned their trade before the Revolution. "Soviet publishers"—I quote from the Russian edition of *International Literature*, issue 2 of 1936— "are bringing out Hemingway and Proust not merely in order to demonstrate bourgeois decay." Every genuine work of art—and such are the productions of Hemingway and Proust—enriches the writer's knowledge of life and heightens his esthetic sensibility and his emotional culture—in a word, it figures, in the broad sense, as a factor of educational value. Liberated socialist humanity inherits all that is beautiful, elevating and sustaining in the culture of previous ages. The truth is that the talk in Soviet Russia about proletarian literature and art has resulted from the persistence of the same situation which led Tolstoy under the old regime to put on the muzhik's blouse and to go in for carpentry, cobbling and plowing, the difficulty experienced by an educated minority, who were only about 20 per cent of the people, in Vetting in touch with the illiterate majority. In America the situation is quite different. The percentage of illiterates in this country is only something like 4 per cent; and there is relatively little difficulty of communication between different social groups. Our development away from England, and from the old world generally, in this respect—in the direction of the democratization of our idiom—is demonstrated clearly in H. L. Mencken's *The American Language*; and if it is a question of either the use for high literature of the language of the people or the expression of the dignity and importance of the ordinary man, the country which has produced *Leaves of Grass* and *Huckleberry Finn* has certainly nothing to learn from Russia. We had created during our pioneering period a literature of the common man's escape, not only from feudal Europe, but also from bourgeois society, many years before the Russian masses were beginning to write their names. There has been a section of our recent American literature of the last fifteen years or so—the period of the boom and the depression—which has dealt with our industrial and rural life from the point of view of the factory hand and the poor farmer under conditions which were forcing him to fight for his life, and this has been called proletarian literature; but it has been accompanied by books on the white-collar worker, the storekeeper, the well-to-do merchant, the scientist and the millionaire in situations equally disastrous or degrading. And this whole movement of critical and imaginative writing—though with some stimulus, certainly, from Russia—had come quite naturally out of our literature of the past. It is curious to observe that one of the best of the recent strike novels, *The Land of Plenty* by Robert Cantwell, himself a Westerner and a former mill worker, owes a good deal to Henry James.

Yet when all these things have been said, all the, questions have not been answered. All that has been said has been said of the past; and Marxism is something new in the world: it is a philosophical system which leads directly to programs of action. Has there ever appeared before in literature such a phenomenon as M. Andre Malraux, who alternates between attempts, sometimes brilliant, to write long-range fiction on revolutionary themes, and exploits of aviation for the cause of revolution in Spain? Here creative political action and the more complex kind of imaginative writing have united at least to the extent that they have arisen from the same vision of history and have been included in the career of one man. The Marxist vision of Lenin—Vincent Sheean has said it first—has in its completeness and its compelling force a good deal in common with the vision of Dante; but, partly realized by Lenin during his lifetime and still potent for some years after his death, it was a creation, not of literary art, but of actual social engineering. It is society itself, says Trotsky, which under communism becomes the work of art. The first attempts at this art will be inexpert and they will have refractory material to work with; and the philosophy of the Marxist dialectic involves idealistic and mythological elements which have led too often to social religion rather than to social art. Yet the human imagination has already come to conceive the possibility of recreating human society; and how can we doubt that, as it acquires the power, it must emerge from what will seem by comparison the revolutionary "underground" of art as we have always known it up to now and deal with the materials of actual life in ways which we cannot now even foresee? This is to speak in terms of centuries, of ages; but, in practicing and prizing literature, we must note unaware of the first efforts of the human spirit to transcend literature itself.

From *The Triple Thinkers* by Edmund Wilson. First published in 1938, by Harcourt, Brace and Company, Inc; and in a revised edition by the Oxford University Press, 1948, from which the essay is here reproduced by permission of the author and publishers, first published in *The Atlantic Monthly*, Vol. CLX (December, 1937), pp. 741-750.

Lionel Trilling

Freud and Literature

[1940-1947]

The Freudian psychology is the only systematic account of the human mind which, in point of subtlety and complexity, of interest and tragic power, deserves to stand beside the chaotic mass of psychological insights which literature has accumulated through the centuries. To pass from the reading of a great literary work to a treatise of academic psychology is to pass from one order of perception to another, but the human nature of the Freudian psychology is exactly the stuff upon which the poet has always exercised his art. It is therefore not surprising that the psychoanalytical theory has had a great effect upon literature. Yet the relationships reciprocal, and the effect of Freud upon literature has been no greater than the effect of literature upon Freud. When, on the occasion of the celebration of his seventieth birthday, Freud was greeted as the "discoverer of the unconscious," he corrected the speaker and disclaimed the title. "The poets and philosophers before me discovered the unconscious," he said. "What I discovered was the scientific method by which the unconscious can be studied." A lack of specific evidence prevents us from considering the particular literary "influences" upon the founder of psychoanalysis; and, besides, when we think of the men who so clearly anticipated many of Freud's own ideas—Schopenhauer and Nietzsche, for example—and then learn that he did not read their works until after he had formulated his own theories, we must see that particular influences cannot be in question here but that what we must deal with is nothing less than a whole *Zeitgeist*, a direction of thought. For psychoanalysis is one of the culminations of the Romanticist literature of the nineteenth century. If there is perhaps a contradiction in the idea of a science standing upon the shoulders of a literature which avows itself inimical to science in so many ways, the contradiction will be resolved if we remember that this literature, despite its avowals, was itself scientific in at least the sense of being passionately devoted to a research into the self.

In showing the connection between Freud and this Romanticist tradition, it is difficult to know where to begin, but there might be a certain aptness in starting even back of the tradition, as far back as 1762 with Diderot's *Rameau's Nephew*. At any rate, certain men at the heart of nineteenth-century thought were agreed in finding a peculiar importance in this brilliant little work: Goethe translated it, Marx admired it, Hegel—as Marx reminded Engels in the letter which announced that he was sending the book as a gift—praised and expounded it at length, Shaw was impressed by it, and Freud himself, as we know from a quotation in his *Introductory Lectures*, read it with the pleasure of agreement. The dialogue takes place between Diderot himself and a nephew of the famous composer. The protagonist, the younger Rameau its a despised, outcast, shameless fellow; Hegel calls him the "disintegrated consciousness" and credits him with great wit, for it is he who breaks down all the normal social values and makes new combinations with the pieces. As for Diderot, the deuterogamist, he is what Hegel calls the "honest consciousness," and Hegel considers him reasonable, decent, and dull. It is quite clear that the author does not despise his Rameau and does not mean us to. Rameau is lustful and greedy, arrogant yet selfabasing, perceptive yet "wrong," like a child. Still, Diderot seems actually to be giving the fellow a kind of superiority over himself, as though Rameau represents the elements which, dangerous but wholly necessary, lie beneath the reasonable decorum of social life. It would perhaps be pressing too far to find in Rameau Freud's *id* and in Diderot Freud's *ego*; yet the connection does suggest itself; and at least we have here the perception which is to be the common characteristic of both Freud and Romanticism, the perception of the hidden element of human nature and of the opposition between the hidden and the visible. We have too the bold perception of just what lies hidden: "If the little savage [i.e., the child] were left to himself, if he preserved all his foolishness and combined the violent passions of a man of thirty with the lack of reason of a child in the cradle, he'd wring his father's neck and go to bed with his mother."

From the self-exposure of Rameau to Rousseau's account of his own childhood is no great step; society might ignore or reject the idea of the "immorality" which lies concealed in the beginning of the career of the "good" man, just as it might turn away from Blake struggling to expound a psychology which would include the forces beneath the propriety of social man in general, but the idea of the hidden thing went forward to become one of the dominant notions of the age. The hidden element takes many forms and it is not necessarily "dark" and "bad"; for Blake the "bad" was the good, while for Wordsworth and Burke what was hidden and unconscious was wisdom and power, which work in despite of the conscious intellect.

The mind has become far less simple; the devotion to the various forms of autobiography—itself an important fact in the tradition—provides abundant examples of the change that has taken place. Poets, making poetry by what seems to them almost a freshly discovered faculty, find that this new power may be conspired against by other agencies of the mind and even deprived of its freedom; the names of Wordsworth, Coleridge, and Arnold at once occur to us again, and Freud quotes chiller on the danger to the poet that lies in the merely analytical reason. And it is not only the poets who are threatened; educated and sensitive people throughout Europe become aware of the depredations that reason might make upon the affective life, as in the classic instance of John Stuart Mill.

We must also take into account the preoccupation—it began in the eighteenth century, or even in the seventeenth—with children, women, peasants, and savages, whose mental life, it is felt, is less overlaid than that of the educated adult male by the proprieties of social habit. With this preoccupation goes a concern with education and personal development, so consonant with the historical and evolutionary bias of the time. And we must certainly note the revolution in morals which took place at the instance (we might almost say) of the *Bildurgsroman*, for in the novels fathered by *Wilhelm Meister* we get the almost complete identification of author and hero and of the reader with both, and this identification almost inevitably suggests a leniency of moral judgment. The autobiographical novel has a further influence upon the moral sensibility by its exploitation of all the modulations of motive and by its hinting that we may not judge a man by any single moment in his life without taking into account the determining past and the expiating and fulfilling future.

It is difficult to know how to go on, for the further we look the more literary affinities to Freud we find, and even if we limit ourselves to bibliography we can at best be incomplete. Yet we must mention the sexual revolution that was being demanded—by Shelly, for example, by Schlegel of *Lucinde*, by George Sand, and later and more critically by Ibsen; the belief in the sexual origin of art, baldly stated by Tieck, more subtly by Schopenhauer; the investigation of sexual maladjustment by Stendhal, whose observations on erotic feeling seem to us distinctly Freudian. Again and again we see the effective, utilitarian ego being relegated to an inferior position and a plea being made on behalf of the anarchic and self-indulgent *id*. We find the energetic exploitation of the idea of the mind as a divisible thing, one part of which can contemplate and mock the other. It is not a far remove from this to Dostoevski's brilliant instances of ambivalent feeling. Novalis brings in the preoccupation with the death wish, and this is linked on the one hand with sleep and on the other hand with the perception of the perverse, self-destroying impulses, which in turn leads us to that fascination by the horrible which we find in Shelley, Poe, and Baudelaire. And always there is the profound interest in the dream—"Our dreams," said Gerard de Nerval, "are a second life"—and in the nature of metaphor, which reaches its climax in Rimbaud and the later Symbolists, metaphor becoming less and less communicative as it approaches the relative autonomy of the dream life.

But perhaps we must stop to ask, since these are the components of the Zeitgeist from which Freud himself developed, whether it can be said that Freud did indeed produce a wide literary effect. What is it that Freud added that the tendency of literature itself would not have developed without him? If we were looking for a writer who showed the Freudian influence, Proust would perhaps come to mind as readily as anyone else; the very title of his novel, in French more than in English, suggests an enterprise of psychoanalysis and scarcely less so does his method—the investigation of sleep, of sexual deviation, of the way of association, the almost obsessive interest in metaphor; at these and at man other points the "influence" might be shown. Yet I believe it is true that Proust did not read Freud. Or again, exegesis of *The Waste Land* often reads remarkably like the psychoanalytic interpretation of to dream, yet we know that Eliot's methods were prepared for him not by Freud but by other poets.

Nevertheless, it is of course true that Freud's influence on literature has been very great. Much of it is so pervasive that its extent is scarcely to be determined; in one form or another, frequently in perversions or absurd simplifications, it has been infused into our life and become a component of our culture of which it is now hard to be specifically aware. In biography its first effect was sensational but not fortunate. The early

Freudian biographers were for the most part Guildensterns who seemed to know the pipes but could not pluck out the heart of the mystery, and the same condemnation applies to the early Freudian critics. But in recent years, with the acclimatization of psychoanalysis and the increased sense of its refinements and complexity, criticism has derived from the Freudian system much that is of great value, most notably the license and the injunction to read the work of literature with a lively sense of its latent and ambiguous meanings, as if it were, as indeed it is, a being no less alive and contradictory than the man who created it. And this new response to the literary work has had a corrective effect upon our conception of biography. The literary critic or biographer who makes use of the Freudian theory is no less threatened by the dangers of theoretical systematization than he was in the early days, but he is likely to be more aware of these dangers; and I think it is true to say that now the motive of his interpretation is not that of exposing the secret shame of the writer and limiting the meaning of his work, but, on the contrary, that of finding grounds for sympathy with the writer and for increasing the possible significances of the work.

The names of the creative writers who have been more or less Freudian in tone or assumption would of course be legion. Only a relatively small number, however, have made serious use of the Freudian ideas. Freud himself seems to have thought this was as it should be: he is said to have expected very little of the works that were sent to him by writers with inscriptions of gratitude for all they had learned from him. The Surrealists have, with a certain inconsistency, depended upon Freud for the "scientific" sanction of their program. Kafka, with an apparent awareness of what he was doing, has explored the Freudian conceptions of guilt and punishment, of the dream, and of the fear of the father. Thomas Mann, whose tendency, as he himself says, was always in the direction of Freud's interests, has been most susceptible to the Freudian anthropology, finding a special charm in the theories of myths and magical practices.

James Joyce, with his interest in the numerous states of receding consciousness, with his use of words as things and of words which point to more than one thing, with his pervading sense of the interrelation and interpenetration of all things, and, not least important, his treatment of familial themes, has perhaps most thoroughly and consciously exploited Freud's ideas.

II

It will be clear enough how much of Freud's thought has significant affinity with the anti-rationalist element of the Romanticist tradition. But we must see with no less distinctness how much of his system is miliantly rationalistic. Thomas Mann is at fault when, in his first essay on Freud, he makes it seem that the "Apollonian," the rationalistic, side of psychoanalysis is, while certainly important and wholly admirable, somehow secondary and even accidental. He gives us a Freud who is committed to the "night side" of life. Not at all: the rationalistic element of Freud is foremost; before everything else he is positivistic. If the interpreter of dreams came to medical science through Goethe, as he tells us he did, he entered not by way of the Walpurgisnacht but by the essay which played so important a part in the lives of so many scientists of the nineteenth century, the famous disquisition on Nature.

This correction is needed not only for accuracy but also for any understanding of Freud's attitude to art. And for that understanding we must see how intense is the passion with which Freud believes that positivistic rationalism, in its golden-age pre-Revolutionary purity, is the very form and pattern of intellectual virtue. The aim of psychoanalysis, he says, is the control of the night side of life. It is "to strengthen the ego, to make it more independent of the super-ego, to widen its field of vision, and so to extend the organization of the *id*." "Where *id* was," —that is,

where all the irrational, non-logical, pleasure-seeking dark forces were—
"there shall ego be," that is, intelligence and control. "It is," he concludes,
with a reminiscence of Faust, "reclamation work, like the draining of the
Zuyder Zee." This passage is quoted by Mann when, in taking up the
subject of Freud a second time, he does indeed speak of Freud's
positivistic program; but even here the bias induced by Mann's artistic
interest in the "night side" prevents him from giving the other aspect of
Freud its due emphasis. Freud would never have accepted the role which
Mann seems to give him as the legitimizer of the myth and the dark
irrational ways of the mind. If Freud discovered the darkness for science
he never endorsed it. On the contrary, his rationalism supports all the ideas
of the Enlightenment that deny validity to myth or religion; he holds to
simple materialism, to a simple determinism, to a rather limited sort of
epistemology. No great scientist of our day has thundered so articulately
and so fiercely against all those who would sophisticate with metaphysics
the scientific principles that were good enough for the nineteenth century.
Conceptualism or pragmatism are anathema to him through the greater
part of his intellectual career, and this, when we consider the nature of his
own brilliant scientific methods, has surely an element of paradox in it.

From his rationalistic positivism comes much of Freud's strength and
what weakness he has. The strength is the fine, clear tenacity of his
positive aims, the goal of therapy, the desire to bring to men a decent
measure of earthly happiness. But upon the rationalism must also be
placed the blame for the often naive scientific principles which
characterize his early thought—they are later much modified—and which
consist largely of claiming for his theories a perfect correspondence with
an external reality, a position which, for those who admire Freud and
especially for those who take seriously his views on art, is troublesome in
the extreme.

Now Freud has, I believe, much to tell us about art, but whatever is suggestive in him is not likely to be found in those of his works in which he deals expressly with art itself. Freud is not insensitive to art—on the contrary—nor does he ever intend to speak of it with contempt. Indeed, he speaks of it with a real tenderness and counts it one of the true charms of the good life. Of artists, especially of writers, he speaks with admiration and even a kind of awe, though perhaps what he most appreciates in literature are specific emotional insights and observations; as we have noted, he speaks of literary men, because they have understood the part played in life by the hidden motives, as the precursors and coadjutors of his own science.

And yet eventually Freud speaks of art with what we must indeed call contempt. Art, he tells us, is a "substitute gratification," and as such is "an illusion in contrast to reality." Unlike most illusions, however, art is "almost always harmless and beneficent" for the reason that "it does not seek to be anything but an illusion. Save in the case of a few people who are, one might say, obsessed by Art, it never dares make any attack on the realm of reality." One of its chief functions is to serve as a "narcotic." It shares the characteristics of the dream whose element of distortion Freud calls a "sort of inner dishonesty." As for the artist, he is virtually in the same category with the neurotic. By such separation of imagination and intellectual capacity Freud says of the hero of a novel, "he is destined to be a poet or a neurotic, and he belongs to that race of beings whose realm is not of this world."

Now there is nothing in the logic of psychoanalytical thought which requires Freud to have these opinions. But there is a great deal in the practice of the psychoanalytical therapy which makes it understandable that Freud, unprotected by an adequate philosophy, should be tempted to take the line he does. The analytical therapy deals with illusion. The patient comes to the physician to be cured, let us say, of a fear of walking in the street. The fear is real enough, there is no illusion on that score, and it produces all the physical symptoms of, a more rational fear, the sweating palms, pounding heart, and shortened breath. But the patient knows that there is no cause for the fear, or rather that there is, as he says, no "real cause": there are no machine guns, man traps or tigers in the street. The physician knows, however, that there is indeed a "real" cause for the fear, though it has nothing at all to do with what is or is not in the street; the cause is within the patient, and the process of the therapy will be to discover, by gradual steps, what this real cause is and so free the patient from its effects.

Now the patient in coming to the physician, and the physician in accepting the patient, make a tacit compact about reality; for their purpose they agree to the limited reality by which we get our living, win our loves, catch our trains and our colds. The therapy will undertake to train the patient in proper ways of coping with this reality. The patient, of course, has been dealing with this reality all along, but in the wrong way. For Freud there are two ways of dealing with external reality. One is practical, effective, positive; this is the way of the conscious self, of the ego which must be made independent of the super-ego and extend its organization over the id, and it is the right way. The antithetical way may be called, for our purpose now, the "fictional" way. Instead of doing something about, or to, external reality, the individual who uses this way does something to, or about, his affective states. The most common and "normal" example of this is daydreaming, in which we give ourselves a certain pleasure by imagining our difficulties solved or our desires gratified. The, too, as Freud discovered, sleeping dreams are, in much more complicated ways, and even though quite unpleasant, at the service of this same "fictional" activity. And in ways yet more complicated and yet snore unpleasant, the actual neurosis from which our patient suffers deals with an external reality which the mind considers still more unpleasant than the painful neurosis itself.

For Freud as psychoanalytic practitioner there are, we may say, the polar extremes of reality and illusion. Reality is an honorific word, and it means what is *there*; illusion is a pejorative word, and it means a response to what is *not there*: The didactic nature of a course of psychoanalysis no doubt requires a certain firm crudeness in making the distinction; it is after all aimed not at theoretical refinement but at practical effectiveness. The polar extremes are practical reality and neurotic illusion, the latter judged by the former. This, no doubt, is as it should be; the patient is not being trained in metaphysics and epistemology.

This practical assumption is not Freud's only view, of the mind in its relation to reality. Indeed what may be called the essentially Freudian view assumes that the mind, for good as well as bad, helps create its reality by selection and evaluation. It this view, reality is malleable and subject to creation; it is not static but is rather a series of situations which are dealt with in their own terms. But beside this conception of the mind stands the conception which arises from Freud's therapeutic-practical assumptions; in this view, the mind deals with a reality which is quite fixed and static, a reality that is wholly "given" and not (to use a phrase of Dewey's) "taken." In his epistemological utterances, Freud insists on this second view, although it is not easy to see why he should do so. For the reality to which he wishes to reconcile the neurotic patient is, after all, a "taken," and not a "given" reality. It is the reality of social life and of value, conceived and maintained by the human mind and will. Love, morality, honor, esteem—these are the components of a created reality. If we are to call most of the activities and satisfactions of the ego illusions then we must call art an illusions; Freud, of course, has no desire to call them that.

What, then, is the difference between, on the one hand, the dream and the neurosis, and, on the other hand, art? That they have certain common elements is of course clear; that unconscious processes are at work in both would be denied by no poet or critic; they share too, though in different degrees, the element of fantasy. But there is a vital difference between them which Charles Lamb saw so clearly in his defense of the sanity of true genius: "The ... poet dreams being awake. He is not possessed by his subject but he has dominion over it."

That is the whole difference; the poet is in command of his fantasy, while it is exactly the mark of the neurotic that he is possessed by his fantasy. And there is a further difference which Lamb states; speaking of the poet's relation to reality (he calls it Nature), he says, "He is beautifully loyal to that sovereign directress, even when he appears most to betray her"; the illusions of art are made to serve the purpose of a closer and truer relation with reality. Jacques Barzun, in an acute and sympathetic discussion of Freud, puts the matter well: "A good analogy between art and dreaming has led him to a false one between art and sleeping. But the difference between a work of art and a dream is precisely this, that the work of art *leads us back to the outer reality by taking account of it.*" Freud's assumption of the almost exclusively hedonistic nature and purpose of art bar him from the perception of this.

Of the distinction that must be made between the artist and the neurotic Freud is of course aware; he tells us that the artist is not like the neurotic in that he knows how to find a way back from the world of imagination and "once more get a firm foothold in reality." This however seems to mean no more than that reality is to be dealt with when the artist suspends the practice of his art; and at least once when Freud speaks of art dealing with reality he actually means the rewards that a successful artist can win. He does not deny to art its function and its usefulness; it has a therapeutic effect in releasing mental tension; it serves the cultural purpose of acting as a "substitute gratification" to reconcile men to the sacrifices they have made for culture's sake; it promotes the social sharing of highly valued emotional experiences; and it recalls men to their cultural ideals. This is not everything that some of us would find that art does, yet even this is a good deal for a "narcotic" to do.

III

I started by saying that Freud's ideas could tell us something about art, but so far I have done little more than try to show that Freud's very conception of art is inadequate. Perhaps, then, the suggestiveness lies in the application of the analytic method to specific works of art or to the artist himself? I do not think so, and it is only fair to say that Freud himself was aware both of the limits and the limitations of psychoanalysis in art, even though he does not always in practice submit to the former or admit the latter.

Freud has, for example, no desire to encroach upon the artist's autonomy; he does not wish us to read his monograph on Leonardo and then say of the "Madonna of the Rocks" that it is a fine example of homosexual, autoerotic painting. If he asserts that in investigation the "psychiatrist cannot yield to the author," he immediately insists that the "author cannot yield to the psychiatrist," and he warns the latter not to "coarsen everything" by using for all human manifestations the "substantially useless and awkward terms" of clinical procedure. He admits, even while asserting that the sense of beauty probably derives from sexual feeling, that psychoanalysis "has less to say about beauty than about most other things." He confesses to a theoretical indifference to the form of art and restricts himself to its content. Tone, feeling, style, and the modification that part makes upon part he does not consider: "The layman," he says, "may expect, perhaps too much from analysis … for it must be admitted that it throws no light upon the two problems which probably interest him the most. It can do nothing toward elucidating the nature of the artistic gift, nor can it explain the means by which the artist works—artistic technique."

What, then, does Freud believe that the analytical method can do? Two things: explain the "inner meanings" of the work of art and explain the temperament of the artist as man.

A famous example of the method is the attempt to solve the "problem" of *Hamlet* as suggested by Freud and as carried out by Dr. Ernest Jones, his early and distinguished follower. Dr. Jones's monograph is a work of painstaking scholarship and of really masterly ingenuity. The research undertakes not only the clearing up of the mystery of Hamlet's character, but also the discovery of "the clue to much of the deeper workings, of Shakespeare's mind." Part of the mystery in question is of course why Hamlet, after he had so definitely resolved to do so, did not avenge upon his hated uncle his father's death. But there is another mystery to the play—what Freud calls "the mystery of its effect," its magical appeal that draws so much interest toward it. Recalling the many failures to solve the riddle of the play's charm, he wonders if we are to be driven to the conclusion "that, its magical appeal rests solely upon the impressive thoughts in it and the splendor of its language." Freud believes that we can find a source of power beyond this.

We remember that Freud has told us that the meaning of a dream, is its intention, and we may assume that the meaning of a drams is its intention, too. The Jones research undertakes to discover what it was that Shakespeare intended to say about Hamlet. It finds that the intention was wrapped by the author in a dreamlike obscurity because it touched so deeply both his personal life and the moral life of the world; what Shakespeare intended to say is that Hamlet cannot act because he is incapacitated by the guilt he feels at his unconscious attachment to his mother. There is, I think, nothing to be quarreled with in the statement that there is an Oedipus situation in *Hamlet*; and if psychoanalysis has indeed added a new point of interest to the play, that is to its credit. And just so, there is no reason to quarrel with Freud's conclusion when he undertakes to give us the meaning of *King Lear* by a tortuous tracing of the mythological implications of the theme of the three caskets, of the relation of the caskets to the Norns, the Fates, and the Graces, of the connection of these triadic females with Lear's daughters, of the transmogrification of the death goddess into the love goddess and the identification of Cordelia with both, all to the conclusion that the meaning of *King Lear* is to be found in the tragic refusal of an old man to "renounce love choose death, and make friends with the necessity of dying." There is something both beautiful and suggestive in this, but it is not *the* meaning of *King Lear*, any more than the Oedipus motive is *the* meaning of *Hamlet*.

It is not here a question of the validity of the evidence, though that is of course important. We must rather object to the conclusions of Freud and Dr. Jones on the ground that their proponents do not have an adequate conception, of what an artistic meaning is. There is no single meaning to any work of art; this is true not merely because it is better that it should be true, that is, because it makes art a richer thing, but because historical and personal experience show it to be true. Changes in historical context and in personal mood change the meaning of a work and indicate to us that artistic understanding is not a question of fact but of value. Even if the author's intention were, as it cannot be, precisely determinable, the meaning of a work cannot lie in the author's intention alone. It must also lie in its effect. We can say of a volcanic eruption on an inhabited island that it "means terrible suffering" but if the island is uninhabited or easily evacuated it means something else. In short, the audience partly determines the meaning of the work. But although Freud sees something of this when he says that in addition to the author's intention we must take into account the mystery of *Hamlet*'s effect, he nevertheless goes on to speak as if, historically, *Hamlet*'s effect had been single and brought about solely by the "magical" power of the Oedipus motive to which, unconsciously, we so violently respond. Yet there was, we know, a period when *Hamlet* was relatively in eclipse, and it has always been scandalously true of the French, a people not without filial feeling, that they have been somewhat indifferent to the "magical appeal" of *Hamlet*.

I do not think that anything I have said about the inadequacies of the Freudian method of interpretation limits the number of ways we can deal with a work of art. Bacon remarked that experiment may twist nature on the rack to wring out its secrets, and criticism may use any instruments upon a work of art to find its meanings. The elements of art are not limited to the world of art. They reach into life and whatever extraneous knowledge of them we gain— for example, by research into the historical context of the work—may quicken our feelings for the work itself and even enter legitimately into those feelings. Then, too, anything we may learn about the artist himself may be enriching and legitimate. But one research into the mind of the artist is simply not practicable, however legitimate it may theoretically be. That is, the investigation of is unconscious intention as it exists apart from the work itself. Criticism understands that the artist's statement of his conscious intention, though it is sometimes useful, cannot finally determine meaning. How much less can we know from his unconscious intention considered as something apart from the whole work? Surely very little can be called conclusive or scientific. For, as Freud himself points out, we are not in a position to question the artist; we must apply the technique of dream analysis to his symbols, but, as Freud says with some heat, those people do not understand his theory who think that a dream may be interpreted without the dreamer's free association with the multitudinous details of his dream.

We have so far ignored the aspect of the method which finds the solution to the "mystery" of such a play as *Hamlet* in the temperament of Shakespeare himself and then illuminates the mystery of Shakespeare's temperament by means of the solved mystery of the play. Here it will be amusing to remember that by 1935 Freud had become converted to the theory that it was not Shakespeare of Stratford but the Earl of Oxford who wrote the plays, thus invalidating the important bit of evidence that Shakespeare's father died shortly before the composition of *Hamlet*. This is destructive enough to Dr. Jones's argument, but the evidence from which Dr. Jones draws conclusions about literature fails on grounds more relevant to literature itself. For when Dr. Jones, by means of his analysis of *Hamlet*, takes us into "the deeper workings of Shakespeare's mind," he does so with a perfect confidence that he knows what *Hamlet* is and what its relation to Shakespeare is. It is, he tells us, Shakespeare's "chief masterpiece," so far superior to all his other works that it may be placed on "an entirely separate level." And then, having established his ground on an entirely subjective literary judgment, Dr. Jones goes on to tell us the *Hamlet* "probably expresses the core of Shakespeare's philosophy and outlook as no other work of his does." That is, all the contradictory or complicating or modifying testimony of the other plays is dismissed on the basis of Dr. Jones's acceptance of the peculiar position which, he believes, *Hamlet* occupies in the Shakespeare canon. And it is upon, this quite inadmissible judgment that Dr. Jones bases his argument: "It may be expected *therefore* that anything which will give us the key to the inner meaning of the play will *necessarily* give us the clue to much of the deeper workings of Shakespeare's mind." (The italics are mine.)

I should be sorry if it appeared that I am trying to say that psychoanalysis can have nothing to do with literature. I am sure that the opposite is so. For example, the whole notion of rich ambiguity in literature, of the interplay between the apparent meaning and the latent— not "hidden"—meaning, has been reinforced by the Freudian concepts, perhaps even received its first impetus from them. Of late years, the more perceptive psychoanalysts have surrendered the early pretensions of their teachers to deal "scientifically" with literature. That is all to the good, and when a study as modest and precise as Dr. Franz Alexander's essay on

Henry IV comes along, an essay which pretends not to "solve" but only to illuminate the subject, we have something worth having. Dr. Alexander undertakes nothing more than to say that in the development of Prince Hal we see the classic struggle of the ego to come to normal adjustment, beginning with the rebellion against the father, going on to the conquest of the super-ego (Hotspur, with his rigid notions of honor and glory), then to the conquests of the *id* (Falstaff, with his anarchic self-indulgence), then to the identification with the father (the crown scene) and the assumption of mature responsibility. An analysis of this sort is not momentous and not exclusive of other meanings; perhaps it does no more than point up and formulate what we all have already seen. It has the tact to *accept* the play and does not, like Dr. Jones study of *Hamlet*, search for a "hidden motive" and a "deeper working," which implies that there is a reality to which the play stands in the relation that a dream stands to the wish that generates it and from which it is separable; it is this reality, this "deeper working," which, according to Dr. Jones, produced the play. But *Hamlet* is not merely the product of Shakespeare's thought, it is the very instrument of his thought, and if meaning is intention, Shakespeare did not intend the Oedipus motive or anything less than *Hamlet*; if meaning is effect then it is *Hamlet* which affects us, not the Oedipus motive. *Cariolanus* also deals, and very terribly, with the Oedipus motive, but the effect of the one drama is very different from the effect of the other.

IV

If, then we can accept neither Freud's conception of the place of art in life nor his application of the analytical method, what is it that he contributes to our understanding of art or to its practice? In my opinion, what he contributes outweighs his errors; it is of the greatest importance, and it lies in no specific statement that he makes about art but is, rather, implicit in his whole conception of the mind.

For, of all mental systems, the Freudian psychology is the one which makes poetry indigenous to the very constitution of the mind. Indeed, the mind, as Freud sees it, is in the greater part of its tendency exactly a poetry-making organ. This puts the case too strongly, no doubt, for it seems to make the working of the unconscious mind equivalent to poetry itself, forgetting that between the unconscious mind and the finished poem there supervene the social intention and the formal control of the conscious mind. Yet the statement has at least the virtue of counterbalancing the belief, so commonly expressed or implied, that the very opposite is true, and that poetry is a kind of beneficent aberration of the mind's right course.

Freud has not merely naturalized poetry; he has discovered its status as a pioneer settler, and he sees it as a method of thought. Often enough he tries to show how, as a method of thought, it is unreliable and ineffective for conquering reality; yet he himself is forced to use it in the very shaping of his own science, as when he speaks of the topography of the mind and tells us with a kind of defiant apology that the metaphors of space relationship he is using are really most inexact since the mind is not a thing of space at all, but that there is no other way of conceiving the difficult idea except by metaphor. In the eighteenth century Vico spoke of the metaphorical, imagistic language of the early stages of culture; it was left of Freud to discover how, in a scientific age, we still feel and think in figurative formations, and to create, what psychoanalysis is, a science of tropes, of metaphor and its variants, synecdoche and metonymy.

Freud showed, too, how the mind, in one of its parts, could work without logic, yet not without that directing purpose, that control of intent from which, perhaps it might be said, logic springs. For the unconscious mind works without the syntactical conjunctions which are logic's essence. It recognizes no because, no *therefore*, no but; such ideas as similarity, agreement, and community are expressed in dreams imagistically by compressing the elements into a unity. The unconscious mind in its struggle with the conscious always turns from the general to the concrete and finds the tangible trifle more congenial that the large abstraction. Freud discovered in the very organization of the mind those mechanisms by which art makes its effects, such devices as the condensations of meanings and the displacement of accent.

All this is perhaps obvious enough and, though I should like to develop it in proportion both to its importance and to the space I have given to disagreement with Freud, I will not press it further. For there are two other elements in Freud's thought which, in conclusion, I should like to introduce as of great weight in their bearing on art.

Of these, one is a specific idea which, in the middle of his career (1920), Freud put forward in his essay *Beyond the Pleasure Principle*. The essay itself is a speculative attempt to solve a perplexing problem in clinical analysis, but its relevance to literature is inescapable, as Freud sees well enough, even though his perception of its critical importance is not sufficiently strong to make him revise his earlier views of the nature and function of art. The idea is one which stands besides Aristotle's notion of the catharsis, in part to supplement, in part to modify it.

Freud has come upon certain facts which are not to be reconciled with his earlier theory of the dream. According to this theory, all dreams, even the unpleasant ones, could be understood upon analysis to have the intention of fulfilling the dreamer's wishes. They are in the service of what Freud calls the pleasure principle, which is opposed tithe reality principle. It is, of course, this explanation of the dream which had so largely conditioned Freud's theory of art. But now there is thrust upon him the necessity for reconsidering the theory of the dream, for it was found that in cases of war neurosis—what we once called shellshock—the patient, with the utmost anguish, recurred in his dreams to the very situation, distressing as it was, which had precipitated his neurosis. It seemed impossible to interpret these dreams by any assumption of a hedonistic intent. Nor did there seem to be the usual amount of distortion in them: the patient recurred to the terrible initiatory situation with great literalness. And the same pattern of psychic behavior could be observed in the play of children; there were some games which, far from fulfilling wishes, seemed to concentrate upon the representation of those aspects of the child's life which were most unpleasant and threatening to his happiness.

To explain such mental activities Freud evolved a theory for which he at first refused to claim much but to which, with the years, he attached an increasing importance. He first makes the assumption that there is indeed in the psychic life a repetition-compulsion which goes beyond the pleasure principle. Such a compulsion cannot be meaningless, it must have an intent. And that intent, Freud comes to believe, is exactly and literally the developing of fear. "These dreams," he says, "are attempts at restoring control of the stimuli by developing apprehension, the pretermission of which caused the traumatic neurosis." The dream, that is, is the effort to reconstruct the bad situation in order that the failure to meet it may be recouped; in these dreams there is no obscured intent to evade but only an attempt to meet the situation, to make a new effort of control. And in the play of children it seems to be that "the child repeats even the unpleasant experiences because through his own activity he gains a far more thorough mastery of the strong impression than was possible by mere passive experience."

Freud, at this point, can scarcely help being put in mind of tragic drama; nevertheless, he does not wish to believe that this effort to come to mental grips with a situation is involved in the attraction of tragedy. He is, we might say, under the influence of the Aristotelian tragic theory which emphasizes a qualified hedonism through suffering. But the pleasure involved in tragedy is perhaps an ambiguous one; and sometimes we must feel that the famous sense of cathartic resolution is perhaps the result of glossing over terror with beautiful language rather than an evacuation of it. And sometimes the terror even bursts through the language to stand stark and isolated from the play, as does Oedipus's sightless and bleeding face. At any rate, the Aristotelian theory does not deny another function for tragedy and for comedy, too, which is suggested by Freud's theory of the traumatic neurosis—what might be called the mithridatic function, by which tragedy is used as the homeopathic, administration of pain to inure ourselves to the greater pain which life will force upon us. There is in the cathartic theory of tragedy, as it is usually understood, a conception of tragedy's function which is too negative and which inadequately suggests the sense of active mastery which tragedy can give.

In the same essay in which he sets forth the conception of the mind embracing its own pain for some vital purpose, Freud also expresses a provisional assent to the idea (earlier stated, as he reminds us, by Schopenhauer) that there is perhaps a human drive which makes of death the final and desired goal. The death instinct is a conception that is rejected by many of even the most thoroughgoing Freudian theorists (as, in his last book, Freud mildly noted); the late Otto Fenichel in his authoritative work on the neurosis argues cogently against it. Yet even if we reject the theory as not fitting the facts in any operatively useful way, we still cannot miss its grandeur, its ultimate tragic courage in acquiescence to fate. The idea of the reality principle and the idea of the death instinct form the crown of Freud's broader speculation on the life of man. Their quality of grim poetry is characteristic Freud's system and the ideas it generates for him.

And as much as anything else that Freud gives to literature, this quality of his thought is important. Although the artist is never finally determined in his work by the intellectual systems about him, he cannot avoid their influence; and it can be said of various competing systems that some hold more promise for the artist than others. When, for example, we think of the simple humanitarian optimism which, for two decades, has been so pervasive, we must see that not only has it been politically and philosophically inadequate, but also that it implies, by the smallness of its view of the varieties of human possibility, a kind of check on the creative faculties. In Freud's view of life no such limitation is implied. To be sure, certain elements of his system seem hostile to the usual notions of man's dignity. Like every great critic of human nature—and Freud is that—he finds in human pride the ultimate cause of human wretchedness, and he takes pleasure in knowing that his ideas stand with those of Copernicus and Darwin in making pride more difficult to maintain. Yet the Freudian man is, I venture to think, a creature of far more dignity and far more interest than the man which any other modern system has been able to conceive. Despite popular belief on the contrary, man, as Freud conceives him, is not to be understood by any simple formula (such a sex) but is rather an inextricable tangle of culture and biology. And not being simple, he is not simply good; he has, as Freud says somewhere, a kind of hell within him from which rise everlastingly the impulses which threaten his civilization. He has the faculty of imagining for himself more in the way of pleasure and satisfaction that he can possibly achieve. Everything that he gains he pays for in more than equal coin; compromise and the compounding with defeat constitute his best way of getting through the world. His best qualities are the result of a struggle whose outcome is tragic. Yet he is a creature of love; it is Freud's sharpest criticism of the Adlerian psychology that to aggression it gives everything and to love nothing at all.

One is always aware in reading Freud how little cynicism there is in his thought. His desire for man is only that he should be human, and to this end his science is devoted. No view of life to which the artist responds can insure the quality of his work, but the poetic qualities of Freud's own principles, which are so clearly in the line of the classic tragic realism, suggest that this is a view which does not narrow and simplify the human world for the artist but on the contrary opens and complicates it.

From *The Liberal Imagination* by Lionel Trilling. Viking Press. Copyright 1950, by Lionel Trilling. Reprinted by permission of the author and publishers. Originally published as "The Legacy of Sigmund Freud: Literary and Aesthetic," in *The Kenyon Review,* Vol. II (Spring, 1940), pp. 152-173; and, in a revised version, as "Freud and Literature" in *Horizon* (London), Vol. XVI (September, 1947), pp. 182-200.

William Barrett

The End of Modern Literature: Existentialism and Crisis

[1949]

We are told that this is the century when man has become for the first time fully and thoroughly problematic to himself. If so, it would only seem natural that literature too should be posed as a new and extreme kind of problem for literary men. Natural and inevitable too, that this problem should be raised particularly by the French, whose literature, whatever its rank, has always been the most programmatic of all literatures, and the most self-consciously attached to critical theory. For sometime now French critics have been talking about a "crisis" in their literature. "Crisis" is a violent word, and there has possibly been some over-dramatization in its use; but there can be no doubt about the seriousness of the situation that has evoked this word. French literature suggests countryside overrun by generations of industrious cultivators until the point of diminishing returns seems reached, where the soil continues to yield crops only after exacting very much more drastic methods of cultivation and ever more painful labor. By the turn of the century some traditional genres already looked exhausted, and recently some French writers have been declaring that the language itself (so much narrower in its range of effects than our protean English) demands new means of expression. American literature is very far from reaching this stage, and perhaps we are wrong to bother our heads at all with asking any extreme or ultimate questions of literature; we are primitives and perhaps for the time being we shall do better to remain such;

but if we do choose to think about the problem of literature as a total one, then we can learn much from seeing this problem raised within the French context, which may very well represent the extreme state toward which modern literature, so long as it still remembers its ambitions, is tending everywhere in the world.

The background of Sartre's book [*What Is Literature?*] is this continuing crisis in French literature. But he is also beset by another and much more urgent crisis—the condition of French and European society after the Second World War—which penetrates so much of European life now that it places the writer in a precarious relation even to his craft. It is very useful to us to have a writer like tempts to realize his own projects for literature; and only too if we read a little between the lines in the present work, observing the writers to whom he makes most frequent and essential reference. Sartre once said that Dos Passos was the greatest modern novelist; in the present work his admiration for American writers is more cautious than in the past, but we notice repeated reference to Richard Wright as a great writer. This is entirely natural, for Wright's books, dealing with the Negro question in America, satisfy Sartre's demand that literature be directed at changing the fundamental conditions of social existence. The highbrow critic in America is likely to settle on altogether different names in any fundamental literary discussion: Joyce or Elior or Proust are the names that remind us of the possible ambitions of literature. Sartre, however, is interested in a very practical program for literature, and his point would seem to be effectively this; that in the crisis of exhaustion, or threatened exhaustion, in which French literature now seems to find itself, the way out may be just to propose the second-rate as an ideal. Perhaps, being second-rate, it is something within reach, and therefore a thoroughly practicable goal for literature. In the sense that his book represents a deliberate abnegation from the great ambitions of modern literature, Sartre is in effect announcing the end of a whole literary period.

For the fact is that the one thing that distinguishes modern literature as a whole from the literature of previous periods is its extraordinary, and perhaps even overweening, ambition. We are now at the mid-point of the century, and looking back on the half-century of writers who will eventually give their names to the period, we seem to see them in retrospect as belonging almost to a vanished culture, so different were the conditions of their existence from those of the period into which we are now entering. If they inherited the nineteenth-century view of the writer as a separate and anointed being, a kind of priest, they were able to hold on to this role only with the tensions of an irony that provide it with a new human content. Proust, Joyce, Mann and the others, all exist in the full plenitude of a tradition, of which they sought to lose no part, so that their work in its richness already carries the seeds of disorder and dissolution. Probably a moment like this in literary history could not be prolonged any further. Sartre's is perhaps the first conscious announcement that the conditions of literature must return to a lower and less ambitious level; but even if the program did not become conscious, the attitude has already begun to prevail generally. We are now able to understand our surprise at the evolution of Sartre's career. The discrepancy between thievery abstract and involved philosophy and the rudimentary and plodding fiction is no longer a puzzle. It was something of a shock, after the intellectual sophistication and complexity of *L'etre et le neant*, to descend upon the first volume of Sartre's trilogy, not because his creative gifts were lacking but because he was willing to aim so low in the novel. But all this Sartre confront this double crisis. By this time it seems clear that he is not, nor is likely to become, a great writer: clever, enormously, furiously energetic, he does not possess the authentic gifts of a really first-rate creative talent. But in the present case this may be no disadvantage: a greater writer, for whom literature itself might never become a question, might be less sensitive to the historic forces that now push the literary man into such an odd and difficult place in the world. And what we can always count on in Sartre is the prodigious intelligence (however it may miscarry in details) with which he plunges into any problem. Sartre divides the problem of literature into three questions: *What is writing? Why write? For whom does one write?* These questions themselves breathe the air of crisis, for they are not the kinds of question that enter the writer's head during his periods of fertility and overflow, they become urgent and sometimes paralyzing for him only when he has descended into the pits of silence, anguish, artistic nihilism; when he exists on the margins of literature where language itself seems to become impossible. But since the writer cannot exist without descending from time to time into these waste places, these are questions that cannot be shirked, and it is better to raise and try to answer them whenever we can than to wait till the heavy silence descends and makes their answer seem hopeless.

Coming out of this double crisis in the French situation, Sartre's book is really a revolutionary one, though he himself gives the rather odd impression of not quite grasping the real revolution he announces. He hardly presents us any radically new theory of literature: most of Sartre's views had their antecedents in the Marxist theorizing of the 'thirties, though he gives them a new philosophical color. The revolutionary import of Sartre's message lies in his complete acceptance of the conditions under which, it appears, the writer may soon have to work, even though to accept these conditions may imply a radical break with the whole tradition of literature in France. Thus his book is revolutionary as a symptom of what is happening to literature, culture, and human society in this epoch—and not only in France.

Sartre attempts to give a historical answer to the three questions that divide his book by reviewing the conditions of author, public, and society during the major periods of French literature. This history is sketched in large rapid strokes: the seventeenth, eighteenth, nineteenth or bourgeois century; the present period (the situation of the writer in 1947) and Sartre's hope for the future. Inevitably the treatment of history shows more of the influence of Marx and Hegel than of Existentialism. Sartre has obviously profited a good deal from a sympathetic reading of Hegel, but the Hegelian apparatus often seems unnecessary and cumbrous, and his use of it an exuberant but self-indulgent practice of virtuosity. The influence of Marxism shows itself in another direction: it actually forms Sartre's judgments of taste at certain points. Thus he undervalues the literature of the seventeenth century because it was aristocratic, actually preferring the comedies of Beaumarchais, which belong to the more democratic eighteenth century, to those of Moliere, and going so far as to describe Moliere's *Le Misanthrope* as a comedy dealing only with the trivial subject of manners. The trouble is not that Sartre lacks taste—the whole book is evidence of his passionate addiction to literature—but that, as usual, he is driven too furiously by his ideas into the violation of perceptible fact—here the perceptible facts of taste. The result is that the brilliance of his insights on the past is often spoiled by extreme and doctrinaire judgments.

This lack of critical balance has its most serious consequences when Sartre is dealing with the bourgeois literature of the nineteenth century. Here Sartre's judgments are obviously colored by his passionate hatred of the bourgeois class itself, and in this respect he reveals the state of mind of France, and indeed of all Europe, where the bourgeoisie is so discredited that the unpleasant associations of the word reflect back on the whole century of civilization dominated by that class. We in America who have not yet had to live through the ruin of that class are still permitted another point of view: as bourgeois civilization—in France, England, and elsewhere—disappears, it is possible to regret its passing and to question very seriously the superiority of the culture that is replacing it. Though Sartre makes some telling points against bourgeois literature, they are usually directed at its weakest side and hardly do justice to its main bulk of significant work. Sartre's error is the familiar one of seeking to convert political and social sympathies too directly into literary judgment, so that he accepts much too simply and wholeheartedly the plebeian or populist taste embedded in the Marxist mind. In general, it can be said of Sartre that he has come to Marxism too late, that he has not lived through it and beyond it, so that he still sees political and cultural realities under the too drastic Marxist simplifications. The facts, however, are always more complex. Flaubert, to take one example, has always been a target for Sartre, and in this book Sartre attempts to justify his severity by citing long passages from Flaubert's letters that express an aristocratic hatred of the mob. This is all very well; but then we are suddenly reminded of the human complications of literary composition when we recall that Flaubert, despite his correspondence, has produced in the few pages of *Un Coeur Simple* a more profound and sympathetic picture of the poor than in all the thousand pages of Sartre's recent trilogy. And if we are going to insist at all on the social role of literature, we may as well remember that it was the bourgeois epoch which first produced the conception of a literature embracing the whole of society in a single understanding vision.

All this brings us now to the core of Sartre's message, which is of course his now well-known concept of *literature engagee*, where we will also be dealing with some of the hazy notions left in the American mind by the "social consciousness" of the 'thirties. ("Engaged literature," by the way, is a piece of linguistic nonsense that the translator might have spared us; if some of the literal force of the French is to be kept, he might have rendered it as "enlisted literature," which is the connotation to French ears; but, all told, "engagement" is probably best done into English as *commitment*.) Sartre complains that he has been misunderstood, but despite all his efforts in this book his idea of commitment still remains somewhat unclear. He has still not dealt adequately with the kinds and degrees of commitment, nor with the question of the necessary *artistic* detachment that must accompany the writer's *human* commitments. It is easy to be sympathetic to the causes that prompt Sartre's doctrine. The most eloquent pages in this book are those on the French experience under the German occupation, which make it quite clear that after such experiences the writer could no longer immure himself in an aestheticism for which neither concentration camps, executioners, nor victims would exist. We can very well accept the decisive force of such experiences for the young men of Sartre's generation. But then, can this experience be generalized for the writer everywhere and allowed to circumscribe his material, methods, and attitudes?

The point is, again, that the writer's involvement is a more complicated matter than Sartre allows. Commitment may work on various levels and in various degrees: the detached writer sometimes turns out to be the most committed at a deeper level, and the most blatantly committed writer to have only a transitory connection with the deeper issues of history, society, and literary tradition. Proust complains in one of his letters of the criticism (made after the first volumes of his novel had already appeared and been acclaimed) that his was the work of a snob, showing no recognition of social (by which was meant socialist) ideas. The criticism was in fact just, in the sense that the socialist ideology plays no role at all in the work of Proust. Yet, by some curious irony of detachment not at all unusual in works of art, *A La Recherche du Temps Perdu* is a profounder study of the breakdown of a social class than anything given us by proletarian or "social realist" literature. No modern writer seems to offer us a more fanatical example of detachment than Joyce. Certainly, during the seventeen years in which he was composing his last work, withdrawn from the ideological battles of the 'twenties and 'thirties, he seemed a curiously eccentric and private figure. Yet the appearance of *Finnegans Wake* in 1939 coincided portentously with the outbreak of a war that seemed the destruction of the whole civilization so laboriously embedded in Joyce's pages, and by some miracle of literary creation the book seemed to sum up a whole epoch. Was Joyce a committed writer? It depends, of course, on what kinds of commitment one has in mind. Joyce was committed in the deepest sense to the fact of human language, and consequently to the whole literary tradition in which he was working; he drew deeply upon the modern consciousness in matters like anthropology and psychoanalysis; and beyond all these, he had a human commitment, which became also the writer's deepest message, to the most primitive and universal emotions of familial life. In the face of such formidable commitments, the absence of political ideology looks like a rather superficial deficiency in Joyce. The examples could be multiplied, but the point that emerges from them is already clear: we demand of the writer a commitment to his time in the sense that his work incorporate contemporary mind and feeling at their deepest levels; but to exist deeply in one's time is not the same as to exist in the spotlight, to pass oneself off as a political leader of sage, and to lose oneself in all the more violently public currents. Withdrawal and silence may open to the writer resources that reflect his time at a profounder level that those works which—in their insistence on being relevant, committed, or conscripted—are only a step beyond the daily newspaper. Some of Sartre's recent work gives the impression of a man writing with the Zeitgeist breathing hotly down his neck.

In the broad human sense, no doubt, Sartre is in the right direction. His doctrine is an insistence upon the reintegration of literature into life, against the idea of the priesthood of letters that germinated during the whole of the nineteenth century to come to full and final bloom in Flaubert and the symbolists. Mallarme put it perfectly when he said, "Everything exists in order to get into a book," willing to countenance the inversion of existence that would subordinate the man to the writer. Our own period hardly permits this attitude: we have to insist that the writer is a man, that he never leaves humanity, and that, living in his period, he has political opinions like everybody else. But expecting the writer to be a citizen, we should not also expect that the literary profession gives him any special privileges of trespass into politics. Politics is usually considered fair game for everybody, and literary men have sometimes been the worst offenders, confusing their vaguest feelings with facts, their rhetoric with logic, and their will to belong with moral heroism. Sartre's own forays into politics show a good deal of this naïveté and confusion. It is time we recognized that there is such a thing as "literary" politics, to be taken no more seriously than "literary" philosophizing, "literary" psychology, and the rest of these adulterated products. During the 'thirties, of course, "literary" politics was the universal pastime; the mood of the period was some excuse, but that period has now passed, and literary men and fellow travelers ought to be told that politics is a special discipline, with its own data and rules, concerning which one ought occasionally to think before one talks.

But the real revolution that Sartre announces for literature is not a matter chiefly of politics. He hardly states this revolution in so many words; we glimpse it only if we measure his theory his practice, taking the present book along with his novels and plays, which are, after all, his deliberate at now turns out to have been intentional: the deliberate aiming at the second-rate is part of Sartre's program for literature. The committed writer disdains the creation of masterpieces, and even the very concept of the masterpiece, with whatever silence, exile, or cunning it may exact, no longer seems to have any connection with that act of writing that aims essentially at making an impact, just as one might strike a blow or fire a pistol.

Sartre is therefore entirely consistent with himself when he proposes that the writer neglect none of the mass media, like radio and cinema, available in this period. He notes with satisfaction that the modern writer is able to reach a much vaster audience than his predecessor of the nineteenth century: for Sartre this is the great opportunity in the present situation. It is true that he also observes the other side of the coin—that when Gide, for example, becomes known through the cinema to thousands who have not read him, the writer also becomes inseparable from the face of Michele Morgan—but he fails to consider what will happen if this process continues unchecked. The cultural process in modern society (which, whatever its form of economy, is everywhere becoming a mass society) is precisely this watering down of content as the writer reaches larger masses of people, and usually not through his own written word but through the mechanical image that an advanced technology substitutes for the printed page. Sartre accepts the process, in fact seeks to assist it; for in his view the writer should aim essentially at addressing the concrete collectivity, which is the total mass of mankind, and eventually this mass is a classless society. This is as utopian as most of Sartre's politics; but programs—and a program for literature is no exception—should deal with present possibilities, and the contemporary writer who seeks to reach this mass audience will inevitably find himself rejecting his own essential difficulties, his complications and subtleties, and indeed the very limitations of personality that have in the past defined his most authentic themes. Here again we have nothing less than a proposal to put and end to modern literature. For the qualities that define modern literature have been in great part the result of a desperate effort to preserve itself by a deliberate escape from a mass audience.

It would be a mistake, however, to discount too easily Sartre's attitudes toward literature as simply the result of his own unhappy will to have a political vocation. We would be right in part, but we would be wrong to forget the more significant question why the writer today should be so furiously haunted by the need to search for such a vocation. Sartre's position might be very different without the large and vocal presence of the Communists upon the French scene: the writer of *La Nausee*, in becoming the leader of a school, has had to sacrifice himself to the public figure who is drawn into competition with the Communists and has had consequently to offer a message emphasizing more and more the "positive" and social role of literature. It is very significant, thus, that the discussion of the present situation of the writer in 1947, with which this book concludes, should be in large part an unequivocal attack upon communism as a moral and intellectual phenomenon (a section which, along with his destruction of the literary theories of surrealism, represents Sartre at his polemic best); but it is even more significant of the ambiguous situation of the French writer now that Sartre's anticommunism on the political level has been so very much less equivocal. Communism and communist ideology do not play the same role in America; but in this respect the French situation may not be so much different as simply in advance of our own, and what we must be prepared for all over the world is a literature produced under the conditions of a mass society, whatever may be the political regime imposed upon this mass base. The end of modern literature, however, does not mean the end of literature. We may regret the passing of a period, but lamentation cannot become the content of a critical doctrine. In the new period which we are now entering the literary medium may discover new forms and adventures for itself: for one thing, the social process in which the writer is now caught up may put an end to his famous alienation in our time, and a literature with very different possibilities may result. Unfortunately all this is still very much in the future, while right now. I do not think there can be much doubt that these new conditions are producing, and will probably produce for some time, a literature that is plainly inferior to the old.

From *The Partisan Review*. Vol. XVI (September, 1949), pp. 942-950. Reprinted by permission of the author and editors.

David Perkins

Contemporary American Poetry

14.

THE POSTWAR PERIOD: INTRODUCTION

During the 1950s poets both in England and the States rejected the styles that were then established. In the continuity of poetry from generation to generation, there had been no comparably sharp break for forty years, since the advent of Modernist poetry just before and after the First World War. The beginning of this new period might be pinpointed in 1954, when Philip Larkin's *Poems* appeared and when, in a completely unrelated event, Allen Ginsberg gave the first public performance of his *Howl*. Other points of departure were Robert Lowell's *Life Studies* (1959) and Charles Olson's 1950 manifesto "Projective Verse" which voiced premises shared by many of the younger poets.

As a name for this period I adopt the term Postmodernism. It is not more satisfactory than similar terms in literary history, such as Modernism, Romanticism, and the Baroque, and I shall briefly discuss the word and the problems it creates. But it is better than other names that have been suggested, for it highlights a central fact about poetry since the 1950s, namely, that it is shaped by the poets' reception of Modernism.

The term "Modernism" derived from poets in the 1910s. It named the new style they hoped to create. In its current senses "Postmodernism" was invented by critics in the 1950s and 1960s. So far as I know, Charles Olson, Robert Creeley, and Robert Duncan are the only poets who often referred to contemporary poetry as "Postmodern." They meant that they and their fellow poets in the 1950s and 1960s were basing their work on the styles of the 1910s and 1990s. Olson's influential essay "Projective Verse" emphasized that this verse develops as a next step from what Olson called the revolution of 1910. As Creeley put it in 1951, "Any movement poetry can now make beyond the achievement of Pound, Williams, et al. must make use of the fact of their work and, further, of what each has stressed as the main work now to be done." Olson also meant by the term that after the Second World War a new human consciousness was developing. At present the term retains both these implications along with many others, and has, as is normal with such terms, no agreed meaning. It may refer, as it does for Olson, to a new mentality, which is being formed, so the argument goes, by contemporary history and technology — by such influences as the memory of concentration camps, Dresden, and Hiroshima, by travel, cultural eclecticism, ecological activism, communes, the use of drugs, television, computers, and the exploration of space. Those who use the term in this sense believe that there has been a radical break with the past in human sensibility, imagination, and morality. Or the term may be used to refer only to a style in the arts. In the latter case, Postmodernism may be thought to characterize all the arts or only some, and in any one art, such as poetry, it may be applied to the contemporary period as a whole or only to some tendencies within it. Critics variously date the beginnings of Postmodernism from the 1950s, 1960s, or 1970s. Some maintain that Postmodernism is a more radical Modernism and others that it negates Modernism, and still others hold that Postmodernism is an altogether different style which flourishes along with Modernism.

I use the term as *a pis aller*. If contemporary American poetry can, as I believe, no longer be called Modernist, we need a name for our different period. Postmodernism is a more or less accepted term, and highlights, to repeat, a central fact about contemporary poetry, namely, that the most strongly shaping factor in it is the Modernist achievement from 1910 to 1950. Reasons for thinking that our poetry should no longer be called Modernist have already been indicated and this and future chapters will elaborate them. I shall also argue that contemporary poetry has a period style or styles of its own, and shall thus reject the interpretation of Postmodernism as a radical perspectivism. According to this interpretation, which derives from contemporary architecture, a Postmodernist artist is one who neither continues from Modernism nor negates it. Instead, he regards Modernism as one historical style among others; he may draw motifs and methods from it, but for him Modernism has no special prestige. If our poets were Postmodernist in this sense, their work might be eclectic, using and combining a variety of past styles, and would not be more closely related to Modernist styles than to others. This is not what we find.

Since the Second World War the prevailing style of poetry in Great Britain has been unlike that in the United States, yet it may equally be called Postmodern. For the term Modernism, like all such terms, covers many moments and tendencies, and, on the whole, the contemporary poetries of England and America have been formed in relation to different moments in the Modernist period. In England the new poetry of the 1950s was created in antagonism to the revived Romanticism of Dylan Thomas and of much poetry written during the Second World War, and it was equally created by a decisive rejection of the high Modernism of Eliot and Pound. (Yeats was repudiated more as a belated Romantic than as a Modernist, and Stevens and Williams were hardly known.) The values that inspired the new poetry from Larkin to Geoffrey Hill included rational thought and communication and introspective honesty, with the complexity of perception and attitude that inevitably attends the honesty of the intelligent. These values were associated with the "academic" New

Criticism in the United States, but in England they were regarded as elements of native tradition to which English poetry should return.

. In the United States, in contrast, the feeling of impasse and crisis, which so many poets experienced in the 1950s, was caused by the dominance of the New Criticism. As I said in Chapter 5, the New Criticism was established in university English departments, widespread as a method of instruction in classrooms, and reflected in a style of poetry. This style was exemplified in the 1950s by, among others, Allen Tate, Adrienne Rich, Robert Lowell, Randall Jarrell, Richard Wilbur, Melvin Tolson, and Howard Nemerov.

The literary values of the New Critics derived in important respects from the criticism of T. S. Eliot, and so did the canon of authors they admired. One of the reasons the New Criticism had achieved its great influence was that it provided criteria for the defense of Modernist poetry—of Eliot, Yeats, and, in lesser degree, Pound—from conservative attacks. Essentially the New Criticism was a rationalizing of the Modernist legacy. The New Critics retained basic Modernist values—economy, wit, irony, impersonality, scrupulous handling of form—but abandoned, without saying so, specific technical features of Modernist poetry, such as the extreme ellipsis, fragmentation, and discontinuity of *The Waste Land* and the *Cantos* and the density of symbolism and overlapping myth in *The Waste Land* and *The Bridge*. As a result the New Critical style was cautious and traditional in comparison with the high Modernism it descended from, and, unlike high Modernism, it did not seem in the least disorienting, grand, or revolutionary. To many of the younger poets the New Critical message was similar to that James Merrill later attributed to the batlike voices in his *Mirabell:* "ALL ENERGY SOURCES MUST BE KEPT COVERD/ THAT IS OUR PRINCIPAL TASK THE DAM BURSTS AS IT ERODES." When they rebelled against the New Critical mode, American poets did not repudiate the high Modernism of the 1920s, but in fact returned to it, and especially to Pound, Williams, and Stevens, for sources of a breakthrough. As they rejected the New Criticism, American poets took many different paths from Whitmanian prophecy to the style of William Carlos Williams, pop, Surrealism, Dada, confession, and collage.

THE CONCEPT OF A PERIOD STYLE

In every age only a small number of the techniques and conventions that are possible in poetry are actually used. The others are not adopted because they would be inconsistent with those which are, or because they involve moral or metaphysical assumptions the poet does not share, or because (in ages that prize originality) they would remind readers of some past style or other poet and are thus suited only for allusion or parody. Our time is unusually open, tolerant, and eclectic, but even so a poet cannot now write "ere" or "hist!" except for comic purposes, cannot use Miltonic blank verse, as eighteenth-century poets could, cannot compose a panegyric, and so forth. And of course in every period much has not yet been conceived. Keats could not have deliberately violated grammar, created collages, or used free verse; if such techniques had occurred to him, they would not have seemed appropriate to poetry, in fact, they would have seemed uneducated and ludicrous.

What we mean by a "convention" in art ranges from an accepted distortion of reality, as when a character speaks in meter, to an expected system of feeling. Petrarchan love in the Renaissance and love of nature in the nineteenth century were conventions of the latter kind. Good poems violate convention in some respects, but all poems follow conventions more than they do not. Otherwise they would be too difficult for the poet to write and too disorienting for readers. In these considerations—that poetry is largely made out of conventions, that the number of conventions available for use at any particular time is limited, and that different conventions are available at different times—we have part of the explanation for a period style, for the fact that poems by different poets who lived in the same age and place are likely to resemble one another in style and content.

Why conventions of art change over time can be debated forever, but in the long run conventions reflect premises about reality and change because these do. Thus, for example, the "beauty" of imagery and sound in the poetry of the Romantic period was not merely pleasurable and escapist. It reflected Romantic Platonism and transcendentalism; beyond the veil of phenomenal experience there was, according to Romantic beliefs, the reality of Harmony and Love, to which poetry lifted the soul. The "happy ending," the closing note of uplift, consolation, reconciliation, or promise for the future, which in one form or another pervades nineteenth-century art, was related to this metaphysical and religious premise and also to Christian beliefs. As acceptance of the underlying ideas waned, the "beauty" of Romantic poetry lost much of its sanction, and it persisted in Tennyson, Rossetti, William Morris, and later poets as something unrelated to reality but expected of poetry. The Modernist movement involved, in part, an acceptance in poetry of a naturalistic view of reality which had long been present in novels. In this transition the more obviously conventional was replaced by the less obviously so. Thus meter, rhyme, stanza, archaic or otherwise "poetic" diction, "beauty" of sound and imagery, formal closure, and the figure of the poet as apart from ordinary life gave way to free verse, colloquial diction, images of everyday experience, open form, and, in one famous example, the figure of the poet as New Jersey doctor.

Conventions normally linger for a while in art even though the beliefs they once embodied are gone. Developments in philosophy and intellectual *Weltanschauung* are assimilated into emotion and imagination with a time lag. The audience, to the degree that the writer composes for an audience, is a conservative influence; the larger the audience intended, the more this is the case. But the main reason is the one I have stressed: literature resists change because it is made out of previous literature.

Sometimes the transformation of conventions is initiated by external events; the Romantic revolution in the arts is commonly associated, for example, with the French Revolution and the upheaval it caused in every realm of thought. Frequently, however, the moment of change seems to come just after the familiar conventions have been associated with an obviously weak literature. We see this in the poetry of the United States at the end of the nineteenth century, just prior to the Modernist period, and in the late Augustan poetry of England before the Romantic creativity. At such moments the distance between conventions and realities is either greater or more visible than usual, forcing a reconstruction. The argument presupposes that poets seek to disclose or convey "reality." The reality intended may be naturalistic, archetypal, unconscious, transcendent, or whatever; the means of rendering it may be relatively direct or by detour, as in fantasy; but "truth" is always the object.

Hegel is the main source for the assumption that every "period" has its own style, an ensemble of qualities that are coherent with one another because they reflect an underlying spirit of the age. But we may accept that period styles exist, and prefer more empirical explanations of them. Poets have worked with the same or similar conventions because they inherited them, were exposed to the same cultural and intellectual influences, lived through the same historical events, and imitated one another. Whether it is appropriate to speak of a period style that does not embrace all the important writers (or even all the arts) of a time and place, or whether the term may also apply to a style shared by many but not all, is a matter of definition; in practice, the term is used in either sense. And though I would not use the term unless the qualities I discerned were logically or psychologically integrated with one another, the extent to which this must be the case is open to dispute.

We would expect a period style of the present to seem less integrated than one in the past, if only because our culture is less coherent. Since there is no longer any authority or consensus to determine what languages, books, phonograph records, films, art reproductions, and so forth an educated person should know, and since all these media are available in overwhelming quantity, the cultural experience of different individuals has less in common than in the past. Especially in the United States, moreover, there are enormous differences in cultural experience that stem from race, ethnic background, region, and political allegiance to a cause, such as ecology, Black power, gay rights, or feminism. And though in any age since the Renaissance artists have been ambivalently motivated both to imitate one another, if only to be up-to-date, and also to depart from the currently fashionable, if only to attract notice, the latter motive urges more powerfully in the twentieth century than ever before.

Nevertheless, since the Second World War we can observe period styles in the poetry of both Great Britain and the United States. They are different styles, but in each country there is a nexus of interrelated tendencies. That their interrelation is often by opposition does not distinguish our time from others. Styles and periods are not usefully to be compared with persons, but they have one point in common with them: they are best understood by their tensions and polarities. Not only what we do or affirm, but also the inner doubt or opposite impulse our words and actions strive to silence, reveals who we are. In this chapter I shall describe the contemporary period style in American poetry and trace its historical development since the Second World War. Except incidentally for purposes of comparison, I shall postpone characterizing the different period style in England until Chapters 18 and 19, which are devoted to that subject.

POETRY IN THE UNITED STATES

Since generalizations lie inert without examples, I may begin by citing verses from various poets. My point, for the moment, is only that they could not have been written in the 1940s and 1950s during the heyday of the New Criticism. Consider these quotations: from John Ashbery's "The Skaters" (1966), where he speaks of a political revolution:

> in Argentina! Think of it! Bullets flying
> through the air, men on the move!

From John Berryman's *Love & Fame* (1970):

> I drink too much. My wife threatens separation.
> She won't "nurse" me. She feels "inadequate."
> We don't mix together.

From Sylvia Plath's "Lesbos" (1962):

> You say I should drown my kittens. Their smell!
> You say I should drown my girl.
> She'll cut her throat at ten if she's mad at two.

From Galway Kinnell's *The Book of Nightmares* (1971):

> learn to reach deeper
> into the sorrows
> to come—to touch
> the almost imaginary bones
> under the face, to hear under the laughter
> the wind crying across the black stones. Kiss
> the mouth
> which tells you, *here,*
> *here is the world.* This mouth. This laughter. These temple
> bones.
> The still undanced cadence of vanishing.

From James Merrill's *The Changing Light at Sandover* (1982), which I cite with the reminder that Merrill is a very sophisticated artist:

NOW LET US BANISH GLOOMY DREAMS

FOR HEAVEN ON EARTH MOST LIKELY SEEMS.

In later chapters I shall comment on most of these passages. I am not yet arguing that they have much relation to one another, and I am not asserting their worth as poetry. My point is merely that they are characteristic of our period, and could not have come from the 1940s and 1950s.

A comparison of these extracts to the earlier poetry of high Modernism, however, shows both continuities and differences. Stevens could never have written the lines from Ashbery, but he almost could have. The Berryman passage might have been one of the fragments quoted in *The Waste Land*. The bit from Merrill's parodic masque has distant precedents in Auden. The verses from Kinnell sound more like Rilke than like any predecessor in English, and Plath's style is too mannered and percussive to recall any other poet.

The salient characteristics of contemporary American poetry are, in general, that it is or seems spontaneous, personal, naturalistic, open in form and antagonistic to the idea of form, intellectually skeptical yet morally concerned and sometimes even righteous, and imbued with feelings of vulnerability, yet with the humor of resignation, acknowledging helplessness. These generalizations, which I shall soon elaborate, naturally require innumerable qualifications and exceptions, and the rest of this book will make them, but first I must, since I observe a period style, try to describe it plainly.

In comparison with most previous poetry, this characteristically seems directly spontaneous. Spontaneous utterance—or the illusion of it—descends to American poets from Whitman and Williams. It may seem easy and swift, as in Gary Snyder; or hysterical, as in Sylvia Plath; or impassioned, as in Allen Ginsberg. Most frequently it seems casual, relaxed, and conversational: "All the untidy activity continues," writes Elizabeth Bishop at the conclusion of "The Bight," "awful but cheerful." "I had a most marvelous piece of luck," says John Berryman in Dream Song 26— "I died." "I could say it's the happiest period of my life," John Ashbery begins "The Ongoing Story"; "It hasn't got much competition!" Such speech attracts because it overcomes the sense of artifice produced by New Critical formality and compression. Its risk is dilution. Spontaneous talk may take too many words. The cost may be greater when the emotion is low-keyed; for the conversational and unexcited may seem dull.

This spontaneous speech has its theoretical justification in a prevalent concept of art in our period, one I mentioned in connection with William Carlos Williams and shall discuss again in Chapter 21, when I come to contemporary ideas of open form. In the 1890s "art" implied primarily the work as finished object-fictional, constructed, closed, perfected, and posed—and the term also referred to the mental powers and acts by which such an object is produced. The work of art was to be created laboriously through repeated revisions. But contemporary concepts of art may stress the process of creation, and may interpret this process as immediate mastery exhibited in appropriate motions. Art, in this sense, is less the painting than the sequence of touches and strokes, one balancing or completing another, by which the painting comes into being and of which it is the record. Analogies to express this sense of art usually involve a creature in action—a bird on the wing, a man diving into water, a shortstop fielding a grounder—and the art lies in the sequence of complexly integrated motions. At least in theory, revision is discouraged, and so is closure, for each particular act is part of an immediate, ongoing process.

Though the natural, spontaneous speech of contemporary poetry is often low-keyed, it need not be. Especially in the 1950s and 1960s, many poets eagerly wished to be directly and strongly emotive, if only to distance themselves further from the New Critical mode, which was intellectual and oblique. But in order to feel and express emotional fervor, a person must normally be in a relatively undivided state of mind, and since poets, like other reflective persons in our time, are alert to the Freudian ambivalence of emotion and prone to intellectual skepticism and perspectivism, they can seldom speak with fervent conviction. Of course, emotion may be intense yet still qualified, and usually we find this in the poetry of Robert Lowell, John Berryman, Allen Ginsberg, and Sylvia Plath, where ambivalence and humor are present amid remorse, disgust, or anguish. Emotions that are strong, direct, and also unqualified are voiced especially in connection with certain subjects, such as the unconscious and myth. In archetypal poetry and in Surrealism the poem is by convention to be read as an expression of the unconscious mind, and in this case the emotion may be complexly qualified at the unconscious level, but is not devitalized by the criticism of the intellect and ego awareness. Poetry of this kind has been written by Robert Bly, James Wright, W. S. Merwin, James Tate, Mark Strand, and many others; in fact, it was a vogue of the 1960s. Poetry about myth is not necessarily emotive, needless to say, but when a poet seeks to recapture and possess the myth-believing mind of ancient or primitive peoples or of the worshipper, he similarly escapes irony and intellectual inhibition. Such passages are frequent in, among others, Robert Duncan, Charles Olson, Allen Ginsberg, Gary Snyder, and Galway Kinnell. These poets may perceive lovers, enemies, parents, children, animals, and landscape in terms of myths, and in form their poems may be incantations based on mythical beliefs, such as spells, litanies, and mantras. In the poetry of Surrealism, archetype, and myth there is frequently a willed simplicity and even sentimentality. This too appeals as a relief from the sophisticated wit of the New Critical mode, but contemporary poets are not genuinely simple; they merely long to be and may write as though they were. James Wright's famous "A Blessing" offers one example. Here the sentimental view of nature is psychologically self-defensive. The poem represses the appalled awareness of modern urban reality that Wright articulates in other poems.

In poetry of social protest, which has been widespread since the 1960s, tentativeness, speculativeness, skepticism, and humor are frequently short-circuited. If the subject is race relations, atomic armaments, the war in Vietnam, environmental pollution, nuclear energy, patriarchy, or the like, the attitude may be morally certain, righteous, denunciatory, and prophetic. Genre offers one explanation; a poet writing to rally and inspire a political cause cannot express doubts. Often, moreover, the poets of protest—Bly, Merwin, Ginsberg, Rich, Levertov—are not the same ones who are otherwise most committed to a skeptical, open-minded way of thinking. To this generalization, however, there are notable exceptions. Robert Lowell was Hardyesque on religious questions but morally convinced on the Vietnam war; Robert Duncan is profoundly speculative, but not on the Vietnam war or environmental issues; James Merrill is eagerly open to diverse meanings in his experience, but closed and prophetic on ecological problems. For poets, like most intellectuals, are genuinely frightened by the dangers of war and environmental pollution, and they are also buoyed into certitude by the support of others, the heady sense of swimming with a political crowd. The opportunity to indulge in feelings of conviction tempts all the more because of the intellectual uncertainty in which we usually languish. And finally, to assail timber companies and nuclear power plants provides a cover and outlet for emotions that are less focused and more problematic. I am alluding to the way in which sensitive contemporaries are turning in disgust against what man is and does.

In his critical essays T. S. Eliot stressed that good poetry is always "impersonal," and the New Critics, elaborating this opinion, argued that in reading we must always distinguish between the speaker and the poet, since the poet has invented the speaker as the appropriate person to utter the poem. No matter how closely the speaker or "persona" seems to approximate the poet in character and biographical circumstances, there is, in principle, a difference, and a reader who ignores this is naive. Though the New Critics were surely right, their view emphasizes that a poem is art—fabricated, fictitious, and illusionistic—and thus distances poetry from "life." For this reason contemporary American poets have rejected it. Their repudiation of the "persona" is consistent with their general antagonism to art, in any sense of art except spontaneous rightness in action, and with their commitments to naturalism and immediacy.

In reading contemporary American poetry, therefore, the convention is usually that the poet is speaking. The so-called Confessional poetry of W. D. Snodgrass, Ginsberg, Lowell, Plath, Anne Sexton, and John Berryman established this convention in a dramatic way, but the grounds of it are wider. At the present time, a personal voice does not in the least imply a confessional subject or emotion. It is the voice of the poet, spontaneously uttering his or her thoughts or emotions. In Denise Levertov's "Triple Feature," for example, we are to suppose that Levertov is watching a poor Mexican family and trying to imagine their experiences in going to the movies. In Richard Wilbur's "Cottage Street, 1953" the poet looks back on an occasion when he had tea with Sylvia Plath. We are not, on reading this poem, to suppose that the 'I' speaking is an invented character, a "persona." And so with poems of James Merrill, Gary Snyder, Adrienne Rich, James Wright, Frank O'Hara, James Schuyler, Robert Hayden, James Dickey, Elizabeth Bishop, and many others. Unless the poem indicates a different convention, as with dramatic monologues, parodies, and some collages, contemporary American poetry is, to repeat, to be read as though it were the immediate utterance or interior monologue of the poet; the circumstances narrated or implied are to be taken as autobiographical.

Contemporary American poetry is naturalistic primarily in this sense. Its subject is the emotions and experiences of the poet, and the poet presents himself as living much as other Americans do—making love, raising children, drinking with friends, camping out, getting sick. In Confessional poetry the subject matter is particularly intimate and harrowing. These poets describe aspects of their lives that most people would conceal, such as impulses to suicide, abject humiliations and lusts, and hatred of their families. The most frequent subject of Confessional poetry is the family interpreted in a Freudian perspective: the family is a nexus of rivalry and emotional ambivalence; parents and children view each other through distorting psychological projections. Even though contemporary poetry is naturalistic, the emphasis on the life of the poor, which was present in the naturalistic novel of the nineteenth century, is absent, and so is the attempt to report with a scientific precision that excludes subjectivity. Since few poets now believe in a transcendent reality, and since the post-Marxist, post-Freudian, post-Hitler vision of this world offers little consolation, the image of life is bleak, or would be except for the redeeming power most poets find in their own minds, in creativity, meditative energy, and memory. The spontaneous, colloquial language of most contemporary poetry is also naturalistic, needless to say, and is part of a more general antagonism to form, which I shall soon discuss. Modernist techniques such as fragmentation, ellipsis, and allusion are present in contemporary American poetry, and sometimes are used heavily, but bear an uneasy relation to its naturalistic tendency, and are seldom as prominent as they were in Eliot and Pound. Of course, much contemporary poetry is not naturalistic, particularly that which is formalist, Surrealist, Dada, archetypal, mythical, or collage.

In its image of life much of our poetry might be more suggestively described not as naturalistic but as "creatural." The term, which is usually employed in connection with the art and literature of the late Middle Ages, refers to an emphasis on man's vulnerable and suffering body and mortality as these unite all human beings. The iconography of the Dance of Death is one well-known example of "creatural" realism, but unlike such work in the fourteenth and fifteenth centuries, the stark, detailed presentation of bodily sufferings, aging, and death in modern poetry is seldom intended to disengage the emotions from earthly existence, since the poet can hope for no other, and is, therefore, seldom wholly unrelieved. John Berryman's "Homage to Mistress Bradstreet" is perhaps the most powerful modern poem of this "creatural" realism, but one thinks also of images of vomiting, hospital operations, sexual impotence, senility, and the like in, among others, Lowell, Plath, Sexton, Ginsberg, James Wright, and Frank Bidart. To which we may add the sense of man's psychological vulnerability and sickness, as in Ginsberg's "Kaddish." "Creatural" realism is especially associated with Confessional poetry, but spreads into other kinds as well, and was much less present in the high Modernist era.

The "creatural" vision of man in our poetry reflects the contemporary weakening of humanism and of religion. "Creatural" man has no greatness or even dignity. Of course this anti-humanist vision of man coalesces with the revelations about human nature given in Freudian depth psychology, and the sense of bodily and psychological vulnerability intertwines with the revulsion from man motivated by images of concentration camps, bombings, torture chambers, and the holocaust—images imprinted on the imagination of every child in our time—and by instances of ecological pollution, exterminations of animal species, and fears of nuclear devastation. In sensitive persons, therefore, the human mind is turning in moral anguish and disgust against itself, against mankind, human nature, and what man has done and will do. That most poets, like most Americans, are living in relatively comfortable circumstances and are not immediately threatened does not mitigate feelings of vulnerability and disgust, and may intensify them. Whether the states of mind of intellectuals and writers reflect those of society at large is always doubtful, but ours is not the poetry of people who feel in control of their lives or hopeful about them. In some poets—for example, in Olson, Merwin, Snyder, Ginsberg, Merrill, and Wright, there is a compensatory assertion that nature is good. For these poets man is no longer primary, either in moral rank or as an object of emotional identification, but is an element in an ecological field that has no moral center apart from the whole.

The forms used in the contemporary poetry of the United States include traditional and free verse in narrative, dramatic monologue, long meditation, list, catalogue, and lyric, including sonnet, song, chant, litany, spell, and mantra. There is also collage, as in early poems by John Ashbery and some by Robert Duncan, and concrete poetry, of which the work of Michael Phillips offers witty examples. Different forms permeate one another in innumerable combinations. Since expectations associated with genres are now much less definite than they used to be, our poets tend to orient their readers by invoking analogies. The poem may resemble a prose essay, conversation, meditation, interior monologue, dream, prayer, primitive myth, diary, notebook, photograph album, film, painting, or musical composition. Such analogies help the reader to understand and accept the poem's tone, content, method of procedure, and purpose.

Generally speaking, our poets repudiate "closed" forms, and many of them are antagonistic to the idea of form. The period style of the present, then, is characterized less by the forms that are used than by the way they are handled, the techniques and procedures that keep form "open" or even abolish it in the same moment that it is being created. I discuss these techniques in Chapter 2, and the purpose here is merely to note their general, underlying motivations. The New Critical poem of the 1940s and 1950s was formally "closed," in other words, metrical, rhymed, and organized into stanzas, tightly integrated in images and figures, and completed in the "curve" or "plot" enacted. Eventually such poems seemed artificial, as I said, and were rejected for that reason. Spontaneous immediacy in expression was prized because of its "truth," "sincerity," or "naturalness," because it enacted a concept of art as motion or becoming rather than being, and because it seemed democratic. For since the New Critical poem was compressed and ironical, it was also difficult and implied an elite audience of especially qualified readers; to create an opposite style was a political gesture.

Poets, furthermore, have become uneasy with the very idea of form because of our modern awareness of the relativism, perspectivism, multiplicity, and swift transition of our mental experience. Such awareness also characterized the Modernist period, needless to say, and no poems more reflect it in their forms than *The Waste Land* and the *Cantos*. But *The Waste Land* and the *Cantos* were formally radical in their day, and they would not seem so now. To impose a form on an experience or a thought is to put it into a context and perspective, and thus to repress other contexts or perspectives that might be no less valid. From instant to instant our thoughts are innumerable, complex, and changing in their interrelations. We doubt that we have a continuing identity. Since experience is a deluge no form can contain, the poet's truth inheres in his stance, in his openness to whatever comes immediately as it comes, in his refusal to impose a form or his readiness to destroy whatever form he has imposed. Not all postwar poetry in the United States is shaped by such considerations. Wilbur, Bishop, Plath, Bly, Wright, Merwin, John Hollander, and Kinnell are generally little influenced by them. But such considerations underlie the notebook or diary poems of Lowell, Berryman, Creeley, Rich, and Levertov; the "I do this I do that" poems of Frank O'Hara; the poems Ginsberg dictated into a tape recorder while riding along the road; the open sequences of Olson in the Maximus Poems, of Duncan in "Passages," and of Gary Snyder, Ed Dorn, Jack Spicer, and many other poets; the collages of Robert Duncan and the "montage succession" of

David Antin and Robert Kelly; and the continually changing onwardness of meditation in the long poems of A. R. Ammons and John Ashbery.

Our poets are, to repeat, deeply alienated from our imperialist, bureaucratic, consumerist, commercially manipulative civilization. "Moloch," as Allen Ginsberg calls it, is the vast, entrenched system of economic, political, and ideological power: the government, armed forces, police, business corporations, labor unions, and media. Disgust and fear of this and its manifestations are voiced by approximately half of our contemporary poets; the others are not of an opposite opinion, but are too urbane in style or too personal in subject matter to voice such emotions directly and strongly. But of course "Moloch" seems quite impervious to the fulminations of poets. As one of a huge population, caught like everyone else in the toils of history, of the bureaucratic state, and of the large institutions in which we work, shop, and amuse ourselves, the poet cannot feel that his or her ideas and desires make any difference. What we experience as our own ideas and desires may, in any case, have been instilled in us by propaganda and advertising.

Given the degree to which individuals in the modern world feel vulnerable and helpless, it is not surprising that humor is almost omnipresent in our poetry as a defense. The humor of contemporary American poetry is usually of a kind that acknowledges powerlessness. We find clowning, camp, Dada, parody, but seldom, except in Lowell, the savage disgust of Eliot, or the grand, satiric contempt of Yeats, or the unmitigated invective of Lawrence, or the fury of Pound's Hell Cantos. Even when our poets are prophetically denunciatory, they are also comic, and their comedy undermines their attack. The poet is a buffoon, as in camp humor; or is deliberately, wildly ineffective in his gestures of protest, as in Dada; or is amusing only to intellectuals, as in parody. That our poets do not think themselves a serious threat is one of the reasons why they often seem strangely good humored as well as humorous. In fact, the poet frequently characterizes himself as a more or less ineffectual person. (Significantly, women poets rarely adopt this pose.) He is the perplexed man of Robert Lowell's late sonnets, or the helpless, self-mocking compulsive of Berryman's Dream Songs, or the laconic worrier of Robert Creeley, or the politely self-deprecating Merrill, or Ginsberg, the crank and nonstop yammerer, or Ashbery, contemplating his can of worms and blandly, resignedly, even cheerfully making the best of it. Ours is a humor expressing the fatuity of our struggles in the very moment that we are struggling.

THE DEVELOPMENT OF CONTEMPORARY POETRY

The chapters that follow trace the history of contemporary poetry from the 1950s to the present. I begin with older poets such as Robert Penn Warren, Theodore Roethke, and Elizabeth Bishop. They were of the same generation as Auden, Spender, MacNeice, Dylan Thomas, and other British poets who were famous in the 1930s, but they developed more slowly and did not bring out their first important books until the 1940s. The chapter entitled "Breaking Through the New Criticism" expresses the dominance of the New Criticism in the United States at the end of the Second World War, and describes the careers of a number of poets, including John Berryman and Randall Jarrell, who began to write in this style and gradually rejected it. (One chapter cannot include all the poets whose careers followed this course, and many of them, such as Sylvia Plath, Adrienne Rich, and W S. Merwin, are discussed elsewhere in other connections, while Robert Lowell is considered in a separate chapter.) In each poet much the same general ideas and influences motivated the transition. These were too complex to be summarized here, and later chapters go into them at length, but they ranged from metaphysical assumptions—that reality is open, multiple, in swift transition, and ungraspable—to considerations of morality and taste. The ethos of the New Criticism came, as I said, to seem repressive and elitist, and the dense, intellectual idiom and closure of New Critical poetry seemed artificial. These literary reactions were of course supported by developments in society at large, especially in the 1960s. Beatniks, drugs, communes, feminism, gay liberation, black pride and power, Zen, and other manifestations of cultural eclecticism, and the protest against the war in Vietnam had an impact on the subject matter and style or poetry, which generally rejected "high" culture, "closed" and therefore "strict" forms, tradition, and other embodiments of authority. But the most immediate reason for the reaction against the New Criticism was, I believe, its acceptance within the classroom. Once it was being taught to students as a dogma, it was doomed. Here, however, I should distinguish between poets such as Allen Ginsberg, Robert Duncan, and Frank O'Hara, who rejected the New Critical mode as students, and somewhat older poets, such as Robert Lowell, who had written brilliantly in it for years. As these older poets changed their styles, they did not abandon their rigorous artistry, but merely concealed it. This is one of the reasons why Lowell in *Life Studies* (1959) Berryman in his Dream Songs, and Elizabeth Bishop in *Poems* (1955) and subsequent volumes are among the greatest poets of our time.

Meanwhile in England during the 1950s poets broke with the high Modernist tradition, and they also reacted strongly against Dylan Thomas, who was then at the height of his fame. They emphasized such values as clarity, realism, empirical honesty, and rationalism, and they looked with favor on past styles, such as that of the later eighteenth century and of Thomas Hardy and Georgian poetry in the early part of this century, to which such values could be attributed. The language of British poetry was sober, low-keyed, exact, and reflective. Philip Larkin is the great poet of this phase. He and several others were associated in the 1950s in a group called the Movement, but most English poets, whether numbered in the

Movement or not, shared a similar ethos. They expressed a rather drab, painful sense of existence. Outwardly their eyes focused on weedy railroad embankments, littered back lots, hospital waiting rooms, and the like, and inwardly on boredom, envy, fear, and darker emotions. Moral self-scrutiny was common, though moral judgments were baffled by honesty. To what extent this poetry was shaped by postwar English history is a difficult question. Deflated emotions, anti-romantic ennui, and a questioning, as in Robert Frost's poem "The Oven Bird" of "what to make of a diminished thing" seem appropriate in the aftermath of the Second World War. They might also be related, as we shall see, to the Labourite social revolution in postwar England, which left many liberal intellectuals feeling that they must now accept what they had made.

In the 1960s the type of poetry associated with Larkin and the Movement began to be challenged in England, and poets again opened themselves to American and Continental examples. Robert Lowell had a vogue in England; Geoffrey Hill formed his style partly on the New Critical mode of the United States; Sylvia Plath learned from her husband, Ted Hughes; Thom Gunn from his teacher, Yvor Winters; Donald Davie was fascinated by the style of Ezra Pound; and Charles Tomlinson by that of Wallace Stevens. Poets also experimented with the Surrealism of central Europe and with Poundian discontinuity. Basil Bunting's *Briggflatts* (1966), though quintessentially English in its regional diction, is in form a *symboliste* poem, and the favorable reception it received would have been less probable in Great Britain ten years earlier. The poetry of Ireland, though quite different from that of Great Britain, resembles it much more than it does American poetry, and I shall describe it immediately after the poetry of England, though in a separate chapter.

Despite what I have just said, English and American poetry have, on the whole, developed independently of each other in the last forty years and are quite different in style. There has been nothing comparable to the transatlantic impact of Eliot, Yeats, and Auden during the first half of the century. The present difference between English and American poetry helps us to see each more clearly.

Since the three connected chapters on England and Ireland bring us to Geoffrey Hill and Seamus Heaney, I violate chronology by returning, in the chapter entitled "Open Form," to developments in the United States during the 1950s and 1960s. I also move without transition into a very different milieu and ethos. The remaining chapters are devoted to poetry in the United States. Thus the organization of Part Four of this history reflects the fact that English and American poetry have followed relatively separate, national lines during the postwar period.

The 1950s were the formative decade of postwar American poetry. As this new poetry was more widely read, appreciated, and imitated during the 1960s, it established itself as the dominant American style or nexus of styles. Though the social upheavals of the 1960s conduced to the favorable reception of this poetry, it was created during the Eisenhower era, when social protest and innovation were less widespread and less visible. During the 1950s William Carlos Williams first became an important influence on younger poets, teaching them his natural, American speech rooted in the immediate, local, and particular. In Ginsberg's *Howl* and Lowell's *Life Studies* the Beat and Confessional movements produced their respective masterpieces. The camp, pop poetry of Frank O'Hara and others dates originally from the 1950s, and Charles Olson and Robert Duncan began then to adopt and revise the methods of Pound's *Cantos* and to transmit them to younger poets. In the 1950s Olson also began to influence younger poets by the energy of his theorizing in manifestoes and personal letters. In the chapter "Open Form" I discuss his theories and those of others associated with him, especially Robert Duncan, Robert Creeley, and Denise Levertov, keeping in mind that although Olson expressed his theories in an extreme, provocative, and mannered way, the theories themselves were broadly representative. What Olson said, other American poets also assumed.

The perception of postwar American poetry was greatly influenced by Donald Allen's 1960 anthology, *The New American Poetry*. Allen intended to show that many of the younger American poets had been developing along similar lines. But gathering so many poets into his anthology, Allen was naturally under the necessity of dividing them into subgroups—Black Mountain Poets, New York Poets, Beat Poets, San Francisco Poets, and so forth. In literary conversations and critical essays thereafter these classifications enjoyed a great career. They were irresistibly tempting, not only because they organized a scene that seemed confused, but because they allowed readers to feel and seem *au courant*. Moreover, Allen's classifications reflected networks of personal acquaintance among his poets, and personal acquaintance had led in many cases to similarities in style. Anyone discussing the poets Allen presented is still likely to group them in similar ways, the more so since Allen's classifications are well known. Two of his classifications are adopted here in the chapter entitled "Poetry in New York and San Francisco," where the work of a New Yorker, Allen Ginsberg, who also lived in San Francisco, is used to represent the Beat poetry that flourished there, and Frank O'Hara exemplifies the quite different style of Allen's New York School. The poetry of John Ashbery, whom readers once associated with this school, now transcends this identification, and I discuss Ashbery in a later chapter with A. R. Ammons, the other important "meditative" poet of our period.

Though postwar American poetry is, on the whole, naturalistic and personal, opposing styles arose in the 1960s. One of these was Surrealist, and poets in this vein included Frank O'Hara, Robert Bly, James Wright, W. S. Merwin, Mark Strand, Gregory Orr, and James Tate. Most of these poets have been Surrealist only at times, and partly for this reason I have not dwelt on the American Surrealist movement in a separate chapter.

Though it was a flourishing vogue, it was transient both in the careers of most of its adherents and in the poems it produced. Another style grounded itself in the presentation of myth and archetypal symbol. Bly, Merwin, Gary Snyder, Galway, Kinnell, and Louise Gluck are among the poets of this tendency. The poetry of myth and archetype shares with Surrealism an impulse to escape from the limitations of a personal voice and of naturalistic immediacy, to speak from a deeper, more universal level of feeling and experience. These different types of poetry naturally interfuse, and they also combine with the personal and naturalistic, as in poems of Charles Wright and Frank Bidart that include or center on dreams. The dreams reflect the poet's personality and experience, but they also have the disorienting, phantasmagorical qualities of Surrealist verse. The poems of Charles Simic are terse, disturbing metaphors, many of them drawn from memories of his childhood in wartime Europe, in which the personal and naturalistic becomes Surrealist or mythical. Many of these poets do not fall within our chronological limits, and therefore are not discussed at any length. The others are here grouped in the chapter entitled "Against Civilization." They voice hostility to our urban-militarist- industrialist society and a compensatory primitivism and sympathy with "nature."

The final chapters of the book deal at length with the most difficult, formally complex, intellectually sophisticated, and brilliant of contemporary American poets, John Ashbery and James Merrill. Before coming to them, however, I take up the poetry of women's experience and of blacks. These are distinct types of poetry because of their subject matter, and one of the characteristics of our period is the new freedom and boldness of self-expression in these groups. Poetic tradition and social convention obviously inhibited women poets more than men in the past, since the social conventions governing women were more restrictive. So far as postwar women poets have escaped these inhibitions, the personal, Confessional tendencies in American poetry have helped them to do so.

These tendencies interacted with the feminist movement in American society, for both the Confessional style and feminism demanded the overthrow of inner censors, internalized representatives of social convention and authority. Feminism helped inspire the breakthrough of some women poets directly, as with Adrienne Rich, but for others who were not themselves feminists, such as Sylvia Plath and Anne Sexton, the feminist movement was nevertheless a strong, indirect support, both psychologically and in bringing them an audience. The audience feminism helped create was of women who no longer shrank from confronting their authentic emotions, even when these emotions were not what social convention dictated. In Rich, Plath, Sexton, Denise Levertov, Muriel Rukeyser, Diane Wakoski, and others, women readers especially welcomed the strong, direct truth to experience. These poets might voice hatred outweighing love for their fathers, resentment of their children, sexual lusts, and similar emotions that had, for the most part, previously been buried in silence. The Black poetry of America was liberated by a similar combination of a political cause, the Confessional movement in poetry, and the general, cultural revolt in the 1960s against authority, of which the Beats and Hipsters were the most visible symbol. In a poet such as Baraka the Beat ethos merges with modern avant-gardism.

An Excerpt on Contemporary Poetry from Chapter 14 of David Perkins' *A History of Modern Poetry: Modernism and After*. Cambridge, MA: Harvard University Press, 1987.

C. W. E. Bigsby

Twentieth-Century American Drama

INTRODUCTION

The theatre is the most public of arts. It offers the opportunity of acting out anxieties and fears which are born in the conflict between private needs and public values. In America in the 1930s it staged the battle between capital and labour, reflected a desperate pacifism, and dramatised the diminishing space allowed the individual by the encroaching city and an increasing mechanisation. Frequently utopian or visionary in spirit, it tended to pitch love against the sheer density of social experience and the coercions of an economic system which seemed to find no place for the self. The mere placing of the individual on the stage was an assertion of priorities while the co-operative nature of theatre implied a possible social strategy. The post-war theatre, by contrast, seemed more intensely psychological, less convinced that experience could be subordinated to idea, altogether less assured. It seemed to reflect a sense of basement, the war having apparently drawn a line across a particular kind of historical development. And yet, of course, those who emerged as playwrights after 1945 had, in a sense, been shaped by the assumptions of the previous decade. It was there that they found their images no less than a language of liberal possibility often curiously at odds with the social reality which they chose to render as simple threat.

Tennessee Williams and Arthur Miller, who dominated the American theatre for nearly a decade and a half, both began their careers as political playwrights. Formed by the 1930s, they responded to the economic and social realities of the age. Though their first works appeared on Broadway in the 1940s, they had both been writing for more than a decade, and in the case of Tennessee Williams those early works were actually staged by a radical theatre company in St. Louis. There seemed to be a simple coherence to the world which they dramatised then. It resolved itself into contending forces in which the necessities of justice seemed clear, and evil was an unexamined force expressing itself through a wayward capitalism or an inherent corruption. And in that they scarcely differed from those whose work dominated the public stage, people like Sidney Kingsley, Clifford Odets, Maxwell Anderson and William Saroyan. Though these all differed from one another in many ways, they seemed to share a radically simplified vision of human relations and social process.

The war changed this. For Arthur Miller, a Jew, the enormity of the events in Europe challenged equally his model of human nature and his sense of history as an account of progress. For Williams it intensified his feeling of society as threat; it deepened a sense of insecurity rooted in private experience but intensified by the new realities of a post-nuclear age. The pieties of pre-war America no longer seemed capable of sustaining the individual or the culture—though both writers were capable of invoking them, ironised by their own deepening sense of unease. The new materialism bred its own discontents and the word 'alienation' infiltrated the language of sociologist and literary critic alike. Affluence, proudly proclaimed as a value, seemed to locate the individual primarily as consumer. Babbitt was welcomed back into the clan after two decades of naive rebellion. After all, was this not the America which possessed most of the world's consumer goods? It was a period of conspicuous consumption. It is, thus, not for nothing that Willy Loman makes his car and refrigerator criteria of value, and is dismissed from his job by a man distracted by his pride in possession of a new wire recorder (precursor of the tape recorder). For much the same reason Tennessee Williams, in *Cat on a Hot Tin Roof,* uses as a central prop and metaphor:

> a monumental monstrosity peculiar to our times, *a huge* console combination of radio-phonograph (Hi-Fi with three speakers) vv set *and* liquor *cabinet,* bearing and containing many glasses and bottles, all in one piece, which is a composition of muted silver tones, and the opalescent tones of reflecting glass, a chromatic link, this thing, between the sepia (tawny gold) tones of the interior and the cool (white and blue) tones of the gallery and sky. This piece of furniture (? !), this monument, is a very complete and compact little shrine to virtually all the comforts and illusions behind which we hide from such things as the characters in the play are faced with.

In both cases the stance is more than a little informed with nostalgia for an older, gentler America, more lyrical, more in touch with the reality of human need. And if that time also had its betrayals then at least the individual had seemed more in tune with his environment. Now that environment was changing. The countryside was giving way to suburbia and suburbia to the city (though that is a world for the most part ignored by Tennessee Williams). Nor was the individual invited to assume a personal relationship to his society, to play an active role in the moral and political issues of the age. New Deal liberalism was deferring to a conservatism which, following the explosion of the Soviet bomb in 1949, sought to expose and punish those whose Americanness seemed suspect or whose loyalty might be in question. Indeed in many ways the principal victims were those who had been most closely associated with Roosevelt's policies, and those in the arts and education unwilling to disavow values not immediately compatible with the orthodoxies of the moment. It is perhaps not altogether strange that total disaffection, a determined bohemianism, should have emerged as a principal literary stance in the decade. It was a tactic which seemed culturally subversive but which was safely apolitical.

There is, of course, something entirely familiar in this role of alienated intellectual (Irving Howe discusses precisely this in his essay, 'The Age of Conformity'), while the romantic stance of the poet in a prosaic age is a comfortable one, springing from a natural sense of superiority. But in the 1940s and 1950s these positions were not without a certain *subversivefrisson*. The moral and spiritual charge to be derived from a stance of alienation (in Miller's case still with vague Marxist overtones, in Williams's with equally vague Freudian ones) was not without its attraction. Unsurprisingly, neither Miller nor Williams had much time for the new model citizen: an organisation man (in the words of William Whyte); a member of the lonely crowd (according to David Reisman), who made a virtue of submerging his identity in the team: a consumer, a realist, a conformist, prepared to trade independence of mind and spirit for immunity from social pressure. It was, indeed, a period which distrusted the idealist (had he not turned traitor?), the artist (on the one hand a hopeless dreamer; on the other perversely critical of the society which protected him), and the non-conformist (by definition un-American). Writing in the 1950s, James Thurber became convinced that McCarthyism had turned the word 'security' into a term to be 'employed exclusively in a connotation of fear, uncertainty and suspicion'. He felt that the world was faced with 'the smokescreen phrases of the political terminologists 'which left it threatened with a menacing Alice in Wonderland meaninglessness. And not the least of Miller's concerns was the necessity of rescuing language from its debasement: to make his characters responsible for the words they uttered no less than the deeds they committed. Not the least of Williams's obsessions was the need to restore a sense of poetry to lives rendered void by the banality of the world in which they were nurtured.

For a time it seemed that the only legitimate stance for an intellectual to take was one of resolute rejection of public values. But, denied a retreat to the radical ideology of the 1930s, they had relatively little purchase on those values. Miller did adopt a forthright stance, denouncing informers, refusing to be infected by hysteria, and forcibly expressing a distrust of materialism, but he was rather less sure of what could replace it, beyond a kind of instinctively felt existentialism allied to a sense of natural decency. At the heart of his work was an insistence that the individual had to acknowledge responsibility for his actions and that the past could make legitimate demands on the present. But that present seemed to leave remarkably little space for the social conscience to operate. For Williams the past was more problematic, involving, as it did, racial guilt and corruption. His response to the crude coercions of the social world was to see them as evidence of other determinisms and seek to transmute them into tragedy.

To Erich Fromm, writing in the 1950s, modern capitalist society was an assault equally on the integrity of the individual and the social contract which sustains that individual in his relations with others. It had eroded a sense of the self and hence the notion of society as a group of autonomous selves subscribing to shared values: 'That is the way he experiences himself, not as a man, with love, fear, convictions, doubts, but as that abstraction, alienated from his real nature, which fulfils a certain function in the social system. His sense of value depends upon his success: on whether he can sell himself favourably.... If the individual fails in a profitable investment of himself, he feels that *he* is a failure; if he succeeds, *he* is a success. No wonder he regarded Miller's *Death of a Salesman* as an exemplary text. For Willy Loman's problem is precisely that he has internalised these values. Much the same is true of the figures in the early plays of Edward Albee——the third of the triumvirate who dominated the post-war American theatre. And Tennessee Williams's characters are so often destroyed because they offer love in a world characterised by impotence and sterility. And both Miller and Albee would also have agreed with Fromm's contention that 'man can fulfil himself only if he remains in touch with the fundamental facts of his existence, if he can experience the exaltation of love and solidarity, as well as the tragic facts of his aloneness and of the fragmentary character of his existence'—as they would with his conviction that drama is itself a primary attempt to 'get in touch with the essence of reality by artistic creation'.

But if alienation erodes a sense of the real and breeds a mode of conformity as an apparent solution to the problems of isolation, it also creates a sense of guilt, nebulous, unrelated, as Fromm again has pointed out, to any sense of a religious sanction but prompted by a sense of inadequacy, an acknowledgement of that very failure of community and organic relationship which is itself the essence of alienation. And it would be hard to think of a writer who has made this theme more central to his work than Arthur Miller, though the notion of a private betrayal to be expiated by art is also clearly visible in Williams's *The Glass Menagerie*. Albee, on the other hand, is less interested in guilt than responsibility (though Miller has claimed much the same about his own work). In the early part of his career be seemed concerned with identifying the means whereby the individual can terminate his self-imposed exclusion and resist the process which otherwise erodes will, identity and imagination, and thereby destroys the basis for moral action. But both Miller and Albee unite in their assumption that alienation is a product of decisions taken, action deferred, myths endorsed, a freedom denied, rather than a simple consequence of capitalism.

While Williams retained his central theme of the romantic in an unromantic world, a theme derived in part from D. H. Lawrence whom he greatly admired, he largely turned away from a direct concern with social structures, seeing them simply as images of the facticity which threatened the necessary fictions of his characters. Increasingly he described those desperate attempts to hold the world at bay with alcohol, illusion, and fragile sexuality which, as he indicates in his *Memoirs,* came to characterise his own life. Miller, on the other hand, after writing two plays which seemed to admit of no wholly satisfactory response to public and private betrayals—*All My Sons* and *Death of a Salesman*—was stung into a defence of liberal values by the political persecutions of the 1950s. Both *The Crucible* and *A View from the Bridge* were responses to what Miller saw as the collapse of individual integrity and life under the assaults of the social system; they were assertions of the need to play socially responsible roles. Willy Loman never knew who he was or what the connection between himself and his society could be. John Proctor, in *The Crucible,* takes on total responsibility for himself and for his world. But more profound questions lie behind the immediate issues of political coercion and moral instability.

At the heart of Miller's work, partly concealed and only inadequately expressed in the early plays but fully articulated in the later ones, is a concern with guilt, a guilt directly related to his experience as a Jew who had survived the Holocaust, and as an individual who had discovered his own potential for betrayal. The apparent clarity of the clash between the free individual and a politically malevolent system had merely served to conceal the subtlety of a problem which had become increasingly central to his work, and which he perceived as having metaphysical rather than social origins. Now he tended to see the pieties of his 1930s plays as a form of sentimentality.

Tennessee Williams is hardly immune to charges of sentimentality. But in his best work the note of self-pity, which is never entirely absent, is contained by a rigorous honesty about the desperate self-deceptions practised by his characters and the fundamental evasions which may be implied by art. His broken figures appeal, partly because they are victims of history—the lies of the old South no longer being able to sustain the individual in a world whose pragmatics have no place for the fragile spirit—and partly because they hint at a spiritual yearning which Williams sees as being extinguished by the processes of life no less than by those of society. In other words, the social and the metaphysical meet in Williams's work as they do in Miller's. His protagonists in the major plays are close kin to those other 1950s romantics, the Beats, restlessly moving on, afraid of stasis and extolling a love which is curiously androgynous. His plays are highly charged. They deal in violence, in sexual tensions, in violations of the body and spirit. His South is another country, elemental, crudely Manichean, suggestive, in a sense, of a kind of Freudian war between body and mind. On occasion he was capable of a genuine poetry, and if he was equally capable of a reduction of experience to simplistic symbol he could also, in a play like *The Glass Menagerie,* demonstrate a fine control of language and image, a precisely sustained tension between the poetic sensibility and a prosaic setting which still makes that deceptively simple play one of the best works to have come out of the American theatre.

Though he, too, often failed to maintain the tension in his work, and was capable of permitting a destructive slide into sentimentality—the simplistic ironies of *The Rose Tattoo* doing nothing to prevent this—Williams at his best was from the beginning a genuinely original voice in a way that Miller, so heavily dominated by Ibsen, seemed at first not to be. Yet both remained desperately committed to the idea of an identifiable and functioning moral self, and as a consequence their doubts about individual and social coherences tended to be deflected into style. For Beckett the public and private are mutually interpenetrated with absurdity; for Miller and Williams the erosion of private space and the consequent social collapse are born out of a failure of courage and imagination on a private and public level. Needing to believe in the integrity of a resistant self they shift the threat of collapse onto the form of the play (*Death of a Salesman* and *Camino Real*) or onto a dramatic symbol which must stand for that collapse (the unicorn in *The Glass Menagerie,* the dried-up fountain in *Camino Real,* the concentration camp in *After the Fall*). But both men at times recognised the ambiguous nature of their own craft, late in their career acknowledging the potentially hermetic and deceptive nature of art—Miller with *The Archbishop's Ceiling* and Williams with *Out Cry.*

The American theatre is eclectic. It lacks stylistic consistency. And in a way its energy derives precisely from its refusal to accept conventional restraints. O'Neill writes, on occasion, interminable and, indeed, unstageable works in a wide variety of styles; Williams, in *Camino Real,* invades the audience and deliberately projects experience to extremes, exposing the generative power of sexuality and elaborating images to the point at which they assume a threatening literalness (as in *Suddenly Last Summer*). Miller opens up the mind, allowing a neurotically deluded self to recreate the past, to flow with a freedom which potentially denies stylistic unity as it does temporal logic. To Williams, indeed, there was a special virtue in the theatre's capacity to sustain conflicting pressures, to dissolve the literal in search of animating principles. And he saw the stylistic tension of many of his plays as expressive of the moral and even spiritual tension which is their subject. As he said in the note to *The Glass Menagerie:*

> The straight realistic play with its genuine frigidaire and authentic ice cubes, its characters that speak exactly as its audience speaks, corresponds to the academic landscape and has the same virtue of a photographic likeness. Everyone should know nowadays the unimportance of the photographic in art; that truth, life, or reality, is an organic thing which the poetic imagination can represent or suggest in essence only through transformation, through changing into other forms than those which merely present appearances.

'These remarks', he added,

> are not meant as a preface only to this particular play. They have to do with a conception of a new plastic theatre which must take the place of the exhausted theatre of realistic conventions if the theatre is to resume vitality as a part of our culture.

Clearly in making such a statement he was ignoring a number of developments in the American and European theatre over the previous thirty years. But his main point of reference was the Broadway play which clung to realism for reasons only partly to do with a consistent social and aesthetic position. Both Miller and Williams regarded themselves as experimenters. It is true that their fundamental impulse was mimetic; the 'continuous present' of *Death of a Salesman* being designed to present a mind in a state of collapse, and the expressionistic devices of *Camino Real* the distorting power of a prosaic world. But they were concerned to develop a theatrical style which reflected their desire to dissolve a confident realism and to trace the social and psychological origins of cultural anxiety. And his notion of a plastic theatre was not without its value, for the American theatre, at its best, has proved remarkably malleable. In particular, it has charged the apparently naturalistic setting with a metaphysical rather than simply a social significance. Writers like Wilder, O'Neill, Eliot, Miller and Albee have not merely stretched the surface fabric until opacity becomes translucence, revealing thereby a social and psychological mechanism; they have attempted to forge powerful dramatic metaphors out of a setting which stands both as a threat to fragile identity and the defining boundary of the world in which their characters must move. O'Neill's strictures against a naturalism which simply held the family Kodak up to ill nature reflected his desire to penetrate behind the private and public masks, but it was equally an assertion about the nature of reality and the role of art. The world which their characters inhabit is not simply given; it is also in large part invented by them, as memory redesigns their lives and the imagination resists the pressures of the real. From the very beginning, then, their work has in part been reflexive; it has been concerned with the tension between the apparently substantial nature of historical, economic and social realities, and the individual's necessity to transform those supposed realities.

At times O'Neill, Miller, Williams and even Albee all seem to have believed that this process of transformation was a literal one, involving political action, reform, the restoration of a natural and manifest justice. They have all written plays which either directly or indirectly insist on the need to change the world in such a way as to accommodate the needs of the individual or the mass. But by degrees they shifted their ground and saw this process as a continuing effort by the imagination to resist the apparently implacable. Thus their work becomes reflexive to the degree that their subject becomes the process of imaginative reshaping which is in essence the one in which they are themselves engaged. The inhabitants of Harry Hope's bar (in *The Iceman Cometh*), Blanche Dubois (in *A Streetcar Named Desire*), Willy Loman (in *Death of a Salesman*), George and Martha (in *Who's Afraid of Virginia Woolf?*) are all engaged in recreating the world. They all confront, consciously or unconsciously, the paradox that while this process is possibly a necessary act of rebellion, a resistance which is perhaps not without its heroism, it is also potentially destructive. The cost of indulging the imagination may be the loss of a grasp on the moral world. The act of rebellion may also be an act of betrayal and desertion. The need to project a world in which the self plays a central role, and there is a natural consonance between that self and its setting, may ultimately be the source of irony. For Beckett it was wholly so. For the American playwright the issue was never that clear. Beckett simply accepted the paradox which made his own work further evidence of a reductive irony. The coherences of his own plays were inevitably self-mocking. For O'Neill, as for Miller and Williams, and, to some degree,

Albee, the tension is sustained. For the most part the self-doubt of the writer is implicit, though real enough. But in the later works it tends to surface more directly. It is there to some degree in *Long Day's Journey into Night*; it is there very clearly in Tennessee Williams's *Out Cry* and in Edward Albee's *Box*. And it is there in Miller's confessional *After the Fall* and *The Archbishop's Ceiling*. These are all writers who have chosen to foreground style because they are all writers whose plays concern characters who display the writer's defence against the world. Their work is in some fundamental sense about the ambiguous battle of the imagination to sustain the self. It was not for nothing that Williams's favourite Chekhov play was *The Seagull*. But it was Albee, whose first works were staged just at the moment when Miller's and Williams's careers seemed to be faltering, who made this concern with the nature of the real most central to his work.

Albee's real achievement has always lain in his control of, and sensitivity to, language, particularly at a time when Off-Broadway was in flight from the spoken word, seeing it as a tool of power and a rational restraint on the intuitive and the spontaneous. The moral fervour of the early plays and the simple distinction between illusion and the real gave way first to a complex, if not always dramatically satisfying, debate about the nature of reality, and subsequently to intelligent if at times arcane experiments with form and language. His plays no longer tend to be confidently located in time and space; the world he presents is theatrically, socially, and morally reified, as voices, detached from personal and public histories, test emotional propositions, conduct experiments in dissonance and harmony, and reveal something of the mechanisms of control which Albee seems to imply are the real source of the ethical questions with which he had begun his career. Despite his Broadway productions Albee has remained committed to experiment, to the values and objectives of the Off-Broadway theatre from which he sprang. The very nature of these experiments implies a refusal to accept the crown as successor to Miller and Williams so eagerly thrust upon him in the early 1960s, and now as precipitately withdrawn by those anxious for the emergence of a writer who can satisfactorily bridge the gulf between Broadway and Off-Broadway. But he remains one of the most intelligent and fascinating of America's playwrights.

When he first appeared, he was seen as and, indeed, was a liberal voice recalling the individual to his moral and even spiritual responsibility. Fundamentally that remains his stance but his confidence has slowly been eroded, his sense of human potential qualified by the evidence of further decline. The verbal oratorios of the early plays, the splendid articulateness, has given way to fragmented speeches, brief snatches of language located in lengthening silences, dialogue which is little more than a series of statements, the ironies and oblique references of which mirror his sense of a loss which he sees as the central fact of modern existence. His, like Beckett's, has become an entropic art, a reflection and ironic presentation of the world which he observes and which, in *The Zoo Story* and *Who's Afraid of Virginia Woolf?*, he still believed could be saved with compassion, a liberal respect for reality, and a language which, if wilfully deceptive, could still offer hints for the restoration of harmony. That presumption has gradually been displaced by a more reified vision. And character too has collapsed. In *Tiny Alice* the characters have already become baroque creations, figures moved around with an eye to the arabesques of language and symbolic function rather than moral enquiry. Albee is here more interested in defining the contours of the real than with identifying the moral content of an assured if threatened social structure. But the allegorical dimension of that play did imply the persistence of a sense of structure, an underlying confidence in the pattern-forming power of art, though reality has already begun to dislocate, to shatter into a disturbing flux of shifting roles and competing fictions.

Even that surviving confidence has since been leached away. *Quotations from Chairman Mao Tse-Tung, Listening* and *Counting the Ways* show evidence of his interest in words detached from their social function, in the movement of minds no longer confidently located in time and space. *Quotations from Chairman Mao Tse-Tung* mixes time-scales as it blends the apparently fictive with the ostensibly real until the two become simply alternative fictions—systems of words and images which offer an explanation for a sense of apocalypse. Indeed the reality which he had urged on his characters with such assurance in the early plays has now splintered until the Chinese box, the interweaving of different levels and kinds of experience, the simple fact of the simultaneity and experiential equivalence of events, becomes the only model which he can sustain. And so the dramatist becomes a sculptor of language, a collagist, a creator of images, a choreographer, a composer for whom character and words are found objects and the process of interaction as interesting and authentic as the ostensible but probably delusory object of that interaction. Mao exists on the same plane and at the same time as avowedly fictional characters. There is apparently no more than a simple correspondence between these experiences which are not linked by causal process but merely coexist. Albee's use of Mao is in fact a gesture of refusal. And by that I don't mean a rejection of Mao's message but a refusal to be coerced by public fictions. Albee struggles to fictionalise the public world as it attempts to fictionalise him, reducing him to number, function and role. Much the same, of course, could be said of *Slaughterhouse 5, V, Gravity's Rainbow* and *The Painted Bird* which equally imply an exact equivalence between various fictions, including the fiction which is the novel, and the society in which it exists.

But who, after all, is a greater manipulator of others, a greater plotter, than the novelist or the dramatist? Implicit in Albee's later work, as in the work of Coover, Pynchon and others, is a suspicion of art. In a sense, of course, that is a central quality of literature, certainly of American literature. What, after all, are *The Narrative of Arthur Gordon Pym, Moby Dick, The Confidence Man, Tender is the Night, The Day of the Locust,* if not confessions of the cruelly deceptive coherences implied in the act of writing? It is a dilemma which can perhaps only be adequately expressed by silence (sometimes even suicide), by the deployment of a self-destructing language whose assurances will crumble even as the book or play proceeds, or, as with Albee in *Quotations,* by the surrender of some small element of his control as author—letting the arbitrary seep into his work through spaces deliberately left open.

So, if all of Albee's characters are struggling to retain possession of a world, to imprint their own meaning on it, they are in a sense mimicking the activity of the artist as he mimics that of life. The precision with which they and he use words—they frequently correct one another's usage, try for precisely the right nuance—parody of the writer's conviction that language is indeed a net which can successfully trap experience and hence reality (though at times, it remains 'an unconscious attempt to make people aware that they must listen more carefully').

In *Counting the Ways* and *Listening,* rather as in Pinter's and Beckett's most recent work, the word 'reality' has lost all meaning. We are left with a present which is no more than the recalling of a past which may never have happened. Even the substance of the physical surroundings has shrunk to a space which offers no clue as to meaning or time. There is a chilling moral detachment in *Listening* and, to a lesser extent, in *Counting the Ways* which is reminiscent of Kosinski's *Steps* and *The Painted Bird.* For Jerzy Kosinski the natural analogue for human experience is the scientific experiment. His protagonists are often literally plotters writing scenarios for other people's lives. Albee, too, is interested in the process whereby people seek to gain control over experience, their own and that of others, through their fiction-making skills.

This is in effect a drama of exhaustion—not in the sense that John

Barth uses a similar phrase of a particular form of literature but to the degree that this is a theatre concerned with the entropic nature of the human machine, the defeat of the conscience, the loss of control over experience, the collapse of language and that sense of structure which it implies. Just as Pynchon's characters pursue their parodic quest for meaning through trying to track down the lexically defined but finally intangible V, or Joseph Heller's protagonist in *Something Happened* tries to sieve experience through the finer filter of his emotional responses in order to understand his situation, so Albee's characters, in his most recent plays, try to perceive their doubtful past through a language which has itself become attenuated. But, for all this, Albee will not surrender his fundamental conviction that change is possible, that some kind of intervention may be made in the logic which he identifies. Like Arthur Miller he will not relinquish his grasp on the moral world and perhaps in some respects that is a characteristic of their work and in some degree of the American dramatist. Some final redemptive possibility remains.

It would be less than generous to see Miller and Williams as facilitating the processes against which they were ostensibly in revolt but there is something of that. They both write about failed adjustments. They both run the risk of sentimentalising the misfit. The individual who cannot adjust to the new materialism is celebrated and deplored simultaneously. He or she is associated with a simpler, and, indeed, as both writers admit, even a simplistic model of society. Theirs is thus a tainted lyricism. Indeed such characters are often seen as verging on the psychotic. The fault lies not only with the system which destroys them but also with the individual who clings to myths and dreams discarded by history. Thus what is wrong with society, in Miller's view, is not that capitalism has betrayed some organic relationship between people or between the individual and his setting, but that capitalism has betrayed its own principles. So Joe Keller is attacked in *All My Sons* not as an industrialist but as a bad industrialist.

Similarly, Willy Loman comes up against a brash young employer who casually discards him, but is anyway presented as a man who has betrayed his own father's capitalist principles. And, as his career advanced, Miller was prone to locate social evil in a deeply flawed human nature rather than in any system of social organisation. Accommodation to that fact becomes a moral virtue, albeit an accommodation which implies a continuous resistance to what must now be acknowledged as inevitable. Much the same is true of Williams and Albee. It is not always apparent how that can transfigure the world which menaces their characters.

In the case of Williams we are asked to celebrate the individual in a state of neurotic recoil, the person who refuses to resist the forces to which he seems to grant an implacable power. And yet the fragility of such figures, maimed, broken, destroyed in spirit and in body, ensures that our sympathy is never likely to go beyond a certain wistful regret. They are presented as ahistorical, resisting the flow of time and experience. They represent what seems a childlike response to pain, anguish and reality. Thus while we are asked to sympathise with them, to recognise the loss involved in their defeat, there is an inevitability about that defeat in which we are asked to acquiesce. A brutal or simply careless capitalism provides the context for their lives; it shapes their environment and defines and severely limits their freedom. But since that seems no more than a name for the modern there is a perverse sense in which the audience is invited to collaborate, if not in the conscious cruelty, then at least in the regrettable need to lay aside dreams and to compromise on visions which are tainted by their seemingly adolescent origins or by the risk of insanity if they are persisted in the face of a prosaic reality. There is a sense in which the man who began as a highly political playwright quickly became not merely apolitical but even anti-political as his characters were invited to retreat into personal relationships or to flee from causalities altogether. His puritan conscience survives in the high price they pay for their non-involvement but, perhaps because, professionally, he was committed to a world of fiction, he found it difficult to condemn them. Certainly his imagination for the most part found itself unequal to the task of locating them in that ongoing world of social and political exchanges to which he thereby seemed to grant some ultimate authority. In a not unfamiliar gesture he opposes the modern only by celebrating what it destroys but in doing so historicises those victims and conceals the power and logic of the forces that would crush them. He seems less concerned with pleading for a humanising of the present, for the survival of qualities and values of fundamental importance, than with regretting the passing of an age in which they had been a natural expression of human life. But to be sure, on some fundamental level, he, too, suspects that if one were willing to press the action back into the past that conflict between the material and the spiritual would always have been relevant. For the force of history is associated with a physical and material drive; the transcendent vision which justifies that history with a spiritual impulse. The war between them seems unavoidable both within the individual sensibility and, externalised, in the public world beyond. And that inevitability implies a certain level of acquiescence in the process which he seems to deplore. His protagonist-victims are not, finally, destroyed by capitalism, political corruption or a new brutalism, but by life's own internal tensions—that sacrifice of the spiritual to the material which is the motor force of history and, to Williams, as, I suspect, to Miller, the root of the tragic.

And, despite his invocations to change, Albee, too, can be accused of precisely that accommodation against which he rails so consistently. George and Martha, in *Who's Afraid of Virginia Woolf?*, in effect learn the necessity to adjust to the real. And though George speaks of the need to defend freedom and oppose what he sees as a drift towards a conformist culture this remains at the level of rhetoric. Here, as elsewhere in his work, the only available model for the society which he proposes lies in the

American past. He repeatedly invokes American revolutionary principles and the virtues of a lost individualism. But since access to those principles seems to have been closed off by time he substitutes a faith in human relationship and a restored sense of community which his characters advocate but do not live by. He deplores the drift towards totalitarianism and the nullity of consensus and yet, like Miller, the reality to which he urges his characters is one of a human imperfection which explains both personal and national failure. His analysis of social collapse is so generalised, however, as to make it difficult to see precisely how the renewed commitment to which he urges his characters can operate. His rhetoric implies the possibility of change; the logic of his plays suggests a certain inevitability. And if resistance is presented as a necessary stance then the terms of that resistance have to be negotiated with a singularly unyielding reality.

Certainly if these writers are concerned with revolt the scope for radical change seems slight. But slight or not it plainly remains crucial to all three, and resistance a central theme. Their characters may be required to accommodate to the realities of time and to the diminishing space available for moral action but they ultimately refuse to capitulate to social process or the simple pragmatics of a material life. Apocalypse has become an ever more present possibility and this has exerted a pressure on character and language by no means so apparent earlier in their careers. The structures of art are themselves now thoroughly infiltrated by irony. A confident collusion between artist and audience has shown acute signs of collapse. And yet the notion of an alliance between that artist and his audience continues to be offered as a model of a social contract with some ultimate power to neutralise a destructive privatism and an equally corrosive moral conformity. When consensus disintegrated, as it did in the mid 1960s, the moral focus diffused. An anxious liberalism no longer claimed attention any more than did an apologetic bohemianism. For a brief moment the radical and the romantic anarchist seemed to have obtained some purchase on the system. Indeed the outcast, the artist and the poet now felt entirely capable of challenging the public world and deflecting the course of national policy. But neither Miller nor Williams seemed to address this new concern with political action, cultural identity or sensual liberation. The sexuality of Williams's plays had seemed subversive only so long as society had been excessively puritanical. When sexual liberation became normative it was Williams who seemed the puritan. Albee's Jerry in *The Zoo Story* was more clearly a figure of the age, deploying a necessary violence and preaching a renewed community. But Albee, too, came to seem outside the central concerns of the decade as he sought his models in T. S. Eliot and generated a drama which seemed increasingly hermetic. And when the pendulum swung, in the 1970s, although their own work did reflect a growing self-consciousness and, in the case of Miller and Williams, a pull towards autobiography equally evident elsewhere in theatre, they did so with work which no longer had the kind of assurance which had once made them primary interpreters of national hopes and fears.

Nonetheless Williams, Miller and Albee all succeeded in bringing to Broadway a moral seriousness and an aesthetic sensitivity which has hardly marked that theatre over the years and which certainly can't be said to do so today when it is dominated by comedies, musicals and foreign imports. Certainly no other writers have commanded the popular and critical following which all three have achieved. There can, indeed, be little doubt that with the single exception of Eugene O'Neill theirs is the outstanding achievement of the American theatre. These were playwrights who addressed the anxieties of their age. All three have been concerned with the state of their society and with examining the fate of fundamental American myths having to do with liberal individualism, a sense of community and a utopian vision. For all three America had lost a crucial innocence. In a sense they have said of the country what Stella says of her sister, Blanche: 'You should have known her when she was a girl.' What they chiefly seem to regret is the decay of a metaphor—the metaphor which once linked history with the notion of growth and located the individual in a natural cycle which pulled him or her into harmony with the world he or she inhabited and with those who shared that fate. Like O'Neill before them they have registered some fundamental disturbance, a breaking of the natural rhythm. Their characters no longer belong, and that sense of loss, addressed through different languages and distilled into different symbols, is their theme as it has been the theme of America's major dramatists from O'Neill through to Odets and Wilder. They lament the decline of the moral self and the slow fading of a vision but in doing so they implicitly make a case for the possibility of change and indeed see in the theatre itself a principal agent of transformation and a paradigm of the social, moral and spiritual community whose decline they regret.

An Excerpt from C. W. E. Bigsby's *A Critical Introduction to Twentieth-Century American Drama*. Cambridge, England: Cambridge University Press, 1984.

C. W. E. Bigsby

Modern American Drama

CHAPTER ONE

The Absent Voice: American Drama and the Critic

In recent years attempts have been made to fill some of the more obvious absences in the literary canon. The battle for the future, as ever, begins with the past. First blacks and then women chose to define present reality in terms of a redefined tradition. The project was an implicit critique of a critical practice that had filtered out experiences not felt to be normative, that had denied a voice to those marginalised by the social or economic system—hence the significance of the title of Tillie Olsen's book *Silences* and the potency of Richard Wright's image of laboratory dogs, their vocal chords cut, silently baying to the moon, in *American Hunger*. Language is power, the shaping of language into art is power, and the codification of that literature in the form of literary history is also a source of power.

It is, however, not merely the literary expression of the experiences of particular sections of American society that have fallen below the threshold of critical attention. There is also another surprising absence, another silence, another example of critical reticence. Whatever happened to American drama? Why is it that literary critics, cultural historians, literary theorists, those interested in the evolution of genre, in discourse and ideology, find so little to say about the theatre in general and the American theatre in particular? Can it really be that an entire genre has evaded the critic who was once drawn to the poem and then the novel and who, more recently, has chosen to concentrate on literary theory? There are, of course, honourable exceptions, but on the whole the silence has been remarkable.

Any account of American drama must begin by noting the casual disregard with which it has been treated by the critical establishment. There is no single history of its development, no truly comprehensive analysis of its achievement. In the standard histories of American literature it is accorded at best a marginal position. Why should this be? Is it perhaps the nature of drama which takes it outside the parameters of critical discourse, unless, like Shakespeare, its canonical status as scholarly text has been established by time? After all, is drama, and the theatre in which it takes place, not inherently ideological? Does the transformation of the word on the page into the mobility of performance not raise questions about discourse and text? Is the stage, the most public of the arts, not a place to see dramatised the tensions and concerns of a society? Is a concern with the reception of a work, with the way in which it is 'read', not of special significance to an art in which that reception may profoundly modify the work in question? May questions of authorship not have special bearing on an art which might be thought to be collaborative? Is the very nature and status of criticism not challenged by work which to a large degree incorporates a critical reading in the very processes of its transmission? These might be thought to be rhetorical questions, but the history of literary criticism and cultural studies suggests otherwise.

It was Umberto Eco who reminded us that though the intervention of the actor complicates the act of reception, the process remains the same in that every 'reading', 'contemplation' or 'enjoyment' of a work of art represents a tacit form of 'performance': and every performance a reading.

That reader may, of course, be in the theatre. He or she may be on their own, confronted with the printed word. It could even be argued that the latter may, in a perverse way, be in a more privileged if exposed position in that the individual imagination is not coerced by the interpretative strategy of director and actor. As David Mamet has said, 'the best production takes place in the mind of the beholder'. But of course the theatre's attraction lies in its power to transcend the written word. That is the key. It is physical, three-dimensional, immediate, and perhaps that very fact has itself intimidated the critic. It should instead have challenged him. Too often, we are offered reductive versions, even by those who acknowledge drama as an aspect of literature. Thus, in his diatribe against the American playwright, Robert Brustein, as a young critic, had denounced Eugene O'Neill as a 'charter member of a cult of inarticulacy' who perversely suggested that the meaning of one of his plays might lie in its silences, and Tennessee Williams for emphasising 'the incontinent blaze of live theatre, a theatre meant for seeing and feeling', a plastic theatre which did not reward the literary critic. This view, expressed in *Harper's* magazine in 1959, has been echoed sufficiently widely since then to merit consideration.

Roland Barthes describes the author as a man who radically absorbs the world's *why* in a *how to write*, by enclosing himself in the *how to write,* the author ultimately discovers the open question, par excellence! Why the world? What is the ultimate meaning of things? In short, it is precisely when the author's work becomes its own end that it regains a mediating character: the author conceives of literature as an end, the world restores it to him as a means: and it is in this perpetual inclusiveness that the author rediscovers the world, an alien world, since literature represents it as a question—never finally as an answer.

But who more than Eugene O'Neill was engaged in this restless search? No other playwright has committed himself so completely to the 'how' of literature, restlessly testing every style, strategy, concept of character, linguistic mode, theatrical device. And the 'how' does indeed lead him towards the 'why'.

The process of O'Neill's *The Emperor Jones* is one in which style is substance, in which the theatricalised self is left disabled by its own imaginative projections. It is like the film of a life run backwards, from sophistication and power to innocence and total vulnerability; the portrait of a social world unmaking itself, of a language dislocated and in retreat from coherence, of a civilisation reverting to origins, of an individual stripping off the accretions of logic and civility, of a society tracing its roots back to myth.

In so far as language is power, the absence of language is an index of relative powerlessness. So it is that Brutus Jones's language slips away with his loss of social control as the lowly night porter, in O'Neill's *Hughie,* barely contributes a coherent sentence. On the other hand a steady flow of language does not of itself imply a confident control of experience. Indeed in this latter case the hotel guest's articulate accounts of personal triumph merely serve to underline the social silence which is his life. What is spoken betrays the centrality of what is not. The truth of his life is what can never make its way into language. He keeps alive by the stories he tells. He is a down-market Scheherazade. The dramas he invents are his defence against the world and his own insignificance. They are also all that stands between him and despair.

The theatre is unique in its silences. In the literary text such spaces close. Even the blank page of a Laurence Sterne can be turned in a second. In the theatre silence is not merely kinetic potential. It may teem with meaning. We are used to the notation 'silence' in a Beckett or Pinter play, but Susan Glaspell and Eugene O'Neill were fully alive to the possibilities of reticence forty years earlier. In *The Outside* Susan Glaspell created a character stunned into silence by experience; but the aphasia of Anna

Christie and the inarticulateness of Yank in O'Neill's *The Hairy Ape* equally compacted meaning into those moments when language is inadequate to feeling.

If the word, spoken or withheld, is a central and potent fact of theatre, so, too, is space and the occupation of that space by the body. Nor is it simply a matter of proxemics, of the meaning generated by gesture or appearance; it is that the word is made flesh. The theatre is by its nature sensuous. Even didactic drama alchemises its arguments through the mind made body. The severity of words on the page is corrupted by the mouth which articulates them. The minimalism of the printed word gives way to plenitude. That seduction, implicit in the text, becomes explicit in production. It cannot be extirpated. The Puritans were right to close the theatres. However irreproachable the sentiments, their theatricalising required a waywardness the elect were bound to suspect. For Tennessee Williams, for example, that sensuousness was crucial, since theatre is not merely the condition of his art but also his subject.

Thus *A Streetcar Named Desire* is pre-eminently aware of its own constitutive conventions; that is to say it is concerned, in the Russian formalist Viktor Schlovsky's terms, with the generation of plot from story. It foregrounds the processes of theatre, the elaboration of a structure of meaning out of mere events. It defamiliarises the real by dramatising the extent to which, and the manner in which, that reality is constituted. Blanche is self-consciously her own playwright, costume designer, lighting engineer, scenic designer and performer. You could say of her world what Roland Barthes says of the actor: it is artificial but not factitious. The dramas which she enacts—southern belle, sensitive virgin, sensuous temptress, martyred daughter, wronged wife—are all carefully presented performances embedded in their own narrative contexts. In Fredric Jameson's terms, it is a play that speaks of its own coming into being, of its own construction. If, to Jameson, all literary works emit a kind of lateral message about their own process of formation, in *Streetcar* it seems more central and more deliberate. And not here alone. Laura, in *The Glass Menagerie,* enters the theatre of her glass animals, making mobile in her imagination what is immobile in a world of mere facticity, just as Tennessee Williams himself enters his own drama, charging the words on the page with a kind of static potential which gives them the energy to be discharged in performance. There is, indeed, a real sense in which Williams is a product of his work. When he began to write he was plain Tom, poor Tom. The invention of Tennessee was not merely coterminous with the elaboration of theatrical fictions; it was of a piece with it. In that sense it is not entirely fanciful to suggest that he was the product of the discourse of his plays. Indeed he created female alter egos, such as Blanche in *Streetcar* and Alma in *Summer and Smoke,* before he began, as he did in later life, to dress up as a woman. Later he even turned performer, stepping into one of his own plays as actor in a work called *Small Craft Warning* where the part he played, that of a failed doctor who had lost his licence to practice, was in effect itself an expression of his sense of his own disintegrating powers. Where did the work end and the life begin? The man who consigns Blanche to insanity later found himself in a straitjacket. Later still he wrote a play set in an empty theatre in which two characters fill the emptiness of their lives by speaking lines from a play generated out of those lives, a metadrama of fascinating intellectual and ontological complexity. And if by that stage of his career there was a terrible appositeness in a play in which characters address an empty auditorium, is there not another significance to it, for though America's playwrights have found huge and appreciative audiences around the world and though their plays are reviewed and widely published and read, the academic critic, the cultural historian, the literary theorist for the most part has turned his or her head away.

Tennessee Williams saw himself as a poet. Why, then, turn to the stage? I think because the body had a significance to him beyond the homosexual reveries which recur in his *Memoirs*. It—the body—was everything the world was not. It was warm; it was animate; it was three-dimensional. It inscribed its own meaning; it generated its own discourse, independent of and at a tangent to a verbal language which threatens to pull the self into history. It was its own act of resistance in a world in which the mechanical dominated. And how could that body's violations, its temporary alliances, its vulnerabilities, its resistances be better communicated than on the stage? So much of the tension of his work (as of O'Neill's) comes from placing the body in a situation essentially oppressive to and at odds with its needs. The immobility towards which he presses his characters, the catatonia which awaits them, derives its impact precisely from their earlier manifest motility—a motility most easily invested with immediacy and meaning in the theatre. Then again the protean gesture of pluralising the self and, indeed, meaning itself—not as in a novel where a narrator controls and contains the multiple self—offers a protection against being too completely known and hence vulnerable. For a man for whom the concealment of his true sexual identity was for long a literal necessity the fragmentation of the self into multiple roles offered a possible refuge.

A novel is more fixed, more stolid, more resistant to subversion by its own form (though of course we have the evidence of *Tristram Shandy* that such subversion is perfectly possible). Since Williams is the poet of the unauthorised, the unsanctioned, the outlawed, it seems logical that he should choose a form which more easily releases its pluralism of meanings under the pressure of actors, director, audience than does the poem or the novel. It is not that novels have restrictive meanings but that the incompletions of the theatrical text are readily apparent, indeed implicit in the form. If Roland Barthes is right in saying 'Who *speaks* is not who *writes,* and who *writes* is not who *is'*, it is equally true to say of the theatrical text that what is *written* is not what is *spoken,* and what is *spoken* is not what *is.* In the theatre language is deliberately played against gesture, *mise en scone,* appearance; the mouth which shapes the word also subverts the word, as facial expression, tone, inflection, volume offer a counter-current. It is uttered in a social context, the silent receiver of language on the stage communicating with no less force than its transmitter. Meaning is communicated proxemically, annihilated by its own expressive gestures. In the novel, speech is sequential, part of a serial logic in which one word replaces or supersedes another; actions which may be simultaneous have to be recreated in a way which denies their simultaneity and simultaneity is a crucial virtue of the theatre. Theatre is the only genre which habitually operates in the present tense and which makes that presentness an acknowledged part of its own methodology. It is the only genre which unavoidably foregrounds its processes. The lighting scaffold, the conscious frame of the proscenium arch—abandoned in the sixties and resurrected in the eighties—the co-presence of other members of the audience underlines one's own status as 'reader' of the text of the performance. The curtain separating the performance on stage from that off, the ticket you hold in your hand (the sign of your entry into otherness and itself a text inscribed with meaning), the whole paraphernalia involved in visiting the theatre, is part of the process of defamiliarising, which is what theatre is about. The novel can be put down, picked up, interleaved with other experiences; the theatre makes its demands. The price of entry in terms of energy and commitment and sometimes financial cost is high. We go to the theatre as ourselves part of a ceremony knowing that our own involvement will be central to the meanings which proliferate.

Mikhail Bakhtin argues for the primacy of the novel on the grounds that its generic skeleton 'is still far from having hardened, and we cannot foresee all its plastic possibilities'. While the other genres are older than written literature, 'it has no canon of its own... it alone is ... receptive to...

reading'. This sounds to me a little like special pleading. In Tennessee Williams's *Camino Real* there is a gypsy girl whose virginity is restored by every full moon. It's a good trick if you can pull it off, but the theatre is a little like that. It is surely the most sensuous, the most alluring, the most unformed of the genres. Each production restores a kind of innocence only to take pleasure in violating it. When Bakhtin argues that in drama 'there is no all-encompassing language that addresses itself dialogically to separate languages, there is no second all-encompassing plotless (non-dramatic) dialogue outside of the (non-dramatic) plot', this, too, seems to me a virtue. In the theatre I am in fact more free from the author's discourse, which in the novel invites me to align my imagination with his. For Bakhtin, 'The fundamental condition, that which makes a novel a novel, that which is responsible for its stylistic uniqueness, is the *speaking person and his discourse...* [which] is an object *of verbal* artistic representation.' In contrast to drama it is represented by means of 'authorial discourse'. Since there is clearly such a thing as an implied author as well as an implied reader the distinction he draws is perhaps rather too sharp but in so far as he is correct to suggest an instability in drama, a plurality of possibilities, this is surely one of its strengths. Indeed in some ways it is the author's loss of control which constitutes something of the attraction of theatre. For the playwright, at any rate, it may offer a means of breaking with an aestheticism that has overtones of inauthenticity. And that leads us in the direction of ideology.

In 'Authors and Writers' Roland Barthes insists that for the author, *to write* is an intransitive verb; hence it can never explain the world, or at least, when it claims to explain the world, it does so only the better to conceal its ambiguity: once the explanation is fixed in a work, it immediately becomes an ambiguous product of the real, to which it is linked by perspective. Barthes distinguishes between the author and the writer, for the latter the verb 'to write' being transitive. Thus, the notion of a committed author is a contradiction in terms. As he says, it is absurd to ask an author for 'commitment': a 'committed' author claims simultaneous participation in two structures, inevitably a source of deception... whether or not an author is responsible for his opinions is unimportant; whether or not an author assumes, more or less intelligently, the ideological implications of his work is also secondary; the author's true responsibility is to support literature as a failed commitment, as a Mosaic glance into the Promised Land of the real.

But frequently, of course, those impulses are indeed contained in the same sensibility. There *is* an ambiguity about the committed author/ writer whose commitment is necessarily a double one—to the word and to the word's transparency. Commitment requires that the word should dissolve into its own social fulfilment, declare its own ultimate irrelevance, its second-order status, as the writer serves a cause whose demands go beyond his own imagining. But the author also wants to refashion language, ease it away from its history, separate it from the social world which exercises its restraints.

James Baldwin was all too aware of this ambivalence and seized on the theatre as a way of resolving the tension. Drama offered a way to loosen his grip on aestheticism. The balanced sentences, the carefully sculpted prose that had distinguished his essays, and which many blacks in America felt were distancing him from his own and their experience and aligning him with an alien literary tradition rather than a social cause, were broken open by the glossalalia, the profusion of voices which is the essence of theatre. He turned to the theatre precisely because he needed to deny himself a controlling voice, because he wished to subvert his own authority. It was almost as though the surrender of total responsibility implicit in theatre was in some way a guarantee that subject had primacy over style, that he was not allowing aesthetic issues to dominate experiences whose authenticity could only be diminished by the transformations of art. LeRoi Jones plainly felt much the same, his change of name coinciding with a retreat from metaphor into a literalism which intensified as black nationalism gave way to Marxist-Leninism and the dense and profoundly ambiguous images of *Dutchman* and *The Slave* led first to the crude melodrama of his black revolutionary plays and then to works such as SI and *The Motions of History*, in which social reality was allowed primacy. Ultimately, he followed his own logic and abandoned the stage for the factory gate and the dramatic text for the political leaflet. It was a logic followed, too, by a number of politically motivated theatre groups whose distrust of the ideology implicit in the fact of the theatre building took them onto the streets, and whose distrust of what Barthes called 'fine writing' led them to the communal creation of texts which were an assault on the authority of the writer and whose openness to audience participation was another antidote to a self-referring art.

As Baraka has his black protagonist confess in *Dutchman* there is a seductive quality in language. Words have a detachment from experience. They are not the thing itself. They stand in the place of action. They have a coherent structure which may be at odds with the unregulated passion which generates them. To that extent they are a betrayal, representing a kind of sanity when a holy madness is required. In the case of Clay, in *Dutchman,* the safety that he seeks in words is finally only securable in action. He dies because he cannot relinquish his grasp on the detachment that language brings—the detachment of the writer. It is a debate that Baraka continued in *The Slave* in which the intellectual leader of a black revolt remains enslaved to his own articulateness no less than his emotions. So the battle rages outside the window while he engages in debate with a white professor, husband to the white wife he had abandoned. Since Baraka, university educated, separated from his white wife and drawn to the literary world which showed every sign of responding to his talent, was himself caught in just such a dilemma, it is hard not to see the play as a debate in which he engages himself, a debate whose power derives, at least in part, from the honesty with which he confesses to and dramatises his own ambivalence. What the theatre offers is a social context for language, a language now energised as it becomes the action it invokes.

Literature requires and is an act of renunciation. The condition of its creation is withdrawal. Its nature implies abstinence. But the theatre offers a special grace. Drama may be privately conceived but it is publicly created. It is a re-entry into the world. The word becomes action, albeit action drained of true risk. It gives back to the writer what he has sacrificed in order to write. It restores in the public action of the play the power to act, to offer the body as a sign of authenticity. What is conceived in a denial of community ends with a restoration of community. A word silently inscribed sounds forth in confident expectation of communication. The act of distributing that language between characters and the actors who articulate them is itself a confident sign of shared experience and of the possibility of sharing language.

The actor who speaks another's words and endeavours to mould them to his own shape, to bend the language to his own reality and accommodate himself to the language (a compromise without which he would lack all conviction) mirrors our own relationship to the words that we speak, words we do not devise but which we struggle to make our own. His attempt to negotiate the terms on which necessity and freedom, the given and the created, can co-exist is a model of those other such negotiations in which we participate daily. For the black writer there is a special irony in deploying a language which was the instrument and sign of slavery. To distrust the words you speak, words which have a history, is to place yourself at odds with your own articulateness, and the theatre, which never carries the voice of the writer, only his or her characters, offers a release from that paradox which can then become subject rather than means.

Roland Barthes has suggested that 'literature is always unrealistic' since language 'can never explain the world, or at least, when it claims to explain the world, it does so only the better to conceal its ambiguity; once the explanation is fixed in a work, it immediately becomes an ambiguous product of the real, to which it is linked by perspective'. And there is, indeed, a revealing suspicion of language not merely on the part of the avant-gardist, disassembling his art in a radical gesture of defamiliarisation, but also on the part of the committed playwright for whom that language is a barrier between the urgencies of a tangible world and those he would make aware of those realities. More than that, the gap between act and word is a reproach, that between fact and word an irony; the disproportion between need and its expression is a constant reminder of the impossible project in which the writer chooses to engage. In becoming itself, a 'product of the real', the play simultaneously submits to the condition it would resist and becomes a rival for attention with the circumstance which inspired its creation but to which it is only analogically connected. Those who left Clifford Odets's *Waiting for Lefty* shouting out the need to 'Strike! Strike! Strike!' re-entered a world whose social structure and political arrangements lacked the ordered logic and casual resolutions of the play, a world in which character and action were more profoundly ambiguous, a world, indeed, in which theatre itself is regarded as marginal and as implicated in the values of the system it purports to challenge. At base it was its lack of realism that was its most noticeable characteristic and perhaps its redemption. The same logic would apply with equal force to the committed writing of the fifties, sixties, seventies and eighties. The most striking aspect of this theatre is its naivety, a willed innocence that conceives of character, language and action as elements in a dialectic, as compressed images of oppression or revolt. Amira Baraka's *Four Black Revolutionary Plays* offered a catechism of revolutionary faith which divided the world not so much into contending racial forces as into platonic models of rebel or collaborator. These were agit-prop gestures, a theatre of praxis designed to intervene in the political system at the level of personal epiphany, to be achieved through group experience. But it was always an uneasy theatre, acutely aware of the inadequacy of its own gestures, expressive and direct, preferable to an inert prose contained and constrained by the page, but still disproportionate to the fact.

There is a poem by the Czechoslovak poet Miroslav Holub which explains something of this desire to *show* in theatre rather than *tell* in the novel. The poem is called 'Brief Reflection on the Word Pain':

> Wittgenstein says the words 'It hurts' have replaced tears and
> cries of pain.
> The word 'Pain' does not describe the expression of pain but
> replaces it.
> Replaces and displaces it.
> Thus it creates a new behaviour pattern in the case of pain.
> The word comes between us and the pain like a pretence of
> silence.
> It is a silencing. It is a needle unpicking the stitch between
> blood and clay.

It is not that the theatre can wholly close this gap but that it can remind us of its existence by pitching word against dramatised experience. Perhaps that is one reason why the committed writer has been drawn to the theatre. It is out of a desire to replace that stitch which will reconnect blood and clay. Either way the aesthetic and literary implications of committed theatre, particularly in the American context, have barely even been registered let alone addressed with any sophistication or theoretical concern.

And what of those critics attracted by theory in recent years? After all, Derrida takes a brief look at the theatre of cruelty and Roland Barthes at Brecht and Bunraku theatre. On the whole, theatre has commanded very little interest from the major theorists or those who have taken up their theories. Not even the question of authorship seems to have stirred much interest, except among those most immediately involved. Antonin Artaud believed that no one had the right to call himself author, that is to say creator, except the person who controls the direct handling of the stage. In the 1960s even this claim on behalf of the director was challenged in the name of the group. Texts were deliberately broken open and invaded by actors who chose thereby to imprint themselves more directly on the performance. In one of the Open Theatre's productions the actors literally spelt out words with their bodies, in revolt against the canonical text. When the Wooster Group chose to do this to Arthur Miller's *The Crucible* in their work, *LSD,* he threatened to go to law, as did Samuel Beckett, over the American Repertory Theatre's version, in that same year, *of Endgame,* and Harold Pinter, over an Italian version of *Old Times,* which presented that play as a lesbian tryst. In an earlier production the Wooster Group stirred up the Thornton Wilder Estate by playing selections from *Our Town* on video monitors juxtaposed with pornographic images. What was at stake was copyright. What was at stake was ownership. It was in effect a debate about authority and authorship. The authors were in effect asserting the significance of the printed text. Granted that in order to move from page to stage a series of transformations, of interpretations, were necessary but the authors wished, as a bare minimum, to insist on the retention of the words as written, on the right to define the limits of an interpretive range. And that of course raises questions entirely familiar in other genres but scarcely addressed at all in theatre criticism. What constitutes the text, who could be said to write it, how do we describe it or define its reception? It may make legal sense to demand that a play be performed 'without changes or alterations'—a phrase from legal contracts but it scarcely makes theatrical let alone epistemological sense. Beckett's own response was to suggest that the best possible play was one in which there are no actors, only text, adding, perhaps only partly ironically, that he was trying to write one. It is hard to resist the thought that he almost made it. Can critics, though, afford to be equally cavalier? Can they, moreover, continue to regard the American theatre as socially and culturally marginal, peripheral to the concerns of the critic, whether that critic be committed to an exploration of the structure of language, the generation of character, the elaboration of plot, the nature of readership or the aesthetic response to ideological fact.

After all, could Barthes's description of a text of bliss, of jouissance—the text that imposes a state of loss, the text that discomforts, unsettles the reader's historical, cultural, psychological assumptions, the consistency of his tastes, values, memories, brings to a crisis his relations with language—not be said to apply to O'Neill's *The Emperor Jones,* Williams's *Outcry* and even *Streetcar,* Miller's *The Archbishop's Ceiling,* Albee's *Listening,* Mamet's *American Buffalo,* or Shepard's *Icarus's Mother.*

The conditions of theatre do radically disrupt accustomed readings. It may be indeed that this insecurity over the object of study is the real reason for critical withdrawal. Should it not, however, rather be a reason for critical engagement? The aim is not to arrest that mobility, to deny drama's protean quality by generating normative versions, critical models which are stable because inert, but to acknowledge the legitimacy of analysis, of readings of a text which is in truth only a pretext for a performance that will in turn constitute a new text.

An Excerpt from C. W. E. Bigsby's *Modern American Drama.* Cambridge, England: Cambridge University Press, 1984.